FIFTH EDITION

Marketing

Basic Concepts and Decisions

FIFTH EDITION

Marketing

Basic Concepts and Decisions

William M. Pride
Texas A & M University

O. C. Ferrell
Texas A & M University

Houghton Mifflin Company   *Boston*

Dallas ■ *Geneva, Illinois* ■ *Lawrenceville, New Jersey* ■ *Palo Alto*

Cover Photography: Martin Paul
Illustrations: Boston Graphics, Inc.

Credits for Company Logos: p. 105, Kinder-Care Learning Centers Inc.; p. 157, Jacuzzi is a registered trademark of Jacuzzi Inc.; p. 260, Saab-Scania of America; p. 311, registered trademark of Ralston Purina Company; p. 369, the service mark 'Federal Express' is used pursuant to a license agreement with Federal Express Corporation, the owner of the service mark; p. 398, 'Coca-Cola,' 'Coke,' and the Dynamic Ribbon are registered trademarks of the Coca-Cola Company and are used with permission; p. 563, reprinted with permission of Campbell Soup Company; p. 566, Sigma Marketing Concepts, Jacksonville, Florida.

Library of Congress Catalog Card Number: 86-81102

ISBN: 0-395-35710-1

BCDEFGHIJ-VH-8987

To Nancy, Michael, and Allen Pride

To James Collins Ferrell

Contents

2 The Marketing Environment   34

3 Target Markets: Segmentation and Evaluation   72

6 Marketing Research and Information Systems   160

Part II *Product Decisions* 198

7 Product Concepts 200

8 Developing and Managing Products 234

Part III Distribution Decisions 262

9 Marketing Channels 264

10 Wholesaling 292

11 Retailing 314

14 Advertising and Publicity   402

15 Personal Selling and Sales Promotion   440

Part VI *Marketing Management* 528

18 Strategic Market Planning 530

21   Services and Nonbusiness Marketing   626

22   International Marketing   664

Preface

Marketing is a relevant, challenging, and exciting field to study. Our economy, our lifestyles, and our physical well-being are directly or indirectly influenced by marketing activities. We believe that *Marketing: Basic Concepts and Decisions* is widely used because it provides comprehensive coverage and effectively stimulates student interest with its readable style and extensive use of interesting, real-life examples. The depth of coverage in this text provides students with a full understanding of the marketing discipline.

To provide insight to the practice of marketing in a changing environment, this book presents a comprehensive framework that integrates traditional concepts with the realities of today. *Marketing: Basic Concepts and Decisions* presents the concepts and applications that are most relevant to the marketing decision maker. While our view is broad enough to encompass marketing in both business and nonbusiness situations, our focus is on the universal concerns of managers who are responsible for marketing decisions.

The study of the dynamic world of marketing requires continuous review, revision, and updating. After careful consideration of suggestions from reviewers and adopters, we have made a number of content changes in this edition that will provide students with a greater depth of knowledge of the marketing field. We have included two new chapters: one on organizational buying behavior and the second on the marketing of services. We have condensed two environmental chapters into one chapter and we have positioned it in the front of the text. It is now Chapter 2. In Chapter 1, we have revised our definition of marketing and we have included discussions of a number of key topics in the area of strategic marketing management.

The marketing research chapter in this edition includes more thorough coverage of shopping mall intercept studies, telephone interviewing, and the changing nature of personal interviewing. The first pricing chapter has been totally revised and updated. Some of the topics covered include non-price competition and a discussion of numerous factors that have an impact on marketers' pricing decisions. In the international marketing chapter, new sections on global marketing strategies and on trading companies have been added.

As in earlier editions, the Fifth Edition contains numerous real-world examples, illustrations, cases, and applications. In this edition a vast majority of the longer applications that are set off in the main portion of the chapter are new. These new applications illustrate or extend the discussions of topics presented in the chapter. Half of the end-of-chapter cases are new; many of the others have been revised. Most of them focus on real, recognizable products and organizations.

In making improvements to this new edition, we have not lost sight of our original primary objective—to provide an introductory marketing textbook that is comprehensive, readable, teachable, full of real-world examples and illustrations, and interesting to students. Our book provides numerous features to facilitate student learning.

- Learning objectives at the beginning of each chapter inform the student about what should be achieved by reading the chapter.
- An opening vignette for each chapter provides a marketing situation that relates to issues discussed in the chapter.
- Many real-world examples about familiar products and organizations aid in illustrating and explaining concepts and issues.
- Two longer applications in each chapter provide examples of concepts and decisions. These applications are current and focus on recognizable firms and products.
- Numerous figures, tables, and photographs are used to facilitate learning.
- A complete summary in each chapter covers the major topics discussed.
- A list of important terms alerts the student to the major concepts and issues discussed in the chapter. These terms are highlighted in the text.
- Discussion and review questions are provided not only for review but also for thoughtful exploration of the topics covered in each chapter.
- Two concise and provocative cases appear at the end of each chapter.
- A visual framework for organizing the text is repeated at the beginning of each part to tell students how information in that part is related to other material in the text.
- Full color design makes the book come alive and emphasizes the real-world practical theme. Full color provides better contrast between art and prose and facilitates the ease of learning.
- A glossary appears at the end of the text to provide students with convenient access to definitions of over 625 important marketing terms.
- The appendices on financial analysis in marketing and on marketing careers provide additional insights to two important areas.
- The name index and the subject index aid in quickly finding topics of interest.

In addition to numerous instructor support materials discussed in the front of the instructor's manual, the package for this text includes a number of components to aid in both teaching and learning. A study guide, *Understanding Marketing*, is available for use with the text. A casebook, entitled *Marketing Cases*, is also available. It contains 42 short-to-medium length cases designed to facilitate an understanding of how marketing decisions are made. *Marketer: A Simulation* provides student teams with experience in making marketing decisions and is designed for use with most popular microcomputers. MICRO-STUDY, a computerized, self-instructional program for use on microcomputers, aids students' mastery of key marketing concepts.

The seven parts of *Marketing: Basic Concepts and Decisions* are organized around a managerial framework to give students both an understanding of marketing concepts and an understanding of how to apply them when making decisions and managing marketing activities. In Part I, we discuss general concepts and present an overview of marketing. We also consider the marketing environment, types of markets, target market analysis, buyer behavior, and marketing research. Part II presents product concepts and the development and management of products. In Part III, we examine marketing channels, institutions, and physical distribution. In Part IV, we analyze promotion decisions and methods, such as advertising, personal selling, sales promotion, and publicity. The chapters in Part V are devoted to pricing decisions. Part VI focuses on marketing management and includes discussions of strategic market planning and organization, implementation, and control. The chapters in Part VII explore strategic decisions in the areas of industrial, service, nonbusiness, and international marketing.

Over the years we have received a number of very helpful suggestions for improving the text from professors and students. We invite your comments, questions, or criticisms. We want to do our best to provide materials that enhance the teaching and learning of basic marketing concepts and decisions. Your suggestions will be sincerely appreciated.

William M. Pride

O. C. Ferrell

Acknowledgments

Like most textbooks, this one reflects the ideas of a multitude of academicians and practitioners who have contributed to the development of the marketing discipline. We appreciate the opportunity to present their ideas in this book.

A number of individuals have made many helpful comments and recommendations in their reviews of this or earlier editions. We appreciate the generous help of these reviewers.

Timothy Hartman
Ohio University

Sheldon Somerstein
City University of New York

Linda K. Anglin
Mankato State University

Winston Ring
University of Wisconsin–Milwaukee

William Lundstrom
Old Dominion University

Shanna Greenwalt
Southern Illinois University

Philip Kemp
DePaul University

Ernest F. Cooke
Memphis State University

Paul N. Bloom
University of North Carolina

George C. Hozier
University of New Mexico

Jay D. Lindquist
Western Michigan University

Robert F. Dwyer
University of Cincinnati

David R. Rink
Northern Illinois University

John Buckley
Orange County Community College

Thomas Ponzurick
West Virginia University

Barbara Unger
Western Washington University

Harrison L. Grathwol
University of Washington

Robert D. Hisrich
Boston College

Charles L. Hilton
Eastern Kentucky University

Roy Klages
State University of New York at Albany

William G. Browne
Oregon State University

Poondi Varadarajan
Texas A & M University

Lee R. Duffus
University of Tennessee

Glen Riecken
East Tennessee State University

W. R. Berdine
California State Polytechnic Institute

Charles L. Lapp
University of Dallas

Thomas V. Greer
University of Maryland

Patricia Laidler
Massasoit Community College

Stan Madden
Baylor University

Elizabeth C. Hirschman
New York University

Peter Bloch
Louisiana State University

Linda Calderone
State University of New York Agricultural and Technical College at Farmingdale

Barbara Coe
North Texas State University

Alan R. Wiman
Rider College

Donald L. James
Fort Lewis College

Terrence V. O'Brien
Clarkson College

Joseph Guiltinan
University of Kentucky

Kent B. Monroe
Virginia Polytechnic Institute

William Staples
University of Houston—Clear Lake

Richard J. Semenik
University of Utah

Pat J. Calabro
University of Texas at Arlington

James F. Wenthe
University of Georgia

Richard C. Becherer
Wayne State University

Thomas E. Barry
Southern Methodist University

Mark I. Alpert
University of Texas at Austin

Richard A. Lancioni
Temple University

Steven Shipley
Governor's State University

Paul J. Solomon
University of South Florida

Michael Peters
Boston College

Terence A. Shimp
University of South Carolina

Kenneth L. Rowe
Arizona State University

Allan Palmer
University of North Carolina at Charlotte

Stewart W. Bither
Pennsylvania State University

John R. Brooks, Jr.
West Texas State University

Carlos W. Moore
Baylor University

Charles Gross
Illinois Institute of Technology

Hugh E. Law
East Tennessee University

Dillard Tinsley
Stephen F. Austin State University

John R. Huser
Illinois Central College

David J. Fritzsche
University of Portland

David M. Landrum
Central State University

Robert Copley
University of Louisville

Robert A. Robicheaux
University of Alabama

Sue Ellen Neeley
University of Houston—Clear Lake

Otto W. Taylor
State University of New York Agricultural and Technical College at Farmingdale

Acknowledgments

Michael L. Rothschild
University of Wisconsin—Madison

Thomas Falcone
Indiana University of Pennsylvania

William L. Cron
Southern Methodist University

Sumner M. White
Massachusetts Bay Community College

Del I. Hawkins
University of Oregon

Ralph DiPietro
Montclair State College

Norman E. Daniel
Arizona State University

Bruce Stern
Portland State University

Beheruz N. Sethna
Clarkson College

Stephen J. Miller
Oklahoma State University

Dale Varble
Indiana State University

William M. Kincaid, Jr.
Oklahoma State University

John McFall
San Diego State University

James D. Reed
Louisiana State University—Shreveport

Ken Jensen
Bradley University

Arthur Prell
Lindenwood College

David H. Lindsay
University of Maryland

Claire Ferguson
Bentley College

Joseph Hair
Louisiana State University

Roger Blackwell
Ohio State University

James C. Carroll
University of Southwestern Louisiana

Guy Banville
Creighton University

Jack M. Starling
North Texas State University

Lloyd M. DeBoer
George Mason University

Dean C. Siewers
Rochester Institute of Technology

Benjamin J. Cutler
Bronx Community College

Gerald L. Manning
Des Moines Area Community College

Hale Tongren
George Mason University

Lee Meadow
University of Lowell

Ronald Schill
Brigham Young University

Don Scotton
Cleveland State University

George Glisan
Illinois State University

Jim L. Grimm
Illinois State University

John I. Coppett
Iowa State University

Roy R. Grundy
College of DuPage

Steven J. Shaw
University of South Carolina

Melvin R. Crask
University of Georgia

J. Paul Peter
University of Wisconsin—Madison

Bert Rosenbloom
Drexel University

Terry M. Chambers
Appalachian State University

Rosann L. Spiro
Indiana University

For contributing cases we are indebted to Scott Markham, University of Central Arkansas; David Loudon, C. W. McConkey, and Maynard M. Dolecheck, Northeast Louisiana University; James Kennedy, Navarro College; Donald Sapit, Sigma Marketing Concepts; and Terry Trudeau, Howard University. We especially thank Jim L. Grimm for drafting the appendix on financial analysis in marketing.

We wish to express a great deal of appreciation to Donna Legg, American Airlines, and Valarie A. Zeithaml, Duke University, for playing a major role in developing the services and nonbusiness marketing chapter. Our special thanks go to Charles W. Lamb, Texas Christian University, for developing the casebook, *Marketing Cases*. For creating *Marketer: A Simulation*, we wish to thank Jerald R. Smith, University of Louisville. We would also like to thank Steven Skinner, University of Kentucky, for creating the original CARE (Computer-Assisted Review and Evaluation) program. A great deal of thanks also go to Edwin C. Hackleman for preparing MARKETS and for creating the current version of MICROSTUDY for personal computers. For many types of technical assistance we thank Gary Bryant, John Ermer, Jean Kin, and Steve Lacy.

Acknowledgments

FIFTH EDITION

Marketing

Basic Concepts and Decisions

Part I
An Analysis of Marketing Opportunities

In Part I, we introduce the field of marketing and provide a broad perspective from which to explore and analyze various components of the marketing discipline. In the first chapter, we define marketing and discuss why an understanding of it is useful in many aspects of everyday life, including one's career. We provide an overview of general strategic marketing issues such as market opportunity analysis, target markets, and marketing mix development. Marketers should understand how environmental forces can affect customers and their responses to marketing strategies. In Chapter 2 we discuss political, legal, regulatory, societal, economic and competitive, and technological forces in the environment. Chapter 3 focuses on one of the major steps in the development of a marketing strategy—selecting and analyzing target markets. Understanding elements that affect buying decisions enables marketers to better analyze customers' needs and evaluate how specific marketing strategies can satisfy those needs. In Chapter 4, we discuss consumer buying decision processes and factors that influence buying decisions. Chapter 5 focuses on organizational markets, organizational buyers, the buying center, and the organizational buying decision process. In Chapter 6, we analyze the role of a marketing information system, and we describe the basic steps in the marketing research process.

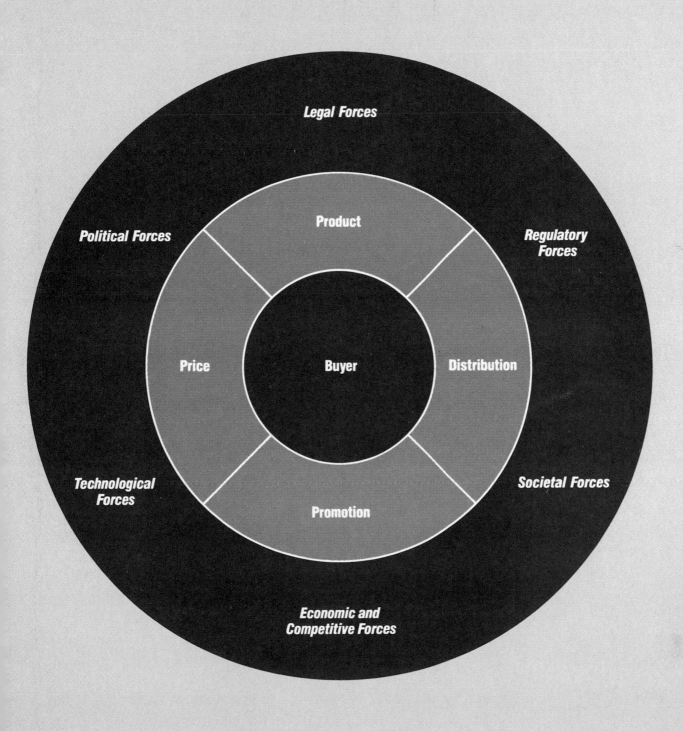

1 / An Overview of Strategic Marketing

Objectives

- ■ To learn some representative definitions of marketing, and to understand the definition used in this text.

- ■ To understand why a person should study marketing.

- ■ To gain insight into the basic elements of the marketing concept and its implementation.

- ■ To understand the major components of a marketing strategy.

- ■ To acquire an overview of general strategic marketing issues such as market opportunity analysis, target market analysis, and marketing mix development.

Figure 1.1
Stew Leonard's dairy store (Source: Courtesy of Stew Leonard's)

Stew Leonard's (Figure 1.1) is the world's largest selling dairy store. The Norwalk, Connecticut, store sells ten times more products per square foot than does the average U.S. supermarket. Although it carries only 700 items (an average supermarket carries 14,000 items), Stew Leonard's sells enormous quantities of them each year: 10 million quarts of milk, 1 million pints of cream, 29 million quarts of orange juice, 500 tons of freshly ground hamburger, 350 tons of baked-fresh-daily chocolate chip cookies, 1 million dozen eggs, 3 million croissants, and 100 tons of cottage cheese.

Stew Leonard's overall strategy is to provide fresh, high-quality products at low prices in a friendly, fun atmosphere. Prices are about 25 percent below those of other grocery stores, and Stew Leonard's store is sometimes viewed as the Disneyland dairy store because shopping there is fun. Employees wear animal or cartoon-character costumes to amuse children. In the parking lot, a farm features over 100 barnyard animals, including goats, cows, chickens, sheep, and geese. The 450 employees, called "team members," are friendly, highly motivated workers. They are treated like family members, and in fact two-thirds are related to at least one other store employee. Stew Leonard's believes that hiring employees who are related to each other is effective, because each puts pressure on the other to do a good job.

The store's retail philosophy is that the customer is king. A sign at the store entrance lists the house rules.

Rule #1 says, "The customer is always right." Rule #2 is "If the customer is ever wrong, go back and reread rule #1." Other signs in the store read "If you won't take it home to your mother, don't put it out for our customers," and "When in doubt throw it out." Store management continually seeks input from customers. The suggestion box receives over 100 suggestions from customers per week.

People Express Airlines began operations from Newark International Airport in 1980 with only a few aircraft and several flights a day. Today sales exceed $1 billion and the firm has over 80 airplanes. People Express offers a simple product: "no frills" air transportation. The philosophy is that a customer should not have to pay for unwanted services. Thus, the ticket price includes transportation only. A traveler who wants a meal or a drink or to check baggage pays a small additional fee. The ticket prices at People Express are quite low, and there are no restrictions on when tickets may be purchased or used. The price structure is designed so that customers can understand it easily. Another major emphasis of the People Express philosophy is people. The airline believes that if it treats its employees well, employees will treat customers well.

The obvious similarity between Stew Leonard's and People Express—two very different types of organizations—is that both have implemented well-defined marketing strategies. The marketing efforts have been effective, allowing each firm to compete successfully against leading firms in its industry.

In this first chapter, we provide an overview of the marketing concepts and decisions covered in the text. Initially, we develop a definition of marketing and explain each element of the definition. Then we look at several reasons why people should study marketing and point out that marketing activities pervade our everyday lives. We introduce the marketing concept and consider some of the issues associated with implementing it. Then we discuss the major tasks of strategic marketing management—market opportunity analysis, target market selection, marketing mix development, and management of marketing activities. We conclude our overview by discussing the organization of this text.

Marketing Defined

If you asked several people what **marketing** is, they would probably respond with a variety of descriptions. Marketing encompasses many more activities than most people think. Remember, though, that any definition is merely an abstract description of a broad concept. No definition perfectly describes the concept to which it refers. Like most developing disciplines, marketing has been, and continues to be, defined in many ways. Here are several definitions:

Marketing is the process of planning and executing the conception, pricing, promotion, and distribution of ideas, goods, and services to create exchanges that satisfy individual and organizational objectives.[1]

Marketing is a total system of business activities designed to plan, price, promote, and distribute want-satisfying products and services to present and potential customers.[2]

Marketing encompasses all activities involving exchange and the cause and effect phenomena associated with it.[3]

Marketing is the process in a society by which the demand structure for economic goods and services is anticipated or enlarged and satisfied through the conception, promotion, exchange, and physical distribution of such goods and services.[4]

Although these definitions of marketing may be acceptable to some academicians and practitioners, we believe that each has limitations for one or more of the following reasons. First, one of the definitions states that marketing consists of business activities; however, marketing also occurs in nonbusiness situations and is practiced by nonbusiness organizations. Second, one definition is so broad that it is difficult to know what is not a part of marketing. Third (as we will see), marketing deals not only with goods and services, but also with ideas. Finally, none of the definitions state that marketing decisions and activities occur in a dynamic environment.

To avoid such limitations, we prefer a broader definition:

Marketing consists of individual and organizational activities that facilitate and expedite satisfying exchange relationships in a dynamic environment through the creation, distribution, promotion, and pricing of goods, services, and ideas.

This definition views marketing as a diverse group of activities directed at a varied set of products and performed within a wide range of organizations. In marketing exchanges, any product may be involved. We assume only that individuals and organizations expect to gain a reward in excess of the costs incurred. To fully understand this definition, let us examine its components more closely.

Marketing Consists of Activities

A multitude of activities are required to market products effectively. Some activities can be performed by producers. Some can be accomplished by intermediaries, who buy from producers or other intermediaries in order to resell the products. And some may even be performed by purchasers. Marketing does not include all human and organizational activities. It encompasses only those activities aimed at facilitating and expediting exchanges. Table 1.1 (page 8) lists several major categories of marketing activities and provides a number

1. "AMA Board Approves New Marketing Definition," *Marketing News,* March 1, 1985, p. 1.
2. William J. Stanton, *Fundamentals of Marketing,* 7th ed. (New York: McGraw-Hill, 1984), p. 7.
3. Richard P. Bagozzi, "Marketing As Exchange," *Journal of Marketing,* Oct. 1975, p. 32.
4. Marketing Staff of the Ohio State University, "A Statement of Marketing Philosophy," *Journal of Marketing,* Jan. 1965, p. 43.

Table 1.1 *Possible decisions and activities associated with marketing mix variables*

Marketing Mix Variables	Possible Decisions and Activities
Product	Develop and test-market new products; modify existing products; eliminate products that do not satisfy customers' desires; formulate brand names and branding policies; create product warranties and establish procedures for fulfilling warranties; plan packages, including materials, sizes, shapes, colors, and designs
Distribution	Analyze various types of distribution channels; design appropriate distribution channels; design an effective program for dealer relations; establish distribution centers; formulate and implement procedures for efficient product handling; set up inventory controls; analyze transportation methods; minimize total distribution costs; analyze possible locations for plants and wholesale or retail outlets
Promotion	Set promotional objectives; determine major types of promotion to be used; select and schedule advertising media; develop advertising messages; measure the effectiveness of advertisements; recruit and train salespersons; formulate compensation programs for sales personnel; establish sales territories; plan and implement sales promotion efforts such as free samples, coupons, displays, sweepstakes, sales contests, and cooperative advertising programs; prepare and disseminate publicity releases
Price	Analyze competitors' prices; formulate pricing policies; determine method or methods used to set prices; set prices; determine discounts for various types of buyers; establish conditions and terms of sales

of examples for each. This general enumeration should not be considered all-inclusive. Each of the activities listed could easily be subdivided into numerous, more specific activities.

Marketing Is Performed by Individuals and Organizations

Marketing pervades many relationships between individuals, groups, and organizations. All types of organizations perform marketing activities to facilitate exchanges. Business organizations obviously do so, but so do nonbusiness organizations such as universities, charitable organizations, political parties, civic clubs, community theaters, hospitals, and religious organizations. (The application on page 11 discusses how the U.S. Army uses marketing efforts to attract recruits.) The sole owner and operator of a small neighborhood store performs a variety of marketing activities to facilitate exchanges. He or she decides which products will satisfy customers, arranges to have the products delivered to the store, prices them, decides how many to keep in storage and how many to display, advertises, assists customers, and at times even gift wraps and delivers purchases.

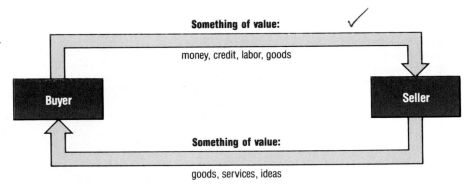

Figure 1.2

Exchange between buyer and seller

Something of value: ✓

money, credit, labor, goods

Buyer

Seller

Something of value:

goods, services, ideas

Colleges and universities and their students engage in exchanges. To receive knowledge, entertainment, room, board, and a degree, students give up time, money, effort, perhaps services in the form of labor, and opportunities to do other things. In return, the institution provides instruction, food, medical services, entertainment, recreation, and the use of land and facilities.

Marketing Facilitates Satisfying Exchange Relationships

For an **exchange** to take place, four conditions must exist. First, an exchange requires participation by two or more individuals, groups, or organizations. Second, each party must possess something of value that the other party desires. Third, each must be willing to give up its "something of value" to receive the "something of value" held by the other. The objective of a marketing exchange is to receive something that is desired more than what is given up to get it, that is, a reward in excess of costs. Fourth, the parties to the exchange must be able to communicate with each other to make their "somethings of value" available.[5] The process of exchange is illustrated in Figure 1.2. As the arrows indicate, the two parties communicate to make their "somethings of value" available to each other. Note, though, that an exchange will not necessarily take place just because these four conditions exist. However, even if there is no exchange, marketing activities still have occurred. The "somethings of value" held by the two parties are most often products and/or financial resources such as money or credit. When an exchange occurs, products are traded for either other products or financial resources.

The word *satisfying* is included in the definition because the exchange needs to be satisfying to both the buyer and the seller. For the buyer, satisfaction may come in the form of being satisfied with the product or being satisfied by the transaction itself. That is, the behavior of the seller may be viewed in a very favorable way by the buyer, thus allowing the buyer to derive satisfaction from the transaction. For instance, a seller may have a good sense of humor or an especially pleasing personality.

A seller's satisfaction may derive from doing business with a particular customer or customer group; from making a profit through a particular exchange relationship; or perhaps from achieving another organizational objective.

5. Philip Kotler, *Marketing Management: Analysis, Planning, and Control*, 6th ed. (Englewood Cliffs, N.J.: Prentice-Hall, 1984), p. 8.

Figure 1.3

The Travelers promotes
its long-lasting relationship with customers
(Source: Courtesy of The
Travelers)

A marketer must take care that customers receive levels of satisfaction that ensure future exchanges. Most organizations rely on repeat business, which requires a relationship with a buyer. Loyalty toward products, brands, or organizations derives from a satisfying relationship between buyer and seller, and it can benefit both. The seller benefits because customer loyalty is the cornerstone of repeat business. The buyer benefits from the security of knowing that expectations of product quality and performance will be fulfilled. For example, a customer wants to go to a bank, an auto repair center, a department store, or a bakery knowing that the people there will be helpful in rendering satisfying products. The message in Figure 1.3 is that The Travelers Corporation has developed long-lasting, satisfying relationships with its customers and plans to do the same in the future.

Maintaining a positive relationship with buyers is an important goal for a seller regardless of whether the seller is marketing cereal, laundry equipment, financial services, or an electric generating plant. Through buyer-seller interaction the buyer develops expectations about the seller's future behavior. To fulfill these expectations, the seller must deliver on promises made. Over time, a healthy buyer-seller relationship results in interdependencies between the two.

By 1995 there will be 4.5 million fewer young adults aged eighteen to twenty-one than there were in 1980. The decline in this age group will require the U.S. Army to recruit 55 percent of the young adult group, as compared to only 42 percent today.

The army will face tough competition for a decreasing number of young people. It will be competing not only with civilian industry and colleges but also with the other branches of the armed forces. Attracting the best-qualified men and women will be especially difficult. Recruits who score high on the Armed Forces Qualification Test generally make the air force their first choice.

To attract the higher-scoring recruits, the army is implementing an $8-million advertising campaign to introduce the new G.I. Bill and Army College Fund. This new campaign offers qualified recruits $17,000 to $25,000 for use toward a college education. Army recruiters recognize, however, that the promise of college funding is not enough. Young people seek personal challenges and skills training.

Thus, in commercials and advertisements the army campaign stresses the opportunity to learn skills and face new challenges through the testimonials of outstanding young soldiers. To be more selective in who receives its advertising messages, the army will also use direct mail advertising targeted toward potential recruits. (*Source: Brad Edmondson, "Tight Years Ahead for the Army,"* American Demographics, *Sept. 1985, pp. 20–21.*)

The buyer depends on the seller to provide information, parts, and service; to be available; and to provide satisfying products in the future. The seller depends on the buyer to continue to make purchases from the seller and to seek information.

There is a growing trend among consumer goods companies to establish communication channels with buyers to maintain long-term relationships. For example, many such companies now have toll-free numbers through which customers can make inquiries, make complaints, ask for information, or the like. Large projects or products, such as a weapons system, require considerable interaction between the buyer and the seller after the sale and before and after delivery. Sellers of such products must be prepared to maintain favorable relationships with the buyer for a long period. The sale, in this case, is just the beginning of the relationship.[6]

Marketing Occurs in a Dynamic Environment

The marketing environment consists of many changing forces: laws, regulations, actions of political officials, societal pressures, changes in economic conditions, and technological advances. Each of these dynamic forces has an impact on how effectively marketing activities can facilitate and expedite exchanges. We explore such environmental forces later in this chapter and in Chapter 2.

6. Theodore Levitt, "After the Sale Is Over," *Harvard Business Review,* Sept.–Oct. 1983, pp. 87–93.

Marketing Involves Product Development, Distribution, Promotion, and Pricing

Marketing is more than just advertising or selling the product. Marketing people get involved with designing and developing a product. Marketing focuses on making the product available at the right place at the right time at a price that is acceptable to customers, and on informing customers in a way that helps them determine if the product is consistent with their needs. Later in this chapter we discuss in more detail the areas of product development, distribution, promotion, and pricing.

Marketing Focuses on Goods, Services, and Ideas

We already have used the word *product* a number of times in this chapter. For purposes of analysis in this text, a **product** is viewed as being a good, a service, or an idea. A **good** is a physical entity one can touch. A **service** is the application of human and mechanical efforts to people or objects. Services such as bank services and long-distance telephone services are just as real as goods, but an individual cannot actually touch them. Examples of marketers that deal in services include airlines, dry cleaners, beauty shops, financial institutions, hospitals, day-care centers, and carpet cleaners. **Ideas** include concepts, philosophies, images, and issues. For instance Weight Watchers, for a fee, provides its members with ideas to help them lose weight and control their eating habits. Other marketers of ideas include political parties, churches, and schools.

Why Study Marketing?

After considering the definition of marketing, one can understand some of the obvious reasons why the study of marketing is relevant. In this section we will discuss several perhaps less obvious reasons why one should study marketing.

Marketing Activities Are Used in Many Organizations

From 25 to 33 percent of all civilian workers in the United States perform marketing activities. A variety of interesting and challenging career opportunities is available in the marketing field. Some of these are personal selling, advertising, packaging, transportation, storage, marketing research, product development, wholesaling, and retailing. In addition, many individuals who work for nonbusiness organizations are involved in marketing activities. Marketing skills are used to promote political, cultural, church, civic, and charitable activities. The advertisement in Figure 1.4 is a joint marketing effort by the American Cancer Society and the United Way of Massachusetts Bay, both of which are nonprofit organizations. Whether a person earns a living through marketing activities or performs them without compensation in nonbusiness settings, marketing knowledge and skills are likely to be a valuable asset.

Marketing Activities Are Important to Businesses and the Economy

A business organization must sell products to survive and to grow. Marketing activities directly or indirectly help to sell the organization's products. By doing so, they generate financial resources that can be used to develop innovative products. New products allow a firm to better satisfy customers' changing needs, which in turn allows the firm to generate more profits. Procter & Gamble exemplifies this process. It does an excellent job of understanding consumers, creating products to meet their needs, and using innovative marketing.

United Way of Massachusetts Bay and the American Cancer Society, Massachusetts Division:
partners in education and fundraising in business and industry.

Figure 1.4 *Joint marketing effort by two nonprofit organizations (Source: Courtesy of United Way)*

Our highly complex, industrialized economy depends heavily on marketing activities. They help produce the profits that are essential not only to the survival of individual businesses, but also to the health and ultimate survival of the economy as a whole. Profits are essential to economic growth. Without them, businesses find it difficult, if not impossible, to buy added raw materials, hire more employees, attract more capital, and produce the additional products that in turn make more profits.

Marketing Knowledge Enhances Consumer Awareness

Besides contributing to the well-being of our nation, marketing activities pervade our everyday lives. In fact, they help us to achieve many improvements in the quality of our lives. Still, critics contend that commonplace products are marketed so zealously that they get attention out of all proportion to their merit.[7]

Studying marketing activities allows us to weigh their costs, benefits, and flaws more effectively. We can see where they need to be improved and how to accomplish that goal. For example, if you have had an unsatisfactory experience with a warranty, you may have wished that laws were enforced more

7. "In Today's Marketplace, It's Hype, Hype, Hype," *U.S. News and World Report,* Dec. 5, 1983, p. 51.

strictly to make sellers fulfill their promises. In the same vein, you may have wished that you had more information about a product—or more accurate information—before you made the purchase. Understanding marketing enables us to evaluate the corrective measures (such as laws, regulations, and industry guidelines) that may be required to stop unfair, misleading, or unethical marketing practices. The results of a national survey presented in Table 1.2 indicate that there is a considerable lack of knowledge about marketing activities as reflected by the sizeable proportion of respondents who agree with the myths in the table.

Marketing Costs Consume a Sizable Part of Buyers' Dollars

The study of marketing will make you aware that many marketing activities are necessary to provide people with satisfying goods and services. Obviously, these marketing activities cost money. In fact, about one-half of a buyer's dollar goes for marketing costs. A family that has a monthly income of $2,000 and allocates $400 to taxes and savings spends about $1,600 for goods and services. Of this amount, $800 goes for marketing activities. Clearly, if marketing expenses consume that much of your dollar, you should know how this money is used.

✓The Marketing Concept

During World War II, the U.S. Air Force established a supply base on a South Pacific island. The islanders watched the service personnel build the runway, install landing lights, set up a control tower, and erect storage buildings. After the base was completed, the natives enjoyed watching the aircraft land and take off. They especially liked to see supplies being unloaded, because they had developed ways of getting food and other supplies from the storage areas.

After the war was over, the supplies were removed, the facilities were torn down, the landing lights were taken out, and the runway was destroyed. When the last of the U.S. military personnel left the island, the islanders—who had become dependent on the supplies—decided that if they could rebuild the base, then the large silver birds would return. So they built crudely thatched storage huts, cleared and smoothed a makeshift runway, and erected a tower-like structure close to it. They lit torches on both sides of the runway at night to guide the silver birds to the island. Although the islanders waited day after day, the large silver birds never returned.

Some business organizations face a similar problem. They build or acquire facilities, hire personnel, obtain equipment, and make or buy products; yet— like the Pacific islanders—they fail to attract people with what they have to offer. However, a business that adopts and properly implements the marketing concept should not experience this problem.

The marketing concept is not a second definition of marketing. It is a way of thinking—a management philosophy about an organization's entire activities. This philosophy affects all efforts of the organization, not just the marketing activities.

Table 1.2 *National survey results regarding marketing myths*

Myths	Strongly Agree	Somewhat Agree	Neither Agree Nor Disagree	Somewhat Disagree	Strongly Disagree	No Response
Marketing and selling are about the same thing	11.9% (245)	31.4% (645)	23.2% (476)	21.0% (431)	11.4% (234)	1.2% (24)
A grocery store owner takes home at least $3.00 for every $10.00 bag of groceries sold	19.5% (400)	23.8% (486)	30.3% (619)	14.9% (305)	11.0% (226)	0.4% (9)
Products that are advertised a great deal cost more	30.5% (625)	36.1% (741)	13.7% (282)	13.1% (270)	5.7% (117)	1.0% (20)
Wholesalers make high profits which significantly increase prices consumers pay	35.4% (725)	37.7% (771)	15.9% (326)	8.0% (164)	2.4% (49)	0.5% (10)
Marketing is the same thing as advertising	12.9% (265)	35.7% (734)	22.7% (465)	19.8% (406)	7.7% (157)	1.3% (28)

Source: William M. Pride and O. C. Ferrell; a national survey of U.S. households. © 1985.

Basic Elements of the Marketing Concept

According to the **marketing concept,** an organization should try to satisfy the needs of customers or clients through a coordinated set of activities that also allows the organization to achieve its goals. Customer satisfaction is the major aim of the marketing concept. First, a business organization must find out what will satisfy customers. GTE Sprint clearly expresses this basic element of the marketing concept in the advertisement in Figure 1.5. With this information, the business can create satisfying products. But that is not enough. The business then must get these products into the hands of customers. Nor does the process end there. The business must continue to alter, adapt, and develop products to keep pace with customers' changing desires and preferences. For example, consumers' snack-food preferences have changed toward lower-calorie foods. General Foods is offering reduced-calorie snacks to serve the needs of people with this preference. The marketing concept stresses the importance of customers and emphasizes that marketing activities begin and end with them.

In attempting to satisfy customers, businesses must consider not only short-run, immediate needs but also broad, long-term desires. Trying to satisfy customers' current needs by sacrificing their long-term desires will only create strong dissatisfaction in the future. For example, people want efficient, low-cost energy to power their homes and automobiles. Yet they clearly react adversely to energy producers who pollute the air and water, kill wildlife, or cause disease or birth defects in future generations. To meet these short- and long-run needs and desires, a firm must coordinate all its activities. Production, finance, accounting, personnel, and marketing departments must work together.

Please do not think that the marketing concept is a highly philanthropic philosophy aimed at helping customers at the expense of the business organization. A firm that adopts the marketing concept must not only satisfy its customers' objectives but also achieve its own goals. Otherwise, it will not stay in business

Figure 1.5

GTE's expression of its marketing philosophy (Source: Courtesy of GTE Sprint)

for long. The overall goals of a business might be directed toward increasing profits, market shares, sales, or a combination of the three. The marketing concept stresses that a business organization can best achieve its goals by providing customer satisfaction. Implementing the marketing concept should benefit the organization as well as its customers. A firm can only be successful through coordination of all the organization's activities with the aim of meeting its objectives.

Evolution of the Marketing Concept

The marketing concept may seem like an obvious and sensible approach to running a business. However, business people have not always believed that the best way to make sales, and profits, is to satisfy customers. This philosophy emerged in the third major era in the history of U.S. business. It was preceded by the production era and the sales era. Surprisingly, thirty years after the marketing era began, many businesses still have not adopted the marketing concept.

The Production Era

During the second half of the nineteenth century, the Industrial Revolution came into its own in the United States. Electricity, rail transportation, the division of labor, the assembly line, and mass production made it possible to manufacture products more efficiently. As a result of new technology and new ways of using labor, products streamed out of factories into the marketplace, where consumer demand for manufactured goods was strong. This **production orientation** continued into the early part of this century, encouraged by the scientific management movement which, to increase worker productivity, championed rigidly structured jobs and pay based on output.

The Sales Era

Beginning in the 1920s, the strong consumer demand for products subsided. Businesses realized that products, which by this time could be made relatively efficiently, would have to be "sold" to consumers. From the mid-1920s to the early 1950s, businesses looked on sales as the major means of increasing profits. As a result, this period came to have a **sales orientation.** Business people believed that the most important marketing activities were personal selling and advertising.

The Marketing Era

By the early 1950s, some business people began to recognize that efficient production and extensive promotion of products did not guarantee that customers would buy them. These businesses, and many others since then, found that they must first determine what customers want and then produce it, rather than simply make products and try to change customers' needs to fit what is produced. As more and more organizations realized that the measurement of customers' needs is where everything begins, U.S. business moved into the marketing era, the era of **customer orientation.**

Implementing the Marketing Concept

A philosophy may look good on paper. It may sound reasonable and even noble. But that does not mean it can be put into practice easily. The marketing concept is a case in point. To implement it, an organization must focus on some general conditions. It must also be cognizant of several problems. Because of these conditions and problems, the marketing concept has yet to be fully accepted by American business.

Since the marketing concept affects all types of business activities, not only marketing activities, the top management of an organization must adopt it wholeheartedly. High-level executives must incorporate the marketing concept into their personal philosophies of business management so completely that it serves as the basis for all the goals and decisions they set for their firms. They must convince other members of the organization to accept the changes in policies and operations that flow from their acceptance of the marketing concept.

As the first step, management must establish an information system that enables it to discover customers' real needs and to use that information internally to create satisfying products. Since an information system of this sort is almost always expensive, management must be willing to commit a substantial amount of money and time for development and maintenance. Without an adequate information system, an organization cannot be customer oriented.

Management's second major task may well be restructuring the organization. We have already pointed out that if a firm is to satisfy customers' objectives as well as its own, it must coordinate all activities. To achieve this coordination, the internal operations and the overall objectives of one or more departments may need restructuring. If the head of the marketing unit is not a member of the organization's top-level management, the situation should be rectified. Some departments may have to be abolished and new ones created. Implementing the marketing concept demands the support not only of top management but also of managers and staff at all levels in the organization.

Even when the basic conditions of establishing an information system and reorganizing the firm are satisfied, it is not certain that the firm's new marketing approach will function perfectly. First of all, there is a limit on a firm's ability to satisfy customers' needs for a particular product. In a mass production economy, most business organizations cannot tailor products to fit the exact needs of each customer. Second, although a firm may try to learn what customers want, it may be unable to do so. Even when a firm correctly identifies customers' needs, the firm's personnel often have a hard time actually developing a product to satisfy those needs. Many companies spend considerable time and money to research customers' needs and yet still create some products that do not sell well. Third, by satisfying one segment of society, a firm sometimes contributes to the dissatisfaction of other segments. Government and nonbusiness organizations also experience this problem. Fourth, a firm may have trouble maintaining employee morale during any restructuring that may be required to coordinate the activities of various departments. Management must clearly enunciate the reasons for the changes and communicate its own enthusiasm for the marketing concept.

Strategic Marketing Management

Marketing management is a process of planning, organizing, implementing, and controlling marketing activities to facilitate and expedite exchanges effectively and efficiently. Effectiveness and efficiency are important dimensions of this definition. *Effectiveness* refers to the degree to which an exchange helps to achieve an organization's objectives. The quality of exchanges relative to an organization's objectives may range from highly desirable to highly undesirable. One major purpose of the marketing management process is to facilitate desirable exchanges. *Efficiency* refers to the minimization of the resources that an organization must spend to achieve a specific level of desired exchanges. Thus, the overall goal of marketing management is to facilitate highly desirable exchanges and to minimize, as much as possible, the costs of doing so.

Our definition of marketing states that activities are performed to facilitate and expedite exchanges. When marketing managers are attempting to properly manage marketing activities, they must deal with two broad sets of variables: those relating to the marketing mix and those that make up the marketing environment. The marketing mix decision variables—product, distribution, promotion, and price—are factors over which an organization has control. As shown in Figure 1.6, these variables are constructed around the buyer. The marketing environment variables are political, legal, regulatory, societal, economic and competitive, and technological forces. These factors are subject to less control by an organization, but they affect buyers and marketing managers' decisions regarding the marketing mix variables.

To achieve the broad goal of facilitating and expediting desirable exchanges, marketing management in an organization is responsible for developing and managing marketing strategies. Strategy—a word derived from the ancient

Figure 1.6

Components of the marketing mix and marketing environment

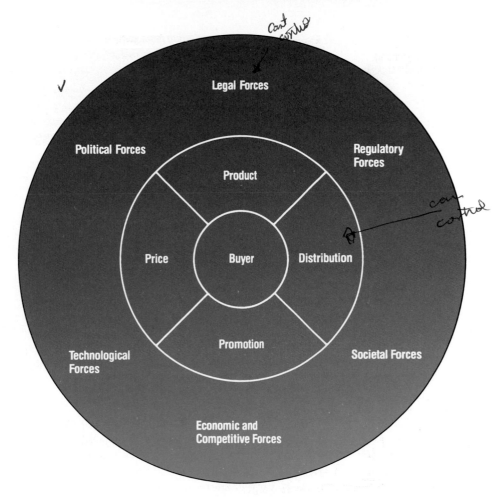

Greek *strategia*, meaning "the art of the general"—is concerned with the key decisions required to reach an objective or set of objectives. A marketing strategy articulates a plan for the best use of the organization's resources and advantages to meet its objectives. Specifically, a **marketing strategy** encompasses selecting and analyzing a target market (the group of people whom the organization wants to reach) and creating and maintaining an appropriate **marketing mix** (product, distribution, promotion, and price) that will satisfy those people.

The development and management of marketing strategies requires an organization's marketing management to focus on several generic marketing management tasks. The tasks are market opportunity analysis, target market selection, marketing mix development, and management of marketing activities. They are shown in Figure 1.7 along with the chapters of this book in which these tasks are discussed.

Market Opportunity Analysis

Customer desire for almost any product diminishes over time. Few organizations can assume that products popular today will be of interest to buyers ten years from now. It is critical for an organization's long-term survival to find new products and markets.

Figure 1.7

Generic marketing
management tasks

Generic marketing management tasks

Market opportunity analysis and target market selection
The Marketing Environment (Chapter 2)
Target Market Evaluation (Chapter 3)
Consumer Markets and Buying Behavior (Chapter 4)
Organizational Markets and Buying Behavior (Chapter 5)
Marketing Research and Information Systems (Chapter 6)

Marketing mix development
Product Decisions (Chapters 7 and 8)
Distribution Decisions (Chapters 9, 10, 11, and 12)
Promotion Decisions (Chapters 13, 14, and 15)
Price Decisions (Chapters 16 and 17)

Management of marketing activities
Strategic Market Planning (Chapter 18)
Organization, Implementation, and Control (Chapter 19)

An organization can consider a variety of alternatives through which to grow and sustain itself. An organization can modify existing products, introduce new products, and delete some that customers no longer desire. A firm may attempt to market its products to a greater number of individuals in its existing markets. Various efforts may be initiated to convince current customers to use more of a product, or marketing managers may decide to expand the geographic boundaries of a market. Diversification into new product offerings through internal efforts or through acquisitions of other organizations may be viable options for a firm.

The ability of an organization to pursue any of these alternatives successfully depends on the organization's internal characteristics and the forces in the marketing environment.

Internal Organizational Factors

The primary factors inside an organization that should be considered when analyzing market opportunities are organizational objectives, financial resources, managerial skills, organizational strengths and weaknesses, and cost structures. Most organizations that plan to flourish over time have overall objectives. Some market opportunities may be consistent with these objectives, while others are not. To pursue opportunities that are inconsistent with the firm's overall objectives is hazardous. Frequently, the pursuit of such opportunities ends in failure or forces the firm to alter its long-term objectives.

Obviously, a firm's financial resources place a constraint on the type of market opportunities that can be pursued. An organization typically does not develop projects that can result in an economic catastrophe. However, there are situations in which the firm has little choice but to invest in a high-risk opportunity because the costs of not pursuing the project are so high.

The skills and experience of management place limits on the types of opportunities that an organization can pursue. Especially when a firm is exploring the possibility of entering unfamiliar markets with new products, a good deal of caution should be exercised. When managerial experience and skills are lacking, they sometimes can be acquired by hiring managerial personnel.

Most organizations have certain strengths and weaknesses. Because of the types of operations that a firm has engaged in, it normally has employees with specialized skills and technological information. These characteristics can be a strength when launching marketing strategies that require them. However, they may be a weakness if the firm tries to compete in new, unrelated product areas.

An organization's cost structure may be advantageous if certain opportunities are pursued and disadvantageous if other market opportunities are pursued. The cost structure can be affected by such factors as geographic location, employee skill mix, access to raw materials, and type of equipment and facilities.

Marketing Environment Forces

The **marketing environment** of political, legal, regulatory, societal, economic and competitive, and technological forces surrounds the buyer and the marketing mix (see Figure 1.6). The forces in the marketing environment affect in three general ways a marketer's ability to facilitate and expedite exchanges. First, the marketing environment influences customers. It affects lifestyles, standards of living, and preferences and needs for products. Since a marketing manager tries to develop and adjust the marketing mix to satisfy consumers, the effects of environmental forces on customers also have an indirect impact on the marketing mix components. Second, forces in the marketing environment directly influence whether and how a marketing manager can perform certain marketing activities. Third, the environmental forces may affect a marketing manager's decisions and actions by influencing buyers' reactions to the firm's marketing mix.

Although forces in the marketing environment sometimes are considered "uncontrollables," a marketing manager may be able to influence one or more of them. However, marketing environment forces fluctuate quickly and dramatically, which is one reason why marketing is so interesting and challenging. Since these forces are highly interrelated, a change in one of them may cause others to change.

Even though environmental changes produce uncertainty for marketers and, at times, have severe adverse effects on marketing efforts, they also can create opportunities. Thus a marketer must be aware of changes in environmental forces not only to adjust to and influence them, but also to capitalize on the opportunities they provide. The remainder of this section briefly describes environmental forces. In Chapter 2 we explore each of the major environmental forces in greater depth.

Our political institutions enact laws and create regulatory units that affect business organizations. More broadly, **political forces** strongly influence the economic and political stability of our country. They do so through decisions that affect domestic matters as well as through their authority to negotiate trade agreements and determine foreign policy. If government officials have negative opinions about a firm or an industry, they may pass and enforce laws that place severe constraints on its ability to market products. In addition, the government purchases many products in tremendous quantities and offers several kinds of loans that can aid businesses. Political officials thus may affect the financial position of firms by awarding or failing to award government contracts or loans.

Legislation and the interpretation of laws give rise to **legal forces.** Marketing decisions and activities are restrained and controlled by a multitude of laws, many enacted either to preserve a competitive atmosphere or to protect consumers. Laws tend to influence marketing activities directly, but their real effects on the marketing mix components depend largely on how marketers and the courts interpret the laws. For example, wide-open competition in the drug market is one result of a unanimous decision of the U.S. Supreme Court in favor of generic medications. This decision permits pharmacists to substitute a less expensive form of a drug for a brand-name medication when filling prescriptions.[8]

Regulatory forces arise from regulatory units at the local, state, and federal levels. These units create and enforce numerous regulations that affect marketing decisions. At times government regulatory agencies, especially at the federal level, sponsor meetings to encourage firms in a particular industry to develop guidelines to stop questionable practices. Industry leaders usually cooperate in such cases, for they recognize that the next step may be government regulation. Government is not the only source of regulations affecting marketers, however. Individual firms and trade organizations also exert regulatory pressures on themselves and their members.

Most American consumers seek a high standard of living and an enjoyable quality of life. **Societal forces** pressure marketers to provide such living standards and lifestyles through socially responsible decisions and activities. Today, thirty to forty thousand local consumer groups are well prepared and educated to monitor and, if need be, fight industries on an issue-by-issue basis.[9] This proliferation is just one example of how people in our society form interest groups to let marketers know what they want. In general, such groups desire not only a high standard of living but also a high-quality environment. In addition, they insist on honest marketing and attention to product safety. For example, pressure from consumer groups claiming McDonalds' Chicken McNuggets and Filet-O-Fish sandwiches were too fatty resulted in the company switching from beef and vegetable shortening to pure vegetable shortening, which has a considerably lower fat content.[10]

To a large extent **economic forces** determine the strength of a firm's competitive atmosphere. The intensity of competition is affected by three primary factors: the number of businesses that control the supply of a product; how easily a firm can enter the industry; and how much demand there is for the product relative to supply. Economic factors affect the impact of marketing activities because they determine the size and strength of demand for products. Two general determinants of demand are buyers' ability to purchase and their willingness to purchase. Changes in general economic conditions have a great bearing on these two factors.

8. Pravet Choudhury, "High Court Clears the Way for Generic Drug Competition," *Marketing News,* March 4, 1983, p. 6.
9. John Elkins, "Social Trends Dictate Changes in American Approach to Business," *Marketing News,* June 24, 1983, p. 16.
10. Jonathan Dahl, "McDonald's to Fry Its Kettle of Fish in a Different Fat," *Wall Street Journal,* May 9, 1986, p. 21.

There are two ways in which **technological forces** influence marketers' decisions and activities. First, they have great impact on people's everyday lives. Technology affects our lifestyles and standards of living which, in turn, influence our desires for products and our reactions to the marketing mixes offered by business organizations. Second, technological developments may have a direct impact on creating and maintaining a marketing mix, because they may affect all its variables: product, distribution, promotion, and price. The technologies of communication, transportation, computers, energy, medicine, fabrics, metals, and packaging have influenced the types of products produced as well as advertising, personal selling, marketing research, pricing, storage, and the use and processing of credit.

This brief description of marketing environment forces suggests some of their possible effects on marketing decisions and activities. If marketers hope to create and maintain effective marketing strategies, they must recognize that dynamic environmental forces can create both marketing problems and marketing opportunities. They must therefore be able to adjust marketing strategies to major changes in the marketing environment.

Marketing Strategy: Target Market Selection

A **target market** is a group of persons for whom a firm creates and maintains a marketing mix that specifically fits the needs and preferences of that group. When choosing a target market, marketing managers try to evaluate possible markets to see how entering them would affect the firm's sales, costs, and profits. Furthermore, marketers attempt to determine whether the organization has the resources to produce a marketing mix that meets the needs of a particular target market and whether satisfying those needs is consistent with the firm's overall objectives. They also analyze the size and number of competitors who already are selling in the possible target market.

Marketing managers may define a target market to include a relatively small number of people, or they may define it to encompass a vast group of people. For example, women are the newest target market of sports marketers. Over half of all women participate in sports and there has been a dramatic increase in the number of women athletes. Moreover, women hold 65 percent of health club memberships. Miller Lite is attempting to use this information in aiming advertisements at women involved in sports.[11] Although it may focus its efforts on one target market through a single marketing mix, a business often focuses on several target markets by developing and employing multiple marketing mixes.

Target market selection is crucial to generating productive marketing efforts. On numerous occasions a business has failed because its management did not identify the specific customer group at which the organization was aiming its products and marketing efforts. Business organizations that try to be "all things to all people" typically end up not satisfying the needs of any customer group very well. It is important for an organization's management to designate which customer groups the firm is trying to serve and to have some information about these customers. The identification and analysis of a target market provides a foundation on which a marketing mix can be developed.

11. Carol Kleiman, "Women are Newest Target Group of Sports Marketing," *Eagle,* May 11, 1986, p. 5E.

Marketing Strategy: Marketing Mix Development

The marketing mix consists of four major components: product, distribution, promotion, and price. As discussed earlier, these components are called marketing mix decision variables because a marketing manager can vary the type and amount of each element. One primary goal is to create and maintain a marketing mix that satisfies consumers' needs for a general product type. Notice in Figure 1.6 that the marketing mix is built around the buyer (as is stressed by the marketing concept). Also, bear in mind that the marketing mix variables are affected in many ways by the marketing environment variables.

Marketing mix variables often are viewed as "controllable" variables because they can be changed. However, there are limits to how much these variables can be altered. For example, because of economic conditions or government regulations, a manager may not be free to adjust prices from one day to the next. Changes in sizes, colors, shapes, and designs of most tangible goods are expensive; therefore such product features cannot be altered very often. In addition, promotional campaigns and the methods used to distribute products ordinarily cannot be changed overnight.

Marketing managers must develop a marketing mix that precisely matches the needs of the people in the target market. Before they can do this, they have to collect in-depth, up-to-date information about those needs. (The application on page 26 deals with a firm that incorrectly assessed buyers' needs in one case and yet was able to accurately assess needs in another situation.) The information might include data regarding the age, income, race, sex, and educational level of people in the target market; their preferences for product designs, features, colors, and textures; their attitudes toward competitors' products, services, advertisements, and prices; and the frequency and intensity with which they use the product. With these kinds of data, marketing managers are better able to develop a product, distribution, promotion, and price that satisfy the people in the target market.

Now let us look more closely at the decisions and activities related to each marketing mix variable (product, distribution, promotion, and price). Table 1.1 shows a partial list of the numerous decisions and activities associated with each marketing mix variable.

The Product Variable

As noted earlier, a product can be a good, a service, or an idea. The actual physical production of products is not a marketing activity. However, marketers do research consumers' product wants and design products to achieve the desired characteristics. They may also create and alter packages and brand names. This aspect of the marketing mix is known as the **product variable.** Repair and warranty services also may be a part of the decisions included in the product variable (see Figure 1.8).

Product variable decisions and related activities are important because they are involved directly with creating want-satisfying products. To maintain a satisfying set of products that will help an organization to achieve its goals, a marketer must be able to develop new products, modify existing ones, and eliminate those that no longer satisfy buyers and yield acceptable profits. For example, the Delco Electronics Division of General Motors and Bose Corporation spent $12 million to develop a new automobile stereo system because they perceived that there was high demand for studio-sound quality in an automobile system. The new system is available for approximately $895 on many General

Put a $25 lid on major car repair costs.

With Ford ESP Plus,™ you never pay more than $25—whether it's for a $600 repair or a $60 repair. You pay no parts or labor charges. Just a $25 deductible each repair visit. No matter how many different covered parts need to be fixed.

ESP Plus covers thousands of parts—even high tech components—for up to five years or 60,000 miles, whichever comes first.

ESP Plus is only one of the Ford Extended Service Plans available. There's even a plan that provides scheduled maintenance and no

deductible. That's ESP Care.™

If you own (or plan to own soon) a new Ford car or light truck, Mercury, Lincoln or Merkur, find out more about the peace of mind that ESP protection brings. See one of the over 6,100 Ford and Lincoln-Mercury dealers throughout the U.S. and Canada who offer the Ford Extended Service Plan. Or call toll-free 1-800-FORD-ESP. The Ford Extended Service Plan—it's the only plan with the Ford name on it.

Buckle up—together we can save lives.

Ford Extended Service Plan (Ford)

Motors automobiles. In the first year, it exceeded General Motors sales estimates, with 25 percent of Oldsmobile buyers and 84 percent of Corvette buyers ordering the unit.[12]

The Distribution Variable

To satisfy consumers, products must be available at the right time in a convenient and accessible location. In dealing with the **distribution variable,** a marketing manager attempts to make products available in the quantities desired to as many customers as possible and to hold the total inventory, transportation, and storage costs as low as possible. A marketing manager may become involved in selecting and motivating intermediaries (wholesalers and retailers), establishing and maintaining inventory control procedures, and developing and managing transportation and storage systems.

As an example of the importance of the distribution variable in the marketing mix, management at Adolph Coors Company dramatically increased sales when it expanded its distribution into six southeastern states, which represented the fastest-growing beer market in the United States. Instead of relying on inex-

12. Thomas Pezinge, Jr., "GM Wins Back Music Fans by Developing a High-Quality Stereo for Its Automobiles," *Wall Street Journal,* Aug. 29, 1983, p. 15.

Chapter 1 / An Overview of Strategic Marketing

25

Significant changes in demographic variables can have a decisive impact on the success or failure of a product. Marketers must engage in research both to analyze and anticipate such changes, but important trends in consumer behavior may be overlooked, causing product failure.

Stouffer, a company that produces frozen prepared foods, conducted research several years ago showing that purchases by larger families, defined as having two or more children, made up a significant portion of its sales. Stouffer then developed the Family Casserole line, packages that served four or more people. This line flopped; Stouffer's research had failed to detect "split-menu dining"—a growing trend among larger, active families. Such families are not always able to eat together, and even when they do, family members do not necessarily eat the same thing. Thus, when consumers bought Stouffer products, they tended to purchase the smaller packages, suitable for one- or two-person servings. Nevertheless, a flop can be "profitable." It was the failure of the Family Casserole line that alerted Stouffer to the split-menu trend.

By contrast, Stouffer's Lean Cuisine line has been a success. This time Stouffer's research located major demographic changes indicating that women, smaller families, and single-person households would purchase the line. The interest of working women, Stouffer found, would be stimulated by their desire to watch their weight and to serve their families nourishing meals that required minimal preparation. The success and failure of the two Stouffer lines illustrate the necessity of both research and accurate assessment of buyers' needs. (*Source: Based on Ann Lloyd, "The Lean Cuisine Story,"* American Demographics, December, 1984, p. 16.)

perienced wholesalers, Coors tapped into an existing network of Schlitz distributors that needed extra business. This distribution strategy allowed Coors to gain 10 percent of the Florida market in a very short time.[13]

The Promotion Variable

The **promotion variable** is used to facilitate exchanges by informing one or more groups of people about an organization and its products. Promotion is used for various reasons. For example, it might be used to increase public awareness of an organization, a new product, or a new brand. In addition, promotion is used to educate consumers about product features or to urge people to adopt a particular position on a political or social issue. It may also be used to renew interest in a product whose popularity is waning. The International Coffee Organization and the National Coffee Association recently spent $20 million in advertising to encourage the 18–34 age group to drink coffee. Lately, people between the ages of 20 and 29 have averaged only 1.3 cups of coffee daily, compared with 3.4 cups twenty years ago. In this promotional campaign, television advertising shows celebrities drinking coffee, working hard, and pursuing goals and achievements. The advertisements indicate that coffee gives both serenity and vitality.[14]

13. John J. Curran, "Beer Stocks with Yeasty Promise," *Fortune,* Oct. 17, 1983, pp. 179–180.
14. Kathleen A. Hughs, "Coffee Makers Hope New Ads Will Reverse Declining Sales," *Wall Street Journal,* Sept. 1, 1983, p. 21.

Figure 1.9

Advertisement for Chanel No. 5 perfume (Source: Courtesy of Chanel Inc.)

Part 4 looks closely at such promotion activities as advertising, publicity, personal selling, and sales promotion.

The Price Variable

In the area of the **price variable,** marketing managers usually have a hand in establishing pricing policies and determining product prices. Price is important to consumers because they are concerned about the value obtained in an exchange. Thus, price is a critical component of the marketing mix. It often is used as a competitive tool; in fact, extremely intense price competition sometimes leads to "price wars." Airlines such as People Express, Continental, and Southwest have touched off air-fare price wars that have caused some larger, higher-cost airlines to go bankrupt or lose millions of dollars.

Price also helps to establish a product's image. For instance, if the makers of Chanel No. 5 (see Figure 1.9) tried to sell that perfume in a 1-gallon jug for $3.95, consumers probably would not buy it. The price would destroy the image of Chanel No. 5.

Developing and maintaining an effective marketing mix is a major requirement for having a strong marketing strategy. Thus, as indicated in Figure 1.7, a considerable portion of this text (Chapters 7 through 17) focuses on the concepts, decisions, and activities associated with the components of the marketing mix.

Management of Marketing Activities

Managing marketing activities involves planning, organizing, implementation, and control. Marketing planning is a systematic process that focuses on the assessment of opportunities and resources, the determination of marketing objectives, the development of a marketing strategy, and the development of plans for implementation and control. Planning determines when and how marketing activities will be performed and who is to perform them. It forces marketing managers to think ahead, to establish objectives, and to consider future marketing activities. Effective planning also reduces or eliminates daily crises.

Organizing marketing activities involves developing the internal structure of the marketing unit. This structure is the key to directing marketing activities. The marketing unit can be organized by functions, products, regions, or types of customers. An organization may use one of these forms or a combination of them.

Proper implementation of marketing plans depends on the coordination of marketing activities, the motivation of marketing personnel, and effective communication within the unit. Marketing managers must coordinate the activities of marketing personnel and integrate these activities both with those in other areas of the firm and with the marketing efforts of personnel in external organizations such as advertising agencies and research firms. Marketing managers also must motivate marketing personnel. The communication system of an organization must allow the marketing manager to communicate with high-level management, with managers of other functional areas in the firm, and with personnel involved in marketing activities both inside and outside the organization.

The marketing control process consists of establishing performance standards, evaluating actual performance by comparing it with established standards, and reducing the difference between desired and actual performance. An effective control process has several requirements. It should assure a rate of information flow that allows the marketing manager to detect quickly differences between actual and planned levels of performance. It must accurately monitor different kinds of activities and be flexible enough to accommodate changes. The control process must be economical so that its costs are low relative to the costs that would arise if there were no controls. Finally, the control process should be designed so that both managers and subordinates can understand it. To maintain effective marketing control, an organization needs to develop a comprehensive control process that evaluates marketing operations at regular intervals.

The Organization of This Book

Figure 1.7 is a table of the overall organization of this book. Chapter 2 discusses the marketing environment variables listed in the outer portion of Figure 1.7. We then focus on the center of Figure 1.7, analyzing markets, buyers, and marketing research (in Chapters 3, 4, 5 and 6, respectively). Chapters 7 through 17 explore the marketing mix variables, starting with the product variable and moving clockwise around Figure 1.7. Chapters 18 and 19 discuss strategic market planning, organization, implementation, and control. Decisions and activities that are unique to industrial marketing, international marketing, and services and nonbusiness marketing are considered in Chapters 20, 21, and 22. If, as you are reading, you wonder where the text is leading, look again at Figure 1.7.

Summary

Marketing consists of individual and organizational activities that facilitate and expedite satisfying exchange relationships in a dynamic environment through the creation, distribution, promotion, and pricing of goods, services, and ideas. Four conditions must exist for an exchange to occur: (1) an exchange requires participation by two or more individuals, groups, or organizations; (2) each must have something of value desired by the other; (3) each must be willing to give up what it has to receive the value item held by the other; and (4) the parties to the exchange must be able to communicate with each other to make their "somethings of value" available. In an exchange, products are traded either for other products or for financial resources, such as cash or credit. Products can be goods, services, or ideas.

About half of each consumer dollar is spent in marketing activities. You should be aware of what marketing is because its activities permeate our lives. They are performed by business firms and also by nonbusiness organizations such as political, social, church, cultural, and civic groups. Moreover, marketing activities help business organizations to generate profits, the lifeblood of a capitalist economy. Finally, the study of marketing will help you evaluate marketing activities.

The marketing concept is a management philosophy that affects all activities of a business organization. According to this philosophy, a business organization should try to satisfy customers' needs through a coordinated set of activities that, at the same time, allows the organization to achieve its goals. Customer satisfaction is the major objective of the marketing concept. The organization first must determine consumers' needs and then try to satisfy those needs through a coordinated set of activities. An organization achieves its own goals by satisfying customers. To make the marketing concept work, top management must accept it as an overall management philosophy. Implementing the marketing concept always requires an efficient information system and sometimes the restructuring of the organization.

Strategic marketing management attempts to facilitate and expedite exchanges effectively and efficiently. Marketing managers focus on several generic marketing management tasks to achieve set objectives. These generic marketing management tasks are (1) market opportunity analysis, (2) target market selection, (3) marketing mix development, and (4) management of marketing activities.

Conducting a market opportunity analysis involves reviewing several organizational factors to identify internal characteristics. Primary factors that need consideration are organizational objectives, financial resources, managerial skills, organizational strengths, organizational weaknesses, and cost structures. In addition to performing an internal evaluation, the marketing manager needs to be aware of environmental forces. The marketing environment variables include political, legal, regulatory, societal, economic and competitive, and technological forces. The forces in the marketing environment affect a manager's strategic decisions in general ways. The environmental forces affect consumers' wants and needs, buyer reactions to the firm's marketing mix, and the extent to which a marketing manager can perform certain marketing activities. Marketers must recognize that dynamic environmental forces can create marketing opportunities as well as problems. They must be able to adjust marketing strategies to the rapid changes in the environment.

The development of a marketing strategy encompasses two steps: (1) selecting and analyzing a target market and (2) creating and maintaining an appropriate marketing mix. Target market selection is not only the foundation on which a marketing mix is developed; it is crucial to productive marketing efforts. Cost/benefit analysis as well as determination of available resources can determine whether entrance into a particular target market is a feasible alternative. The four variables that make up the marketing mix are product, price, promotion, and distribution. These components can be altered as they are affected by fluctuating environmental variables. Marketers research consumer wants in their effort to create want-satisfying products. To achieve customer satisfaction, products must be made accessible at the right time and place in the quantities desired—the distribution variable. The promotion variable applies to informing the target group about an organization and its products. Because price is important to the consumer, it is a critical component of the marketing mix. Developing and maintaining an effective marketing mix is the basis for having a strong marketing strategy. Within limits, a marketing manager can alter marketing mix variables as consumers' preferences and needs change.

The marketing management process includes planning, organizing, implementing, and controlling marketing activities. This systematic process focuses on assessing opportunities and resources, setting goals and objectives, developing strategic and tactical marketing plans, and establishing steps for implementation and control. Planning determines when, how, and who is to perform marketing activities. Organizing deals with internal structure, which can be defined by function, product, region, or type of customers. Implementing the plans depends on the coordination of marketing activities, the motivation of marketing personnel, and communication flow. To maintain control, performance standards are set, and actual performance is evaluated against standards at regular intervals. Whatever difference exists between the two must be eliminated.

Important Terms

Marketing
Exchange
Product
Good
Service
Idea
Marketing concept
Production orientation
Sales orientation

Customer orientation
Marketing management
Marketing strategy
Marketing mix
Marketing environment
Political forces
Legal forces
Regulatory forces
Societal forces

Economic forces
Technological forces
Target market
Product variable

Distribution variable
Promotion variable
Price variable

1. In what important ways does the definition of marketing used in this text differ from the other definitions given? How did you define marketing before you read this chapter?
2. Why should someone study marketing?
3. Discuss the basic elements of the marketing concept. Which businesses in your area employ this concept? In your opinion, have these businesses adopted the marketing concept? Why or why not?
4. Identify several business organizations in your area that obviously have not adopted the marketing concept. What characteristics of these organizations indicate nonacceptance of the marketing concept?
5. Describe the major components of a marketing strategy. What is the relationship among the components?
6. Identify the generic marketing management tasks.
7. What are the primary issues that marketing managers consider when doing a market opportunity analysis?
8. What are the variables in the marketing environment? How much control does a marketing manager have over environmental variables?
9. Why is the selection of a target market such an important issue?
10. Why are the elements of the marketing mix known as variables?
11. What types of management activities are involved in the process of marketing management?
12. What is the relationship between a marketing strategy and the generic marketing management tasks?

Cases

Case 1.1 Levi Strauss & Co. Introduces Women's 501® Jeans[15]

Levi Strauss & Co.'s Womenswear Division markets several lines of casual sportswear, including jeans, slacks, knit and woven tops, blazers, and skirts. Although new products are continuously being introduced by Levi Strauss & Co., the recent introduction of the Women's 501® jeans was particularly successful.

The marketing strategy for the new product launch was based on studies identifying two consumer clusters as primary targets. The first consumer group consisted of women whose median age was 25, who had sophisticated tastes and were appreciative of the latest styles, and who had progressive lifestyles and a high degree of brand consciousness. The second group consisted of women whose median age was 28, who followed a traditional lifestyle, and who preferred practical clothes. Research showed that the product attributes most important to these two consumer groups were quality, value, comfort, and fit.

The product was a new version of the original Levi's® jeans that set apparel

15. Many of the facts in this case are based on the *1982 Levi Strauss & Co. Annual Report.*

standards for gold-seeking forty-niners more than 100 years ago. The new garment retains all features of the original, including copper rivets on the front pockets, metal buttons on the fly, and the all-cotton denim fabric that in three washings shrinks to fit individual body contours. With additional washings the 501® jean becomes lighter in color, softer and more comfortable, yet retains its durability.

In contrast with the general practice of advertising after product distribution was completed, "consumer-pull" advertising and intense promotion stimulated distribution. Good communication with retailers also facilitated distribution. For example, although quality and value were inherent in the product, fit testing needed to be more rigorous than usual because a garment designed for the male figure was being converted for women. Since the product actually does "shrink when washed," the consumer education program was also more intensive than usual, with much of the information based on advance interviews with major retailers.

Promotional references to the company's origin and the aura surrounding the Old West were strong selling features. The advertising—"designed to create a sensation"—did. Most memorable was a TV commercial which featured an attractive, self-assured young woman in 501® jeans. Photographed against a backdrop of stark Texas countryside, she says only six words: "Travis, you're a year too late!" This cryptic statement generated such intense public interest that it proliferated dramatically through word-of-mouth and frequent editorial mentions. Letters and phone calls inquiring about the identity of Travis deluged the company.

The Levi image was maintained in competitive pricing to provide an image of quality, durability, and good value for the money. The Women's 501® jeans rapidly became a new product success, with first-year shipments more than doubling optimistic projections. The successful promotional efforts for the Women's 501® also generated renewed interest in the entire women's denim line. Individuals closely involved in the product's inception say that the launch was outstanding because of superb teamwork by all involved.

Questions for Discussion

1. How did Levi Strauss & Co. make the marketing concept work in launching Women's 501® jeans?
2. Define the target market and marketing mix used in the Levi's® Women's 501® jeans marketing strategy.
3. Why do you think that a contemporary product that was physically similar to the 100-year-old original Levi's® jeans was so successful?

Case 1.2 Pillsbury Restaurants[16]

The Pillsbury Company is a diversified international food company operating in three major segments of the food industry: consumer foods, restaurants, and agriproducts. Included in the area of consumer foods is the entire line of Pillsbury brand products, Green Giant vegetables, and Häagen-Dazs ice cream. Pillsbury's restaurant group includes Steak and Ale, Bennigans Tavern and

16. Facts in this case are from the *Pillsbury 1983 Annual Report.*

Restaurant, and Burger King. The agriproducts division is involved with grain merchandising and the production of industrial foods such as flour and bakery products.

Pillsbury's restaurants prospered in the early 1980s. Steak and Ale, for instance, experienced a 22-percent sales increase in 1982. Management programs focused on maintaining continued sales growth. New menu items were added to satisfy continuing customer demand for quality and variety, and wine sales were strongly promoted, with an emphasis on premium brands. New television advertising was developed featuring "lifestyle" themes. Sixty-two restaurants were remodeled and 22 were sold as part of an ongoing asset-management program. High-potential locations, in terms of sales and returns on investment, were identified for expansion of the chain.

Bennigans restaurants experienced a 65-percent rate of expansion with 43 new restaurant openings last year. This rapid expansion was achieved through high-quality site selection and the recruiting and training of management personnel. Both television and radio advertising were used to support sales. A major feature of Bennigans was its broad menu that emphasized price and value. Menu changes were made continuously to ensure satisfaction of consumers' evolving needs. Bennigans successfully promoted the celebration of certain holidays (for example, Halloween) to increase patronage.

Burger King, promoted as a high-quality fast-food restaurant chain, attained a 19-percent sales increase in 1982. During that year, Pillsbury opened 270 new restaurants, achieving a worldwide total of 3,502. Burger King franchises were responsible for 227 of the 270 new restaurant openings, which demonstrates the company's strong support of the franchise system. New restaurants were smaller, to take advantage of current demographic and economic trends, and required fewer operators and less construction time. Yet they could produce yearly sales of $1 million per unit and could be expanded as increased sales warranted.

Television advertising increased sales and awareness of Burger King restaurants. The company distributed coupons that made a free Whopper available when a customer purchased one and said, "The Whopper beat the Big Mac." Many restaurants reported 100-percent increases in sales due to this promotion.

New product introductions also helped sales. The Bacon Double Cheeseburger, the Whopper, and the 23-item salad bar were offered as new menu alternatives. Emphasis also was placed on operating excellence, with Burger King's "Shape-Up" program concentrating on new standards of quality, training, and service.

While Burger King has maintained a highly successful domestic concept, its international operations have produced substantial operating losses. Executive management is concentrating on transferring to Canada and other international markets basic marketing, operations, franchising, and financial strategies that have proved successful in the United States.

Questions for Discussion

1. Has Pillsbury been practicing the marketing concept?
2. What societal or economic trends may have caused Pillsbury to sell some restaurants—such as Poppin' Fresh, featuring desserts and sandwiches—and expand others, such as Burger King?
3. Identify the differences in the target market for Burger King versus Bennigans.

2 / The Marketing Environment

Objectives

- ■ To understand the importance of environmental scanning and analysis.

- ■ To identify the types of political forces in the marketing environment.

- ■ To understand the influence of laws and their interpretation on marketing practices.

- ■ To determine how government regulations and self-regulatory agencies affect marketing activities.

- ■ To identify social and ethical issues that marketers must deal with as they make decisions.

- ■ To identify the tools by which firms compete.

- ■ To understand how economic and competitive factors affect organizations' abilities to compete and customers' buying power and willingness to spend.

- ■ To explore the effects of technological knowledge on society.

- ■ To understand how technology can influence marketing activities.

Figure 2.1

Promotion of AT&T products (Source: © AT&T 1984. UNIX is a trademark of AT&T)

The dissolution of the mammoth Bell System left AT&T with mounting headaches: increased competition from rival long-distance services, shortages of certain products, and a $1.1 billion shortfall in projected annual new earnings. To counterbalance lost market shares, AT&T decided to seek increased sales growth in several areas, including automated office equipment.

Unfortunately, AT&T's plunge into the business computer waters amounted to a painful bellyflop. The first year after divestiture, AT&T introduced the PC 6300 microcomputer but sold only 30,000 units. That same year IBM sold 1.5 million personal computers. AT&T's 3B series of minicomputers fared even worse. The minis were built with outdated technology, could not communicate with IBM mainframes (which house most corporations' computing instructions and financial information), and used UNIX, an operating system that could not run the applications software familiar to most business customers and available on other microcomputers.

After its painful bellyflop, AT&T created a new marketing strategy that highlights the corporation's major strength: communications. AT&T leads the market in simultaneous voice and data communications and in long-distance communications. With UNIX, developed by AT&T's own Bell Labs, the company also has the technology to move computing jobs from mainframes to smaller computers. So AT&T is stressing these combined capabilities. Instead of representing its systems as general-

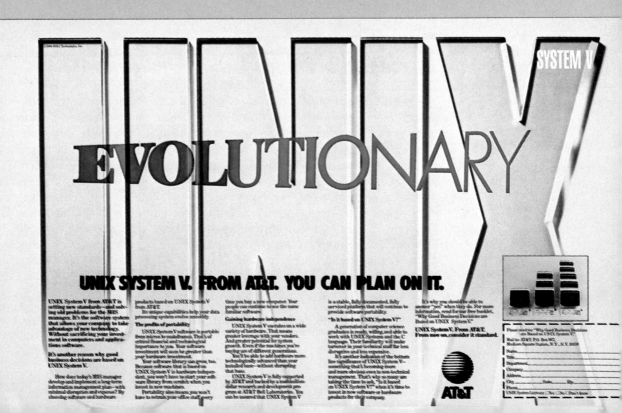

purpose tools, it is marketing them as instruments of superior communications and integration.

AT&T feels the key to success in the computer market is effective communications, both among the smaller computers and between those units and the mainframes within a company. IBM is weakest at precisely this point: distributed data processing. AT&T's emphasis on the integrative potential of UNIX in this arena has already brought success in approaching large accounts. However, although this new strategy seems promising, AT&T marketers must wait to see if further strategic shifts are needed.

AT&T has been forced to cope with several unfavorable marketing environment forces over the last few years. Deregulation of the telecommunications industry and adverse court decisions forced a major internal reorganization of the corporation. Deregulation and rapidly advancing technology led to the development of numerous new competitors who exerted major pressures. In addition, general U.S. economic conditions have not been favorable.

Initially, in this chapter we consider why it is critical to scan and analyze the environment. Next, we discuss political forces, which provide the foundation for government actions that influence marketing activities. Then we consider the effects of laws and regulatory actions on marketing activities. Next we describe the general societal forces in the marketing environment and focus on some of the social and ethical issues facing marketers. Then we explore several types of economic forces that influence firms' abilities to compete and consumers' willingness and ability to buy. We also consider the effects of general economic conditions—prosperity, recession, depression, and recovery. Finally, we analyze the major dimensions of the technological forces in the environment.

Examining and Dealing with the Marketing Environment

The **marketing environment** consists of external forces that directly or indirectly influence an organization's acquisition of inputs and generation of outputs. Examples of inputs include skilled personnel, financial resources, raw materials, and information. The outputs could be information (such as advertisements), packages, goods, services, or ideas. As indicated in Chapter 1 and as shown in Figure 1.8, we view the marketing environment as consisting of six categories of forces: political, legal, regulatory, societal, economic and competitive, and technological. Although there are numerous environmental factors, most fall into one of these six categories. Whether they fluctuate rapidly or slowly, environmental forces are always dynamic. For an organization, the changes in the marketing environment create uncertainty, threats, and opportunities. Marketing managers who fail to recognize environmental changes leave their

1. "The New AT&T Struggles to Get to Its Feet," *Business Week,* Dec. 3, 1984, pp. 92–100; "AT&T Makes a Second Stab at the Computer Market," *Business Week,* April 1, 1985, p. 92; and "It's IBM vs. AT&T in a Clash of the Titans," *U.S. News & World Report,* June 10, 1985, pp. 86–88.

organizations unprepared to capitalize on marketing opportunities or to cope with adverse environmental pressures. The inability to cope with an unfavorable environment can result in an organization's demise. Thus, monitoring the marketing environment is crucial to an organization's survival and to the long-term achievement of its goals.

Environmental Scanning and Analysis

To monitor changes in the marketing environment effectively, marketers must engage in environmental scanning and analysis. **Environmental scanning** is the collection of information regarding the forces in the marketing environment. Scanning involves observation; perusal of secondary sources such as business, trade, and government publications; and marketing research efforts. It is important to gather useful information on the environment. However, managers must be careful not to gather so much information that sheer volume makes analysis impossible.

Environmental analysis is the process of assessing and interpreting the information gathered through scanning. A manager evaluates the information for accuracy, tries to resolve inconsistencies in the data, and assigns significance to the findings, if warranted. Through analysis, a marketing manager attempts to define current environmental changes and, if possible, to predict future changes. By evaluating these changes, a marketing manager should be able to determine possible threats and opportunities associated with environmental fluctuations. Knowledge of current and predicted environmental changes aids a marketing manager in assessing the performance of current marketing efforts and in developing marketing strategies for the future.

Responding to Environmental Forces

There are two general approaches that marketing managers can employ when responding to environmental forces. One approach views environmental forces as totally uncontrollable and difficult to predict and the organization as passive and reactive toward the environment. In this approach, the organization does not try to influence forces in the marketing environment. Marketing managers attempt to adjust current marketing strategies to changes in the environment, and market opportunities discovered through environmental scanning and analysis are approached cautiously.

A second approach is to take an aggressive stance toward environmental forces.[2] Rather than viewing forces in the environment as totally uncontrollable, a practitioner of this proactive approach attempts to influence and shape environmental forces. For example, a firm might lobby lawmakers to try to ensure that the provisions of a bill will be consistent with the firm's interests. Similarly, the advertisement in Figure 2.2, sponsored by two insurance trade organizations, encourages citizens to write to lawmakers about the proposed tax on insurance accumulations.

Management may try to influence environmental forces so as to create market opportunities or to extract greater benefits relative to costs from existing market opportunities. When using this approach, managers must recognize that there are limits on how much an environmental force can be influenced and

2. Carl P. Zeithaml and Valarie A. Zeithaml, "Environmental Management: Revising the Marketing Perspective," *Journal of Marketing,* Spring 1984, pp. 46–53.

Figure 2.2

Message encouraging
citizens to take action
(Source: American Council
of Life Insurance and
Health Insurance Associa-
tion of America)

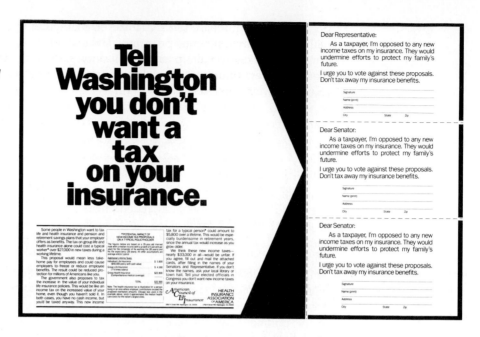

that these limits vary across environmental forces. For example, while an organization may be able to influence the shape of legislation through lobbying, it is quite unlikely that a single organization can significantly increase the national birthrate or move the economy from recession to prosperity!

We cannot generalize and say that one of these approaches to environmental response is superior to the other. For some organizations, the passive, reactive approach is most appropriate, while for other firms the aggressive approach leads to better performance. The selection of a particular approach is affected by an organization's managerial philosophies, objectives, financial resources, markets, and human skills and by the composition of the set of environmental forces within which the organization operates.

Politics and the Marketing Environment

Political and legal forces are closely interrelated aspects of the marketing environment. Legislation is enacted, legal decisions are interpreted by the courts, and regulatory agencies are created and operated, for the most part, by persons who occupy government positions.

When political officials have positive feelings toward particular firms or industries, they are less likely to create or enforce laws and regulations that are unfavorable to those business organizations. For example, political officials who believe that oil companies are making honest efforts to control pollution are not likely to create and enforce highly restrictive pollution control laws. There is another reason why business organizations need to be concerned about making a favorable impression on political officials. As we point out in Chapter 3, governments are big buyers, and people who hold political office can influence how much a government purchases and from whom. Still another reason to seek political favor is that political officials can play key roles in helping organizations secure foreign markets.

Many marketers view political forces as beyond their control; therefore, they simply try to adjust to conditions that arise from those forces. However, some firms attempt to influence political events by helping to elect certain individuals to political offices. Much of this help is in the form of campaign contributions. Although laws restrict direct corporate contributions to campaign funds, corporate money is channeled into campaign funds as personal contributions of corporate executives or stockholders. Not only do such actions violate the spirit of the corporate campaign contribution laws, but they are also unethical. A sizable contribution to a campaign fund may carry with it an implicit understanding that the elected official will perform "political favors" for the contributing firm.

It is not unusual for a corporation to make contributions to the campaign funds of several candidates who seek the same position. Occasionally, it is so important to ensure favorable treatment that certain businesses make direct illegal corporate contributions to campaign funds. Indeed, a former official of American Airlines admitted that the firm illegally contributed $55,000 from corporate funds, not to purchase political favors, but because executives feared what might happen if a contribution were not made. Governments can and do take actions aimed at specific industries or companies. However, many markets concern themselves with the political environment primarily because of its strong influence on the legal forces with which they must deal.

Laws and Their Interpretation

Since the passage of the landmark Sherman Act in 1890, a number of laws have been enacted that influence marketing decisions and activities. These laws affect pricing, advertising, personal selling, distribution, product development, and product warranty and repair policies. For purposes of analysis, laws that directly affect marketing practices can be divided into two categories: (1) procompetitive legislation and (2) consumer protection laws.

Procompetitive Legislation

Table 2.1 briefly describes several major procompetitive laws. **Procompetitive legislation** is enacted to preserve competition. As the Industrial Revolution gained momentum in the mid-1800s, many people were fascinated by new production techniques, the introduction of mass production, and the use of new equipment driven by new sources of power. Although the Industrial Revolution and the rapid growth in business enterprises may have had some beneficial effects on society in the long run, these changes were often devastating to individuals. Masses of workers toiled long, hard hours for little money under bad working conditions, while a few industrialists amassed tremendous wealth. Eventually, public resentment in the United States became so strong that the Sherman Act was passed.

The Sherman Act

The **Sherman Act** was passed in 1890 to prevent businesses from restraining trade and monopolizing markets. Section 1 of the act condemns "every contract,

Table 2.1 *Major federal procompetitive laws affecting marketing decisions*

Act	Purposes
Sherman Act (1890)	Prohibits contracts, combinations, or conspiracies to restrain trade; establishes as a misdemeanor monopolizing or attempting to monopolize
Clayton Act (1914)	Prohibits specific practices such as price discrimination, exclusive dealer arrangements, and stock acquisitions in which the effect may substantially lessen competition or tend to create a monopoly
Federal Trade Commission Act (1914)	Created the Federal Trade Commission; gives the FTC investigatory powers to be used in preventing unfair methods of competition
Robinson-Patman Act (1936)	Prohibits price discrimination that lessens competition among wholesalers or retailers; prohibits producers from giving disproportionate services or facilities to large buyers
Wheeler-Lea Act (1938)	Prohibits unfair and deceptive acts and practices regardless of whether competition is injured; places advertising of foods and drugs under the jurisdiction of the FTC
Celler-Kefauver Act (1950)	Prohibits any corporation engaged in commerce from acquiring the whole or any part of the stock or other share of the capital or assets of another corporation when the effect substantially lessens competition or tends to create a monopoly
Consumer Goods Pricing Act (1975)	Prohibits the use of price maintenance agreements among manufacturers and resellers in interstate commerce
Trademark Counterfeiting Act (1980)	Provides civil and criminal penalties against those who deal in counterfeit consumer goods or any counterfeit goods that can threaten health or safety

combination, or conspiracy in restraint of trade." Section 2 prohibits monopolizing or attempting to monopolize. Enforced by the Antitrust Division of the Department of Justice, the Sherman Act applies to firms operating in interstate commerce and to U.S. firms operating in foreign commerce.

The Clayton Act

The Sherman Act was written in general terms, and the courts have not always interpreted it as its creators intended. For this reason, the second major pro-competitive act, the **Clayton Act,** was passed in 1914. The Clayton Act prohibits price discrimination (section 2), tying and exclusive agreements (section 3), and the acquisition of stock in another corporation (section 7) "where the effect may be to substantially lessen competition or tend to create a monopoly." In addition, interlocking directorates are deemed unlawful under section 8. Sections 6 and 20 exempt farm cooperatives and labor organizations from antitrust laws.

The Federal Trade Commission Act and the Wheeler-Lea Amendment

The Federal Trade Commission, established by the **Federal Trade Commission Act** (1914), today regulates the greatest number of marketing practices. Like the Clayton Act, the FTC Act was written to strengthen antimonopoly provisions of the Sherman Act. Whereas the Clayton Act prohibits specific practices, the FTC Act more broadly prohibits unfair methods of competition. This act also empowers the FTC to work with the Department of Justice to enforce the provisions of the Clayton Act. Later sections of this chapter discuss the FTC's regulatory activities.

The creators of the FTC Act, like the authors of the Sherman Act, found that the courts did not always interpret it as they had intended. In the Raladam case (1931) the Supreme Court held that a producer's misrepresentation of an obesity cure was not an unfair method of competition because the firm's action did not injure competition.[3] This ruling—among others—spurred Congress in 1938 to enact the **Wheeler-Lea Act,** which amended section 5 of the FTC Act. Essentially, the Wheeler-Lea Act makes unfair and deceptive acts or practices unlawful, regardless of whether or not they injure competition. It specifically prohibits false advertising of foods, drugs, therapeutic devices, and cosmetics and provides penalties for violations and procedures for enforcement. "False advertising" means an advertisement, other than labeling, that is misleading in any respect.

The Robinson-Patman Act

During the early 1930s, when the Depression was at its peak, the FTC was alarmed by the buying practices and lower prices of some chain stores. The commission reported to the Senate that many of the low prices that suppliers offered to chains could not be justified on the basis of cost savings arising from quantity purchases. Eventually, after several years of economic hardship, pressure from the FTC and popular political support for further legislation led to the enactment of the Robinson-Patman Act in 1936.

The **Robinson-Patman Act** is significant because it directly influences pricing policies. The major provisions of the Robinson-Patman Act include the following:

1. Price discrimination among different purchasers of commodities of like grade and quality is prohibited if the effect of such discrimination may lessen competition substantially or tend to create a monopoly.

---

3. *Federal Trade Commission* v. *Raladam Company,* 283 U.S. 643, 1931.

2. Price differentials are legal if they can be justified as cost savings or as meeting competition in good faith. Price differentials per se are not illegal.
3. Paying, receiving, or accepting anything of value as a commission, brokerage, or other compensation—except for actual services rendered—is prohibited.
4. It is unlawful to knowingly induce or receive discriminatory prices when prohibited by this law.
5. The furnishing of services or facilities to purchasers upon terms not accorded to all purchasers on proportionately equal terms is illegal.[4]

The Robinson-Patman Act deals only with discriminatory price differentials. Price differentials become discriminatory when one reseller, who is competing against other resellers, can acquire similar quantities of commodities of like grade and quality at lower prices than can other purchasers dealing with the same supplier. Such price differentials give that reseller an unfair advantage in the market.

Consumer Protection Legislation

The second category of regulatory laws, **consumer protection legislation,** is not a recent development. During the mid-1800s, lawmakers in many states enacted laws to prohibit the adulteration of food and drugs. However, consumer protection laws at the federal level mushroomed in the mid-1960s and early 1970s. A number of the federal laws are designed to provide consumer safety. For example, the food and drug acts, the flammable fabric law, the child protection acts, and the product safety law were enacted to protect people from actual and potential physical injuries.

To help buyers become better informed, Congress has passed several laws concerning the disclosure of information. Some laws deal with information about specific products such as textiles, furs, cigarettes, and automobiles. Others focus on particular marketing activities—product development and testing, packaging, labeling, advertising, and consumer financing, for example.

Interpreting Laws

Many laws have the potential to influence marketing activities, but their actual effects are determined by the interpretations of marketers and the courts. At first glance, laws seem to be quite specific because they contain many complex clauses and subclauses. In reality, however, many laws and regulations are stated in vague terms that force marketers to rely on legal counsel rather than their own understanding and common sense. Because of this vagueness, an organization may operate in a legally questionable way to see how much it can get away with before it is prosecuted under the law. On the other hand, some marketers interpret regulations and statutes very conservatively to avoid violating a vague law.

When firms are charged with violations, the courts must interpret the law. Although the provisions of existing laws do not change over the years, court interpretations do. Businesses—and lawyers—have often asked, "What constitutes a monopoly?" The Sherman Act remains the same, but the judicial answer to the question, in the form of court rulings, has changed radically over the years.

4. E. T. Grether, *Marketing and Public Policy* (Englewood Cliffs, N.J.: Prentice-Hall, 1966), pp. 60–61. Used by permission of the author.

Although court rulings have a direct effect on businesses that are being tried for violations, they also have broader, less direct effects on other businesses. When marketers try to interpret laws in relation to specific marketing practices, they often analyze recent court decisions. By being aware of current court interpretations, marketers acquire a better understanding of what the law is intended to do and how the courts are likely to interpret the law in the future.

Regulatory Forces

Interpretation alone does not determine the effectiveness of laws. The level of enforcement by regulatory agencies significantly influences a law's effectiveness. Some regulatory agencies are created and administered by government units; others are sponsored by nongovernmental sources. Here we first discuss federal, state, and local government regulatory units. Then we examine the forces of self-regulation.

Federal Regulatory Agencies

Federal agencies influence many marketing activities, including product development, pricing, packaging, advertising, personal selling, distribution, and storage.

Regulatory units usually have the power to enforce specific laws, as well as some discretion in establishing operating rules and drawing up regulations to guide certain types of industry practices. Because of this discretion and overlapping areas of responsibility, confusion or conflict as to which agencies have jurisdiction over specific types of marketing activities is not uncommon.

In recent years the federal government has attempted to deregulate some industries. Airline routes and fares are one well-known example. The Treasury Department, in accordance with President Reagan's policies, is eager to dismantle its programs to regulate alcoholic beverage advertising and trade practices. However, the alcoholic beverage industry seems to prefer the regulations. Industry executives claim that only full-time specialists, such as those at the Treasury's Bureau of Alcohol, Tobacco, and Firearms, are capable of understanding their problems.[5]

The Federal Trade Commission (FTC)

Of all the federal regulatory units, the Federal Trade Commission has the broadest powers to influence marketing activities. The **Federal Trade Commission** consists of five commissioners, each appointed for a term of seven years by the president of the United States with the consent of the Senate. Not more than three commissioners may be members of the same political party. Their terms of office are staggered to ensure continuity of experience in the judgment of cases. The FTC has many administrative duties under existing laws, but the policy underlying all of them is the same: "To prevent the free enterprise system from being stifled or fettered by monopoly or anti-competitive practices and to provide the direct protection of consumers from unfair or deceptive trade practices."[6]

5. "Liquor Ad Rules: Regulation Hangover," *Advertising Age,* Nov. 23, 1981, p. 18.
6. "Your Federal Trade Commission" (Washington, D.C.: Federal Trade Commission, 1977), pp. 8–9.

One major function of the FTC is to enforce laws and regulatory guidelines falling under its jurisdiction. When it has reason to believe that a firm is violating a law, the commission issues a complaint stating that the business is in violation. If the company continues the questionable practice, the FTC can issue a cease and desist order, which is simply an order for the business to stop doing whatever caused the complaint in the first place. The firm can appeal to the federal courts to have the FTC order rescinded. The FTC itself has no direct power or authority to imprison or fine. However, provisions added to the Trans-Alaska Pipeline Act of 1973 empowered the FTC to seek civil penalties in the courts. Before passage of the Trans-Alaska Pipeline Act, the FTC had to seek action indirectly through the Justice Department. The maximum penalty is $10,000 a day for each violation if a cease and desist order is violated; previously, the maximum was $5,000 per day. In addition, the amendment allows the FTC to obtain preliminary injunctions or temporary restraining orders to stop firms from engaging in deceptive or unfair practices.

The FTC is obligated to provide assistance and information to businesses so that they will know how to comply with laws. Because marketing is continuously changing, many new marketing methods are evaluated every year. As new commissioners are appointed and as other personnel changes occur, FTC decisions as to what is legal and what is not also change. Although the FTC is intended to be a law enforcement agency, its broad powers allow commissioners and lawyers not only to prosecute through the courts but also to explain to businesses what is considered to be unfair, deceptive, or illegal. The FTC also investigates industry trade practices. When general sets of guidelines are needed to improve business practices in a particular industry, the FTC sometimes encourages the firms in that industry to establish a set of trade practices voluntarily. The FTC may even sponsor a conference to bring industry leaders and consumers together for this purpose. Although the FTC regulates a variety of business practices, it allocates a large portion of its resources to curbing false advertising, misleading pricing, and deceptive packaging and labeling.

Other Federal Regulatory Units

The FTC has broad powers to regulate a variety of business practices. The powers of other regulatory units are limited to specific products, services, or business activities. For example, the Federal Communications Commission (FCC) licenses radio and television stations and develops and enforces regulations regarding their operations. In one case, the FCC revoked the license of WJIM-TV in Lansing, Michigan, for reasons of misrepresentation and fraud. Table 2.2 outlines the major areas of responsibility of several federal agencies.

As marketing activities become more complex, some of the responsibilities of federal units overlap. When authority over a specific product or marketing practice cannot be assigned to a single federal unit, marketers must try to comply with many different regulations.

State and Local Regulatory Agencies

All states—as well as numerous towns and cities—have agencies that enforce laws and rules regarding marketing practices. State and local regulatory agencies try hard not to establish and enforce regulations that conflict with the actions of national regulatory agencies. State and local agencies enforce specific laws dealing with the production and/or sale of particular goods and services.

Table 2.2 Major federal regulatory agencies

Agency	Major Areas of Responsibility
Federal Trade Commission (FTC)	Enforces laws and guidelines regarding business practices; takes action to stop false and deceptive advertising and labeling
Food and Drug Administration (FDA)	Enforces laws and regulations to prevent distribution of adulterated or misbranded foods, drugs, medical devices, cosmetics, veterinary products, and particularly hazardous consumer products
Consumer Product Safety Commission	Ensures compliance with the Consumer Product Safety Act; protects the public from unreasonable risk of injury from any consumer product not covered by other regulatory agencies
Interstate Commerce Commission (ICC)	Regulates franchises, rates, and finances of interstate rail, bus, truck, and water carriers
Federal Communications Commission (FCC)	Regulates communication by wire, radio, and television in interstate and foreign commerce
Environmental Protection Agency (EPA)	Develops and enforces environmental protection standards and conducts research into the adverse effects of pollution
Federal Power Commission (FPC)	Regulates rates and sales of natural gas producers, thereby affecting the supply and price of gas available to consumers; also regulates wholesale rates for electricity and gas, pipeline construction, and U.S. imports and exports of natural gas and electricity

Industries that are commonly regulated by state agencies include banking, savings and loan, insurance, utilities, and liquor.

Nongovernmental Regulatory Forces

In the absence of governmental regulatory forces and in an attempt to prevent government intervention, some businesses try to regulate themselves. Trade associations in a number of industries have developed self-regulatory programs. Even though these programs are not a direct outgrowth of laws, many are established as an indirect result of legal action or proposed legislation. That is, numerous self-regulatory programs are created to stop or stall the development of laws and governmental regulatory groups that would regulate marketing practices. Sometimes, these programs deal with ethical and social issues. For example, many firms in the cigarette industry agreed, through a code of ethics, not to advertise cigarettes to children and teen-agers.

Self-regulatory programs offer several advantages over governmental laws and guidelines. They are usually less expensive to establish and implement, at least in comparison to government programs, and their guidelines are generally more realistic and operational. In addition, industry self-regulatory programs reduce the need to expand government bureaucracy.

Nongovernmental self-regulatory programs do have some limitations. When a trade association creates a set of industry guidelines, nonmember firms do not have to follow the guidelines. Many self-regulatory programs lack the tools or the authority to enforce guidelines. Finally, guidelines in self-regulatory programs often are less strict than those established by government agencies.

Better Business Bureaus

The **Better Business Bureau** is perhaps the best-known nongovernmental regulatory group. It is a local regulatory agency that is supported by local businesses. Today there are over 140 bureaus that help settle problems between consumers and specific business firms. They also act to preserve good business practices in a locality, although they usually do not have strong enforcement tools to use in dealing with firms that employ questionable practices. When a firm continues to violate what the Better Business Bureau believes to be good business practices, the bureau warns consumers through local newspapers that a particular business is operating unfairly.

National Advertising Review Board

The Council of Better Business Bureaus, a national organization, and three advertising trade organizations have created a self-regulatory unit called the **National Advertising Review Board.** In addition to screening national advertisements to check for honesty, the NARB processes complaints about deceptive advertisements. The National Advertising Division (NAD) of the Council of Better Business Bureaus serves as the investigative arm of the NARB. The following describes a typical case handled by NAD/NARB:

> A spaghetti sauce, made to be extra thick, was demonstrated alongside a competitor's regular spaghetti sauce by pouring them through kitchen strainers. The NAD found that this was misleading because the competition also made extra thick sauce under the same brand name, a fact not disclosed in the advertising.[7]

The NARB has no official enforcement powers. However, if a firm refuses to comply with its decision, the NARB publicizes the questionable practice and files a complaint with the FTC.

Societal Forces

Societal forces comprise the structure and dynamics of individuals and groups and the issues with which they are concerned. The public raises questions about the activities of marketers when the consequences of those activities are felt to be inconsistent with the goals of individuals or of society in general. Even when marketers do a good job of satisfying society, letters of praise or positive evaluation rarely follow. Society expects marketers to provide a high

7. Report of NARB Panel #34, p. 4.

standard of living and to protect the general quality of life that we enjoy. In this section, we examine some of society's expectations, the vehicles used to express those expectations, and the problems and opportunities that marketers experience as they try to deal with society's often contradictory wishes.

Living Standards and Quality of Life

In our society, we want much more than just the bare necessities required to sustain life—shelter, food, and clothing. Our homes, schools, factories, stores, and other buildings must provide not only protection from the elements but also comfort and aesthetic satisfaction. Our food must give us the nutrients necessary for life and good health, but almost all of us also want it to be readily available in large quantities, in wide varieties, and in easily prepared forms. We use our clothing to cover, protect, and warm our bodies, but most of us also think it necessary to provide ourselves with a variety of clothing for adornment and to project an "image" to others.

We have many other wants, too, beyond the necessities of life. We want vehicles that provide rapid, convenient, and efficient transportation when and where we want to go. We want communication systems that allow us to talk to anyone in the world and that quickly provide us with information from around the globe. We want sophisticated medical services that prolong our life span, make our lives more tolerable, and improve our physical appearance. And we expect our education to equip us both to acquire and to enjoy a higher standard of living.

Our society's high material standard of living is not enough. We also want a high degree of quality in our lives. We do not want to spend all our waking hours working. We seek leisure time for recreation, entertainment, amusement, and relaxation. Nor do we wish to spend our lives in a dirty environment. We cannot enjoy the benefits of a high living standard when the water is polluted with raw sewage and industrial wastes or when the air is full of smoke, foul odors, and loud noises. The quality of life is enhanced by leisure time, clean air and water, and unlittered earth, conservation of wildlife and natural resources, and security from radiation and poisonous substances.

Our society seeks a multitude of goods and services in addition to healthy environmental conditions. It expects business to provide many elements necessary to both a high standard of living and a satisfying quality of life. Since marketing activities are a vital part of the total business structure, marketers have a responsibility to help provide what societal members want and to minimize what they do not want.

Consumer Movement Forces

The **consumer movement** is a diverse group of independent individuals, groups, and organizations that attempts to protect the rights of consumers. The major issues of the consumer movement fall into three categories: environmental protection, product performance and safety, and information disclosure. A recent study, for example, reported that consumers are seeking simpler, gentler, and safer health and beauty aids such as analgesics and shampoos.[8] The major forces of the consumer movement are individual consumer advocates, consumer organizations, consumer education, and consumer laws. Consumer advocates,

8. Bill Abrams, "Hair Care Fears ... License Plates Locate Customers ... Sex and Sales," *Wall Street Journal,* Feb. 5, 1981, p. 29.

such as Ralph Nader, take it upon themselves to protect the rights of consumers. They inform and organize other consumers, help businesses develop consumer-oriented programs, and pressure lawmakers to enact consumer laws. More often, however, consumer advocates band together into consumer organizations, either voluntarily or under government sponsorship. Some organizations operate nationally, while others are active at state and local levels.

Consumer organizations aid the consumer movement by encouraging consumers to get involved, advising and pressuring legislators to pass stronger consumer laws, encouraging enforcement of existing consumer laws, and establishing consumer education programs. Educating consumers to make wiser purchasing decisions will perhaps be one of the most far-reaching aspects of the consumer movement. Consumer education is increasingly becoming a part of high school and college curricula and adult education programs.

Ethical Issues and Social Responsibility

The advertisement in Figure 2.3 reflects an organization's desire to behave in a socially responsible manner. R. J. Reynolds Tobacco Company is encouraging young people to not smoke.

The changing values of society have placed more pressure on marketers to act responsibly and ethically. Such issues as racial injustice, malnutrition, human rights, poverty, and unethical marketing behavior have increased public concern about the role of marketing in society. Payoffs, bribes, and coverups of defective products have eroded public confidence in marketers.

For an organization to behave ethically, it must be guided by decision makers who make ethical decisions. Trying to define an ethical decision precisely is difficult. However, a manager can raise several questions when assessing the ethics of a decision or action. Will anyone be deceived? Will human or property rights be violated? Will some people benefit at the expense of others? Will elements in the natural or civic environment be damaged? Other questions may also need to be raised.

The factors that affect people's propensity to make ethical or unethical decisions are not fully understood. There is speculation that three general sets of factors influence the ethics of one's decisions.[9] First, individual factors such as values, knowledge, attitudes, and intentions are believed to influence a person's decisions. Second, opportunity resulting from the absence of professional codes of ethics, corporate policies regarding ethics, or punishment may encourage unethical decision making. Third, the values, attitudes, and behavior of significant others such as peers, supervisors, and top management affect the ethics of one's decisions.

Society does not want products that are faulty or unsafe. It does not want product warranties that are misleading or that are not backed up by sellers. It does not want durable goods for which replacement parts and repair services cannot be obtained easily. Deceptive packages that are misleading in terms of quantity, size, color, shape, or uses of products are also undesirable, as are labels that inaccurately describe or fail to describe the contents of products. Nor does society want deceptive advertisements that cause consumers to spend money unwisely and to lose confidence in advertising generally; equally objec-

9. O. C. Ferrell and Larry G. Gresham, "A Contingency Framework for Understanding Ethical Decision-Making in Marketing," *Journal of Marketing,* Summer 1985, pp. 87–96.

Does smoking really make you look more grown up?

It's a crazy world.

Most adults we know would love to look younger than they really are. While most young people are busy trying to look more adult.

This is one reason why many young people take up smoking.

Well, we wish they wouldn't.

For one thing, it doesn't work. A fifteen-year-old smoking a cigarette looks like nothing more or less than a fifteen-year-old smoking a cigarette.

Even though we're a tobacco company, we don't think young people should smoke. There is plenty of time later on to think about whether or not smoking is right for you.

Besides, when you think about it, being grown up is highly overrated. You have to go to work, pay taxes, wear normal clothes and raise kids who grow up to be teenagers.

Why be in such a hurry?

R.J. Reynolds Tobacco Company

tionable are deceptive selling practices, including dishonest personal selling techniques, unfair consumer contests, and deceptive premium offers. And because prices to some degree determine how far people can stretch their dollars, consumers do not want to be abused by misleading or exploitative prices that yield excessive profits to sellers. In addition to all of these constraints on the marketing mix variables, products or packages that increase problems of pollution, litter, or solid waste disposal are undesirable.

Some firms are recognizing that ethical issues and social responsibility find their expression in the daily decisions of marketers rather than in abstract ideals. According to this view, to preserve their ethical and socially responsible behavior while they accomplish their goals, organizations must monitor changes and trends in society's values. Also, marketers must develop control procedures to ensure that a few unethical employees do not damage their company's relations with the public. An organization's top management must assume some responsibility for the ethical conduct of employees by establishing and enforcing policies.

Being socially responsible may be a noble and necessary endeavor, but it is not a simple one. To be socially responsible, marketers must confront certain major problems. They must determine what society wants and then predict the long-run effects of their decisions, often by turning to specialists such as lawyers, doctors, and scientists. However, specialists do not necessarily agree with each other, and the fields in which they work can yield findings that undermine previously acceptable marketing decisions. Forty years ago, marketers promoted cigarettes as being good for one's health. Scientists had not yet discovered that cigarette smoking is linked to cancer. Since society is made up of many diverse groups, finding out what "society" as a whole wants is difficult, if not impossible. In trying to satisfy the desires of one group, marketers may dissatisfy others. Moreover, costs are associated with many of the demands of society. Marketers must evaluate the extent to which members of society are willing to pay for what they want. For example, consumers may desire more information regarding a product yet be unwilling to pay the costs that the firm sustains in providing it. Thus, marketers who want to make socially responsible decisions may find the task difficult.

Economic and Competitive Forces

The economic and competitive forces in the marketing environment influence both marketers' and customers' decisions and activities. Here we will explore the effects of broad economic and competitive forces, specifically, competition, buying power, willingness to spend, spending patterns, and general economic conditions.

Assessment of Competitive Forces

Few firms, if any, operate free of competition. Broadly speaking, all firms compete with each other for the buying power of consumers. From a more practical viewpoint, however, a business generally views as **competition** those firms that market products similar to, or substitutable for, its products in the same geographic area. For example, a local supermarket manager views all grocery stores in town as competitors but almost never thinks of all other local or out-of-town stores as competitors. Several factors affect the strength—and thus the importance—of the competitive forces acting on a firm. Let us explore a few of them.

Types of Competitive Structures

The number of firms that control the supply of a product may affect the strength of competition. When only one or a few firms control supply, competitive factors will exert a different sort of influence on marketing activities than when there are many competitors. Table 2.3 presents four general categories or models of competitive relationships.

A **monopoly** exists when a firm produces a product that has no close substitutes. The organization has complete control over the supply of the product. In this case, a single seller can erect barriers to potential competitors.

Table 2.3 Selected characteristics of competitive structures

Type of Structure	Number of Competitors	Ease of Entry into Market	Product	Knowledge of Market	Example
Monopoly	One	Many barriers	Almost no substitutes	Perfect	Dayton (Ohio) Power and Light (gas and electricity service)
Oligopoly	Few	Some barriers	Homogeneous or differentiated (real or perceived differences) products	Imperfect	Philip Morris (cigarettes)
Monopolistic competition	Many	Few barriers	Product differentiation with many substitutes	More knowledge than oligopoly; less than monopoly	Levi Strauss (jeans)
Perfect competition	Unlimited	No barriers	Homogeneous products	Perfect	Vegetable farm (sweet corn)

An **oligopoly** exists when a few sellers control the supply of a large proportion of a product. In this case, each seller must consider the reactions of other sellers to changes in marketing activities. Products facing oligopolistic competition may be homogeneous, such as aluminum, or differentiated, such as cigarettes and automobiles. There usually are some barriers that make it difficult to enter the market and compete with oligopolies. Few companies or individuals could enter the oil refining or steel industries, for example, because of the tremendous financial resources that are necessary. Moreover, some industries require special technical or marketing skills that block the entry of many potential competitors.

Monopolistic competition exists when a firm with many potential competitors attempts to develop a differential marketing strategy to establish its own market share. For example, Levi's has established a differential advantage for its jeans through a well-known trademark, design, advertising, and a quality image. Although many competing brands of jeans are available, this firm has carved out its market share through use of a differential marketing strategy.

Perfect competition, if it existed at all, would entail a large number of sellers, no one of which could significantly influence price or supply. Products would be homogeneous, and there would be full knowledge of the market and easy entry into it. The closest thing to an example of perfect competition would be an unregulated agricultural market.

Few, if any, marketers operate in a structure of perfect competition. Rather, perfect competition is an ideal at one end of the continuum, with monopoly at the other end. Most marketers function in a competitive environment that falls somewhere between these two extremes.

The Tools of Competition

Another set of factors that influences the level of competition is the number and types of competitive tools used by competitors. To survive, a firm uses one or several available competitive tools to deal with competitive economic forces. Once a firm has analyzed its particular competitive environment and decided which factors in that environment it can or must adjust to or influence, it can choose among the variables it can control to strengthen its competitive position.

Probably the first competitive tool that occurs to most of us is price. Recognizing this phenomenon, Bic produces disposable products that are similar to competing products but less expensive. There is, however, one major problem with using price as a competitive tool. Frequently competitors will either match or beat your price. This threat is one of the primary reasons for employing nonprice competitive tools that are based on the differentiation of market segments, product offering, promotion, distribution, or enterprise.[10] For example, Caterpillar charges at least 10 percent more than the competition for its earthmoving equipment, but its customers are willing to pay for a reliable product and the best parts and service system in the industry.

By focusing on a specific market segment, a marketer sometimes gains a competitive advantage. Timex is an example. One primary reason it gained a competitive advantage is that it concentrated its intial marketing efforts on a single market segment—people who wanted an inexpensive, durable watch that was reasonably accurate. Many marketers compete by differentiating their product offerings. Producers often attempt to gain a competitive edge by incorporating product features that make their brands, to some extent, distinctive. Stores sometimes use services as competitive tools. To compete with a large discount store like K mart, a locally owned independent hardware dealer may offer free delivery, gift wrapping, and credit services. Firms employ distinguishing promotional methods to compete, such as advertising and personal selling. A number of marketers use gifts, stamps, and discounts as competitive tools. Competing producers sometimes use different distribution channels to gain competitive advantage over each other. Merchants may compete by placing their outlets in locations that are convenient for a large number of shoppers and by creating unique and appealing atmospheres that make their stores distinctive.

Monitoring Competition

Marketers in an organization need to be aware of the actions of major competitors. They should monitor what competitors are currently doing and assess the changes that are occurring in competitive actions. For example, a marketer should determine if major competitors are changing features such as prices, product designs, warranty and service policies, packages, advertising, distribution methods, sales-force size, and use of sales promotion efforts like coupons or free samples. This type of information aids marketers in making adjustments to current marketing strategies and in planning new ones. Information about these issues may come from direct observation or from sources such as salespeople, customers, trade publications, syndicated marketing research services, distributors, and marketing studies.

10. Wroe Alderson, *Dynamic Marketing Behavior* (Homewood, Ill.: Irwin, 1965), pp. 195–197.

An organization also needs information about competitors that will allow its marketing managers to assess the performance of the firm's marketing efforts. Comparison of performance relative to competitors helps marketing managers to recognize strengths and weaknesses in their own marketing strategies. Data about market shares, product movement, sales volume, and expenditure levels can be quite useful. However, accurate information regarding these issues often is difficult to obtain.

Consumer Demand and Spending Behavior ✓

Marketers must understand the factors that determine whether, what, where, and when people buy. In Chapters 4 and 5 we look at behavioral factors underlying these choices. Here, we focus on economic aspects of buying behavior. Specifically, we analyze buying power and consumers' willingness to purchase, as well as their spending patterns.

Buying Power

One of the requirements for a market is that people have buying power. The strength of a person's **buying power** depends both on the size of the resources that give that individual the ability to purchase and on the state of the economy. The resources that make up buying power are goods, services, and financial holdings. The state of the economy affects buying power because it influences price levels. During inflationary periods, when prices are rising, buying power is reduced because more dollars are required to buy products. For example, products today cost almost three times as much as they did in 1967. Conversely, in periods of declining prices, the buying power of a given set of resources increases.

The major financial sources of buying power are income, credit, and wealth. From an individual's viewpoint, **income** is the amount of money received through wages, rents, investments, pensions, and subsidy payments for a given period, such as a month or a year. Normally, this money is used for three purposes—paying taxes, spending, and saving. The average annual family income in the United States is approximately $24,000. However, because of the differences in people's educational levels, abilities, occupations, and wealth, income is not equally distributed in this country (or in other countries). Income distribution is discussed further in Chapter 4.

Marketers are most interested in the amount of money that is left after taxes are paid. After-tax income is called **disposable income** and is used for spending or saving. Because disposable income is a ready source of buying power, the total amount available in our country is important to marketers. Several factors affect the size of total disposable income; one, of course, is the total amount of income. Total national income is affected by wage levels, rate of unemployment, interest rates, and dividend rates. These factors, in turn, affect the size of disposable income. Since disposable income is the income left after taxes are paid, the number of taxes and their amount directly affects the size of total disposable income. When taxes rise, disposable income declines; when taxes fall, disposable income increases.

Disposable income that is available for spending and saving after an individual has purchased the basic necessities of food, clothing, and shelter is called **discretionary income.** People use discretionary income to purchase entertainment, vacations, automobiles, education, lawn supplies, pets and pet supplies, furniture, appliances, and so on. Changes in total discretionary income affect the sales of these products, especially of automobiles, furniture, large appliances, and other durable goods.

Credit transactions allow people to spend future income now or in the near future. Credit increases current buying power at the expense of future buying power. Several factors determine whether consumers use or forgo credit. First, of course, credit must be available to consumers. Interest rates, too, affect consumers' decisions to use credit, especially for expensive purchases such as homes, appliances, and automobiles. When credit charges are high, consumers are more likely to delay purchases of expensive items. Because of high interest rates on home loans in the early 1980s, for example, many people decided not to purchase homes. These decisions hurt the sales of related industries—building materials, appliances, furniture, carpet, and real estate. Credit usage also is affected by credit terms such as the size of the down payment and the amount and number of monthly payments. On page 56, current trends in credit usage are discussed in an application.

A person can have a high income and very little wealth. It is also feasible, but not likely, for a person to have great wealth but not much income. **Wealth** is the accumulation of past income, natural resources, and financial resources. It may exist in many forms, including cash, securities, savings accounts, jewelry, art, antiques, real estate, minerals, machinery, and even animals. Like income, wealth is unevenly distributed among people in this country. The significance of wealth to marketers is that as people become more wealthy, they gain buying power in three ways. They can use their wealth not only for current purchases but also to generate income and to acquire large amounts of credit.

Marketers need to analyze buying power because it has a tremendous impact on consumers' reactions to firms' marketing strategies. Marketing managers can use buying power analysis for many purposes: evaluating opportunities in various markets, forecasting sales, establishing sales quotas, and budgeting marketing expenditures, to name only a few. Buying power information is available from government sources, trade associations, and research agencies.

One of the most current and comprehensive sources of buying-power data is the *Sales and Marketing Management Survey of Buying Power,* published annually by *Sales and Marketing Management* magazine. As shown in Table 2.4, the *Survey of Buying Power* presents data for specific geographic areas including states, counties, and most cities with populations in excess of forty thousand. The *Survey of Buying Power* also contains population and retail sales data for the same geographic areas.

The most direct indicators of buying power in the *Survey of Buying Power* are "effective buying income" (EBI) and "buying power index" (BPI). **Effective buying income** is similar to what we call disposable income; it includes salaries, wages, dividends, interest, profits, and rents, less federal, state, and local taxes. The **buying power index** is a weighted index consisting of population, effective buying income, and retail sales data.[11] The higher the index number, the greater the buying power. Like other indexes, the buying power index is most useful for comparative purposes. Marketers can use buying power indexes for a particular year to compare the buying power of one area with the buying power of another area. Or they can analyze trends for a particular area by comparing the area's buying power indexes for several years.

11. *Sales Management 1985 Survey of Buying Power,* July 22, 1985, pp. C-3 and C-4.

Table 2.4 *Examples of information in the Survey of Buying Power*

Kansas			**Effective Buying Income 1984**				
			% of hslds. by EBI group: (A) $10,000–$19,999 (B) $20,000–$34,999 (C) $35,000–$49,999 (D) $50,000 & over				
Metro Area *County* *City*	*Total EBI ($000)*	*Median hsld. EBI*	*A*	*B*	*C*	*D*	*Buying power index*
Kansas City	**18,253,339**	**29,826**	**18.2**	**28.7**	**22.8**	**17.4**	**.7014**
Johnson	4,960,331	40,198	11.0	24.3	25.9	33.5	.1733
• Olathe	616,452	36,023	13.9	27.8	29.4	22.7	.0230
Overland Park ..	1,517,711	41,950	9.4	23.5	27.3	35.6	.0598
Leavenworth......	605,062	29,483	18.4	29.5	25.3	13.3	.0211
• Leavenworth ..	358,090	27,357	20.2	29.5	23.4	11.7	.0136
Miami............	240,479	25,923	22.0	30.4	20.9	11.5	.0085
Wyandotte	1,812,712	26,241	20.3	28.8	21.0	12.4	.0667
• Kansas City ...	1,680,329	25,880	20.6	28.8	20.7	12.0	.0621
Cass, Mo..........	537,790	26,844	20.3	32.9	21.4	10.5	.0200
Clay, Mo..........	1,688,580	30,802	17.1	32.4	26.9	13.6	.0702
Jackson, Mo.	7,398,503	27,258	20.3	28.4	21.2	14.8	.3058
Independence...	1,365,581	30,640	18.0	29.1	26.7	14.4	.0546
• Kansas City ...	5,074,672	25,587	21.3	28.6	19.3	13.7	.2151
Lafayette, Mo......	280,409	22,461	24.6	32.8	16.5	6.3	.0104
Platte, Mo.........	543,208	28,387	19.1	36.2	23.7	9.4	.0184
Ray, Mo.	186,265	21,690	25.1	34.3	15.2	4.8	.0070
Suburban total ...	10,523,796	32,688	15.9	28.8	24.7	20.7	.3876
Lawrence	**776,981**	**24,617**	**23.0**	**26.7**	**17.8**	**14.5**	**.0291**
Douglas	776,981	24,617	23.0	26.7	17.8	14.5	.0291
• Lawrence.....	597,277	22,992	24.2	26.2	15.9	13.8	.0239
Suburban total ...	*179,704*	*30,758*	*18.6*	*28.5*	*25.0*	*16.8*	*.0052*
Topeka	**2,141,127**	**30,753**	**18.1**	**28.9**	**23.0**	**19.1**	**.0774**
Shawnee	2,141,127	30,753	18.1	28.9	23.0	19.1	.0774
• Topeka.......	1,592,979	28,177	20.4	30.1	20.7	16.4	.0618
Suburban total ...	*548,148*	*39,708*	*9.9*	*24.8*	*31.3*	*29.0*	*.0156*

Source: Survey of Buying Power, Copyright 1985, *Sales and Marketing Management.* Reprinted by permission.

Income, wealth, and credit equip consumers to purchase goods and services. Marketing managers should be aware of current levels and expected changes in buying power in their own markets, because buying power directly affects the types and quantities of goods and services that consumers purchase, as we shall see later in our discussion of spending patterns. Just because consumers have buying power, however, does not mean that they will buy. They must also be willing to use their buying power.

Consumers' Willingness to Spend

A person's **willingness to spend** is, to some degree, related to his or her ability to buy. That is, a person is sometimes more willing to buy if he or she has

Application

Consumer Use of Credit

Home mortgages represent a large portion (about 75 percent) of total consumer debt. However, only about one-third of all U.S. households owe on home mortgages. Most of the remaining households rent their living accommodations. Slightly over one-third of U.S. households owe on credit cards. The average credit card balance is about $500. Almost half of all households owe on installment loans.

Approximately two-thirds of American households have at least one credit card. This proportion has not changed much over the last ten years, but the types of credit cards held by Americans have. The number of gasoline company credit cards has declined considerably, while the number of bank credit cards such as Visa and MasterCard (Figure 2.4) has increased significantly. The use of travel and entertainment credit cards, such as Diners Club and American Express cards (Figure 2.4), has grown moderately over the last few years. In addition, over half of all households have at least one retail store credit card.

The travel and entertainment card is the credit card of young upwardly mobile individuals—people under thirty-five in white-collar occupations. They have the highest incomes, the greatest liquid assets, and the largest outstanding debts relative to holders of other types of cards. Holders of gasoline credit cards tend to have higher incomes and greater liquid assets than do holders of bank credit cards. This is explained by the fact that the gasoline credit card user tends to be older than the bank credit card holder. The types of credit cards held by individuals influence how they use credit cards and, to some extent, what they buy on credit. (*Source: Robert B. Avery, Gregory E. Elliehausen, and Thomas A. Guastafson, "How People Use Financial Services,"* American Demographics, *Sept. 1985, pp. 34–37.*)

the buying power. However, a number of other elements also influence willingness to spend. Some affect specific products; others influence spending in general. A product's absolute price and its price relative to the price of substitute products influence almost all of us. At times, the total dollar outlay for an item may seem too great, or a consumer may know of a similar, substitutable item with a much lower price. The amount of satisfaction currently received or expected in the future from a product already owned may also influence a consumer's desire to buy other products. Satisfaction depends not only on the quality of the functional performance of the currently owned product but also on numerous psychological and social forces.

Factors that affect a person's general willingness to spend are expectations about future employment, income levels, prices, family size, and general economic conditions. If a person is unsure whether or how much he or she will be employed, willingness to buy ordinarily declines. Willingness to buy may increase if a person is reasonably certain of a higher income in the future. Expectations of rising prices in the near future may also increase the willingness to spend. For a given level of buying power, the larger the family, the greater the willingness to buy. One reason for this relationship is that as family size increases, a greater number of dollars must be spent to provide the basic

Figure 2.4 *MasterCard and American Express credit cards (Source: Ad on left courtesy of MasterCard International. Ad on right courtesy of American Express Travel Related Services Company, Inc. Copyright 1986)*

necessities of life to sustain the family members. Lastly, perceptions of future economic conditions influence willingness to buy.

√ Consumer Spending Patterns

Marketers must be aware of the factors that influence consumers' ability and willingness to buy, but they should also analyze how consumers actually spend their disposable incomes. Marketers obtain this information by studying consumer spending patterns.

Consumer spending patterns indicate the relative proportions of annual family expenditures or the actual amount of money that is spent on certain kinds of goods and services. Families are usually categorized on the basis of one of several characteristics, including income, age of the household head, geographic area, and family life cycle. There are two types of spending patterns: comprehensive spending patterns and product-specific spending patterns.

The percentages of family income allotted to annual expenditures for general classes of goods and services constitute **comprehensive spending patterns.** Comprehensive spending patterns or the data to develop them are available in government publications and in reports by the Conference Board. In Table 2.5, comprehensive spending patterns are classified by family life cycle. Note

Table 2.5 *Spending patterns based on family life cycle*

Item	All Consumer Units	Total Husband and Wife Families	Husband and Wife Only	Oldest child under 6	Oldest child 6 to 17	Oldest child 18 or over	Other Husband and Wife Families	One Parent, At Least One Child Under 18	Single Person and Other Families
Total Expenditures	$17,144	$21,173	$17,959	$18,605	$23,054	$26,146	$23,993	$12,066	$11,417
Food	18.8%	18.7%	17.6%	17.1%	19.5%	19.9%	19.9%	22.8%	18.4%
Alcoholic Beverages	1.6%	1.3%	1.6%	1.3%	1.2%	1.3%	1.2%	1.0%	2.7%
Housing	16.4%	15.4%	16.3%	19.5%	15.8%	11.8%	13.3%	20.0%	19.0%
Fuels, Utilities, & Public Services	7.4%	7.3%	7.3%	6.9%	7.2%	7.4%	7.5%	9.2%	7.4%
Housefurnishings, Equipment, & Supplies	5.7%	5.8%	6.2%	7.3%	5.8%	4.3%	6.1%	5.5%	5.3%
Apparel	5.5%	5.5%	5.1%	5.0%	5.8%	5.7%	5.9%	7.0%	5.2%
Transportation	20.1%	20.7%	20.1%	20.9%	19.7%	23.0%	21.2%	16.0%	19.1%
Health Care	4.4%	4.4%	5.8%	3.6%	3.7%	4.0%	4.2%	2.9%	4.3%
Entertainment	4.4%	4.5%	4.3%	4.3%	5.3%	4.1%	4.3%	3.9%	4.3%
Personal Care	0.9%	0.9%	1.1%	0.6%	0.8%	1.0%	1.0%	0.8%	0.9%
Reading	0.7%	0.7%	0.8%	0.7%	0.6%	0.6%	0.6%	0.5%	0.8%
Education	1.3%	1.3%	0.7%	0.3%	1.5%	2.6%	1.1%	1.2%	1.2%
Tobacco & Smoking Supplies	1.0%	1.0%	1.0%	1.0%	1.0%	1.0%	1.2%	1.2%	1.1%
Miscellaneous	1.5%	1.5%	1.3%	1.5%	1.3%	1.5%	2.7%	1.4%	1.6%
Cash Contributions	2.9%	2.9%	3.6%	1.5%	2.5%	3.6%	2.4%	1.5%	3.1%
Personal Insurance and Pensions	7.4%	8.0%	7.5%	8.5%	8.3%	8.4%	7.5%	5.0%	5.8%

Source: U.S. Department of Labor, Bureau of Labor Statistics, *Consumer Expenditure Survey: Interview Survey, 1980–81,* Bulletin 2225, pp. 31–32.

the variation in expenditures between husband and wife families and single parent families.

Product-specific spending patterns indicate the annual dollar amounts spent by families for specific products within a general product class. Information sources used to construct product-specific spending patterns include government publications, the Conference Board, trade publications, and consumer surveys. Table 2.6 illustrates a product-specific spending pattern. Notice the differences between this type of spending pattern and the comprehensive ones. The products listed fall into one general product category, and the figures are stated in terms of dollars.

A marketer uses spending patterns to analyze general trends in the ways that families spend their incomes for various kinds of products. For example, an individual who is considering opening a bakery might use the data in Table 2.6 to estimate the demand for various categories of bakery products. Analyses of spending patterns yield information that a marketer can use to gain perspec-

Part I / An Analysis of Marketing Opportunities

Table 2.6 *Annual dollar expenditures for nonfrozen bakery products by various household incomes*

		Household Income							
		Under $5,000	$5,000–$10,000	$10,000–$15,000	$15,000–$20,000	$20,000–$25,000	$25,000–$35,000	$35,000–$50,000	$50,000 & Over
	Total								
Households (millions)	70.0	12.5	12.5	10.2	8.7	8.0	10.7	5.4	2.1
Distribution of Households	100.0%	17.9	17.9	14.5	12.4	11.4	15.3	7.7	3.1
Average Household Size	2.6	1.9	2.1	2.4	2.8	3.0	3.1	3.4	3.3
Distribution of Persons	100.0%	13.0	14.7	13.4	13.5	13.0	18.6	10.0	3.9
Distribution of Income	100.0%	2.5	7.4	10.2	12.2	14.3	25.4	17.8	10.2
Expenditures in Dollars	**Average**								
Nonfrozen bakery products	144.79	98.01	112.89	117.98	151.22	165.77	192.42	215.82	210.64
White Bread	40.64	31.68	33.81	37.66	41.99	48.22	49.42	50.62	44.26
Bread other than white	16.98	11.91	14.52	15.45	17.27	17.67	21.14	23.00	28.60
Fresh Biscuits, Rolls, etc.	17.55	9.51	11.37	13.14	19.13	20.57	24.43	33.40	29.55
Cakes and Cupcakes	16.29	9.57	14.10	11.50	18.23	17.44	22.44	25.38	25.21
Cookies	19.52	12.31	13.62	14.95	19.87	22.71	29.16	29.99	29.78
Crackers	11.23	7.79	8.59	9.66	10.70	13.03	14.50	16.65	19.74
Bread and Cracker Products	2.11	1.06	1.25	1.70	2.19	2.51	2.42	5.16	4.14
Doughnuts, Sweetrolls, etc.	15.81	11.46	11.58	10.59	15.76	18.48	22.78	24.72	23.62
Fresh Pies and Tarts	4.67	2.72	4.05	3.32	6.09	5.16	6.12	6.90	5.73

Source: Consumer Research Center, *How Consumers Spend Their Money* (New York: Conference Board, 1984), pp. 20, 44. Used by permission.

tive and background for decision making. However, spending patterns reflect only general trends and thus cannot be used as the only basis for making specific decisions.

General Economic Conditions

The overall state of the economy fluctuates in all countries. These changes in general economic conditions affect (and are affected by) the forces of supply and demand, buying power, willingness to buy, consumer expenditure levels, and the intensity of competitive behavior. Therefore, present-day economic conditions and changes in the economy have a broad impact on the success of organizations' marketing strategies.

Fluctuations in our economy follow a general pattern that is often referred to as the "business cycle." In the traditional view, the business cycle consists of four stages: prosperity, recession, depression, and recovery. To understand some of the effects of the general economic climate, let us explore certain characteristics of the four stages.

During **prosperity,** unemployment is low and aggregate income is relatively high. Assuming a low inflation rate, this combination causes buying power to be high. To the extent that the economic outlook remains prosperous, consumers generally are willing to buy. In the prosperity stage, marketers often expand their product mixes to take advantage of the increased buying power. They sometimes capture a larger market share by intensifying distribution and promotion efforts.

Since unemployment rises during a **recession,** total buying power declines. The pessimism that accompanies a recession often stifles spending by both consumers and businesses. Because of decreased buying power, many consumers become more price and value conscious—they look for products that are basic and functional. For instance, people ordinarily reduce their consumption of the more expensive convenience foods and exert greater effort to save money by growing and preparing more of their own food. Individuals buy fewer durable goods and more repair and do-it-yourself products. During a recession some firms make the mistake of drastically reducing their marketing efforts and thus damage their ability to survive. Obviously, marketers should consider some revision of their marketing activities during a recessionary period. Because consumers are more concerned about the functional value of products, a firm must focus its marketing research on determining precisely what product functions are important to buyers and then make certain that these functions are included in the firm's products. Promotional efforts should emphasize value and utility.

A **depression** is a period in which there is extremely high unemployment, wages are very low, total disposable income is at a minimum, and consumers lack confidence in the economy. The federal government has used both monetary and fiscal policies in an attempt to offset the effects of recession, depression, and inflation. Monetary policies are employed to control the money supply, which in turn influences spending, saving, and investment by both individuals and businesses. Through fiscal policies, the government can influence the amount of savings and expenditures by altering the tax structure and by changing the levels of government expenditures. Some experts believe that effective use of monetary and fiscal policies can eliminate depressions from the business cycle.

Recovery is the business cycle stage in which the economy moves from recession to prosperity. During this period, the high unemployment rate begins to decline, total disposable income increases, and the economic gloom that lessened consumers' willingness to buy subsides. Both the ability and the willingness to buy rise. Marketers face some problems during recovery. One is the difficulty of ascertaining how quickly prosperity will return. It can also be difficult to forecast the level of prosperity that will be attained. In the recovery stage, marketers should maintain as much flexibility in their marketing strategies as possible to be able to make the needed adjustments as the economy moves from recession to prosperity.

Technological Forces

The impact of technology on society and businesses is a major factor in the success—or failure—of a business enterprise. Economic forces are related to technology because the pursuit and existence of technological information may affect income, taxation, prices, and consumers' willingness to spend. The effects of technology are broad in scope and today exert a tremendous influence on our lives.

The rapid technological growth of the last several decades is expected to continue through the 1980s. Areas that hold great technological promise include solid-state electronics, artificial intelligence, materials research, biotechnology, and geology. Current research is investigating new forms of chips, computers that are a hundred times faster than current models, and optical computers that use video images rather than digital codes. By 1990, a single chip may be able to hold one million bits of data as compared to the current level of 65,000 bits. Special artificial intelligence systems are presently being used in industry and medicine. These systems mimic human experts with astonishing precision. New "microscience" equipment allows scientists to explore the innermost structure of matter and to modify the ninety-two basic elements of the periodic table. Research has been done, for example, with ceramics that can conduct electricity and with plastics that are derived from nonpetroleum sources. Research in biotechnology has yielded new drugs and chemicals by altering the hereditary characteristics of bacteria. Amazing developments in the modification of plant, animal, and human genetics may profoundly affect food production, human health, and medical science.[12]

These and other technological developments will have a definite impact on buyers and on marketers' decisions. Let us, therefore, take the time to define technology and to consider some of its effects on society and on marketers. Then, we will discuss several factors that influence the adoption and use of technology.

Technology Defined

The word *technology* brings to mind creations of progress such as spaceships, computers, synthetic fibers, laser beams, and heart transplants. Even though such items are outgrowths of technology, none of them *is* technology. **Technology** is the knowledge of how to accomplish tasks and goals.[13] Often this knowledge comes from scientific research.

Technology is credited with providing the machines, buildings, materials, and processes that allow us to achieve a high standard of living. Yet it is also blamed for pollution, unemployment, crime, and a number of other social and environmental problems. Technology itself is neither good nor bad. Its effects are determined largely by how it is applied. Technology has been used to improve health care so that people can live longer. It has also been used to kill masses of people. It enabled the Nazis, for example, to exterminate millions of people during World War II. In addition, although the potential effects of technology may be significant, the actual effects of certain types of technology are nonexistent unless the technology is used. For example, some technological knowledge that has come out of our space explorations has not yet been put to use.

Technology grows out of research performed by businesses, universities, and nonprofit organizations. Much of this research—in fact, over half of it— is paid for by the federal government, which supports investigations in a variety of areas including health, arms, agriculture, energy, and pollution. Because much federally funded research requires the use of specialized machinery,

---

12. "Technologies for the '90s," *Business Week*, July 6, 1981, pp. 48–56.
13. Herbert Simon, "Technology and Environment," *Management Science*, June 1973, p. 1110.

personnel, and facilities, a sizable proportion of this research is done by large business organizations that already possess the necessary specialized equipment and people.

The Impact of Technology

Marketers must be aware of new developments in technology and their possible effects, because technology can and does affect marketing activities in many different ways. Consumers' technological knowledge influences their desires for goods and services. To provide marketing mixes that satisfy consumers, marketers must be aware of these influences. Technological developments can put some people out of business while opening up new business opportunities to others. The introduction and general acceptance of synthetic fabrics drove some sheep raisers, cotton growers, and dry cleaners out of business. Yet this technology provided new market opportunities for synthetic fabric producers, clothing manufacturers, retail clothiers, and self-service laundries. Technology definitely affects the types of products that are offered to consumers. The items that follow are only a few of the thousands of existing products that were not available to consumers twenty years ago.

Solar-powered pocket calculators
Microwave ovens
Supersonic airliners
Videotape recorders for home use
Tuning-fork and quartz-crystal wrist
  watches

Calorie-reduced beer, wine, and
  pasta
Felt-tipped and nylon-tipped pens
Low-cost personal computers

The various ways in which technology affects marketing activities fall into two broad categories. It affects consumers and society in general, and it influences what, how, when, and where products are marketed.

The Effects of Technology on Society

When you stop to think about it, technology influences whether you are born, how you live, and how and when you die. (See related examples in the application on page 64.) In fact, it is difficult to think of any aspect of human life that is untouched by technological developments; we are engulfed by them. One measure of the increasing magnitude of technological applications is the general increase in the number of patents issued (see Figure 2.5). Except during the 1930s and 1940s, the number of patents issued has increased substantially from decade to decade.

Technology determines how we satisfy our physiological needs. In various ways and to varying degrees, eating and drinking habits, sleeping patterns, sexual activities, and health care are all influenced both by existing technology and by changes in technology. For example, freeze-dried foods, birth control pills, and computerized health information systems have had a definite impact on how people satisfy physiological requirements.

Technological developments definitely have improved our standard of living. Through technology, workers are more productive, do less physical labor, and earn larger incomes with which to purchase the extremely large number of technologically improved goods and services available where and when they want them. Technological knowledge also allows producers and manufacturers to create products that help people perform ordinary tasks more easily, thus

Figure 2.5

Growth in the number of patents issued (Source: Adapted from Statistical Abstract of the United States, *1949, 1964, 1972, 1977)*

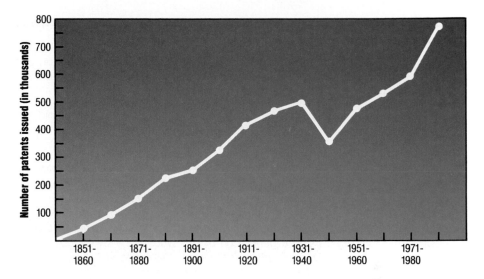

giving us more leisure time. Education, information, and entertainment have been improved through technology.

Nevertheless, technology can detract from the quality of life through undesirable side effects such as unemployment, polluted air and water, and other health hazards. These unfavorable aspects of technology arise from the physical production of goods and services and from the ways in which society uses products. Some people believe that further applications of technology can soften or eliminate these undesirable side effects. Others argue that the best way to improve the quality of our lives is to reduce the use of technology.

The Impact of Technology on Marketing Activities

Technology affects the types of products that marketers can offer. Technological improvements in production processes and materials sometimes result in more durable, less expensive products. When color television sets, for example, were introduced, they did not work very well and were quite expensive. Over the years, technological advances (and competitive pressures) have led to higher-quality, lower-priced sets.

Technology has altered the ways in which marketers inform consumers about goods and services. Because of technological changes in communications, marketers now can reach large masses of people through a variety of media including newspapers, magazines, direct mail, radio, television, transit, and billboards. Also, technology is helping marketers to be more efficient. GTE and other firms offer worldwide telemail service. This service allows people in the same organization but in different locations to communicate. It can be used for entering orders, managing salespeople, and other marketing activities.

Technological advances in transportation allow consumers to travel farther and more often to shop at a larger number of stores. The greater mobility of consumers has, in turn, affected the sizes and locations of stores. Thirty years ago the owner of a large furniture store would have been reluctant to build a store at the edge of a city. Today, this practice is common. Technological changes in transportation also have affected the producers' ability to get products to retailers and wholesalers. The ability of present-day manufacturers of relatively lightweight products to reach any of their dealers within twenty-four hours (through air freight) would astound their counterparts of fifty years ago.

The following passage by Linda Peterson focuses on how technology has changed childhoods and parenting in this generation compared to the last generation. When reading these comments, consider how technology has changed your daily life since you were growing up.

If this piece were appearing in a supermarket tabloid instead of these pages, the headline might read: "Trekkies Raise Techies. Havoc Results."

After failing, once again, to follow my seven-year-old's most rudimentary VCR instructions on how to watch one channel, record on another, and switch back and forth to blip out commercials, I've decided the generation gap is about technology. What we're talking here, those of us in the child-rearing biz, is a bunch of aging Trekkies (people who grew up on Captain Kirk and the gang) raising a generation of kids who take answering machines, VCRs, ATMs, and VDTs as matter-of-factly as PB&J (peanut butter and jelly).

Except in California, where people at parties talk about the price of real estate or where you can get the consummate coffee bean, parental party talk hasn't changed in hundreds of years. It still centers on how different things are for the kids than they were for us. And what seems to make them different, this generation out? Technology. Just a few examples: Long-distance calling is now so affordable that kids think nothing of twice-weekly chats with Grandma across the continent. When we were kids, long distance still had the feel of "special occasion," something reserved for announcements of births, deaths, and particularly inappropriate marriages.

Remember banks? When we were kids, they featured marble floors, pillars, and velvet ropes. Today those places are rarer than the snow leopard. What we've got instead is the "money machine," that dispenser of green largesse and pesky little paper slips.

And spelling tests. We studied for those at the formica table in the kitchen, while Mom (yes, Mom) grated cheese (by hand) for the tuna casserole and called out the words. My kid studies for his spelling test at the word processor in the breakfast room accompanied by the whine of the food processor.

Are we complaining about how technologically sophisticated our kids are? Not really. We're bewitched, a little bothered, and definitely bewildered. It's not just technology that makes these kids sophisticated, but a degree of affluence as well. The American Economic Dream may need overhauling, but it's still producing the hardware—and software—of our lives.

What's more, I think we're over our first mindless dazzle with technology. Computers were once heralded as likely replacements for teachers in the classroom because machines, unlike cantankerous Miss Philpott, were consistent and predictable, never wearied of repetition, never got nasty about mistakes. Today, according to the gaggle of journals devoted to educational software, computers are just another tool that teachers can use to coach kids who have learning problems and enrich kids who move ahead too fast.

There's a group of conscientious educators scrutinizing just what all this technology buys us. Neil Postman, professor of media ecology (uh-huh, media ecology—you read it here first) and author of The Disappearance of Childhood, *says: "The computer opened up the 'Age of Information' . . . but information for what and for whom? We're training our kids to be information junkies, who believe that access to information is an end in itself." Then, there's teacher Stan Silverman, who points out, "Good teachers don't always follow a line from a to b to c. If a student goes off on a tangent, a creative teacher can help him benefit from his detour. Computers can't think tangentially."*

Besides that, computers aren't very good at making mistakes. By and large, they're never wrong. And being wrong some of the time, goofing up and learning from those goof-ups, is an important part of childhood. As physician/biologist Lewis Thomas notes in his essay "To Err Is Human": "Mistakes are the very base of human thought, embedded there, feeding the structure like root nodules. If we were not provided with the knack of being wrong, we could never get anything useful done."

Where does that leave us mistake-ridden, low-tech Trekkies? Still in our kids' thrall, that's where. As they get older, they'll explain more and more things to us—UNIX, Pascal (not the French philosopher), how to access a hacker's bulletin board, the best buys in fishing rods and stocks and bonds by phone.

But, here's the good news. As they grow up, they're in our thrall, too. We can explain why the law of odds makes Marvin Gardens a better place to buy than Park Place and Boardwalk, what a roadster is (remember? Nancy Drew drove a red one), and where the owl and the pussycat were heading.

I'll tell you something else. There's nothing finer than an afternoon of taped Star Trek reruns with those commercials blipped right out. "Beam me up, Scotty. This Trekkie is willing to go higher-tech with the kids." (Source: Linda Peterson, "High Tech Tykes," AT&T Magazine, *Vol. 2, No. 3, 1985, p. 45. © 1985 by AT&T. Used by permission.)*

Adoption and Use of Technology

As we implied earlier, businesses will not necessarily use all available technologies. There are a number of reasons why. A firm must be capable of using technological information, and consumers must be able and willing to buy the resulting products. Consumers have rejected a variety of new products: cereals with freeze-dried fruits, certain types of automobile safety equipment, and improved mousetraps—among others.

Through a procedure known as **technology assessment,** managers try to foresee the effects of new products and processes on their firm's operation, on other business organizations, and on society in general. With the information gained through a technology assessment, management tries to estimate whether or not the benefits of using a specific kind of technology outweigh the costs to the firm and to society generally. The degree to which a business is technologically based also will influence how its management responds to technology. Firms whose products and product changes are outgrowths of recent technology are very much concerned with gathering and using technological information. At the same time, although technology may exist that could radically improve a firm's products or other parts of the marketing mix, the firm may not apply the technology as long as its competitors do not attempt to use it. In addition, the extent to which a firm can protect inventions that arise from research influences its use of technology. How secure a product is from imitation depends on how easily the product can be copied without violating its patent. If new products and processes cannot be protected through patents, a firm is less likely to market them and make the benefits of its research available to competitors.

How a firm uses (or does not use) technology is important for its long-run survival. A firm that makes the wrong decisions may well lose out to its competitors. Poor decisions may also affect a firm's profits by requiring expensive corrective actions. Poor decisions about technological forces may even drive a firm out of business.

Summary

The marketing environment is made up of constantly changing environmental forces that marketing managers must monitor to secure organizational survival. To monitor the changes in these forces, marketers can practice environmental scanning and analysis, which involve observation and information gathering. By gathering useful information and making accurate observations, marketing managers should be able to predict opportunities and threats associated with environmental fluctuation. Marketing management may assume either a passive, reactive approach or an active, aggressive approach in responding to these environmental fluctuations. There is no best method of response. The choice depends on an organization's structure and needs and on the composition of the environmental forces that affect it. The marketing environment contains political, legal, regulatory, societal, economic and competitive, and technological forces that marketers must understand in order to operate successfully. Political and legal forces are closely interrelated aspects of the marketing environment. The atmosphere in which legal and regulatory forces are developed and implemented is strongly shaped by political forces. The current political outlook of lawmakers is reflected in legislation or the lack of it.

Federal legislation covers all major areas of marketing activities and can be divided into two categories: procompetitive legislation and consumer protection laws. Beginning with very broad procompetitive legislation such as the Sherman Act, these laws have gradually focused more directly on specific marketing practices. The apparent vagueness of the Sherman Act allowed the courts to apply its provisions to a variety of situations that had the common characteristic of being harmful to competition. Subsequent legislation such as the Clayton Act, the Federal Trade Commission Act, the Wheeler-Lea Act, and the Robinson Patman Act were directed more toward specific practices. Awareness of laws alone is not enough; marketers must also consider court interpretation of them.

Regulatory agencies exert considerable force on marketing practices. Often these agencies generate regulatory guidelines that carry considerable weight in the marketplace. For example, the FTC has been active in several areas, including the monitoring and regulation of advertising practices. Marketers must not overlook state and local laws and regulatory agencies when considering the legal forces in the marketing environment.

Industry self-regulation provides another source of concern for marketers. However, marketers view this type of regulation more favorably than government action because they have more opportunity to participate in the creation of the guidelines. Self-regulatory groups provide a more operational and often a less expensive regulatory structure. However, they generally cannot enforce compliance as effectively as government agencies.

Marketers are subjected to a variety of societal forces that express what society wants and what it does not want. Members of our society want a high standard of living and a high quality of life. People expect business organizations to help them obtain what they want. As they attempt to provide what society wants, marketers must also avoid transgressions that society does not desire— faulty and unsafe products, misleading and unsupported warranties, deceptive packages and labels, misleading advertisements, fraudulent selling practices, or unfair and exploitative prices. In trying to be socially responsible, marketers experience two general problems. It is difficult, if not impossible, to determine what society as a whole wants, because its various groups have diverse and often contradictory desires. Marketers also have a tough job in attempting to estimate their decisions' long-run effects on society.

The economic factors that can strongly influence marketing decisions and activities are competitive forces, buying power, willingness to spend, spending patterns, and general economic conditions. Although all business organizations compete for consumers' dollars, a business usually views its competitors as the businesses in its geographic area that market products similar to, or substitutable for, its own products. Several factors influence the intensity of competition in a firm's environment, including the type of competitive structure in which a firm operates and the kinds of competitive tools employed by the organizations in that particular industry.

Consumer demand is affected by consumers' buying power and by their willingness to purchase. Consumers' goods, services, and financial holdings make up their buying power, that is, their ability to purchase. The financial sources of buying power are income, credit, and wealth. Just because consumers have buying power, however, does not mean that they will use it; they also must be willing to spend. Factors that affect the willingness to spend are the product's price; the level of satisfaction that is obtained from currently used products; family size; and expectations about future employment, income, prices, and general economic conditions.

The general economic conditions in our country affect the forces of supply and demand, buying power, the willingness to buy, consumer expenditure levels, and the intensity of competitive behavior. The overall state of the economy fluctuates in a general pattern known as a business cycle. The stages of the business cycle are prosperity, recession, depression, and recovery.

Technology is the knowledge of how to accomplish tasks and goals. Technological knowledge grows out of research—much of it paid for by the federal government—performed by businesses and nonprofit organizations such as universities. Technology today exerts a tremendous influence on our lives, including our work, recreation, eating and drinking, sleep, and sexual behavior.

Like all other aspects of our society, marketing decisions and activities are affected by technology. Product development, packaging, promotion, prices, and distribution systems are all influenced directly by technology. Not all businesses, however, are affected in the same way or to the same degree. Several factors determine how much and in what way a particular business will make use of technology. They include the firm's ability to use it, consumers' ability and willingness to buy technologically improved products, the firm's perception of the long-run effects of applying technology, the extent to which it is technologically based, the degree to which technology is used as a competitive tool, and the extent to which the business can protect technological applications through patents.

Important Terms

Environmental scanning
Environmental analysis
Procompetitive legislation
Sherman Act

Clayton Act
Federal Trade Commission Act
Wheeler-Lea Act
Robinson-Patman Act
Consumer protection legislation

Federal Trade Commission (FTC)
Better Business Bureau
National Advertising Review Board (NARB)

Societal forces
Consumer movement
Competition
Monopoly
Oligopoly
Monopolistic
  competition
Perfect competition
Buying power
Income
Disposable income

Discretionary income
Wealth
Effective buying
  income
Buying power index
Willingness to spend
Consumer spending
  patterns
Comprehensive
  spending patterns

Product-specific
  spending patterns
Prosperity
Recession
Depression
Recovery
Technology
Technology
  assessment

Discussion and Review Questions

1. How are political forces related to legal and governmental regulatory forces?
2. Describe marketers' attempts to influence political forces.
3. What types of procompetitive legislation directly affect marketing practices?
4. What was the major objective of most procompetitive laws? Do these laws generally accomplish this objective? Why or why not?
5. What are the major provisions of the Robinson-Patman Act? Which marketing mix decisions are influenced directly by this act?
6. What types of problems do marketers experience as they try to interpret legislation?
7. What are the goals of the Federal Trade Commission? List the ways in which the FTC affects marketing activities. Do you think a single regulatory agency should have such broad jurisdiction over so many marketing practices? Why or why not?
8. Name several nongovernmental regulatory forces. Do you feel that self-regulation is more or less effective than governmental regulatory agencies? Why?
9. How does society expect marketers to handle social responsibility and ethical matters?
10. Describe the consumer movement. Analyze some active consumer forces in your area.
11. Define income, disposable income, and discretionary income. How does each affect consumer buying power?
12. How is consumer buying power affected by wealth and consumer credit?
13. How is buying power measured? Why should it be evaluated?
14. What factors influence a consumer's willingness to buy?
15. In what ways can each of the business cycle stages affect consumers' reactions to marketing strategies?
16. What business cycle stage are we experiencing currently? How is this stage affecting business firms in your area?
17. What does the term *technology* mean to you?
18. How does technology affect you as a member of society? Do the benefits of technology outweigh its costs and dangers?
19. Discuss the impact of technology on marketing activities.
20. What factors determine whether a business organization adopts and uses technology?

Cases

Case 2.1 Eli Lilly's Oraflex[14]

Millions of Americans suffer from arthritis. For these people, a simple task like opening a jar can be difficult. Eli Lilly and Company, a large manufacturer of pharmaceuticals, developed a drug called Oraflex to help sufferers of arthritic pain. In April, 1982, the FDA gave Lilly approval to market Oraflex.

Less than three months later, Lilly pulled the medication off the market. It had come under pressure from consumer protection groups and regulatory forces who claimed the drug had adverse side effects. This recall cost Lilly $11.4 million. The Justice Department has been conducting an investigation, and a product liability suit against Lilly is pending.

The chemical name for Oraflex is benoxaprofen. Oraflex is an oral prescription medication that is taken once daily. The 400-milligram tablets cost about 94 cents apiece. This is significantly cheaper than another antiarthritic drug, Feldome, that sells at $1.11 for a 20-milligram tablet.

U.S. officials are considering suing Lilly on the grounds that the FDA was ill-informed about the adverse side effects associated with Oraflex. Shortly after FDA approval, benoxaprofen was associated with sixty-one deaths in Britain (where it was sold under the name of Opien). The drug allegedly causes liver and kidney damage that can be fatal. In the United States, eleven deaths are under investigation. Although this adverse publicity has hurt Oraflex, nothing definite about the deaths has been proven. Lilly still maintains that if proper dosage is followed, Oraflex is safe and effective.

Lilly claims that the only side effects it was aware of before marketing the drug were increased sensitivity to the sun of the skin and nails. Lilly had submitted an application to the FDA for new-drug approval on January 17, 1980. Twenty-eight months later, the FDA, after a routine review process, gave its approval for the marketing of Oraflex. Lilly had estimated that sales of Oraflex would be about $100 million annually.

Although it now takes less time than it did in the past, FDA approval is still a lengthy process. In 1981, a relaxed approval program was put into effect, reducing the previous review time by 20 percent. Now, any applicant seeking approval of a medication containing a previously approved drug is not required to conduct primary research; instead, a report of 50–200 pages summarizing available technical data can be submitted. This has reduced the manufacturer's cost considerably, allowing some generic producers to enter the market. (Previously, generic producers could not afford to reproduce studies of the innovator.)

The new program also allows the FDA to approve competitive brands at the same time. For example, Oraflex was approved along with two similar oral antiarthritic drugs. In the past, the FDA had released only one of a group of similar drugs, watched its effects, and then a year later approved competitive drugs. The FDA also may begin accepting the results of foreign tests that follow U.S. regulations. This new, relaxed process has only been in effect for a short time. If the Department of Justice uncovers evidence that Oraflex caused fatal

---

14. The facts in this case are from Lou LaMarca, "FDA Sets Faster Pace for New Drug Review," *Advertising Age,* Sept. 27, 1982, pp. M24, M27; "An Arthritis Drug's Sudden Exit," *Newsweek,* Aug. 16, 1982, p. 59; "Oraflex: Behind the Headlines," *Consumers' Research Magazine,* Dec. 1982, pp. 11–14; and Howard Banks, "The Oraflex Fiasco," *Forbes,* Oct. 25, 1982, pp. 41–42.

effects, the old FDA approval process will be reinstituted and Lilly's new drug application will certainly undergo extensive analysis by the FDA if Lilly seeks re-approval of an Oraflex-type product.

Questions for Discussion

1. What kinds of environmental forces does Eli Lilly have to deal with that may not be as strong for firms in many other types of industries?
2. What types of risks does Eli Lilly (and other pharmaceutical firms) bear when developing and introducing a new drug such as Oraflex?
3. How could a pharmaceutical product like Oraflex pass through all the testing conducted by Eli Lilly, pass all of the FDA tests and requirements, and still have to be recalled after less than three months?

Case 2.2 Xerox Corporation Adjusts to a Changing Environment[15]

Xerox's phenomenal growth started with its introduction of the 914 copier. The 914 was one of the most successful products in the history of American business. For the first three-fourths of its life, Xerox Corporation had a virtual monopoly in the plain-paper copier business. Its basic corporate strategy through the first half of the 1970s was to focus on high-profit high- and medium-output copiers. At that time the growing market of offices that needed less expensive, low-output copiers was not served adequately.

In the mid-1970s Japanese firms realized that the needs of this significant market segment were not being met. In a joint venture, Savin designed a lower-cost yet efficient plain-paper copier. Ricoh manufactured the Savin-designed copiers, and Savin and Nashua marketed them. Working together, they captured the low-priced end of the copier industry.

Reducing Xerox's market share still further, IBM introduced a medium-volume copier in the late 1970s. The market shares of firms in the copier industry for the early 1980s are shown in Figure 2.6.

By 1985 Xerox had halted erosion and stabilized market share in the low and high end of the market and had dramatically increased market share in the mid-range copier market by developing new products for this area. Xerox is in a U.S. industry sector that is doing battle, without trade protection, against strong Japanese companies. Xerox has been successful in the battle and has made significant strides with lower costs, high quality, and highly functional fundamental products. A major objective of Xerox is to improve its operating margin.

Several factors make it likely that Xerox will attain its objective. In 1981, an FTC ruling was lifted that had previously required Xerox to maintain uncompetitively high prices to prevent it from acting as a monopoly. Xerox's products are now more competitively priced. It is hoped that some smaller competitors in the low-priced end of the copier market will have their market shares reduced by Xerox's presence, making it ultimately possible for Xerox to build a stronger margin into its sales.

---

15. Some of the facts in this case are from "Competition Heats Up in Copiers," *Business Week,* Nov. 5, 1979, p. 115; and from "Xerox Zooms Toward the Office of the Future," *Fortune,* May 18, 1981, p. 45; and 1983, 1984, and 1985 Xerox Annual Reports.

Figure 2.6

Estimated 1980 market
share for copiers

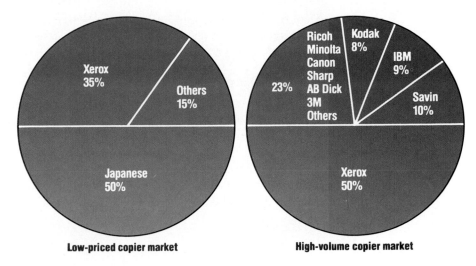

Low-priced copier market   **High-volume copier market**

Another important factor is that Ricoh, Nashua, and Savin have ended their partnership. Each of them is going after its own share of the market. Individually they are less threatening than they were when acting as a unit. Also, Xerox is expanding its marketing force of company employees through use of dealers and part-time salespeople in areas not regularly covered by its full-time staff.

Finally, Xerox has enlarged its product mix to include text and data processing machines. The Star, a management-oriented information processing computer, is now the leader in automated office work stations. Xerox's Ethernet, another information systems product, allows integration of terminals, printers, plotters, and processors into one network.

Memorywriter electronic typewriters now capture over 20 percent of the U.S. market for this product. Sales of electronic printers and electronic typewriters have grown rapidly. In both areas, Xerox claims to be the market leader. The company is confident that a steady stream of new products will allow it to stay in the forefront of these growing markets.

By a combination of environmental factors (the lifted FTC ruling and the Savin, Ricoh, and Nashua breakup) and new strategies (expanded marketing and product innovation), Xerox hopes to maintain its dominance of the high-volume segment and increase its low-volume market share. Xerox's objectives for the future include

To remain the leader in reprographics, the base for all other business
  growth
To expand its preeminent position in electronic printing
To become a major factor in office information systems
To expand its base in the financial services business

Questions for Discussion

1. Discuss the competitive structure in which Xerox has participated.
2. How has Xerox's changing corporate and marketing strategies been influenced by changes in the environment?
3. What types of laws and government regulation impact on Xerox's ability to achieve its objectives?

3 / Target Markets: Segmentation and Evaluation

Objectives

- To understand the definition of a market.
- To find out what types of markets exist.
- To learn how firms identify target markets.
- To gain an understanding of market potential.
- To understand the definition of a company sales forecast.
- To become familiar with sales forecasting methods.

Figure 3.1

Advertisement aimed at a specific customer group (Source: Courtesy of the Stride-Rite Corporation)

The product in Figure 3.1 is not directed at you unless you are the parent of young children. This advertisement helps the sponsor to zero in on a particular customer group. By focusing on one group, this organization is not trying to be all things to all people.

PRETTY, TOUGH SHOES
FOR PRETTY TOUGH KIDS.

Funny, they don't look practical. But don't let the stylish look fool you. Because the new Scuff Tuff™ leather shoes from Stride Rite® are tough. Very tough.

The uppers are made with our new Scuff Tuff leather, which undergoes a special process to make it scuff-resistant. The soles are made of Dura-5™ to make them durable, flexible and lightweight.

What's more, the shoes are available in a variety of styles and colors with the same quality and comfort offered in all Stride Rite leather shoes. Plus lots of sizes and widths (B to EEE) to ensure a proper fit every time.

So if you have a kid who's pretty tough on shoes, Scuff Tuff leather shoes are the answer to your problem.

Stride Rite®
AMERICA'S FIRST PAIR OF SHOES™

A company identifies or singles out groups of customers for its products and directs some or all of its marketing activities at those groups. It develops and maintains a marketing mix consisting of a product, a distribution system, promotion—such as the advertisement in Figure 3.1—and price that effectively meets customers' needs.

In this chapter, we initially discuss the characteristics of a market and the major types of markets. Then, we examine two approaches to selecting target markets. Next, the major issues associated with market measurement and evaluation are considered. Finally, we describe the primary techniques used in sales forecasting.

What Are Markets?

The word *market* has a number of meanings. People sometimes use the word to refer to a specific location where products are bought and sold. A large geographic area may also be called a market. Sometimes "market" refers to the relationship between the demand and supply of a specific product. It has this meaning, for example, in the question, "How is the market for diamonds?" At times "market" is used to mean the act of selling something.

As used in this book, a **market** is an aggregate of people who, as individuals or as organizations, have needs for products in a product class and who have the ability, willingness, and authority to purchase such products. In general use, "market" sometimes refers to the total population—or mass market— that buys products in general. However, our definition is more specific; it refers to persons seeking products in a specific product category. Obviously, there are many different markets in our complex economy. In this section, we will identify and describe several general groups of markets.

Requirements of a Market

✓For an aggregate of people to be a market, it must meet four requirements.

1. The people must need the product. If the people in the aggregate do not desire the particular product, then that aggregate is not a market.
2. The people in the group must have the ability to purchase the product. Ability to purchase is a function of their buying power, which consists of resources such as money, goods, and services that can be traded in an exchange situation.
3. The people in the aggregate must be willing to use their buying power.
4. Individuals in the group must have the authority to buy the specific products.

Individuals can have the desire, the buying power, and the willingness to purchase certain products but may not be authorized to do so. For example, young teen-agers may have the desire, the money, and the willingness to buy liquor. However, a liquor producer does not consider them a market because they are not authorized by law or social custom to buy alcoholic beverages. An aggregate of people that lacks any one of the four requirements thus does not constitute a market.

Types of Markets

Markets fall into one of two categories—consumer markets and organizational or industrial markets. These categories are based on the characteristics of the individuals and groups that make up a specific market and the purposes for which they buy products. A **consumer market** consists of purchasers and/or individuals in their households who intend to consume or benefit from the purchased products and who do not buy products for the main purpose of making a profit. Each of us belongs to numerous consumer markets. The millions of individuals with the ability, willingness, and authority to buy make up a multitude of consumer markets for such products as housing, food, clothing, vehicles, personal services, appliances, furniture, and recreational equipment. In Chapter 4 we discuss consumer markets in detail.

An **organizational or industrial market** consists of individuals or groups who purchase a specific kind of product for one of three purposes: resale, direct use in producing other products, or use in general daily operations. For example, a lamp producer who buys electrical wire to use in the production of lamps is a part of the industrial market for electrical wire. This same firm purchases dust mops to clean its office areas. Although the mops are not used in the direct production of lamps, they are used in the operations of the firm; thus, this manufacturer is part of the industrial market for dust mops. There are four categories of organizational or industrial markets: producer, reseller, government, and institutional. These four types are discussed in Chapter 5.

Selecting Target Markets

In Chapter 1, we said that a marketing strategy has two components: (1) the selection of the organization's target market and (2) the creation and maintenance of a marketing mix that satisfies the market's needs for a specific product. Regardless of what general types of markets a firm focuses on, marketing management must select the firm's target markets. We will now examine two general approaches to identifying target markets—the total market approach and the market segmentation approach.

Total or Undifferentiated Market Approach

An organization sometimes defines the total market for a particular product as its target market. When a company designs a single marketing mix and directs it at an entire market for a particular product, it is using a **total market** (or **undifferentiated**) **approach.** Notice in Figure 3.2 that the organization is aiming a single marketing mix at the total market for the product. This approach assumes that individual customers in the target market for a specific kind of product have similar needs and, therefore, that the organization can satisfy most customers with a single marketing mix. This single marketing mix consists of one type of product with no (or very little) variation, one price, a promotional program aimed at everyone, and one distribution system to reach all customers in the total market. Products that can be marketed successfully with the total market approach include staple food items such as sugar and salt, certain kinds of farm produce, and some other products that most customers think of as homogeneous (no different from any other product of the same type). Morton's

Figure 3.2 ✔

Total market approach

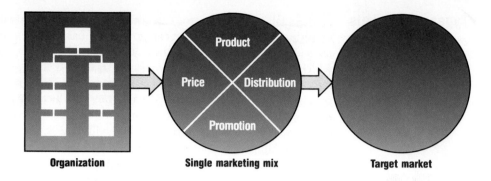

| Organization | Single marketing mix | Target market |

table salt, for instance, is aimed at the total market. One marketing mix can satisfy most consumers of this product.

The total market approach can be effective under two conditions. First, a large proportion of customers in the total market must have similar needs for the product. A marketer who uses a single marketing mix for a total market of customers with a variety of needs will find that the marketing mix satisfies very few people. Anyone could predict that a "universal shoe" that "fits everyone" would satisfy very few customers' needs for shoes because it would not fit most people. Second, the organization must be able to develop and maintain a single marketing mix that satisfies customers' needs. The company must be able to identify a set of product needs that are common to most customers in a total market, and it must have the resources and managerial skills to reach a sizable portion of that market. If customers' needs are dissimilar or if the organization is unable to develop and maintain a satisfying marketing mix, then a total market approach is likely to fail.

Companies that take the total market approach frequently attempt to use promotional efforts to differentiate their own products from competitors' products. They hope to establish in customers' minds that their products are superior and preferable to competing brands. This strategy is called **product differentiation** because a marketer tries to differentiate the product, in consumers' minds, from competitive brands.[1] Premium Saltines are promoted as "The All Goodness Family Cracker." The reclosable bags that help keep the crackers fresh are promoted to differentiate the product.

A marketer who uses product differentiation rarely designs a product that is very different physically from other brands. After all, consumers have relatively similar needs for the product. Because the product actually is not much different from competing brands, marketers rely heavily on promotional efforts to emphasize one or several small differences. Unleaded gasoline, for example, has a broad appeal. Millions of consumers need and use it. Yet most unleaded gasolines are not much different physically from other unleaded gasolines. Therefore, oil companies differentiate their unleaded gasolines from competing brands by promoting greater mileage, additives, or economy. The effectiveness of product differentiation is determined largely by whether the features used to distinguish one brand from another are credible and important to a large number of customers in the total market.

1. Wendell R. Smith, "Product Differentiation and Market Segmentation as Alternative Marketing Strategies," *Journal of Marketing*, July 1956, pp. 3–4.

Part I / An Analysis of Marketing Opportunities

Figure 3.3 ✔

Market segmentation approach

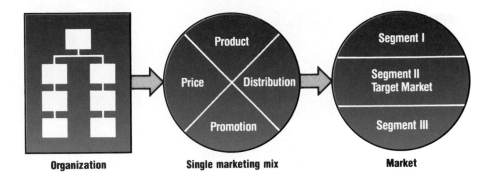

Although customers' needs for some products, such as staple food items, may be similar, there are a multitude of products for which customers' needs are decidedly different. In these cases, a company should not use the total market approach; instead, it should use the market segmentation approach.

Market Segmentation Approach

Markets made up of individuals with diverse product needs are called **heterogeneous markets.** Not everyone wants the same type of car, house, furniture, or clothes. If you were to ask fifty people what type of home each would like to have, you probably would receive fifty different answers, many of them quite distinct. The automobile market is another example of a heterogeneous market. Some individuals want a car that is economical, some see a car as a status symbol, and still others seek an automobile that is roomy and comfortable for travel. For such heterogeneous markets, the market segmentation approach is appropriate.

As shown in Figure 3.3, **market segmentation** is the process of dividing a total market into market groups consisting of people who have relatively similar product needs. The purpose is to design a marketing mix (or mixes) that more precisely matches the needs of individuals in a selected segment (or segments). Market segments arise from the segmentation process. A **market segment** is a group of individuals, groups, or organizations who share one or more similar characteristics that cause them to have relatively similar product needs.

The principal rationale for using the segmentation approach is that in a heterogeneous market, an organization is better able to develop a marketing mix that satisfies a relatively homogeneous portion of a total market than it is to design a marketing mix that meets the product needs of all people. The segmentation approach differs from the total approach because it aims one marketing mix at one segment of a total market rather than directing a single marketing mix at a total market.

The market segmentation approach is widely used. We will therefore analyze several of its most important features, including types of market segmentation strategies, conditions required for effective segmentation, selection of segmentation variables, and types of variables used to segment consumer and industrial markets.

Figure 3.4

Rolls-Royce advertisement (Source: Reprinted by permission of Rolls-Royce Motors Inc.)

Rolls-Royce. Simply the best motor car in the world.

New York
Carriage House Motor Cars, Ltd.
(212) 688-4650

Mount Kisco
Marty Cadillac Oldsmobile
(914) 241-3800

Glen Cove
Rallye Motors, Inc.
(516) 671-4622

Montclair, NJ
Regency Motors
(201) 746-4500

Greenwich, CT
Imported Cars of Greenwich, Inc.
(203) 869-2850

For information, contact your local authorized dealer or the national Rolls-Royce office (1-800-851-8576). © Rolls-Royce Motors, Inc. 1985.
The names "Rolls-Royce" and "Silver Spur" and the mascot, badge, and radiator grille are registered trademarks, as are the Bentley name, mascot, and badge.

Market Segmentation Strategies

There are two major segmentation strategies: the concentration strategy and the multisegment strategy.

Concentration Strategy

When an organization directs its marketing efforts toward a single market segment through one marketing mix, it is following a **concentration strategy.** This strategy is used, for example, by Rolls-Royce, which concentrates on only the luxury segment of the automobile market (see Figure 3.4).

The concentration strategy has advantages and disadvantages. A primary advantage is that it allows a firm to specialize. By concentrating all marketing efforts on a single segment, the firm has an opportunity to analyze the characteristics and needs of a distinct customer group. The firm can then direct all its efforts toward satisfying that group's needs. A firm can generate a large sales volume by reaching a single segment. In addition, concentrating on a single segment allows a firm with restricted resources to compete with much larger organizations. However, specialization can be a disadvantage too, because the firm puts "all its eggs in one basket." If a company's sales depend on a single segment and that segment's demand for the product declines, then the

Figure 3.5

Multisegment strategy ✔

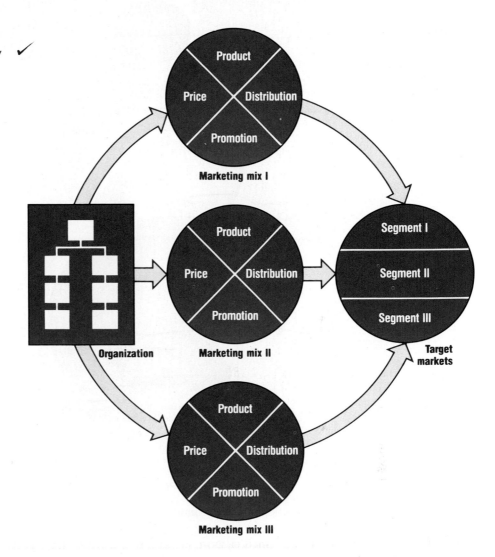

Marketing mix I

Organization   **Marketing mix II**   **Target markets**

Marketing mix III

company's financial strength also declines. Moreover, when a firm penetrates one segment and becomes well entrenched, its popularity may keep it from moving into other segments. For example, in the automobile market, Ferrari would have trouble moving into the economy-car segment, whereas Volkswagen would have difficulty entering the luxury-car segment.

Multisegment Strategy

After a firm uses a concentration strategy successfully in one market segment, it sometimes focuses on several segments. A **multisegment strategy** (see Figure 3.5) is one in which an organization directs its marketing efforts at two or more segments by developing a marketing mix for each selected segment. For example, designer fragrances have traditionally been aimed at one segment— women. However, as shown in the ad in Figure 3.6, Halston Enterprises, Inc. markets designer fragrances for men as well as women. The marketing mixes used for a multisegment strategy may vary in terms of product differences, distribution methods, promotion methods, and prices.

Chapter 3 / Target Markets: Segmentation and Evaluation   79

Figure 3.6

Designer fragrance for men (Source: Halston, 1–12, and Z–14 are registered trademarks. © 1986 Halston Enterprises, Inc. Advertising agency: Korey, Kay & Partners)

A business using the multisegment strategy can usually increase its sales in a total market by focusing on more than one segment, because the firm's mixes are being aimed at more people. A firm with excess production capacity may find the multisegment approach advantageous because the sale of products to additional segments may absorb excess capacity. However, because the multisegment strategy often requires a greater number of production processes, materials, and skills, production costs may be higher than with the concentration strategy. Keep in mind, also, that a firm using the multisegment approach ordinarily experiences higher marketing costs. Because the approach usually requires several different promotion plans and distribution methods, the costs of planning, organizing, implementing, and controlling marketing activities increase.

✓Conditions for Effective Segmentation

Whether a firm uses the concentration approach or the multisegment approach, several conditions must exist for market segmentation to be effective. First, a company must find out whether consumers' needs for the product are heterogeneous. If they are not, there is little need to segment the market. Second, the segments must be identifiable and divisible. The company must find some basis for effectively separating individuals in a total market into groups, each of which has a relatively uniform need for the product. Third, the total market should be divided in such a way that the segments can be compared with respect to estimated sales potential, costs, and profits. Fourth, at least one segment must have enough profit potential to justify developing and maintaining a special marketing mix. Finally, the firm must be able to reach the chosen segment with a particular marketing mix.

Some market segments may be difficult or impossible to reach because of legal, social, or distribution constraints. For instance, marketers of rock music recordings or jeans are not permitted to sell to a large market in the Soviet Union because of political and trade restrictions. For similar reasons, the strong demand in the United States for Cuban cigars is not met.

Choosing Segmentation Variables

Segmentation variables are the dimensions or characteristics of individuals, groups, or organizations that are used for dividing a total market into segments. For example, location, age, sex, or rate of product usage can be used for segmentation purposes. Here we will discuss how marketers determine a single segmentation variable. Later in the chapter we will examine multivariable segmentation.

Several factors are considered in selecting a segmentation variable. The segmentation variable should be related to customers' needs for, uses of, or behavior toward the product. That is, people's needs, uses, and actions should vary according to the chosen segmentation characteristic. Automobile producers use income as one means of segmenting the automobile market, but they do not use religion, because one person's automobile needs are not much different from those of persons of other religions. In addition, to classify individuals or organizations in a total market accurately, the segmentation variable must be measurable. For example, age, location, and sex are measurable. Such information can be obtained through observation or questioning. But trying to divide a market on the basis of intelligence would be extremely difficult because this characteristic is harder to measure accurately.

Choosing a segmentation variable is a critical step in segmenting a market. Selecting an inappropriate variable limits the chances of developing a successful strategy. To gain a better understanding of possible segmentation variables, we will consider the major types of variables in more detail.

Variables for Segmenting Consumer Markets

A marketer who uses a segmentation strategy to reach a consumer market can select one or several variables from a broad assortment of possible ones. As shown in Figure 3.7, segmentation variables can be grouped into four categories: (1) demographic, (2) geographic, (3) psychographic, and (4) product-related.

Demographic Variables

A demographer studies aggregate population characteristics such as the distribution of age and sex, fertility rates, migration patterns, and mortality rates. Marketers typically consider a broader range of socioeconomic characteristics as "demographic variables." Demographic characteristics that marketers commonly use to segment markets include age, sex, race, ethnicity, income, education, occupation, family size, family life cycle, religion, and social class. Marketers use demographic characteristics frequently because they are closely related to customers' product needs and purchasing behavior and because they can be readily measured.

Figure 3.7

Segmentation variables
for consumer markets

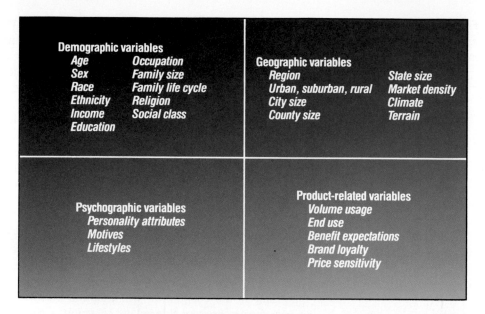

Demographic variables
Age   Occupation
Sex   Family size
Race   Family life cycle
Ethnicity   Religion
Income   Social class
Education

Geographic variables
Region   State size
Urban, suburban, rural   Market density
City size   Climate
County size   Terrain

Psychographic variables
Personality attributes
Motives
Lifestyles

Product-related variables
Volume usage
End use
Benefit expectations
Brand loyalty
Price sensitivity

Figure 3.8

U.S. age distribution
and projected changes

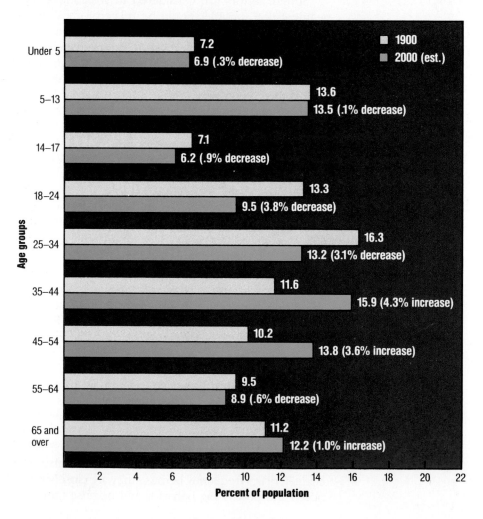

Part I / An Analysis of Marketing Opportunities

Figure 3.9 ✓

Segmentation of the toy
market

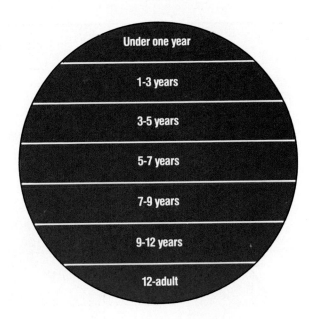

Since age is often used for segmentation purposes, marketers need to be aware of the distribution of age and how that distribution is changing. Figure 3.8 shows the proportion of the U.S. population in various age groups for 1980 and projections for 2000. The under-5 age group will increase, while the remaining age groups under 25 are expected to decline. All age groups that include persons now 25 years or older are expected to increase. In 1970, the average age of a U.S. citizen was 27.9 and it is currently about 32; it is projected that the average age will be 35.5 in the year 2000.

Consider the types of markets that are segmented according to age. Some examples are clothing, toys, automobiles, and diet foods. (See the application on page 86 for a discussion of how sports participation varies across age groups.) Figure 3.9 shows a possible segmentation scheme for the toy market. Notice that with the exception of the 12-to-adult segment, the age ranges that define the segments are relatively narrow because children's needs for toys change rapidly. A toy that entertains children at age 2 rarely interests them at age 5.

A firm's resources and capabilities affect the number and size of segment ranges used. The type of product and the degree of variation in consumers' needs also dictate the number and size of segment categories for a particular firm's marketing approach. For example, the number and size of the segments in Figure 3.9 may be appropriate for dividing the toy market. Clearly, however, the same age ranges would not be satisfactory for segmenting the market for dairy products.

Sex is commonly employed to segment a number of markets, including clothes, soft drinks, nonprescription medications, deodorants, magazines, soaps, and even cigarettes. The product in Figure 3.10 is definitely aimed at women. The *1980 U.S. Census of Population* indicated that there are about 6 million more females than males in the United States. Females represent 51.3 percent of the total population.

Figure 3.10

Advertisement for a product aimed at women (Source: Halston, © 1986 Halston Enterprises, Inc. Advertising agency: Korey, Kay & Partners)

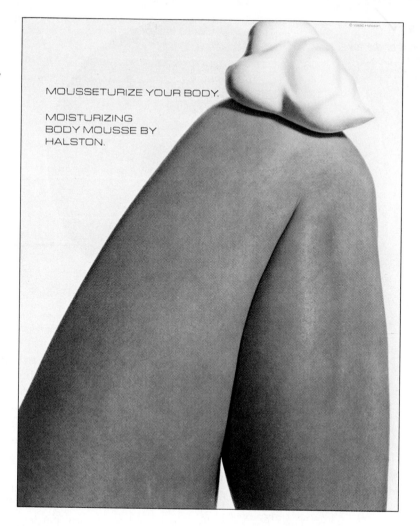

A variety of markets are divided on the basis of income. Beginning in 1950 real family income rose steadily for thirty years, almost doubling during that time. The distributions of annual family income for 1960, 1970, and 1980 are presented in Figure 3.11. In 1960 over one-fourth (27.5 percent) of the families earned incomes of less than $10,000, while in 1980 only about one out of five (18.9 percent) had incomes below $10,000. Less than 20 percent of the families in 1960 earned over $25,000 annually. By 1980 almost 40 percent did.

Income is often used to divide markets because it strongly influences people's product needs. It affects their ability to buy (discussed in Chapter 2) and their aspirations for a certain style of living. Examples of product markets segmented by income include housing, furniture, clothing, automobiles, food, and certain kinds of sporting goods.

Ethnicity, too, is used to segment markets for goods such as food, music, and clothing and for services such as banking and insurance. A striking example of the importance of ethnicity as a segmentation variable is the U.S. Hispanic population. Made up of people with Mexican, Cuban, and Puerto Rican ancestry and other people of Central and South American heritage, this ethnic group

Part I / An Analysis of Marketing Opportunities

Figure 3.11

Distribution of the U.S.
population by annual
family income, 1960,
1970, and 1980

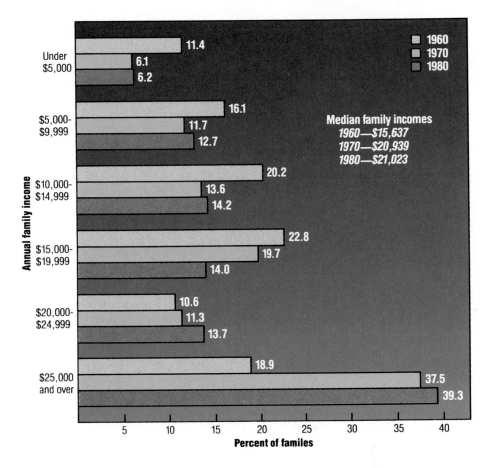

is growing six times faster than the general population. The Hispanic population is concentrated in nine states, as indicated in Table 3.1. If it continues to grow at its current rate, it will be the largest ethnic group in the country by the year 2020.

The product needs of a household also vary according to marital status and the presence and age of children. These characteristics can be combined into a single variable, sometimes called the family life cycle. Housing, appliances, food, automobiles, and boats are a few of the numerous product markets sometimes segmented by family life cycle stages. The family life cycle has been broken down in several different ways, one of which follows:

1. Young
    a. Single without children
    b. Married without children
    c. Single with children
    d. Married with children
2. Middle-aged
    a. Single without children
    b. Married without children
    c. Single with children
    d. Married with children

Application

Age and Sports Participation

Consider the different types of organizations that are directly affected by individuals' participation in sports-related activities: producers of sports equipment, shoes, and clothing; providers of commercial sports facilities; local parks and recreation departments; and retail sporting goods stores.

Age is a major demographic factor that influences people's participation in sports. Recent survey results show sports participation to be at record highs, partly because 30 percent of Americans are aged 18 to 29. This age group is twice as likely as other groups to participate in sports. A subgroup, aged 18 to 24, enjoys swimming, bowling, fishing, jogging, and softball; and this age group is twice as likely as others to participate in touch football, tennis, soccer, water skiing, scuba diving, windsurfing, and skateboarding. People aged 25 to 29 are more likely than others to fish, camp, and hike; they are also more likely to swim and twice as likely to go jogging and play pool, softball, and volleyball. Racketball, snow skiing, and weight lifting are more popular in this age range than in other age groupings.

Americans aged 30 to 49 tend to stay away from the more strenuous activities, preferring swimming, fishing, camping, gardening, hiking, bowling, softball, and jogging. Those between the ages of 50 and 64 prefer gardening as well as swimming, camping, fishing, hiking, hunting, motorboating, and bowling. However, compared to the share of all adults that participate in these sports, their share is smaller. People over 65 are least likely to participate in sports. Elderly Americans who do participate most enjoy gardening but also like to fish, hike, golf, bowl, swim, camp, and hunt. (*Source: Martha Farnsworth Riche, "Americans at Play,"* American Demographics, *Aug. 1985, pp. 38–39.*)

    e. Single without dependent children
    f. Married without dependent children
3. Older
    a. Single
    b. Married[2]

The number of single-person households has increased from 17 percent in 1970 to about 25 percent in the mid-1980s. The "typical" American family of two adults (with one being the bread winner) and two children makes up only 6 percent of all U.S. households. Almost 60 percent of all adult women work outside the home. Of these women, 40 percent have children under 6 years of age. Over two-thirds of all adults are married. However, people are waiting longer to get married and are having fewer children. About half of all families do not have children under 18 years of age.

People of the same age may have diverse product needs because they are in different stages of the family life cycle. Individuals in a particular life cycle stage may have very specific needs that can be satisfied by precisely designed marketing mixes. Young, educated single adults may desire small but well-appointed apartments or condominiums. Some can afford expensive clothing, stereo systems, and appliances such as microwave ovens. Divorced females

2. Adapted with permission from Patrick E. Murphy and William A. Staples, "A Modernized Family Life Cycle," *Journal of Consumer Research,* June 1979, p. 16.

Table 3.1 Nine states that contain 85 percent of U.S. Hispanics

State	1970	1980	Percent of 1980 Hispanics in USA
California	2,369,292	4,544,331	31.1
Texas	1,840,648	2,985,824	20.4
New York	1,351,982	1,659,300	11.4
Florida	405,036	858,158	5.9
Illinois	393,204	635,602	4.4
New Jersey	288,488	491,883	3.4
New Mexico	308,340	477,222	3.3
Arizona	264,770	440,701	3.0
Colorado	225,506	339,717	2.3

Source: U.S. Census Bureau.

with children may be seeking life insurance. A middle-aged couple, with children no longer at home, has more discretionary income for entertainment, expensive restaurants, and travel.

We have discussed only a few demographic variables among many. Publishers of encyclopedias and dictionaries use education level to segment markets, while brewers sometimes aim their products at broad occupational categories. Producers of cosmetics and hair-care products sometimes segment markets based on race. Certain types of foods and clothing are directed toward people of specific religious sects.

Geographic Variables · coffee

Geographic variables—climate, terrain, natural resources, population density, and subcultural values—also influence consumer product needs. Markets may be divided into regions because one or more geographic variables cause customers to differ from one region to another. A company that markets products to a national market might divide the United States into the following regions: Pacific, Southwest, Central, Midwest, Southeast, Middle Atlantic, and New England. A firm operating in one or several states might regionalize its market by counties, cities, zip code areas, or other units.

Marketers sometimes segment on the basis of state populations, and they use population figures in estimating demand. Between 1970 and 1980 the U.S. population grew by 11.4 percent, but the population in all geographic areas did not grow proportionally. The South and the West increased significantly, while the Midwest and East experienced only minor gains. However, New York, Rhode Island, and the District of Columbia lost population. The map in Figure 3.12 indicates the projected population growth (or loss) of each state between 1980 and 2000. Note that the heaviest growth will be in Florida and the western states. Nine states and the District of Columbia are expected to decline in population. For segmentation and market analysis purposes, marketers must be aware of both current population patterns and projected changes in these patterns.

City size can be an important segmentation variable. Some marketers want

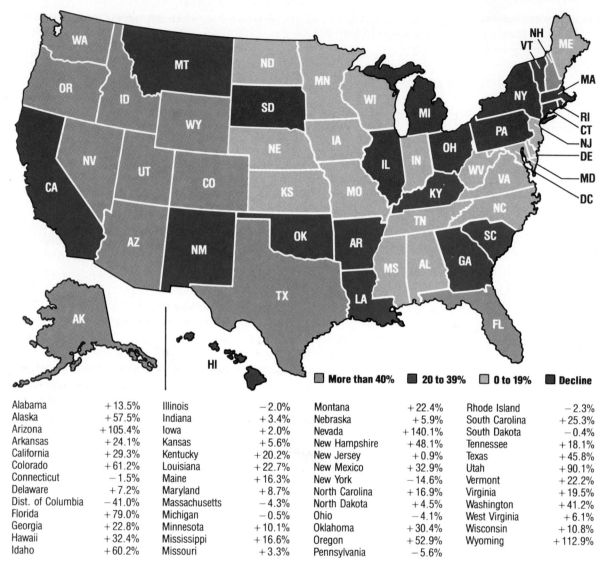

More than 40%		**20 to 39%**		**0 to 19%**	**Decline**

State	%	State	%	State	%	State	%
Alabama	+13.5%	Illinois	−2.0%	Montana	+22.4%	Rhode Island	−2.3%
Alaska	+57.5%	Indiana	+3.4%	Nebraska	+5.9%	South Carolina	+25.3%
Arizona	+105.4%	Iowa	+2.0%	Nevada	+140.1%	South Dakota	−0.4%
Arkansas	+24.1%	Kansas	+5.6%	New Hampshire	+48.1%	Tennessee	+18.1%
California	+29.3%	Kentucky	+20.2%	New Jersey	+0.9%	Texas	+45.8%
Colorado	+61.2%	Louisiana	+22.7%	New Mexico	+32.9%	Utah	+90.1%
Connecticut	−1.5%	Maine	+16.3%	New York	−14.6%	Vermont	+22.2%
Delaware	+7.2%	Maryland	+8.7%	North Carolina	+16.9%	Virginia	+19.5%
Dist. of Columbia	−41.0%	Massachusetts	−4.3%	North Dakota	+4.5%	Washington	+41.2%
Florida	+79.0%	Michigan	−0.5%	Ohio	−4.1%	West Virginia	+6.1%
Georgia	+22.8%	Minnesota	+10.1%	Oklahoma	+30.4%	Wisconsin	+10.8%
Hawaii	+32.4%	Mississippi	+16.6%	Oregon	+52.9%	Wyoming	+112.9%
Idaho	+60.2%	Missouri	+3.3%	Pennsylvania	−5.6%		

Figure 3.12 *Projected U.S. population growth in 1980–2000 (percent) (Source: U.S. Census Bureau)*

to focus their efforts on cities of a certain size. For example, a certain franchised restaurant organization will not locate in cities of less than 200,000 because it takes at least that many people to generate enough sales volume to provide the profit potential for a successful operation. Other firms seek opportunities in smaller towns. Initially, Wal-Mart Stores, Inc., a rapidly growing discount chain with over seven hundred stores in eighteen states, would locate only in towns with less than 25,000 people.

Since cities often cut across political boundaries, the U.S. Census Bureau developed a system to classify metropolitan areas (any area with a city of at least 50,000 or with an urbanized area of at least 50,000 and a total metropolitan population of at least 100,000). Metropolitan areas are categorized as one of the following: a metropolitan statistical area (MSA), a primary metropolitan statistical area (PMSA), or a consolitated metropolitan statistical area (CMSA). A MSA is an urbanized area encircled by nonmetropolitan counties and neither socially nor economically dependent on any other metropolitan area. A metropolitan area within a complex of at least one million inhabitants can elect to be named a PMSA. A CMSA is a metropolitan area of at least one million consisting of two or more PMSAs. CMSAs total twenty-three, including one in Puerto Rico (see Figure 3.13). The five largest CMSAs, New York, Los Angeles, Chicago, Philadelphia, and San Francisco, account for 20 percent of the U.S. population. The federal government provides a considerable amount of socioeconomic information about MSAs, PMSAs, and CMSAs that is useful for market analysis and segmentation purposes.

Market density refers to the number of potential customers within a unit of land area, such as a square mile. Although market density is related generally to population density, the correlation is not exact. For example, in two different geographic markets of approximately equal size and population, the market density for denture cleaners might be much higher in one area than in another if one area contains a significantly greater proportion of older people. That low-density markets often require different sales, advertising, and distribution activities than high-density markets explains why market density is used as a segmentation variable.

Climate is commonly used as a geographic segmentation variable because it has such a broad impact on people's behavior and product needs. The wide variety of product markets that are affected by climate include air-conditioning and heating equipment, clothing, yard tools, sports equipment, and building materials.

Psychographic Variables

Many psychographic factors could be used to segment markets, but the three most common are personality characteristics, motives, and lifestyles. A psychographic dimension can be used by itself to segment a market, or it can be combined with other types of segmentation variables.

Examples of personality characteristics used to segment markets are gregariousness, compulsiveness, competitiveness, extroversion, introversion, ambitiousness, and aggressiveness. Personality characteristics are useful when a product is similar to many competing products and consumers' needs are not affected significantly by other segmentation variables.

When attempting to segment a market on the basis of a personality characteristic, marketers face two major problems. First, personality characteristics are difficult, if not impossible, to measure accurately. Existing personality tests were developed for clinical use, not for segmentation purposes. Second, even though it seems reasonable that personality characteristics affect buyers' actions, research has yielded little evidence to support this assumption.

When appealing to a personality characteristic, a marketer almost always selects one that is valued positively by many people in our culture. Individuals with this characteristic, as well as those who would like to have it, may be influenced to buy that marketer's brand. For example, a brand may be promoted as "not for everyone" but for those who are "independent," "strong-minded," or "outgoing." Marketers who take this approach do not worry about measuring

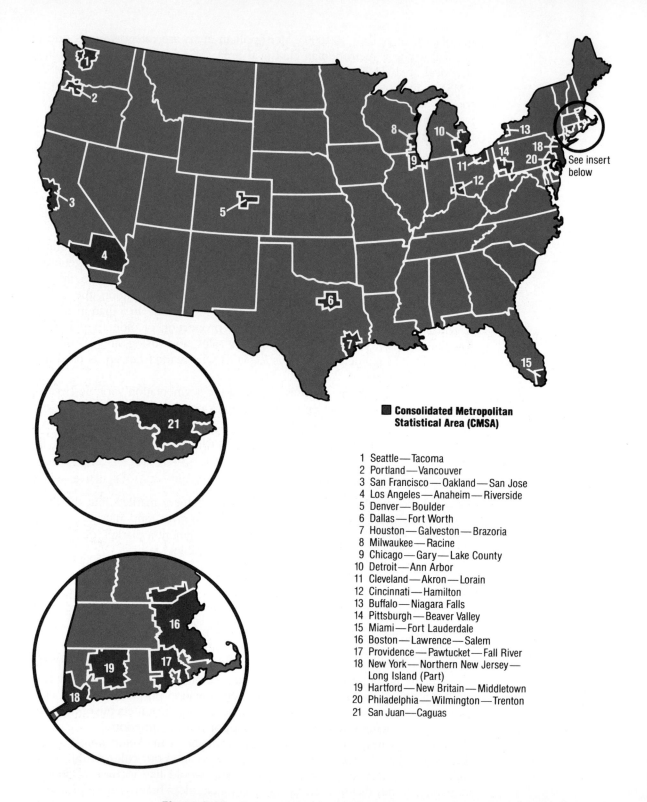

Consolidated Metropolitan Statistical Area (CMSA)

1 Seattle—Tacoma
2 Portland—Vancouver
3 San Francisco—Oakland—San Jose
4 Los Angeles—Anaheim—Riverside
5 Denver—Boulder
6 Dallas—Fort Worth
7 Houston—Galveston—Brazoria
8 Milwaukee—Racine
9 Chicago—Gary—Lake County
10 Detroit—Ann Arbor
11 Cleveland—Akron—Lorain
12 Cincinnati—Hamilton
13 Buffalo—Niagara Falls
14 Pittsburgh—Beaver Valley
15 Miami—Fort Lauderdale
16 Boston—Lawrence—Salem
17 Providence—Pawtucket—Fall River
18 New York—Northern New Jersey—
   Long Island (Part)
19 Hartford—New Britain—Middletown
20 Philadelphia—Wilmington—Trenton
21 San Juan—Caguas

Figure 3.13 *Consolidated metropolitan statistical areas and projected growth (Source: U.S. Census Bureau)*

how many people have the positively valued characteristic, because they assume that a sizable proportion of people in the target market either have it or want to have it.

A motive is an internal energizing force that moves an individual toward a goal. To some degree, motives influence what people buy. Despite the difficulty of measuring them, motives are occasionally used to divide markets. Product durability, economy, convenience, and status are all motives that may affect the types of products purchased and the choice of stores in which they are bought. When a market is segmented according to a motive, it is divided on the basis of consumers' reasons for making a purchase. For example, one motive for the purchase of soft drinks in nonreturnable containers is convenience.

Lifestyle analysis provides a broad view of buyers because it encompasses numerous characteristics related to people's activities, interests, and opinions. Lifestyle segmentation divides individuals into groups on the basis of how they spend their time, the importance of things in their surroundings (their homes or their jobs, for example), their beliefs about themselves and broad issues, and some socioeconomic characteristics such as income and education.[3] Obviously, the manner in which people live affects their product needs. Revlon (see Figure 3.14) couples age with lifestyle characteristics to divide the cosmetic market into seven segments. Each segment is served by one of the following Revlon product lines: Classic Revlon, Moon Drops, Natural Wonder, Charlie, Ultima II, Princess Marcella Borghese, and Etherea Fine Fragrances. Charlie is directed at aspiring, self-assured women who are out to shape their own lives and develop their careers. Revlon portrays the Charlie woman as exciting, adventurous, rule-breaking, and earthshaking. The Princess Marcella Borghese line is directed at the fulfilled (rather than aspiring) woman who is very much concerned with fashion, status, and class. This expensive product line is for the "select few." It is promoted by word of mouth and by a limited number of distinctive, subtle advertisements in upscale women's magazines. Compare how these two lifestyles are portrayed in the Revlon advertisements in Figure 3.14.

Psychographic dimensions can effectively divide a market. However, their use has been limited, and probably will continue to be, for several reasons. First, they are more difficult than other types of segmentation variables to measure accurately. Second, the relationships among psychographic variables and consumers' needs are sometimes obscure and unproven. Third, segments that result from psychographic segmentation may not be reachable. For example, a marketer may determine that highly compulsive individuals desire a certain type of clothing. However, no specific stores or specific media vehicles—such as television or radio programs, newspapers, or magazines—appeal precisely to this group and this group alone.

Product-related Variables

Marketers can divide a market on the basis of a characteristic of the consumer's relationship to the product. These characteristics commonly involve some aspect of product use. Thus, a total market may be divided into users and nonusers. Users may then be classified as heavy, moderate, or light. To satisfy a specific group, such as heavy users, a marketer may have to create a distinctive product, set special prices, and initiate special promotion and distribution activities.

3. Joseph T. Plummer, "The Concept and Application of Life Style Segmentation," *Journal of Marketing,* Jan. 1974, p. 33.

How customers use or apply the product may also be a basis for segmenting the market. To satisfy customers who use a product in a certain way, some feature—say packaging, size, texture, or color—may have to be designed precisely to make the product easier to use, safer, or more convenient. In addition, special distribution, promotion, or pricing activities may have to be created.

Another product-related characteristic is the benefit that consumers expect from the product. **Benefit segmentation** is the division of a market according to the benefits that customers want from the product. Although most segmentation variables imply a purported relationship between the variable and customers' needs, benefit segmentation is different in that the benefits sought by customers *are* their product needs. That is, individuals are segmented directly according to their needs. By determining the benefits that consumers want, marketers may be able to divide people into groups that are seeking certain sets of benefits.

The effectiveness of benefit segmentation depends on several conditions. The benefits sought by people must be identifiable. Using these benefits, marketers must be able to group people into recognizable segments, and one or more of the resulting segments must be accessible to the firm's marketing efforts.

As this brief discussion shows, consumer markets can be divided on the basis of numerous characteristics. However, some of these variables are not particularly helpful for segmenting industrial or organizational markets.

Variables for Segmenting Organizational Markets

Industrial or organizational markets, like consumer markets, must sometimes be segmented to satisfy organizations' needs for products. Marketers make this segmentation on the basis of geographic factors, type of organization, customer size, and product use.

Geographic Location

We have noted that the demand for some consumer products varies considerably from one geographic area to another as a result of differences in climate, terrain, customer preferences, or similar factors. For example, the producers of certain types of lumber divide their markets geographically because their customers' needs vary regionally. Geographic segmentation may be especially appropriate for reaching industries that are concentrated in certain locations. Furniture producers, for example, are concentrated in the Southeast, while most iron and steel producers are located in the Great Lakes area.

Type of Organization

A company sometimes segments a market on the basis of the types of organizations in that market. Different types of organizations often require different product features, distribution systems, and price structures. Because of these variations, a firm either may concentrate on a single segment with one marketing mix or may focus on several groups with multiple mixes. A carpet producer could segment potential customers into several groups, including auto makers, commercial carpet contractors (firms that carpet large commercial buildings), apartment-complex developers, carpet wholesalers, and large retail carpet outlets.

Buying procedures in various kinds of organizations may be sufficiently different that they require special marketing efforts. Marketers who sell to

Wear an original.

Charlie

REVLON

If you're going to do something about beauty care,
do it very, very well.

Princess Marcella **B**orghese

Special beauty treatment and uncommon colour. Available internationally.

Figure 3.14 *Lifestyles associated with two Revlon perfume lines (Source: Courtesy of Revlon)*

governments, for example, must know how to prepare proposals, bids, and contracts. One or more of a variety of individuals—including chief executives, purchasing agents, and engineers—may have a hand in the buying decisions of a manufacturing organization. Selling to a committee is quite different from selling to an individual.

Customer Size

An organization's size may affect purchasing procedures and the types and quantities of products desired. Size can thus be an effective variable for segmenting an organizational market.

To reach a particular-sized segment, marketers may have to adjust one or more marketing mix components. For example, customers who buy in extremely large quantities sometimes are charged lower prices. In addition, marketers often have to provide greater personal selling efforts to serve larger organizational buyers properly. Because the needs of larger and smaller buyers tend to be quite distinct, marketers frequently employ different marketing practices to reach various customer groups.

Use of Product

Some products—especially basic raw materials such as steel, petroleum, plastics, and lumber—are used in numerous ways. How a firm uses products affects the types and amounts of the products purchased as well as the method of making the purchase. For example, computers are used for engineering purposes,

Figure 3.15

*Single-variable
segmentation*

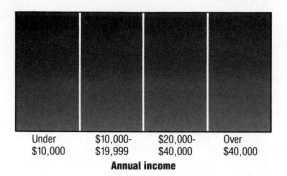

| Under $10,000 | $10,000-$19,999 | $20,000-$40,000 | Over $40,000 |

Annual income

for performing basic scientific research, and for business operations such as telephone service and airline reservations. A computer producer may segment the computer market by types of use because needs for computer hardware and software depend on the purpose for which the products are purchased.

Selecting the appropriate variable for market segmentation is an important marketing management decision because the variable is the primary factor in defining the target market. So far, we have discussed segmentation by one variable. In fact more than one variable can be used, and marketers must decide on the number of variables to include.

Single-variable or Multivariable Segmentation

A marketer can divide a market in terms of one variable or several. **Single-variable segmentation** is achieved by using only one variable. The segmentation shown in Figure 3.15 uses only income. (Although the areas shown on the graph are the same size, this does not mean that the segments are the same size or equal in sales potential.) Single-variable segmentation, the simplest form of segmentation, is the easiest to perform. However, a single characteristic affords marketers only moderate precision in designing a marketing mix to satisfy individuals in a specific segment.

Multivariable segmentation is achieved by using more than one characteristic to divide a total market (see Figure 3.16). Notice in the figure that the market is segmented by three variables—income, population density, and volume usage. The people in the darkly shaded segment earn over $40,000, are urban dwellers, and are heavy users. Multivariable segmentation provides more information about the individuals in each segment than does single-variable segmentation. More is known about the people in each segment of Figure 3.16 than about those in the segments of Figure 3.15. This additional information may allow a marketer to develop a marketing mix that will satisfy customers in a given segment more precisely.

The major disadvantage of multivariable segmentation is that the larger the number of variables used, the greater the number of segments. This proliferation reduces the sales potential of many of the segments. Compare, for example, the number and size of the segments in Figure 3.15 with the number and size of those in Figure 3.16.

The use of additional variables can help to create and maintain a more precise and satisfying marketing mix. However, when deciding on single- or multivariable segmentation, a marketing manager must consider whether using additional variables actually will help improve the firm's marketing mix. If

Figure 3.16

Multivariable segmentation

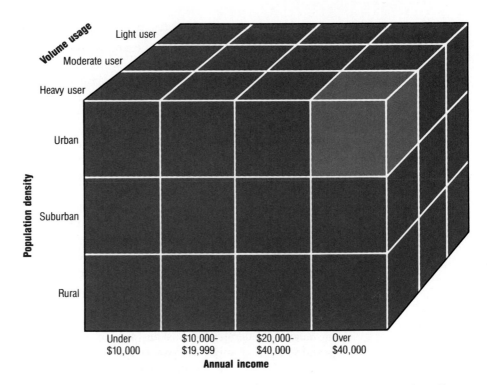

using a second or third variable does not provide useful information that allows greater precision, there is little reason to spend more money to gain information about the extra variables.

Evaluating Markets and Forecasting Sales

Whether single-variable segmentation or multivariable segmentation is used, a marketer must be able to measure the sales potential of the segment or segments. Developing and maintaining a marketing mix normally consumes a considerable amount of a firm's resources. The target market or markets selected must have enough sales potential to justify the cost of developing and maintaining one or more marketing mixes.

A marketer must evaluate the sales potential in possible target markets as well as in the target markets that the firm currently serves. Moreover, a marketing manager must determine the proportion of this potential that the firm can capture relative to its objectives, resources, and managerial skills. He or she must ponder the question, "To what extent can our company tap this market if the potential is there?"

Demand can be measured along several dimensions, including product level, competitive level, geographic area, and time.[4] With respect to product level, demand can be estimated for specific product items (such as frozen orange juice) or for a product line (such as frozen foods). The competitive level specifies whether sales are being measured for one firm or for an entire

4. Philip Kotler, *Marketing Management: Analysis, Planning, and Control,* 5th ed. (Englewood Cliffs, N.J.: Prentice-Hall, 1984), p. 225.

industry. A manager must also decide on the geographic area to be included in an evaluation of demand. For example, demand could be measured for a neighborhood, town, county, state, or nation. In relation to time, demand measurements can be short range (one year or less), medium range (one to five years), or long range (longer than five years).

Market and Company Sales Potentials

Market sales potential refers to the amount of a product that would be purchased by specific customer groups within a specified period at a specific level of industrywide marketing activity. Market sales potential can be stated in terms of dollars or units and can refer to a total market or to a market segment. When analyzing market sales potential, it is important to specify a time frame and to indicate the relevant level of industry marketing activities.

Note here that marketers have to assume a certain general level of marketing effort in the industry when they estimate market sales potential. The specific level of marketing effort varies, of course, from one firm to another, but the sum of all firms' marketing activities equals industry marketing efforts. A marketing manager also must consider whether and to what extent industry marketing efforts will change.

Company sales potential is the amount of a product that an organization could sell during a specified period. Several general factors influence a company's sales potential. First, the market sales potential places absolute limits on the size of the company's sales potential. Second, the intensity of industrywide marketing activities has an indirect but definite effect on the company sales potential. Those activities have a direct bearing on the size of the market sales potential. When Texas Instruments advertises calculators, for example, it indirectly promotes calculators in general; it may, in fact, help to sell competitors' calculators. Third, the intensity and effectiveness of a company's marketing activities in proportion to the total industry's marketing efforts affect the size of the company's sales potential. If a company is spending twice as much as any of its competitors on marketing efforts, and if each dollar spent is more effective in generating sales, the firm's sales potential will be quite high compared with its competitors'.

There are two general approaches to measuring company sales potential—the breakdown approach and the buildup approach. In the **breakdown approach,** the marketing manager initially develops a general economic forecast for a specific time period. The market sales potential is estimated on the basis of this economic forecast. The company sales potential then is derived from the general economic forecast and the estimate of market sales potential. Thus, this approach is called the breakdown approach because the marketer starts with broad, comprehensive estimates of general economic activity and ends up with an estimate of a single firm's sales of a specific product.

In the **buildup approach,** an analyst begins by estimating how much of a product a potential buyer in a specific geographic area, such as a sales territory, will purchase in a given period. Then the analyst multiplies that amount by the total number of potential buyers in that area. He or she does the same thing for each geographic area in which the firm sells products and then adds the totals for each area to calculate the market potential. To determine the company sales potential, the analyst must estimate, on the basis of specific levels of marketing activities, the proportion of the total market potential that the firm can obtain.

For example, the marketing manager of a regional paper company with three competitors might estimate the company sales potential for bulk gift-wrapping paper using the buildup approach. The manager might determine that each of sixty-six paper buyers in a single sales territory purchases an average of 10 rolls annually. Thus, for that sales territory, the market potential is 660 rolls annually. The analyst follows the same procedure in each of the firm's other nineteen sales territories. He or she then totals the sales potential for each sales territory. Assume that this total market potential is 18,255 rolls of paper (the quantity expected to be sold by all four paper companies). Then the marketing manager would estimate the company sales potential by ascertaining what percentage of the estimated 18,255 rolls the firm could sell, assuming a certain level of marketing effort. The marketing manager might develop several company sales potentials, based on several levels of marketing effort.

Notice that regardless of whether marketers use the breakdown or buildup approach, they depend heavily on sales estimates. To get a clearer idea of how these estimates are arrived at, we need to explore sales forecasting.

Developing Company Sales Forecasts

A **company sales forecast** is the amount of a product that the company actually expects to sell during a specific period at a specified level of marketing activities. When analyzing sales potential, marketers consider what sales amounts are possible at various levels of marketing activities, assuming that certain environmental conditions will exist. However, when marketers develop a sales forecast, they concentrate on what the actual sales will be at a certain level of marketing effort.

Many operating units use the company sales forecast for planning, organizing, implementing, and controlling their activities. Managers use sales forecasts when purchasing raw materials, scheduling production, securing financial resources, considering plant or equipment purchases, hiring personnel, and planning inventory levels. The success of numerous activities depends on the accuracy of the company sales forecast. (The application on page 98 discusses two firms that lacked accurate sales forecasts.)

A sales forecast must be time specific. As indicated earlier, sales estimates can be short range (one year or less), medium range (one to five years), or long range (longer than five years). The length of time chosen for the sales forecast depends on what the forecast will be used for, how stable the market is, and what the firm's objectives and resources are.

To forecast company sales, a marketer can choose from a number of forecasting methods. Some forecasting methods are rather arbitrary; others are more scientific, complex, and time consuming. The method or methods that a firm uses depend on the costs involved, the type of product, the characteristics of the market, the time span of the forecast, the purposes for which the forecast is used, the stability of the historical sales data, the availability of required information, and the expertise and experience of the forecasters.[5] For purposes of analysis, common forecasting techniques can be grouped into five categories: executive judgment, surveys, time series analysis, correlation methods, and market tests. We will explore each of these techniques.

5. David Hurwood, Elliott S. Grossman, and Earl Bailey, *Sales Forecasting* (New York: Conference Board, 1978), p. 2.

Application

Importance of Accurate Sales Forecasts

The accuracy of sales forecasts is important to the long-term economic health of an organization. Consider the two following examples.

When IBM introduced its PC*jr* home computer, forecasted sales did not materialize. Company strategists went to work. In addition to upgrading the keyboard and investing $40 million in Charlie Chaplin ads, IBM cut prices by 20 percent. However, the slashed prices failed to generate the 40 percent gross margin IBM expects from its products. IBM attempted to raise margins several months later by lifting the rebate that had permitted dealers to sell PC*jr*'s for less than $1,000, but as soon as the company took this action, sales came to a standstill. Having sold only 30,000 units, IBM could either settle for unacceptable margins by cutting prices again or discontinue the PC*jr*. IBM chose the latter alternative.

Although marketers would much prefer sales to exceed rather than fall short of forecasts, it is nonetheless true that a product moving faster than projected can cause lost revenues. Pillsbury's refrigerated Soft Breadsticks sold so fast that sales exceeded projected figures by 40 percent only months after national distribution began. Because Pillsbury was caught off guard, the high-volume purchases emptied the shelves throughout the Thanksgiving and Christmas holidays. This "stockout" condition created customer dissatisfaction at the retail store level, which made grocers and distributors unhappy. Also, the empty shelves meant that customers who wanted to try the product for the first time could not do so, thus slowing consumer exposure to the new product. Pillsbury had to move fast to supply the demand and prevent further loss of resources. (*Sources: "Junior Was Too Expensive, Even for IBM,"* Business Week, *April 1, 1985, pp. 34–35; William Pat Patterson, "IBM Price Cut Signals New Line,"* Industry Week, *June 25, 1984, pp. 25–26; and Julie Frary, "New Pillsbury Dough Looks Like It'll Stick,"* Advertising Age, *April 8, 1985, p. 82.*)

Executive Judgment

At times, a company forecasts sales primarily on the basis of **executive judgment**—the intuition of one or more executives. This approach is highly unscientific, but it is expedient and inexpensive. Executive judgment may work reasonably well when product demand is relatively stable and the forecaster has years of market-related experience. However, because intuition is swayed most heavily by recent experience, the forecast may be overoptimistic or overpessimistic. Another drawback to intuition is that the forecaster has only past experience as a guide for deciding where to go in the future.

Surveys

A second way to predict sales is to question customers, sales personnel, or experts regarding their expectations about future purchases.

Customer surveys Through a **customer forecasting survey,** marketers can ask customers what types and quantities of products they intend to buy during a specific period. This approach may be useful to a business that has relatively few customers. For example, a transistor producer with fewer than two hundred potential buyers could conduct a customer survey. PepsiCo, Inc., though, has millions of customers and cannot feasibly employ a customer survey to forecast future sales.

Customer surveys have several drawbacks. Customers must be able and willing to make accurate estimates of future product requirements. Although industrial buyers can sometimes estimate their anticipated purchases accurately from historical buying data and their own sales forecasts, many customers cannot make such estimates. For a variety of reasons, customers may not want to participate in a survey. Occasionally, a few respondents give answers that they know are incorrect, making survey results inaccurate. In addition, customer surveys reflect buying intentions, not actual purchases. Customers' intentions may not be well formulated, and even when potential purchasers have definite buying intentions, they do not necessarily follow through on them. Finally, customer surveys consume a great deal of time and money.

Sales-force surveys In a **sales-force forecasting survey,** members of the firm's sales force are asked to estimate the anticipated sales in their territories for a specified period of time. The forecaster combines these territorial estimates to arrive at a tentative forecast.

Let us trace this process in one manufacturing organization—Ex-Cell-O Corporation, which manufactures machine tools. Machine tools usually are sold through open proposals. These bids are submitted to specific customers for certain types of products. The data in the proposals go into the firm's marketing information system. When the forecast is being prepared, each salesperson receives a summary of his or her proposals, reviews this summary, updates it as needed, and then prepares the forecast for his or her territory for the next five quarters. The sales representatives then send their forecasts to regional managers, who review them and make necessary refinements. The regional managers send the forecasts to the marketing staff at corporate headquarters, where the forecasts are processed. The new forecast is transmitted to Ex-Cell-O's eight manufacturing plants to aid in production and inventory control.[6]

A marketer may survey the sales staff for several reasons. The most important one is that the sales staff is closer to customers on a daily basis than are other company personnel and therefore should know more about customers' future product needs. Moreover, when sales representatives assist in developing the forecast, they are more likely to work toward its achievement. Another benefit of this method is that forecasts can be prepared for single territories, for divisions consisting of several territories, for regions made up of multiple divisions, and then for the total geographic market. This method readily provides sales forecasts from the smallest geographic sales unit to the largest.

Despite these benefits, a sales-force survey has certain limitations. Salespeople can be too optimistic or pessimistic because of recent experiences. Their estimates may be either inflated or low. In addition, salespeople tend to underestimate the sales potential in their territories when they believe that their sales goals will be determined by their forecasts. Finally, salespeople usually dislike paperwork because it consumes time that could be spent selling. If the preparation of a territorial sales forecast is time consuming, the sales staff may do an inadequate job on it.

Nonetheless, sales-force surveys can be effective under certain conditions. If, for instance, the salespeople as a group are accurate—or at least consistent—estimators, the overestimates and underestimates should counterbalance each

6. Ibid., pp. 40–41.

other. If the aggregate forecast is consistently over or under actual sales, then the marketer who develops the final forecast can make the necessary adjustments. Assuming the survey is well administered, the sales force can really believe that it is making a definite contribution to developing reasonable sales goals. Alternatively, the sales force can be assured that its forecasts are not used to set sales quotas.

Expert surveys In an **expert forecasting survey,** a company uses experts to help prepare the sales forecast. These experts are usually economists, management consultants, advertising executives, college professors, or other persons outside the firm who have much experience in a specific market. Drawing on their experience and their analysis of available information about the company and the market, these experts prepare and present their forecasts or attempt to answer questions regarding a forecast.

The use of experts is expedient and relatively inexpensive. However, since they work outside the firm, they may not be as motivated as company personnel to do an effective job.

Time Series Analysis

Time series analysis is a technique in which the forecaster, using the firm's historical sales data, tries to discover a pattern or patterns in the firm's sales volume over time. If a pattern is uncovered, it can be used to forecast sales. This forecasting method assumes that the past sales pattern will continue in the future. The accuracy, and thus the usefulness, of time series analysis depends heavily on the validity of this assumption.

In a time series analysis, a forecaster usually performs four types of analysis: trend, cycle, seasonal, and random factor.[7] **Trend analysis** focuses on aggregate sales data, such as a company's annual sales figures, from a period of many years to determine whether annual sales are generally rising, falling, or staying about the same. Through **cycle analysis** a forecaster analyzes sales figures (often monthly sales data) over a period of three to five years to ascertain whether sales fluctuate in a consistent, periodic manner. When performing **seasonal analysis,** the analyst studies daily, weekly, or monthly sales figures to evaluate the degree to which seasonal factors such as climate and holiday activities influence the firm's sales. **Random factor analysis** is an attempt to attribute erratic sales variations to random, nonrecurrent events such as a regional power failure, a natural disaster, or the death of a president of the United States. After performing each of these analyses, the forecaster combines the results to develop the sales forecast.

Time series analysis is an effective forecasting method for products that have reasonably stable demand, but it is not very useful for products that have highly erratic demand. Joseph E. Seagram & Sons, Inc., an importer and producer of liquor and wines, uses several types of time series analyses for forecasting purposes and has found them to be quite accurate. For example, Seagram's forecasts of industry sales volume have proved correct within ±1.5 percent, and the firm's company sales forecasts have been accurate within ±2 percent. However, time series analysis is not always so dependable.[8]

7. Norbert L. Enrick, *Market and Sales Forecasting: A Quantitative Approach* (San Francisco: Chandler, 1969), pp. 39–40.
8. Hurwood, Grossman, and Bailey, *Sales Forecasting,* p. 61.

Correlation Methods

Like time series analysis, correlation methods are based on historical sales data. When **correlation methods** are used, the forecaster attempts to find a relationship between past sales and one or more variables such as population, per capita income, or gross national product. To determine whether a correlation exists, the analyst uses regression analysis, which analyzes the statistical relationships among changes in past sales and changes in one or more variables. The objective of regression analysis is a formula that accurately describes a mathematical relationship between the firm's sales and one or more variables, but the formula indicates only an associational relationship, not cause-and-effect. Once an accurate formula has been established, the forecaster plugs the necessary information into the formula to derive the sales forecast.

Correlation methods are useful when a precise relationship can be established. However, a forecaster seldom finds a perfect correlation. In addition, this method can be used only when the available historical sales data are extensive. Ordinarily, then, correlation techniques are useless for forecasting the sales of new products.

Market Tests

A **market test** consists of making a product available to buyers in one or more test areas and measuring purchases and consumer responses to distribution, promotion, and price. Even though test areas are often cities with populations of 200,000 to 500,000, test sites can be larger metropolitan areas or towns with populations of 50,000 to 200,000. A market test provides information about consumers' actual purchases rather than about their intended purchases. In addition, purchase volume can be evaluated in relation to the intensity of other marketing activities—advertising, in-store promotions, pricing, packaging, distribution, and the like. On the basis of customer response in test areas, forecasters can estimate product sales for larger geographic units.

When considering the use of a market test, a marketer must weigh the advantages and disadvantages. A market test is an effective tool for forecasting the sales of new products or the sales of existing products in new geographic areas, because it does not require historical sales data. It provides the forecaster with information about customers' real actions rather than about intended or estimated behavior. A market test also gives a marketer an opportunity to test various elements of the marketing mix. But these tests are often time consuming and expensive. In addition, a marketer cannot be certain that the consumer response during a market test represents the total market response or that such a response will continue in the future.

Using Multiple Forecasting Methods

Although some businesses depend on a single sales forecasting method, most firms employ several techniques. At Rockwell International, for example, division managers are encouraged to use multiple forecasting methods and are even sent manuals describing numerous sales forecasting methods.[9] A firm is sometimes forced to use several methods when it markets diverse product lines, but even for a single product line, several forecasts may be needed, especially when the product is sold in different market segments. For example, a producer of

9. Ibid., p. 216.

automobile tires may employ one technique for forecasting new car tire sales and another to forecast the sales of replacement tires. Variation in the length of the needed forecasts may require the use of several forecast methods. A firm that employs one method for a short-range forecast may find it inappropriate for long-range forecasting. Sometimes a marketer verifies the results of one method by employing one or several other methods and comparing results.

Summary

A market is defined as an aggregate of people who, as individuals or as organizations, have needs for products in a product class and who have the ability, willingness, and authority to purchase such products. There are two types of markets: consumer markets and organizational or industrial markets. A consumer market consists of purchasers and/or individuals in their households who intend to consume or to benefit from the purchased products. An organizational or industrial market consists of individuals and groups that purchase a specific kind of product for resale, for direct use in producing other products, or for use in day-to-day operations. The four major categories of organizational markets are producer, reseller, government, and institutional.

Marketers use two general approaches to identify their target markets—the total market approach and the market segmentation approach. A firm using a total market approach designs a single marketing mix and directs it at an entire market for a particular product. The total market approach can be effective under two conditions: a large proportion of individuals in the total market must have similar needs for the product, and the organization must be able to develop and maintain a single marketing mix to satisfy them.

Companies taking the total market approach frequently employ a product differentiation strategy. They aim one type of product at the total market and attempt to establish in customers' minds that their product is superior and preferable to competing brands.

The market segmentation approach divides the total market into groups consisting of people who have relatively similar product needs. The purpose is to design a marketing mix (or mixes) that more precisely matches the needs of individuals in a selected segment (or segments). There are two major types of market segmentation strategies. In the concentration strategy, the organization directs its marketing efforts toward a single market segment through one marketing mix. In the multisegment strategy, the organization develops different marketing mixes for two or more segments.

Certain conditions must exist for market segmentation to be effective. First, consumers' needs for the product should be heterogeneous. Second, the segments of the market should be identifiable and divisible. Third, the total market should be divided in such a way that the segments can be compared with respect to estimated sales potential, costs, and profits. Fourth, at least one segment must have enough profit potential to justify developing and maintaining a special marketing mix for that segment. Fifth, the firm must be able to reach the chosen segment with a particular marketing mix.

A segmentation variable serves as the basis for dividing a total market into segments. The segmentation variable should be related to customers' needs for, uses of, or behavior toward the product. Segmentation variables for consumer markets can be grouped into four categories: socioeconomic, geographic, psychographic, and product related. Segmentation variables for industrial and reseller markets include geographic factors, type of organization, customer size, and product use. Besides selecting the appropriate segmentation variable, a marketer also must decide how many variables to use.

A marketer must be able to evaluate the sales potential in possible target markets as well as in target markets that the firm currently serves. There are two general approaches to measuring company sales potential: the breakdown approach and the buildup approach. Several methods are used to forecast company sales. The executive judgment method—the intuition of one or more company executives—is inexpensive and expedient, but unscientific. Businesses that use the survey method question customers, experts, or salespeople regarding their expectations about future purchases. Time series analysis is a sales forecasting method based on ascertaining sales patterns over time. Forecasters who use correlation methods develop a mathematical relationship between past sales and one or more variables such as population, per capita income, or gross national product. Finally, a market test can be used to forecast sales. It consists of making a product available to buyers in one or more test areas and measuring purchases and consumer response to distribution, promotion, and price.

Important Terms

Market
Consumer market
Organizational or
  industrial market
Total (or undifferentiated)
  market approach
Product differentiation
Heterogeneous markets
Market segmentation
Market segment
Concentration strategy
Multisegment strategy
Segmentation variables
Market density
Benefit segmentation
Single-variable
  segmentation

Multivariable segmentation
Market sales potential
Company sales potential
Breakdown approach
Buildup approach
Company sales forecast
Executive judgment
Customer forecasting survey
Sales-force forecasting survey
Expert forecasting survey
Time series analysis
Trend analysis
Cycle analysis
Seasonal analysis
Random factor analysis
Correlation methods
Market test

Discussion and Review Questions

1. What is a market? What are its requirements?
2. In your local area, is there a group of people with unsatisfied product needs who represent a market? Could this market be reached by a business organization? Why or why not?
3. Identify and describe two major types of markets. Give examples of each.
4. What is the total market approach? Under what conditions is it most useful? Describe a present market situation in which a firm is using a total market approach. Is the business successful? Why or why not?

5. Explain the basic characteristics of the product differentiation strategy. What companies are currently using this approach? Is it working for them? Why or why not?
6. What is the market segmentation approach? Describe the basic conditions required for effective segmentation. Identify several firms that employ the segmentation approach.
7. List the differences between the concentration strategy and the multisegment strategy. Describe the advantages and disadvantages of each.
8. When choosing a segmentation variable, what major factors should marketers consider?
9. Identify and describe four major categories of variables that can be used to segment consumer markets. Give examples of product markets that are segmented by variables in each category.
10. What dimensions are used to segment industrial or organizational markets?
11. How do marketers decide whether to use single-variable or multivariable segmentation? Identify examples of product markets that are divided through multivariable segmentation.
12. Why is a marketer concerned about sales potential when trying to find a target market?
13. Describe the relationship between market sales potential and company sales potential.
14. What is a company sales forecast and why is it important?
15. Identify five major types of sales forecasting methods.
16. What are the advantages and disadvantages of using executive judgment as a sales forecasting technique?
17. Explain three types of surveys used for sales forecasting. Compare their benefits and limitations.
18. Compare and contrast correlation forecasting methods with time series analysis.
19. Under what conditions are market tests useful for sales forecasting? Discuss the advantages and disadvantages of market tests.

Cases

Case 3.1 Kinder-Care Segments Child-care Market[10]

Of the 30,000 day-care centers in the United States, Kinder-Care Learning Centers operates 900 facilities in forty-two states and additional facilities in two Canadian provinces. Kinder-Care, a publicly owned chain that was founded in Montgomery, Alabama, in 1969, cares for about 100,000 children daily. The organization provides a full day of child care for preschoolers and after-school programs for older children under thirteen years of age. Its overall goal is to provide educationally stimulating programs of uniform quality in clean, secure facilities. Kinder-Care does not want to be viewed as a baby sitter.

Most of Kinder-Care's competitors are small, single-unit operations. However, there are several other corporate care providers, such as La Petite Academy with 385 units and DayBridge Learning Centers with 150 units. Additional enterprises with multiple units include Children's World, Mary Moppet's Day Care Schools, and Gerber Products. On a local level, these proprietary child-care operations are facing competition from religious institutions, charitable groups, and other nonprofit organizations. Businesses like Polaroid Corporation in Cambridge, Massachusetts, are also starting to address the need for child care by funding referral services to help employees find day care, subsidizing part of child-care costs, or actually providing day-care centers where the firms are headquartered.

Kinder-Care uses demographic and geographic characteristics as variables for segmenting markets. In locating new facilities, the organization seeks recently built housing developments or neighborhoods with new homes. It wants to serve families having two incomes, and it figures that new homes require two working adults to make the mortgage payments. The company looks for areas populated by couples with children and a combined annual income of $20,000 or more. The firm avoids areas with apartment buildings that house primarily young singles or older people. For that reason, it seeks not only regions that are growing in population, such as the West Coast and Southwest, but also areas that are growing in working class and family income.

Kinder-Care has several reasons to believe that the market potential for its child-care services will increase. At present, the entire child-care industry serves only 20 percent of children under age five, while over 50 percent of all mothers are working outside of the home. By 1990, marketers expect that two-thirds of all mothers with children of age six or under will have jobs. In addition, recent publicity regarding child abuse in in-home facilities has made parents distrustful of such centers; approximately 95 percent of reported cases have occurred in these types of facilities. Thus, Kinder-Care anticipates that parents will probably be more likely to use larger, commercial facilities like its own.

10. This case is based on information from William Dunn, "Kinder-Care Sets Its Sites," *American Demographics,* May 1985, pp. 20–21; Peter Hall, "Bringing Child Care Back Into Focus," *Financial World,* Oct. 17, 1984, pp. 29–30; and David Wiessler with Jeannye Thornton, "Who'll Watch the Kids? Working Parents' Worry," *U.S. News & World Report,* June 27, 1983, pp. 67–68.

Table 3.2 *Bay State's actual and forecasted sales (in millions of dollars)*

Year	Actual Annual Sales	Sales Forecasts			
		Sales-force Survey	Correlation Method	Executive Judgment	Expert Opinion
10	42.0	41.1	44.5	37.2	44.1
9	46.2	43.9	48.0	50.4	46.6
8	54.3	52.7	51.0	53.9	58.1
7	57.8	56.6	56.1	54.0	61.3
6	72.4	70.2	77.5	81.9	75.3
5	98.7	93.7	100.1	107.9	99.7
4	114.0	111.9	107.1	113.0	122.0
3	131.8	129.1	127.8	120.7	133.1
2	152.9	148.3	160.5	170.1	159.0
Last year	184.4	180.2	195.4	175.0	189.9

Questions for Discussion

1. Which types of segmentation variables is Kinder-Care using? Is multivariable segmentation appropriate for Kinder-Care? Explain.
2. The number of single-parent households with children is sizable and increasing. Assess Kinder-Care's decision not to direct its marketing efforts toward these households.
3. If you were asked to develop a long-range estimate of national demand for child-care services, what factors would you consider?

Case 3.2 Sales Forecasting at Bay State Machine Company

Bay State Machine Company is a medium-sized producer of portable rigs that are used in drilling oil or water wells. Bay State manufactures several standardized models and also custom-designs rigs. Although Bay State began as a small machine shop in 1918, its primary business activities have focused for over forty years on building high-quality portable drilling rigs. Bay State's sales force of thirty-six is managed by three regional sales managers and a national sales director.

For a number of years, Bay State managers have employed several types of sales forecasting techniques, including sales-force surveys, correlation methods, executive judgments, and expert opinions. The annual sales forecasts arrived at with each method for the last ten years are shown in Table 3.2, along with actual sales figures for each year.

Bay State managers have recently begun to question whether it is really necessary to use four different sales forecasting methods, given that the costs associated with each method have been escalating, especially during the last few years.

Questions for Discussion

1. How does Bay State management benefit from using several sales forecasting techniques?

2. Given Bay State's experience over the last ten years, which sales forecasting method should be used if the managers decide to rely on a single method? Explain your answer and be sure to enumerate the major advantages and disadvantages of the method that you recommend.
3. Which combination of sales forecasting methods should Bay State Management use if multiple methods are employed? Why?

People — specific
A. demographic
B Situation

Psychographic
perception   4 learning
2 motive   5 attitude
3 motive   6 personality
social
1. Role + Fam.
2 Reference groups
3 Social class
4. culture

4 / Consumer Buying Behavior

Objectives

■ To understand the types of decision behaviors employed by consumers when making purchases.

■ To become aware of the stages of the consumer buying decision process.

■ To become familiar with the major factors that influence the consumer buying decision process.

Figure 4.1

Hershey introduces a new line of healthful snack bars (Source: Courtesy of Hershey Foods Corporation)

Consumers are showing an increasing concern about health and physical fitness, and this awareness is changing their perceptions and attitudes toward a variety of foods. Although most people have not altered their diets, one-third of the population, particularly well-educated professionals of the upper-middle class, have significantly dropped their intake of foods high in fat or cholesterol (eggs, butter, whole milk, and meat, for instance), regular coffee, and sugar. Members of the food industry—including farmers, major food manufacturers, supermarkets, fast-food chains, and restaurants—have been closely monitoring the shift in consumers' buying attitudes and responding accordingly. As a result, health foods, nutritional substitutes, and vitamins have moved from the shelves of health-food stores and supermarket diet sections into the main aisles of retail food stores. The $30 billion business for fitness foods now constitutes the fastest-growing segment of the $300 billion retail-food industry.

Although consumers are looking for more nutritious snacks, the sales of chocolate and confectionery products have not been adversely affected. In fact, the annual per capita consumption of chocolate products has risen. Peo-

ple continue to find a place in their diets for treats with that chocolate taste.

Well aware of that age-old preference as well as the trend toward more nutritious content, Hershey Foods Corporation has introduced several products since 1978 that contain smaller percentages of chocolate than its traditional Hershey Kisses and Krackel. Among the offerings are Reeses Pieces candy, Whatchamacallit candy bar, Skor toffee candy bar, and New Trail granola bars (see Figure 4.1). More recently, a chocolate-covered line of the New Trail granola bars has hit the market. In 1963, 80 percent of Hershey Chocolate Company's sales came from products that were predominantly (70 percent or more) chocolate. By 1985 that percentage had dropped to 45 percent on a substantially larger sales base. [1]

Being able to recognize and adjust to changes in customers' preferences is required to provide customer satisfaction, as illustrated by the Hershey example. A firm's ability to establish and maintain satisfying exchange relationships requires an understanding of buying behavior. **Buying behavior** is the decision processes and acts of people involved in buying and using products.[2] **Consumer buying behavior** refers to the buying behavior of ultimate consumers—those persons who purchase products for personal or household use, not for business purposes. Marketers should analyze buying behavior for several reasons. First, buyers' reactions to a firm's marketing strategy have great impact on the firm's success. Second, as indicated in Chapter 1, the marketing concept stresses that a firm should create a marketing mix that satisfies customers. To find out what satisfies buyers, marketers must examine the main influences on what, where, when, and how consumers buy. Third, by gaining a better understanding of the factors that affect buyer behavior, marketers are in a better position to predict how consumers will respond to marketing strategies.

Marketers may attempt to understand and influence buying behavior, but they cannot control it. Even though some critics credit them with the ability to manipulate buyers, marketers have neither the powers nor the knowledge to do so. Their knowledge of behavior comes from what psychologists, social psychologists, and sociologists know about human behavior in general. Even if marketers wanted to manipulate buyers, the lack of laws and principles in the behavioral sciences would prevent them from doing so.

In this chapter, we initially examine the types of decision making that consumers use. Next, we analyze the major stages of the consumer buying decision process. Finally, we explain some of the factors that are believed to influence the consumer buying decision process.

1. Based on Brad Edmondson, "The Market for Medical Self-Care," *American Demographics,* June 1985, pp. 35–37, 51; Jane E. Brody, "America Leans to a Healthier Diet," *The New York Times Magazine,* Oct. 13, 1985, pp. 32, 34, 38, 77–79; and Lewis J. Lord, "Fitness Food Makes Good Business," *U.S. News & World Report,* Jan. 20, 1986, p. 69.
2. James F. Engel and Roger D. Blackwell, *Consumer Behavior* (Hinsdale, Ill.: Dryden Press, 1986), p. 5.

Types of Consumer Decision Behavior

As we analyze buyer behavior, we will think of buyers as decision makers. Consumers usually have the general objective of creating and maintaining a collection of goods and services that provides current and future satisfaction. To accomplish this objective, buyers make many purchasing decisions. For example, an average adult must make several decisions daily regarding food, clothing, shelter, medical care, education, recreation, or transportation. As they make these decisions, buyers use different decision-making behaviors.

Although the types of consumer decision making vary considerably, they can be classified into one of three broad categories—routine response behavior, limited decision making, and extensive decision making.[3] A consumer uses **routine response behavior** when buying frequently purchased, low-cost items that require very little search and decision effort. These items are sometimes called low-involvement products. When buying them, a consumer may prefer a particular brand, but he or she is familiar with several brands in the product class and views more than one as being acceptable. Products bought through routine response behavior are purchased quickly with very little mental effort. Most buyers, for example, do not stand at the detergent shelf pondering the detergents for twenty minutes. Instead, they walk by, grab a box, and proceed down the aisle.

Limited decision making is employed for products that are purchased occasionally and when a buyer needs to acquire information about an unfamiliar brand in a familiar product category. This type of decision making requires a moderate amount of time for information gathering and deliberation.

A consumer uses **extensive decision making** when purchasing an unfamiliar expensive product or an infrequently bought item. This process is the most complex type of consumer decision-making behavior. A buyer uses a large number of criteria for evaluating alternative brands and spends a great deal of time seeking information and deciding on the purchase.

The type of decision making that an individual uses when buying a specific product does not necessarily remain constant. In some instances, the first time we buy a certain kind of product we might use extensive decision making. Limited decision making might be used for subsequent purchases of that product. Also, when a routinely purchased, formerly satisfying brand no longer satisfies, we may use limited or extensive decision processes to switch to a new brand.

The Consumer Buying Decision Process

As defined earlier, a major part of buying behavior is the decision process used in making purchases. Figure 4.2 is a simplified model of the **consumer buying decision process.** It also shows the major factors believed to affect this process. The five major stages of the consumer buying decision process are problem recognition, information search, evaluation of alternatives, purchase, and postpurchase evaluation. Before examining each stage, we should consider

3. John A. Howard and Jagdish N. Sheth, *The Theory of Buyer Behavior* (New York: Wiley, 1969), pp. 27–28.

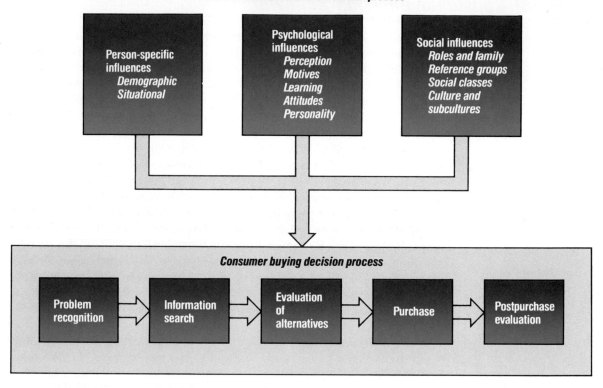

Figure 4.2 *Consumer buying decision process and possible influences on the process*

several important points. First, note that the actual act of purchasing is only one stage in the process and that the process is initiated several stages prior to the actual purchase. Second, even though, for discussion purposes, we indicate that a purchase occurs, not all decision processes lead to a purchase. The individual may terminate the process during any stage. Finally, not all consumer decisions always include all five stages. Persons engaged in extensive decision making usually employ all stages of this decision process; while those engaged in limited decision making and routine response behavior may omit some stages.

Problem Recognition

Problem recognition occurs when a buyer becomes aware that there is a difference between a desired state and an actual condition. For example, a consumer may desire an automobile that is reliable. When her car will not start in the morning for the third time in a week, she may recognize that a difference exists between the desired state—a reliable car—and the actual condition—a car that refuses to start.

Sometimes, a person has a problem or need but is unaware of it. Marketers use sales personnel, advertising, and packaging to aid in triggering the recognition of such needs or problems. The speed of consumer problem recognition can be rather slow or quite rapid.

Information Search

After becoming aware of the problem or need, the consumer (if continuing the decision process) searches for information. Information search can focus on availability of brands, product features, seller characteristics, warranties, operating instructions, prices, and the like. The duration and intensity of search efforts depend on the consumer's experience in purchasing the product and on the importance of the purchase to the consumer. If the woman with the unreliable car moves into the information search stage, she is likely to engage in a rather lengthy search. However, if she is buying a blouse, her information search stage will probably be shorter.

When seeking information, a consumer may turn to one or several major sources. One primary source of information is experience. Direct experience with a product can provide selected kinds of needed information that a consumer may not be able to acquire in other ways. Marketers sometimes attempt to help customers experience products through free samples, demonstrations, and temporary use, such as a test drive of an automobile. Personal contacts—friends, relatives, and associates—can also act as sources of information. Since they tend to trust and respect these sources, consumers view them as credible. A third category of information sources is called marketer-dominated sources, which include salespersons, advertising, packaging, and displays. These sources typically do not require the consumer to expend much effort to receive the information. Finally, buyers can use public sources of information, such as government reports, news presentations, and reports from product-testing organizations. Because of its factual and unbiased nature, consumers frequently view information from public sources as being quite credible.

A successful information search yields a group of brands that a buyer views as possible alternatives. This group of products is sometimes called the buyer's evoked set. For example, an evoked set of imported station wagons might include Peugeot, Mercedes-Benz, and Volvo.

Evaluation of Alternatives

To evaluate the products in the evoked set, a consumer establishes a set of criteria against which to compare the products' characteristics. These criteria are characteristics or features that are desired (or not desired) by the buyer. For example, one car buyer might want a red car, whereas another might have no preference about color except for an intense dislike for red. The buyer also assigns a certain level of importance to each criterion; some features and characteristics are more important than others. Using the criteria and considering the importance of each one, a buyer rates and eventually ranks the brands in the evoked set. Evaluation may yield no brand that the buyer is willing to purchase. In this case, further search may be required. If the evaluation yields one or more brands that the consumer is willing to buy, he or she is ready to move on to the next stage of the decision process.

Purchase

The consumer selects the product or brand to be bought during the purchase stage. The choice is based on the outcome of the previous evaluation stage and on other dimensions. Product availability may influence which brand is purchased. For example, if the brand that ranked the highest during evaluation is not available, the buyer may purchase another acceptable brand. During this stage, the consumer determines from which seller he or she will buy the product. The choice of the seller may influence the final product selection. So might the terms of sale which, if they are negotiable, are determined during the purchase decision stage. Issues such as price, delivery, warranties, maintenance agreements, installation, and credit arrangements are discussed and settled. Finally, the actual act of purchase occurs during this stage, unless, of course, the consumer terminates the buying decision process prior to purchase.

Postpurchase Evaluation

After purchase a buyer will begin to evaluate the product. Shortly after the purchase of an expensive product, postpurchase evaluation may result in cognitive dissonance. **Cognitive dissonance** is dissatisfaction that occurs because the buyer questions whether he or she should have purchased the product at all or would have been better off purchasing another brand that was evaluated very favorably. A consumer who feels cognitive dissonance may attempt to return the product or may seek positive information about it to justify that choice.

As the product is used, the consumer evaluates it to determine if its actual performance meets expected levels. Many of the criteria used in the evaluation-of-alternatives stage are used during postpurchase evaluation. The outcome of this stage is either satisfaction or dissatisfaction, which feeds back to other stages of the decision process and influences subsequent purchases.

Influences on the Consumer Buying Decision Process

As shown in Figure 4.2, there are three major categories of factors that are believed to influence the consumer buying decision process: person-specific, psychological, and social. Although we discuss each major factor separately, keep in mind that they are interrelated in their effects on the consumer decision process.

Person-specific Influences

A **person-specific factor** is one that is unique to a particular individual. Numerous person-specific characteristics can affect purchasing decisions. In this section, we consider two categories of person-specific factors—demographic and situational.

Demographic Factors

Demographic factors are individual characteristics such as age, sex, race, ethnicity, income, family, life cycle state, and occupation. (These and other characteristics are discussed in Chapter 3 as possible variables for segmentation purposes.) Demographic factors can influence who is involved in family decision making. For example, findings of a study several years ago indicated that there is more joint decision making by husbands and wives without children than by those with children.[4] Demographic attributes may influence the speed at which a person moves through the consumer buying decision process. Also, behavior during a specific stage of the decision process is partially determined by

---

4. Pierre Filiatrault and J. R. Brent Ritchie, "Joint Purchase Decisions: A Comparison of Influence Structure in Family and Couple Decision-Making Units," *Journal of Consumer Research,* Sept. 1980, p. 139.

demographic factors. For example, during the information stage, a person's age and income may affect the number and types of information sources used and the amount of time devoted to seeking information.

Demographic factors also affect the extent to which a person uses products in a specific product category. For example, the singles demographic group, which is growing rapidly in the United States, accounts for 12.5 percent of consumer spending. Yet singles account for 15 percent of total vacation expenditures, 15.5 percent of expenditures for eating away from home, 15.5 percent of car sales, and 20 percent of alcohol sales.[5] Brand preferences, store choice, and timing of purchases are other areas influenced by selected demographic factors. Consider, for example, how differences in occupation result in variations in product needs.

A college professor may earn almost as much income annually as a plumber does. Yet, these incomes will be spent quite differently because the product needs that arise from these two occupations vary considerably. Both occupations require the purchase of work clothes. Yet a professor and a plumber purchase quite different types of clothes, and the types of vehicles they drive surely will vary to some extent. What they eat for lunch and where they eat are likely to be different. Finally, the "tools" that they purchase and use in their work clearly are not the same.

Many demographic factors result in variations in consumer buying behavior. These factors are very closely associated with people's needs, product expectations, and behavior toward products. Demographic characteristics of the "baby-boomers" are discussed in the application on page 116.

Situational Factors

Situational factors are the set of circumstances or conditions that exist when a consumer is making a purchase decision. Sometimes, a consumer engages in buying decision making as a result of an unexpected situation. For example, an individual may be buying an airline ticket hurriedly to spend the last few days with a relative who is terminally ill. Or a situation may arise that lengthens or causes a person to terminate the buying decision process. A consumer who is considering the purchase of a personal computer, for example, may be laid off during the evaluation-of-alternatives stage. The job loss would certainly slow the buying decision process and might cause the person to reject the purchase entirely. However, if the same person experienced a different circumstance, say a 20-percent raise in salary, then the buying decision process might be completed more quickly than if no pay increase had been received.

Situational factors can influence a consumer's actions during any stage of the buying decision process and in a variety of ways. If the time for selecting and purchasing a product is short, an individual may make a quick choice and purchase a brand that is readily available. Uncertainty about future marital status may influence a consumer's purchases. A couple who is experiencing marital difficulties will probably delay the purchase of durable goods. A single person who is contemplating marriage also might delay the purchase of durables such as appliances and furniture. People who believe the supply of necessary products to be sharply limited are more likely to make a purchase. For example, people have purchased and hoarded gasoline and toilet paper when these

5. Gay Jerrey, "Y & R Study: New Life to Singles," *Advertising Age,* Oct. 4, 1982, p. 14.

Between 1946 and 1964, 78 million Americans were born. This group is known as the baby-boom generation and has frequently been characterized as one large body having common characteristics. However, it is becoming apparent that there is a wide diversity of traits among baby-boomers.

The individual ages of baby-boomers vary considerably. The younger boomers, ages 21 to 29, outnumber the older boomers, who are 30 to 39. The older boomers have higher average incomes and represent a larger number of household heads than the younger boomers. A greater portion of older boomers were able to buy homes prior to the real estate inflation of a few years ago. Thus, younger boomers have higher mortgage payments.

There are 34 million single and 44 million married boomers. Approximately nine out of ten boomers in their twenties have never been married, while about 50 percent of the single boomers in their thirties have never been married. Approximately 75 percent of the 20 million married couples have at least one child and expect to have another.

About one-half of the baby-boom generation have a partial or complete college education; only 10 percent are high school dropouts. The high school dropouts earn roughly $12,000 annually, while the college graduates earn over $32,000 annually. However, the higher incomes do not translate into a higher volume of personal consumption. For the average thirty-year-old professionals usually have sizable school debts to pay off, and the older boomers have to worry about the cost of their kids' higher education. The boomers that have postponed first marriages and assumed more debt spend a greater fraction of their income on luxury items.

Differences in demographic characteristics lead to differences in consumer attitudes, preferences, and perceptions that account for variations in what people buy, where they buy it, and how they buy it. Thus, the differences in the demographic characteristics of boomers should make marketers aware that the baby-boom generation cannot be treated as a single market. (*Sources: "The Big Chill Revisited: Whatever Happened to the Baby Boom?"* American Demographics, *Sept. 1985, pp. 24–29; Cheryl Russell, "Why the Baby Boom Is Gone, and When It Will Be Back,"* American Demographics, *Sept. 1985, p. 7; Maria Fisher, "The Last Yuppie Story You Will Ever Have to Read,"* Forbes, *Feb. 25, 1985, pp. 134–135.)*

products were believed to be in short supply. When a product is viewed as a necessity and it shows signs of malfunctioning, a consumer is more likely to consider making a purchase. These and other situational factors can change rapidly, and the effects on purchase decisions can arise or subside quickly.

Psychological Influences

Psychological influences operating within individuals partly determine their general behavior and thus influence their behavior as consumers. The primary psychological influences on consumer behavior are (1) perception, (2) motives, (3) learning, (4) attitudes, and (5) personality. Even though these behavioral factors operate internally, later in this chapter we will see that they are very much affected by social forces outside the individual.

Perception

In Figure 4.3, are the birds flying to the left, or to the right? It could be either way depending on how the birds are perceived. Different people perceive the same thing at the same time in different ways. Likewise, the same individual at different times may perceive the same item in a number of ways.

Perception is the process of selecting, organizing, and interpreting information inputs in order to produce meaning. A person receives information through the senses: sight, taste, hearing, smell, and touch. **Information inputs** are the sensations that we receive through sense organs. When we hear an advertisement, see a friend, smell polluted air or water, or touch a product, we receive information inputs.

As the definition indicates, perception is a three-step process. Although we receive numerous pieces of information at once, only a few of them reach awareness. We select some inputs and ignore many others because we do not have the ability to be conscious of all inputs at one time. This phenomenon is sometimes called **selective exposure** because we select inputs that are to be exposed to our awareness. If you are concentrating on this paragraph, you probably are not aware that people or cars are outside making noise, that the light is on, or that you are touching this book. Even though you are receiving these inputs, you ignore them until they are mentioned.

There are several reasons why some types of information reach awareness while others do not. An input is more likely to reach awareness if it relates to an anticipated event. Stuckey's, a chain of roadside snack-food stores, uses a series of billboards to encourage travelers to anticipate seeing a Stuckey's store. Even though some motorists may not stop, there is a good chance that they will at least notice the store. A person also is likely to allow an input to reach consciousness if the information helps to satisfy current needs. For example, you are more likely to notice food commercials when you are hungry. Conversely, if you have just eaten a large pizza and you hear a Burger King commercial, there is a good chance that the advertisement will not reach your awareness. Finally, if the intensity of an input changes significantly, it is more likely to reach awareness. When a store manager reduces a price slightly, we may not notice because the change is not significant. However, if the manager cuts the price in half, we are much more likely to recognize the reduction.

The selective nature of perception leads to two other conditions: selective distortion and selective retention. **Selective distortion** is the changing or twisting of currently received information. This condition can occur when a person receives information inconsistent with his or her feelings or beliefs. For example, upon seeing an advertisement promoting a brand that he or she dislikes, a person may distort the information to make it more consistent with prior views. This distortion substantially lessens the effect of the advertisement on the individual. **Selective retention** is a phenomenon in which a person remembers information inputs that support his or her feelings and beliefs and forgets inputs that do not. After hearing a sales presentation and leaving the store, a customer may forget many of the selling points if they contradict prior beliefs.

The information inputs that do reach awareness are not received in an organized form. To produce meaning, an individual must organize them. Ordinarily, this organizing is done rapidly. How a person organizes information affects the meaning obtained. For example, depending on how you organize the input in Figure 4.3, you could perceive one of two different forms.

As Figure 4.3 illustrates, an individual can organize inputs in more than one way and obtain more than one meaning. Thus, interpretation—the third step in the perceptual process—is needed to reduce mental confusion. A person bases interpretation on what is familiar. For this reason, a manufacturer that changes a package design faces a major problem. People look for the product in the old, familiar package, and they might not recognize it in the new one.

Several years ago Du Pont test-marketed in several cities a new package design for one of its established automobile polishes. Sales declined significantly because consumers interpreted a different container to mean a different polish. They did not interpret the product as the same polish in a container with a new package design. Unless a package change is accompanied by a promotional program that makes people aware of the change, a firm may lose sales.

Not only does one form perceptions of packages, products, brands, and organizations, a buyer also has a perception of himself or herself. That perception is called the person's **self-concept** or self-image. Some behavioral scientists believe that the self-concept is a combination of the actual self-concept and the ideal self-concept. The actual self-concept is how a person actually perceives himself or herself, while the ideal self-concept is the way he or she would like to be perceived. One's self concept is a function of experiences and hereditary traits. An individual changes his or her self-concept over time.

It is reasonable to believe that a person's self-concept affects purchase decisions and consumption behavior. The results of some studies have suggested that buyers purchase products that reflect and enhance their self-concepts.

Figure 4.4

Advertisement aimed at changing buyers' perceptions (Source: The Potato Board)

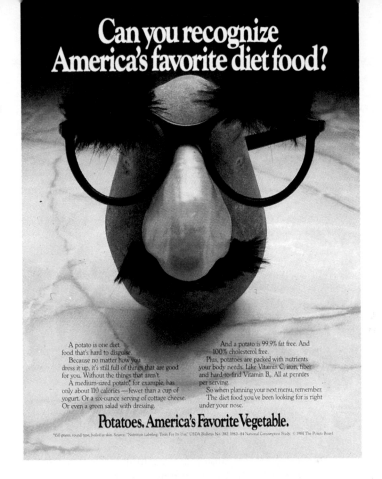

Although marketers cannot control people's perceptions, they often try to influence them. Several problems may arise in this attempt. First, a consumer's perceptual process may operate in such a way that a seller's information never reaches that person. For example, a consumer may block out a store clerk's sales pitch. Second, a buyer may receive a seller's information and perceive it differently than was intended. For example, when a toothpaste producer states in an advertisement that "35 percent of the people who use this toothpaste have fewer cavities," a customer could take the statement to mean that 65 percent of the people who use the product have more cavities. Third, a buyer who perceives information inputs that are inconsistent with prior beliefs is likely to forget the information quickly. Thus, if a salesperson tells a prospective car buyer about a highly favorable EPA mileage rating, but the customer does not believe it, the customer probably will not retain the information very long.

It is obvious that how and what consumers perceive strongly affect their behavior toward products, prices, package designs, salespeople, stores, advertisements, and manufacturers. With good reason, then, marketers often concern themselves with how their organizations and products are perceived by consumers. (The application on page 120 focuses on J.C. Penney's and K mart's attempts to influence customers' perceptions.) As is illustrated in Figure 4.4, organizations sometimes attempt to change customers' perceptions of products. In this advertisement, the Potato Board is saying that the potato should be perceived as nutritious, low-calorie food.

Application
Changing Store Perceptions

Two large major retailers, K mart and J.C. Penney, have recently tried to change how consumers perceive them. To compete with Target and Wal-Mart, K mart is trying to keep customers in its stores longer with the hope that they will buy more merchandise. K mart researchers determined that its customers' views of value included not only price but also quality. K mart's image as a low-price retailer was well established. However, it needed to convince its customers that it was a high-quality retailer as well.

K mart has moved toward more attractive department store type merchandise displays. Since customers associate quality with national brand names, K mart is offering name brand products in its home electronic centers and providing designer label clothing in its apparel centers. K mart also plans to offer in-store financial services as Sears has done. In changing its image, K mart has had to be careful not to alienate customers who are mainly price oriented. As the upgrading has continued, promotional efforts have aimed at accenting value through low price and high quality.

J.C. Penney determined that its image was rather drab and uninteresting to buyers. Researchers for Penney's discovered that consumers tend to associate department stores with higher-quality merchandise. Thus, J.C. Penney decided to change its image by upgrading its stores, making them appear to be department stores. In doing so, the retailer eliminated a considerable number of its hard-good lines in areas such as appliances and hardware. Today, about three-fourths of its merchandise is in soft goods and about one-fourth in hard goods. Penney's has also placed considerable emphasis on fashion. Fashion-related lines like Halston and Armani were introduced to show customers that Penney is in the fashion business. In all, over $60 million has been spent to help change the J.C. Penney image.

Changing consumers' images of organizations such as K mart and J.C. Penney requires time and financial resources. J.C. Penney's management believes that the changes are already having a very positive impact through increased sales and profits. At K mart, marketers are in the process of measuring the effects of their attempts to change their image. (*Sources: "K-mart Assumes New Posture,"* Chain Store Executive, *Aug. 1984, pp. 25–29; Jesse Synder, "K-mart Says Come On Down,"* Advertising Age, *Feb. 11, 1985, pp. 1 and 84; Pat Sloan, "Penney's Saying Ciao to Staid Image,"* Advertising Age, *April 9, 1984, p. 4; and David Main, "Penney's: Big Chain Reaction for Italy,"* Women's Wear Daily, *April 2, 1984, p. 6.*)

Motives and Motivation Research

A **motive** is an internal energizing force that orients a person's activities toward a goal. A buyer's actions at any time are affected by a set of motives rather than just one motive. At a single point in time, some motives in the set are stronger than others, but the strengths of motives vary from one time to another. For example, a person's motives toward having a cup of coffee are much stronger right after waking up than just before going to bed.

Motives can reduce or build tension. When motives drive us toward our goals, they reduce tension. But if some motives impel us toward one goal while other motives pull us toward a different goal, tension may increase because we cannot accomplish either goal.

Many different motives influence buying behavior at once. For example, a person who is purchasing a sofa might be attracted by several characteristics, such as durability, economy, and styling. If a marketer appeals to customers by emphasizing only one attractive characteristic, the effort may fail to generate a satisfactory sales level.

Motives that influence where a person purchases products on a regular basis are called **patronage motives.** A buyer may shop at a specific store because of such patronage motives as price, service, location, honesty, product variety, or friendliness of salespeople. To capitalize on patronage motives, a marketer should try to determine why regular customers patronize a store and then emphasize these characteristics in the store's marketing mix.

Motivation research lets marketers analyze the major motives that influence consumers to buy or not buy their products. Motives, which often operate at a subconscious level, are difficult to measure. People ordinarily do not know what motivates them. Therefore, marketers cannot simply ask them about their motives. Most motivation research relies on interviews or projective techniques.

When researchers study motives through interviews, they may use depth interviews, group interviews, or a combination of the two. In a **depth interview** the researcher tries to get the subject to talk freely about anything to create an informal atmosphere. The researcher may ask general, nondirected questions and then probe the subject's answers by asking for clarification. A depth interview may last for several hours. In a **group interview,** the interviewer—through leadership that is not highly structured—tries to generate discussion on one or several topics among the six to twelve people in the group. Through what is said in the discussion, the interviewer attempts to uncover people's motives relating to some issue such as the use of a product. The researcher usually cannot probe as deeply in a group interview as in a depth interview. To determine the subconscious motives reflected in the interviews, motivation researchers must be extremely well trained in clinical psychology. Their skill in uncovering subconscious motives from what is said in an interview determines the effectiveness of their research. Both depth and group interview techniques can yield a variety of information. For example, they might discover why customers do not like prunes or why they select high-calorie desserts.

Projective techniques are tests in which subjects are asked to perform specific tasks for particular purposes while, in fact, they are being evaluated for other purposes. Such tests are based on the assumption that subjects unconsciously will "project" their motives as they perform the required tasks. Researchers who are trained in projective techniques can analyze the materials produced by a subject and can make predictions about the subject's subconscious motives. Some common types of projective techniques are word-association tests, sentence-completion tests, and balloon tests.

Motivation research techniques can be reasonably effective. They are, however, far from perfect. Marketers who want to research people's motives should obtain the services of professional psychologists who are skilled in the methods of motivation research.

Learning

Learning consists of changes in one's behavior that are caused by information and experience. Variations in behavior that result from psychological conditions such as hunger, fatigue, physical growth, or deterioration are not considered to be learning. Learning refers to the effects of direct and indirect experiences on future behavior.

The response to an individual's behavior strongly influences the learning process. If an individual's actions bring about rewarding or satisfying results, the person may behave in the same way in a subsequent, similar situation. However, when behavior leads to unsatisfying outcomes, a person is likely to behave differently in future situations. For example, when a consumer buys a specific brand of candy bar and likes it, that person is more likely to buy the same brand the next time. In fact, he or she will probably continue to purchase that brand until it no longer provides satisfaction. When the effects of the behavior are no longer satisfying, the person will switch to a different brand, perhaps, or stop eating candy bars altogether!

For a firm to market products successfully, it must help consumers to learn about them. Consumers learn about products directly by experiencing them. As noted earlier, many marketers try to provide consumers with direct experiences before the consumers purchase products. Consumer learning is also affected by experiencing products indirectly through information from salespersons, advertisements, friends, and relatives. Through sales personnel and advertisements, marketers provide information before (and sometimes after) purchases to influence what consumers learn and to create a more favorable attitude toward the products.

Although marketers may attempt to influence what a consumer learns, their attempts are seldom fully successful. Marketers experience problems in attracting and holding consumers' attention, in providing consumers with the kinds of information that are important for making purchase decisions, and in convincing them to try the product.

Attitudes

An **attitude** consists of knowledge and positive or negative feelings about an object. We sometimes say that a person has a "positive attitude," but that statement is incomplete. It has no meaning until we know what the positive attitude relates to. The objects toward which we hold attitudes may be tangible or intangible, living or nonliving. For example, we have attitudes about sex, religion, and politics, just as we do about flowers and beer.

An individual learns attitudes through experience and interaction with other people. Just as attitudes are learned, they can also be changed. However, an individual's attitudes remain generally stable and do not change from moment to moment. Likewise, at any one time, a person's attitudes do not all have equal impact; some are stronger than others.

Consumer attitudes toward a firm and its products greatly influence the success or failure of the firm's marketing strategy. When consumers have strong negative attitudes about one or more aspects of a firm's marketing practices, they may not only stop using the firm's product, but may also implore their relatives and friends to do the same. Since attitudes can play such an important part in determining consumer behavior, marketers should measure consumer attitudes toward such dimensions as prices, package designs, brand names, advertisements, salespeople, repair services, store locations, and features of existing or proposed products.

Not long ago, General Foods realized that consumers' changing attitudes toward desserts affected its dessert line. Consumption of Jell-O pudding and gelatin was declining. Research revealed that consumers wanted quick, low-calorie desserts. To take advantage of this attitude, General Foods created

Pudding Pops. They require no preparation time, and a two-ounce Pudding Pop has 100 calories, versus 170 calories in a three-ounce, chocolate-covered vanilla ice-cream bar.[6]

Marketers have several methods available to measure consumer attitudes. One of the simplest ways is to question people directly. An attitude researcher for a watch manufacturer, for example, might ask respondents what they think about the styling and design of the firm's new digital watch. Projective techniques used in motivation research can also be employed to measure attitudes. Marketers sometimes use attitude scales to evaluate attitudes. An **attitude scale** usually consists of a series of adjectives, phrases, or sentences about an object. Subjects are asked to indicate the intensity of their feelings toward the object by reacting to the adjectives, phrases, or sentences in a certain way. For example, if a marketer were measuring people's attitudes toward cable television, respondents might be asked to state the degree to which they agree or disagree with a number of statements such as "Cable television is too expensive." Several computer-assisted analytic approaches currently are being developed. They hold great promise for future attitude research. However, a discussion of these analytic approaches is beyond the scope of this text.

A marketer can gather many types of information by researching attitudes. One food processor researched dog owners' attitudes toward their dogs and dog foods and found that dog owners could be categorized into three attitudinal groups. One group viewed their dogs as performing a utilitarian function such as protecting the family or household, playing with children, or herding farm animals. These consumers wanted a low-priced, nutritious dog food. They weren't interested in a wide variety of flavors. People in the second group were quite fond of their dogs and treated them as companions and as family members. These buyers were willing to pay a relatively high price for dog food and wanted a wide variety of types and flavors so that their dogs would not get bored. Persons in the third group had negative feelings and, in fact, were found to hate their dogs. These customers wanted the cheapest dog food that they could buy and were not concerned with nutrition, flavor, or variety. Because this research determined that other firms were serving these three groups quite effectively, the processor decided not to enter the dog food market after all.

When marketers determine that a significant number of consumers have strong negative attitudes toward an aspect of a marketing mix, they may try to change consumer attitudes to make them more favorable. This task is generally long, expensive, and difficult and may require extensive promotional efforts. When they first entered the U.S. motorcycle market, Honda discovered that many people in this country had negative attitudes toward motorcyclists. People believed that most motorcycle riders were thugs or hoodlums. Honda also determined that people associated motorcyclists with such negative images as crime, black leather jackets, and knives. Knowing this, Honda was able to develop and launch a massive advertising campaign with the general theme "You meet the nicest people on a Honda." Although this campaign required considerable effort, time, and money, Honda became a leader in the U.S. motorcycle market. In the same vein, both business and nonbusiness organizations

6. Janet Guyon, "General Foods Gets a Winner with Its Jell-O Pudding Pops," *Wall Street Journal*, March 10, 1983, p. 27.

try to change people's attitudes about many things, from health and safety to product prices and features.

Personality

Some personalities are not as noticeable as others, but everyone does have one. **Personality** is an internal structure in which both experience and behavior are related in an orderly way. The manner in which they are organized within each individual makes each of us unique. Our uniqueness arises from heredity and our experiences.

Personalities typically are described as having one or more of such characteristics as compulsiveness, ambitiousness, gregariousness, dogmatism, authoritarianism, introversion, extroversion, aggressiveness, and competitiveness. Marketing researchers attempt to find relationships among such characteristics and buying behavior. Even though a few relationships among several personality characteristics and buyer behavior have been determined, the results of many studies have been inconclusive. Nevertheless, some marketers believe that a person's personality does influence the types and brands of products purchased. For example, the type of clothing, jewelry, or automobile that a person buys may reflect one or more personality characteristics.

At times, marketers aim advertising campaigns at general types of personalities. In doing so, they use positively valued personality characteristics such as gregariousness, independence, or competitiveness. Products that are promoted in this way include beer, soft drinks, cigarettes, and sometimes clothing. In Figure 4.5, for example, Hathaway is appealing to the personality characteristics of individualism and a sense of well being.

Social Influences

So far we have examined the person-specific and the psychological forces that can influence the consumer buying decision process. Now let us consider how other people influence buying decisions.

The forces that other people exert on buying behavior are called **social influences.** As shown in Figure 4.2, they can be grouped into four major areas: (1) roles and family influences, (2) reference groups, (3) social classes, and (4) culture and subcultures.

Roles and Family Influences

All of us occupy positions within groups, organizations, and institutions. Associated with each position is a **role**—a set of actions and activities that a person in a particular position is supposed to perform, based on the expectations of both the individual and surrounding persons. For example, even though family roles have changed a good deal, traditionally a married male parent has held two positions in the family: husband and father. The behaviors and activities that make up a man's role as father are determined by the expectations that he, his wife, and his children have regarding the behavior of a father.

Since people occupy numerous positions, they also have many roles. The male in our example not only performs the roles of husband and father but also may perform the roles of plant supervisor, church deacon, Little League coach, and student in an evening college class. In this way several sets of expectations are placed on each person's behavior.

Figure 4.5

Advertisement directed at a specific personality type (Source: C. F. Hathaway)

John Naisbitt, the man in the Hathaway shirt.

Every man has his own management style.
Take <u>Megatrends</u> author John Naisbitt. Imaginative, influential, with the insight to draw conclusions.
And there's a Hathaway shirt to match. Does that mean there's a Hathaway shirt for every management style?
No, only successful ones. **Management Style. Hathaway.**

An individual's roles influence not only general behavior but also buying behavior. The demands of a person's many roles may be inconsistent and confusing. To illustrate, assume that the father we have been discussing is thinking about buying a boat. His wife wants him to buy it next year. His fourteen-year-old daughter is hoping for a high-powered skiing boat. His eighteen-year-old son wants a sailboat. His fellow deacons are casually suggesting that he increase his monetary contribution to the church. Several classmates at the college are urging him to buy a specific brand of boat. A coworker indicates that he should buy a different brand, one known for high performance. Thus, an individual's buying behavior is partially affected by the input and opinions of significant others (family and friends).

Family roles relate directly to purchase decisions. The male head of household is likely to be involved heavily in the purchase of products like liquor and tobacco. And although female roles have changed, research shows that women still make buying decisions related to many household items, including health-care products, laundry supplies, paper products, and foods.[7] Husband and wife participate jointly in the purchase of a variety of products, especially durable goods. When two or more family members participate in a purchase, their roles may dictate that each is responsible for performing certain tasks: initiating the idea, gathering information, deciding on whether to buy the product, or

7. *Purchase Influence: Measures of Husband/Wife Influence on Buying Decisions* (New Canaan, Conn.: Haley, Overholser, and Associates, 1975), pp. 13–22.

Table 4.1 Relative influence of husband and wife when purchasing selected durable goods and services

| | Purchase Decision Influence[a] | | | |
| | Product Decision | | Brand Decision | |
	Wife	Husband	Wife	Husband
Automotive				
Automobiles	38	62	33	67
Automobile tires	20	80	18	82
Small Appliances				
Electric blender	59	41	53	47
Coffee maker	64	36	64	36
Vacuum cleaner	60	40	60	40
Home Furnishings				
Broadloom carpet	60	40	59	41
Mattress	58	42	59	41
Vinyl flooring	59	41	59	41
Insurance (new policy or increase in coverage)				
Automobile	33	67	31	69
Homeowners'	40	60	39	61
Life	36	64	34	66

[a] Wives' and husbands' influences on purchase decisions = 100 percent (read table across).

selecting the specific brand. The particular tasks performed depend on the types of products being considered. The results of a 1975 national survey (see Table 4.1) show the amount of influence that the husband and wife have in certain decisions and tasks related to the purchase of selected durable goods. Children's influence on the purchase of numerous items also must be considered, for it is substantial. In the table, *purchase decision* refers to the decision regarding whether or not to buy a general type of product, such as a typewriter. *Brand decision* deals with the selection of a specific brand.

Marketers need to be aware of how roles affect buying behavior. To develop a marketing mix that precisely meets the needs of the target market, they need to know not only who does the actual buying but what other roles influence the purchase. For example, the data in Table 4.1 indicate that a high proportion of women are the information gatherers for the purchase of carpet. Thus, a carpet producer should design a marketing mix in which much of the advertising is directed toward women. However, because sex roles are changing so rapidly in our country, marketers must be cautious when using data like those in Table 4.1. They must be sure that the information is current and accurate.

Reference-group Influence

A group is a **reference group** when an individual identifies with the group so much that he or she takes on many of the values, attitudes, or behaviors of group members. The person who sees a group as a reference group may or

Initiation				Information Gathering			
Product Decision		Brand Decision		Product Decision		Brand Decision	
Wife	*Husband*	*Wife*	*Husband*	*Wife*	*Husband*	*Wife*	*Husband*
22	78	21	79	18	82	18	82
12	88	11	89	13	87	14	86
67	33	50	50	53	47	52	48
73	27	68	32	64	36	66	34
80	20	69	31	66	34	65	35
82	18	74	26	72	28	69	31
74	26	70	30	67	33	68	32
77	23	66	34	63	37	65	35
21	79	22	78	30	70	28	72
34	66	26	74	37	63	36	64
25	75	23	77	27	73	27	73

Source: Purchase Influence: Measures of Husband/Wife Influence on Buying Decisions (New Canaan, Conn.: Haley, Overholser, and Associates, Inc., 1975), pp. 27–29. Reprinted by permission.

may not know the actual size of the group. Most people have several reference groups—families, fraternities, civic organizations, and professional groups like the American Medical Association are examples.

A group can be a negative reference group for an individual. Someone may have been a part of a specific group at one time but later rejected the group's values and members. Also, one can specifically take action to avoid a particular group.[8] However, in this discussion we refer to reference groups as those that are viewed positively by the individual involved.

A reference group may act as a point of comparison and as a source of information for an individual. A customer's behavior may change to be more in line with the actions and beliefs of group members. For example, a person might stop buying one brand of cold medication and switch to another on the advice of members of the reference group. Similarly, an individual may seek information from the reference group about one or more factors affecting a purchase decision, such as where to buy a certain product.

The degree to which a reference group affects a purchase decision depends on an individual's susceptibility to reference-group influence and the strength of involvement with the group. In addition, reference-group influence may affect the purchase decision, the brand decision, or both. For example, the

8. Henry Assael, *Consumer Behavior and Marketing Action* (Boston: Kent Publishing Company, 1981), p. 318.

Table 4.2 Characteristics and buying behavior of persons in various social classes

Class (percentage of population)	General Characteristics	Patterns of Buying Behavior
Upper (0.2)	Socially prominent; possess inherited wealth; may live in large family mansions in mature, exclusive neighborhoods; investors, merchants, and high-level professionals; college degrees from major institutions	Are not conspicuous consumers; purchase or inherit large homes; buy conservative clothes; patronize exclusive shops and avoid mass merchandisers; travel extensively; purchase expensive, unique products
Upper-middle (10–15)	Well educated and career oriented; professionals and middle management; gregarious and socially at ease; have high expectations of their children; tend to join organizations	Buy expensive homes to indicate social position; purchase products such as insurance to achieve financial security; consumption may be conspicuous but cautious to ensure that purchases are socially acceptable; buy high-quality products in pursuit of gracious living
Lower-middle (35)	Respectability is major objective; live in suburban tract homes; owners of small businesses, office workers, semiprofessionals, and white-collar workers	To be respectable, own rather than rent houses; houses are well maintained through purchase of do-it-yourself products; furniture bought one piece at a time, likely to be moderately priced and of standard design; highly price sensitive; shopping done in a wide variety of stores but not in exclusive stores; joint shopping by husband and wife more common in this class than in others

purchase decision for frozen prepared dinners is affected by reference-group influence, while the brand decision for this product is not. Generally, the more conspicuous a product is, the more likely the brand decision will be influenced by reference groups.

A marketer sometimes tries to use reference-group influence in advertisements by suggesting that people in a specific group buy a product and are highly satisfied with it. In this type of appeal, the advertiser hopes that a large number of people use the suggested group as a reference group and that they will buy (or react more favorably to) the product. The success of this kind of advertising depends on the advertisement's effectiveness in communicating the message, on the type of product, and on the individual's susceptibility to reference-group influence.

Social Classes

Within all societies, people rank others into higher and lower social positions of respect. This ranking results in social classes. A **social class** is an open group of individuals who have similar social rank. A class is referred to as "open"

Table 4.2 *(continued)*

Class (percentage of population)	General Characteristics	Patterns of Buying Behavior
Upper-lower (35–40)	Blue-collar, semiskilled workers, seeking job security; want to improve social position; reside in older, less expensive neighborhoods, or suburban tracts; earn good incomes	Live in small houses or apartments; favor national brands and tend to be brand loyal; spend less than other classes on housing and more on household items such as kitchen appliances; spend smaller proportion of income on travel; prefer to shop at nonexclusive department stores and at discount houses; heavy users of credit
Lower-lower (15–20)	Poorly educated, poverty stricken; welfare recipients; unskilled workers plagued by high unemployment; live in substandard and slum areas; children expected to be obedient, quiet, and servile; loyal to family and kinfolk; pessimistic about future; apathetic about politics; belong to very few organizations	Purchases are impulsive rather than planned; often pay high prices and interest rates; compared with other classes, spend a larger proportion of income on products to improve personal appearance and less on formal education and cars; prefer to shop in local stores where they know the owner and can get easy credit terms

Sources: Harold M. Hodges, Jr., "Pennisula People: Social Stratification in a Metropolitan Complex," in *Permanence and Change in Social Class: Readings in Stratification,* W. Clayton Lane, ed. (Cambridge, Mass.: Schenkman, 1968), pp. 5–36; James F. Engel and Roger D. Blackwell, *Consumer Behavior* (Hinsdale, Ill.: Dryden Press, 1986), pp. 348–358; and Harold W. Berkman and Christopher C. Gilson, *Consumer Behavior: Concepts and Strategies* (Boston: Kent, 1981), pp. 158–165.

because people can move into and out of it. The criteria used to group people into classes vary from one society to another. In our society, we use many factors, including occupation, education, income, wealth, religion, race, ethnic group, and possessions. A person who is ranking someone does not necessarily apply all of a society's criteria. The number and the importance of the factors chosen depends on the characteristics of the individual being ranked and on the values of the person who is doing the ranking.

To some degree, individuals within social classes develop and take on common patterns of behavior. They may have similar attitudes, values, language patterns, and possessions. Social class influences many aspects of our lives. For example, it affects our chances of having children and their chances of surviving infancy. It influences our occupation, religion, childhood training, and educational attainment. Because social class affects so many aspects of a person's life, it also influences buying decisions.

Analysts of social class commonly divide people in our country into five or six classes. The five-class system is outlined in Table 4.2. Note that social class determines to some extent the type, quality, and quantity of products that

Figure 4.6

Bathroom accessories targeted at upper social class (Source: Sherle Wagner, New York)

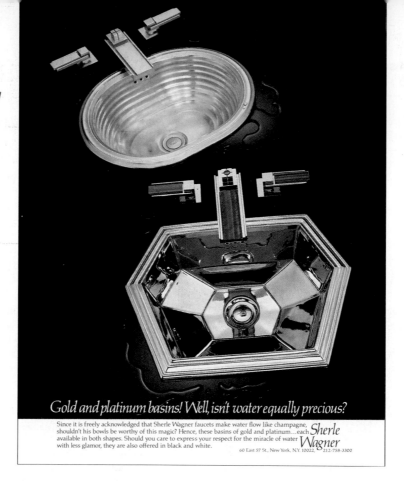

Gold and platinum basins! Well, isn't water equally precious?

Since it is freely acknowledged that Sherle Wagner faucets make water flow like champagne, shouldn't his bowls be worthy of this magic? Hence, these basins of gold and platinum...each available in both shapes. Should you care to express your respect for the miracle of water with less glamor, they are also offered in black and white.

Sherle Wagner

60 East 57 St., New York, N.Y. 10022, 212-758-3300

a person buys and uses. Social class also affects an individual's shopping patterns and the types of stores patronized. Advertisements, such as the one in Figure 4.6, sometimes are based on an appeal to a specific social class.

Cultural and Subcultural Influences

Culture is everything in our surroundings that is made by human beings. It consists of tangible items such as foods, furniture, buildings, clothing, and tools and intangible concepts such as education, welfare, and laws. Culture also includes the values and broad range of behaviors that are acceptable within a specific society. The concepts, values, and behavior that make up a culture are learned and are passed on from one generation to the next.

Cultural influences have broad effects on buying behavior because they permeate our daily lives. Our culture determines what we wear and eat, where we reside and travel. It broadly affects how we buy and use products, and it influences our satisfaction from them. For example, in our culture, the problem of time scarcity is increasing because of the increase in the number of females who work and because of the current emphasis we place on physical and mental self-development. Many people do time-saving shopping and buy time-saving products to cope with this scarcity.[9]

Since culture, to some degree, determines how products are purchased and used, it in turn affects the development, promotion, distribution, and

9. Leonard L. Berry, "The Time Sharing Consumer," *Journal of Retailing,* Winter 1979, p. 69.

pricing of products. Food marketers, for example, have had to make a multitude of changes in their marketing efforts. Thirty years ago most families in our culture ate at least two meals a day together, and the mother devoted four to six hours a day to preparing those meals. Today, over 60 percent of the women in the 25–54 age group are employed outside the home, and average family incomes have risen considerably. These two changes have led to changes in the national per capita consumption of certain foods.

When U.S. marketers sell products in other countries, they often see the tremendous impact that culture has on the purchase and use of products. International marketers find that people in other regions of the world have different attitudes, values, and needs, which in turn call for different methods of doing business, as well as different types of marketing mixes. Some international marketers fail because they do not or cannot adjust to cultural differences. The effect of culture on international marketing programs is discussed in greater detail in Chapter 22.

On the basis of geographic regions or human characteristics, such as age or ethnic background, a culture can be divided into **subcultures.** In our country, we have a number of different subcultures: West Coast, teen-age, and German, for example. Within subcultures there are even greater similarities in people's attitudes, values, and actions than within the broader culture. Relative to other subcultures, individuals in a certain subculture may have stronger preferences for certain types of clothing, furniture, or foods. For example, there is a greater per capita consumption of rice among Southerners than among New Englanders or Midwesterners.

Marketers must recognize that even though their operations are confined to the United States, to one state, or even to one city, subcultural differences may dictate considerable variations in what, how, and when people buy. To deal effectively with these differences, marketers may have to alter their product, promotion, distribution systems, or price to satisfy members of particular subcultures.

Understanding Consumer Behavior

Many marketers try to understand buyer behavior so that they can provide greater satisfaction to consumers. Yet there is still a certain amount of customer dissatisfaction. Some marketers have not adopted the marketing concept. Therefore, they are not consumer oriented and do not regard customer satisfaction as a primary objective. Also, since the tools for analyzing consumer behavior lack precision, marketers may not be able to determine accurately what is highly satisfying to buyers. Finally, even if marketers know what increases consumer satisfaction, they may not be able to provide it.

Understanding consumer behavior is an important task for marketers. Even though consumer behavior research has not provided all the knowledge that marketers need, progress has been made over the last twenty years and is likely to continue in the next twenty years. Not only will refinements in research methods yield more information about consumer behavior, but the pressure of an increasingly competitive business environment will increase marketers' needs for a greater understanding of consumer decision processes.

Summary

Buyers' reactions to a firm's marketing strategy or strategies have great impact on the firm's success. Understanding buying behavior is thus essential to create a marketing mix that satisfies customers.

Consumer buying behavior refers to the behavior of ultimate consumers—those who purchase products for personal or household use, not for business purposes. The three types of consumer decision making are (1) routine response decision making, used for frequently purchased, low-cost items that require very little search and decision effort; (2) limited decision making, used for products that are purchased occasionally or when a buyer needs to acquire information about an unfamiliar brand in a familiar product category; and (3) extensive decision making, used for purchasing an unfamiliar expensive product or an infrequently bought item.

The five parts of the consumer buying decision process are problem recognition, information search, evaluation of alternatives, purchase, and postpurchase evaluation. Problem recognition occurs when a buyer becomes aware that there is a difference between a desired state and an actual condition. Consumers search for information on such factors as availability of brands, product features, seller characteristics, warranties, and prices. To evaluate alternatives, the consumer establishes criteria based on the information search and uses them to compare product characteristics. When the consumer buys the product, the purchase is completed. After the purchase, the buyer uses postpurchase evaluation to assess the product. The buyer may experience cognitive dissonance—dissatisfaction occurring because the buyer questions whether or not the purchase should have been made at all.

The consumer buying decision process can be affected by three categories of factors: person-specific, psychological, and social. A person-specific factor is one that is unique to a particular individual. Two categories of person-specific factors are demographic factors, such as age, sex, race, and nationality, and situational factors, which are the set of circumstances or conditions that exist when a consumer is making a purchase decision.

Psychological influences are perception, motives, learning, attitudes, and personality. Perception is the process by which an individual selects, organizes, and interprets information inputs to create meaning. Motives are internal energizing forces that orient a person's activities toward his or her goals; they sometimes are researched through interviews and projective techniques. Learning consists of changes in one's behavior that are caused by information and experience. An attitude consists of knowledge and positive or negative feelings about an object. Personality is an internal structure in which experience and behavior are related in an orderly way.

The main social influences on consumer behavior are roles and family influences, reference groups, social classes, and cultural and subcultural forces. A role is a set of actions and activities that a person in a particular position is supposed to perform. A reference group is a group with which an individual identifies so much that he or she takes on the values, attitudes, and behaviors of group members. A social class is an open aggregate of people with similar social rank. Culture is everything in our surroundings that is made by human beings. A culture consists of several subcultures. Both cultural and subcultural forces influence people's buying behavior.

Important Terms

Buying behavior
Consumer buying behavior
Routine response behavior
Limited decision making
Extensive decision making
Consumer buying decision
  process
Cognitive dissonance
Person-specific influences
Demographic factors
Situational factors

Psychological influences
Perception
Information inputs
Selective exposure
Selective distortion
Selective retention
Self-concept
Motive
Patronage motives
Depth interview
Group interview

Projective techniques
Learning
Attitude
Attitude scale
Personality
Social influences
Role
Reference group
Social class
Culture
Subculture

Discussion and Review Questions

1. Why do we think of consumers as decision makers when we analyze buyer behavior?
2. What are the types of decision making used by consumers?
3. What are the major stages in the consumer buying decision process? Are all of these stages used in all consumer purchase decisions?
4. How do person-specific influences affect the consumer buying decision process?
5. How does perception influence buyer behavior?
6. How do motives influence a person's buying decisions?
7. What is the role of learning in a consumer's purchasing decision process?
8. How do marketers attempt to shape consumers' learning?
9. Why are marketers concerned about consumer attitudes?
10. How do roles affect a person's buying behavior?
11. Describe reference groups. How do they influence buying behavior?
12. In what ways does social class affect a person's purchase decisions?
13. What is culture? How does it affect a person's buying behavior?
14. Describe your own subculture. Identify buying behavior that is unique to your subculture.

Cases

Case 4.1   First Bank & Trust

First Bank & Trust is located in a medium-sized city. In total deposits, First Bank is third among the six banks in the trade area. Top-level managers of First Bank are not happy about being number three. They want to attract new accounts and have placed much of the responsibility for this on Sandra Stinson, vice president of marketing.

To develop a strategy to attract new customer accounts, Stinson, with the help of an independent research company, conducted a telephone survey of residents in the trade area. The group of respondents included both First Bank customers and customers at other banks. The survey focused on (1) residents' attitudes regarding general features of the banks in the area and (2) residents'

Table 4.3 *Percent of responses regarding general bank characteristics*

General Features	American State Bank	Citizens Bank	Capital Bank	City National Bank	First Bank & Trust	Guaranty National Bank	Other	Don't Know	Total
Largest bank	17.0	0.4	1.4	3.2	7.0	59.8	0.4	10.8	100.0
Strongest bank	18.0	1.0	1.6	3.8	5.8	37.4	0.4	32.0	100.0
Bank with most convenient locations	14.2	2.4	7.2	11.2	15.2	33.2	2.2	14.4	100.0
Most progressive bank	19.0	2.6	3.0	2.8	8.2	41.0	0.6	22.8	100.0
Bank catering to the young	24.0	19.8	6.6	3.0	10.6	12.0	0.8	23.2	100.0
Bank for everyone	10.6	2.0	1.4	3.0	6.0	20.0	4.2	52.8	100.0

attitudes regarding the relative importance of several characteristics when selecting a bank. Table 4.3 shows the percentage of respondents who answered with various banks' names when questioned about several general features such as size and strength. Responses regarding the importance of certain characteristics when selecting a bank are shown in Table 4.4.

Questions for Discussion

1. Will the information in Tables 4.3 and 4.4 be useful to Stinson in her efforts to attract new customers? What additional information does she need? Why?
2. Which data in Tables 4.3 and 4.4 are most important for developing a strategy to attract new accounts? Why?
3. On the basis of these findings, what recommendations might Stinson make?

Case 4.2 Crown Clothing and Accessories

Crown Clothing, Inc., is the maker of clothing and accessories bearing an unusual crown emblem. Although Crown manufactures a line of men's and women's athletic swimwear, the company focuses primarily on producing and marketing sportswear for the entire family.

Over the last five years, the overwhelming popularity of its crown-emblazoned products caused Crown's sales to quadruple. However, within the last year, sales of its products leveled off and even showed signs of a decline. Some business analysts believe that by the end of the year, sales may be down 25 percent from the previous year.

There are several possible explanations for this. During the five years that sales were climbing rapidly, Crown spent most of its resources and efforts emphasizing the crown symbol and spent little time monitoring changes in buyer trends or preferences. Also, competitors were quick to produce their own emblemized sportswear products, which detracted from the uniqueness

Table 4.4 *Percent of responses regarding the importance of selected bank characteristics*

Bank Features	Very Important	Somewhat Important	Not Important	Don't Know	Total
Convenient to home	76.0	14.8	9.2	0.0	100.0
Convenient to work	46.4	21.8	31.6	0.2	100.0
New building	11.0	15.4	72.8	0.8	100.0
Travel department	8.8	17.6	67.2	6.4	100.0
Financial counseling	37.4	28.6	31.4	2.6	100.0
Financial strength	66.2	16.8	12.4	4.6	100.0
Weekend banking services	37.2	24.6	37.2	1.0	100.0
Evening banking hours	48.4	29.6	21.8	0.2	100.0
Drive-in windows	59.0	23.8	16.6	0.6	100.0
Bank credit card	31.6	22.8	43.8	1.8	100.0
Free checking accounts	56.2	19.8	22.8	1.2	100.0
Gives premiums such as stamps or gifts	14.6	15.6	68.8	1.0	100.0
Ease in acquiring loans	44.4	26.4	26.8	2.4	100.0
24-hour cash machines	25.6	19.8	47.8	6.8	100.0

of the crown emblem. To make matters worse, some companies Crown had licensed to use the crown emblem did not maintain the high quality level that they had promised, and an image problem was created.

Recently, a research firm conducted a study for Crown to help it determine the kinds of changes that needed to be made in its sportswear. There were several findings that Crown marketers believed to be important. First, teenagers' and adult females' purchases of sportwear seemed to be heavily influenced by close friends and associates. When asked how they found out about new clothing styles, these respondents reported that they often talked about clothes with friends and that friends often went shopping with them. Second, the findings indicated that clothing buyers had strong feelings about external emblems that clearly identified a brand. Some of the respondents strongly preferred to purchase clothes with an emblem, while others reported that they would not buy a garment bearing an emblem even if they liked all the other features of the garment. Third, the results showed that 40 percent of the respondents preferred clothes without brand emblems. Four years ago in a similar study, the findings suggested that 20 percent of sportswear buyers disliked brand emblems.

Currently, Crown is making several changes in its marketing mix. Although it is still producing clothes with the crown emblem, it is also making sportswear without emblems. Looser fitting styles in soft fabrics with multicolored stripes are being introduced. To make buyers aware of these new designs, the firm's advertising expenditures have doubled, and Crown's sales force has increased.

Questions for Discussion

1. What type of buyer decision making do most people use when purchasing sportswear?
2. In what ways do roles influence the purchase of sportswear?
3. How do a person's reference groups influence buying decisions for sportswear?
4. Do you feel that Crown's product adjustments are advisable?

5 / Organizational Markets and Buying Behavior

Objectives

■ To become aware of the various types of organizational markets.

■ To identify the major characteristics of organizational buyers and transactions.

■ To understand some of the attributes of organizational or industrial demand.

■ To become familiar with the major components of a buying center.

■ To understand the major stages of the organizational buying decision process and the factors that affect this process.

Figure 5.1

The F. G. Montabert Company (Source: Courtesy of F. G. Montabert Company)

Calvin Klein, Levi, Sasson, Wrangler, and Izod are all familiar names. But do the makers of these brands produce the labels on which their names appear? No! The labels for these popular brands, as well as hundreds of others, are made by F. G. Montabert Company, located in New Jersey. With a 50 percent increase in sales last year, Montabert is one of the largest clothing label makers in the country (see Figure 5.1).

Only a few years ago, Montabert was very unprofitable and was experiencing declining sales. The firm's looms were old and inefficient. A new CEO assumed the major leadership role. He equipped the Montabert Company with new computer-aided design equipment and high-speed automated looms. The technologically advanced equipment enabled the firm to produce innovative labels with intricate designs and dramatic color combinations.

This organization, which began operations in 1914, has become a successful, effective marketer because it is able to provide labels that are unique and distinctive. Its labels are not cheap. Marketers at Montabert argue that the labels are nonetheless a very good value for clothing manufacturers because they help to upgrade the image of clothing lines. Most clothing manufacturers agree and are willing to pay the higher prices to provide a distinctive image for their clothing.[1]

1. Robert A. Mamis, "Silver Threads Among the Gold." Reprinted with permission, *Inc.* magazine (Nov. 1985). Copyright © 1985 by INC. Publishing Company, 38 Commercial Wharf, Boston, MA 02110.

Montabert is an example of a company that serves organizational markets. It does not deal with consumers directly. An organizational market is defined in Chapter 3 as consisting of individuals or groups that purchase a specific type of product for resale, for use in producing other products, or for use in day-to-day operations. In this chapter we take a closer look at organizational markets and organizational buying decision processes. We first discuss the various kinds of organizational markets and the types of buyers that make up these markets. Next, we explore several dimensions of organizational buying, including the attributes of organizational transactions, the characteristics and concerns of organizational buyers, the methods of organizational buying, and the characteristics of demand for products sold to organizational purchasers. Finally, we examine organizational buying decisions by considering who makes organizational purchases and how the decisions are made.

Types of Organizational Buyers

In Chapter 3, we identify four major kinds of organizational markets: producer, reseller, government, and institutional. In the following section we discuss the characteristics of the customers that make up these markets.

Producer Markets

Individuals and business organizations that purchase products for the purpose of making a profit by using them to produce other products or by using them in their operations are classified as **producer markets.** Producer markets include buyers of raw materials as well as purchasers of semifinished and finished items used to produce other products. For example, grocery stores and supermarkets are part of the producer markets for numerous support products such as paper bags, counters, scanners, and floor-care products. Farmers are part of the producer markets for farm machinery, fertilizer, seed, and livestock. A broad array of industries make up producer markets, including—besides agriculture—forestry, fisheries, mining, construction, transportation, communications, and utilities. As indicated by the data in Table 5.1, the number of business units in national producer markets is enormous.

Table 5.1 Number of firms in industry groups	
Industry	**Number of Firms**
Agriculture, forestry, fishing	3,486,000
Mining	181,000
Construction	1,412,000
Manufacturing	569,000
Transportation, public utilities	570,000
Finance, insurance, real estate	2,179,000
Services	4,777,000

Source: Statistical Abstract of the United States, 1986, p. 518.

Manufacturers are geographically concentrated. Over half of them are located in only seven states: New York, California, Pennsylvania, Illinois, Ohio, New Jersey, and Michigan. This geographic concentration sometimes allows an industrial marketer to serve customers more efficiently. Within certain states, production in only a few industries may account for a sizable proportion of total industrial output.

Reseller Markets

Reseller markets consist of intermediaries, such as wholesalers and retailers, who buy finished goods and resell them to make a profit. (Wholesalers and retailers are discussed in Chapters 10 and 11.) Other than minor alterations, resellers do not change the physical characteristics of the products they handle. With the exception of items that producers sell directly to consumers, all products sold to consumer markets are first sold to reseller markets.

Wholesalers purchase products for resale to retailers, to other wholesalers, and to producers, governments, and institutions. Of the 337,943 wholesalers in the United States a large percentage are located in New York, California, Illinois, Texas, Ohio, Pennsylvania, and New Jersey.[2] Although some expensive, highly technical products are sold directly to end users, many products are sold through wholesalers who, in turn, sell products to other firms in the distribution system. Thus, wholesalers are very important in helping a producer's product to be accepted by users. Wholesalers often carry a huge number of products—perhaps as many as 250,000 items. When inventories are vast, the reordering of products normally is automated and the wholesaler's initial purchase decisions are made by professional buyers and buying committees.

Retailers purchase products and resell them to final consumers. There are approximately 1,330,000 retailers in the United States. They employ about 16 million people and generate close to $1 trillion in annual sales.[3] Some retailers carry a large number of items. Drug stores, for example, may stock up to 12,000 items, and some supermarkets may handle as many as 20,000 different products. In small family-owned retail stores, the owner frequently makes purchasing decisions. Large department stores have one or more employees in each department who are responsible for buying products for that department. For chain stores, a buyer or buying committee in the central office frequently decides whether a product will be available in the firm's stores. But, for most products, local store management makes the actual buying decisions for its particular store.

When making purchase decisions, resellers consider several factors. They evaluate the level of demand for a product to determine in what quantity and at what prices the product can be resold. They assess the amount of space required to handle a product relative to its potential profit. Retailers, for example, sometimes evaluate products on the basis of sales per square foot of selling area. Often, customers depend on a reseller to have a product when they need it, so a reseller typically evaluates a supplier's ability to provide adequate quantities when and where needed. Resellers also consider the ease of placing orders and the availability of technical assistance and training programs from the producer. (The Zenith advertisement in Figure 5.2 is aimed at resellers and addresses some of these issues.) More broadly, when resellers consider

2. *Statistical Abstract of the United States,* 1986, p. 785.
3. Ibid, p. 778.

Figure 5.2

Promotion aimed at resellers (Source: Zenith Data Systems; Agency: Foote, Cone and Bending/Direct Market)

the purchase of a product not previously carried, they try to determine whether the product competes with or complements products currently being handled by the firm. These types of concerns distinguish reseller markets from other markets. Markets dealing with reseller markets must recognize these needs and be able to serve them.

Government Markets

Federal, state, county, and local governments make up **government markets.** They spend billions of dollars annually for a variety of goods and services to support their internal operations and to provide citizens with such products as highways, education, water, national defense, and energy. For example, in 1983 the federal government spent over $229 billion on defense, about $16

Table 5.2 Annual expenditures by government units for selected years (in billions of dollars)

Year	Total Government Expenditures	Federal Government Expenditures	State and Local Expenditures
1960	151	90	61
1970	333	185	148
1975	560	292	268
1980	959	526	432
1981	1,110	625	485
1982	1,233	710	523
1983	1,351	786	565

Source: *Statistical Abstract of the United States,* 1986, p. 262.

billion on health, and about $25 billion on education.[4] Governmental expenditures annually account for about 20 percent of this country's gross national product.

In addition to the federal government there are 50 state governments, 3,041 county governments, and 82,290 other local governments.[5] The amount spent by federal, state, and local units over the last thirty years has increased rapidly because the total number of government units and the services they provide have both increased. In addition, the costs of providing these services have increased. In Table 5.2, notice that the federal government spends over half of the total amount spent by all governments.

The types and quantities of products purchased by government markets reflect societal demands on various government agencies. As citizens' needs for government services change, so does the demand for products by government markets. Because government agencies spend public funds to buy the products needed to provide services, they are accountable to the public. This accountability explains their relatively complex set of buying procedures. Some firms don't even try to sell to government buyers because they don't want to deal with so much red tape. However, many marketers learn to deal efficiently with government procedures and don't find them to be a stumbling block. For certain products such as defense-related items, the government may be the only customer. The U.S. Government Printing Office publishes and distributes several documents explaining buying procedures and describing the types of products purchased by various federal agencies.

Government purchases are made through bids or through negotiated contracts. To make a sale under the bid system, a firm must appear on a list of qualified bidders. When a government unit wants to buy, it sends out a detailed description of the products to qualified bidders. Businesses that wish to sell such products submit bids. The government unit usually is required to accept the lowest acceptable bid.

4. *Statistical Abstract of the United States,* 1986, p. 264.
5. Ibid, p. 262.

When buying nonstandard or highly complex products, a government unit often uses a negotiated contract. Under this procedure, the government unit selects only a few firms and then negotiates specifications and terms; it eventually awards the contract to one of the negotiating firms. Most large defense-related purchases are made through negotiated contracts.

Although government markets can be complicated in their requirements, they can also be very lucrative. When the Postal Service, Social Security Administration, and other government agencies modernize obsolete computer systems, successful bidders can gain a billion dollars over the life of a contract, usually five years or more. One computer service company, Electronic Data Systems Corp., a subsidiary of General Motors, is trying to use federal contracts to make itself the industry leader.[6] Some firms have established separate departments to facilitate marketing to government units.

Institutional Markets

Organizations that seek to achieve goals other than normal business goals such as profit, market share, or return on investment constitute **institutional markets.** Members of institutional markets include churches, private schools, some hospitals, civic clubs, fraternities, sororities, charitable organizations, and foundations. Institutions purchase millions of dollars' worth of products annually to provide goods, services, and ideas to congregations, students, patients, club members, and others. Because institutions often have different goals and fewer resources than other types of organizations, marketers may employ special marketing activities to serve these markets.

Dimensions of Organizational Buying

Having gained an understanding of the different types of organizational customers, we need to consider several dimensions of organizational buying. In this part of the chapter we examine some characteristics of organizational transactions. Then we discuss several attributes of organizational buyers and some of their primary concerns when making purchase decisions. After that we consider methods of organizational buying and the major types of purchases. We conclude the section with a discussion of how the demand for industrial products differs from the demand for consumer products.

Characteristics of Organizational or Industrial Transactions

Organizational or industrial transactions differ from consumer sales in several ways. Orders by organizational buyers tend to be much larger than individual consumer sales. Suppliers often must sell their products in large quantities to make profits; they therefore prefer not to sell to customers who place small orders.

Organizational purchases are generally negotiated less frequently than are consumer sales. Some purchases involve large, expensive items, such as capital equipment, that are used for a number of years. Other products, such as raw materials and component items, are used continuously in production and may have to be supplied frequently. However, the contract regarding the terms of

6. "Ross Perot's Raid on Washington," *Fortune,* Oct. 31, 1983, p. 124.

sale and supply for these items is likely to be a long-term agreement, requiring negotiations, for example, every third year.

In addition to infrequent sales negotiations, long negotiating periods may be needed to complete organizational sales. Purchasing decisions are often made by a committee, orders are frequently large and expensive, and products may be custom-built. There is a good chance that several people or departments in the purchasing organization will be involved. While one department might express a need for a product, a second department might develop its specifications, a third might stipulate the maximum amount to be spent, and a fourth might actually place the order.

One practice that is unique to organizational sales is **reciprocity,** an arrangement in which two organizations agree to buy from each other. Reciprocal agreements that threaten competition are illegal. The Federal Trade Commission and the Justice Department take action to stop reciprocal practices judged to be anti-competitive. However, a considerable amount of "innocent" reciprocal dealing occurs among small businesses, especially in the service industries. Some larger corporations engage in informal reciprocity to a lesser extent.[7] Because reciprocity forces or strongly influences purchasing agents to deal only with certain suppliers, its use can lower morale among agents and lead to less than optimal purchases.

Attributes of Organizational Buyers

We usually think of organizational or industrial buyers as being more rational than ultimate consumers in their purchasing behavior. The basis for this view is that compared with ultimate consumers, organizational buyers are informed about the products they purchase or they seek more information before purchasing. This assumption is not unfounded. To make purchasing decisions that fulfill an organization's needs, organizational buyers demand detailed information about functional features and technical specifications of products.

Marketers may try to appeal to the assumed rationality of organizational buyers. Despite the assumption of rational behavior, however, personal goals still influence organizational buying behavior. Most organizational purchasing agents seek the psychological satisfaction that comes with organizational advancement and financial rewards. Agents who consistently exhibit rational organizational buying behavior are likely to obtain these personal goals because they are performing their jobs in ways that help their firms achieve organizational objectives. Suppose, though, that an organizational buyer develops a close friendship with a certain supplier. If the buyer values friendship more than organizational promotion or financial rewards, he or she may behave irrationally from the firm's point of view. Dealing exclusively with that supplier regardless of better prices, product qualities, or services offered by competitors may indicate an unhealthy alliance between the buyer and seller.

Primary Concerns of Organizational Buyers

Organizational customers consider a variety of factors when they make purchasing decisions. Many of their primary considerations relate to quality level, service, or price.

Most organizational customers try to achieve and maintain a specific level of quality in the products they offer to their target markets. (See the application

---

7. E. Robert Finney, "Reciprocity: Gone but Not Forgotten," *Journal of Marketing,* Jan. 1978, p. 55.

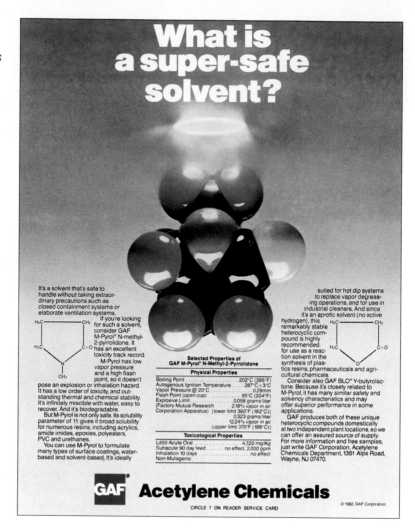
on page 146 regarding AT&T's concern about quality.) To accomplish this goal, they often buy their products on the basis of a set of expressed characteristics, commonly called specifications. Thus, an organizational buyer evaluates the quality of the products being considered to determine whether they meet specifications.

Meeting specifications is extremely important to organizational customers. The advertisement in Figure 5.3 details a solvent's uses, characteristics, and properties so that a potential customer can more adequately evaluate the product relative to required specifications. If a product fails to meet specifications and its use results in a final product that malfunctions for the ultimate consumer, the organizational customer may become disenchanted with the product and switch to a different supplier. On the other hand, organizational customers are ordinarily cautious about buying products that exceed specifications, because such products frequently cost more and thus increase an organization's production costs.

Service is also important to organizational buyers. The services offered by suppliers directly and indirectly influence organizational customers' costs, sales,

Figure 5.4

Message that emphasizes fast on-time delivery (Source: Reprinted with permission of First Software Corporation, Lawrence, Massachusetts)

Now you can order extra late, and get your delivery extra early.

Introducing *Extra Early Delivery*.
If our free overnight delivery on orders for $300 or more opened your eyes, our new *Extra Early Delivery* will really give you something to wake up to.

Because now the fastest delivery in software distribution is even faster.

Now every overnight delivery order you place with First Software will be shipped to your doorstep before noon the next morning. Automatically, for no extra charge.

So when you tell your customers, "I'll have it for you by lunchtime tomorrow", you will.

Just call your sales consultant at First Software, and ask for *"Extra Early Delivery."* And wake up to fastest delivery experience ever!

Introducing *Extra Late Ordering*.
Need software the next morning, and it's already 4:00 p.m.? No sweat.

Just call First Software and take advantage of our new *Extra Late Ordering* service. Even if it's after your normal order deadline, you can still place an overnight order — as late as 7:30 p.m. EST. We'll ship as many as 5 product lines, for the minimal charge of $20.

So your order is packed and on the way to you the same day — for *Extra Early Delivery* the next morning. Talk about fast turnaround.

FIRST SOFTWARE
DISTRIBUTOR OF AMERICA'S LEADING SOFTWARE

17-21 Ballard Way, Lawrence, MA 01843 (617) 689-0077
Boston • Los Angeles • Miami • Houston • Minneapolis
For free overnight delivery, call:
(800) 343-1290
In Massachusetts Call: (800) 322-3077
Software and accessories for Apple, IBM and Commodore 64

and profits. When tangible goods are the same or quite similar—as is the case with most raw materials—the goods may be sold at the same price in the same kind of containers and may have the same specifications. Under such conditions the mix of supplier services is likely to be the major avenue by which an organizational marketer can gain a competitive advantage. Specific services vary in importance, but those commonly desired include market information, inventory maintenance, on-time delivery, repair services and replacement parts, and credit. Organizational buyers are likely to need technical product information, data regarding demand, information about general economic conditions, or supply and delivery information. Maintaining an inventory is critical because it helps to make products accessible when an organizational buyer needs them and reduces the buyer's inventory requirements and costs. On-time delivery is crucial to organizational buyers because it is usually their responsibility to have the products available and ready for use when needed. The advertisement in Figure 5.4, aimed at organizational buyers, emphasizes rapid, on-time delivery. By providing reliable, on-time delivery, organizational marketers enable customers to carry less safety stock, thus reducing the customers'

Application

Quality Awareness at AT&T

Marketers at AT&T recognize that providing high-quality products to organizational buyers is the quickest and best way to achieve the company's overarching goal: customer satisfaction. Working from the premise that it is the customer's definition of quality that determines manufacturing standards and marketing procedures, AT&T companies traditionally have implemented extremely rigorous quality control programs.

Competition and evolving technology, however, are forcing standards of quality ever higher, and customers' definitions of quality vary among different markets and among different countries. To contend with this, and to avoid the overwhelming costs associated with less-than-adequate products, AT&T has established a policy of continuous quality improvement to govern every aspect of the business. This policy emphasizes "doing it right the first time" by investing resources to design and build high-quality products from the very start. Such a philosophy, practiced at AT&T's Oklahoma City plant, dramatically increased production of digital switches, which resulted in significant cost savings.

With the help of computerized quality-management control methods, AT&T's Bell Labs has decreased its amount of software maintenance problems (bugs) by 67 percent. The Network Systems Division manufactures and markets network equipment for local telephone companies and long distance carriers. New, statistically-based quality control methods saved that division $28 million in the first half of last year. At the Network Systems' cable plant in Atlanta, improved quality control methods so effectively reduced defects that production of guide cable increased by 500 percent.

AT&T's Information Systems and Network Systems divisions have established customer satisfaction feedback programs. Interviews are conducted with customers over the telephone and in person to ascertain how well AT&T products and services have met customer expectations. This information is promptly transferred to action teams, and the speed of their response is measured as a part of the systemized quality control effort. All of these examples illustrate that AT&T is attempting to provide higher quality products with the hope of improving relationships with customers. (*Source: Bruce Brackett, "Nothing But the Best,"* AT&T Magazine, *2, no. 3, pp. 2–5; James E. Olson, "The Quality Challenge,"* Quality Progress, *vol. 19, no. 2, Feb. 1986, pp. 12–14; and "Customer Contact Enables AT&T to Communicate Quality Message,"* Marketing News, *vol. 19, no. 24, Nov. 22, 1986, p. 14.*)

costs. Organizational purchasers of machinery are especially concerned about obtaining repair services and replacement parts quickly because inoperable equipment is costly.

Availability of credit can improve an organizational customer's cash flow and reduce the peaks and valleys of capital requirements which, in turn, lowers the firm's cost of capital. Although a single supplier cannot provide every possible service to its organizational customers, a marketing-oriented supplier strives to create the service mix that best satisfies the target market.

Price is obviously important to an organizational customer because it influences operating costs and costs of goods sold, and these costs affect the customer's selling price and profit margin. When purchasing capital equipment, an industrial buyer views the price as the amount of investment necessary to obtain a certain

level of return or savings. Thus, an organizational purchaser is likely to compare the price of a machine with the value of the benefits that the machine will yield. For example, the quartz conveyor oven in Figure 5.5 is being promoted on the basis of low cost, speed, efficiency, and control. Remember, however, that an organizational buyer does not compare alternative products strictly on the basis of price. Other factors, such as product quality and supplier services, are also important elements of the purchase decision. A study of more than one hundred business and medical equipment markets (including copying and data-processing) found that the most important factors in user selection of equipment involved customer service, including equipment reliability, quality of performance, ease of operation, field service response time, and cost of service.[8]

8. Dick Berry, "Industrial Marketers Use 'Secret Weapon' Consumer Services for Marketing Success," *Marketing News,* May 1, 1981, p. 8.

Methods of Organizational Buying

Although no two organizational buyers go about their jobs in the same way, most use one or more of the following purchase methods: description, inspection, sampling, or negotiation.

When the products being purchased are commonly standardized on the basis of certain characteristics (e.g., size, shape, weight, and color) and are normally graded using such standards, an organizational buyer may be able to purchase simply by describing or specifying quantity, grade, and other attributes. Agricultural commodities often fall into this category. Purchases through description are especially common between a buyer and seller who have established an ongoing relationship built on trust.

Certain products—large industrial equipment, used vehicles, and buildings, for example—have unique characteristics and may vary in terms of their condition. A particular used truck might have a bad transmission. Thus, organizational buyers of such products must base their purchase decisions on inspection.

In buying based on sampling, a sample of the product is taken from the lot and evaluated. It is assumed that the characteristics of this sample represent the entire lot. This method may be appropriate when the product is highly homogeneous—grain, for example—and examination of the entire lot is not technically or economically feasible.

Some industrial purchasing relies on negotiated contracts. In certain instances an organizational buyer describes exactly what is needed and then asks sellers to submit bids. The buyer may take the most attractive bids and negotiate with those suppliers. In other cases, the buyer may not be able to identify specifically what is to be purchased but can only provide a general description. This might be the case for a special piece of custom-made equipment. A buyer and seller might negotiate a contract that specifies a base price and contains provisions for the payment of additional costs and fees. These contracts are most likely to be used for one-time projects such as buildings and capital equipment.

Types of Organizational Purchases

Most organizational purchases are one of three types: new-task purchase, modified rebuy purchase, or straight rebuy purchase. A **new-task purchase** is one in which an organization is making an initial purchase of an item to be used to perform a new job or to solve a new problem. A new-task purchase may require the development of product specifications, vendor specifications, and procedures for future purchases of that product. To make the initial purchase, the organizational buyer usually needs a great deal of information. A new-task purchase is important to a supplier because, if the organizational buyer is satisfied with the product, the supplier may be able to sell the buyer large quantities of the product over a period of years.

A **modified rebuy purchase** is one in which a new-task purchase is changed the second or third time it is ordered, or in which the requirements associated with a straight rebuy purchase are modified. For example, an organizational buyer might seek faster delivery, lower prices, or a different quality level of product specifications. A modified rebuy situation may cause regular suppliers to become more aggressive and competitive in order to keep the account. Other competing suppliers may have the opportunity to obtain the business.

A **straight rebuy purchase** occurs when a buyer purchases the same products routinely under approximately the same terms of sale. Buyers require little information for these routine purchase decisions. The buyer tends to use familiar suppliers that have provided satisfactory service and products in the past. These suppliers try to set up automatic reordering systems to make reordering easy and convenient for organizational buyers. A supplier may even monitor the organizational buyer's inventory and indicate to the buyer what needs to be ordered.

Demand for Industrial Products

Products sold to organizational customers are called industrial products. The demand for these products is referred to as industrial demand. Industrial demand differs from consumer demand in that industrial demand is (1) derived, (2) inelastic, (3) joint, and (4) more fluctuating. As we discuss each of these characteristics, remember that the demand for different types of industrial products varies.

Derived Demand

The demand for industrial products is **derived demand** because organizational customers purchase products to be used directly or indirectly in the production of goods and services to satisfy consumers' needs. Therefore, the demand for industrial products derives from the demand for consumer products. In the long run, no industrial demand is totally unrelated to the demand for consumer goods.

The derived nature of industrial demand is usually multilevel. Industrial sellers at different levels are affected by a change in consumer demand for a particular product. For example, a few years ago, fiber makers were turning out large quantities of doubleknits. When consumers stopped buying doubleknits, the demand for equipment used in manufacturing doubleknits also dropped. Therefore, factors influencing consumer buying of doubleknit fabrics affected fiber makers, equipment manufacturers, and other suppliers. Changes in derived demand are the result of a chain reaction. When consumer demand for a product changes, a wave is set in motion that affects the demand for all firms involved in the production of that consumer product.

Inelasticity of Demand

The demand for many industrial products at the industry level is **inelastic demand.** This simply means that a price increase or decrease will not significantly affect demand for the item. Since a lot of industrial products contain a great many parts, price increases that affect only one or two parts of the product may yield only a slightly higher per-unit production cost. Of course, when a sizable price increase for a component part represents a large proportion of the product's cost, then demand may become more elastic because the price increase of the component part causes the price at the consumer level to rise sharply.

The inelasticity characteristic applies only to market or industry demand for the industrial product, not to the demand for an individual supplier. Suppose, for example, that a sparkplug producer increases the price of sparkplugs sold to small-engine manufacturers, while its competitors continue to maintain their same lower prices. The sparkplug company probably would experience reduced sales because most small-engine producers would switch to lower-priced brands. A specific firm is quite vulnerable to elastic demand, even though industry demand for a particular product is inelastic.

Joint Demand

The demand for certain industrial products, especially raw materials and component parts, is affected by joint demand. **Joint demand** occurs when two or more items are used in combination to produce a product. For example, a firm that manufactures axes needs the same number of ax handles as it does ax blades; these two products are demanded jointly. If the supplier of ax handles cannot furnish the required number of handles and the ax producer cannot obtain them elsewhere, the producer will stop buying ax blades.

Understanding the effects of joint demand is particularly important for a marketer that sells multiple, jointly demanded items. Such a marketer must realize that when a customer begins purchasing one of the jointly demanded items, a good opportunity exists to sell other related products. Likewise, when customers purchase a number of jointly demanded products, the producer must exercise extreme caution to avoid shortages of any item because such shortages jeopardize the marketer's sales of all the jointly demanded products.

Demand Fluctuations

The demand for industrial products may fluctuate enormously because it is derived demand. In general, when particular consumer products are in high demand, producers of those products buy large quantities of raw materials and component parts to ensure that long-run production requirements can be met. In addition, these producers may expand their production capacity, which entails the acquisition of capital goods.

A fall in the demand for certain consumer goods works in the same way to significantly reduce the demand for industrial products used to produce those goods. In fact, under such conditions, a marketer's sales of certain products may come to a short-run standstill. When consumer demand is low, industrial customers cut their purchases of raw materials and component parts and stop purchasing equipment and machinery, even for replacement purposes.

A marketer of industrial products may notice substantial changes in demand when its customers change their inventory policies—perhaps because of expectations about future demand. For example, if several dishwasher manufacturers who buy timers from one producer increase their inventory of timers from a two-week to a one-month supply, the timer producer will have a significant immediate increase in demand.

Sometimes, price changes can lead to surprising short-run changes in demand. A price increase for an industrial item may initially cause organizational customers to buy more of the item because they expect the price to rise further. Similarly, demand for an industrial product may be significantly lower following a price cut, because buyers are waiting for further price reductions. Fluctuations in demand can be significant in industries in which price changes occur frequently.

Organizational Buying Decisions

Organizational (or industrial) **buying behavior** refers to the purchase behavior of producers, resellers, government units, and institutions. Although some of the same factors that influence consumer buying behavior (discussed in Chapter 4) also influence organizational buying behavior, a number of factors are unique to the latter. In this section we discuss who participates in making organizational purchase decisions by analyzing the buying center. Then we focus on the stages of the buying decision process and the factors that affect it.

The Buying Center

Relatively few organizational purchase decisions are made by just one person. Instead, they are made through a buying center. Typically, the **buying center** consists of individuals who participate in the purchase decision process, including users, influencers, buyers, deciders, and gatekeepers.[9] One person may perform several of these roles. These participants share some goals and risks associated with their decisions.

Users are the organization members who actually use the product being acquired. They frequently initiate the purchase process and/or generate the specifications for the purchase. After the purchase, they also evaluate the product's performance relative to the specifications. Influencers have a definite impact on the purchase decision process. Often, they are technical personnel, such as engineers, who help develop the specifications and evaluate alternative products. Technical personnel are especially important influencers when the products being considered involve new, advanced technology.

Buyers are responsible for selecting suppliers and actually negotiating the terms of purchase. They may also get involved in developing specifications. Buyers are sometimes called purchasing agents or purchasing managers. Their choices of vendors and products are heavily influenced by persons occupying other roles in the buying center, especially for new-task purchases. For straight rebuy purchases, the buyer plays a major role in the selection of vendors and in negotiations with them. Deciders actually choose the products and vendors. Although buyers may be the deciders, it is not unusual for these roles to be occupied by different people. For routinely purchased items, buyers usually are the deciders. However, a buyer may not be authorized to make purchases that exceed a certain dollar limit. In this case, higher-level management personnel are the deciders. Gatekeepers, such as secretaries and technical personnel, control the flow of information to and among the persons who occupy the other roles in the buying center. Buyers who deal directly with vendors also may be gatekeepers since they can control the flow of information. The flow of information from supplier sales representatives to users and influencers often is controlled by personnel in the purchasing department.

The number and structure of an organization's buying centers are affected by the organization's size and market position, by the volume and types of products being purchased, and by the firm's overall managerial philosophy regarding exactly who should be involved in purchase decisions. A marketer attempting to sell to an organizational customer should determine who is in the buying center, the types of decisions made by each individual, and which individuals are the most influential in the decision process. Since, in some instances, a large number of people make up the buying center, marketers cannot contact all participants. Instead they must be certain to contact a few of the most influential individuals in the buying center.

9. Frederick E. Webster, Jr., and Yoram Wind, *Organizational Buyer Behavior* (Englewood Cliffs, N.J.: Prentice-Hall, 1972), pp. 78–80.

Figure 5.6

Organizational buying decision process and factors that may influence the process (Source: Adapted from Frederick Webster/Yoram Wind, Organizational Buying Behavior, *1972, pp. 33–37. Adapted by permission of Prentice-Hall, Englewood Cliffs, New Jersey)*

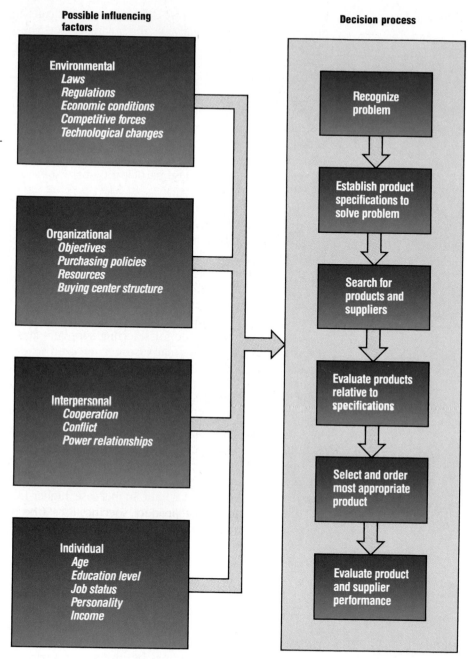

Possible influencing factors

Environmental
Laws
Regulations
Economic conditions
Competitive forces
Technological changes

Organizational
Objectives
Purchasing policies
Resources
Buying center structure

Interpersonal
Cooperation
Conflict
Power relationships

Individual
Age
Education level
Job status
Personality
Income

Decision process

Recognize problem

Establish product specifications to solve problem

Search for products and suppliers

Evaluate products relative to specifications

Select and order most appropriate product

Evaluate product and supplier performance

Stages of the Organizational Buying Decision Process

The stages of the organizational buying decision process are shown on the right side of Figure 5.6. In the first stage, one or more individuals in the organization recognize that a problem or need exists. Problem recognition may arise under a variety of circumstances, for instance, when a machine malfunctions or when a firm is modifying an existing product or introducing a new one. Individuals in the buying center, such as users, influencers, or buyers, may be involved in problem recognition, but it may be stimulated by external sources, such as sales representatives.

Figure 5.7

Promotion of supplier as source of research chemicals (Source: Courtesy of Kjell B. Sandved. Client/company: Alfa Products Division of Morton Thiokol, Inc. Agency: SGM & Co., Inc.)

The development of product specifications (the second stage) requires organizational participants to assess the problem or need and determine what will be necessary to satisfy it. During this stage, users and influencers, such as technical personnel and engineers, often provide information and advice used in developing product specifications. By assessing and describing needs, the organization should be able to establish product specifications.

Searching for possible products to solve the problem and locating suppliers is the third stage in the decision process. Search activities may involve looking in company files and trade directories, contacting suppliers for information, soliciting proposals from known vendors, and examining catalogs and trade publications. The industrial advertisement in Figure 5.7 is an example of information that is available in trade publications. Some vendors may not be viewed as acceptable because they are not large enough to supply the needed quantities. Others may have poor records of delivery and service.

If all goes well, the search stage will result in a list of several alternative products and suppliers. The fourth stage is that of evaluating the products on the list to determine which ones (if any) meet the product specifications developed in the second stage. Also, during this stage various suppliers are evaluated based on multiple criteria such as price, service, and ability to deliver.

Application

Cogenic Energy Systems Markets through Savings

A growing company, Cogenic Energy Systems Inc. (CESI), has resurrected a hundred-year-old energy-saving method and reinstated it for use in today's energy-hungry society. In cogeneration heat that is given off as an engine produces electricity is captured and used to simultaneously heat water. In the past, cogeneration was used to produce heat and electricity in individual buildings, but the practice fell into disuse as utility companies began building power grids. The resurgence of cogeneration in the United States was stimulated by the 1978 Public Utilities Regulatory Policies Act (PURPA), which exempted cogeneration marketers from regulation.

Richard Nelson, president of CESI, claims his company's cogeneration system can save a user 60 percent on its monthly utility bill. CESI faced a tremendous challenge in marketing cogeneration systems in the $10,000 to $100,000 price range. When CESI sells a system to a customer such as a factory, hotel, or hospital, the buyer does not pay for the equipment at the time of the sale. Instead, over a ten-year period the customer pays CESI a percentage of the money saved from reduced utility bills.

CESI was disappointed with sales in the first three years of operations. The firm has switched from a five-person direct sales force to a dealer distributor network. CESI uses a number of promotional techniques, including magazine advertisements, direct mailings, product training seminars, and feasibility studies comparing local utility rates with the costs of cogeneration. Word-of-mouth testimonials from cogeneration users seem to be a very effective promotional tool.

In spite of CESI's marketing struggles, the company is growing and its future outlook is good. Because of CESI's small capacity, it is a likely takeover candidate for larger firms entering the cogeneration market. (*Source: Larry Riggs, "A Pay-As-You-Save Plan Sells 19th-Century Technology,"* Sales and Marketing Management, *Oct. 7, 1985, pp. 39–40. Reprinted by permission of* Sales and Marketing Management.)

The results of the deliberations and assessments in the fourth stage are used during the fifth stage to select the product to be purchased and the supplier from whom to buy it. In this stage the product is actually ordered. Specific details regarding terms, credit arrangements, delivery dates and methods, and technical assistance are worked out during this stage. (As illustrated in the application on this page, the terms of payment may be crucial to the buyer.) During the sixth stage the product's performance is evaluated. Actual performance is compared to specifications. Sometimes, it is determined that although the product met the specifications, its performance did not adequately satisfy the problem or need recognized in the first stage. In this case, product specifications must be adjusted. In addition, during the sixth stage the supplier's performance is evaluated, and if it is found to be unacceptable, the organizational purchaser seeks corrective action from the supplier or searches for a new supplier. The results of the evaluation in this stage become feedback for the other stages and influence future organizational purchase decisions.

This organizational buying decision process is used in its entirety primarily for new-task purchases. Several of the stages, but not necessarily all of them, are employed for modified rebuy and straight rebuy situations.

Influences on Organizational Buying

As shown in Figure 5.6, there are four major categories of factors that appear to influence organizational buying decisions: environmental, organizational, interpersonal, and individual.

Environmental factors are uncontrollable forces such as laws, regulatory actions and guidelines, activities of interest groups, inflation, competitors' actions, and technological changes. These forces generate a considerable amount of uncertainty for an organization, which can make individuals in the buying center rather apprehensive about certain types of purchases. Changes in one or more environmental forces can create new purchasing opportunities and also can make yesterday's purchase decisions look terrible.

Organizational factors include the buying organization's objectives, purchasing policies, and resources, as well as the size and composition of its buying center. An organization may have certain buying policies to which buying center participants must conform. For instance, a firm's policies may mandate long-term contracts, perhaps longer than most sellers desire. The nature of an organization's financial resources may require special credit arrangements. Any of these conditions could affect the firm's purchase decision processes.

The interpersonal factors are the relationships among the people in the buying center. The use of power and the level of conflict among buying center participants, for example, influence organizational buying decisions. Certain persons in the buying center may be better communicators than others and may thus be more convincing. These interpersonal dynamics frequently are hidden, making them difficult for marketers to assess.

Individual factors are the personal characteristics of individuals in the buying center, such as age, education, personality, position in the organization, and income. How influential these factors are varies according to the buying situation, the type of product being purchased, and whether the purchase is new-task, modified rebuy, or straight rebuy. The negotiating styles of people will vary within an organization and from one organization to another. To be effective, a marketer must know customers well enough to be aware of these individual factors and the effects they may have on purchase decisions.

Summary

In this chapter we initially focused on the various types of organizational markets. Organizational markets consist of producers, resellers, governments, and institutions that purchase a specific kind of product for resale, for direct use in producing other products, or for use in day-to-day operations. Producer markets consist of individuals and business organizations that purchase products for the purpose of making a profit by using them to produce other products or by using them in their operations. Reseller markets consist of intermediaries who buy finished products and resell them for the purpose of making a profit. Government markets consist of federal, state, and local governments. These government units spend billions of dollars annually for a variety of goods and services to support their internal operations and to provide citizens with such products as highways, education, health protection, water, waste disposal, national defense, fire and police protection, and energy. Institutional markets consist of organizations that seek to achieve goals other than normal business goals such as profit, market share, or return on investment. Institutions purchase millions of dollar's worth of products annually to provide goods, services, and ideas to congregations, students, patients, club members, and others.

Organizational customers are usually viewed as being more rational than ultimate consumers and as more likely to seek more information about a product's features and technical specifications. When purchasing products, organizational customers are concerned especially about quality, service, and price. Quality is important to an organizational buyer because it directly affects the quality of products the buyer's firm produces. Because services can have such a direct influence on a firm's costs, sales, and profits, such things as market information, on-time delivery, availability of parts, and credit can be crucial to an organizational buyer. Although an organizational customer does not depend solely on price to decide which products to buy, price is of prime concern because it directly influences a firm's profitability.

Organizational transactions differ from consumer transactions in several ways. The orders tend to be considerably larger. Negotiations occur less frequently but are often lengthy when they do occur. Organizational transactions sometimes involve more than one person or one department in the purchasing organization.

Organizational buyers use several purchasing methods, including description, inspection, sampling, and negotiation. Most purchases are one of three types: new task, modified rebuy, or straight rebuy.

Industrial demand differs from consumer demand along several dimensions. Industrial demand derives from the demand for consumer products. At the industry level, industrial demand is inelastic; if the price of an industrial item changes, demand for the product will not change as much proportionally. In some cases, an industrial product is demanded jointly with another product. The demand for industrial products can fluctuate widely.

Organizational buying behavior refers to the purchase behavior of producers, resellers, government units, and institutions. Organizational purchase decisions are made through a buying center—a group of several people with multiple roles in the organization, such as users, influencers, buyers, deciders, and gatekeepers. Users are those in the organization who actually use the product. Influencers help develop the specifications and evaluate alternative products for possible use. Buyers are responsible for selecting the suppliers and negotiating the terms of the purchases. Deciders are those who choose the products and vendors. Gatekeepers control the flow of information to and among persons who occupy the other roles in the buying center.

Stages of the organizational buying decision process are problem recognition, establishing product specifications to solve the problem, the search for products and suppliers, evaluation of products relative to specifications, selection and ordering of the most appropriate product, and evaluation of the product's and the supplier's performance. Four categories of factors appear to influence organizational buying decisions: environmental, organizational, interpersonal, and individual.

Important Terms

Producer markets	Institutional markets
Reseller markets	Reciprocity
Government markets	New-task purchase

Modified rebuy purchase
Straight rebuy purchase
Derived demand
Inelastic demand

Joint demand
Organizational buying behavior
Buying center

Discussion and Review Questions

1. Identify and describe four major types of organizational markets. Give examples of each.
2. In terms of purchasing behavior, why are organizational buyers generally considered to be more rational than ultimate consumers?
3. What are the primary concerns of organizational buyers?
4. List some characteristics that differentiate organizational transactions from consumer sales.
5. What are the commonly used methods of organizational buying?
6. Why is so much less information required by buyers in a straight rebuy purchase than in a new-task purchase?
7. How does industrial demand differ from consumer demand?
8. What are the major components of a buying center?
9. Identify the stages of the organizational buying decision process. How is this decision process used when making straight rebuys?
10. How do environmental, organizational, interpersonal, and individual factors affect organizational purchases?

Cases

Case 5.1   Jacuzzi Incorporated[10]

In 1920 the Jacuzzis, manufacturers of airplane propellers, incorporated and diversified into airplane repairing and remodeling. Several years later, the brothers decided to enter private airplane manufacturing, first with a small, single seater. They then designed and built the first multipassenger, enclosed-cabin, high-wing monoplane in the United States. One of the brothers, Giocondo, was killed testing the plane, and the surviving brothers decided against further production.

As agriculture was a major industry in California, the brothers decided to combine their knowledge of propellers and wind currents with agricultural needs. They developed a "frost machine" to fan the air over plants and trees, keeping frost from forming in cold, still weather. The brothers also developed an oil-burning furnace at this time, and they began research on steam water injectors, or jets, as they would later become known.

By 1926 the Jacuzzis were ready to test their water-jet idea in connection with a one-horsepower, centrifugal pump, but they could not find a pump that met their specifications. They manufactured their own. The purpose of the

---

10. This case was contributed by Scott Markham, Department of Marketing and Management, University of Central Arkansas. Reprinted by permission of the author.

system was to pump water (or other liquids) from 20 to 30 feet below the level in which the pump and water jet were installed, something that had not been accomplished up to that time. The pumps would prove especially efficient in agricultural water wells, as they required no moving parts in the well itself.

Candido Jacuzzi took off his "production hat," replacing it with his "marketing" one and hit the road to sell the newly developed liquid-jet injector pumps. Forty units were sold and installed in a short period. Requests began to come in for larger-capacity units. Three- and five-horsepower models were thus developed. Not able to keep up with demand themselves, the brothers began selecting dealers in large western cities to handle sales. Business was humming. Disinclined to rest on their laurels, the brothers proceeded to test and develop other types of pumps, including those operated by turbines.

The company began printing price lists and specification sheets, along with one-year guarantee policies after their dealers began requesting them. At this time, other pump companies began to generate unfavorable and untrue publicity about the "unproved" scientific principle on which Jacuzzi pumps were based. As a result, the sales force met strong opposition in some geographic locales. Lengthening the guarantee to four years helped overcome much resistance.

In 1978 the firm began exploring the possibility of selling out. A deal was initially struck with Textron, Inc., in 1979, but it fell through. Later that same year Walter Kidde and Company offered about $70 million on the condition that at least 60 percent of Jacuzzi's approximately 4.6 million shares be tendered. Kidde offered $15.35 per share. This time the deal was completed, with 100 percent of the shares being tendered.

Depending upon size and specifications, pumps for industrial application currently range in price from $1,000–$5,000. Jacuzzi claims from 10 to 12 percent of the U.S. small-pump market. Pumps for industrial applications are sold through builder-supply houses and plumbing-supply wholesalers. Jacuzzi spends approximately 90 percent of its promotional dollars on personal selling. The remaining promotional dollars are spent primarily in trade journals such as *Hardware Age, Wholesale Plumbing Monthly, Groundwater Age,* and *Wholesaler Magazine.*

By the early 1980s, Jacuzzi, Inc., was smoothly operating as a wholly owned subsidiary of Kidde, Inc. Ray Horan, President of Jacuzzi, Inc., reported in the 1980s that the company "has shown growth every year since its establishment in 1920. In the last 10 years the company's sales have grown by an average of 15% compounded annually with net after tax profits in the 5–10% range. Volume in the 1980's is not projected to be as rapid as the growth of the 60's and 70's. Sales in the $100,000,000–$150,000,000 range are expected. The decade of the 1990's is expected to bring the company sales in the $175–$200,000,000+ range. Net after tax profits are projected to continue in the 5–10% range."

Questions for Discussion

1. What types of individuals are included in the buying centers of Jacuzzi's customers?
2. What are the major concerns of Jacuzzi's customers?
3. The demand for Jacuzzi pumps derives from consumer demand for what types of products?

Case 5.2 IBM Serves Organizational Customers[11]

International Business Machines (IBM) is the premier manufacturer, marketer, and service company in the computer industry. It employs 400,000 people and in 1984 grossed $46 billion in sales. By 1994 sales are expected to reach $185 billion. In the past five years, IBM has invested $28 billion in land, buildings, equipment, and research and development; in the next five years, it plans to invest an additional $56 billion.

IBM makes one out of every four mainframe computers sold in the United States. Its dominance of the mainframe market has given IBM its number-one position in the computer industry. Mainframes are high-profit products, represented over 25 percent of IBM's total sales revenues in 1984, and give the company a solid customer base. Even though personal computers are becoming a mainstay of the office, mainframes are still the central hub of large computer operations for financial (banking and insurance), factory (computer-aided design and manufacturing), and scientific and engineering applications. As IBM's customers prosper, they continue to need and ask for more powerful systems to meet their growth.

In response to this demand, IBM recently introduced a new family of fifth-generation mainframes. Called the Sierra computers, they are available in two versions, Models 200 and 400. The Model 200 costs about $5 million, and the Model 400, over $9 million—plus minimum monthly maintenance fees of about $6,000 and $9,000, respectively. By targeting the Sierras at scientific research and engineering users, IBM is heightening its competition and reinforcing its dominance in the mainframe business.

The challenge ahead for IBM is to provide its customers with the systems software for adequate networking and communications between mainframes and other computers. The key to office and factory automation is linking mainframes to less powerful machines, and IBM must provide the means for this integration if it is to lead in these arenas.

Questions for Discussion

1. What types of organizations purchase large mainframe computers such as those in the Sierra family?
2. What type of organizational purchase is the purchase of a large computer?
3. What types of people make up IBM customers' buying centers?
4. What are IBM customers' major concerns when purchasing a large computer?

11. Frank Barbetta, "IBM Debuts Two Sierras," *Electronic News,* Feb. 18, 1985, pp. 1, 8; Jeff Moad, "Price/Performance Upgrades in Sierra Called 'Moderate,'" *Electronic News,* p. 8; and "High Sierra," *The Economist,* Feb. 16, 1985, p. 68.

6 / Marketing Research and Information Systems

Objectives

- To understand the relationship between research and information systems in marketing decision making.

- To distinguish between research and intuition in solving marketing problems.

- To learn five basic steps for conducting a marketing research project.

- To understand the fundamental methods of gathering data for marketing research.

- To understand questionnaire construction, sampling, and the design of experiments.

Figure 6.1

One of Kodak's major innovations—the disc camera (Source: Courtesy of Eastman Kodak Company)

To understand target markets and make marketing decisions, detailed information is needed. Consider the following questions and the answers gained through research:

Do husbands and wives buy the same brand of beer? No: if spouses go to a store separately to buy beer, there is a 90-percent chance they will buy different brands.

How much do American families actually use a vacuum cleaner? When surveyed, families claimed to vacuum their homes one hour per week. When timers were hooked to their vacuum cleaners, the data revealed that people actually spent an average of thirty-five minutes per week vacuuming.

What is the annual per capita consumption of familiar food products? Americans consume 156 hamburgers, 95

"Smile!"

You're gonna get 'em with the Kodak disc!

Life doesn't wait for you to focus your camera, advance the film and adjust the flash. So the Kodak disc camera does it for you. There's nothing to set. Just push the button.

Slip a Kodak disc camera in your pocket—and don't you miss another doggone shot! Get great shots with the Kodak disc 3100 and 4100 cameras, and great close-ups like the one above with the Kodak disc 6100 camera.

Kodak
Kodacolor VR film
for color prints
disc

© Eastman Kodak Company, 1984

hot dogs, 283 eggs, 5 pounds of yogurt, 9 pounds of cereal, and 2 pounds of peanut butter per year.

What kind of person drives a Volvo? Volvo has found that their buyers are thoughtful, secure, and self-reliant. When purchasing a car they seek safety, comfort, performance, and value. Most Volvo drivers are not primarily concerned with status but like the car's understated image of quality and excellent engineering.

How detailed is Coca-Cola's research-based understanding of its customers? The average customer puts 3.2 ice cubes in a glass of Coke. The average American sees sixty-nine Coca-Cola television commercials per year. And, one million people drink Coca-Cola for breakfast every day.

How did Eastman Kodak use marketing research to develop the disc camera? Marketing research indicated that amateur photographers snap 2 billion pictures a year. Kodak examined 10,000 photos to see what commonly goes wrong. Based on this data a prototype disc camera was developed to help eliminate out-of-focus and underexposed shots (see Figure 6.1). Marketing researchers then asked consumers in households to comment on the prototype. The final outcome was a camera that has been one of the most successful products in Kodak's history.[1]

Marketing research and systematic information gathering increase the probability of successful marketing. In fact, the failure of companies, and even entire industries, has been attributed to a lack of marketing research.[2] Research findings are essential in planning and developing marketing strategies. Information about target markets provides vital input in planning the marketing mix and in controlling marketing activities. In addition, marketing research helps to determine what product lines deserve the bulk of a company's efforts and resources.[3] In short, the marketing concept—the marketing philosophy of customer orientation—can better be implemented when adequate information about customers is available.

Marketing research and information systems provide the insight for carrying out the marketing concept. Without adequate information and research, the marketing concept cannot be effectively implemented. With the intense com-

---

1. Some facts adapted from John Koten, "You Aren't Paranoid If You Feel Someone Eyes You Constantly," *Wall Street Journal,* March 29, 1985, pp. 1 and 12.
2. Bernie Whalen, "An Executive Charges: Marketing Research Killed Salesmanship," *Marketing News,* March 15, 1985, p. 1.
3. David K. Hardin, "Research State-of-Art: Today and Tomorrow," *Marketing Times,* March–April 1983, p. 38.

petition in today's marketplace, it is difficult to develop an ingenious invention and then look for a market where it can be profitably sold. The increasing inability of U.S. products to compete successfully with product innovations from other parts of the globe may have its roots in a lack of understanding and application of the marketing concept.[4]

This chapter focuses on the approaches to and processes of gathering information needed for marketing decisions. It distinguishes between managing information within an organization (a marketing information system) and conducting marketing research projects. We discuss the role of marketing research in decision making and problem solving and compare it with intuition. Next, we examine individual steps in the marketing research process. We look at sampling and experimentation as approaches to reducing error in gathering information. Finally, we describe the three major methods of obtaining data.

Defining Marketing Research and Marketing Information Systems

Marketing intelligence is a broad term that includes all data available for marketing decisions. **Marketing research** is the part of marketing intelligence that involves specific inquiries into problems. Its purpose is to guide marketing decisions by gathering information that is not available to decision makers. It is conducted on a special-project basis, and research methods are adapted to the problems studied and to changes in the environment. General Motors, for example, conducts interviews of more than 130,000 consumers annually to determine consumer behavior, consumer satisfaction, reasons for purchase, loyalty trends, and demographics. The information gathered by marketing research is used in planning the company's marketing activities.[5]

Dr Pepper provides another example of marketing research conducted on a special project basis. Dr Pepper's market share had been sliding in the 1980s. Research in 1982 indicated that Dr Pepper drinkers were "inner-directed" people who followed their own values rather than the values of others. This consumer profile was in conflict with the current advertising theme "Be a Pepper." These results led the company to drop the "Be a Pepper" theme in favor of a more individualistic theme, "Hold out for the out of the ordinary."[6]

A **marketing information system (MIS)** is the framework for the day-to-day managing and structuring of information gathered regularly from sources both inside and outside an organization. As such, an MIS provides a continuous flow of information about prices, advertising expenditures, sales, competition,

---

4. A. Parasuraman, "Hang On to the Marketing Concept," *Business Horizons,* Sept.–Oct. 1981, p. 40.
5. "Panelists Provide a Glimpse of Automotive Marketing Research," *Marketing News,* Sept. 30, 1983, p. 3.
6. Ronald Alsop, "Dr Pepper Is Bubbling Again After Its 'Be a Pepper' Setback," *Wall Street Journal,* September 26, 1985, p. 33.

Figure 6.2

An organization's marketing information system

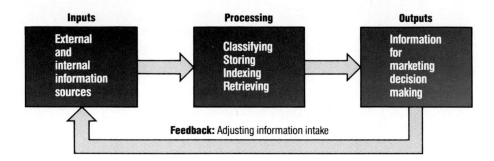

Inputs	Processing	Outputs
External and internal information sources	Classifying Storing Indexing Retrieving	Information for marketing decision making

Feedback: Adjusting information intake

and distribution expenses. Figure 6.2 illustrates the chief components of an MIS.

MIS inputs include those information sources inside and outside the firm that are assumed to be useful for future decision making. Processing of information involves classifying information and developing categories for meaningful storage and retrieval. Marketing decision makers determine which information is useful for making decisions. This data makes up the outputs shown in Figure 6.2. Finally, feedback enables those who are responsible for gathering internal and external data on a systematic basis to adjust the information intake.

Nabisco handles 235,000 consumer contacts each year. Usually they are inquiries about product usage, nutrition, and ingredients. This consumer feedback is computerized and available on demand throughout Nabisco's operating divisions.

Regular reports of sales by product or market categories, data on inventory levels, and records of the activities of salespersons are all examples of information flows. In the MIS, the means of gathering data receive less attention than do the procedures for expediting the flow of information. The main focus of the system is on data storage and retrieval, as well as on computer capabilities and the information requirements of management.

Marriott Corporation, for example, places an evaluation card signed by Bill Marriott himself in each room. The message on the card urges customers to report both positive and negative aspects of their stay. This information provides a continuous flow of data that can be used to evaluate the ongoing operations of the firm and its individual units. In addition, it leads to timely corrective actions. Figure 6.3 is an example of the questionnaire used by the Kansas City Marriott.

Whereas an MIS provides a continuous data input for an organization, marketing research is an information gathering process for specific situations. Nonrecurring decisions that deal with the dynamics of the marketing environment often call for a data search structured according to the problem and decision. Marketing research is usually characterized by in-depth analyses of major problems or issues. Often, the needed information is available only from sources outside an organization's formal channels of information. For example, an organization may want to know something about its competitors or may want to gain an objective, unbiased understanding of its own customers. Such information needs may require an independent investigation by a marketing research firm. Table 6.1 shows the top ten U.S. marketing research organizations by revenues.

Kansas City Marriott
OCA 726

1. How would you rate our hotel on an *overall* basis?
   ☐ Excellent ☐ Good ☐ Average ☐ Fair ☐ Poor

2. Was your room reservation in order at check in?
   ☐ Yes   ☐ No

3. How would you rate the following?

	Excellent	Good	Average	Fair	Poor
Check in, speed/efficiency	☐	☐	☐	☐	☐
Cleanliness of room on first entering	☐	☐	☐	☐	☐
Cleanliness and servicing of your room during stay	☐	☐	☐	☐	☐
Decor of your room	☐	☐	☐	☐	☐
Check out, speed/efficiency	☐	☐	☐	☐	☐
Value of room for price paid	☐	☐	☐	☐	☐

4. Was everything in working order in your room?
   ☐ Yes   ☐ No
   If you checked NO, would you please tell us what was *not* in working order?
   ☐ Room air conditioning
   ☐ Room heating
   ☐ Bathroom plumbing
   ☐ Television
   ☐ Light bulbs
   ☐ Other _____

5. How would you rate the following in terms of their friendly and efficient services?

	Excellent	Good	Average	Fair	Poor
Reservation staff	☐	☐	☐	☐	☐
Front desk clerk	☐	☐	☐	☐	☐
Bellstaff	☐	☐	☐	☐	☐
Housekeeping staff	☐	☐	☐	☐	☐
Telephone operators	☐	☐	☐	☐	☐
Gift shop staff	☐	☐	☐	☐	☐
Engineering staff	☐	☐	☐	☐	☐
Front desk cashier	☐	☐	☐	☐	☐

If any members of our staff were especially helpful, please let us know who they are and how they were helpful so that we can show them our appreciation.
Name _____
Position/Comments _____
_____
_____

6. Please rate the following which you have used on this visit:

A. Restaurant
Please indicate name of restaurant.
_____

☐ Breakfast   ☐ Lunch   ☐ Dinner

	Yes	No
Were you seated promptly?	☐	☐
Was your order taken promptly?	☐	☐
Was your food served promptly?	☐	☐

	Excellent	Good	Average	Fair	Poor
Friendly service	☐	☐	☐	☐	☐
Quality of food	☐	☐	☐	☐	☐
Menu variety	☐	☐	☐	☐	☐
Value for price paid	☐	☐	☐	☐	☐

B. Room Service

	Excellent	Good	Average	Fair	Poor
Prompt service	☐	☐	☐	☐	☐
Friendly service	☐	☐	☐	☐	☐
Quality of food	☐	☐	☐	☐	☐
Menu variety	☐	☐	☐	☐	☐
Value for price paid	☐	☐	☐	☐	☐

C. Cocktail Lounge

	Excellent	Good	Average	Fair	Poor
Prompt service	☐	☐	☐	☐	☐
Friendly service	☐	☐	☐	☐	☐
Quality of drinks	☐	☐	☐	☐	☐
Value for price paid	☐	☐	☐	☐	☐

D. Banquet/Convention Event

	Excellent	Good	Average	Fair	Poor
Prompt service	☐	☐	☐	☐	☐
Friendly service	☐	☐	☐	☐	☐
Quality of food	☐	☐	☐	☐	☐

7. Did you use "The Marriott Hot Line" to register any dissatisfaction with our hotel?
   ☐ No
   ☐ Yes . . . problem was resolved.
   ☐ Yes . . . but problem was *not* resolved.

Please explain any problem which remains unresolved.
_____
_____
_____
_____
_____
_____
_____
_____
_____
_____
_____
_____

8. What was the primary purpose of your visit?
   ☐ Pleasure
   ☐ Convention/group meeting/banquet
   ☐ Business (other than above)

9. Have you stayed at this hotel previously?
   ☐ Yes   ☐ No

10. If in the area again, would you return to this Marriott?
    ☐ Yes   ☐ No

PLEASE PRINT THE FOLLOWING INFORMATION
Departure date: _____
Length of stay: _____ days. Room number _____
☐ Mr.   ☐ Mrs.   ☐ Miss   ☐ Ms.
Name _____
Home address _____
_____ Zip _____
Company or organization _____
_____
Business address _____
_____ Zip _____

THANK YOU VERY MUCH FOR YOUR RESPONSE.
YOUR EVALUATION *WILL* MAKE A DIFFERENCE.

Figure 6.3 An evaluation card used by the Marriott Corporation (Source: Courtesy of Marriott Corporation)

Table 6.1 The top 10 U.S. marketing research organizations

Rank	Organization	Research Revenues (millions)
1	A. C. Nielsen Co.	$491.0
2	IMS International	151.4
3	SAMI	118.4
4	Arbitron Ratings Co.	105.8
5	Burke Marketing Services	66.0
6	M/A/R/C	37.6
7	Market Facts	35.9
8	Information Resources	35.8
9	NFO Research	29.5
10	NPD Group	29.2

Source: *Advertising Age,* May 23, 1985, p. 17. Reprinted with permission from *Advertising Age,* May 23, 1985. Copyright © 1985 Crain Communications Inc.

However, data brought into the organization through marketing research do become part of its **marketing data bank,** a file of data collected through both the MIS and marketing research projects. Figure 6.4 is an advertisement for a marketing research firm that maintains extensive consumer product data bases.

The marketing data bank permits researchers to retrieve information that is useful in addressing problems quite different from those that prompted the original data collection. For example, the Miles Laboratories data bank contained information that people were not overeating as much as in the past. The result was a change in the Alka-Seltzer slogan from one that stressed relief from overeating to "For the symptoms of stress that come with success." Often, a research study developed for one purpose will be very useful in developing a research method or indicating problems in researching a particular topic. For example, research may show that in consumer surveys respondents most frequently select a pink bar of soap as their favorite, even though pink is rarely a top-selling color. Such knowledge permits those interested in marketing soap to be cautious when interpreting research findings. Thus, marketers should make sure that data from marketing research and the MIS are classified and

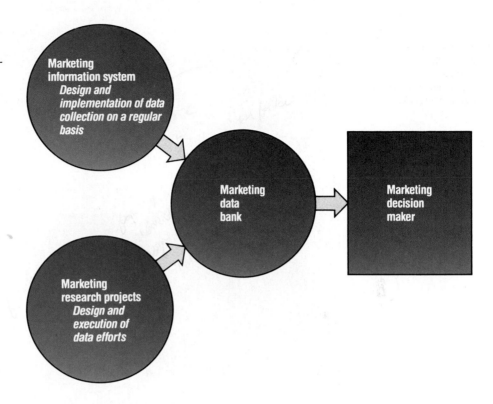

stored in the data bank, so that the information's usefulness in future marketing decision making can be identified.

Data banks vary widely from one organization to another. In a small organization, the data bank can simply be a large notebook, but in many organizations a computer storage and retrieval system is needed to handle the large volume of data. Figure 6.5 illustrates how marketing decision makers combine research findings with data from an MIS to develop a data bank. Although many organizations do not use the term *data bank*, they still have some system for storing information for later use. While the terms *MIS* and *marketing research* may not be used by smaller organizations, they usually do perform these marketing activities.

After a marketing information system—of whatever size and complexity—has been established, information needs to be related to marketing planning. In the next section, we will see how marketers use marketing information, experience, and judgment in making decisions.

Information Needs and Decision Making

The real value of marketing research and the systematic gathering of information that supports it is measured by improvements in a marketer's ability to make decisions. For example, marketing research has guided the marketing and advertising of Mercedes Benz automobiles since 1965. Before 1965, the company knew nothing about its buyers, and marketing was a hip-shot affair. Research

indicated that Mercedes customers had little in common with buyers of other luxury models. Mercedes buyers wanted a car with distinct quality, engineering, design, and performance values.[7] Figure 6.6 shows how Nielsen can assist manufacturers of grocery products by providing weekly access to marketing information.

Research and information systems provide customer feedback to the organization. Without feedback, a marketer cannot understand the dynamics of the marketplace. The role of marketing information in decision making is increasing as managers recognize its benefits. The application on page 169 describes how the red meat industry is using research to improve its marketing efforts.

As we will discuss in Chapter 18, strategic market planning involves developing objectives, assessing opportunities, formulating strategies, and planning for implementation and control. Table 6.2 lists some basic information needs that arise during these phases of the planning process. This list is not exhaustive, of course. The specific information needs of any organization will depend on its unique situation and environment.

Although uncertainty is inherent to decision making, research can make the process more objective and systematic. The increase in marketing research

7. "Research Played Role in Launch of Baby Benz," *Marketing News,* Jan. 4, 1985, p. 20.

Application

Research Gives Meat Industry a Leaner Image

Red meat producers have been plagued in recent years by flat consumption rates and a generally poor image in the marketplace. In a focus group setting, an industry-sponsored study of consumer's beef-purchasing habits revealed great concern over issues such as chemicals, hormones, and additives. Red meat production is a $63-billion industry, but it is losing market share to chicken and seafood products.

To combat this loss in share, additional marketing research has been conducted to determine a potential solution. Research by Yankelovich, Skelly, and White revealed that the blue-collar, traditionally food-oriented group's red meat consumption had fallen from 22 to 12 percent of the total population in two years. And "active lifestyle" and "health-oriented" consumers, who are least likely to consume red meat, increased from 33 to 50 percent of those surveyed. Thus, an increasing number of individuals are using less red meat. To exacerbate the problems for meat producers, research also reveals that the industry's traditional production and merchandising methods are undermining beef's image. Fresh meat with a half-inch or more of fat accentuates beef's negative image. When consumers see less fat on that same meat, sales increase.

In light of the research findings, several courses of action are now being pursued. To make people aware of beef's nutritional value, a massive television and magazine campaign has been developed for beef producers with the theme, "Beef. Good news for people who eat." The campaign seeks to assure consumers that beef is a sound nutritional choice. The advertisements make the point that 4 ounces of beef is lower in fat and cholesterol than people might think.

Supermarkets, such as Kroger and Safeway, are acknowledging the research findings and are adopting a more customer-oriented approach to merchandising red meat. Both stores are developing programs to trim the fat on red meat from a half-inch to a quarter-inch. In addition, select grocery stores are offering "natural" meat. Natural meat is produced without artificial chemicals, growth hormones, or other feed additives that might affect the meat's quality or healthfulness.

It was stated last year that the red meat industry was ten years behind the times in marketing. After implementing the results of the research described here, the beef industry should be more up-to-date. (*Source: Candace Talmadge, "Red Meat: Image at Steak," Adweek, March 31, 1986, pp. 1, 8; CNN (Cable News Network) Report, April 8, 1986; and Jean Carper, "Mix and Match Foods for a Better Diet," U.S. News & World Report, Jan. 20, 1986, p. 68.)*

activities represents a transition from intuitive to scientific problem solving. In relying on **intuition,** marketing managers do not look for any information other than personal knowledge or experience. However, in **scientific decision making,** managers take an orderly and logical approach to gathering information. They seek facts on a systematic basis; they apply methods other than trial and error or generalization from experience.

Despite the obvious value of formal research, marketing decisions often are made in its absence. It is true that relatively minor problems requiring immediate attention can and should be handled on the basis of personal judgment and common sense. But limited research is valuable when it appears that complete data are not needed for good decisions and would be too

Table 6.2 *Information needs during different phases of the marketing planning process*[a]

Type of Marketing Intelligence	Development of Objectives	Assessment of Opportunities
Marketing information system (MIS)	Organizational goals Activities of functional departments such as production, finance, and personnel Resources of the firm	Dissatisfactions, needs in relevant market segments Size, trend of demand Industry/market structure and composition, competition, market shares, profitability Technological, materials innovations Supply conditions, prices
Marketing research	Research projects to assess when and if an objective can be accomplished	Research project; for example, when a new opportunity or environmental threat suddenly arises

[a]This list of information needs is offered only as an example and is not exhaustive.

expensive in relation to the data's usefulness to decision makers. As the number of solutions to a problem, the expected economic or social payoffs, and the possible risks multiply, the use of full-scale research in planning becomes more desirable and rewarding.

We are not suggesting here that intuition has little or no value. Successful decisions blend both research and intuition. Statistics, mathematics, and logic are tools that contribute to problem solving and provide information that decreases the uncertainty of predictions based on limited experience. However, these tools do not necessarily produce all the answers, or even the right ones. Consider one extreme example. A marketing research study conducted for Xerox Corporation in the late 1950s indicated that there was a very limited market for an automatic photo copier. Xerox management judged that the researchers had drawn the wrong conclusions from the study and decided to launch the product anyway. That product, the Xerox 914 copier, was an instant success. An immediate backlog of orders developed, and the rest is sales history.

Thus, a proper blend of research and intuition is required to make a correct decision. Table 6.3 distinguishes between the roles of research and intuition in decision making.

Table 6.2 (continued)

Type of Marketing Intelligence	Formulation of Marketing Strategies	Developing Plans for Implementation and Control
Marketing information system (MIS)	Identifying, tracking target markets by product category Identifying, tracking market behavior toward products, promotion, distribution, prices	The costs, effectiveness of firm's marketing efforts Firm's sales by product and market Total industry, product-class sales Compilation, aggregation of operating data for an accurate picture of performance
Marketing research	In-depth evaluation of existing or potential target markets Testing the appeal of potential product attributes Testing current marketing effectiveness, developing new promotion or price alternatives Evaluating the needs and attitudes of marketing channel members Selecting the most efficient, effective physical distribution alternative	Surveys of consumer awareness, trial, attitudes, preferences, and repurchase rates Research projects when unforeseen events occur or problems develop

Source: Some of this material has been adapted from Harper W. Boyd, Jr., Ralph Westfall, and Stanley F. Stasch, *Marketing Research: Text and Cases,* 6th ed. (Homewood, Ill.: Irwin, 1985), p. 9. © 1985 by Richard D. Irwin, Inc.

Table 6.3 Distinction between research and intuition in marketing decision making

	Research	Intuition
Nature	Formal planning, predicting based on scientific approach	Preference based on personal feelings
Methods	Logic, systematic methods, statistical inference	Experience and demonstration
Contributions	General hypotheses for making predictions, classifying relevant variables, carrying out systematic description and classification	Minor problems solved quickly through consideration of experience, practical consequences

Marketers determine when research is needed and design projects that will provide useful information to decision makers. They must develop practical and understandable procedures to guide the research and to provide a framework for its conduct. Above all, marketers approach marketing research logically to maintain the control necessary to obtain accurate data. The difference between good research and bad research depends on the input, including effective control over the entire marketing research process.

The five steps shown in Figure 6.7 should be thought of as an overall approach to conducting research rather than as a rigid set of rules to be followed in each project. When they plan research projects, marketers must think about each of the five major steps and how they can best be tailored to fit a particular problem.

Defining and Locating Problems

Initially, marketers center their attention on how best to discover the nature and boundaries of a problem. This **problem definition** is the first step toward finding a solution or launching a research study. The problem definition stage should occupy researchers and decision makers until they are very clear about what they want from the research and how they will use it.[8] Fuzzy, inconclusive studies are a waste of time and money.

The first sign of a problem is usually a departure from some normal function, such as conflicts between or failures in attaining objectives. If a corporation's objective is a 12-percent return on investment and the current return is 6 percent, this discrepancy should act as a warning flag. It is a symptom that something inside or outside the organization has blocked the attainment of the desired goal or that the goal could be unrealistic. Decreasing sales, increasing expenses, or decreasing profits are also broad indications of problems. To get at the specific causes of the problem through research, however, marketers must define the problem and its scope in a way that goes beneath its superficial symptoms.

The interaction between the marketing manager and the marketing researcher should result in a clearly defined problem. Depending on the abilities of the manager and the marketing researcher, various methods may be used to help define problems. Traditionally the problem formulation process has been assumed to be a subjective, creative process. Today, however, more objective and systematic approaches are being used. For example, the delphi method for problem definition consists of a series of interviews with a panel of experts. With repeated interviews, the range of responses converges toward a "correct" definition of the problem.[9] This method introduces structure as well as objectivity into the process of problem definition.

The research objective specifies the information required to achieve the research purpose. Deciding how to refine a broad, indefinite problem into a

8. Bruce R. Dreisbach, "Marketing: The Key to Successful Research Management," *Marketing News,* Jan. 4, 1985, p. 3.
9. Raymond E. Taylor, "Using the Delphi Method to Define Marketing Problems," *Business,* Oct.– Dec. 1984, p. 17.

Figure 6.7 *The five steps of the marketing research process*

clearly defined and researchable statement is a prerequisite for the next step in planning the research—developing the type of hypothesis that best fits the problem.

Developing Hypotheses

The objective statement of a marketing research project should include hypotheses drawn from previous research and from expected research findings. A **hypothesis** is a guess or assumption about a certain problem or set of circumstances. It is based on all the insight and knowledge available about the problem from previous research studies and other sources. As information is gathered, a researcher can test the hypothesis. Sometimes, several hypotheses are developed during the actual study; the hypotheses that are accepted or rejected become the study's chief conclusions.

Collecting Data

Two types of data are available to marketing researchers. **Primary data** are observed and recorded or collected directly from respondents. **Secondary data** are compiled inside or outside the organization for some purpose other than the current investigation. Examples of secondary data include general reports supplied to an enterprise by various data services. Such reports might concern market shares, retail inventory levels, and consumers' purchasing behavior. Figure 6.8 illustrates how primary and secondary sources differ. Secondary data are usually already available in private or public reports or have been collected and stored by the organization itself. Primary data must be gathered by observing phenomena or surveying respondents.

The nature and type of the hypothesis being tested determines the choice of a general data gathering approach: exploratory, descriptive, or causal investigations. When more information is needed about the problem and the tentative hypothesis must be made more specific, marketers conduct **exploratory studies.** For instance, a review of information in the organization's data bank or a review of publicly available data may be helpful. By questioning knowledgeable people inside and outside the organization, marketers may get additional insight into the problem. An advantage of the exploratory approach is that it permits marketers to conduct ministudies with a very restricted data base.

Descriptive studies are undertaken when marketers recognize that they must understand the characteristics of certain phenomena to solve a particular problem. Marketers may plan to conduct surveys of consumers' education, occupation, or age; they may find out how many consumers purchased Ford Escorts last month; or they may determine how many adults between the ages of eighteen and thirty drink coffee at least three times a week.

Figure 6.8

Approaches to
collecting data

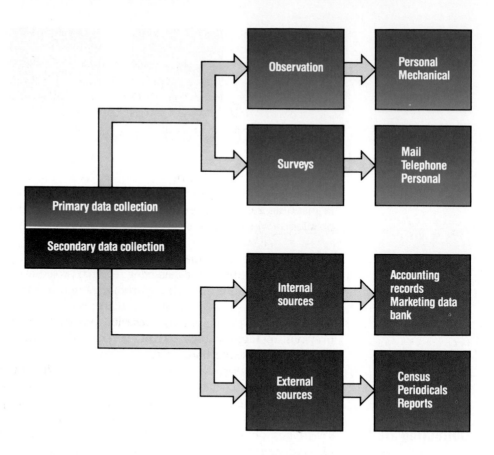

Descriptive studies may call for statistical analysis and predictive tools. A researcher trying to find out how many people will vote for a certain political candidate, for example, may have to use sampling, questionnaires, computer tabulations, and estimates of error to predict the correct answer. Descriptive studies generally require much prior knowledge and assume that the problem is clearly defined. The marketers' major task is to find adequate methods for collecting and measuring data.

Hypotheses about causal relationships require a more complex approach than those that can be tested by a descriptive study. In **causal studies,** it is assumed that a particular variable X is the cause of the variable Y. Marketers must plan the research so that the data collected prove or disprove that X causes Y. To do so, marketers must try to hold constant all variables except X and Y. For example, to find out whether premiums increase the number of new accounts in a savings and loan association, marketers must try to keep all variables constant except premiums and new accounts.

Interpreting Research Findings

After collecting data to test their hypotheses, marketers are ready to interpret the research findings. Interpretation is easier if marketers carefully plan their data analysis methods early in the research process. They should also allow for continual evaluation of the data during the entire collection period. They can then gain valuable insight into areas that ought to be probed during the formal interpretation.

The first step in drawing conclusions from most studies is tabulation of the data. If marketers intend to apply the results to individual categories of the things or people being studied, then cross-tabulation may be quite useful, especially in tabulating joint occurrences. For example, a cross-tabulation could show how men and women differ in some behavior, such as purchasing automobile tires.

After the data are tabulated, they must be analyzed. **Statistical interpretation** focuses on what is typical or what deviates from the average. It indicates how widely responses vary and how they are distributed in relation to the variable being measured. This interpretation is another facet of marketing research that calls for marketers to apply judgment or intuition. Also, when they interpret statistics, marketers rely on estimates of expected error or deviation from the true values of the population. The analysis of data may lead researchers to accept or reject the hypothesis being studied.

Reporting Research Findings

The final step in the marketing research process is preparing a report of the research findings. Before writing the report, the marketer must take a clear, objective look at the findings to see how well the gathered facts answer the fundamental research question posed in the beginning. In most cases, it is extremely doubtful that the study will provide everything needed to answer the research question. Thus, a lack of completeness will probably have to be pointed out in the report together with reasons for it.[10]

Usually, results are communicated in a formal written report. Marketers must allow time for this task when they plan and schedule the project. Since the purpose of the report is to communicate with the decision makers who will use the research findings, researchers also should decide beforehand how much detail and supporting data to include in their report. Often, they will give their summary and recommendation first, especially if decision makers do not have time to study how the results were obtained. A technical report does allow its users to analyze data and interpret recommendations since it describes the research methods and procedures and the most important data gathered.

A survey of top corporate executives has indicated that they have a low opinion of marketing research reports. Their chief complaints were the impracticality of results and the inefficiency of research reports (inefficient in the sense of the executive time needed to read them). Specifically, executives stated that (1) researchers are captivated by techniques and often fit the problem to a favored technique and (2) researchers prefer complex studies, language, and reports to simple ones.[11] Obviously, the researcher must recognize the needs and expectations of the report user and adapt to them.

When marketing decision makers have a firm grasp of research methods and procedures, they are able to integrate reported findings and personal

10. George E. Breen and Albert B. Blankenship, "How to Present a Research Report That Gets Action," *Marketing Times,* March–April 1983, p. 33.
11. Joseph H. Rabin, "Top Executives Have Low Opinion of Marketing Research, Marketers' Role in Strategic Planning," *Marketing News,* Oct. 16, 1981, p. 3.

experience. If marketers can spot limitations in research from reading the report, then personal experience assumes more importance in making decisions. The inability of some marketers to understand basic statistical assumptions and data gathering procedures causes them to misuse research findings. Thus, report writers should understand the backgrounds and research abilities of those who will use the report to make decisions. Providing adequate explanations in understandable language makes it easier for decision makers to apply the findings and consequently diminishes the likelihood that a report will be misused or ignored entirely. Communicating with potential research users prior to writing a report can help the researcher provide information that will, in fact, improve decision making.

Now that we have looked briefly at the factors to consider in planning a research project, let us explore—in general terms—how marketers design research procedures to fit particular problems. The next section discusses how to collect data that will fulfill the design.

Designing the Research

That marketers must be able to design research procedures and produce reliable and valid data may seem obvious. However, reliability and validity have precise meanings for researchers. A research technique has **reliability** if it produces almost identical results in successive repeated trials. But a reliable technique is not necessarily valid. To have **validity,** the method must measure what it is supposed to measure, not something else. A valid research method provides data that can be used to test the hypothesis being investigated.

Now that we have introduced the basic aims of research, we are ready to examine some of the main concepts of designing research.

Sampling

By systematically choosing a limited number of units to represent the characteristics of a total population, marketers can project the reactions of a total market or market segment from the reactions of the sample. The objective of **sampling** in marketing research is therefore to select representative units from a total population. Sampling procedures must be used in studying human behavior as well as in estimating the likelihood of events not connected directly with an activity. For one thing, it would be almost impossible to investigate all members of a population because the time and resources available for research are limited.

A **population,** or "universe," is made up of all elements, units, or individuals that are of interest to researchers for a specific study. For example, if a Gallup poll is designed to predict the results of a presidential election, all registered voters in the United States would constitute the population. A representative national sample of several thousand registered voters would be selected in the Gallup poll to project the probable voting outcome.

Random Sampling

In simple **random sampling,** all the units in a population have an equal chance of appearing in the sample. Random sampling is basic probability sampling. The various events that can occur have an equal or known chance of taking place. For example, a specific card from a deck should have a 1/52 probability of being drawn at any one time. Similarly, if each student at your university or college were given a sequential number, and these numbers were mixed up in a large basket, each student's number would have a known probability of being selected. Sample units are ordinarily chosen by selecting from a table of random numbers statistically generated so that each digit, zero through nine, will have an equal probability of occurring in each position in the sequence. The sequentially numbered elements of a population are sampled randomly by selecting the units whose numbers appear in the table of random numbers.

Stratified Sampling

In **stratified sampling,** the population of interest is divided into groups according to a common characteristic or attribute. Then a probability sample is conducted within each group. The stratified sample may reduce some of the error that could occur in a simple random sample. By ensuring that each major group or segment of the population receives its proportionate share of sample units, investigators avoid including too many or too few sample units from each of the strata. Usually, samples are stratified when researchers believe that there may be variations among different types of respondents. For example, many political opinion surveys are stratified by sex, race, and age.

Area Sampling

Area sampling involves two stages: (1) selecting a probability sample of geographic areas such as blocks, census tracts, or census enumeration districts; and (2) selecting units or individuals within the selected geographic areas for the sample. This approach is a variation of stratified sampling, with the geographic areas serving as the segments, or primary units, used in sampling. To select the units or individuals within the geographic areas, researchers may choose every nth house or unit, or random selection procedures may be used to pick out a given number of units or individuals from a total listing within the selected geographic areas. Area sampling may be used when a complete list of the population is not available.

Quota Sampling

Quota sampling is different from other forms of sampling in that it is judgmental. That is, the final choice of respondents is left up to the interviewers. A study of consumers who wear eyeglasses, for example, may be conducted by interviewing any person who wears eyeglasses. In quota sampling, there are some controls—usually limited to two or three variables such as age, sex, and education—over the selection of respondents. The controls attempt to ensure that representative categories of respondents are interviewed.

Quota samples are unique because they are not probability samples; not everyone has an equal chance of being selected. Therefore, sampling error cannot be measured statistically. Judgmental samples are used most often in exploratory research, when hypotheses are being developed. Often, a small judgmental sample will not be projected to the total population, although the findings may provide valuable insights into a problem. Quota samples are useful when people with some unusual characteristic are found and questioned on the topic of interest. A probability sample to find people allergic to cats would be highly inefficient.

Figure 6.9

Relationship between
independent and
dependent variables

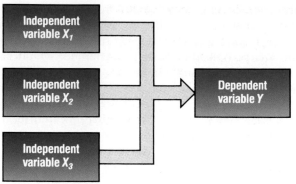

$Y = f(X_1, X_2, X_3)$. (Dependent variable Y is a function of X_1, X_2, and X_3.) The independent variables could be $X_1 =$ advertising expenditures, $X_2 =$ number of salespersons, and $X_3 =$ number of dealers. The dependent variable Y could be sales in a specific time period.

Experimentation

Experimentation is a general term for the approach taken in investigating relationships. Finding out which variable or variables caused an event to occur may be difficult unless researchers adopt an experimental approach. **Experimentation** involves maintaining as constants those factors that are related to or may affect the variables under investigation so that the effects of the experimental variables may be measured. For instance, when Coca-Cola taste tests a new cola formula, all variables should be held constant except the formula of the beverage. **Marketing experimentation** is a set of rules and procedures under which the task of data gathering is organized to expedite analysis and interpretation.

In the experimental approach, an **independent variable** (a variable not influenced by or dependent on other variables) is usually manipulated and changes are measured in a **dependent variable** (a variable contingent on, or restricted to, one or a set of values assumed by the independent variable). Figure 6.9 shows the relationship between these variables. For example, when a book publisher sets the price of a new dictionary, it may want to estimate the number of dictionaries that could be sold at various prices. The dependent variable would be sales, and the independent variable would be price. Researchers would design the experiment so that other independent variables that might influence sales—such as advertising, distribution, and variation of the product—would be controlled. Experiments may be conducted in the laboratory or in the field. Each research setting has advantages and disadvantages.

Laboratory Settings

Participants or respondents in marketing experiments are often invited to a central location to react or respond to experimental stimuli. In such an isolated setting, it is possible to control independent variables that might influence the outcome of an experiment. The features of laboratory settings might include a taste kitchen, video equipment, slide projectors, tape recorders, one-way mirrors, central telephone banks, and interview rooms. In an experiment to determine the influence of price (independent variable) on sales of dictionaries (dependent variable), respondents would be invited to a laboratory—a room with table, chairs, and sample dictionaries—before the dictionary was available in stores. The dictionary would be placed on a table with competitors' dictionaries.

Analysts would then query respondents about their reactions to the dictionaries at various prices.

One problem with a laboratory setting is its isolation from the real world. It is simply not possible to duplicate all the conditions that affect choices in the marketplace. On the other hand, by controlling variables that cannot be controlled in the real world, laboratory simulations can focus on variables that marketers think may be significant for the success of a marketing strategy. Market Facts, Inc., a leading marketing research firm, has reported that test market laboratories are being used more frequently today. Of the largest consumer goods and services companies surveyed by the firm, 37 percent reported using test market laboratories in the preceding year.[12]

Field Settings

The experimental approach also can be used in field or survey research. Market Facts has reported that 36 percent of major consumer goods and services companies use controlled store testing.[13] This procedure tests consumer reaction to new products or product modification in the store under usual shopping conditions. Field settings give the marketer an opportunity to obtain a more direct test of marketing decisions than laboratory settings.

There are several limitations to field experiments. Field experiments can be influenced or biased by inadvertent events such as weather or major economic news. Carryover effects of field experiments are impossible to avoid. What respondents have been asked to do in one time period will influence what they do in the next time period. For example, evaluating competing advertisements may influence attempts to get objective evaluations of new proposals for a firm's future advertising. Respondent cooperation may be difficult because respondents don't understand what role they play in the experiment. Finally, only a small number of variables can be controlled in field experiments. It is impossible, for example, to control competitors' advertising or attempts by competitors to influence the outcome of the experiment. Tactics which competitors can use to thwart field test marketing efforts include couponing, temporary price discounting, and the use of point-of-purchase materials.

Experimentation is used in marketing research design to improve hypothesis testing. However, whether experiments are conducted in the laboratory or in the field, many assumptions must be made to limit the number of factors and isolate causes. Marketing decision makers must recognize that assumptions may diminish the reliability of the research findings. For example, viewing proposed ads on a VCR in a laboratory is different from watching the ads on TV at home.

Simulated test markets for new products can use an experimental approach. For example, one marketing research company, Behavior Scan, has brought a new dimension to experimental research by combining cable television, supermarket scanners, and computers. The company tracks every commercial its panelists watch and every purchase they make in a supermarket or drug store. This procedure permits a projection of the impact of advertising on new product purchases by various consumer groups.[14]

---

12. Based on a survey conducted by Market Facts, Inc., April 28, 1983.
13. Ibid.
14. James S. Figuia, "Simulated Test Markets Are an Oasis in an Era of Marketing Research Which Doesn't Deliver," *Marketing News,* Jan. 20, 1984, p. 3.

Gathering Research Data

The two types of data available to marketing researchers are primary and secondary. Primary data are observed and recorded or collected directly from respondents; secondary data are compiled inside or outside the organization for some purpose other than the current investigation. Firsthand information obtained to test a hypothesis is primary data. Survey results of consumer attitudes toward Coca-Cola's Diet Coke are an example. Secondary data may be internal accounting records and other information stored in the company's marketing data bank or information collected by such external organizations as the Census Bureau and trade associations.

Most marketing research investigations use a combination of primary and secondary data sources. A thorough search of internal records and past studies is particularly useful in determining which additional data should be gathered by primary collection methods such as surveys or observation. The application on page 182 discusses how secondary and primary data collection methods can be combined.

Survey Methods

Survey methods include interviews by mail or by telephone and personal interviews. The selection of an interviewing method depends on the nature of the problem, the data needed to test the hypothesis, and the resources, such as funding and personnel, that are available to the researcher. Table 6.4 summarizes and compares the advantages of the various methods. Researchers must know exactly what type of information is needed to test the hypothesis and what type of information can be obtained through interviewing. Table 6.5 lists the most frequently used consumer survey techniques. The data are based on a survey of large American consumer goods and services companies.

Mail Surveys

In a mail survey, questionnaires are sent to respondents who are encouraged to complete and return them. This type of survey is used most often when the individuals chosen for questioning are spread over a wide area and funds for the survey are limited. A mail survey is the least expensive survey method as long as the response rate is high enough to produce reliable results. The main disadvantages of this method are the possibility that the response rate may be low or that the results may be misleading if respondents are significantly different from the population being sampled.

A high response rate usually results when respondents have some motivation to return the questionnaire. They might be regular customers, organization members, or hard-to-interview respondents who have an interest in the topic. Some techniques that have been useful in achieving a 50- to 70-percent response rate include (1) giving advance notification (post card, letter, mailgram, or phone call) prior to mailing the actual questionnaire package; (2) using a questionnaire package that appears to be personalized; (3) letting respondents know the benefits of filling out the questionnaire, making it easy for them to complete, offering them a monetary incentive, and including a self-addressed stamped envelope; (4) sending a follow-up letter two to three weeks after

Table 6.4 Comparison of the three basic survey methods

	Mail Surveys	Telephone Surveys	Personal Interview Surveys
Economy	Potentially the lowest cost per interview if there is an adequate return rate; increased postage rates are raising costs	Avoids interviewers' travel expenses; less expensive than in-home interviews; most common survey method	In-home interviewing is the most expensive interviewing method; shopping-mall, focus-group interviewing may lower costs
Flexibility	Inflexible; questionnaire must be short, easy for respondents to complete; no probing questions; may take more time to implement than other survey methods	Flexible because interviewers can ask probing questions, encourage respondents to answer questions; rapport may be gained, but observations are impossible	Most flexible method; respondents can react to visual materials, assist in filling out questionnaire; since observation is possible, demographic data are more accurate; in-depth probes are possible
Interviewer bias	Interviewer bias eliminated; questionnaires can be returned anonymously	Some anonymity; may be hard to develop trust among respondents	Refusals may be decreased by rapport-building efforts of interviewers; personal attributes of interviewers may bias respondents
Sampling and respondents' cooperation	Obtaining a complete mailing list is difficult; nonresponse is a major disadvantage	Sample must be limited to respondents with telephones and listed numbers; busy signals, no answers, and nonresponse—including refusals—are problems	Not-at-homes are more difficult to deal with; focus-group, shopping-mall interviewing may overcome these problems

Table 6.5 Survey methods used most frequently and survey spending patterns of the largest consumer goods and services companies

	Percent Using This Technique in the Last Year (a) %	Percent Spending Major Budget Share On (b) %
WATS interviewing	91	44
Shopping mall intercept	90	43
Focus groups	90	6
Local telephone interviewing	61	5
Consumer mail panels	57	13
Consumer purchase diaries	48	8
In-home interviewing	47	9
Trade surveys	39	1
Direct mail surveys	33	4
Average number used	5.6	—

(a) Question: Here is a list of a number of research data *collection* methods and techniques. For which of these have you used outside suppliers within the past year?
(b) Question: On which one or two have you spent the most money in the past year?
Source: "A Description of Consumer Market Research Technique Usage Patterns and Attitudes in 1982," a survey conducted by Market Facts, Inc., April 28, 1983. Reprinted by permission.

Application

Survey Car License Plates to Define Retail Trade Area

Many research firms, such as R. L. Polk & Co., use primary and secondary data to define the trade area of retail locations. The primary data involves observing and recording license plate numbers of vehicles at retail establishments. The secondary data involves motor vehicle registration files purchased from state agencies. Observations are matched with vehicle registrations, and summary reports are compiled from this matching process. The reports indicate significant geographic areas for a retail location and can help marketers determine cut-off points for primary and secondary trade areas. It should be noted that the privacy of individual customers is maintained since names and addresses are never released. Reports are summarized by town, zip code, census tract, and census block group. This, of course, illustrates the use of census data as a secondary source in addition to vehicle registration data. More detailed analysis by time, day, or parking lot can give further information on day-of-the-week and time-of-day shopping patterns and on the draw of a major department store in relation to the overall customer base of a regional mall.

There are several advantages associated with the use of this method. First, the results are typically very accurate since the vehicle registration files maintained by state agencies are carefully compiled and up-to-date. Second, the method does not impose on customers. Finally, it is a relatively low-cost method since highly skilled interviewers are not required to record license plate numbers and other facts such as time, date, and parking lot. The major requirement, and limitation, of surveying license plates is that the majority of the customers must arrive by automobile and park in the store's lot. Thus, the method is inappropriate for downtown shopping areas. (*Source: Larry D. Crabtree and James A. Paris, "Survey Car License Plates to Define Retail Trade Area," Marketing News, Jan. 4, 1985, p. 12. Reprinted from* Marketing News, *published by the American Marketing Association.*)

mailing the questionnaire; and (5) making the results of the survey available to the respondents upon request.[15]

Although these techniques have proved useful in increasing response rates, they may introduce sample-composition bias. Sample-composition bias results when those responding to a survey differ in some important respect from those not responding to the survey. In other words, response-enhancing techniques may alienate some portion of the sample and appeal to another, causing the results to be nonrepresentative of the population of interest.[16] Perhaps as a result of these problems and the others discussed earlier, only 4 percent of the firms represented in Table 6.4 spent a major portion of their research funds for direct mail surveys.

15. Milton M. Pressley, "Try These Tips to Get 50% to 70% Response Rate from Mail Surveys of Commercial Populations," *Marketing News,* Jan. 21, 1983, p. 16.
16. Charles D. Parker and Kevin F. McCrohan, "Increasing Mail Survey Response Rates: A Discussion of Methods and Induced Bias," in *Marketing: Theories and Concepts for an Era of Change,* John Summey, R. Viswanathan, Ronald Taylor, and Karen Glynn, eds. (Southern Marketing Association, 1983), pp. 254–256.

Premiums or incentives used to encourage respondents to return questionnaires have been effective in developing panels of respondents who are interviewed repeatedly by mail. Mail panels, which are selected to represent a market or market segment, are especially useful in evaluating new products, providing general information about consumers, and providing records of consumers' purchases. As Table 6.5 indicates, 57 percent of the companies surveyed used consumer mail panels, but these panels represented a major budget share for only 13 percent of the companies. It is interesting that 48 percent of the sample used consumer purchase diaries. (These surveys are similar to mail panels, but consumers only keep track of purchases.) Consumer mail panels and consumer purchase diaries are much more widely used than direct mail surveys.

Telephone Surveys

In a telephone survey, respondents' answers to a questionnaire are recorded by interviewers. A telephone survey has some advantages over a mail survey. The rate of response is higher because it takes less effort to answer the telephone and talk than to fill out a questionnaire and return it. If there are enough interviewers, telephone surveys can be conducted very quickly. Thus, they can be used by political candidates or organizations seeking an immediate reaction to an event. In addition, this survey technique permits interviewers to gain rapport with respondents and to ask probing questions.

WATS (Wide Area Telecommunications Service) significantly reduces the expense of long-distance telephone interviewing. The data in Table 6.4, which are supported by a 1985 American Marketing Association survey, show that virtually all of the surveyed firms used telephone interviewing.[17] Computer-assisted telephone interviewing permits an integration of questionnaire, data collection, and tabulations. Computer-assisted telephone interviewing provides data to aid decision makers in the shortest time possible.

In computer-assisted telephone interviewing, the paper questionnaire is replaced by a video screen, or cathode ray tube (CRT). Responses are entered on a terminal keyboard, or the interviewer can use a light pen, a pen-shaped flashlight, to record a response on a light sensitive screen. On the most advanced devices, the interviewer uses a finger to touch the responses on a touch-sensitive CRT. Open-ended responses can be typed on the keyboard or recorded with paper and pencil.

CRT interviewing saves time and facilitates monitoring the progress of interviews. Entry functions are largely eliminated; the computer determines which question to display on the CRT, skipping questions that are not relevant. Because data are available as soon as they are entered into the system, cumbersome hand computations are eliminated and interim results can be quickly retrieved. With some systems, a microcomputer may be taken to off-site locations for use in data analysis. Some suppliers claim that CRT telephone interviewing—including hardware, software, and operation costs—is less expensive than conventional paper and pencil methods.[18]

Telephone interviews have disadvantages, too, however. They are limited

17. "AMA Outlook Survey Finds Marketing Research Directors Expect More Emphasis on Marketing, Less on Network Advertising," *Marketing News,* April 26, 1985, pp. 1 and 15.
18. Stephen M. Billig, "Go Slow, Be Wary When Considering Switch to Computer-Assisted Interviewing System," *Marketing News,* Nov. 26, 1982, sec. 2, p. 2.

to oral communication; visual aids or observation cannot be included. Interpretation of results must make adjustments for subjects who are not at home or who do not have telephones. Many households are excluded from telephone directories by choice (unlisted numbers) or because the residents moved after publication of the directory. If households with unlisted numbers are systematically excluded, the resulting sample will be somewhat older, more rural, more white, more educated, more retired, and more white-collar than the universe of households with telephone service.[19]

These findings have serious implications for the use of telephone samples in conducting surveys. Some adjustment must be made for groups of respondents that may be undersampled because of a smaller-than-average incidence of telephone listings. Nondirectory telephone samples can overcome such bias. Various methods are available, including random-digit dialing (adding random numbers to the telephone prefix) and plus-one telephone sampling (adding one to the last digit of a number in the directory). These methods make it feasible to dial any working number, whether or not it is listed in a directory.

Telephone surveys, like mail and personal interview surveys, are sometimes used to develop panels of respondents who can be interviewed repeatedly to measure changes in attitudes or behavior. Use of these telephone panels is increasing.

Personal Interview Surveys

Traditionally, marketing researchers have favored the face-to-face interview, primarily because of its flexibility. Various audiovisual aids—pictures, products, diagrams, or prerecorded advertising copy—can be incorporated into a personal interview. Rapport gained through direct interaction usually permits more in-depth interviewing, including probes, follow-up questions, or psychological tests. In addition, because face-to-face interviews can be longer, they can yield more information. Finally, respondents can be selected more carefully, and reasons for nonresponse can be explored.

Shopping mall intercept interviews   In the past, most personal interviews, which were based on random sampling or prearranged appointments, were conducted in the respondent's home. Today, the nature of personal interviews has changed. As Table 6.5 indicates, most personal interviews are conducted in shopping malls. The technique consists of interviewing a percentage of persons passing by certain "intercept" points in a mall. Although there are many variations of this technique, Table 6.5 indicates that shopping mall intercept interviewing is the second most popular survey technique used today, next only to WATS interviewing. Not only did 90 percent of the major consumer goods and services companies use this technique, but 43 percent reported that shopping mall intercept interviewing was their major expenditure on survey research.

As with any face-to-face interviewing method, mall intercept interviewing has many advantages. The interviewer is in a position to recognize and react to nonverbal indications of confusion on the part of the respondent. Respondents can be shown product prototypes, videotapes of commercials, story boards, and the like, and reactions can be sought. The mall environment permits the

19. Patricia E. Moberg, "Biases in Unlisted Phone Numbers," *Journal of Advertising Research,* Aug.–Sept. 1982, p. 55.

researcher to deal with complex situations, such as those requiring taste tests, by ensuring that all the respondents are reacting to the same product, which can be prepared and monitored from the mall test kitchen or some other facility. Lower cost, greater control, and the ability to conduct tests requiring bulky equipment are the major reasons for the popularity of this survey method.[20]

Research has indicated that given a comparable sample of respondents, shopping mall intercept interviewing is a suitable substitute for more traditional telephone interviewing.[21] In addition, there seem to be no significant differences in the completeness of consumer responses between telephone interviewing and shopping mall intercept interviewing. For questions dealing with socially desirable behavior, shopping mall intercept respondents appear to be more honest about their past behavior.[22]

On-site computer interviewing consists of respondents completing a self-administered questionnaire displayed on a computer monitor. General Motors used this technique to ask passersby at auto shows their opinions about the Chevrolet Astro Van. After analyzing the data GM learned that the majority of the eight hundred respondents did not like the placement of the fuel-filler in the middle of the side body panel.[23]

Focus-group interview   The object of a focus-group interview is to observe group interaction when members are exposed to an idea or concept. Often, these interviews are conducted on an informal basis without a structured questionnaire. Consumer attitudes, behavior, lifestyles, needs, and desires can be explored in a flexible and creative manner through focus-group interviews. Researchers approach consumers without preconceived notions. Questions are open ended and stimulate consumers to answer in their own words. Researchers who hear something they do not fully understand or something unexpected and interesting can probe for insights into deeper thoughts and feelings that explain consumer behavior.[24] Table 6.5 indicates that 90 percent of the firms surveyed used focus-group interviewing, and 6 percent of the firms spent the major share of their budgets on this technique.

In-home interviews   While in-home interviews represent only 9 percent of the budget spent on surveys, 47 percent of the largest consumer companies use this technique. Because it may be desirable to eliminate group influence, in-depth interviews offer a real advantage when thoroughness of self-disclosure is important. In a long in-depth interview of 45 to 90 minutes, respondents can be probed to reveal their real motivations, feelings, behaviors, and aspirations. In-depth interviews permit the discovery of emotional "hot buttons" that provide psychological insights.[25]

20. Roger Gates and Paul J. Soloman, "Research Using the Mall Intercept: State of the Art," *Journal of Advertising Research,* Aug.–Sept. 1982, pp. 47–48.
21. Alan J. Bush and A. Parasuraman, "Mall Intercept versus Telephone-Interviewing Environment," *Journal of Advertising Research,* April–May 1985, p. 42.
22. Alan J. Bush and Joseph F. Hair, Jr., "An Assessment of the Mall Intercept as a Data Collecting Method," *Journal of Marketing Research,* May 1985, p. 162.
23. Bernie Whalen, "On Site Computer Interviewing Yields Research Data Instantly," *Marketing News,* Nov. 9, 1984, p. 1.
24. NFO Research Inc., Advertisement, *Marketing News,* Jan. 21, 1983, p. 20.
25. Hal Sokolow, "In-Depth Interviews Increasing in Importance," *Marketing News,* Sept. 13, 1985, p. 26.

Coca-Cola failed to investigate the emotional attachment of consumers to its existing product before launching New Coke. The company only conducted superficial taste tests with 200,000 people in shopping malls, asking, "Do you like it or don't you?" In-depth interviews might have revealed that even if the new formula tasted better, many people might still be suspicious of it.[26]

Questionnaire Construction

A carefully constructed questionnaire is essential to the success of a survey. First of all, questions must be designed to elicit information that meets the data requirements of the study. Questions must be clear, easy to understand, and directed toward a definable objective. Until that objective has been defined, researchers should not attempt to develop a questionnaire, for the composition of the questions depends on the nature of the objective and the detail demanded. One common mistake in questionnaire construction is to ask questions that interest the researchers but do not provide information that helps in deciding whether to accept or reject a hypothesis. Finally, the most important rule is to maintain an unbiased, objective approach in composing questions.

Several kinds of questions can be included: open ended, dichotomous, and multiple-choice. Examples of each follow.

Open Ended Question
What is your general opinion of the American Express Card?

_____

_____

_____

Dichotomous Question
Do you presently have an American Express Card?

                    Yes   _____
                    No   _____

Multiple-Choice Question
What age group are you in?

                    Under 20   _____
                    20–29   _____
                    30–39   _____
                    40–49   _____
                    50–59   _____
                    60 and over _____

Researchers must be very careful about questions that a person might consider too personal or that might result in a respondent's admitting to activities that other people are likely to condemn. Questions of this type should be worded in such a way as to make them less offensive. For example, Table 6.6 shows how a series of questions can be designed to overcome the potentially

26. Mitchell J. Shields, "Coke's Research Fizzles: Fails to Factor in Consumer Loyalty," *Adweek*, July 15, 1985, p. 8.

> **Table 6.6** *A series of questions designed to overcome the objectionable nature of a subject*
>
> **Problem**
> Have you ever shoplifted anything?
>   1 no
>   2 yes
>
> **Revision**
> As you know, there is now a great deal of community concern about shoplifting and how to handle it. Some people feel it is a serious problem, while others feel it is not. How about yourself? How serious a problem do you think shoplifting is in our community?
>   1 serious
>   2 moderate
>   3 slight
>   4 not at all
> During the past few years do you think the frequency of shoplifting has increased, stayed about the same, or decreased in this community?
>   1 increased
>   2 stayed about the same
>   3 decreased
> When you were a teenager, did you personally know anyone who took something from a store without paying for it?
>   1 no
>   2 yes
> How about yourself? Did you ever consider taking anything from a store without paying for it?
>   1 no
>   2 yes
> (If yes) Did you actually take it?
>   1 no
>   2 yes

Source: Don A. Dillman, *Mail and Telephone Surveys: The Total Design Method* (New York: Wiley, 1978), p. 107. Used by permission.

objectionable nature of a question about shoplifting. Even though this approach does not guarantee truthful responses, it should improve their probability of occurring. Note that the series of questions in Table 6.6 asks about the importance of shoplifting as a crime. These questions are designed to measure beliefs or behavior indirectly as well as directly.

Observation Methods

Various methods other than surveys can be used to collect primary data. In using the **observation method,** researchers record the overt behavior of respondents, taking note of physical conditions and events. Direct contact with respondents is avoided; instead, their actions are examined and noted systematically. For example, researchers might use observation methods to answer the question, "How long does the average McDonald's restaurant customer have to wait in line before being served?"

Observation methods can be used to control such retail store factors as inventory, spoilage, and breakage. Observation may also be combined with interviews. For example, during personal interviews, the condition of a respondent's home or other possessions may be observed and recorded, and demographic information such as race, approximate age, and sex can be confirmed by direct observation.

Data gathered through observation sometimes can be biased if the respondent is aware of the observation process. An observer can be placed in a natural market environment, such as a grocery store, without biasing or influencing the actions of shoppers. However, if the presence of a human observer is likely to bias the outcome or if human sensory abilities are inadequate, mechanical means may be used to record behavior. **Mechanical observation devices** include cameras, recorders, counting machines, and equipment to record physiological changes in individuals. For instance, an audiometer is used to record the station to which a television or radio receiver is tuned. Similarly, a special camera can be used to record eye movements of respondents looking at an advertisement. In this way the sequence of reading and the parts of the advertisement that receive greatest attention can be detected. Electric scanners in supermarkets are mechanical observation devices that provide an exciting opportunity for marketing research. Scanner technology can provide accurate data on sales and purchase patterns of consumers. Some supermarket chains are now selling scanner data to marketing researchers.[27]

Observation methods, like survey methods, are used to test hypotheses, discover problems, or provide a continuous flow of information into a data bank. Observation is straightforward and avoids a central problem of survey methods, motivating respondents to state their true feelings or opinions. However, observation tends to be descriptive. When it is the only method of data collection, it may not provide insights into causal relationships. Another limitation is that analyses based on observation are subject to the biases and limitations of the observer or the mechanical device.

Secondary Data Collection

In addition to or instead of collecting primary data, marketers may use available reports and other information to study a marketing problem. An organization's marketing data bank may contain information about past marketing activities, such as sales records and research reports, that can be used to test hypotheses and pinpoint problems.

Secondary data also are found in periodicals, government publications, and unpublished sources. Periodicals such as *Business Week, Sales and Marketing Management,* and *Industrial Marketing* print general information that is helpful in defining problems and developing hypotheses. *Survey of Buying Power,* the annual supplement to *Sales and Marketing Management,* contains sales data for major industries on a county-by-county basis. Many marketers consult federal government publications such as the *Census of Business,* the *Census of Agriculture,* and the *Census of Populations* available from the Superintendent of Documents in Washington, D.C. Table 6.7 summarizes the major external sources of secondary data, excluding syndicated services.

27. Fitzhugh L. Carr, "Scanners in Marketing Research: Paradise (Almost)," *Marketing News,* Jan. 4, 1985, pp. 1 and 15.

Table 6.7 *A guide to external sources of secondary data*

Trade journals	Virtually every industry or type of business has a trade journal. These journals give a feel for the industry—its size, degree of competition, range of companies involved, and problems. To find trade journals in the field of interest, check *Ulrich's*, a reference book that lists American and foreign periodicals by subject.
Trade associations	Almost every industry, product category, and profession has its own association. Depending on the strength of each group, they often conduct research, publish journals, conduct training sessions, and hold conventions. A call or a letter to the association may yield information not available in published sources. To find out which associations serve which industries, check the *Encyclopedia of Associations*.
International sources	Periodical indexes such as the *F&S Index International*, are particularly useful for overseas product or company information. More general sources include the *United Nations Statistical Yearbook* and the *International Labour Organization's Yearbook of Labour Statistics*.
Government	The federal government, through its various departments and agencies, collects, analyzes, and publishes statistics on practically everything. Government documents also have their own set of indexes: the *Monthly Catalog*. Other useful indexes for government-generated information are the *American Statistical Index* and the *Congressional Information Service*.
Books in Print (*BIP*)	*BIP* is a two-volume reference book found in most libraries. All books issued by U.S. publishers and currently in print are listed by subject, title, and author.
Periodical indexes	The library's reference section contains indexes on virtually every discipline. The *Business Periodicals Index,* for example, indexes each article in all major business periodicals.
Computerized literature-retrieval data bases	Literature-retrieval data bases are periodical indexes stored in a computer. Books and dissertations are also included. Key words (such as the name of a subject) are used to search a data base and generate references.

Syndicated data services collect general information that is sold to clients. Their information is available only to subscribers. American Research Bureau (ARB) furnishes television stations and media buyers with estimates of the number of viewers at specific times. Sell Area Marketing, Inc. (SAMI) furnishes monthly information that describes market shares for specific types of manufacturers. The A. C. Nielsen Company Retail Index gathers data about products primarily sold through food stores and drugstores. This information includes total sales in a product category, sales of clients' own brands, and sales of important competing brands. The Market Research Corporation of America (MRCA) collects data through a national panel of consumers to provide information about purchases. MRCA maintains data on sales by brands classified by age, race, sex, education, occupation, and family size.

Similar organizations operate at the local level. Market Search, a marketing research company in Indianapolis, for example, offers "Indyindex." This monthly omnibus study for small Indianapolis businesses contains information gleaned from three hundred consumer telephone interviews about product preferences, prices, stores, and other marketing topics. Small businesses use this research information to plan their marketing activities.[28]

Another type of secondary data available for a fee involves demographic analysis. Companies which specialize in demographic data banks have the special knowledge and computer systems to work with the very complex U.S. census data bank. As a result, they are able to respond to specialized requests that the Census Bureau cannot or will not handle. Such information may be valuable in tracking demographic changes that have implications for consumer behavior.[29]

Internal sources of information can contribute tremendously to research. An organization's accounting records are an excellent source of data but, strangely enough, they are often overlooked. The large volume of data collected by the accounting department does not automatically flow to the marketing area. As a result, detailed information about costs, sales, customer accounts, or profits by product category may not be part of the MIS. This condition is especially true in organizations that do not store marketing information on a systematic basis. As was pointed out early in this chapter, such information—collected systematically and continuously through a carefully constructed marketing information system—is essential to the success of marketing efforts.

Marketing Research Ethics

Clearly, marketing research and information systems are vital to marketing decision making. Today, managers in all types of organizations are recognizing the need for more and better information. One final area of marketing research practice must not go unmentioned. It is imperative that marketers establish acceptable standards of education and ethics. Too often, respondents are unfairly manipulated and research clients are not told about flaws in data. Attempts to stamp out shoddy practices and to establish generally acceptable procedures for conducting research will enhance the professional image of marketing researchers.

Most studies of ethics in marketing research have focused on either delineating responsibilities of researchers to clients and respondents or exploring whether certain marketing research practices are perceived as ethical or unethical. Research integrity, fair treatment of outside clients, and research confidentiality

---

28. "Marketing Research Briefs," *Marketing News,* Jan. 21, 1983, p. 5.
29. Ronald L. Vaughn, "Demographic Data Banks: A New Management Resource," *Business Horizons,* Nov.–Dec. 1984, pp. 38–42.

are the top three ethical issues in marketing research. A recent survey revealed that 61 percent of the surveyed market researchers perceived many opportunities to engage in unethical behavior.[30] Opportunity and the perceived behavior of peers and superiors are major determinants of ethical behavior.[31] There is limited agreement on the uniformity of marketing research and these techniques are performed differently by companies. On the other hand, general codes of marketing research ethics, statements on respondents' rights, and principles of appropriate conduct are available. The American Marketing Association and the Marketing Research Association both have codes to promote marketing research ethics. Improving marketing research ethics helps to insure that data inputs are accurate and useful for marketing decisions.

Summary

Marketing research and information systems are essential to an organization's planning and strategy development. The marketing concept cannot be implemented without information about buyers. As acceptance of the marketing concept in planning efforts has increased, higher levels of management have begun using marketing research.

Marketing research is the design and execution of specific inquiries to yield results for making marketing decisions. The marketing information system (MIS) provides a framework for the day-to-day managing and structuring of information regularly gathered from sources both inside and outside an organization. Marketing research usually is characterized by in-depth analysis of a problem, while the MIS focuses on data storage, retrieval, and classification.

Research and information systems are scientific approaches to decision making in marketing. Intuitive decisions are made on the basis of past experience and personal bias. Scientific decision making is an orderly, logical, and systematic approach. Minor, nonrecurring problems can be handled successfully by intuition. As the number of alternative solutions, payoffs, and risks multiply, the use of research becomes more desirable and rewarding.

The five basic steps of planning marketing research are (1) defining the problems, (2) developing hypotheses, (3) collecting data, (4) interpreting research findings, and (5) reporting the findings. A problem must be stated clearly for marketers to develop a hypothesis, which is a guess or assumption about that problem or set of circumstances. To test the accuracy of hypotheses and to gather data, researchers may use exploratory, descriptive, or causal studies. To apply research to decision making, marketers must interpret and report their findings properly.

Research design involves establishing procedures for obtaining reliable and valid marketing data. A study is valid if it measures what it is supposed to measure. Reliable studies can be repeated with approximately the same results obtained.

Sampling is a method of selecting representative units from a total population. Four basic sampling designs for marketing research are random sampling,

30. Shelby D. Hunt, Lawrence B. Chonko, and James B. Wilcox, "Ethical Problems of Marketing Researchers," *Journal of Marketing Research,* Aug. 1984, pp. 309–324.
31. O. C. Ferrell and Larry Gresham, "A Contingency Framework of Ethical Decision Making," *Journal of Marketing,* Summer 1985, p. 89.

stratified sampling, area sampling, and quota sampling. The first three sampling methods are based on statistical probability; that is, sample units have a known or equal chance of being chosen. Quota sampling depends upon judgmental selection.

Experimentation is a procedure for organizing data to increase the validity and reliability of research findings. Experimentation focuses on controlling some variables and manipulating others to determine cause-and-effect relationships. Laboratory settings provide marketers with maximum control over influential factors. Field settings are preferred when marketers want experimentation to take place in natural surroundings.

There are three fundamental ways to obtain data: surveys, observation, and secondary sources. The three types of surveys—personal interview, telephone, and mail—gather data through interviews or by having respondents fill out questionnaires. Questionnaires are instruments used to obtain information from respondents and to record observations; they should be unbiased and objective.

Attempts to stamp out shoddy practices and to establish generally acceptable procedures for conducting research are enhancing the professional image of marketing researchers.

Important Terms

Marketing research	Validity
Marketing information system (MIS)	Sampling
	Population
Marketing data bank	Random sampling
Intuition	Stratified sampling
Scientific decision making	Area sampling
Problem definition	Quota sampling
Hypothesis	Experimentation
Primary data	Marketing experimentation
Secondary data	Independent variable
Exploratory studies	Dependent variable
Descriptive studies	Survey methods
Causal studies	Observation method
Statistical interpretation	Mechanical observation devices
Reliability	Syndicated data services

Discussion and Review Questions

1. How do the benefits of decisions guided by marketing research compare to those of intuitive decision making? How do marketing decision makers know when it will be worthwhile to conduct research?
2. Give some specific examples of situations in which intuitive decision making would probably be more appropriate than marketing research.
3. What is the MIS likely to include in a small organization? Do all organizations have a marketing data bank?
4. In what ways do marketing research and the MIS overlap?
5. What is the difference between defining a research problem and developing a hypothesis?

6. *Nonresponse* refers to the inability or refusal of some respondents to cooperate in a survey. What are some ways to decrease nonresponse in personal door-to-door surveys?

7. Make some suggestions for encouraging respondents to cooperate in mail surveys.

8. If a survey of all homes with listed telephone numbers is conducted, what sampling design should be used?

9. List some problems of conducting a laboratory experiment on respondents' reactions to the taste of different brands of beer. How would these problems differ from those of a field study on beer taste preferences?

10. Give some examples of marketing problems that could be solved through information gained from observation.

11. What are the major limitations of using secondary data to solve marketing problems?

Cases

Case 6.1 Lady Indian Basketball[32]

Benny Hollis, Athletic Director at Northeast Louisiana University (NLU), was very interested in the results of a survey he had just received. The research had been conducted by his staff in response to his request for information about the women's basketball program at the university. Although the team was becoming very successful, growth in fan attendance was lagging behind. Hollis hoped that the results of a survey to find out what type of person attends women's basketball games might be used to develop a better program for marketing the sport at NLU.

The Lady Indians were gaining much success. They were undefeated in the 1982–83 season in Southland Conference play. In the same season they were ranked among the top twenty teams in the nation in four of the eight team-statistics categories compiled by the NCAA, and they were third in the nation in scoring. However, Hollis was not sure that they had been adequately marketed to the relevant groups of fans who might be attracted. This was true not only at NLU, but also around the country as women's sports were just beginning to grow.

Hollis believed the greatest return for the cost, at that time, was to be found in the promotion of women's basketball. The quality of competition and the level of interest had increased to the point that if the sport were effectively marketed, it could have a significant impact on university athletic income. Additionally, most conferences, including the Southland Conference, had now incorporated women's programs into their conference structures, thus enhancing image and interest. Most of these changes had occurred in just the past three to five years.

It was also apparent to Hollis that there was tremendous room for attendance growth in women's basketball. For instance, the average attendance for all

32. This case was prepared by David Loudon, C. W. McConkey, and Maynard M. Dolecheck, all of Northeast Louisiana University. Copyright © 1986 by David Louden, C. W. McConkey, and Maynard M. Dolecheck. Reprinted with permission.

NCAA Division I women's basketball games (excluding doubleheaders with men) was only 555—up 9.25 percent over the previous year. Yet, a few teams did better: Louisiana Tech (located 30 miles from NLU), Iowa, and Southern California averaged 5,285, 3,381, and 3,159, respectively, during their seasons. NLU averaged only 2,441 at home for the season. However, as recently as five years before, a crowd of 200 was considered good.

Although the potential for increased attendance appeared to be present, Hollis realized that women's basketball had to be properly marketed. Before an effective marketing plan could be developed, however, the market for women's basketball had to be defined and selected. Then a marketing program could be assembled to attract this target market. Thus, the Sports Information Department planned a survey aimed at learning some things about women's collegiate basketball fans to help establish appropriate marketing strategies.

A questionnaire was developed to administer to patrons at one of the well-attended games during the season (see Figure 6.10). The single-page, two-sided questionnaire was designed to obtain general demographic information as well as to gauge what attracts women's fans to the game.

The questionnaire was distributed at the home game between the NLU women and Louisiana Tech University. Almost everyone entering the arena was offered a questionnaire to complete for usher pickup at half time. To assure maximum participation, a pencil was supplied with each questionnaire. A total of 2,200 questionnaires were distributed and 717 were returned. Questionnaires completed by half time were collected by ushers; those not completed by half time could be deposited in boxes provided at all exits.

The questionnaires were tabulated, and findings were significant. Many of the fans were devoted solely to the women's game, and two-thirds of those respondents believed their game was more entertaining because it displays more finesse than physical dominance. Women's fans also tended to be older and female and were more likely to be white. In the fan's mind, the product is not just the sport of women's basketball. It includes elements such as uniforms, music, half-time entertainment, cheerleading, concessions, schedules, and so on.

The results indicate that most women's basketball fans consider the games to be one of the best entertainment values available. Also, special events and premiums such as T-shirt giveaways had little value in boosting game attendance. This was particularly true of nonstudents.

The study also found that getting people to attend a few games is the key to continued attendance. The entire marketing program could be geared to inducing people to attend a couple of games to overcome any misperceptions about the sport. As Hollis evaluated the responses, he now had the challenging job of interpreting their meaning for the future marketing direction of the Lady Indian basketball program.

Questions for Discussion

1. Evaluate the research project conducted to improve attendance at Lady Indian basketball games.
2. What type of basketball fan would have been likely to fill out the questionnaire? What can be said about the nonrespondents?
3. Suggest a marketing strategy for Hollis based on the results of the Lady Indian survey.

Figure 6.10

Women's college basketball survey

Dear Fan:

To learn more about the growing interest in WOMEN'S college basketball please help us by completing this questionnaire. It will take you less than 10 minutes to complete.----THANK YOU.

SECTION 1

For EACH of the statements below, CIRCLE the Number that best describes how much you AGREE with that statement. Please give careful thought to each of the statements.

		Strongly Disagree	Disagree	Neither	Agree	Strongly Agree	
1.	WOMEN'S basketball should be the preliminary game to the MEN'S game so the fans can view two games for a single admission............................	1	2	3	4	5	(5)
2.	Sufficient tax dollars should be spent on athletics to produce a winning program.......................................	1	2	3	4	5	(6)
3.	WOMEN'S basketball is more entertaining than MEN'S basketball because it displays more finesse than physical dominance.........................	1	2	3	4	5	(7)
4.	I select basketball games to attend based on the reputation and ranking of the visiting team..........................	1	2	3	4	5	(8)
5.	WOMEN'S basketball is one of the best entertainment values available.........	1	2	3	4	5	(9)
6.	I attend WOMEN'S basketball because of the urging of my spouse or children...	1	2	3	4	5	(10)
7.	I usually attend WOMEN'S basketball games with a friend or neighbor.........	1	2	3	4	5	(11)
8.	I am personally acquainted with one or more players in tonight's game.........	1	2	3	4	5	(12)
9.	I would be inclined to attend more WOMEN'S basketball games when my team is ranked nationally.	1	2	3	4	5	(13)
10.	I listen to the away games on the radio when I am unable to attend.	1	2	3	4	5	(14)
11.	I enjoy participation in recreational activity.	1	2	3	4	5	(15)
12.	Special event nights (such as T-shirt night) are important to my attending WOMEN'S basketball.........................	1	2	3	4	5	(16)
13.	Quality education is more important for WOMEN athletes because of the lack of professional sports opportunities.	1	2	3	4	5	(17)
14.	A successful athletic program is important for a positive University image in the community....................	1	2	3	4	5	(10)

SECTION 2

Please supply the following information by either filling in the blanks or circling the number of the appropriate reply:

1. SEX: 1. Male 2. Female (18)   2. MARITAL STATUS: 1. Single   (19)
                                                          2. Married

3. NUMBER OF CHILDREN: 0   1   2   3   4   5 or more   (20)

4. THE AGE OF MY YOUNGEST CHILD IS ____.   (21-22)

5. EDUCATION (highest level of education attained):   (23)
      1. Grade   2. High   3. Vo-Tech   4. Attended   5. College
         School   School   College   Graduate

6. MY AGE IS ____. (23-24)   7. RACE: 1. Black 2. White 3. Other   (25)

8. EMPLOYMENT STATUS: (26)
      1. Retired   2. Home-maker   3. Self-employed
      4. Employed (not self)   5. Student

9. I have attended the following universities: (27)
      1. NLU   2. TECH   3. OTHER

10. I am a graduate of the following university: (28)
      1. NLU   2. TECH   3. OTHER

continued next page

Figure 6.10

(continued)

11. My children have attended the following universities: (29)
    1. NLU   2. TECH   3. OTHER

12. Circle all of the following that describe you: (30-35)
    1. College Athletic Club   2. College Alumni Association Member
    Member   4. Country/Tennis Club Member
    3. Civic Club Member   6. Union Member
    5. Fitness Club Member

13. How many miles have you traveled to see tonight's game?   (36)
    1. 10 or less   2. 11-20   3. 21-50   4. More than 50

14. How many WOMEN'S basketball games will you attend
    this season? ____.   (37-38)

15. How many MEN'S basketball games will you attend this
    season? ____.   (39-40)

16. My interest in WOMEN'S basketball started when I was exposed via (41)
    1. Newspaper   2. T.V.
    3. Radio   4. Game Attendance   5. Discussion of friends

17. For sports information, I depend on: (Rank the following
    based on frequency of use--1 most used thru 8 least used)   (42-49)
    _____ KTVE-TV   (42)   _____ Quachita Citizen   (46)
    _____ KNOE-TV   (43)   _____ Ruston News Leader   (47)
    _____ KARD-TV   (44)   _____ Monroe News-Star World (48)
    _____ KNLU   (45)   _____ Word of Mouth   (49)

18. Which radio format do you listen to most often?   (50)
    1. Country   2. Soft Rock   3. Hard Rock   4. Easy Listening

19. Other than basketball, which WOMEN'S sport would you most
    enjoy viewing?   (51)
    1. Softball   2. Tennis   3. Swimming   4. Track   5. Volleyball

20. Do you plan to attend the NLU vs TECH MEN'S basketball game
    on Feb. 9?   (52)
    1. Yes   2. No   3. Undecided

21. Which team are you "rooting" for tonight? 1. TECH   2. NLU   (53)

> WE NEED YOUR HELP ! ! ! !
> WOULD YOU BE WILLING TO SPEND 15-30 MINUTES TO COMPLETE AN IN-
> DEPTH QUESTIONNAIRE, CONCERNING COLLEGE ATHLETICS? IF SO, PLEASE
> PRINT YOUR NAME AND ADDRESS BELOW. THOSE SELECTED WILL BE MAILED
> A QUESTIONNAIRE (NO ONE WILL CALL). UPON COMPLETION AND RETURN OF
> THE QUESTIONNAIRE YOU WILL RECEIVE A COUPON WORTH $10.00 OFF THE
> PURCHASE PRICE OF EACH 1984-1985 NLU WOMEN'S BASKETBALL SEASON
> TICKET AS AN EXPRESSION OF OUR APPRECIATION.

        NAME: _____
     ADDRESS: _____
              _____

PLEASE PASS THE COMPLETED QUESTIONNAIRE TO THE END OF THE ROW FOR
COLLECTION AS INSTRUCTED BY THE PUBLIC ADDRESS ANNOUNCER----THANK YOU.

Case 6.2   A. C. Nielsen Company[33]

A. C. Nielsen Company and its subsidiaries provide worldwide business services that help clients to make factually based decisions on matters relating to marketing, production, distribution, product and package design, and sales and promotional programs.

33. The facts in this case are based on the A. C. Nielsen Company *1983 Annual Report.*

The company's major resources include the Marketing Research Group which provides continuous measurement of consumer response at the point of sale. The Neodata Services Group maintains computerized circulation lists for magazine publishers and others. The Media Research Group provides measurement of national and local television audiences. The Clearing House Group processes merchandise coupons for retailers and manufacturers and provides inquiry services for advertisers and magazine publishers. The Petroleum Information Corporation provides statistical data to make oil and gas exploration more efficient. Dataquest, Inc., provides comprehensive information for use in evaluating technology and marketing developments in industrial markets.

A major service provided by the Marketing Research Group is the measuring of consumer reaction at the actual point of sale. In the U.S. there are more than 7,000 stores equipped with scanners that electronically read the zebra-striped bar codes appearing on most packaged grocery products. Nielsen auditors regularly visit a national sample of retail stores and use these checkout scanners as a source of consumer sales information. The Nielsen auditors also obtain information on retail inventories, brand distribution, out-of-stock conditions, prices, and displays. Since audits are repeated regularly, all important trends are tracked by the Marketing Research Group.

New products or new ideas can be tested on a limited scale to minimize their risk. Nielsen's E.R.I.M. Consumer Research evaluates the performance of brands using a new technique. Special television advertising messages about new products or select brands are transmitted by cable television to certain households in a small geographic area. By scanning cash register data in stores where these sample households shop, information about the effect of these commercials on consumer purchase patterns is obtained. This new technique enhances the value of test marketing research.

Nielsen's clients are continually informed about their products' sales performance and market share either for the entire country or by region, by store type and size, and by package size. The Nielsen Warehouse Inventory Service, also provided by the Marketing Research Group, helps manufacturers of health and beauty aids to gain a more complete knowledge of how their products move through the distribution pipeline from factory to retail stores. The Marketing Research Group also offers a computerized management system to help manufacturers organize the ever-increasing quantities of market data and to utilize these data more effectively.

Nielsen's Marketing Research Group has worldwide sales of $363 million. Its worldwide market review service provides clients with access to market-development information on selected product categories in a large number of countries. All the services provided by A. C. Nielsen Company have a common objective—to help clients market their products more profitably.

Questions for Discussion

1. In what ways does the comprehensive marketing information provided by the Nielsen Marketing Research Group help its clients?
2. How do Nielsen marketing services impact on the ultimate users of products that are surveyed?
3. Is it best for a company to conduct its own marketing research efforts or purchase marketing research services from a firm such as A. C. Nielsen?

Part II
Product Decisions

We now are prepared to analyze the decisions and activities associated with developing and maintaining effective marketing mixes. In Parts II, III, IV, and V we focus on the major components of the marketing mix—product, distribution, promotion, and price. Specifically, in Part II we explore the product ingredient of the marketing mix. Chapter 7 introduces basic concepts and relationships that must be understood in order to make effective product decisions. Branding, packaging, and labeling are also discussed in this chapter. In Chapter 8, we analyze a variety of dimensions regarding product management, such as the ways that a firm can be organized to manage products, the development and positioning of products, product modification, and the phasing out of products.

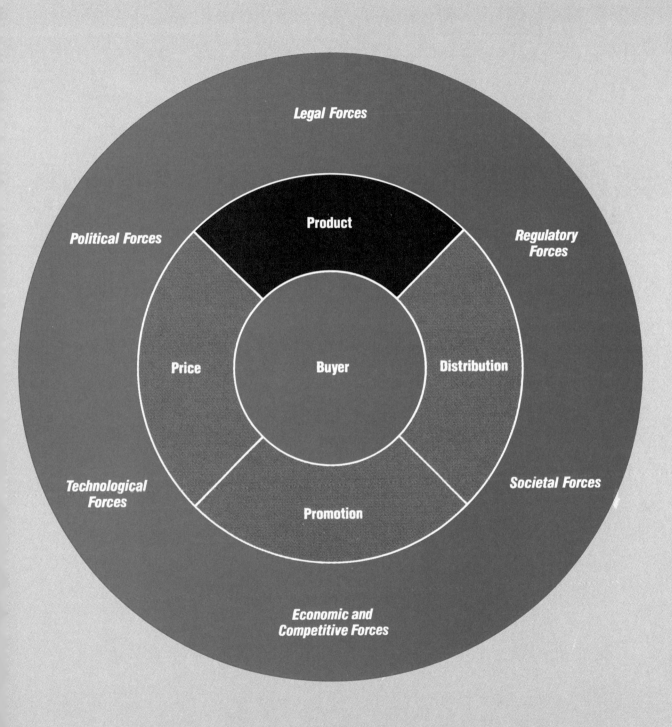

7 / Product Concepts

Objectives

- To learn how marketers define products.

- To understand how to classify products.

- To see how product mix and product line policies are developed.

- To develop an understanding of the concept of product life cycle.

- To grasp the basic product identification concepts as they relate to branding, packaging, and labeling.

Figure 7.1

AT&T emphasizes their product quality over that of their competitors (Source: AT&T)

With the 1984 breakup of "Ma Bell," consultants to the industry were predicting that consumers would rather purchase their telephones than lease them. As a result, many companies saw the home phone market as a major marketing opportunity. Some two hundred companies quickly added telephones to their product lines or expanded their existing lines of phones in hopes of cashing in on this new market (see Figure 7.1). The consultants' estimates have proven to be fairly accurate. Approximately 52 percent of the 146 million phones in service are owned by consumers. Yet despite these impressive figures, manufacturer and distributor losses have run into hundreds of millions of dollars.

Why the losses? Companies jumped into the market without considering what consumers wanted. Many companies, for example, turned to manufacturers in Hong Kong and Taiwan to produce inexpensive phone sets. These cheap phones were often defective, and those that did work produced sounds that were unfamiliar to consumers. It turns out that consumers want reliable telephones and prefer reputable name brands. Although

EVENTUALLY, CHEAP PHONES WILL FIND THEIR PLACE IN HISTORY.

People have a way of figuring out pretty fast what's good and what's not. And it looks like cheap phones aren't good enough. Especially if you're used to AT&T phones.

For over a century, people have counted on our phones to sound right and ring right and feel right. And they have —because we took the time to understand what "right" means to you.

Maybe in another century, you'll find other phones as good as AT&T's. But until then, there's one thing for certain.

You get what you pay for.

AT&T
The right choice.

AT&T guessed right in this respect, they also made a major mistake. AT&T developed 215 styles of telephones, some with fancy features like speakers and displays of the time or last number called, that cost up to $350. Consumers actually prefer more traditional phones like those they used to lease.[1]

Products are among a firm's most important and visible contacts with buyers. If a company's products do not meet the desires and needs of buyers, the company will fail unless adjustments are made. Developing a successful product requires knowledge of fundamental marketing and product concepts. The product is an important variable in the marketing mix, and other variables (promotion, distribution, and price) must be coordinated with product decisions.

The concepts and definitions that we discuss first in this chapter help clarify what a product is and how buyers view products. Product planners must consider what other products their company offers in the marketplace. Thus, an examination of the concepts of product mix and product line will help us understand product planning. However, a product is not created in a vacuum, nor does it exist in one. Therefore, we must look at the stages of product life cycles. Each life cycle stage generally requires a specific marketing strategy, assumes a certain competitive environment, and has its own profit pattern. Finally, since branding and packaging are vital components of a product—in fact, they help create the product—we explore these topics, along with labeling, an important informational device.

What Is a Product?

A **product** is everything, both favorable and unfavorable, that one receives in an exchange. It is a complexity of tangible and intangible attributes including functional, social, and psychological utilities or benefits.[2] A product can be an idea, a service, a good, or any combination of these three. This definition includes supporting services that go with goods, such as installation, guarantees, product information, and promises of repair or maintenance. (Chapter 21 provides a detailed discussion of marketing services.) Goods are tangible and have form utility. Services are intangible and provide facilitating or direct benefits. Ideas provide psychological stimulation that helps us solve problems or adjust to our environment.

When buyers purchase a product, they actually are buying the benefits and satisfaction they think the product will provide. A sports car is purchased for excitement and fun in driving, not merely for transportation. Buyers purchase services—insurance, education, health care, accounting, and air travel—on the basis of promises of satisfaction. Promises, together with the images and appearances of symbols, help consumers make judgments about both tangible and

1. Brian O'Reilly, "Lessons from the Home Phone Wars," *Fortune,* Dec. 24, 1984, pp. 83–86. © 1984 Time Inc. All rights reserved.
2. Part of this definition is adapted from S. H. Rewoldt, J. D. Scott, and M. R. Warshaw, *Introduction to Marketing Management,* 4th ed. (Homewood, Ill.: Irwin, 1981), p. 253.

intangible products.[3] Often symbols and cues are used to make intangible products more tangible or real to the consumer. Exxon has used a tiger for many years to communicate the chemical ingredients that produce power in its gasoline. Although gasoline is itself tangible, the average consumer rarely sees it and may have difficulty judging its performance. The financial services company Merrill Lynch uses a bull to symbolize its investment philosophy. The type of cue depends on the type of benefit to be stressed, regardless of the product or service being provided.[4]

Classifying Products

Products fall into one of two general categories, depending on the buyers' intentions. Products purchased to satisfy personal and family needs are **consumer products.** Those bought for use in a firm's operations or to make other products are **industrial products.** Consumers buy products to satisfy their personal wants, while industrial buyers seek to satisfy the goals of their organizations. Thus, the buyer's intent—or the ultimate use of the product—determines the classification of an item as either a consumer or an industrial product.

The same thing can be both a consumer product and an industrial product. For example, an electric light bulb is a consumer product if it is used in someone's home and an industrial product if it is purchased either to become part of another product or to light an assembly line. After a product is classified as either a consumer or an industrial product, it can be categorized further. In this section, we examine the characteristics of these subcategories and explore the marketing activities associated with some of them.

You may wonder why we need to know about product classifications. The primary reason is that classes of products are aimed at particular target markets, and this affects distribution, promotion, and pricing decisions. Industrial products, for example, usually require less advertising than consumer products do. Also, the types of marketing activities and efforts needed differ among the classes of consumer or industrial products. In short, the entire marketing mix can be affected by how a product is classified.

Classification of Consumer Products

Although there are several approaches to classifying consumer products, the traditional and most widely accepted approach consists of four categories: convenience products, shopping products, specialty products, and unsought products. This approach is based primarily on characteristics of buyers' purchasing behavior. One problem associated with the approach is that not all buyers behave in the same way when purchasing a specific type of product. Thus, a single product can fit into all four categories. To minimize this problem, marketers think in terms of how buyers *generally* behave when purchasing a specific item. In addition, they recognize that a product may fall into more

3. Theodore Levitt, "Marketing Intangible Products and Product Intangibles," *Harvard Business Review,* May–June 1981, pp. 94–102.
4. Kathleen A. Krentler and Joseph P. Guiltinan, "Strategies for Tangibilizing Retail Services: An Assessment," *Journal of the Academy of Marketing Science,* Fall 1984, p. 90.

than one category and that the "correct" classification can be determined only by considering a particular firm's intended target market. With these thoughts in mind, let us examine the four traditional categories of consumer products.

Convenience Products

Convenience products are relatively inexpensive, frequently purchased items for which buyers want to exert only minimal purchasing effort. Examples include bread, gasoline, newspapers, soft drinks, and chewing gum. The buyer spends little time either in planning the purchase of a convenience item or in comparing available brands or sellers. Even a buyer who prefers a specific brand will readily choose a substitute if the preferred brand is not conveniently available.

Classifying a specific product as a convenience product has several implications for a firm's marketing strategy. A convenience product normally is marketed through many retail outlets. Since sellers experience high inventory turnover of a convenience item, per-unit gross margins can be relatively low. Producers of convenience products such as Lays potato chips and Crest toothpaste can expect little promotional effort at the retail level and thus must provide it themselves in the form of product advertising. Packaging is an important element of the marketing mix. The package may have to sell the product, since a majority of convenience items are available only on a self-service basis at the retail level.

Shopping Products

Shopping products are items for which buyers are willing to expend considerable effort in planning and making the purchase. Buyers allocate considerable time for comparing stores and brands with respect to prices, product features, qualities, services, and perhaps warranties. Appliances, upholstered furniture, men's suits, bicycles, and stereos are examples of shopping products. Figure 7.2 shows a Technics compact disc player, an example of a shopping product. These products are expected to last for a fairly long time and thus are purchased less frequently than convenience items. Even though shopping products are more expensive than convenience products, few buyers of shopping products are particularly brand loyal.

To market a shopping product effectively, a marketer should consider several key issues. Shopping products require fewer retail outlets than convenience products do. Because shopping products are purchased less frequently, inventory turnover is lower and middlemen expect to receive higher gross margins. Although rather large sums of money may be required to advertise shopping products, an even larger percentage of resources is likely to be used for personal selling. Usually, a producer and the middlemen expect some cooperation from one another with respect to providing parts and repair services and performing promotional activities.

Specialty Products

Specialty products possess one or more unique characteristics, and a significant group of buyers is willing to expend considerable purchasing effort to obtain them. Buyers actually plan the purchase of a specialty product; they know exactly what they want and will not accept a substitute. A Jaguar automobile is an example of a specialty product. Another specialty product is cancer

Figure 7.2

The Technics compact disc player, an example of a shopping product (Source: Courtesy of Panasonic Co., Division of Matsushita Electric Corporation of America)

treatment at the Mayo Clinic. In searching for specialty products, purchasers do not compare alternatives. They are concerned primarily with finding an outlet that has a preselected product available.

That an item is a specialty product can affect a firm's marketing efforts in several ways. Specialty products are often distributed through a limited number of retail outlets. Like shopping goods, they are purchased infrequently, causing inventory turnover to be lower and thus requiring gross margins to be relatively high.

Unsought Products

Unsought products are purchased because of a sudden problem that needs to be solved or when aggressive selling is used to obtain a sale that otherwise would not take place. In general, the consumer does not think of buying these products on a regular basis. Emergency auto repairs and cemetery plots are classic examples of unsought products. Life insurance and encyclopedias, in contrast, are examples of products that need aggressive personal selling. The salesperson must try to make consumers aware of benefits that can be derived from the purchase of such products.

Industrial Products

Industrial products are purchased to produce other products or for use in a firm's operations. Purchases of industrial products are based on an organization's goals and objectives. Usually, the functional aspects of the product are much more important than the psychological rewards that sometimes are associated with consumer products. On the basis of their characteristics and intended uses, industrial products can be classified into seven categories: raw materials, major equipment, accessory equipment, component parts, process materials, supplies, and services.[5]

Raw Materials

Raw materials are the basic materials that actually become part of a physical product. They are provided from mines, farms, forests, oceans, and recycled solid wastes. Other than the processing required to transport and physically handle the products, raw materials have not been processed when a firm buys them. Raw materials are usually bought and sold according to grades and specifications. Purchasers frequently buy raw materials in relatively large quantities.

Major Equipment

Major equipment includes large tools and machines used for production purposes. Examples are lathes, cranes, and stamping machines. Usually, major equipment is expensive and is intended to be used in a production process for a considerable length of time. Some major equipment is custom made to perform specific functions for a particular organization, but other items are standardized products that perform one or several tasks for many types of organizations. Because of the high cost of major equipment, purchase decisions often are made by high-level management. Marketers of major equipment frequently must provide a variety of services including installation, training, repair and maintenance assistance, and even aid in financing the purchase.

Accessory Equipment

Accessory equipment does not become a part of the final physical product but is used in production or office activities. Figure 7.3 shows the office furniture that Bush sells as an accessory to major computer equipment. Other examples include hand tools, typewriters, fractional-horsepower motors, and calculators. Compared with major equipment, accessory items are usually much less expensive; are purchased routinely, with less negotiation; and are treated as expense items, rather than as capital items, because they are not expected to be used as long. Accessory products are standardized items that generally can be used in several aspects of a firm's operations. More outlets are required for accessory equipment than for major equipment, but sellers do not have to provide the multitude of services expected of major-equipment marketers.

Component Parts

Component parts become a part of the physical product and either are finished items ready for assembly or are products that need little processing before assembly. Although they become part of a larger product, component parts

---

5. Richard M. Hill, Ralph S. Alexander, and James S. Cross, *Industrial Marketing,* 2nd ed. (Homewood, Ill.: Irwin, 1975), p. 37.

often can be identified and distinguished easily. Spark plugs, tires, clocks, and switches are all component parts of the automobile. Buyers purchase such items according to their own specifications or industry standards. They expect the parts to be of specified quality and to be delivered on time so that production is not slowed or stopped. Producers that are primarily assemblers, such as most lawn-mower manufacturers, depend heavily on the suppliers of component parts.

Process Materials

Process materials are used directly in the production of other products. Unlike component parts, however, process materials are not readily identifiable. For example, Reichhold Chemicals, Inc., markets a treated fiber product—a phenolic-resin, sheet-molding compound. This material is used by a major aircraft manufacturer in the production of flight deck instrument panels and cabin interiors. Although the material is not identifiable in the finished panels and interiors, it retards burning, smoke, and toxic-gas formation if molded components are subjected to fire or high temperatures.[6] Like component parts, process materials are purchased according to industry standards or the purchaser's specifications.

6. Reichhold Chemicals, Inc., *Annual Report, 1980,* p. 11.

Supplies

Supplies facilitate production and operations, but they do not become part of the finished product. Paper, pencils, oils, cleaning agents, and paints are examples. Since such supplies are standardized items used in a variety of situations, they are purchased by many different types of organizations. Usually, supplies are sold through numerous outlets and are purchased routinely. To ensure that supplies are available when needed, buyers frequently deal with more than one seller. Because supplies can be divided into three categories—maintenance, repair, and operating (or overhaul) supplies—they are sometimes called **MRO items.**

Industrial Services

Industrial services are the intangible products that many organizations use in their operations. Examples include financial products, legal services, marketing research services, and janitorial services. Purchasers must decide whether to provide their own services internally or obtain them outside the organization. This decision depends greatly on the costs associated with each alternative and on how frequently the services are needed.

Product Mix and Product Line

Marketers must understand the relationships among all of an organization's products if they are to coordinate the marketing of the total group of products. The following concepts help to describe the relationships among an organization's products. A **product item** is a specific version of a product that can be designated as a distinct offering among an organization's products. A **product line** includes a group of closely related products that are considered a unit because of marketing, technical, or end-use considerations.

Consider the Gerber line of baby foods. A single item in the product line is Gerber's strained bananas. Gerber's nonfood baby product line includes clothes, nursery equipment, vaporizers, and hygiene aids. The nonfood baby product line is an interrelated unit because it is usually sold in a single area or department in a retail store. Also, television advertisements and other promotional activities treat the nonfood product line as a distinct group because all the products are used in caring for babies but they have different characteristics than the products in the baby food line. A **product mix** is the composite or total group of products that an organization makes available to consumers. Gerber's total product mix consists of hundreds of items. These products include adult foods and other items that are not made for babies.

The Product Mix

No matter how large an organization is, there is a limit to the number and variety of products that it can offer to buyers. Figure 7.4 illustrates Honda's power equipment product mix, which includes lawn tractors, tillers, snowblowers, generators, outboard motors, and lawn mowers. Usually, the **depth** of a product mix is measured by the number of different products offered in each product line. On the other hand, the **width** of the product mix measures the number

Figure 7.4 *Honda's power equipment product mix (Source: Courtesy of Honda Motor Co., Ltd.)*

of product lines offered by a company. Figure 7.5 illustrates these concepts by showing the width of the product mix (number of product lines) and the depth of each product line (number of items in each product line) for selected Procter & Gamble products.

Some companies such as Perrier have a very narrow and shallow product mix. On the other hand, a company selling only ice cream but offering many flavors, such as Baskin Robbins, has a narrow product mix but much depth.

The Product Line

A product line—that is, a related group of products in a product mix—is developed on the basis of marketing or technical considerations. Marketers must understand buyers' goals if they hope to come up with the optimum product line. Figure 7.6 illustrates the beer product line of Miller Brewing Company. Specific items in a product line usually reflect the desires of different target markets or the different needs of consumers. Look at Figure 7.5 again. Items in Procter & Gamble's toothpaste product line appeal to different target markets. Gleem is aimed at those concerned mainly with appearance and personal appeal; Crest stresses cavity prevention and good dental hygiene.

Procter & Gamble is known for using differential branding, packaging, and consumer advertising to promote individual items in its detergent product line. Tide, Bold, Gain, Bonus, Dash, Cheer, Oxydol, and Duz—all Procter & Gamble detergents—share the same distribution channels and similar manufacturing facilities. Yet each is promoted as distinctive, and this claimed uniqueness adds depth to the product line.

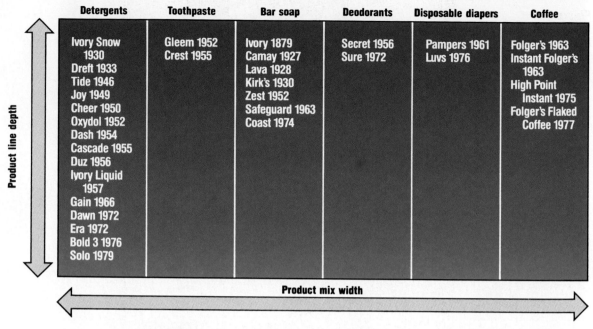

Detergents	Toothpaste	Bar soap	Deodorants	Disposable diapers	Coffee
Ivory Snow 1930 Dreft 1933 Tide 1946 Joy 1949 Cheer 1950 Oxydol 1952 Dash 1954 Cascade 1955 Duz 1956 Ivory Liquid 1957 Gain 1966 Dawn 1972 Era 1972 Bold 3 1976 Solo 1979	Gleem 1952 Crest 1955	Ivory 1879 Camay 1927 Lava 1928 Kirk's 1930 Zest 1952 Safeguard 1963 Coast 1974	Secret 1956 Sure 1972	Pampers 1961 Luvs 1976	Folger's 1963 Instant Folger's 1963 High Point Instant 1975 Folger's Flaked Coffee 1977

(Product line depth — vertical axis; Product mix width — horizontal axis)

Figure 7.5 *The concepts of product mix and product line depth applied to selected Procter & Gamble products*

Product Life Cycles

Products are like living organisms. They are born, they live, and they die. A new product is introduced into the marketplace; it grows; and when it loses appeal, it is terminated. Remember that our definition of a product focuses on both tangible and intangible attributes. Thus, the total product might not be just a good, but also the ideas and services attached to it. Packaging, branding, and labeling techniques alter or help to create products. And just as biological cycles progress through growth and decline, so do the life cycles of products. However, product life cycles can be modified by marketers. (The marketing strategies for different life cycle stages are discussed in Chapter 8.)

As shown in Figure 7.7, a **product life cycle** has four major stages: (1) introduction, (2) growth, (3) maturity, and (4) decline. As a product moves through its cycle, the strategies relating to competition, promotion, distribution, pricing, and market information must be periodically evaluated and possibly changed. Astute marketing managers use the life cycle concept to make sure that the introduction, alteration, and termination of a product are timed and executed properly. By understanding the typical life cycle pattern, marketers can, in theory at least, maintain profitable products and drop unprofitable ones.

Introduction

The **introduction stage** of the life cycle begins at a product's first appearance in the marketplace, when sales are zero and profits are negative. Profits are below zero because initial revenues are low at the same time that the firm usually must cover large expenses for promotion and distribution. Notice in

Figure 7.6

The beer product line of Miller Brewing Company (Source: Courtesy of Miller Brewing Company)

Figure 7.7 how sales should move upward from zero, while profits should move from below zero. In this stage, it is important to communicate product benefits to buyers. Very few new products represent major inventions. The reason is cost; developing and introducing a new product can cost $100 million or even more. The failure rate for new products is quite high, ranging from 33 to 90 percent. For example, L'ORÉAL introduced the first hairstyling mousse. In less than a year it had forty direct competitors. California Cooler marketed the first combination of wine and fruit juices but today is up against approximately forty other companies for the wine cooler business.[7] More typically, product introductions involve a new packaged convenience food, a new automobile model, or a new fashion in clothing, rather than a major product innovation.

During the introduction stage, potential buyers must be made aware of the product's features, uses, and advantages. For example in Figure 7.8, Mousse du Jour is introduced and positioned as an all-natural frozen mousse dessert with packaging similar to that of traditional ice cream. Two difficulties may arise at this point. There may be only a few sellers with the resources, technological knowledge, and marketing know-how to launch the product successfully; and initially, a high product price may be required to recoup expensive marketing research or development costs. Given these difficulties, it is not surprising that many products never get beyond the introduction stage.

7. Carrie Gottlieb, "Products of the Year," *Fortune,* Sept. 9, 1985, p. 107.

Figure 7.7

The four stages of the product life cycle

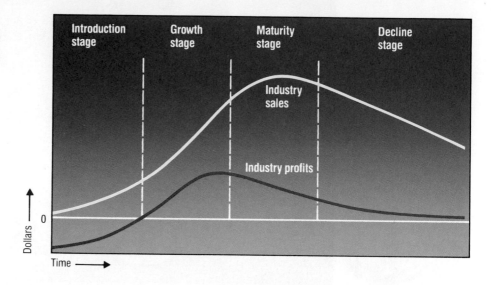

Growth

During the **growth stage,** sales rise rapidly while profits reach a peak and then start to decline (see Figure 7.7). The growth stage is critical to a product's survival because competitive reactions to the product's success during this period will affect its life expectancy. Profits decline late in the growth stage as more firms enter the market, driving prices down and creating the need for heavy promotional expenses. At this point a typical marketing strategy encourages strong brand loyalty and competes with aggressive emulators of the product. During the growth stage an enterprise tries to strengthen its market share by identifying the product's benefits and by emphasizing them to develop a competitive niche.

Aggressive promotional pricing including price cuts is typical during the growth stage. Today, the VCR industry in the United States is in the growth stage. Many competitors have entered the market. By adjusting their prices competitively, firms like Panasonic and RCA are able to maintain their market lead during the growth stage. They thus extend the life expectancy of their product far beyond that of marginal competitors.

Maturity

During the **maturity stage** the sales curve peaks and starts to decline while profits continue to decline (see Figure 7.7). This stage is characterized by severe competition as many brands enter the market. Competitors emphasize improvements and differences in their versions of the product. As a result, during the maturity stage weaker competitors are squeezed out or lose interest in the product. For example, as the jogging boom has leveled off with approximately 20 million runners in the United States, competition has become fierce in the running shoe industry. Nike was once the industry leader with 50 percent of the market, closing out many smaller competitors.[8]

Now, successful European imports such as Reebok have grabbed significant market share. At its lowest point, Nike experienced an inventory backlog of

8. Victor F. Zonana, "Jogging's Fade Fails to Push Nike Off Track," *Wall Street Journal,* March 5, 1981, p. 27.

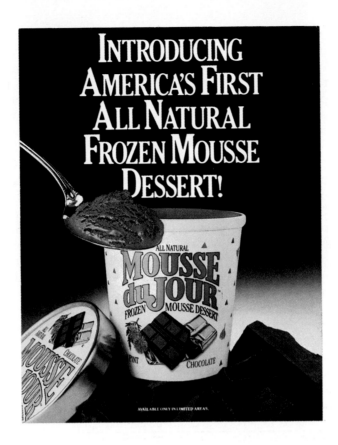

12 million pairs of unsold shoes. To counter this sales slump, Nike developed "Air Jordans," featuring a special gas pocket in the sole that provides a light, springy step. The shoe's namesake is Michael Jordan, a well-known professional basketball player. Nike's new product introduction successfully complemented the mature running shoe segment.[9]

When a product has reached the maturity phase, producers must make fresh promotional and distribution efforts; advertising and dealer-oriented promotions are typical during this stage of the product life cycle.

Those who remain in the market make fresh promotional and distribution efforts; advertising and dealer-oriented promotion are typical during this stage of the product life cycle. Also, as the product reaches maturity, buyers' knowledge of it reaches a high level. Consumers of the product are now no longer inexperienced generalists but experienced specialists. As buyers change, the benefits they seek change, for instance from full service to low price.[10]

Decline

During the **decline stage,** sales fall rapidly (see Figure 7.7). New technology or a new social trend may cause product sales to take a sharp turn downward. When this happens, the marketer considers pruning items from the product line to eliminate those not returning a profit. At this time, the marketer may

9. "Nike's Air Jordan," *Fortune,* Dec. 9, 1985, p. 112.
10. E. Steward De Bruicker and Gregory L. Summe, "Make Sure Your Customers Keep Coming Back," *Harvard Business Review,* Jan.–Feb. 1985, p. 92.

cut promotion efforts, eliminate marginal distributors, and, finally, plan to phase out the product.

Since most enterprises have a product mix, a firm's destiny is rarely tied to one product. A composite of life cycle patterns is formed when various products in the mix are at different cycle stages. As one product is declining, other products are in the introduction, growth, or maturity stages. Marketers must deal with the dual problem of prolonging existing products and introducing new products to meet organizational sales goals. For example, General Mills has prolonged the product life cycle of Bisquick prepared biscuit mix by materially improving the product since it was introduced in the mid-1930s. But General Mills has also continued to introduce new products, such as Betty Crocker's Pop Secret. Pop Secret is shelf-stable microwave popcorn. The new product competes against Pillsbury and Orville Redenbacher's microwave popping corn but has twice the advertising budget of the competition.[11] The microwave brands, which account for approximately one-third of the unpopped popcorn market, are the fastest growing market segment. Today, half of all U.S. households have a microwave oven, versus 19 percent in 1980.[12] General Mills differentiates its brand and its appeal to consumers by promoting that Pop Secret will pop in microwave ovens of any wattage. The competition works best in high-wattage ovens. We examine approaches to developing new products and managing products in their various life cycle stages in the next chapter.

Branding

Marketers must make many product decisions associated with branding, such as brands, brand names, brand marks, trademarks, and trade names. A **brand** is a name, term, symbol, design, or a combination thereof that identifies a seller's products and differentiates them from competitors' products.[13] A **brand name** is that part of a brand which can be spoken—including letters, words, and numbers—such as 7UP. A brand name is often a product's only distinguishing characteristic. Without the brand name, a firm could not identify its products. To consumers, brand names are as fundamental as the product itself. Brand names simplify shopping, guarantee quality, and allow self-expression.[14] The element of a brand that cannot be spoken, often a symbol or design, is called a **brand mark.** An example is the inscribed anchor on Anchor Hocking glassware. Figure 7.9 shows how Nabisco's familiar brand mark has changed over the years. A **trademark** is a legal designation indicating that the owner has exclusive use of a brand or a part of a brand and that others are prohibited by law from using it. In the United States, to protect a brand name or brand mark, an organization must register it as a trademark with the U.S. Patent Office. Finally, a **trade name** is the legal name of an organization, such as Ford Motor Company or Safeway Stores, Inc., rather than the name of a specific product.

11. Janet Neiman, "General Mills Pops Big-Buck Budget," *Adweek,* Nov. 11, 1985, p. 82.
12. "Microwaves Spur Frozen Food Sales," *Duns Business Month,* July 1985, p. 24.
13. Adapted from Committee on Definitions, *Marketing Definitions: A Glossary of Marketing Terms* (Chicago: American Marketing Association, 1960), p. 8. Used by permission.
14. James U. McNeal and Linda Zeren, "Brand Name Selection for Consumer Products," *MSU Business Topics,* Spring 1981, p. 35.

Figure 7.9

Nabisco's trademarks from 1900 to the present (Source: Courtesy of Nabisco Brands, Inc.)

Benefits of Branding

As we note above, branding can provide benefits to both buyers and sellers. Brands aid buyers by identifying specific products that they like and do not like, which in turn facilitates the purchase of items that satisfy individual needs. Without brands, product selection would be rather random since buyers could not be assured that what they purchased was the preferred item. A brand also assists buyers in evaluating the quality of products, especially when a person lacks the ability to judge a product's characteristics. That is, a brand may symbolize a certain quality level to a purchaser, and the person in turn allows that perception of quality to represent the quality of the item.

As an example, a car buyer associates certain quality levels with the automobile brands Plymouth, Ford, and Chevrolet. Although a buyer may go through a "ritual" of slamming doors, kicking tires, and starting the engine to judge a car's quality, this behavior provides little information to most people. Actually, the brand name is among the main indicators of quality to the prospective car buyer.

Another benefit a brand can provide is the psychological reward that comes from owning a brand that symbolizes status. Certain brands of watches (Rolex), automobiles (Mercedes Benz), and shoes (Allen-Edmonds and Nichols), for example, fall into this category.

Sellers benefit from branding because each firm's brands identify its products, which facilitates repeat purchasing by consumers. To the extent that buyers become loyal to a specific brand, the firm's market share for that product achieves a certain level of stability. The application on page 217 discusses how R.J. Reynolds with Nabisco Brands has created success with loyalty to their brands. A stable market share allows a firm to use its resources more efficiently. When a firm develops some degree of customer loyalty to a brand, it can charge a premium price for the product. The producer of Bayer aspirin enjoys this position. Branding also aids an organization in introducing a new product that carries the name of one or more of its existing products, for buyers are already familiar with the firm's existing brands. For example, Coca-Cola is testing a variety of new soft drink flavors such as Vanilla Coke, Lemon Coke, Chocolate Coke, Cream Coke, and a berry-flavored Coke. Carrying the Coke logo would give these potential new products quicker recognition and trial in the marketplace than would an unfamiliar brand name.[15] Finally, branding facilitates promotional efforts because the promotion of each branded product indirectly promotes all other products that are similarly branded.

Types of Brands

There are two categories of brands: manufacturer brands and private distributor brands. **Manufacturer brands** are initiated by producers and make it possible for producers to be identified with their products at the point of purchase. Green Giant, Sylvania, and Exxon are examples. A manufacturer brand usually requires a producer to get involved with distribution, promotion, and, to some extent, pricing decisions. Brand loyalty is created by promotion, quality control, and guarantees; it is a valuable asset to a manufacturer. The producer tries to stimulate demand for the product, which tends to encourage middlemen to make the product available.

Private distributor brands, or **private brands,** are initiated and owned by resellers (marketing organizations that buy products for the purpose of reselling them). The major characteristic of private brands is that manufacturers are not identified on the products. Retailers and wholesalers use private distributor brands to develop more efficient promotion, to generate higher gross margins, and to improve store images. Private distributor brands give retailers or wholesalers freedom to purchase products of a specified quality at the lowest cost without disclosing the identity of the manufacturer.

Wholesaler brands include IGA (Independent Grocers' Alliance) and Topmost (General Grocer). Familiar retailer brand names include Kenmore (Sears, Roebuck) and Penncraft (J. C. Penney). Many successful private brands are distributed nationally. The Sears Die-Hard battery is at least as well known as most manufacturer brands. The private-brand tires sold by such stores as K mart and Montgomery Ward are manufactured by major tire companies—Firestone, Goodrich, Goodyear, Uni-Royal, and others. Sometimes retailers with successful distributor brands start manufacturing their own products in the hope of increasing profits and gaining even more control over their products.

Competition between manufacturer brands and private distributor brands (sometimes called "the battle of the brands") is becoming more intense in several major product categories. For example, Sears' and J. C. Penney's private brands of jeans have half as much market share as does Levi Strauss, the market leader.[16] In the grocery trade, private distributor's brands now account for approximately 28 percent of total turnover in thirty-eight major grocery classes, a growth rate of almost 6 percent over the last four years.[17]

Developing multiple manufacturer brands and distribution systems has been an effective means of combating the increased competition from private brands. Holiday Inn has effectively developed several different brand names appealing to varying lifestyles and needs. Traditionally, lodging was categorized as budget, midscale, and upscale. Now more categories are recognized and appealed to,

---

15. "Coke Testing Tastes for Everyone," *Adweek,* November 11, 1985, p. 85.
16. "It's Back to Basics for Levi's," *Business Week,* March 8, 1982, p. 77.
17. Arthur C. Nielsen, Jr., "The Development of Industry Brands & Distributors' Brands in Europe and the United States: Comparisons and Conclusions for the Future," *The Nielsen Researcher,* no. 2, 1984, pp. 2–19.

Application

**Brands with
Staying Power**

The merger of R.J. Reynolds Industries, Inc. with Nabisco Brands, Inc. has created one of the largest consumer goods producers, with many well-known brand names. Major brands include Del Monte canned fruits and vegetables; Camel, Winston, and Salem cigarettes; Oreo cookies, Ritz crackers, Premium Saltines, and other Nabisco products.

According to R.J. Reynolds, all successful brands have these three characteristics:

1. They satisfy a need or desire.
2. They offer value and provide a reliable and consistent quality.
3. They are continuously updated and repositioned, repackaged, or reformulated as consumer preferences change.

Here is an example of how two major brands have changed over the years.

Camel cigarettes were the first brand to have wide acceptance in the United States. In 1913, the U.S. was told "The Camels are Coming." Camel was a top seller for many years until filter cigarettes gained favor. At this time Camel took the product into the international market. Camel had long been recognized outside the United States as the cigarette of the American soldier. Camels soon became very strong in these markets. Domestic performance also improved as a result of the line's extension to include filter and "light" cigarettes. Camels are just one example of R.J. Reynolds' marketing savvy.

Shortly before Camels were introduced in 1912, the National Biscuit Company offered three versions of their premium quality biscuits, Mother Goose Biscuits, Veronese Biscuits, and the Oreo Biscuit. Nabisco, as the firm was later known, had the highest hopes for the first two products. But it was the Oreo Biscuit which gained national acceptance. This biscuit has changed size many times over the years and has been referred to as a biscuit sandwich, creme sandwich, and chocolate sandwich cookie; Oreos have also experienced numerous packaging changes. The basic product, however, has remained as it was described in 1912, "Two beautifully embossed, chocolate-filled wafers with rich cream filling." Recent line extensions of the successful Oreo cookie include Double Stuff with twice as much filling and Mint Creme Chocolate Sandwich Cookies. (*Source: "The Staying Power of Brand Names,"* RJR Report, *3rd Quarter 1985, p. 56.*)

for example, all-suite, extended stay, and residence hotels. Holiday Inn has expanded into four types of lodging: Hampton Inns, budget; Embassy Suite, all suites; Residence Inn, apartments; and Crown Plaza, upscale.[18] By developing a new brand name, manufacturers can adjust various elements of the marketing mix to appeal to a different target market. For example, Scott Paper has developed lower-priced brands of paper towels. They have tailored their new products to a target market that tends to purchase private brands.

It is difficult for manufacturers to ignore the market opportunities to be gained by producing private distributor brands. Usually, if a manufacturer refuses to produce a private brand, a competing manufacturer will get the

18. "A Variety of Lodging 'Brands' Enables Holiday Inns to Cater to Independent-Minded People," *Marketing News,* Oct. 25, 1985, p. 29.

business. Also, the production of private distributor brands allows the manufacturer to use excess capacity during periods when its own brands are at nonpeak production. The final decision about whether to produce a private or a manufacturer brand depends on an enterprise's resources, production capabilities, and goals.

Selecting and Protecting a Brand

The choice of a brand is a critical decision because the name affects customers' images and attitudes toward a product, and sometimes toward a firm. Thus, it ultimately affects purchase decisions. Nissan Motors Corporation, U.S.A., has dropped its well-known Datsun brand name and replaced it with the Nissan corporate name. *Datsun* had an 85-percent recognition rate compared with 10–15 percent for *Nissan,* but a company representative stated, "It's essential to unify the name of the company and the brand name in order to pursue our global strategy. . . ."[19] At the time, Nissan was selling products under different corporate identities in 130 countries. This situation apparently complicated expanding overseas operations.

Marketers should consider a variety of issues when they select a brand name. The name should be easy for customers to say, spell, and recall (including foreign buyers, if the firm intends to market its products in other countries). Short, one-syllable names like *Cheer* often satisfy this requirement. If possible, the brand name should suggest in a positive way the product's uses and special characteristics. Negative or offensive references should be avoided. For example, a deodorant spray against underarm body odor should not be called *Sweat.* Instead, it should be branded with a name that connotes freshness, dryness, or perhaps long-lasting protection as *Ban, Arid,* and *Ice Blue Secret* do. The name should be descriptive of the product's major benefits. In a recent survey of large, consumer goods producers, almost 60 percent of the respondents reported that the latter issue is a major criterion in brand name selection.[20]

If a marketer intends to use a brand for a product line, it must be designed to be compatible with all products in the line. The manufacturer of Hotpoint products (a brand originally used on kitchen ranges) may have had some misgivings about the name when it introduced Hotpoint room air conditioners. Finally, a brand should be designed so that it can be used and recognized in all types of media.

To protect the firm's exclusive rights to a brand, the company should be certain that the selected brand is not likely to be considered an infringement on any existing brand already registered with the U.S. Patent Office. This task may be complex because infringement is determined by the courts. They base their decisions on whether a brand causes consumers to be confused, mistaken, or deceived about the source of the product.[21] In recent years, the producers of such brands as Ultra Brite, Tylenol, Scrabble, Tic Tac, and Playboy have brought infringement charges against competing brands. Coca-Cola, with a trademark research department of twenty-five people, files forty to sixty suits annually to protect its brands.[22]

19. "A Worldwide Brand for Nissan," *Business Week,* Aug. 24, 1981, p. 104.
20. McNeal and Zeren, "Brand Name Selection," p. 37.
21. George Miaoulis and Nancy D'Amato, "Consumer Confusion and Trademark Infringement," *Journal of Marketing,* April 1978, pp. 48–49.
22. Frank Delano, "Keeping Your Trade Name or Trademark Out of Court," *Harvard Business Review,* March–April 1982, p. 73.

The marketer should also design a brand that can be protected through registration. Because of their designs, some brands can be infringed upon more easily than others. Although registration protects trademarks domestically for twenty years and can be renewed indefinitely, a firm should develop a system that ensures that its trademarks will be renewed as needed. If possible, a marketer must guard against allowing a brand name to become a generic term used to refer to a general product category. Generic terms cannot be protected as exclusive brand names. For example, names such as *cellophane, linoleum,* and *shredded wheat*—all brand names at one time— eventually were declared to be generic terms that refer to product classes; thus, they no longer could be protected.

To keep a brand name from becoming a generic term, the firm should spell it with a capital letter and should use it as an adjective to modify the name of the general product class, as in *Lysol Disinfectant.*[23] Including the word *brand* just after the brand name is also helpful. An organization can deal with this problem directly by advertising that its brand is a trademark and should not be used generically. The firm can also indicate that the brand is trademarked with the symbol ®.

A U.S. firm that tries to protect a brand in a foreign country frequently encounters problems. In many foreign countries, brand registration is not possible; the first firm to use a brand in such a country has the rights to it. In some instances, a U.S. company has actually had to buy its own brand rights from a firm in a foreign country because the foreign firm was the first user in that country. In Italy (one of the world's biggest producers of counterfeit brands) one can purchase fake Cartier watches, Marlboro brand cigarettes, and Levi's jeans (the fake Levi's do not fade). None of the products are made by the U.S. firms that own these brands. But not all of the fake merchandise is manufactured in foreign countries. Roughly 20 percent of the bogus merchandise is made in the U.S. The Counterfeit Intelligence Bureau in London estimates that roughly $60 billion in annual world trade involves counterfeit merchandise.[24]

Branding Policies

In attempting to establish branding policies, the first decision to be made is whether the firm should brand its products at all. When an organization's product is homogeneous and is similar to competitors' products, it may be difficult to brand. Raw materials, such as coal, sand, and farm produce, are hard to brand because of the homogeneity of such products and also because of their physical characteristics.

Some marketers of products that have traditionally been branded have embarked on a policy of not branding, often called generic branding. A **generic brand** indicates only the product category (such as aluminum foil) and does not include the company name or other identifying terms. Many supermarkets are selling generic brands at lower prices than they sell comparable branded items. Purchasers of generic-branded grocery items tend to be concentrated in middle income, large households that are price conscious and predisposed to select regularly low-priced alternatives, as opposed to temporarily lower-priced products. Much of the growth in generic grocery brand sales has thus

23. "Trademark Stylesheet," U.S. Trademark Association, No. 1A.
24. Thomas C. O'Donnell and Elizabeth Weiner, "The Counterfeit Trade," *Business Week,* December 16, 1985, pp. 64–68, 72.

been at the expense of private distributor brands.[25] It is estimated that in 1985 generic brands represented 10 percent of all grocery sales.[26]

Assuming that a firm chooses to brand its products, marketers may opt for one or more of the following branding policies: individual branding, overall family branding, line family branding, and brand-extension branding.

Individual branding is a policy of naming each product something different. A major advantage of individual branding is that when an organization introduces a poor product, the negative images associated with it do not contaminate the company's other products. An individual branding policy may also facilitate market segmentation when a firm wishes to enter many segments of the same market. Separate, unrelated names can be used, and each brand can be aimed at a specific segment. As mentioned earlier, Procter & Gamble relies on an individual branding policy for its line of detergents, which includes Tide, Bold, Dash, Cheer, and Oxydol.

In **overall family branding,** all of a firm's products are branded with the same name or at least part of the name. Examples include *Sealtest* and *General Electric.* In some cases, a company's name is combined with other words to brand items. Arm & Hammer has used its name on all of its products along with a generic description of the product. Arm & Hammer Heavy Duty Detergent, Arm & Hammer Pure Baking Soda, and Arm & Hammer Carpet Deodorizer are examples.[27] Unlike individual branding, overall family branding means that the promotion of one item with the family brand promotes the firm's other products.

Sometimes an organization uses family branding only for products within a line rather than for all its products. This policy is called **line family branding.** The same brand is used within a line, but the firm does not use the same name for a product in a different line. Colgate-Palmolive Co., for example, produces a line of cleaning products including a cleanser, a powdered detergent, and a liquid cleaner, all of which carry the name *Ajax.* Colgate also produces several brands of toothpaste, none of which carry the Ajax brand.

Brand-extension branding occurs when a firm uses one of its existing brand names as part of a brand for an improved or new product that is usually in the same product category as the existing brand (the application on Coca-Cola illustrates how Coke has dropped its individual branding strategy in favor of brand-extension branding). The makers of Arrid deodorant eventually extended the name *Arrid* to Arrid Extra-Dry and Arrid Double-X. There is one major difference between line family branding and brand-extension branding. With the former, all products in the line carry the same name, but with the latter, this is not the case. The producer of Arrid deodorant, for example, also makes other brands of deodorants.

An organization's marketers are not limited to a single branding policy. Instead, branding policy is influenced by the number of products and product

25. Martha R. McEnally and Jon M. Hawes, "The Market for Generic Brand Grocery Products: A Review and Extension," *Journal of Marketing,* Winter 1984, pp. 75–83.
26. "Metamorphosis: Now They're with Names, Colorful Labels," *Marketing News,* April 30, 1985, p. 1.
27. Gerald Schoenfeld, "Line Extensions: Milking a Name for All It's Worth," *Adweek,* Nov. 18, 1985, pp. 44, 46.

The Coca-Cola Company always followed a strict individual branding strategy—
Coke was the name of its regular cola, and *Tab* was the name of its diet cola.
But, since the mid-seventies, Pepsi has come on so strong that today Coke and
Pepsi have an almost equal share of supermarket shelf space and the soft-drink
market. In response to Pepsi's challenge, Coke has dropped its individual
branding in favor of brand extension. By using the name *Coke* on numerous
new soft drinks, the firm is hoping that consumers will associate the quality
image of Coke with the new line. The famous trademark now graces the labels
of six Coke versions—New Coke, Caffeine-Free Coke, Diet Coke, Caffeine-Free
Diet Coke, Cherry Coke, and Classic Coke. Most of these products have sold
well, but the success of Diet Coke has hurt the sales of Tab, rather than those
of Pepsi. Since the introduction of Diet Coke, the sales of Tab have dropped by
30 percent, and beverage analysts are waiting to see if Coca-Cola's brand
extension will further erode Tab's market share and also draw from, rather than
add to, Coke's former non-diet audience. Meanwhile, the Coca-Cola Company is
trying to reformulate and market Tab as a tart, dry-tasting alternative for diet-
soda drinkers. *(Sources: "Trying to Recapture Tab's Sweet Success*, Business
Week, *June 11, 1984, p. 174; Monci Jo Williams, "Soft Drink Wars: The Next
Battle,"* Fortune, *June 24, 1985, pp. 71–72; and Barbara Kallen, "Cola Clones,"*
Forbes, *May 7, 1984, p. 133.)*

lines produced by the firm, the characteristics of its target markets, the number
and types of competing products available, and the size of the firm's resources.
Anheuser-Busch, for example, employs both individual and brand-extension
branding. Most of the brands are individual brands. However, the Michelob
Light brand is an extension of the Michelob brand.

A more recent trend in branding strategies involves the licensing of trademarks.
Companies will allow approved manufacturers to use their trademark on other
products for a licensing fee. Royalties may be as low as 2 percent of wholesale
revenues or better than 10 percent. As recently as 1980, only a few firms such
as Playboy licensed their corporate trademarks. Today, licensing is a $6-billion
business and growing. Harley-Davidson has authorized use of its name on such
unrelated products as cologne, wine coolers, gold rings, and polo shirts. Coca-
Cola, however, has moved into licensing in hopes of protecting its trademark.
The Coca-Cola name appears or is scheduled to appear on products in fourteen
different product areas, including glassware, radios, trucks, and clothing.[28] The
major advantages of licensing include the following: extra revenues, little cost,
free publicity, new images, and trademark protection. The major disadvantages
include a lack of manufacturing control, which could hurt the company's name,
and bombarding consumers with too many unrelated products bearing the
same name.

28. Frank E. James, "I'll Wear the Coke Pants Tonight; They Go Well with My Harley-Davidson
Ring," *Wall Street Journal,* June 6, 1985, p. 31.

Packaging

Packaging involves the development of a container and a graphic design for a product. A package can be a vital part of a product. It can make the product more versatile, safer, or easier to use. Like a brand name, a package can also influence customers' attitudes toward a product, which in turn affects their purchase decisions. For example, Noxell is introducing its traditional Noxzema Skin Cream in a new package, the pump container (see Figure 7.10).

Buyers' impressions of a product, formed at the point of purchase or during use, are significantly influenced by package characteristics. In this section, we examine the major functions of packaging and consider several major packaging decisions. We also analyze the role of the package in a market strategy.

Packaging Functions

Effective packaging involves more than simply putting products in containers and covering them with wrappers. Packaging materials serve several primary functions. First, they protect the product or maintain its functional form. Product tampering recently has become a problem for marketers of many types of products, and several packaging techniques are being used to counter the problem. Fluids such as milk, orange juice, and hair spray need packages that preserve and protect them. The protection of the product should be effective in reducing damage that could affect its usefulness and increase costs. Another function of packaging is to offer the convenience that consumers often look for. For example, aseptic packages, individual-sized boxes or plastic bags that contain liquids, have had the strongest appeal among children and young adults who have active lifestyles. Juice manufacturers have benefited greatly from this packaging development. Formerly, their target market was 25–54-year-olds; the convenience of the package makes their product more appealing to a much younger market. For example, when Ocean Spray introduced its Cranberry juice in aseptic packaging, sales rose 20 percent.[29] The size or shape of a package may relate to the product's storage, convenience of use, or replacement rate. Small, single-serving cans of vegetables, for instance, may prevent waste and facilitate storage. A third function of packaging is to promote a product by communicating its features, uses, benefits, and image.

Major Packaging Considerations

Marketers must consider many factors as they develop packages. Obviously, one major consideration is cost. Although a variety of packaging materials, processes, and designs are available, some are rather expensive. In recent years buyers have shown a willingness to pay more for improved packaging, but there are limits. Marketers should try to determine through research just how much customers are willing to pay for packages.

Marketers must also decide whether to package the product singly or in multiple units. Multiple packaging is likely to increase demand because it increases the amount of the product available at the point of consumption (in one's home, for example). However, multiple packaging is not appropriate for infrequently used products since buyers do not like to tie up their dollars or

29. "Knowing a Drink by Its Cover," *American Demographics*, April 1985, p. 16.

Figure 7.10

Noxell has packaged its traditional skin cream in a new pump (Source: Courtesy of Noxell Corporation)

Figure 7.10

Noxell has packaged its traditional skin cream in a new pump (Source: Courtesy of Noxell Corporation)

store these products for a long time. Multiple packaging *can*, however, make products easier to handle and store (just think of six-packs used for soft drinks); and special price offers, such as a two-for-one sale, are facilitated through multiple packaging. In addition, multiple packaging may increase consumer acceptance of a product by encouraging the buyer to try it several times. On the other hand, since they must buy several units when multiple packaging is used, customers may hesitate to try the product in the first place.

Marketers should consider how much continuity among an organization's package designs is desirable. No continuity may be the best policy, especially if a firm's products are unrelated or are aimed at vastly different target markets. To promote an overall company image, a firm may decide that all packages are to be similar or are to include one major element of the design. This approach is called **family packaging.** Sometimes, this approach is used only for lines of products, as can be seen with Campbell's soups, Weight Watchers' foods, and Planter's nuts.

The promotional role of a package should be considered. It can be used to attract customers' attention and encourage them to examine the product.

Through verbal and nonverbal symbols, the package can inform potential buyers about the product's content, features, uses, advantages, and hazards. A firm can create desirable images and associations by its choice of color, design, shape, and texture. Many cosmetics manufacturers, for example, design their packages to create impressions of richness, luxury, and exclusiveness. A package may perform a promotional function when it is designed to be safer or more convenient to use if such characteristics help stimulate demand.

To develop a package that has a definite promotional value, a designer must consider size, shape, texture, color, and graphics. Beyond the obvious limitation that the package must be large enough to hold the product, a package can be designed to appear taller or shorter. Thin vertical lines, for example, make a package appear taller, while wide horizontal stripes make it look shorter. In some cases a marketer may want a package to appear taller because many people perceive something that is taller as being larger.

The shape of the package can help communicate a particular message. Research and successful promotions have led marketers to stereotype the sexes. They offer men packages with angular shapes and wood or burlap textures. Women's packages, on the other hand, have rounded, curved shapes and soft, fuzzy textures.

Colors on packages are often chosen to attract attention. People associate certain feelings and connotations with specific colors. Red, for example, is linked with fire, blood, danger, and anger; yellow suggests sunlight, caution, warmth, and vitality; blue can imply coldness, sky, water, and sadness.[30] When selecting packaging colors, marketers must first decide whether a particular color will evoke positive or negative feelings when it is used with a specific type of product. Rarely, for example, do processors package meat or bread in green materials because customers may associate green with mold. A sunburn ointment is more likely to appear in a soothing blue package than in a fiery red one. Marketers must also decide whether a specific target market will respond favorably or unfavorably to a particular color. Cosmetics for women are much more likely to be sold in pastel packaging than are personal care products for men. Packages designed to appeal to young children often use primary colors and bold designs.

Packaging and Marketing Strategy

Packaging can be a major component of a marketing strategy. A unique cap or closure, a better box or wrapper, or a more convenient container size may give a firm a competitive advantage. Packaging of consumer products is extremely important at the point of sale. Manufacturers of beer, detergents, and most packaged foods spend a great deal of money to research consumers' reactions to packages. Usually, however, there is a direct relationship between a product's package and its cost. The marketer must manage this trade-off to provide the desired benefits.

As package designs improve, it is harder for any one product to dominate on the basis of packaging. For example, Stouffer's decided to package its frozen

30. James U. McNeal, *Consumer Behavior: An Integrative Approach* (Boston: Little, Brown, 1982), pp. 221–222.

foods in orange boxes so that they would visually dominate the frozen food section where they compete.[31] As competitors have developed more eye-catching packaging, Stouffer's advantage has eroded. The typical large store stocks fifteen thousand items. Thus, the product that "stands out" is more likely to be purchased. Today skilled artists and package designers, who have experience in marketing research, test packaging to see what sells well, not just what is aesthetically appealing.[32]

Packaging must also take into account the needs of middlemen. Resellers (wholesalers and retailers) consider whether a package facilitates transporting, storing, and handling of the product. In some cases, resellers refuse to carry certain products because their packages are too troublesome.

Labeling

Labeling, too, is an important dimension related to packaging, not only for promotional and informational reasons, but also from a legal perspective. The Food and Drug Administration and the Consumer Product Safety Commission can require products to be labeled or marked with warnings, instructions, certifications, and manufacturer's identifications. Federal laws require disclosure of such data as textile identifications, potential hazards, and nutritional information. Del Monte Corp. introduced nutritional labeling before it was required by federal law. In this case, the eventual legal requirement worked to the advantage of the marketer. Consumers responded favorably to the nutritional information, and Del Monte gained a competitive edge over manufacturers who did not disclose nutritional values. Yet, despite the fact that consumers have responded favorably to the inclusion of this type of information on labels, there is little evidence that they actually use it. In fact, research results have been mixed—several studies indicate that consumers do not use nutritional information, while others indicate that the information is useful.[33] Labels also can be used to promote other products of the manufacturer or to encourage proper use of products and therefore greater satisfaction with them.

Color and eye-catching graphics on labels overcome the jumble of words—known to designers as "mouse print"—that have been added to satisfy government regulations. More direct cues about what a product is or does, often a striking photograph of the product itself, are now found on the front panel.[34] Since so many similar products are available, an attention-getting device, or "silent salesperson," is needed to attract interest. As one of the most visible parts of a product, the label is an important element in the marketing mix.

31. Bill Abrams and David P. Garino, "Package Design Gains Stature as Visual Competition Grows," *Wall Street Journal,* Aug. 6, 1981, p. 25.
32. Ibid.
33. Jeffrey W. Totten, "The Effect of Nutrition Information on Brand Rating—An Extension," in *Marketing Comes of Age,* David M. Klein and Allen E. Smith, eds. (Southern Marketing Association, 1984), pp. 48–50 and Jim L. Grimm and James B. Spalding, Jr., "Shoppers' Perceptions and Use of Nutritional Label Information," in *Marketing: Theories and Concepts for an Era of Change* (Southern Marketing Association, 1983).
34. "Packaging Design Seen as Cost-Effective Marketing Strategy," *Marketing News,* Feb. 20, 1981, p. 1.

Other Product-related Characteristics

When developing products, marketers make many decisions. Some of these involve the physical characteristics of the product, while others focus on less tangible supportive services that are very much a part of the total product.

Physical Characteristics of the Product

A major question that arises during product development is how much quality to build into the product. A major dimension of a product's quality is its durability. Frequently, higher quality calls for better materials and more expensive processing, which increase production costs and, ultimately, the product's price. In determining the specific level of quality, a marketer must know or ascertain approximately what price the target market views as acceptable. In addition, a marketer usually tries to set a level for a specific product that is consistent with the firm's other products that carry a similar brand. Obviously, the quality of competing brands is a consideration.

A product's physical features require careful consideration by marketers. The prime basis for decisions about them should be the desires of target market members. If marketers do not know what physical features people in the target market want in a product, then it will be an accident if the product is satisfactory. Even a firm whose existing products have been designed to satisfy target market desires should assess these desires periodically to determine whether they have changed enough to require alterations in such features as textures, colors, or sizes. (Product modification is discussed in Chapter 8.)

Supportive Product-related Services

All products, whether they are goods or not, possess intangible qualities: "When prospective customers can't experience the product in advance, they are asked to buy what are essentially promises—promises of satisfaction. Even tangible, testable, feelable, smellable products are, before they're bought, largely just promises."[35] Here, we provide a brief discussion of three product-related services: warranties, repairs and replacements, and credit. There are, of course, many other product-related services and product intangibles.

The type of warranty a firm provides can be a critical issue for buyers, especially when expensive, technically complex products such as appliances are involved. A **warranty** specifies what the producer will do if the product malfunctions. In recent years, government actions have required a warrantor to state more simply and specifically the terms and conditions under which the firm will take action. Because warranties must be more precise today, marketers are using them more vigorously as tools to give their brands a competitive advantage.

A marketer must be concerned with establishing a system to provide replacement parts and repair services. This support service is especially important for expensive, complex products that buyers expect to last a long time. Although the producer may provide these services directly to buyers, it is more common for the producer to provide such services through regional service centers or through middlemen. Regardless of how services are provided, it is important to customers that they be performed quickly and correctly.

35. Levitt, "Marketing Intangible Products and Product Intangibles," p. 96.

Finally, a firm must sometimes provide credit services to customers. Even though doing so places financial burdens on an organization, it can yield several benefits. Providing credit services can help a firm obtain and maintain a stable market share. Many major oil companies, for example, have competed effectively against gasoline discounters by providing credit services. For marketers of relatively expensive items, offering credit services allows a larger number of people to buy the product, thus enlarging the market for the item. Another reason for offering credit services is to earn interest income from customers. The types of credit services offered depend on the characteristics of target market members, the firm's financial resources, the type of products sold, and the types of credit services offered by competitors.

Summary

A product is much more than a physical object or a service rendered. It includes everything that a customer receives in an exchange. It is a complex set of tangible and intangible attributes including functional, social, and psychological utilities or benefits. When buyers purchase a product, they actually are buying the benefits and satisfaction they think the product will provide.

Products fall into one of two general categories: consumer products and industrial products. Consumer products satisfy personal and family needs. Industrial products are purchased for use in a firm's operations or to make other products. Consumer products can be subdivided into convenience, shopping, specialty, and unsought products. Industrial products can be divided into raw materials, major equipment, accessory equipment, component parts, process materials, supplies, and industrial services.

The product mix is the composite or total group of products that an organization makes available. The product line refers to a related group of products within the product mix. Product lines are based on marketing, technical, or end-use considerations. The product item within the product line is a unique offering.

The product life cycle describes how product items in an industry move through (1) introduction, (2) growth, (3) maturity, and (4) decline. The life cycle concept is used to evaluate product strategy and adjust the marketing strategy to particular situations. The sales curve is at zero at introduction, rises at an increasing rate during growth, peaks at maturity, and then declines. Profits peak toward the end of the growth stage of the product life cycle. The life expectancy of a product is based on buyers' wants, the availability of competing products, and other environmental conditions. Products move through various stages of their life cycles according to saturation of market potential. Some enterprises have a composite of life cycle patterns for various products. A major marketing task is to manage existing products and to develop new products to keep the overall sales performance at a desired level.

A brand is a name, term, symbol, design, or a combination thereof that identifies a seller's products and differentiates them from competitors' products. Branding can benefit both marketers and customers. A manufacturer brand is initiated by a producer and makes it possible for producers to be identified with their products at the point of purchase. A private distributor brand is initiated and owned by a reseller. When selecting a brand, a marketer should choose one that is easy to say, spell, and recall and that alludes to the product's uses, benefits, or special characteristics. Major branding policies are individual branding, overall family branding, line family branding, and brand-extension branding.

Packaging serves the functions of protection, economy, convenience, and promotion. When developing a package, marketers must consider packaging costs relative to the needs of target market members. Other considerations include both whether or not to employ multiple packaging and family packaging and how to design the package so that it is an effective promotional tool. Labeling is used on packages to provide instructions, information on the contents, certifications, and manufacturer identifications. Labels can perform both informational and promotional functions.

When creating products, marketers must take into account other product-related considerations such as physical characteristics and less tangible supportive services. Specific physical product characteristics that require attention are the level of quality, product features, textures, colors, and sizes. Supportive services that may be viewed as part of the total product include warranties, repairs and replacements, and credit services.

Important Terms

Product	Product life cycle
Consumer products	Introduction stage
Industrial products	Growth stage
Convenience products	Maturity stage
Shopping products	Decline stage
Specialty products	Brand
Unsought products	Brand name
Raw materials	Brand mark
Major equipment	Trademark
Accessory equipment	Trade name
Component parts	Manufacturer brands
Process materials	Private distributor brands
Supplies	Generic brand
MRO items	Individual branding
Industrial services	Overall family branding
Product item	Line family branding
Product line	Brand-extension branding
Product mix	Family packaging
Depth (of product mix)	Labeling
Width (of product mix)	Warranty

Discussion and Review Questions

1. List the tangible and intangible attributes of a bottle of mouthwash. Compare the benefits of mouthwash with those of an intangible product like life insurance.
2. Products have been referred to as a "psychological bundle of satisfaction." Is this a good definition of a product?
3. Is a roll of shag carpeting in a store a consumer product or an industrial product? Defend your answer.

4. How do convenience products and shopping products differ? What are the distinguishing characteristics of each?
5. Would a stereo tape deck that sells for $869 be a convenience, shopping, or specialty product?
6. In the category of industrial products, how do component parts differ from process materials?
7. How does an organization's product mix relate to its development of a product line? When should an enterprise add depth to its product lines rather than width to its product mix?
8. How do industry profits change as a product moves through the four stages of its life cycle?
9. What is the relationship between the concepts of product mix and product life cycle?
10. What is the difference between a brand and a brand name? Compare and contrast the terms *brand mark* and *trademark*.
11. How does branding benefit an organization?
12. What are the distinguishing characteristics of private distributor brands?
13. Given the competition between private distributor brands and manufacturer brands, should manufacturers be concerned about the increasing popularity of private distributor brands? How should manufacturers fight back in the brand battle? At what point should a manufacturer make private brands?
14. The brand name *Xerox* is sometimes used generically to refer to photo-copying machines. How can Xerox Corporation protect this brand name?
15. Identify and explain the four major branding policies and give examples of each. Can a firm use more than one policy at a time? Explain.
16. Describe the functions that a package can perform. Which function is most important? Why?
17. Why is the determination of a product's quality level an important decision? What major factors affect this decision?

Cases

Case 7.1 Nike's Product Line Development

In 1972, with forty-five employees, Nike began producing running shoes. Sales for that year were $1.96 million. Well over a decade later Nike's worldwide sales totaled $920 million, and the corporation employs four thousand workers. Nike successfully took advantage of the jogging craze that swept the country in the seventies and early eighties. The number of active runners jumped from five to forty million in just ten years. Production and selling reached a frenetic pace for the athletic shoe and clothing company. But what Nike failed to anticipate was a flattening and ultimate downturn in the running shoe market. Demand and buyers' attitudes had been misread, and Nike found itself overstocked with running shoes and underdeveloped in the way of new products.

Nike had expertise in satisfying the needs of the runner. Running was the number-one fitness hobby well into the eighties. Shoes that provided exceptional durability, lightness in weight, and special injury-reduction design features were Nike's trademark. But the shoemaker had not recognized the major market changes that were occurring. Not only was the number of runners declining, but the variety of sports and fitness activities was broadening. People who before had concentrated on running were now diversifying into swimming, weightlifting, aerobics, bicycling, tennis, racquetball, and soccer. This change in fitness activities also led to a decline in the use of running shoes for casual wear. Court and aerobic shoes became fashionable leisure wear.[36] Reebok, one of Nike's newest competitors, recognized the shift in consumers' needs and increased sales from $66 million in 1984 to $307 million in 1985. Reebok shoes offered more than comfort and performance. They offered brilliant colors, soft leather, and interesting styles. According to Brenda L. Gall, a Merrill Lynch, Pierce, Fenner & Smith vice-president, "at least 70% of the shoes designed for basketball and aerobics exercise are used for street wear."[37] Reebok successfully took advantage of this trend. But many market analysts speculate that Reebok's success could be short-lived. The shoemaker has yet to prove that it can move from providing women's fashion shoes to providing dependable basketball and running shoes.

Nike has evaluated its products in light of the changing market and has made several adaptations in its product line. The company is "returning to its roots—sports and fitness—and away from competing with Esprit and Levi's."[38] New-product development is to be based on a functional approach—meeting the needs of athletes—instead of attempting to meet fashion demands with new colors and styles, as many of Nike's competitors are doing. Although the company will strive to provide products that appeal to the increasingly diversified fitness requirements of consumers, it does not intend to relinquish its 50 percent share of the running shoe market. Most importantly, Nike's impressive group of new products can be defined as follows:

Creating demand
Providing functional innovation and unique design
Driven by the marketing concept
Developed around and with athletes
Leading to other new successful products

Nike's new-product development has been responsible for both the Air Jordan line of shoes and apparel, endorsed by Chicago Bulls' NBA star Michael Jordan, and the John McEnroe line of tennis apparel. Other new products are the Air Conditioner shoe, which has a spring-sole cushioning system; bicycle touring and off-road bicycling shoes; and a complete line of aerobic shoes with three designs: for the instructor, for the serious athlete, and for the newcomer. The Air Jordan line generated sales of $80 million in less than six months, representing one of Nike's biggest successes. Nike is expanding its apparel offerings with lines for running and fitness activities, including weight training, aerobics, and cross-country skiing.[39]

One of Nike's strategies will be to limit the number of athletic stars signed as product endorsers. The company had been eating up advertising dollars by signing college and professional athletes at a healthy clip. At one time it had

36. 1985 Nike Annual Report.
37. Lois Therrien and Amy Borrus, "Reeboks: How Far Can a Fad Run?" *Business Week,* Feb. 24, 1986, pp. 89, 90.
38. Lynn Strongin Dodds, "Heading Back on the Fast Track," *Financial World*, Aug. 21–Sept. 3, 1985, pp. 90–91.
39. 1985 Nike Annual Report.

130 NBA players contracted as Nike endorsers. The corporation has selectively cut the roster to approximately 40 big-name athletes. It intends to attach some of these star athletes' endorsements and signatures to newly developed sports-specific product lines. Minimizing the number of these endorsements and making them apply to specific products, rather than the brand name *Nike*, will allow the company to alter its advertising technique. Its ads can use more creativity and subtlety to capitalize on the individual athletes' personalities and popularity.

Although Nike has experienced recent losses, the firm appears to have developed an improved understanding of athletic consumers' needs. Nike is now providing a broad product line that appeals to many different sports enthusiasts. Now that a variety of needs have been defined, Nike is also continuing to innovatively develop and improve existing lines and to identify potential opportunities for new products. Nike is lending credence to its leadership position in the athletic shoe market by successfully managing and developing product lines.

Questions for Discussion

1. What stage of the product life cycle are Nike's running shoes in compared to the life cycle stage of the Air Jordan basketball shoes?
2. Evaluate Nike's decision to produce shoes catering to the athlete's needs, as opposed to Reebok, whose initial strategy was to produce fashionable, colorful shoes.
3. Evaluate and categorize the depth and width of Nike's product lines.

Case 7.2 Recovering from Tylenol's Product Tampering Problems[40]

McNeil Labs, Inc., a subsidiary of Johnson & Johnson, introduced adult-strength Tylenol in 1961. McNeil launched Tylenol's first major consumer advertising campaign in 1976, after its first nonaspirin competitor, Datril, was introduced by Bristol-Myers Co. McNeil promoted only Extra-Strength Tylenol in tablet and capsule form. By 1978 Tylenol had 24 percent of the pain-reliever market, with worldwide sales nearing $500 million. By 1982, the Tylenol name was on twelve different pain-relieving products. It was the number-one analgesic, dominating 35 percent of the $1-billion pain-reliever market.

On September 30, 1982, multiple deaths in the Chicago area were traced to Extra-Strength Tylenol capsules that had been laced with cyanide. Immediately McNeil tried to determine at what point in the product's life the tampering had occurred. When the firm was sure that it had not taken place during the manufacturing process, and therefore could not be traced to one particular plant, McNeil spent approximately $100 million to buy back Tylenol products

---

40. The facts in this case are from "Johnson & Johnson Reincarnates a Brand," *Sales and Marketing Management,* Jan. 16, 1984, p. 63; Thomas Moore, "The Fight to Save Tylenol," *Fortune,* Nov. 29, 1982, pp. 44–49; "The Rise—and Fall?" *Advertising Age,* Oct. 11, 1982, p. 78; "Tylenol Firm Abandoning All Capsules," *Houston Post,* Feb. 18, 1986, p. 1; William J. Hampton, "Scherer Is Ready to Try New Medicine," *Business Week,* March 10, 1986, pp. 58, 62; and Rebecca Fannin, "Diary of an Amazing Comeback," *Marketing & Media Decisions,* Spring 1983, pp. 129–134.

from retailers and consumers and to dispose of the recalled merchandise. Tylenol sales dropped by 80 percent.

Some market analysts and marketing experts would have advised McNeil against attempting to retain the Tylenol brand. However, marketers at Johnson & Johnson and those at McNeil Labs believed a product that had once been so successful could be revived.

As a result of the Tylenol incident, the federal government required that over-the-counter medicines be sold in tamper-resistant packages. The new Tylenol package included glued end flaps, a plastic neck seal, and an inner foil seal, although any one of these precautions would have complied with the government regulation. In addition, on every package a warning label read, "Do not use if safety seals are broken." A massive production and distribution effort was launched to make the newly packaged products available in a short time.

To help rebuild consumer confidence in the product and to remarket it, the maker of Tylenol created and implemented an intensive promotional program on television and in print. Newspaper advertisements offered consumers a $2.50 coupon to replace products they might have discarded. (A survey had shown that over 35 percent of Tylenol users had discarded their Tylenol products.) Consumers also could call a toll-free number to receive a coupon. Advertisements carried the theme "Continue to trust Tylenol." In addition, McNeil resumed the use of feature-oriented advertisements similar to those employed prior to the crisis.

Johnson & Johnson closely monitored public sentiment regarding important dimensions associated with the Tylenol incident. At about the point that the new promotional program was being launched, a survey revealed several issues. Of all adults in the United States, 94 percent knew about the Tylenol incident and 90 percent believed that it was not the fault of the product's makers. Of those surveyed, 93 percent felt that the tragedy could have occurred with any brand of over-the-counter capsule, and 90 percent were aware that only capsules were involved.

Within sixty days after the Tylenol incident Johnson & Johnson had relaunched the Tylenol brand. Within six months, Tylenol's market share had rebounded to 27 percent, and within a year Tylenol had a 32-percent market share. Although the cost had exceeded $100 million, the maker of Tylenol was able to recover from the tampering "bushwhack" and save a brand that grossed over $500 million in annual sales.

Johnson & Johnson appeared to have successfully restored consumer confidence until a similar tampering episode in early 1986 resulted in the death of a twenty-three-year-old White Plains, New York, woman. Nearly three years after the initial tragedy, cyanide-laced capsules were once again turning up on drug store and supermarket shelves. Johnson & Johnson took a very public and visible stand regarding the crisis. Nine days after the incident, without any pressure from the U.S. Food and Drug Administration, Johnson & Johnson discontinued production of all over-the-counter medication in capsules, even though capsules accounted for 30 percent of Tylenol sales. According to James E. Burke, chairman of Johnson & Johnson, "We feel the company can no longer guarantee the safety of these capsules."

At the same time, Tylenol was once again implementing a massive recall and replacement program, costing the company approximately $150 million.

Johnson & Johnson urged consumers to trade in their capsules for caplets, the oval-shaped tablets that had been created as an alternative to the capsules after the first tampering incidents. Caplets are solid and the company feels any tampering would visibly change their composition. A major supplier of Tylenol's two-piece hard capsules, Scherer Corp., has been a firm supporter of a one-piece soft-shelled capsule that is very difficult to tamper with. The industry continues to evaluate the merits and safety of each product form.

Johnson & Johnson is once again confident that its quick, forthright actions will allow Tylenol to remain a leader in the nonaspirin pain-reliever category. Besides abandoning capsules and implementing the product-replacement program, Johnson & Johnson is offering $100,000 for information that might lead to the arrest of anyone involved with the tampering.

Johnson & Johnson's actions have been quick, well-publicized, and influential— causing many drug companies to assess their vulnerability to potential tampering, or even the public's perception of their vulnerability. Johnson & Johnson has made every effort to show strong sensitivity and concern toward consumers— not just in words, but in actions also.

Questions for Discussion

1. What type of branding policy is being used for Tylenol products?
2. To what extent do you believe that the second poisoning tragedy inhibited Johnson & Johnson's ability to continue capsule production? Evaluate the positive and negative aspects of the company's decision to discontinue capsules.
3. What type of contingency plans should be developed for use if product tampering occurs in the future?

8 / Developing and Managing Products

Objectives

- To develop an awareness of organizational alternatives for managing products.

- To understand the importance and role of product development in the marketing mix.

- To become aware of how existing products can be modified.

- To learn that product deletion can be employed to improve product mixes.

- To gain insight into how businesses develop a product idea into a commercial product.

- To acquire knowledge about product positioning and the management of products during the various stages of their life cycles.

Figure 8.1

Hallmark introduces a new line of cards appropriate for contemporary lifestyles (Source: © Hallmark Cards, Inc.)

The two largest greeting card companies in the United States, Hallmark and American Greetings, have come to realize that Americans no longer subscribe to Norman Rockwell's portrait of family life—close-knit families living in two-story clapboard houses filled with traditional furniture. Family relationships have changed. The divorce rate of 2.4 million a year has resulted in a substantial number of single-parent households. In more traditional families, both parents often have full-time jobs. There are even 1.6 million households in which the adult male and adult female are unmarried; one-fourth of these are unmarried parents having children under the age of fifteen living with them. As a result, Hallmark and American Greetings have developed new products that address these nontraditional family relationships (see Figure 8.1). There are now anniversary cards for "Dad and His Wife" and Mother's Day cards that say, "You're Like a Mother to Me." Both Hallmark and American Greetings report sellouts for these new lines of cards.[1]

1. "New Markets, New Products," *Forbes*, July 30, 1984, p. 102.

To compete effectively and achieve its goals, an organization must be able to adjust its product mix in response to changes in buyers' preferences. A firm may learn to modify existing products, introduce new products, or eliminate products that were at one time successful, perhaps only a few years ago. These adjustments and the way a firm is organized to make them are facets of product management.

This chapter examines how enterprises are organized to develop and manage products. We look at several ways to improve a product mix, including product modification, product deletion, and new-product development. We also examine product positioning—how marketers decide where a product should fit into the field of competing products and which benefits to emphasize. Finally, we consider some of the decisions that must be made to manage a product through its life cycle.

Organizing to Manage Products

A firm must often manage a complex set of products and/or markets. It frequently finds that the functional form of organization traditionally used by businesses does not fit its needs. In the functional form, managers specialize in business functions such as advertising, sales, and distribution. A manager—or a group of managers—must find an organizational approach that accomplishes the tasks necessary to develop and manage products. Alternatives to functional organization include the product manager approach, the market manager approach, and a combination approach.

A **product manager** holds a staff position in a multiproduct company in which the number of products makes it difficult to use other organizational forms. Product managers are responsible for a product, a product line, or several distinct products that make up an interrelated group. A **brand manager** is a type of product manager who is responsible for a single brand. General Foods, for example, has one brand manager for Maxim coffee and one for Maxwell House coffee. A product or brand manager operates cross-functionally to coordinate the activities, information, and strategies involved in marketing an assigned product. Product managers plan marketing activities to achieve objectives by coordinating a mix of distribution, promotion (especially sales promotion and advertising), and price. The areas they must consider include packaging, branding, and the coordination of research and development, engineering, and production. Marketing research enables product managers to understand consumers and to find target markets. The product or brand manager form of organization is used by many large, multiple-product companies in the consumer package goods business.[2]

A **market manager** is responsible for managing the marketing activities that serve a particular group or class of customers. This organizational approach is especially useful when a firm uses different types of marketing activities to provide products to diverse customer groups. For example, a firm might have one market manager for industrial markets and another for consumer markets. These broad market categories might be broken down into more limited market responsibilities.

2. Thomas J. Cosse and John E. Swan, "Strategic Marketing Planning by Product Managers—Room for Improvement?" *Journal of Marketing,* Summer 1983, pp. 92–102.

A **venture team** is designed to create entirely new products that may be aimed at new markets. Unlike a product manager or a market manager, a venture team is responsible for all aspects of a product's development: research and development, production and engineering, finance and accounting, and marketing. Venture teams work outside established divisions to create inventive approaches to new products and markets. As a result of this flexibility, new products can be developed to take advantage of opportunities in highly segmented markets.

The members of a venture team come from different functional areas of an organization. When the commercial potential of a new product has been demonstrated, the members may return to their functional areas, or they may join a new or existing division to manage the product. The new product may be turned over to an existing division, a market manager, or a product manager.[3] A venture department is a separate department or division formed to find, develop, and commercialize promising new-product or new-business areas.[4] Innovative organizational forms such as venture teams are necessary for many companies, especially well-established firms operating primarily in mature markets. These companies must take a dual approach to marketing organization. They must accommodate the management of mature products but also encourage the development of new products.[5] The application on page 238 discusses Chesebrough-Ponds' approach to developing innovative products.

Managing the Product Mix

To provide products that satisfy target markets and achieve the organization's objectives, a marketer must develop, alter, and maintain an effective product mix. Seldom can the same product mix be effective for long. An organization's product mix may need several types of adjustments. Because customers' product preferences and attitudes change, their desire for a product may dwindle. People's fashion preferences obviously change quite often, but individuals' preferences and attitudes change with respect to almost all products.

In some cases a firm needs to alter its product mix to adjust to competition. A marketer may have to delete a product from the mix because one or more competitors dominate the market for that product. Similarly, an organization may have to introduce a new product or modify an existing one to compete more effectively. A marketer may expand the firm's product mix to take advantage of excess marketing and production capacity.

Regardless of why a product mix is altered, the product mix must be managed. In strategic market planning the management of the product mix is often referred to as the portfolio approach. The **product portfolio approach** attempts to create specific marketing strategies to achieve a balanced mix of products that will produce maximum long-run profits. In a portfolio analysis, the most time-consuming task is the collection of data on the items in the

---

3. Richard M. Hill and James D. Hlavacek, "The Venture Team: A New Concept in Marketing Organization," *Journal of Marketing,* July 1972, p. 49.
4. Dan T. Dunn, Jr., "Venture Groups Redefined," *Akron Business and Economic Review,* Fall 1980, pp. 7–11.
5. Roger C. Bennett and Robert G. Cooper, "The Product Life Cycle Trap," *Business Horizons,* Sept.–Oct. 1984, pp. 7–16.

Chesebrough-Pond's, Inc., has a unique approach to product development. Each product category (such as lipstick or eye makeup) is assigned a team, whose members perform and coordinate the market research, R&D, and marketing. In 1983 a program was instituted in the Applied Technology Research Group to stimulate product innovation. Called Free Time, the program allowed all R&D staff to put away their assigned projects every Friday at noon to pursue experimental work until 5 p.m. From this program have emerged such product innovations as Aziza's Polishing Pen, a pen that dispenses nail polish, and One Coat nail polish, a one-application nail-color formula.

To perfect the Polishing Pen required a great commitment of resources and R&D. Chesebrough backed this investment with a substantial promotional campaign, including splashy point-of-sale displays. The company felt that functionally modifying the way nail polish is applied—for the convenience of the consumer—could give its product a significant performance advantage. The risk has paid off. Since the product's introduction, Aziza's nail-polish sales have been up by 22 percent, and the company will try to extend this functional modification to other product lines, such as eye makeup. (*Sources: Carrie Muller-Wainwright, "Aziza Lures Impulse Buyer with Color & Convenience," Drug and Cosmetic Industry, April 1986, pp. 24–30; Amy Dunkin, "Want to Wake Up a Tired Old Product? Repackage It," Business Week, July 15, 1985, pp. 130, 134; and Donald F. Heany, "Degrees of Product Innovation," The Journal of Business Strategy, Spring 1983, pp. 3–14.*)

portfolio and on their performance along selected dimensions. This evaluation requires hard data from company records (for instance, on sales and profitability) and from outside sources (for instance, on market share and industry growth). However, management's judgment is a key element of the portfolio approach.[6]

The product portfolio concept is a useful framework for managing the marketing mix. We will examine product portfolio models in Chapter 18 in the discussion of strategic market planning. At this point, we will look into three major ways to improve a product mix: the modification of an existing product, the deletion of a product, and the development of a new product.

Modifying Existing Products

Product modification refers to changing one or more of a product's characteristics. It is most likely to be employed in the maturity stage of the product life cycle to give a brand a competitive advantage. Altering a product mix in this way entails less risk than developing a new product.

Product modification can effectively improve a firm's product mix under certain conditions. First, the product must be modifiable. Second, existing customers must be able to perceive that a modification has been made (assuming that the modified item is still aimed at them). Third, the modification should make the product more consistent with customers' desires so that it provides greater satisfaction. For example, Figure 8.2 shows that Corvette modifies its product yearly to stay ahead of competition.

6. Yoram Wind and Vijay Mahajan, "Designing Product and Business Portfolios," *Harvard Business Review,* Jan.–Feb. 1981, p. 163.

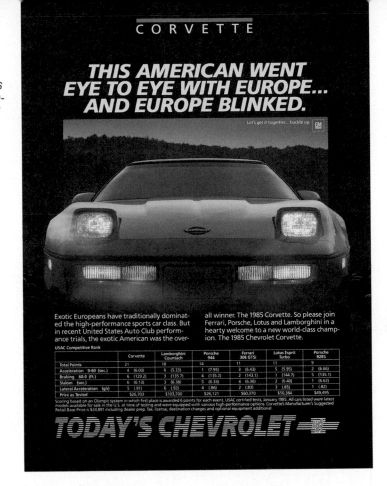

Products can be changed in three major ways: quality modifications, functional modifications, and style modifications.

Quality Modifications

Quality modifications are changes that relate to a product's dependability and durability. They usually are executed by alterations in the materials or production process employed. Reducing a product's quality may allow an organization to lower the price and direct the item at a larger target market.

Increasing the quality of a product may give a firm an advantage over competing brands. In fact, some experts claim that quality improvement is a major means of successfully competing with foreign marketers.[7] Higher quality may allow a firm to charge a higher price by creating customer loyalty and by lowering customer sensitivity to price. On the other hand, higher quality may require the use of more expensive components, less standardized production processes, and other manufacturing and management techniques that force a firm to charge higher prices.[8]

7. Frank S. Leonard and W. Earl Sasser, "The Incline of Quality," *Harvard Business Review,* Sept.–Oct. 1982, p. 171.
8. Lynn W. Phillips, Dae R. Chang, and Robert D. Buzzell, "Product Quality, Cost Position and Business Performance: A Test of Some Key Hypotheses," *Journal of Marketing,* Spring 1983, pp. 26–43.

Functional Modifications

Changes that affect a product's versatility, effectiveness, convenience, or safety are called **functional modifications;** they usually require redesigning the product. Typical product categories in which we have seen considerable functional modifications include kitchen appliances, office and farm equipment, and vacuum cleaners. Functional modifications can make a product useful to more people, which enlarges the market for it. This type of change can place a product in a favorable competitive position by providing benefits not offered by competing items. Functional modifications can also help an organization to achieve and maintain a progressive image.

Style Modifications

Style modifications change the sensory appeal of a product by altering its taste, texture, sound, smell, or visual characteristics. For example, the Nestle Company has increased the size of its Crunch Bar by 10 percent to make the product more appealing to 18–34-year-old men. Commercials for the enlarged crunch bar feature Kareem Abdul-Jabbar, a professional basketball superstar in his late thirties, and thus enhance the adult appeal. Adults 18–34 years old are consuming more chocolate today (20.8 times per year) than in 1977 (15.9 times per year).[9]

Since a buyer's purchase decision is affected by how a product looks, smells, tastes, feels, or sounds, a style modification may have a definite impact on purchases. Hallmark, for example, has had to modify its Valentine's Day cards by replacing Cupid with butterflies, puppies, kittens, birds, rainbows, flowers, and contemporary photographs. Hallmark determined that card buyers now view Cupid as being too traditional and trite.[10]

Through style modifications, a firm can differentiate its product from competing brands and thus gain a sizable market share. The major drawback in using style modifications is that their value is determined subjectively. Although a firm may strive to improve the product's style, customers may actually find the modified product less appealing.

Deleting Products

Generally, a product cannot indefinitely satisfy target market customers and contribute to achieving an organization's overall goals. To maintain an effective product mix, a firm has to get rid of some products, just as it has to modify existing products or introduce new ones. This is called **product deletion.** A weak product is a drain on potential profitability. In addition, too much of a marketer's time and resources are spent trying to revive it. This effort, in turn, reduces the time and resources available for modifying other products or developing new ones. Shorter production runs, which can increase per-unit production costs, may be required for a marginal product. Finally, when a weak product causes unfavorable impressions among customers, the negative ideas may rub off onto some of the firm's other products.

Most organizations find it difficult to delete a product. It was probably a difficult decision for IBM to drop the PC*jr* and admit that it had failed in the

---

9. Ronald Alsop, "Candy Makers Step Up Fight Over America's Sweet Tooth," *Wall Street Journal,* June 13, 1985, p. 29.
10. "Cupid Has Lost the Hearts of the Young," *The Eagle,* Jan. 30, 1983, p. 6D.

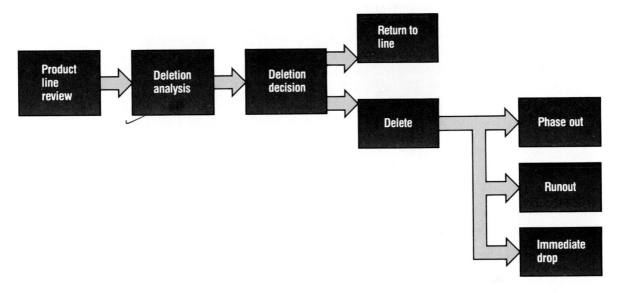

Figure 8.3

Product deletion process (Source: Martin L. Bell, Marketing Concepts and Strategy, *3rd ed., p. 267. Copyright © 1979, Houghton Mifflin Company. Used by permission)*

low end of the personal computer market. A decision to drop a product may be opposed by management and other employees who feel the product is necessary in the product mix. Salespeople who still have some loyal customers are especially upset when a product is dropped. Considerable resources and effort are sometimes spent trying to change the product's marketing mix to improve its sales and thus avoid having to abandon the item.

Some organizations drop weak products only after they have become heavy financial burdens. A better approach is some form of systematic review in which each product is evaluated periodically to determine its impact on the overall effectiveness of the firm's product mix. Such a review should analyze a product's contribution to the firm's sales for a given period. It should include estimates of future sales, costs, and profits associated with the product and a consideration of whether changes should be made in the marketing strategy to improve the product's performance. A systematic review enables an organization to improve product performance and to ascertain when to delete products, thus maximizing the effectiveness of the product mix.

Several alternatives exist for deleting a product, but basically it can be phased out, run out, or dropped immediately (see Figure 8.3). A phase-out approach lets the product decline without changing the marketing strategy. No attempt is made to give the product new life. A runout policy exploits any strengths left in the product. By increasing marketing efforts in core markets or by eliminating some marketing expenditures such as advertising, the product may provide a sudden spurt of profits. This approach is often used for technologically obsolete products, such as calculators, computers, and cassette recorders. Often the price is reduced to get a sales spurt before the product inventory is depleted. An immediate-drop decision results in sudden termination of an unprofitable product. This strategy is appropriate when losses are too great to prolong the life of a product.

Chapter 8 / Developing and Managing Products

Developing New Products

Developing and introducing new products is frequently expensive and risky. Thousands of new products are introduced annually. Depending on how one defines it, the failure rate for new products ranges between 33 and 90 percent. Although it is often reported that 90 percent of new products fail, a recent study of industrial and consumer-oriented firms indicated that only 33 percent of the new products actually introduced to the marketplace fail. This same study, conducted by the Conference Board, reported that medium- and large-sized firms obtain 15 percent of their sales volume from new products introduced in the last five years. Lack of research is the leading cause of new-product failure. Other often-cited causes are technical problems in design or production and errors in timing the product's introduction.[11]

New product development is evidently risky, but so is failure to introduce new products. For example, Those Characters from Cleveland (TCFC), a division of American Greetings that produces toys, has in the past successfully introduced Strawberry Shortcake and the Care Bears. But TCFC has had no recent new-product introduction and has lost share to such products as Coleco Cabbage Patch Kids and Tonka's Pound Puppies. To regain market share, TCFC is putting much of its marketing strength behind a new product called the Popple. A Popple is a stuffed fur animal that folds into its own pouch. Children can make the Popple's arms, legs, and tail disappear easily. To market this product,

11. David Hopkins, "Survey Finds 67% of New Products Succeed," *Marketing News,* Feb. 8, 1980, p. 1.

✓ **Figure 8.5** *Phases of new product development*

American Greetings has chosen Mattel. The firms will spend $10 million in advertising this new product's introduction. Popples will also be supported with a television special and a syndicated cartoon series. But with this costly new product, American Greetings has the opportunity to regain its share of the $10-billion toy and game market.[12] On the other hand, a product failure could leave the company further behind the competition.

The term *new product* can have several meanings. A genuinely new product—such as Crest or the VCR once were—offers innovative benefits. But products that are different and distinctly better are often viewed as new. The following items (listed in no particular order) have been named as the best product innovations of the last twenty-five years: disposable lighters, "Post-it" note pads, Polaroid cameras, the birth control pill, the water pik, felt-tip pens, seat belts, disposable razors, quartz watches, and contact lenses.[13] For our purposes, a new product is one that a given firm has not marketed previously, although similar products may have been available from other organizations. For example, Advil was one of the first new non-aspirin pain relievers marketed over the counter since Tylenol was introduced in 1955. The drug was formerly available on a prescription basis only, but as an over-the-counter drug it was a new product. Figure 8.4 shows another example of a new product, a cereal launched by Ralston Purina Company.

Before a product is introduced, it goes through the six phases of **new-product development** shown in Figure 8.5. The phases are (1) idea generation, (2) screening, (3) business analysis, (4) product development, (5) test marketing, and (6) commercialization. A product can be dropped, and many are, at any stage of development.

Idea Generation

Businesses and other organizations seek product ideas that will help them achieve their objectives. This activity is **idea generation.** The difficulty of the task is illustrated in that only a few ideas are good enough to be commercially successful. Although some organizations get their ideas almost by chance, firms that are trying to maximize product mix effectiveness usually develop systematic approaches for generating new-product ideas. At the heart of innovation is a purposeful, focused effort to identify new ways to serve a market. Unexpected occurrences, incongruities, new needs, industry and market changes, and demographic changes all may indicate new opportunities.[14]

New-product ideas can come from several sources. They may come from internal sources—marketing managers, researchers, engineers, or other organizational personnel. For example, the idea for 3M Post-its adhesive backed yellow notes, came from an employee. As a church choir member, he used

12. Pamela Sherrid, "The Making of a Popple," *Fortune,* Dec. 16, 1985, pp. 174–178.
13. Ellen Brown, "Our Best Innovations of 25 Years," *USA Today,* March 1, 1985, p. D-1.
14. Peter F. Drucker, "The Discipline of Innovation," *Harvard Business Review,* May–June 1985, pp. 67–68.

Chapter 8 / Developing and Managing Products   **243** slips of paper for marking songs in his hymnal. Because they would fall out, he suggested an adhesive-backed note.[15]

New-product ideas may also arise from sources outside the firm—competitors, advertising agencies, management consultants, private research organizations, and customers. For example, customers or users developed 67 percent of the machines employed in the semiconductor industry. The Pillsbury Bake-Off, a recipe contest, has generated several recipes that Pillsbury has commercialized.[16]

Brainstorming and incentives or rewards for good ideas are typical intrafirm devices used to encourage the development of ideas. Sometimes, potential buyers of a product are questioned in depth to discover what attributes would appeal to them.

Screening Ideas

In the process of **screening ideas,** those with the greatest potential are selected for further development. Those that do not match a firm's objectives or that have a limited potential are rejected. Screening product ideas involves a general assessment of the organization's resources. Through forecasting techniques, an early projection of economic payoffs is made. The firm's overall ability to produce and market the product is analyzed. Other aspects of an idea that should be weighed are the nature and wants of buyers, the competition, and environmental factors. The largest number of new product ideas are rejected during this phase of the development process.

At times, a checklist of new-product requirements is used when making screening decisions. It encourages evaluators to be systematic, thereby reducing the possibility that they might overlook some fact. The type of formal research described in Chapter 6 may be needed if a critical checklist factor remains unclear. To screen ideas properly, testing of product concepts may be necessary. A product concept and its benefits can be described or shown to consumers. Several product concepts may be tested to determine which might appeal most to a particular target market.

Business Analysis

Business analysis provides a tentative sketch of a product's compatibility with the marketplace, including its probable profitability. Compatibility factors include the company's manufacturing and marketing capabilities, its financial resources, and its management's attitude toward the product.[17] During a business analysis, evaluators ask such questions as the following:

1. Does the product fit in with the organization's existing product mix?
2. Is demand strong enough to justify entering the market? Will the demand endure?
3. How will the introduction and marketing of this product affect the firm's sales, costs, and profits?
4. What types of environmental and competitive changes can be expected, and how will these changes affect the product's future sales, costs, and profits?

15. Lawrence Ingrassia, "By Improving Scotch Paper, 3M Gets New Product Winner," *Wall Street Journal,* March 31, 1983, p. 27.
16. Eric von Hippel, "Get New Products from Customers," *Harvard Business Review,* March–April 1982, p. 118.
17. Fritz A. Schumacher, "Successful New Product Ideas Require Right Marketing, Financial 'Fit', Corporate 'Champion'," *Marketing News,* Oct. 16, 1981, p. 1.

5. Are the organization's research, development, engineering, and production capabilities adequate?
6. If new facilities must be constructed to manufacture the product, how quickly can they be built? (If it is possible to use existing facilities, the product idea usually has a better chance of survival.)
7. Is the necessary financing for development and commercialization on hand or obtainable at terms consistent with a favorable return on investment?

During business analysis, firms seek information about the market. A poll of consumers, together with secondary data, supplies information for estimating potential sales, costs, and profits. A research budget should explore the financial objectives and related financial considerations for the new product.

Product Development

Product development is a stage in creating new products that moves the product from concept to test stage and also involves the development of other elements of the marketing mix (promotion, distribution, and price).

In the development phase, the company must first find out if it is technically feasible to produce the product and if the product can be produced at costs low enough to result in a reasonable price. If a product idea makes it to the development point, it is then transformed into a model. To test its acceptability, the idea or concept is converted into a prototype or working model. The prototype should reveal tangible and intangible attributes associated with the product in consumers' minds. The design, mechanical features, and intangible aspects of the product must be linked to wants in the marketplace. The development phase of a new product is frequently lengthy and expensive; thus a relatively small number of product ideas are put into development.

However, the development stage is not restricted to mechanical or production aspects of the product. The various ingredients that will make up the marketing mix must also be tested. Management must, for example, review copyrights, preliminary advertising copy, packaging, and labeling to see if there are any legal problems. Management must also plan for personal selling and distribution. The aim is to ensure the effective integration of all marketing mix elements.

Test Marketing

Test marketing is a limited introduction of a product in areas chosen to represent the intended market. Its aim is to determine the reactions of probable buyers. Test marketing is not an extension of the screening and development stages. It is a sample launching of the entire marketing mix. Test marketing should be conducted only after the product has gone through development and after initial plans regarding the other marketing mix variables have been made.

Test marketing is used by companies of all sizes to minimize the risk of product failure. The dangers of introducing an untested product include undercutting already profitable products and, should the new product fail, loss of credibility with distributors and customers. Consider Ocean Spray's development of a liquid concentrate juice that requires no refrigeration and costs 10 percent less than frozen concentrate and 30 percent less than bottled drinks. Concerned that this new entry would take sales from its existing line, Ocean Spray conducted

Table 8.1 Popular test markets for new products

Albany–Schenectady–Troy	Green Bay, WI	Quad Cities: Rock Island, Moline, IL; Davenport, Bettendorf, IA (Davenport–Rock Island–Moline SMSA)[a]
Albuquerque	Houston	
Amarillo	Indianapolis	
Atlanta	Jacksonville, FL	
Binghamton, NY	Kansas City, MO	Rochester, NY
Boston	Lexington, KY	Sacramento–Stockton
Buffalo	Lubbock, TX	San Francisco
Charleston, WV	Memphis	St. Louis
Charlotte	Miami	San Antonio
Chicago	Milwaukee	San Diego
Cincinnati	Minneapolis–St. Paul	Seattle-Tacoma
Cleveland	Nashville	South Bend
Columbus, OH	Oklahoma City	Spokane
Dallas–Forth Worth	Omaha	Syracuse
Dayton	Orlando–Daytona Beach	Tampa–St. Petersburg
Denver	Peoria	Tucson
Des Moines	Phoenix	Tulsa
Erie, PA	Pittsburgh	Wichita
Fargo, ND	Portland, ME	
Fort Wayne	Portland, OR	
Fresno	Providence	

[a]*SMSA* stands for Standard Metropolitan Statistical Area.
Source: "The Nation's Most Popular Test Markets," copyright 1983 *Sales and Marketing Management.* Used by permission.

a five-city test. The company's sales rose 15 percent after the new concentrate was introduced. Ocean Spray therefore proceeded to introduce the product with a $10-million advertising campaign.[18]

Test marketing provides several benefits. It allows marketers to expose a product in a natural marketing environment to obtain a measure of its sales performance. While the product is being marketed in a limited area, it is possible to identify weaknesses in the product or in other parts of the marketing mix. Marketers can experiment with variations in advertising, price, and packaging in different test areas and can measure the extent of brand awareness, brand switching, and repeat purchases that result from alterations in the marketing mix.

A product weakness discovered after a nationwide introduction can be very expensive to correct. Moreover, if initial reactions among consumers are negative, marketers may not be able to convince consumers to try the product again. Thus, making adjustments after test marketing can be crucial to the success of a new product. Examples of variables that can be altered after test marketing are product line extensions; spending and distribution levels; and pricing strategy, product formulation, advertising copy and strategy, package design, and shelf location.[19]

18. Barbara Buell, "How Ocean Spray Keeps Reinventing the Cranberry," *Business Week,* Dec. 2, 1985, p. 142.
19. Joel R. Robinson, "Simulated Test Marketing Reduces Risk in New Brand Introductions, Line Extensions," *Marketing News,* Sept. 18, 1981, p. 3.

Part II / Product Decisions

Table 8.2 *Questions to consider when choosing test markets*

1. Is the area typical of planned distribution outlets?
2. Is the city relatively isolated from other cities?
3. What local media are available, and are they cooperative?
4. Does the area have a dominant TV station; does it have multiple newspapers, magazines, and radio stations?
5. Does the city contain a diversified cross section of ages, religions, and cultural/societal preferences?
6. Are the purchasing habits atypical?
7. Is the city's per capita income typical?
8. Does the city have a good record as a test city?
9. Would testing efforts be easily "jammed" by competitors?
10. Does the city have stable year-round sales?
11. Are retailers that will cooperate available?
12. Are research and audit services available?
13. Is the area free from unusual influences, such as one industry's dominance or heavy tourist traffic?

Source: Adapted from "A Checklist for Selecting Test Markets," copyright 1982 *Sales and Marketing Management.* Used by permission.

Selection of appropriate test areas is a major influence on the accuracy of test-marketing results. Table 8.1 lists some of the most popular test-market cities. The criteria used for choosing test cities depend on the characteristics of the product, the target market's characteristics, and the organization's objectives and resources. Even though the selection criteria will vary from one firm to another, the general issues raised by the questions in Table 8.2 can be useful when assessing a potential test market.

Test marketing is not without risks, however. Not only is it expensive, but a firm's competitors may try to interfere. A competitor may try to "jam" the test program by increasing advertising or promotions, lowering prices, and offering special incentives, all to combat the recognition and purchase of a new brand. Any such devices can invalidate test results. Sometimes, too, competitors copy the product in the testing stage and rush to introduce a similar product. Schick, for example, introduced a double-bladed razor less than six months after Gillette brought out Trac II. It is therefore desirable to move quickly and commercialize as soon as possible after testing.

Because of these risks, many companies are using alternative methods to gauge consumer preferences. One such method is simulated test marketing. Consumers at shopping centers are typically asked to view an ad for a new product and are given a free sample to take home. These consumers are subsequently interviewed over the phone and asked to rate the product. Scanner-based test marketing is another, more sophisticated version of the traditional test-marketing method.[20] (Chapter 6 discusses this type of testing.) The major advantage of simulated test marketing is lower cost. Figure 8.6 indicates that some marketing research firms such as A. C. Nielsen provide test marketing services to help provide independent assessment of products.

20. Eleanor Johnson Tracy, "Testing Time for Test Marketing," *Fortune,* Oct. 29, 1984, pp. 75–76.

Figure 8.6

A. C. Nielsen Company
promotion of its test-
marketing services
(Source: A. C. Nielsen
Company)

Commercialization

During **commercialization,** plans for full-scale manufacturing and marketing must be refined and settled, and budgets for the project must be prepared. Early in the commercialization phase, marketing management analyzes the results of test marketing to find out what changes in the marketing mix are needed before the product is introduced. The results of test marketing may tell the marketers, for example, to change one or more of the product's physical attributes, to modify the distribution plans to include more retail outlets, to alter promotional efforts, or to change the product's price.

The organization gears up for production during the commercialization phase. This may require sizable capital expenditures for plant and equipment, and the firm also may need to hire additional personnel.

The product is introduced into the market during commercialization. During product introduction marketers often spend enormous sums of money for such promotional efforts as advertising, personal selling, and sales promotion. These expenses, together with capital expenditures, can make commercialization extremely costly; such expenditures may not be recovered for several years. For example, when General Mills introduced Fruit Roll-Ups and Fruit Bars, illustrated in Figure 8.7, large expenditures were necessary to communicate product attributes.

Figure 8.7

Communicating product attributes during commercialization (Source: Printed courtesy of General Mills, Inc.)

The Fruit Corners Strawberry

In a State renowned for its beautiful views and natural wonders, few rival the one on the left. The California climate brings out the best in a berry. So, naturally,

that's where we go for the fruit that goes into Fruit Corners Strawberry Fruit Roll-Ups® and Fruit Bars. If you want to end up with a great tasting fruit snack, you have to start out with great fruit.

FRUIT CORNERS®
If it comes from Fruit Corners®, it's made with real fruit.

Commercialization is significantly easier when customers accept the product rapidly. There is a better chance of this if marketers can make customers aware of a product's benefits. The following stages of the **product adoption process** are generally recognized as those that buyers go through in accepting a product:

1. *Awareness.* The buyer becomes aware of the product.
2. *Interest.* The buyer seeks information and is receptive to learning about the product.
3. *Evaluation.* The buyer considers the product's benefits and determines whether to try it.
4. *Trial.* The buyer examines, tests, or tries the product to determine its usefulness.
5. *Adoption.* The buyer purchases the product and can be expected to use it to solve problems.[21]

This adoption model has several implications for the commercialization phase. First, promotion should be used to create widespread awareness of the product and its benefits. Samples or simulated trials should be arranged to

21. Adapted from *Diffusion of Innovations* by Everett M. Rogers (Copyright © 1962 by The Free Press, a Division of Macmillan Publishing Co., Inc.), pp. 81–86.

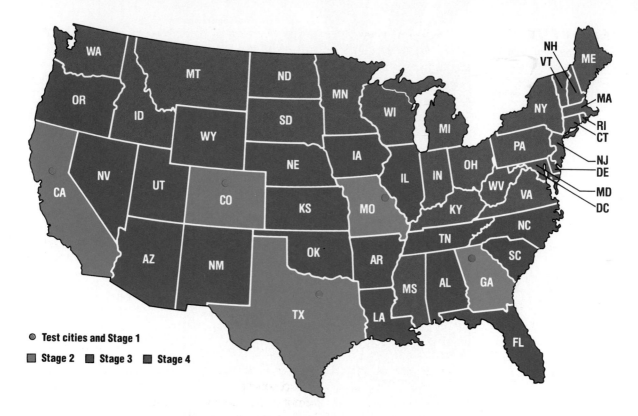

Figure 8.8 *Stages of expansion into the national market during commercialization*
(Source: Adapted from Business: An Involvement Approach, *by Herbert G. Hicks, William M. Pride,
and James D. Powell. Copyright © 1975 by McGraw-Hill. Used with permission of McGraw-Hill Book
Company)*

help buyers make initial purchase decisions. At the same time, marketers should emphasize quality control and provide solid guarantees to reinforce buyer opinion during the evaluation stage. Finally, production and physical distribution must be linked to patterns of adoption and repeat purchases. (The product adoption process is also discussed in Chapter 13.)

Products are not usually introduced nationwide overnight. Most products are introduced in stages, starting in a set of geographic areas and gradually expanding into adjacent areas. It may take several years to market the product nationally. Sometimes, the test cities are used as initial marketing areas, with the introduction being a natural extension of test marketing. For example, a product test-marketed in Sacramento, Denver, Dallas, St. Louis, and Atlanta, as shown on the map in Figure 8.8, could be introduced first in those cities. After the stage 1 introduction is complete, stage 2 could include market coverage of the states in which the test cities are located. In stage 3, marketing efforts could be extended into adjacent states. All remaining states would then be covered in stage 4. Gradual product introductions do not always occur state by state, however; other geographic combinations are used as well.

Gradual product introduction is popular for several reasons. It reduces the risks of introducing a new product. If the product fails, the firm will experience smaller losses when the item has been introduced in only a few geographic areas than when it has been marketed nationally. Furthermore, it is usually impossible for a company to introduce a product nationwide overnight. The system of wholesalers and retailers necessary to distribute a product cannot be established that quickly. The development of a distribution network may take considerable time. Keep in mind, also, that the number of units needed to satisfy the national demand for a successful product can be enormous, and a firm usually cannot produce the required quantities in a short time.

Despite the good reasons for introducing a product gradually, marketers realize that this approach creates some competitive problems. A gradual introduction allows competitors to observe what a firm is doing and to monitor results, just as the firm's own marketers are doing. If competitors see that the newly introduced product is successful, they may enter the same target market quickly with similar products. Also, as a product is introduced on a region-by-region basis, competitors may expand their marketing efforts to offset promotion of the new product.

Product Positioning

The term **product positioning** refers to the decisions and activities intended to create and maintain a firm's product concept in customer's minds. When marketers introduce a product, they attempt to position it so that it seems to possess the characteristics most desired by the target market. This projected image is crucial. *Product position* refers to the customers' concept of the product's attributes relative to their concept of competitive brands. For example, Crest is positioned as a fluoride toothpaste that fights cavities and Close-Up is positioned as a whitening toothpaste that enhances the user's sex appeal.

Product positioning is a part of a natural progression when market segmentation is used. Segmentation allows the firm to aim a given brand at a portion of the total market. Effective product positioning helps to serve a specific market segment by creating an appropriate concept in the minds of customers in that market segment.

A firm can position a product to compete head-on with another brand, as Pepsi has done against Coca-Cola, or to avoid competition, as 7UP has done relative to other soft-drink producers. Head-to-head competition may be a marketer's positioning objective if the product's performance characteristics are at least equal to competitive brands and if the product is lower priced. Head-to-head positioning may be appropriate even when the price is higher if the product's performance characteristics are superior. Conversely, positioning to avoid competition may be best when the product's performance characteristics are not significantly different from competing brands. Also, positioning a brand to avoid competition may be appropriate when that brand has unique characteristics that are important to buyers.

Avoiding competition is critical when a firm introduces a brand into a market in which it already has one or more brands. In this situation, marketers usually want to avoid cannibalizing sales of their existing brands, unless the new brand generates substantially larger profits. When Coca-Cola reintroduced Tab, it attempted to position the cola so as to minimize the adverse effects on

Diet Coke's sales. Tab was positioned as the diet drink containing calcium—catering specifically to a female target market.

If a product has been planned properly, its attributes and its brand image will give it the distinct appeal needed. Style, shape, construction, quality of work, color—all elements of the product component of the marketing mix—assist in creating the image and the appeal. If they can easily identify the benefits, then of course buyers are more likely to purchase the product. When the new product does not offer some preferred attributes, then room exists for another new product or for repositioning an existing product. Ramada Inns, Inc., is experiencing this dilemma currently. Ramada is the third largest lodging chain in the world. Yet it is saddled with many run-down units and an increasingly downscale image. Management is now attempting to buy back many franchise units and either renovate or sell the inns. The sale of some locations will provide capital for renovation of others. Ramada ultimately will be repositioned as a finer, more exclusive lodging environment.[22]

Managing Products After Commercialization

Most new products start off slowly and seldom generate enough sales to produce profits immediately. As buyers learn about the product, marketers should be alert for product weakness and should make corrections quickly. Such actions can prevent the early demise of the product. The marketing strategy should be designed to attract the market segment that is most interested and that has the fewest objections. If any of these factors need to be adjusted, this action, too, must be taken quickly to sustain demand. As the sales curve moves upward and the breakeven point is reached, the growth stage begins.

Marketing Strategy in the Growth Stage

As sales increase, management must support the momentum by adjusting the marketing strategy. The goal is to establish the product's position and to fortify it by encouraging brand loyalty. As profits increase, the organization must brace itself for the entrance of aggressive competitors who may make specialized appeals to selected market segments.

Product ✓

During the growth stage, products might be expanded to appeal to more specialized markets. For example, Wendy's—which has over two thousand hamburger restaurants—views the chicken segment of the fast food business as a good growth area. Wendy's has successfully introduced a chicken sandwich in its hamburger restaurants and is opening Sisters International, Inc., restaurants with more elegant dining rooms than Church's or Kentucky Fried Chicken.[23] Marketers should analyze the product position in terms of competing products and should correct weak or omitted attributes.

22. Stewart Toy, "Ramada: Searching for a Touch of Class," *Business Week,* Dec. 16, 1985, pp. 85–86.
23. Michael King, "Wendy's New Management Cooks Up Plans for Growth and Diversification," *Wall Street Journal,* March 27, 1981, p. 12.

Distribution

Gaps in the marketing channels should be filled during the growth period. It may be easier to obtain new distribution outlets once product acceptance has been established. Sometimes marketers have a tendency to move from an exclusive or selective exposure to a more intensive network of dealers. Marketers must also make sure that the physical distribution system is running efficiently and delivers supplies to distributors before their inventories are exhausted. Since competition increases during the growth period, service adjustments and prompt credit for defective products are important marketing tools.

Promotion

Promotional efforts should stress brand loyalty during the growth stage, but as sales increase, promotion costs should drop as a percentage of total sales. A falling ratio between promotion expenditures and sales should contribute significantly to increased profits.

Price

After recovering development costs, a business may be able to lower prices. As sales volume increases, efficiencies in production can result in lower costs. These savings may be passed on to buyers. If demand remains strong and there are few competitive threats, prices tend to remain stable. Providing price cuts are possible, they can facilitate price competition and discourage new competitors from entering the market. For example, when compact disc players were introduced several years ago, they sported a $1,000 price tag. Primarily because of the price, the product was positioned as a "toy for audiophiles," a very small market segment. To generate mass market demand, compact-disc-player manufacturers dropped their prices to $400 or less, and the cost of discs dropped from $22 to $14. The price is now at a point where the margin is low but the turnover is high. Worldwide sales in 1985 reached approximately $1.3 billion, triple the volume of the previous year. That figure is projected to double in the next several years.[24]

Marketing Strategy for Mature Products

Since many products are in the maturity stage of their life cycles, marketers must deal with these products and must be prepared to improve the marketing mix constantly. During maturity the competitive situation stabilizes, and some of the weaker competitors drop out. It has been suggested that as a product matures, its customers become more experienced and specialized (at least for industrial products). As these customers gain knowledge, the benefits they seek may change as well. Thus, new marketing strategies may be needed.[25]

Product

Marketers may need to alter the product's quality or otherwise modify the product. Wilkinson Sword continues to modify its razors to provide new benefits such as the retractable blade illustrated in Figure 8.9. A product may be rejuvenated through different packaging, new models, or style changes. Sales and market

---

24. Brian Dumaine, "The Compact Disc's Drive to Become King of Audio," *Fortune,* July 8, 1985, pp. 104–107.
25. F. Stewart DeBruicker and Gregory L. Summe, "Make Sure Your Customers Keep Coming Back," *Harvard Business Review,* Jan.–Feb. 1985, pp. 92–98.

Figure 8.9

*An example of a
modification of a
mature product
(Source: Courtesy of
Wilkinson Sword)*

share may be maintained or strengthened by informing buyers about new uses for the product or by encouraging them to use it more frequently. The makers of Noxzema repositioned the product from a medicated skin creme for occasional use to a beauty-care product for routine use.[26]

Distribution

During the maturity stage of the cycle, marketers actively encourage dealers to support the product. Dealers may be offered promotional assistance and help in lowering their inventory costs. In general, marketers go to great effort to serve dealers and provide incentives for selling the manufacturer's brand, in part because private brands are a threat at this time. As we discuss in Chapter 7, private brands present an opportunity as well as a threat to manufacturers, who may be able to sell their product through recognized private brand names as well as their own. However, private brands frequently undermine manufacturers' brands. If manufacturers refuse to sell to private-brand dealers, their competitors usually take advantage of this opportunity.

26. Theodore Karger, "5 Ways to Find Ideas—Re-evaluate Ideas—Re-evaluate Your Old Products," *Marketing Times,* July–Aug. 1981, p. 18.

Promotion

Large advertising expenditures are often necessary during the maturity stage to maintain market share. As competition increases, sales promotion and aggressive personal selling may be potent marketing tools.

Price

There is a greater mixture of pricing strategies during the maturity stage. Marketers develop price flexibility to differentiate offerings in product lines. Markdowns and price incentives are more common, but price increases are likely to occur if distribution and production costs increase.

Marketing Strategy for Declining Products ✓

As a product's sales curve turns downward, profits almost always fall. A business can justify maintaining a product as long as it contributes to profits or enhances the overall effectiveness of a product mix. When a product becomes unprofitable, marketers eventually reduce production. At this stage, marketers must determine when to eliminate the product. This can be an extremely important decision. The application on page 256 discusses a declining product that may still have potential opportunity for its manufacturers.

Product

Usually a declining product has lost its distinctiveness because similar competing products have been introduced. Competition engenders increased substitution and brand switching as buyers become insensitive to minor product differences. For these reasons, marketers do little to change style, design, or other attributes of a product during its decline. New technology, product substitutes, or environmental considerations may also indicate that the time has come to delete a product.

Distribution

During a product's decline, outlets with core sales (the most loyal buyers) are maintained, and unprofitable outlets are weeded out. An entire marketing channel may be eliminated if it does not make an adequate contribution to profits. Sometimes a new marketing channel, such as a factory outlet, will be used to liquidate remaining inventory of an obsolete product. As sales decline, the product tends to become a specialty item, and loyal buyers may seek out dealers who carry it.

Promotion

Promotion loses its importance during the decline stage. However, advertising may slow the rate of decline, and sales incentives, such as coupons and premiums, may temporarily regain buyers' attention. As the product continues to decline, the sales staff shifts its emphasis to more profitable products.

Price

That a product returns a profit may be more important to a firm than maintaining a certain market share through repricing. To squeeze out all possible remaining profits, marketers may maintain the price despite declining sales and competitive

In 1975, Sony introduced the first video cassette recorder (VCR). The product used a system format called beta. Today only two major manufacturers, Sony and Sanyo, still produce beta format VCRs. These manufacturers must deal with the reality that four out of five VCRs purchased are VHS format, not beta. Consumers have become increasingly concerned that beta tapes will not be readily available in the future. Meanwhile, large VHS producers such as RCA, Panasonic, and JVC are bombarding the marketplace with their product. Thus, the beta market is in the decline stage and may have to be abandoned.

Nevertheless, both Sanyo and Sony have developed specific plans to counter the trend. Sanyo's original strategy in reaction to this development was to lower its prices below the lowest VHS competitor. But as acceptance and production of the VHS models grew, their price fell, thus making Sanyo's price concession strategy impractical.

Sanyo then decided to attack the premier VCR market with a product called Super Beta, as did Sony. Super Beta provides a picture significantly better than VHS, along with high fidelity sound reproduction. But not assured of the market's ongoing acceptance of the improved beta VCR, Sanyo also decided to sell VHS VCRs under its own brand name. Sony, on the other hand, has all but abandoned its initial mainstay beta in favor of Super Beta.

Sony and Sanyo both recognized the need to develop and manage their VCR products carefully. Even though sales in the beta segment are declining, VCRs are in approximately 30 percent of American households, and that percentage is growing. As the beta product has moved into the declining phase, both companies are striving to adjust elements of the marketing mix (especially product and price) to stay in this fast-growing home entertainment category. (*Source: Howard Gold, "To the Beta End," Forbes, Dec. 16, 1985, p. 178.*)

pressures. Prices may even be increased as costs rise if a loyal core market still wants the product. In other situations, the price may be cut to reduce existing inventory so that the product can be deleted.

Summary

Developing and managing products is critical to an organization's survival and growth. Although several organizational approaches to product management are possible, they share common activities, functions, and decisions necessary to guide a product through its life cycle. Product managers coordinate marketing efforts for the product in all markets. Market managers focus on products for specific markets. A venture team is sometimes used to develop new products. Members of the venture team come from different functional areas within the organization and are responsible for all aspects of a product's development.

To maximize the effectiveness of a product mix, an organization usually has to alter its mix through new-product development, modification of existing products, or deletion of a product.

Product modification refers to changing one or more of a product's characteristics. This approach to altering a product mix can be effective when the product is modifiable, when customers can perceive the change, and when the modification is desired by customers. Products can be changed in quality, function, or style.

To maintain an effective product mix, a firm has to get rid of weak products. Although a firm's personnel may oppose product deletion, weak products are unprofitable, consume too much time and effort, may require shorter production runs, and can create an unfavorable impression of the firm's other products. A product mix should be systematically reviewed to determine when to delete products. Products to be deleted can be phased out, run out, or dropped immediately.

The six phases of new-product development are generating ideas, screening to determine which ideas to develop, expanding an idea through business analysis, developing a product into a demonstrable concept, test marketing, and commercialization. The decision to enter the commercialization or introduction phase means that full-scale production of the product begins and that a complete marketing strategy is developed. The process that buyers go through in accepting a product includes awareness, interest, evaluation, trial, and adoption.

As a product moves through its life cycle, marketing strategies may require continual adaptation. In the growth stage, it is important to develop brand loyalty and a market position. In the maturity stage, a product may be modified or new market segments may be developed to rejuvenate its sales. A declining product may be maintained as long as it makes a contribution to profits or enhances the product mix.

Important Terms

Product manager
Brand manager
Market manager
Venture team
Product portfolio approach
Product modification
Quality modifications
Functional modifications
Style modifications
Product deletion

New-product development
Idea generation
Screening ideas
Business analysis
Product development
Test marketing
Commercialization
Product adoption process
Product positioning

Discussion and Review Questions

1. What organizational alternatives are available to a firm with two product lines having four product items in each line?
2. When is it more appropriate to use a product manager than a market manager? When might an alternative or combined approach be used?
3. What type of organization might use a venture team to develop new products? What are the advantages and disadvantages of such a team?
4. Do small firms that manufacture one or two products need to be concerned about developing and managing products? Why or why not?
5. Why is product development a cross-functional activity within an organization? That is, why must finance, engineering, manufacturing, and other functional areas be involved?
6. Develop information sources for new product ideas for the automobile industry.

7. Some firms believe that they can omit test marketing. What are some advantages and disadvantages of test marketing?
8. Under what conditions is product modification an appropriate means for changing a product mix? How does a quality modification differ from a functional modification? Can an organization make one without making the other?
9. Why might an organization be unable to eliminate an unprofitable product? Give several reasons.

Cases

Case 8.1   Eastman Kodak's Product Diversification Strategies

Eastman Kodak is best known for its production of photographic products (cameras, films, flashes, and the like). Sales of photographic products account for 80 percent of Kodak's $11 billion in annual revenue.[27] The most profitable item in this category is film. Kodak controls 85 percent of the U.S. market for color film, which provides a 55-percent pretax profit margin for the company. Kodak has also been a leader in the production of what Herbert Keppler, publisher of *Modern Photography,* calls "All other unsophisticated cameras—the Instamatic, the pocket Instamatic and the disk."[28] But now Kodak is struggling to regain its leadership position as market requirements and technology continue to change at a rapid pace.

Kodak has been stagnant while competitors have developed easier-to-use cameras, improved 35-millimeter cameras, better and faster color film, and more efficient processing. Also, Kodak failed to recognize the change in consumer spending habits. According to Eugene G. Glazer, an analyst with Dean Witter Reynolds, Inc., "Excitement that used to be generated by new photographic products has been transferred to consumer electronics products, such as VCRs."[29] Kodak has had another major problem. In the past, it has overlooked new product developments that were offered to its company. For example, Edwin Land made his instant-camera process available to Kodak in the forties—Kodak turned him down and has felt the negative ramifications of this decision ever since.

Polaroid developed Edwin Land's instant camera and successfully became a major producer. The instant camera became popular in the sixties, leaving Kodak scrambling to develop a competitive system. Kodak spent $94 million producing a competitive system, only to see Polariod come out with an improved camera, the SX-70, which produced "litter-free" pictures without the messy film that formerly had to be peeled off. Kodak again was faced with developing a similar competitive system and tried to do so. But by the mid-eighties, that decision and the resulting final product cost the company approximately $800

27. 1985 Kodak Annual Report.
28. Alex Taylor, III, "Kodak Scrambles to Refocus," *Fortune,* March 3, 1986, p. 36.
29. Barbara Buell, "Kodak Just Can't Get Its Giant Feet Moving Fast Enough," *Business Week,* Feb. 24, 1986, p. 37.

million. Polaroid successfully sued Kodak for violation of the former's patent on instant photography. Kodak removed its instant cameras and film from the market and implemented a massive exchange program for customers who had supported the company by purchasing the discontinued products. Kodak offered a disc camera, $50 worth of Kodak film and accessories, or a share of Kodak common stock to anyone who purchased a Kodak instant camera.[30]

Kodak has since established three primary goals: (1) to be a leader in the growing area of imaging technologies, (2) to be among the twenty-five largest companies in the United States, and (3) to increase the return on shareholders' equity by 20 percent. Kodak plans to achieve these goals through diversification and acquisitions. This is a radical change for the film maker, which has been known for being one of the most fully integrated manufacturers in the United States—generating its own electricity at a Rochester, New York, plant; making its own plastic; and even owning cattle yards to provide high-quality gelatin for photographic paper. The acquired products will fill in the gaps in Kodak's lines until it has successfully developed its own technology. For example, Kodak has returned to selling 35-millimeter cameras, but for the time being, these cameras will be manufactured in Japan by Chinon Industries. Such products are designed to give Kodak a quick market presence. The company also hopes the sale of its own cameras will increase the sale of its film.

Kodak will be meeting intense competition as it introduces new products (with which it has limited experience) and redevelops old products. In consumer electronics, Kodak will compete with RCA and G.E.; in the copier and electronic office publishing market, IBM and Xerox; and in the floppy disc market, Memorex and 3M. Kodak's most intense competition will come from foreign competitors for the photographic market. Fuji and Konica in film; Nikon, Canon, and Minolta in still cameras; and Sony, Matsushita, and Toshiba in video cameras and recorders.[31]

Kodak is taking a more proactive view toward the management of existing products and the development of new ones. The film giant is supporting its highly profitable film sales but not relying on them to provide all of its growth. Kodak has recognized emerging technologies and is now trying to take advantage of the corporate strength and resources that result from the company's size and the enormous consumer awareness of the Kodak name. Kodak continues to remain a dominant force in the photographic industry, and with expansions beyond that domain, it may make progress in new areas.

Questions for Discussion

1. What are the potential implications of Kodak's decision to market products that it does not manufacture? Evaluate possible positive and negative effects.
2. Considering that Kodak's recent product developments have been low-cost, mass market items, how should the company position its new products such as 35-millimeter cameras? Bear in mind that these products will be higher priced and technologically superior.
3. Suggest new products for Kodak's expanding product mix.
4. Identify Kodak's mature and declining products and suggest strategies for managing these products.

30. Taylor, "Kodak Scrambles," pp. 35, 36.
31. Taylor, "Kodak Scrambles," pp. 36, 38, 39.

Case 8.2 Saab's Product Positioning

Saab-Scania is a $3-billion "transport technology" company located in Sweden.[32] The corporation was formed in 1969 by a merger of Saab, a car and aircraft maker and Scania-Vabis, a truck manufacturer. Currently trucks and buses account for 52 percent of Saab's sales, cars 34 percent, and aircraft 6 percent.[33] After the merger, the car division produced the weakest products in terms of sales and performance. The early Saab automobile had been called "a homely, underpowered car that only a troll could love."[34] Saab's early automobiles were not very competitive or well known in the world market.

Saab cars had several problems, primarily that their design and performance was "out of touch with the market," according to Robert Sinclair, president of Saab-Scania of America.[35] Saab also had problems recruiting dealers in top markets. But major changes occurred in 1977 when product lines were evaluated and improved with the goal of increasing profit and reducing debt. Engineers were allowed to experiment, with few constraints—except that the end product was to offer high performance and quality. The result—Saab became the first automaker to introduce a turbo-charged engine. Turbo charging involves mixing fuel and air under high pressure to give a car additional power.[36] With a higher-performance engine, Saab realized it had a defensible product benefit. The next step was to redesign the automobile, abandoning its ten-year-old design. The end result was the sleeker line of 900 models. Saab successfully built a technologically and aerodynamically superior product. In addition, Saab pioneered safety features such as seat belts, head rests, crumple zones, and positioning the gas tank above the rear axle to prevent explosion in collisions. To support the high-value position, the list of standard equipment on the 900-series automobiles is impressive, including air conditioning; five-speed or automatic transmission; sun roof; alloy wheels and radial tires; electric door locks, windows, and outside mirrors; electrically heated front seats; full instrumentation, including quartz clock and tachometer; bronze-tinted glass; rear-window defogger; power steering; and front and rear power disc brakes. In addition, the turbo version has an AM/FM stereo radio and cassette player with four speakers, a graphic equalizer, and a retractable antenna.

Saab has positioned its cars to appeal to a small but growing and profitable market niche. Today's average Saab owners are thirty to forty years old, well educated (96 percent are college graduates, of which 40 percent have attended graduate school), with an income between $50,000 and $80,000. Saab takes great pride in its ability to provide effective service to this up-scale segment.[37] Sales personnel thoroughly explain the car's operations and introduce the buyer to the service manager. Saab also follows up on each sale with a questionnaire asking about dealer performance, a thank you from the company's president, and a Saab coffee mug and key ring. As a result of the strong service and

32. Bernie Whalen, "Tiny Saab Drives Up Profits with Market Niche Strategy Repositioning," *Marketing News,* March 16, 1984, p. 14.
33. Ibid., p. 16.
34. Louis Richman, "Saab-Scania Kicks Into High Gear," *Fortune,* Nov. 26, 1984, p. 105.
35. Ibid., p. 106.
36. Ibid.
37. Whalen, "Tiny Saab," p. 16.

product quality, brand loyalty is high. Approximately 75 percent of current owners plan to repurchase a Saab automobile.[38] Saab has moved strategically into one of the fastest-growing areas in the auto industry, the luxury/sport segment.

When Saab redeveloped the 900 and 9000, a joint development effort between Saab and Lancia, marketers had to take strong steps to broaden the consumer's awareness of the Saab automobile. The car was positioned as follows:

A luxurious high-performance automobile
Directly competitive with BMW and Volvo
In the $13,000–$20,000 price range
A tough competitor

But what Saab did not expect was the car's enormous success in the United States. According to a company executive, Saab has become the car of the Yuppies.[39] Saab's successful positioning of its automobiles has created a new problem—how to meet increased consumer demand. Saab's American success shows how a small automaker can develop an expertise, position its product in the consumer's mind, and meet some very specific consumer requirements in one of the most intensely competitive product markets in the United States. In fact, many Saab owners belong to Saab owners clubs, attending annual meetings and picnics to discuss their common denominator: the Saab—"The most intelligent car ever built."[40] As long as this niche continues to believe that claim, Saab will be successful.

Questions for Discussion

1. Based on your own knowledge, how has Saab positioned its 900 series differently from other import automobiles (i.e., Volvo, BMW, Mercedes)?
2. In what way should Saab's new product development support its current market image or position?
3. As a product manager for Saab, would you support a redesign of the 900 model to make it more stylistically competitive with other foreign imports?

38. Ibid., p. 15.
39. "Saab Hitches Its Star to the Yuppie Market," *Business Week,* Nov. 19, 1984, p. 62.
40. Gay Jervey, "Saab Steers into Import-Car Mainstream," *Advertising Age,* Oct. 3, 1983, p. 4.

Part III
Distribution Decisions

Providing customers with satisfying products is important but not sufficient for successful marketing strategies. These products also must be available in adequate quantities in accessible locations at the times when customers desire them. The chapters in Part III deal with the distribution of products and the marketing channels and institutions that provide the structure for making products available. In Chapter 9, we discuss the structure and functions of marketing channels and present an overview of institutions that make up marketing channels. Chapter 10 analyzes the types of wholesalers and the functions that they perform. Then we focus on retailing and retailers in Chapter 11. Specifically, we examine the types of retailers as well as their roles and functions in marketing channels. Finally, in Chapter 12, we analyze the decisions and activities associated with the physical distribution of products, such as inventory planning and control, transportation, warehousing, materials handling, and communications.

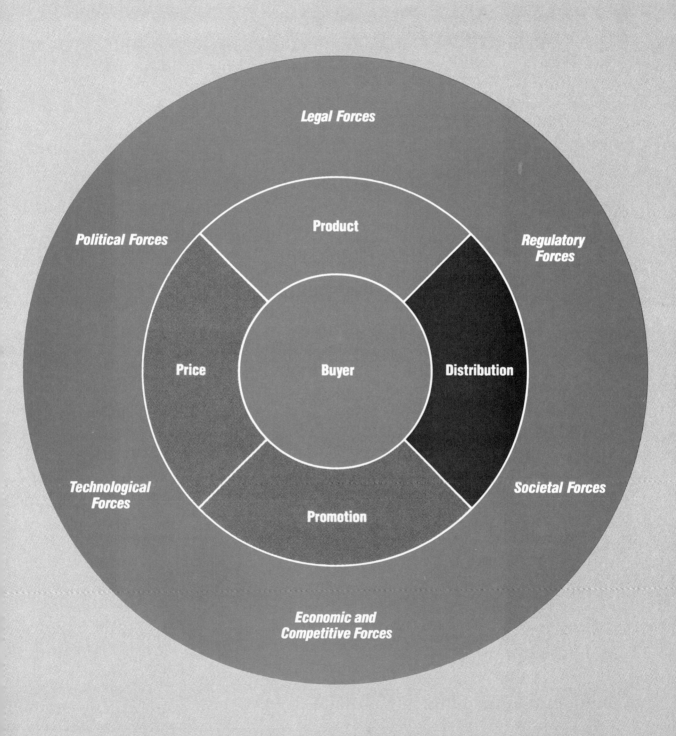

Legal Forces

Political Forces

Regulatory Forces

Product

Price

Buyer

Distribution

Technological Forces

Societal Forces

Promotion

Economic and Competitive Forces

9 / Marketing Channels

Objectives

■ To understand the marketing channel concept and the types of marketing intermediaries in the channel.

■ To discuss the justification of channel members.

■ To examine the structure and function of the channel system.

■ To explore the power dimensions of channels, especially the concepts of cooperation, conflict, and leadership.

Figure 9.1

Hewlett-Packard recognizes the importance of dealers to the distribution of its new line of computers (Source: Hewlett-Packard Company. Hewlett-Packard Vectra Personal Computer shown)

Hewlett-Packard Co. (HP) is known for its computers in the manufacturing, engineering, and scientific environments, but it is more widely known as a maker of scientific instruments. HP is now seeking to become a "computer company" (see Figure 9.1). With that aim in mind, HP has added the small business market to its target market for microcomputers. HP recognizes the importance of dealers and other resellers in reaching the small business market; HP salespeople are working as liaisons between developers or value-added resellers and the manufacturer. HP provides technical information and practical support in systems ordering, merchandising, sales literature, trade-show support, and cooperative advertising allowances. In short, the company is assisting resellers in maintaining profitable margins. To minimize conflict between HP's direct-sales force and dealers, HP encourages its direct sales force to turn over smaller sales to those dealers. In return, the direct sales force receives commissions on those sales.[1]

1. Gerald Frankel, "Hewlett-Packard Plots New Market Course," *Business Marketing*, April 1985, p. 20.

The selection of marketing channels is one of the most critical decisions in developing a marketing strategy. In this chapter, we first present the concepts used to describe and analyze marketing channels. We illustrate the main types of channels and discuss their structures. Then we justify the existence of intermediaries and explain the sorting activities of channel members. Next, we discuss the functions of intermediaries and facilitating agencies, as well as the intensity of market coverage and considerations affecting channel selection. Finally, we examine the behavioral dimensions of channels, including the concepts of cooperation and conflict.

The Nature of Marketing Channels

A **marketing channel,** or **channel of distribution,** is a group of interrelated intermediaries who direct products to customers. The intermediary is a go-between that links producers and buyers. The customer is the ultimate driver of all marketing channel activities. The desires and behavior of buyers are therefore the most important concerns of intermediaries. The marketing intermediary, or middleman, performs the activities described in Table 9.1. There are two major types of **marketing intermediaries,** merchants and agents or brokers. **Merchants** take title to merchandise and resell it, whereas **agents** and **brokers** receive a commission or fee for expediting exchanges.[2]

Both wholesalers and retailers are classified as intermediaries, existing as either merchants or agents. Agents and brokers do not take title to products,

Table 9.1 *Marketing channel activities performed by intermediaries*

Category of Marketing Activities	Possible Activities Required
Marketing information	Analyze information such as sales data; perform or commission marketing research studies.
Marketing management	Establish objectives; plan activities; manage and coordinate financing, personnel, and risk taking; evaluate and control channel activities.
Facilitating exchange	Choose product assortments that match the needs of buyers.
Promotion	Set promotional objectives, coordinate advertising, personal selling, sales promotion, publicity, and packaging.
Price	Establish pricing policies and terms of sales.
Physical distribution	Manage transportation, warehousing, materials handling, inventory control, and communication.

2. Ralph S. Alexander, *Marketing Definitions: A Glossary of Marketing Terms* (Chicago: American Marketing Association, 1960).

California Cooler, a new low-alcohol beverage, was first developed and marketed in the early 1980s. This mixture of white wine and fruit juices was packaged like an imported beer—12-ounce green bottles wrapped at the neck with green foil. The target market of the drink was not imported beer drinkers, but the much larger number of domestic beer and soft-drink buyers.

With distribution in forty-nine states and 1984 sales of $72 million, California Cooler, Inc., is the fourth-largest wine distributor in the United States. The company's strength is its marketing channel strategy. The company decided to use beer distributors to reach the mass market. Besides widespread availability, this channel offered several other advantages. Beer salespeople carry relatively few product items in their line, thus minimizing conflict with direct competitors. Beer distributors also are able to maintain appropriate inventory levels and to communicate effectively with retailers. In addition, few wine products were distributed through this channel when California Cooler began to use it.

To benefit its distributors, California Cooler's superior packaging supported a retail price comparable to that of imported beer. The substantial selling price provided the distributor with an attractive markup.

The widespread availability of the product is significant as competitors invade the market. Heublein, Inc., Joseph E. Seagram & Sons, Inc., and others have done so. Fifty percent of these firms are using beer distributors.

California Cooler developed an appealing product and clever packaging and pulled off a distribution coup by using an existing channel that its competitors had ignored. The competition has responded with similar products and the same distribution strategy. (*Source: Peter Dworkin, "Strange Brew." Reprinted with permission,* Inc. *magazine (Jan. 1985), pp. 99–102. Copyright © 1985 by INC. Publishing Company, 38 Commercial Wharf, Boston, MA 02110.*)

but they do negotiate transfer of ownership or possession of products. Agents and brokers perform fewer marketing activities than most merchants. In this chapter, all wholesalers should be considered merchants unless specifically designated as agents or brokers.

Channel members share certain significant characteristics. Each member has different responsibilities within the overall structure of the distribution system, but mutual profit and success can be attained only if channel members cooperate in delivering products to the market.

Although channel decisions need not precede other marketing decisions, they do exercise a powerful influence on the rest of the marketing mix. Channel decisions are critical because they determine a product's market presence and the efficiency of buyer service. Their strategic significance is further heightened by their inherent long-term commitments. It is much easier to change prices or packaging than distribution systems. The application on this page provides a good example of an effective marketing channel for a new product. Distribution was the pivotal element in determining the marketing mix for California Cooler.

Availability benefits the total product. Marketing channel members make products available at the right time, in the right place, and in the right quantity by providing such product-enhancing functions as transportation and storage. Although consumers do not see the distribution of a product, they evaluate the availability that distribution makes possible. Days Inns of America, Inc.,

Figure 9.2

Typical marketing channels for consumer products

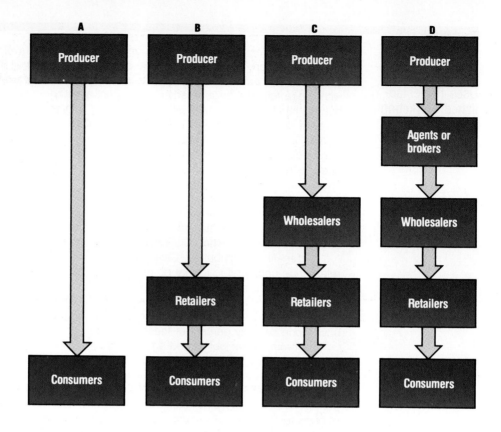

made a location decision to build budget motels along interstate highways from the Northeast and the lower Ohio valley to Orlando, Florida, home of Walt Disney World. Today the Days Inn motels in Orlando are the largest provider of lodging in the area.[3] Now the company has a new distribution strategy designed to push development through the Sun Belt and the remaining parts of the North. Even though motels basically deliver a service, making this service available at particular locations is one of the most important marketing mix decisions, with long-run consequences.

Types of Channels

The marketing channel's structure defines the arrangement and linkage of the channel's members. Consumers may want—and organizations can design—almost any number of different distribution paths. In any channel, however, the various links are the merchants (including producers) and agents who have managerial responsibility for a product as it moves through the channel.

Channels for Consumer Products

Several typical channels for consumer products are depicted in Figure 9.2. Channel A illustrates the direct movement of a product to consumers. Customers who cut their own Christmas trees at a tree farm or pick their own berries or

3. "Days Inns: Looking for a Berth in a Crowded National Field," *Business Week,* Oct. 31, 1983, p. 70.

Figure 9.3

Typical marketing
channels for
industrial products

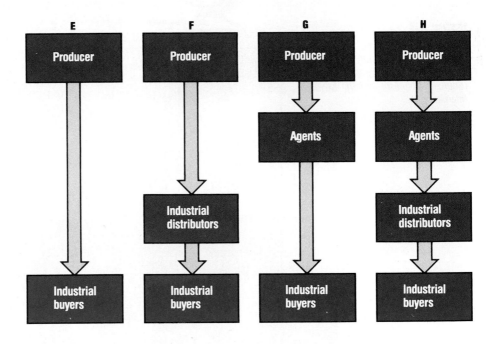

fruit are helping to create a direct channel. Likewise, producers who sell directly from the factory provide a direct marketing channel to consumers.

Channel B—producer to retailers to consumers—is a common choice for products like automobiles. Using such a channel structure, large retailers like J. C. Penney and Sears sell many products such as stereos and tires, which they buy directly from producers.

Channel C—producer to wholesalers to retailers to consumers—is one of the most traditional channels. Typical products distributed on this basis include manufacturer-brand refrigerators, beer, and tobacco products.

Channel D—producer to agents to wholesalers to retailers to consumers— is typically used for products, like candy, that have mass market distribution. Candy often is sold to wholesalers by brokers or agents, who facilitate negotiations by bringing buyers and sellers together. Wholesalers then supply the product to retail stores, vending machines, and other outlets that sell to ultimate consumers.

Channels for Industrial Products

Figure 9.3 illustrates typical channels for industrial products. Products for large industrial buyers are often sold directly to them (Channel E). If the number of customers increases, then direct distribution may not be effective. For example, Mitsubishi Aircraft International, Inc., a Dallas-based subsidiary of Mitsubishi Heavy Industries, sells its Diamond I corporate jet (illustrated in Figure 9.4) direct to corporate buyers (Channel E). In contrast, when Mitsubishi decided to market industrial and construction products such as fork-lift trucks, it used industrial distributors—merchants who take title to products, as shown in Channel F.

Agents are appropriate in industrial channels when products are standardized and when selling functions and information gathering are important. For example, Channel G might be suitable for selling soybeans to animal food processors.

Figure 9.4

The Mitsubishi Diamond I jet, marketed directly to corporate purchasers (Source: Mitsubishi Aircraft International)

Channel H is used, for example, by export agents who sell electronic components from Japan to distributors serving small manufacturers or service dealers in the United States.

Since industrial purchasers use products to produce other products or for operations, retailers rarely appear in the industrial channel. (Industrial buyers may occasionally purchase products in retail stores, though.) However, if an industrial buyer uses the industrial product as a component of a consumer product, then a new marketing channel is created. The final product may pass through wholesalers and retailers on its way to consumers. (More information on industrial marketing channels appears in Chapter 20.)

Multiple Marketing Channels

Multiple marketing channels provide different intermediaries to direct products to customers. Since the buyer is the ultimate concern in designing a marketing channel, different marketing channels may be needed to reach diverse markets or unique market segments. Mitsubishi Motor Sales sells automobiles to Chrysler Corporation for U.S. distribution through Chrysler dealers. Also Mitsubishi and Chrysler are jointly building an assembly plant in Normal, Illinois, that will produce cars for both companies. Mitsubishi products are marketed as the Dodge Colt (as illustrated in Figure 9.5), Plymouth Champ, Plymouth Sapporo, and Dodge Challenger. Mitsubishi began to develop its own U.S. dealership

network to compete directly with Chrysler a few years ago. Mitsubishi developed the dual marketing channels for automobiles because Chrysler now has a full line of its own small cars and because the dealerships will sustain U.S. sales even if Chrysler does not focus its efforts on Mitsubishi products.

In fact, firms that sell only a few products often use multiple marketing channels. For example, in addition to employing a sales force, Xerox established eighty-eight Xerox stores worldwide. More than half the volume from these stores is from the sale of Xerox equipment.[4]

Justifications for Intermediaries

Even if producers and buyers are located in the same city, there are costs associated with exchanges. As shown in Figure 9.6, if five buyers purchased the products of five producers, twenty-five transactions are needed for the buyers to obtain their products. If one intermediary serves both producers and buyers, the number of transactions can be reduced to ten. Intermediaries become specialists in the division of labor. They exercise control and provide

4. David T. Kearns, "Xerox: A Progress Report," *Agenda: 14,* Jan. 1983, p. 5.

Figure 9.6

Efficiency in
exchanges provided
by an intermediary

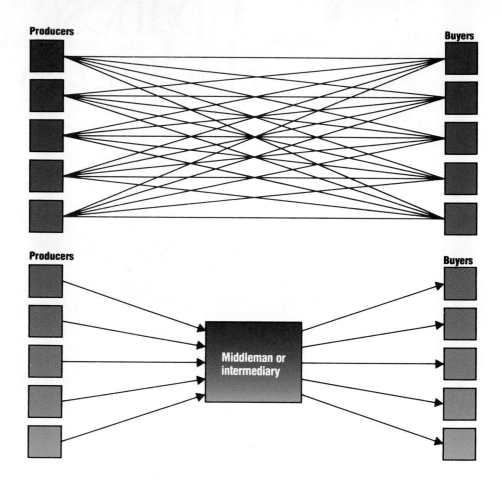

valuable assistance because of their access to, and control over, important resources for the proper functioning of the marketing channel.

Nevertheless, the press, consumers, public officials, and other marketers freely criticize wholesalers. Table 9.2 indicates that in a 1985 national survey of the general public, 74 percent believed that "wholesalers frequently make profits which significantly increase prices that consumers pay." The critics accuse wholesalers of being inefficient and parasitic. Consumers often are obsessed with making the distribution channel as short as possible. They assume that the fewer the intermediaries, the lower the price. Since suggestions to eliminate them come from both ends of the marketing channel, wholesalers must be careful to perform only those marketing activities that are truly desirable. To survive, they must be more efficient and more service oriented than alternative marketing institutions.

Critics who suggest that eliminating wholesalers would result in lower prices for consumers do not recognize that eliminating wholesalers would not do away with the need for the services they provide. Other institutions would have to perform those services, and consumers would still have to pay for them. In addition, all producers would have to deal directly with retailers or consumers, meaning that every producer would have to keep voluminous records and hire enough personnel to deal with every customer. Even in a

Table 9.2 *Consumer misunderstanding about wholesalers*

Statement: Wholesalers frequently make high profits which significantly increase prices that consumers pay.

	Total %	Male %	Female %
Strongly Agree	35.5	33	38
Somewhat Agree	38	40	36
Neither Agree			
nor Disagree	16	14	18
Somewhat Disagree	8	9	7
Strongly Disagree	2.5	4	1

Source: © O. C. Ferrell and William M. Pride. National multi-stage area probability sample of 2,045 households, 1985.

direct channel, consumers might end up paying a great deal more for products because prices would reflect the costs of inefficient producers' operations.

To illustrate the efficient service that wholesalers provide in the market system, assume that all wholesalers were eliminated. Since there are over 1.3 million retail stores, a widely purchased consumer product—say candy— would require an extraordinary number of sales contacts, possibly over a million, to maintain the current level of product exposure. For example, Mars, Inc. would have to deliver its candy, purchase and service thousands of vending machines, establish warehouses all over the country, and maintain fleets of trucks. Selling and distribution costs for candy would skyrocket. Instead of a few contacts with food brokers, large retail organizations, and various merchant wholesalers, candy manufacturers would face thousands of expensive contacts with and shipments to small retailers. Such an operation would be highly inefficient, and its costs would be passed on to consumers. Candy bars would cost more, and they would be harder to find. Wholesalers are more efficient and less expensive not only for manufacturers, but also for consumers.

Functions of Intermediaries

Before we examine the functions of intermediaries, we should define some key terms. An **assortment** is a combination of similar or complementary products put together to provide benefits to a specific market. The lack of consistency or completeness in an assortment calls for sorting activities.[5] **Sorting activities** allow channel members to divide roles and separate tasks. The four main tasks are sorting out, accumulating, allocating, and assorting products (see Figure 9.7).

Consider a supermarket. Meat, frozen vegetables, produce, canned goods, and dairy products come from different producers and require unique handling;

5. Wroe Alderson, *Marketing Behavior and Executive Action* (Homewood, Ill.: Irwin, 1957), p. 216.

Figure 9.7

Sorting activities conducted by intermediaries

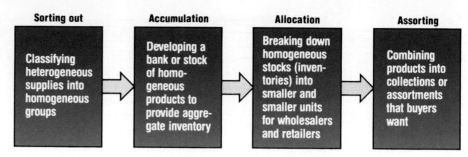

Sorting out	Accumulation	Allocation	Assorting
Classifying heterogeneous supplies into homogeneous groups	Developing a bank or stock of homogeneous products to provide aggregate inventory	Breaking down homogeneous stocks (inventories) into smaller and smaller units for wholesalers and retailers	Combining products into collections or assortments that buyers want

therefore, the supermarket usually depends on different wholesalers for different kinds of supplies. If the supermarket itself attempted to perform the wholesaling function for these diverse products, its risks and investment would increase. Instead, the distribution network makes it possible to develop specialized mass production and yet satisfy the differentiated tastes of consumers.[6] To perform this function, intermediaries perform the four main tasks mentioned above.

Sorting Out

Sorting out is the first step in developing an assortment. It involves breaking down conglomerates of heterogeneous supplies into relatively homogeneous groups. The conglomerates of heterogeneous supplies are so diversified that they are unrelated to one another in functional structure or usefulness to ultimate buyers. Sorting out is the primary step in marketing agricultural and extractive products. Grading eggs exemplifies the sorting process. It makes relatively homogeneous products available for the next step, accumulation.

Accumulation

Through **accumulation,** a bank or inventory is developed of homogeneous products that have similar production or demand requirements. It would be illogical, for example, to develop large inventories of both chain saws and packaged food products because these products come from different manufacturers and usually are sold by different retailers. On the other hand, all power tools manufactured by a company could be developed into an inventory so that the tools could be allocated to stores according to their customers' needs.

Allocation

Allocation is the breaking down of large homogeneous inventories into smaller lots. Wholesalers typically break down large lots and then apportion products to other channel members. Often, a wholesaler buys efficiently in truckload or carload lots and then divides products into case lots. Tobacco wholesalers, for example, provide the bulk-breaking service for competing tobacco companies, affix state tobacco tax stamps, and deliver an entire tobacco assortment to retailers.

Wholesalers serve as a depot and allocate products according to market demand. For example, retailers purchase collections of products from wholesalers; these collections contain competing brands so that retailers can develop suitable assortments for consumers.

6. Ibid., p. 217.

Assorting

Assorting is combining products into collections or assortments that buyers want available at one place. Assorting thus combines products in ways that satisfy buyers, especially at the retail level. Retailers strive to create assortments that match the demands of consumers who patronize their stores. A convenience grocery, for example, is expected to have an assortment of fresh dairy products such as milk, butter, and cheese.

The number and kind of intermediaries in the marketing channel are influenced by the kinds of assortments desired by buyers and by the efficiency of channel arrangements. The assortment of products desired at one location usually relates to some task that buyers want to perform or some problem that they want solved.

Functions of Facilitating Agencies

The total marketing channel is more than a chain linking the producer, intermediary, and buyer. Figure 9.8 illustrates that **facilitating agencies**—transportation companies, insurance companies, advertising agencies, marketing research agencies, and financial institutions—may perform activities that enhance channel functions. Note, however, that any of the functions performed by these facilitating agencies may be taken over by the regular marketing intermediaries in the marketing channel (producers, wholesalers, and retailers).

The basic difference between channel members and facilitating agencies is that members perform the negotiating functions (buying, selling, and transferring title), whereas facilitating agencies do not.[7] In other words, facilitating agencies assist in the operation of the channel but do not sell products. The channel manager may view the facilitating agency as a subcontractor to whom various distribution tasks can be "farmed out" on the principle of specialization and division of labor.[8] Channel members (producers, wholesalers, or retailers) may rely on facilitating agencies because they believe that these independent businesses will perform various activities more efficiently and more effectively than they themselves could.

Marketing research agencies, financial institutions, insurance companies, warehouses, and transportation companies perform essential services that add value and develop benefits that buyers want. Facilitating agencies are functional specialists performing special tasks for channel members without getting involved in directing or controlling channel decisions. They have no control over the path that products take as they move from producers to buyers.

Many people fail to recognize the value added by major channel members and facilitating agencies. For instance, developing assortments of products when and where buyers want them creates important product benefits. Figure 9.9 illustrates transportation services available from a facilitating agency, in this case Norfolk Southern.

Channel functions may be passed on to buyers, or producers may perform the activities themselves instead of passing them on to other channel members. The next section examines how channel members can either combine and

7. Bert Rosenbloom, *Marketing Channels: A Management View* (Hinsdale, Ill.: Dryden Press, 1983), p. 28.
8. Ibid.

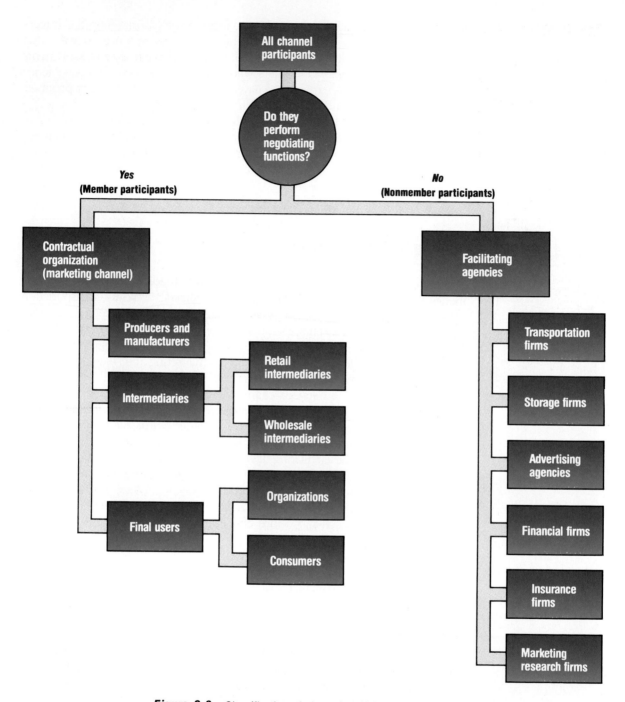

Figure 9.8 *Classification of channel participants (Source:* Marketing Channels: A Management View, *2nd ed., by Bert Rosenbloom. Copyright © 1983 by the Dryden Press. Reprinted by permission of The Dryden Press, CBS College Publishing)*

Figure 9.9 *Norfolk Southern—a facilitating agency assisting firms with transportation*
(Source: Courtesy of Norfolk Southern)

control most activities or pass them on to another intermediary. Remember, though, that the channel member cannot eliminate functions and that unless buyers themselves perform the functions, they must pay for the labor and resources needed to perform them. The statement that "you can eliminate wholesalers but you can't eliminate their functions" is a universally accepted principle of marketing.

Channel Integration

Many marketing channels are determined by consensus. Producers, facilitating agencies, and intermediaries coordinate their efforts for mutual benefit. Some marketing channels, however, are organized and controlled by a single leader, who can be a producer, a wholesaler, or a retailer. The channel leader may establish channel policies and coordinate the development of the marketing mix. Sears, for example, is a channel leader for some of the many products that it sells.

The various links or stages of the channel may be combined under the management of a channel leader either horizontally or vertically. Integration may stabilize supply, reduce costs, and increase coordination of channel members.

Figure 9.10

Promotion showing that The Gap has integrated vertically by producing its own clothes (Source: Courtesy of The Gap, Inc.)

KNOW-HOW

Back in 1969 when we opened the first Gap store in San Francisco, our business didn't take much know-how. We simply offered America the best way to shop for Levi's® blue jeans. Period.

Change

Things aren't so simple now. Over the years we've become experts in our own right. We've learned that if you want just the right shade of blue denim you need to start with the cotton yarn. And dip it eight times in indigo dye. We've learned that when you really know casual clothing, you can even improve on a traditional jean jacket. (Ours has bigger front pockets and we make it longer and fuller, so it's better over sweaters.)

Color

But denim isn't everything. So we offer sweatshirts in 21 great colors. Lambswool vests in 16 colors. Shetland sweaters in 13 colors. And corduroy pants in 8 colors.

Honest Value

We produce most Gap clothes ourselves. That way we can offer you a great price, and still make sure that everything we sell meets our quality standards, and yours. Take a close look as you browse through this catalogue. You'll notice all kinds of special details—double and triple-brushed cotton flannel shirts, full-fashioned sweaters, and rugged heavyweight indigo denim. But words, and even pictures, can't really explain the know-how that goes into Gap clothes. You can't feel how soft the lambswool vests are, or see how great the corduroy trousers fit, but after one visit to the Gap store nearest you, you'll know for yourself.

the gap

Gap Denim . . . available in jeans and jackets for him and her. We guarantee the most functional, authentic denim you can buy.

Vertical Channel Integration

Combining two or more stages of the channel under one management is **vertical channel integration.** For example, Figure 9.10 shows that The Gap has integrated vertically into the production of clothes. One member of a marketing channel may purchase the operations of another member or simply take over the functions that the other member performed. Vertical integration eliminates the need for an intermediary as a separate institution. Esprit de Corp, a maker of youth-oriented fashions, is becoming increasingly vertically integrated. Esprit has traditionally designed and manufactured clothing that "projected an image of a young woman, sexy, vivacious, romantic and flirtatious, a girl who wanted it all."[9] Now Esprit is opening its own retail outlets. President Doug Tompkins commented on his dissatisfaction with department stores which are "famous for cramming a lot of stuff together so that you lose the personality of each line." Through the opening of retail outlets, Esprit hopes to increase sales in department stores by strengthening its overall image and awareness of its label in the marketplace.[10]

Total vertical integration would include control of all functions from production to the final buyer. Some oil companies typify this kind of integration; Mobil owns oil wells, transportation facilities, refineries, and terminals that sell direct to retailers.

9. Joan Kron, "Apparel Firm Makes Profits, Takes Risks by Flouting Tradition," *Wall Street Journal,* June 11, 1985, pp. 1, 10.
10. Amy Dunkin, "Clothing Maker Goes Straight to the Consumer," *Business Week,* April 29, 1985, pp. 114, 115.

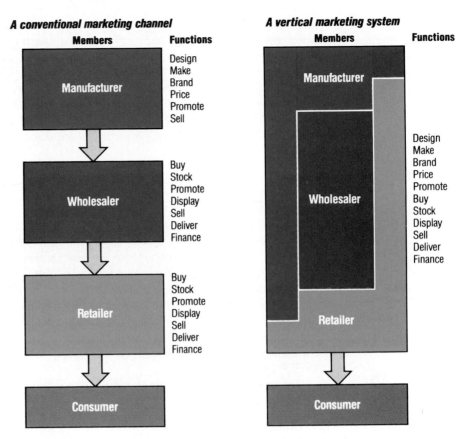

A conventional marketing channel

Members	Functions
Manufacturer	Design Make Brand Price Promote Sell
Wholesaler	Buy Stock Promote Display Sell Deliver Finance
Retailer	Buy Stock Promote Display Sell Deliver Finance
Consumer	

A vertical marketing system

Members	Functions
Manufacturer **Wholesaler** **Retailer**	Design Make Brand Price Promote Buy Stock Display Sell Deliver Finance
Consumer	

Figure 9.11 Comparison of a conventional marketing channel and a vertical marketing system (Source: Strategic Marketing, by David J. Kollat, Roger D. Blackwell, and James F. Robeson. Copyright © 1972 by Holt, Rinehart and Winston, Inc. Reprinted by permission of Holt, Rinehart and Winston, CBS College Publishing)

Integration has proved successful in professionally managed and centrally controlled marketing channels called **vertical marketing systems (VMS).**[11] Most vertical marketing systems are organized with the objective of improving distribution by combining individual efforts. The corporate VMS combines successive channel stages from producers to consumers under one ownership. Figure 9.11 illustrates a shift from the conventional channel to a vertical marketing system. The right side of the figure indicates marketing functions or institutions owned or controlled by the same firm. For example, the manufacturer can own wholesaling operations and control the retailer through a franchise agreement.

In an administered VMS, channel members are independent, but informal coordination brings about a high level of interorganizational management. Decision making takes into account the goals of the system, while authority remains with individual channel members, as it does in conventional marketing channels. Examples of administered marketing channels include Sears (retailer),

11. Bert C. McCammon, Jr., "Perspectives for Distribution Programming," in *Vertical Marketing Systems,* Louis P. Bucklin, ed. (Glenview, Ill.: Scott, Foresman, 1970), p. 43.

Kellogg (cereal), and Magnavox (television and other electronic products). Sears, for example, can strongly influence manufacturers because of the large marketing opportunity that it offers.

Under a contractual VMS, interorganizational relationships are formalized through contracts or other legal agreements. This arrangement is best illustrated by franchise organizations like McDonald's and Kentucky Fried Chicken. Several stages are linked together by legal agreements concerning the rights and obligations of channel members. (Franchisers are discussed in Chapter 11.)

Horizontal Channel Integration

Combining institutions at the same level of operation under one management constitutes **horizontal channel integration.** Store chains such as Dayton-Hudson Corp. illustrate horizontal integration at the retail level. Dayton-Hudson, one of the nation's largest retailers, has expanded from a regional department store chain (Hudson's, Dayton's, Diamond's, John A. Brown) into Target discount stores and B. Dalton bookstores. More recently, Dayton-Hudson has been opening off-price fashion outlets (stores that sell brand-name merchandise at discount prices). Dayton-Hudson is expanding at the same level in a retailing channel.[12]

Horizontal integration allows efficiencies and economies of scale in advertising, marketing research, purchasing, and the employment of specialists. An organization can effect horizontal integration by merging with other organizations or by expanding the number of units (retail stores, for example) at one channel level.

Horizontal integration is not always the best managerial approach to improving distribution. Its limitations include

1. Difficulties in coordinating a large number of units
2. A decrease in flexibility
3. An increase in planning and research to cope with larger-scale operations and more heterogeneous markets

Unless the organization that is combining units can perform the specific channel activities more efficiently than independent stores, horizontal integration will not reduce costs or enhance the competitive position of the organization.

Intensity of Market Coverage

Characteristics of the product and the target market determine the kind of coverage a product should get—that is, the number and kinds of outlets in which it is sold. To achieve the desired intensity of market coverage, distribution must correspond to the behavior patterns of buyers. Chapter 5 divided consumer products into three categories—convenience products, shopping products, and specialty products—according to how consumers make purchases. Consumers view products in terms of replacement rate, product adjustment (services), duration of consumption, searching time to find the product, and similar factors.[13] These variables directly affect the intensity of market coverage.

12. John Curley and Lawrence Ingrassia, "Big Retailer Seeks Profits in Discounting," *Wall Street Journal,* Oct. 26, 1982, p. 29.
13. Leo Aspinwall, "The Marketing Characteristics of Goods," in *Four Marketing Theories* (Boulder: University of Colorado Press, 1961), pp. 27–32.

Three major levels of market coverage are intensive, selective, and exclusive distribution. **Intensive distribution** is a form of market coverage in which all available outlets are used for distributing a product. In **selective distribution,** only some available outlets in an area are chosen to distribute a product. **Exclusive distribution** is a type of market coverage in which only one outlet is used in a relatively large geographic area.

Intensive Distribution

Intensive distribution is appropriate for convenience products such as bread, chewing gum, beer, and newspapers. To consumers, availability means a nearby store location as well as a minimum of searching time for the product at the store. Sales may have a direct relationship to availability. The successful sale of bread and milk at service stations or of gasoline at convenience grocery stores has shown that the availability of these products is more important than the nature of the outlet. Convenience products have a high replacement rate and require almost no service. To meet these demands, intensive distribution is necessary, and multiple channels may be used to sell through all possible outlets.

Consumer packaged products rely on intensive distribution. Intensive distribution is one of the key strengths of Procter & Gamble. It is fairly easy for this company to formulate marketing strategies for many of its products (soups, detergents, food and juice products, and personal care products), since consumers desire availability that is provided quickly on an intensive basis. Under such conditions, a new product line can be made available to almost every consumer in a very short time. For example, Procter & Gamble's Citrus Hill orange juice, in both frozen concentrate and chilled, ready-to-serve form, was launched nationally after only one year of testing in Indiana. Desired market coverage was possible because Procter & Gamble already had an intensive distribution system in place.[14]

Selective Distribution

Selective distribution is appropriate for shopping products. Durable goods such as typewriters and stereos usually fall in this category. Such products are more expensive than convenience goods. Consumers are willing to spend greater searching time visiting several retail outlets to compare prices, designs, styles, and other features.

Selective distribution is desirable when a special effort—such as customer service from a channel member—is important. Shopping products require differentiation at the point of purchase. To motivate retailers to provide adequate presale service, selective distribution and company-owned stores are often used. Many industrial products are sold on a selective basis to maintain a certain degree of control over the distribution process. For example, agricultural herbicides (chemicals that kill weeds) are distributed on a selective basis because dealers must offer services to buyers, such as instructions about how to apply the herbicides safely, or the option of having the dealer apply the herbicide. As illustrated in Figure 9.12, Mariner indicates that its outboard motors are sold by dealers on a selective basis.

14. "P&G Dives into Orange Juice with a Big Splash," *Business Week,* Oct. 31, 1983, p. 50.

Figure 9.12

Mariner Outboards'
selective distribution of
dealerships (Source:
Courtesy of Mariner
Outboards)

Exclusive Distribution

Exclusive distribution is suitable for products that are purchased rather infrequently, that are consumed over a long period of time, or that require service or information to fit them to buyers' needs. Exclusive distribution is used often as an incentive to sellers when only a limited market is available for products. For example, automobiles like the Rolls Royce are sold on an exclusive basis. Customers often seek out the product, but specialized promotion is needed occasionally. For example, a Rolls Royce dealer in Houston, Texas was having difficulty liquidating his previous year's inventory of five Rolls Royce automobiles. To make this select potential target market aware of his inventory, the dealer mailed 30,000 letters to homes with incomes over $100,000.

Behavior of Channel Members

The marketing channel is a social system with patterned and recurrent behavior. Each channel member has a position with rights, responsibilities, rewards, and sanctions for nonconformity. In addition, each channel member has certain expectations of every other channel member. Retailers expect wholesalers to maintain adequate inventories and to provide on-time deliveries. Wholesalers expect retailers to honor payment agreements and to keep them informed about inventory levels. For the channel to function as a social system, role differentiation must result in a division of labor.

Channel Cooperation

Channel cooperation is required if each channel member expects to gain something from other members.[15] It is necessary for the attainment of overall channel goals and individual member goals. Unless a channel member can be replaced, the failure of one link in the chain could destroy the channel. This vulnerability means that policies must be developed to ensure the welfare and survival of all necessary channel members.

An example of channel cooperation would be licensing a product to open up new markets. Miller Brewing Company licensed Carling O'Keefe, Ltd., Canada's fastest-growing brewer, to brew and market Miller beer products. It was estimated that Miller accounted for 9 percent of Canadian consumption after just four months on the market. Since Canada restricts the importation of beer, the licensing agreement was the best way to enter this market, and Carling O'Keefe was able to dramatically increase its market share.[16]

Channel Conflict

Since roles are the means of integration and coordination, role deviance or malfunction is a major source of **channel conflict.** In terms of channel behavior, actual role deviance is not the only source of channel conflict, however. A channel member's perception that goal attainment is being impeded by another channel member will also result in stress or tension. For example, a number of conflicts are developing in the marketing channels for microcomputer software. Many software-only stores are bypassing wholesale distributors and establishing direct relationships with software publishers. Some dishonest retailers are hacking, or making unauthorized copies of software, preventing other channel members from getting their due compensation. These events are causing stress in software marketing channels because of suspicion and lack of trust.[17]

Each role in the channel represents an expected mode of conduct and defines the contribution of that unit in the system.[18] For example, wholesalers expect producers to take care of quality control and production scheduling, and they expect retailers to merchandise products effectively. It is the responsibility of wholesalers, in turn, to conform to the expectations of both retailers and producers by providing coordination, functional services, and communication. If wholesalers or producers fail to deliver products on time, that constitutes channel conflict. A common conflict develops when producers attempt to bypass an intermediary to gain efficiency. Conflicts also develop when dealers decide to place too much emphasis on competing product lines.

Adolph Coors Company has attempted to control both the number of distributors that sell its beer and the territories those distributors can serve. To maintain its proper taste, Coors beer must be refrigerated at all times. Coors

15. Wroe Alderson, *Dynamic Marketing Behavior* (Homewood, Ill.: Irwin, 1965), p. 239.
16. John J. Cunon, "Beer Stocks with Yeasty Promise," *Fortune,* Oct. 17, 1983, p. 180.
17. Lanny J. Ryan, Gaye C. Dawson, and Thomas Galek, "New Distribution Channels for Microcomputer Software," *Business,* Oct.–Dec. 1985, pp. 21–22.
18. Louis W. Stern and Ronald H. Gorman, "Conflict in Distribution Channels: An Exploration," in *Distribution Channels: Behavioral Dimensions,* Louis W. Stern, ed. (Boston: Houghton Mifflin, 1969), p. 157.

believes that unless it exerts tight control over distribution, some beer might be shipped without refrigeration. Channel conflict developed when Coors beer was being sold in Missouri before the brewer had selected its own distributors. The Missouri shipments were made by a distributor that seemed to be more interested in expanding sales than in cooperating with the brewer to maintain quality control. Coors expressed unhappiness publicly and encouraged consumers to boycott its product until proper distribution could be assured.[19]

The following statement summarizes one approach to decreasing conflict and increasing cooperation in marketing channels.

> Two conditions are necessary to minimize and contain conflict and increase cooperation among channel members. First, the role of each channel member has to be specified. In reality, role specification is a specification of performance expectation from each channel member for the functions he performs. Role specification enhances the ability of channel members to predict one another's behaviors. Therefore, role specification, clarification, and agreement enhance the potential of cooperation in channel relations. Role ambiguity and disagreement enhance the potential of conflict among channel members. Second, certain measures of channel coordination have to be undertaken. Coordination in an interorganizational setting requires leadership and the exercise of control. Control is a two-edge sword. If exercised benevolently, it enhances channel member cooperation. Otherwise, it may fuel conflict among the channel members.[20]

Channel Leadership

An important role in marketing channels is **channel leadership.** Figure 9.13 illustrates that different power bases may be used by a channel leader to achieve desired objectives. These power bases include authority, coercion, rewards, referents (reference groups or organizations that channel members try to please), and expertise about products, markets, or technology. **Channel power** relates to the ability of one channel member to influence the goal achievement of another channel member. Sears, for example, is the central power in the marketing of its private-label power tools, paints, tires, motor oil, batteries, and appliances. In this case, Sears exercises two types of power. First, it provides the profit reward to producers that supply the private-label goods. Second, it gains power from its marketing expertise. Many of the producers depend on Sears to perform all marketing activities. Note, too, that to assume leadership, a channel member must want to influence and control overall channel performance. In general, "the amount of power controlled by the producer varies inversely with the number of middlemen, and the amount of competition among producers varies directly with the number of middlemen."[21]

Provision of financing, business advice, ordering assistance, advertising support, and support materials for customers are actions that can help build the power

19. Robert E. Weigand, "Policing the Marketing Channel—It May Get Easier," in *Contemporary Issues in Marketing Channels,* Robert F. Lusch and Paul H. Zinszer, eds. (Norman, Okla.: University of Oklahoma Press, 1979), pp. 105–109.
20. Adel I. El-Ansary, "Perspectives on Channel System Performance," in Lusch and Zinszer, *Contemporary Issues in Marketing Channels,* p. 50.
21. Mary Ann Lederhaus, "Improving Marketing Channel Control Through Power and Exchange," *Journal of the Academy of Marketing Science,* Summer 1984, p. 30.

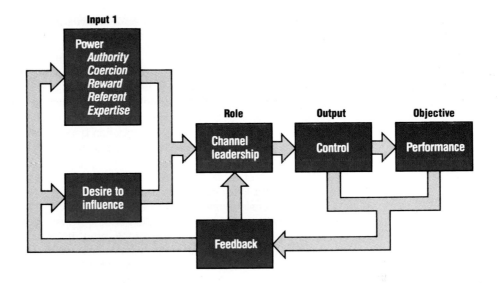

Input 1

Power
Authority
Coercion
Reward
Referent
Expertise

Desire to
influence

Role
Channel
leadership

Output
Control

Objective
Performance

Feedback

Figure 9.13 *Channel leadership: Exercising power to attain desired performance (Source: Adapted from Robert Robicheaux, "Control in a Distribution Channel: A Field Study," Ph.D. Dissertation, Louisiana State University, Baton Rouge, La., 1974)*

of the supplier in the marketing channel. Obviously, a threat to cut off significant support could be viewed as coercive to a retailer or dealer. Exercise of coercive power by a supplier seems to have a strong impact on dealer satisfaction and channel conflict, stronger than just the presence of this power source. In contrast, exercise of rewards has less impact on satisfaction and channel conflict. Therefore, exercise of coercive power can be a major cause of channel conflict.[22]

The following examples illustrate that retailers, producers, or wholesalers can assume the leadership role. The retailers K mart, J. C. Penney, and Sears base their channel leadership on wide public exposure and on consumer confidence in their products. They control many brands and sometimes replace uncooperative producers.

Manufacturers can also exert leadership. Consumer acceptance of Tide, Bold, Cheer, Gain, and other Procter & Gamble detergents allows that manufacturer to structure channel policy and exert considerable control over how retailers make these products available. Many stores traditionally allocated the most desirable positions on display shelves to Procter & Gamble products. The application on page 286 illustrates how competitive pressures are changing Procter & Gamble's dominance over control of marketing channels.

Independent Grocers' Alliance (IGA) is one of the best-known wholesaler-leaders in the United States. Wholesaler-leaders such as IGA assist independent business owners with advertising, pricing, and purchasing. IGA's exercise of power, then, is based on expert knowledge.

22. John F. Gaski and John R. Nevin, "The Differential Effects of Exercised and Unexercised Power Sources in a Marketing Channel," *Journal of Marketing Research,* May 1985, p. 139.

Application

Procter & Gamble's Changing Channel Leadership Role

In the past, the huge success of products such as Tide, Bounty, and Pampers allowed Procter & Gamble to exert considerable pressure on channel members to comply with its wishes. Reportedly, Procter & Gamble at one time restricted the amount of a product that a supermarket could purchase at special discount prices. Furthermore, supermarkets could not even obtain a supply of a discounted product if that product size was not routinely stocked by the supermarket. Times have changed. Procter & Gamble has been stumbling in the past few years, and many competitors have narrowed the quality advantage that the company once maintained.

The results of these changes are simple—premium prices are harder to command, and Procter & Gamble's leverage on retailers has declined. At the same time, retailers have gained power. With the consolidation of the food industry, more sales volume is in the hands of fewer companies. These companies, by controlling shelf space, can now be a major factor in the success of a product. Computerized checkout scanners have also given muscle to retailers. No longer must retailers panic when manufacturers announce a coupon offering. Scanners allow retailers to predict response to such an offering and place their orders accordingly, rather than buying what the manufacturers suggest out of fear of having too little or too much.

Finally, a new product-evaluation technique called Direct Product Profitability (DPP) allows retailers to calculate the handling costs associated with individual products. In other words, retailers are able to determine what it costs to handle a product from warehouse to sale. DPP has shown that very high handling costs are associated with some high-volume products. Retailers view high-volume–high-handling-cost products as less attractive and less deserving of shelf space. Procter & Gamble, as well as its competitors, is now redesigning products to lower handling costs and increase retail profit margins. Procter & Gamble, for example, changed its Ivory Shampoo bottle to a barrel-like shape when DPP data showed that the new shape (which takes less space) would save distributors 29 cents a case. (*Source: Bill Saporito, "Procter and Gamble's Comeback Plan," Fortune, Feb. 4, 1985, pp. 30–35. © 1985 Time Inc. All rights reserved.*)

Summary

A marketing channel is a group of interrelated intermediaries, including wholesalers and retailers, who direct products to customers. Channel members perform functions necessary to move products from producers to customers, and the channel structure delineates the arrangement of members according to their responsibilities in the distribution process. Most producers have dual or multiple channels that adjust the distribution system to various target markets.

Basic tasks of intermediaries are sorting out, accumulating, allocating, and assorting products for buyers. The number and characteristics of intermediaries are determined by the assortments required and by the expertise needed to perform distribution activities. Although intermediaries can be eliminated, the functions they perform are essential in developing product assortments. These activities must either be performed by someone in the marketing channel or be passed on to customers.

Integration of marketing channels brings various activities under the management of one channel member. Vertical integration combines two or more stages of the channel under one management. Horizontal integration combines institutions at the same level of channel operation under a single management. The vertical marketing system is managed centrally and is controlled for the mutual benefit of all channel members.

Channel management concerns product exposure and channel leadership in the division of functional tasks. Intensive distribution strives to make a product available to all possible dealers. Selective distribution screens dealers to select those most qualified to properly expose a product. Exclusive distribution usually gives one dealer exclusive rights to sell a product in a large geographic area.

A marketing channel is a structured behavioral system with an overall goal that links individuals and organizations. The positions of channel members are associated with rights, responsibilities, and rewards for cooperation. The ability of one channel member to facilitate or hinder attainment of other members' goals indicates its channel power. Power can be based on authority, coercion, rewards, referents, or expertise. Role deviance can lead to channel conflict.

Channel leaders exert power over other channel members. Retailers gain channel control through consumer confidence, wide product mixes, and intimate knowledge of consumers. Producers are in an excellent position to structure channel policy and to use technical expertise and consumer acceptance to influence other channel members. Wholesalers become channel leaders when they have expertise valued by other channel members and coordinate functions to match supply with demand.

Important Terms

Marketing channel	Facilitating agencies
Channel of distribution	Vertical channel integration
Marketing intermediaries	Vertical marketing systems (VMS)
Merchants	Horizontal channel integration
Agents and brokers	Intensive distribution
Assortment	Selective distribution
Sorting activities	Exclusive distribution
Sorting out	Channel cooperation
Accumulation	Channel conflict
Allocation	Channel leadership
Assorting	Channel power

Discussion and Review Questions

1. Why do consumers often blame intermediaries for inefficiencies in distribution?
2. When does an organization need multiple distribution channels?
3. "Shorter channels are usually a more direct means of distribution and therefore are more efficient." Comment on this statement.
4. How does the number of intermediaries in the channel relate to the assortments needed by retailers?
5. Can one channel member perform all channel functions?
6. What are the major distinctions between intermediaries and facilitating agencies? Do these units perform different channel functions?
7. Name and describe firms that use (a) vertical integration and (b) horizontal integration in their marketing channels.

8. How does the vertical marketing system (VMS) differ from the traditional marketing channel?
9. Explain the differences among intensive, selective, and exclusive methods of distribution.
10. "Channel cooperation requires that members support the overall channel goals in order to achieve individual goals." Comment on this statement.
11. How do power bases within the channel influence the selection of the channel leader?

Cases

Case 9.1 Developing Marketing Channels for AMF Voit Flying Discs[23]

For over fifty years, AMF Voit, Inc.—the world's largest manufacturer of inflated balls—has made recreational products that have been used by millions of people. W. J. Voit founded the company in 1921 as a small business in a suburb of Los Angeles, California. In 1957, the company became a subsidiary of American Machine and Foundry Co. as part of its leisure products group. Product lines include inflated balls; equipment for exercise, track and field, court sports, and water sports; institutional products; and sport discs.

AMF Voit entered the flying-disc market after research and investigation revealed much potential for growth. Disc throwing has emerged as one of the fastest growing sports in the world. It is estimated that over 20 million people will play with flying discs.

Disc sports have become very competitive throughout the world. Since the 1960s, over twelve competitive sports have been adapted to fit disc capabilities. Some of these sports are Double Disc Court, Ultimate, Guts, Disc Golf, and Freestyle, which are played in fourteen countries. Disc sports do not directly compete with seasonal sports, and tournaments are held throughout the year. Annually, the Pasadena Rose Bowl is filled to capacity as network television covers World Championship and Freestyle competitions, which include the popular dog competitions.

Wham-O Manufacturing Co., makers of Frisbee brand discs, have nearly an 80-percent market share. AMF Voit is challenging Wham-O Manufacturing Co. with a new line of technically advanced discs that covers all major product applications. AMF Voit's patented two-piece disc represents the latest in design and is especially adaptable to freestyle maneuvers. The one-piece product line includes a model for every sports event in the competitive arena. AMF Voit hopes to capitalize on its reputation for quality and on unique disc design.

The majority of disc sales occur during early spring and fall when the college student market is targeted. During summer, the resort- and beach-goer segments have the greatest volume in sales.

Disc users fit into four basic categories. The thousand pro and champion players are the elite of the disc world; they own an average of over a hundred discs each and travel over 5,000 miles a year for tournaments. These players are looking for better products all the time, and new games, techniques, and trends start with them. The weekend players number over a million, own an average of fifteen to fifty discs each, and play three to five times per week.

23. Many of the facts in this case are from the 1982 AMF Voit Fact Sheet on Flying Disc Marketing.

They attend all local and regional tournaments. The next group consists of the average players, who are typically high school and college students. These players number over 3 million, own an average of four to ten discs each, play twice a week, and attend local tournaments. This group is aware of top quality discs and the differences in performance. The fourth category consists of the general public, who are recreational, Sunday afternoon, and novice players. They number over 14 million and each own one to three discs. They play one to three times per month.

The primary target customers for the AMF Voit discs are active users within the United States who have technical knowledge about discs. These customers understand the innovations designed into the AMF Voit disc product line, and they have demonstrated a willingness to buy. They own many discs for many different uses and are continually searching for new and better products. By establishing substantial consumer preference in this key group, AMF hopes to gain the endorsement and crucial word-of-mouth promotion that is needed to sell the product to the secondary market—the recreational and novice disc throwers in the 16-to-25-year-old age category.

Wham-O distributes its Frisbee disc nationally through toy stores, mass merchants, and large sporting goods stores. AMF Voit's goal for its Sport Disc line is to establish nationwide distribution through various channels and gain dealer and player acceptance.

Questions for Discussion

1. What marketing channels should AMF Voit use to reach each of the four categories of disc users? Specify the type of intermediaries.
2. Should AMF Voit use intensive, selective, or exclusive distribution or a combination of distribution approaches?
3. Why are marketing channels so important for AMF Voit in selling sports discs?

Case 9.2 Importance of Distribution for Lowenbrau, Heineken and Other Imports[24]

LÖWENBRÄU

Approximately three hundred imported beers command almost 4 percent of the U.S. beer market. Growth has been impressive in recent years, and most beer importers see no signs of it diminishing as long as the U.S. dollar remains strong. The primary consumers of imported beers are status-conscious, upscale males who choose beer that reflects the self-image they want to portray. Male Yuppies, aged thirty-five and younger, form the core of the group. Most imports are consumed on college campuses or in metropolitan areas. Eighty to 90 percent of all imports are sold to drinking establishments. Import-beer drinkers tend to drink imports at bars and domestic brews at home, and they like to sample a variety of brands. Table 9.3 provides a complete list of the ten top-selling imported beers in the United States, with Heineken the leader, and their growth pattern over a recent five-year period.

24. Kevin T. Higgins, "Beer Importers Upbeat About Future Despite Warning Signs," *Marketing News,* Oct. 25, 1985, pp. 1, 9; Eileen Norris, "Import Uses Novel in Growing Beer Niche," *Advertising Age,* Jan. 31, 1985; Christy Marshall, "Imports: Heineken Sales, Moosehead Charges," *Advertising Age,* Nov. 2, 1981, p. 36; and Theodore Gage, "Import Brands Find Squeeze Is Tighter," *Advertising Age,* July 27, 1981, p. S49.

Table 9.3 Top ten imported beers in 1984

Name	# Cases (millions)	1979 Rank	5-Year Growth
1. Heineken	33.5	1	34.5%
2. Molson	14	2	44.3%
3. Beck's	8.9	5	229.6%
4. Moosehead	6.9	10	666.7%
5. LaBatt	4.6	3	(25.8%)
6. St. Pauli Girl	3.7	8	311.1%
7. Dos Equis	2.4	4	(22.6%)
8. Corona	1.8	—	N/A
9. Guinness	1.7	6	30.8%
10. Tecate	1.6	7	14%

Source: IMPACT, a beverage industry tracking service. The top 10 brands account for 80% of the 98.8 million-case import beer market, IMPACT estimates.

An imported beer may be a good product with a good image, but it will not succeed unless it has quality distribution. There are two basic approaches to importing or exporting beer. The first approach is to develop licensees who pay a commission for the right to produce and distribute the product in a foreign market. For example, Anheuser-Busch uses licensees to brew Budweiser in overseas markets such as Britain, Japan, and Israel. To meet Anheuser's standards, the licensees import ingredients such as yeast from the United States, and the Budweiser production must be approved by Anheuser-Busch's international brew masters. Lowenbrau is a licensee in the United States for Lowenbrau of Munich, Germany. Miller Brewing has agreed to comply with Lowenbrau's quality standards, "The Law of Purity," and is therefore allowed to use the Lowenbrau name, logo, and package to provide the appearance of an imported beer. Lowenbrau in the United States and Budweiser in Britain carry an import brand name, and this method of branding and distribution is the easiest way for a brewer to enter into foreign markets. The licensee usually is an established brewer that can produce and distribute the product through existing relationships with wholesalers and retail establishments.

The second way to export beer to other countries is to physically move the product across national boundaries, with assistance from marketing intermediaries. For example, Karin beer, which sells as well in Japan as Budweiser sells in the United States, has taken this approach. Karin's makers have had to struggle to establish distribution in the United States. While the Japanese beer is served in nearly all Japanese restaurants, there has been difficulty in getting it into other restaurants, drinking establishments; and stores. Distributors do not want to carry an imported beer with a low market share because it could sit on the shelf for a long time before selling, possibly getting old and stale.

To thrive in the United States, an importer needs the financial resources to carve distribution channels through which wholesalers can get the importer's beers into the drinking establishments and onto the retail shelves. That investment in distribution must be backed by big ad dollars. In the U.S. beer market, a domestic brew needs advertising to get sales, but an import needs ads to get distribution. No matter how good an import is or how well advertised, it will not succeed without wholesaler and retailer cooperation.

Van Munching & Company is one company that has made the commitment to advertising *and* distribution. Over the last half-century it has developed a distribution system that makes Holland's Heineken available in volume almost equal to that of domestic beers, and the firm also leads all the import competition in dollars spent on beer advertising. Today Heineken is the country's best-selling imported beer. Analogously, by launching Amstel Light through the same distribution system that it uses for Heineken, Van Munching has been able to boost shipments from 250,000 cases to 1.5 million in a five-year period and has made Amstel Light the best-selling imported light beer in the United States. Clearly, getting wholesalers to make the product available in retail and drinking establishments is the key to success.

Developing a distribution network is even more important for a new imported beer. In some cases the importer sets up its own wholesaler in the United States to develop marketing strategy and to make the product available to distributors. For example, when Warsteiner beer was brought into the United States in 1983, Warsteiner Importers Agency of Aurora, Colorado, was set up by the West German family that owns the Warsteiner Brewery. The company developed its own promotional program and pricing strategy to appeal to an up-scale target market. While Warsteiner has great control over promotion and image development, it has failed to convince distributors and is selling only a very small number of cases compared to the leading imports.

Thus, even a carefully deliberated marketing plan to capture widespread distribution, like Warsteiner's, may not be able to compete with a firmly entrenched distribution system. That seems to be the opinion of some leading domestic brewers. For instance, G. Heileman Brewing Company, the fourth-largest U.S. brewery, is importing Munich's Hacker-Pschorr beer and distributing it through its already established network of 2,200 wholesalers. In addition, Heileman is building a specialty brewery in Milwaukee to produce European-style beers. Stroh Brewing and Anheuser-Busch are two other domestic brewers looking to counter imports with similar foreign import agreements.

Due to beer's perishability and the resulting need for rapid product turnover to maintain quality, distributors may be reluctant to spend their time with an import beer that has no established market. As import-beer sales have grown in recent years, they have attracted the attention of domestic giants that have more resources and better distribution systems to establish their own import brands. Social trends and its continued status image will influence the price that can be charged for imported beer and the profitability of firms that handle its distribution. Still, a company like Anheuser-Busch may need a 3–5-percent market share to make nurturing a brand worthwhile. Some smaller importers, though, are successfully selling in one or two cities to a small number of restaurants or wholesalers. To sum up, independent importers need to find a market niche, establish sound distribution, and if possible avoid all-out competition from the domestic giants and the large, established import distributors.

Questions for Discussion

1. Suggest a distribution strategy for Miller Lite and Bud Light for sales to Japan.
2. Discuss the advantages and disadvantages of using a licensee versus directly exporting a Canadian beer to the United States.
3. Why is the distribution variable important in the marketing strategy for import beers in the United States?

10 / Wholesaling

Objectives

- To understand the nature of wholesaling in the marketing channel.

- To learn about the activities of wholesalers.

- To understand how wholesalers are classified.

- To examine organizations that facilitate wholesaling.

- To explore changing patterns in wholesaling.

Figure 10.1

Super Valu provides efficient warehousing services and low prices to its retail customers (Source: © Al Satterwite)

The five largest food wholesalers in the United States are listed in Table 10.1. Super Valu, Fleming, Wetterau, Malone and Hyde, and Nash Finch are playing key roles in reshaping the food wholesaling industry. Wholesalers provide products and services to other wholesalers and retailers and sometimes operate their own retail stores as well. Wholesalers today are operating more efficiently and increasing the number of services they offer their customers.

Super Valu, in contrast to other wholesalers whose increasing retail activities place them in direct competition with their customers, states that its purpose is to make its retail customers rich and successful (see Figure 10.1). Super Valu continues to upgrade its warehouses, truck fleets, and computer-aided design to respond more rapidly to retailers' needs. Super Valu's Planmark/Studio 70 division helps retailers expand through new store construction and remodeling. The chairman of Super Valu states that his organization has a "total commitment to serving customers more effectively than anyone else could serve them."[1]

1. "Five Top Wholesalers: An Inside Look," *Progressive Grocer*, Nov. 1985, pp. 21–23.

Table 10.1 *Sales and revenues of the five largest food wholesalers*

Company	Total revenues ($ millions)	Wholesale sales ($ millions)	Net earnings ($ millions)
Super Valu	$6,548	$5,590	$107
Fleming	5,512	NA	50
Wetterau	3,131	2,916	27
Malone and Hyde	3,100	NA	40
Nash Finch	1,238	690	12

Source: Progressive Grocer, Nov. 1985, p. 29. © 1985 by *Progressive Grocer.* Used by permission.

Chapter 9 describes the structure and function of the marketing channel. This chapter describes and analyzes wholesaling activities within a marketing channel. In this chapter, wholesaling is viewed as all exchange activities among organizations and individuals in the marketing channel, except for transactions with ultimate consumers. We first examine the importance of wholesalers and their functions in the marketing channel. Then we classify various types of wholesalers and, finally, explore changing patterns in wholesaling.

The Nature and Importance of Wholesaling

Wholesaling includes all marketing transactions in which purchases are intended for resale or are used in making other products.[2] It does not include exchanges with ultimate consumers. Wholesaling establishments are engaged primarily in selling products directly to industrial, reseller, and institutional users, including other wholesalers who act as intermediaries in buying products for, or selling products to, other middlemen.

There are over 337,943 wholesaling establishments in the United States. Wholesale sales increased from $144 billion in 1960 to $1,159 billion in 1982, a 705-percent increase.[3] Retail sales, in comparison, rose from $216 billion in 1960 to $1,296 billion in 1984, a 500-percent increase.[4] Profits of wholesalers have also increased more rapidly than those of retail chain stores.[5]

Wholesalers perform marketing activities, such as transportation, storage, and information gathering, that are necessary to expedite exchanges. They provide marketing activities for organizations above and below them in the marketing channel. Most of the marketing functions discussed in Chapter 1 can be performed by wholesalers.

2. Theodore N. Beckman, William R. Davidson, and W. Wayne Talarzyk, *Marketing,* 9th ed. (New York: Ronald Press, 1973), pp. 286–291.
3. *Statistical Abstract of the United States,* 1986, p. 785.
4. *Statistical Abstract of the United States,* 1986, p. 531.
5. Walter H. Heller, "Business Outlook," *Progressive Grocer,* June 1983, p. 17.

Table 10.2	Major wholesaling activities
Activity	**Description**
Wholesale management	Planning, organizing, staffing, and controlling wholesaling operations
Planning and negotiating supplies	Serving as the purchasing agent for customers by negotiating supplies
Promotion	Providing an outside (field) sales force and inside sales, advertising, sales promotion, and publicity
Warehousing and product handling	Receiving, storing and stockkeeping, order processing, packaging, shipping outgoing orders, and materials handling
Transportation	Arranging local and long-distance shipments
Inventory control and data processing	Controlling physical inventory, bookkeeping, recording transactions, keeping records for financial analysis
Security	Safeguarding merchandise
Pricing	Developing prices and price quotations on value-added basis
Financing and budgeting	Extending credit, borrowing, making capital investments, and forecasting cash flow
Management and merchandising assistance to clients	Supplying information about markets and products and providing advisory services to assist customers in their sales efforts

The Activities of Wholesalers

Over 50 percent of all products are exchanged, or their exchange is negotiated, through wholesaling institutions. Of course, it is important to remember that the distribution of all goods requires wholesaling activities, whether or not a wholesaling institution is involved.[6] Table 10.2 lists some of the major activities performed by wholesalers. The activities listed are not mutually exclusive. Individual wholesalers may perform more or fewer activities shown here.

Services for Producers

Producers have a distinct advantage when they use wholesalers because this distribution link provides accumulation and allocation roles for a number of products. Besides saving them money, this service allows producers to concentrate on producing, assembling, and developing quality products to match consumers' wants.

Ideally, producers would like close, direct contact with retailers and consumers, but wholesalers often have more direct contact.[7] For this reason, many producers have chosen to control promotion and influence the pricing of products while shifting transportation, warehousing, and financing functions to wholesalers.

6. C. Glenn Walters, *Marketing Channels* (Santa Monica, Calif.: Goodyear, 1977), p. 131.
7. Wroe Alderson, *Dynamic Marketing Behavior* (Homewood, Ill.: Irwin, 1965), p. 41.

The following are examples of products whose producers commonly use wholesalers: plumbing supplies, lumber, office furniture, electrical equipment, and construction machinery. In general, wholesalers serve producers of established products. Wholesalers may be slow to introduce new products because of the risks involved and the special product knowledge or service requirements that may be needed. Thus, when a new technical or mechanical product is launched, few wholesalers may be prepared to serve its producer.

Services for Retailers

In most cases, wholesalers specialize in selling. Wholesalers help their retailer-customers select inventory. In industries where obtaining supplies is important, skilled buying is essential. A wholesaler who buys is a specialist in understanding market conditions and an expert at negotiating final purchases. The customer's buyer can thus avoid the responsibility of looking for and coordinating supply sources. Moreover, if the wholesaler makes purchases for several different buyers, expenses can be shared by all customers. Another advantage is that a manufacturer's salespersons can offer retailers only a few products at a time, but independent wholesalers have a wide range of products available.

By buying in large quantities and delivering to customers in smaller lots, a wholesaler can perform physical distribution activities—for example, transportation, materials handling, inventory planning, communication, and warehousing—more efficiently and can provide more service than a producer or retailer could with its own physical distribution system. Furthermore, wholesalers can provide quick and frequent delivery even when demand fluctuates. They are experienced in providing the fastest delivery at the lowest cost. They provide time and place utility, which lets the producer and the wholesalers' customers avoid risks associated with holding large product inventories.

Because they carry products for many customers, wholesalers can maintain a wide product line at a relatively low cost. For example, a small Chrysler-Plymouth dealer in the Midwest discovered that it was cheaper to let wholesale suppliers provide automobile parts than to maintain a parts inventory at the dealership. Often wholesalers can perform storage and warehousing activities more efficiently and can permit retailers to concentrate on other marketing activities. When wholesalers provide storage and warehousing, they generally take on the ownership function as well. This arrangement frees retailers' and producers' capital for other purposes.

Classifying Wholesalers

A wide variety of wholesalers meet the different needs of producers and retailers. In addition, new institutions and establishments develop in response to producers and retail organizations that want to take over wholesaling functions.

Wholesalers adjust their activities as the contours of the marketing environment change. The classification or description of these wholesalers is meaningful only at a point in time; but one fact remains constant: "Wholesaling organizations by nature must count as their most important resource—their intimate knowledge of the product and service requirements of a particular market segment."[8]

8. Richard S. Lopata, "Faster Pace in Wholesaling," *Harvard Business Review,* July–Aug. 1969, pp. 130–143.

Figure 10.2

Types of merchant
wholesalers

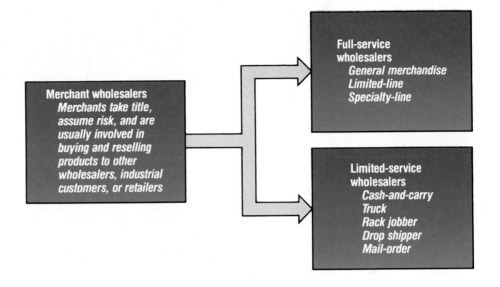

In this section, we will discuss three general categories or types of wholesaling establishments: (1) merchant wholesalers, (2) brokers and agents, (3) manufacturers' sales branches and offices. This classification is based on the activities wholesalers perform.

Merchant Wholesalers

Merchant wholesalers take title to goods and assume risk. They generally are involved in buying and reselling products to industrial or retail customers. The two broad categories of merchant wholesalers are full-service wholesalers and limited-service wholesalers. **Full-service wholesalers** provide most services that can be performed by wholesalers. **Limited-service wholesalers** provide only some marketing services and specialize in a few functions. (They pass other functions on to customers, or the other functions are performed by producers.) Figure 10.2 illustrates the different types of merchant wholesalers discussed in this section.

The *Census of Wholesale Trade* indicates that slightly more than half (53.7 percent) of all wholesale sales are conducted by merchant wholesalers.[9] Two-thirds of all wholesale establishments are merchant wholesalers. Taking title to products is the common criterion that distinguishes merchant middlemen from agent middlemen. Some merchant wholesalers are also involved in branding, packaging, and coordinating the marketing strategy of products they carry. Certified Grocers of California, Ltd. is an example of a merchant wholesaler.

Types of Full-service Merchant Wholesalers

Full-service wholesalers provide numerous services to customers. Delivery, warehousing, credit, promotional assistance, and general information about operations may be available to interested customers. For example, many large grocery wholesalers are offering retailers assistance in store design, site selection, personnel training, financing, merchandising, advertising, coupon redemption,

9. *Census of Wholesale Trade*, June 1980, pp. 52–55.

and scanning.[10] There are three categories of full-service merchant wholesalers: general merchandise, limited-line, and specialty-line.

General Merchandise Wholesalers

General merchandise wholesalers carry a very wide product mix, including such products as drugs, hardware, nonperishable foods, cosmetics, detergents, and tobacco. They typically serve neighborhood grocery stores and small department stores.

Limited-line Wholesalers

Limited-line wholesalers carry only a few product lines, such as groceries, lighting fixtures, or oil-well drilling equipment. Limited-line wholesalers do, however, offer services similar to those of general merchandise wholesalers. Middle East Rug Corporation, illustrated in Figure 10.3, is a wholesaler that imports and

10. "Major Wholesalers," pp. 20–21.

Table 10.3 *Various services provided by limited-service merchant wholesalers*

	Cash and Carry	Truck	Rack Jobber[a]	Drop Shipper[b]	Mail Order
Physical possession of merchandise	Yes	Yes	Yes	No	Yes
Personal sales calls on customer	No	Yes	Yes	No	No
Information about market conditions	No	Some	Yes	Yes	Yes
Advice to customers	No	Some	Yes	Yes	No
Stocking and maintenance of merchandise in customer's store	No	No	Yes	No	No
Credit to customers	No	Some	Yes	Yes	Some
Delivery of merchandise to customers	No	Yes	Yes	No	No

[a]Also called *service merchandiser*.
[b]Also called *desk jobber*.

sells rugs to dealers in the United States. The application on page 300 illustrates the activities of a limited-line wholesaler of computer equipment and supplies.

Specialty-line Wholesalers

Specialty-line wholesalers carry a very limited variety of products. For example, a wholesaler that carries only food delicacies such as shellfish is a specialty-line wholesaler. Generally, to meet their customers' specialized requirements, these merchant wholesalers carry one product line or a few items within a product line.

Types of Limited-service Merchant Wholesalers

Table 10.3 distinguishes the different services provided by various limited-service merchant wholesalers. Cash-and-carry wholesalers, truck wholesalers, rack jobbers, drop shippers, and mail-order wholesalers are typical limited-service wholesalers.

Cash-and-carry Wholesalers

Cash-and-carry wholesalers sell to customers who will pay cash and furnish transportation or pay extra to have products delivered. These middlemen usually handle a limited line of products such as groceries, construction materials, electrical supplies, or office supplies.

Metro Cash and Carry in Hillside, Illinois, is located in a store as large as an airplane hangar. Customers push flatbed carts down 11-foot-wide aisles. This grocery wholesaler caters to small grocery, gas station, and convenience store owners who use Metro to stock their own store shelves. To buy at Metro the customer must be a business owner and pay in cash or by check. The cash-only rule eliminates the need for a credit department, and transportation by customers eliminates the need for delivery people and equipment.[11]

Truck Wholesalers

Truck wholesalers deliver products directly to customers for inspection and selection. Usually, a truck wholesaler has a regular route and calls on retail stores and institutions to determine their needs. These middlemen are often small operators who own and drive their own trucks. They play an important part in supplying small grocery stores with perishables such as fruits and vegetables. Also, meat, potato chips, supplies for service stations, and tobacco products are sometimes supplied by truck wholesalers. Cash purchases and limited services are typical.

Rack Jobbers

Rack jobbers, or service merchandisers, are similar to truck wholesalers, but they provide the extra service of placing products on retailers' shelves. Rack jobbers perform purchasing and stocking functions for retailers. They are unique in that they will take back unsold products. Impulse products that have short life cycles, such as toys, may be supplied by rack jobbers to alleviate the producer's and retailer's risk and the inconvenience to retailers of having to deal with unfamiliar products.

11. Eileen Norris, "Wholesaler Cashes in on Desire to Cut Costs," *Advertising Age,* April 18, 1985, p. 32.

Rack jobbers usually specialize in housewares, hardware, nonprescription drugs, or cosmetics. They physically maintain the goods by refilling shelves, fixing displays, and maintaining inventory records, thus relieving retailers of these chores. Retailers need only furnish the space. These wholesalers usually operate on a consignment or cash basis, and their other services are limited.

Drop Shippers

Drop shippers, or desk jobbers, take title to products and negotiate sales. The distinguishing characteristic of drop shippers is that they do not physically handle products. They are concerned mainly with facilitating exchange through selling activities. A drop shipper assumes title to a certain quantity of products that are produced. If the products are not sold, then the drop shipper assumes the loss. Drop shippers are most commonly used to purchase large quantities of items that do not need to be assorted into groups of related products. The physical inventory may actually remain with the producer or in a public warehouse from which the drop shipper leases space and services.

Drop shippers often deal with products that are inefficient to ship or products that could not be sold at competitive prices if a retailer or wholesaler had to cover the cost of physically handling them. Large supermarkets can use an entire truckload of a product in a short enough period to make drop shipping profitable. Thus, there is a growing trend toward more drop shipping directly from the manufacturer to supermarkets. A drop shipment eliminates unloading of the product into a warehouse and then reloading it for trucking to the store.[12]

Mail-order Wholesalers

Mail-order wholesalers sell through direct mail by sending catalogs to retail, industrial, and institutional customers. Wholesale mail-order houses that feature jewelry, cosmetics, specialty foods, or automobile parts usually serve remote geographical areas where small retailers find mail-order purchasing convenient and efficient. These wholesalers usually sell small products that can be shipped by United Parcel Service (UPS), the U.S. Postal Service, or common carriers. They generally require payment in cash or by credit card, and discounts are given for large orders.

Brokers and Agents

Brokers and agents (see Figure 10.4) negotiate purchases and expedite sales but do not take title to the product. They are **functional middlemen** because they perform a limited number of marketing activities for a commission. Agents in particular perform fewer marketing activities than typical merchant wholesalers, retailers, or manufacturers' wholesale operations. These middlemen account for 10.4 percent of the total sales volume of wholesalers.[13]

Brokers perform fewer functions than other intermediaries; their primary goal is to bring buyers and sellers together. Brokers are not involved in financing or physical possession, and they assume almost no risks. They exist to seek out buyers or sellers and assist in negotiating exchanges. Brokerage fees are paid by whoever seeks the broker's services. **Agents** represent either buyers or sellers on a permanent basis. The services performed by typical

12. "Drop-Shipping Grows to Save Depot Costs," *Supermarket News,* April 1, 1985, pp. 1, 17.
13. *Census of Wholesale Trade,* June 1980, pp. 52–55.

Figure 10.4

Types of agents and brokers

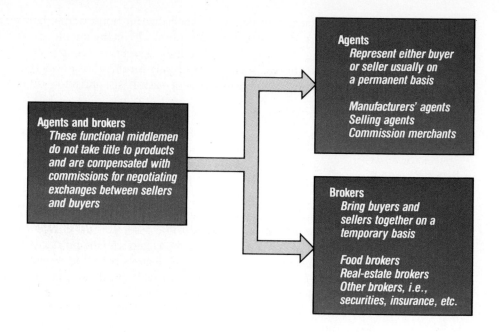

Agents and brokers
These functional middlemen do not take title to products and are compensated with commissions for negotiating exchanges between sellers and buyers

Agents
Represent either buyer or seller usually on a permanent basis

Manufacturers' agents
Selling agents
Commission merchants

Brokers
Bring buyers and sellers together on a temporary basis

Food brokers
Real-estate brokers
Other brokers, i.e., securities, insurance, etc.

agents (manufacturers' agents, selling agents, and commission merchants) and brokers (food brokers, real estate brokers, and others) are summarized in Table 10.4 and explained in the following pages.

Brokers

Brokers specialize in a particular commodity and give their customers the benefit of established contacts. **Food brokers** sell food and other grocery products to retailer-owned and merchant wholesalers, grocery chains, industrial buyers, and food processors. Buyers and sellers use food brokers to cope with fluctuating market conditions and to obtain assistance in grading, negotiating, and inspecting foods. The application on page 305 discusses the benefits that a food broker can provide.

Real-estate brokers bring buyers and sellers together to exchange real estate. The broker is a go-between, not a permanent representative of either the buyer or the seller. Real-estate brokers often seek a compromise in negotiations between the buyer and seller. They often obtain an exclusive contract for a stated period, during which they engage in advertising and other promotional activities.

Manufacturers' Agents

Manufacturers' agents represent several sellers and usually offer a complete product line to customers. They enter into agreements with manufacturers regarding territories, selling price, order handling, and terms of sale relating to delivery, service, and warranties. The relationship between an agent and a seller is detailed explicitly in a written agreement.

Most manufacturers' agents are small establishments with only a few employees. The products they handle must be noncompeting and complementary. These agents are restricted to a particular territory and perform functions for man-ufacturers similar to those of a sales office. Professional salespersons who

Table 10.4 *Various services provided by agents and brokers*

	Brokers	Manufacturers' Agents	Selling Agents	Commission Merchants
Physical possession of merchandise	No	Some	No	Yes
Long-term relationship with buyers or sellers	Some	Yes	Yes	Yes
Representation of competing product lines	Yes	No	No	Yes
Limited geographic territory	No	Yes	No	No
Credit to customers	No	No	Yes	Some
Delivery of merchandise to customers	No	Some	Yes	Yes

contact potential buyers are highly skilled in selling. A good relationship with customers is the most important benefit manufacturers' agents can offer.

By concentrating on a limited number of products, these middlemen are able to provide a sales effort that would be impossible with any other distribution method except producer-owned sales branches and offices. In addition, manufacturers' agents are able to spread operating expenses among noncompeting products and thus can offer each manufacturer lower prices for services rendered. Some agents assist retailers in advertising and in maintaining a service organization. The more services offered, the higher the agent's commission.

Selling Agents

Selling agents market either all of a specified product line or a manufacturer's entire output. Selling agents have full authority with regard to prices, promotion, and distribution. They assume the functions of a sales department for sellers and may be used in place of a marketing department as well.

Selling agents are used most often by small firms or by manufacturers whose seasonal production or other characteristics make it difficult to maintain a marketing department. These middlemen most often distribute canned foods, household furnishings, clothing, and textiles. Selling agents usually assume the sales function for several producers. They avoid conflicts of interest by representing noncompeting product lines. A selling agent is rarely restricted to as narrow a geographical territory as a manufacturer's agent. Selling agents play a key role in advertising, marketing, research, and credit policies, and they may offer advice on product development and packaging.

Commission Merchants

Commission merchants are agents who usually exercise physical control over products and negotiate sales. They may have broad powers regarding prices and terms of sale. Arranging delivery and providing transportation are key services offered by commission merchants, who are found most often in agricultural marketing. A commission merchant takes possession of truckload quantities of commodities and transports them to a central market for sale. These agents specialize in obtaining the best price under market conditions; they deduct a commission plus the expense of making the sale and remit the profits to the shipper.

Businesses—including farms—that use commission merchants face one significant problem: they have extremely limited control over pricing. Because large producers must maintain close contact with the market, they have a limited need for commission merchants.

Manufacturers' Sales Branches and Offices

Manufacturers' sales branches resemble merchant wholesalers in their operations. According to the *Census of Wholesale Trade,* over one-third (38 percent) of wholesale sales volume is developed through these middlemen.[14] **Sales branches** may offer credit, deliver goods, give promotional assistance, and furnish other services. Customers include other wholesalers, retailers, and industrial buyers. Branch operations are common, for example, in electrical supplies (Westinghouse Electric Corp.) and in plumbing (Crane Co. and American Standard).

Sales offices provide service normally associated with agents. These wholesalers are part of the vertically integrated distribution channel of the producer who owns and controls the sales branch or office. Products that enhance the manufacturer's own product line may be sold by the sales office or sales branch. Hiram Walker, Inc., a liquor producer, for example, imports wine from Spain to increase the number of products that its sales offices can offer to wholesalers. United States Tobacco Company imports Borkum Riff smoking tobacco from Sweden to add variety to its chewing tobacco and snuff lines.

The sales office or branch usually is reserved for accounts that need its service. Large retail customers may be served directly by the producer, by-passing the organization's wholesaling operation. For example, a major distiller bottles private-label bourbon for California supermarkets. This operation totally by-passes the company's sales office, which serves other retailers.

Organizations That Facilitate Wholesaling Functions

In addition to the three main categories of wholesalers that have been described, there are other highly specialized organizations that perform wholesaling functions. Certain facilitating organizations make it unnecessary for a manufacturer or retailer to utilize a wholesaling establishment. The following sections show ways in which facilitating agencies can carry out typical wholesaling functions.

Public Warehouses

Public warehouses serve as storage facilities. An organization rents space in a warehouse instead of constructing its own facilities or using a merchant wholesaler's storage services. Public warehouses also provide other wholesaling activities.

14. *Census of Wholesale Trade,* June 1980, pp. 52–55.

A good broker learns the business of clients and this facilitates a continuing business relationship. For example, in one case, when a shipment of frozen grapes arrived, the buyer who wanted to use the grapes in salads refused to accept them. George R. Lyons Company, of Cleveland, the broker, found a winery that could use the grapes. This knowledge of the market helped both the buyer and the seller.

A broker's experience and diplomacy can prevent hard feelings when difficult situations arise. When one retail buyer refused a line of frozen fish, saying that the packages were too big, Arthur H. Froman & Company involved the buyer in developing smaller packages. In the end, the buyer accepted the frozen fish.

A broker's concern for the welfare of his client sometimes results in lower profits. For example, George R. Lyons Company had a major client to whom they were selling a product in drums. Lyons suggested to the client that it would be less expensive to buy in tank quantities, and the savings of one year would offset the cost of tank installation. The client took the suggestion, which reduced the broker's profits from $1,200 to $40. But Lyons regarded the long-term relationship with the client as more important. This decision to focus on long-run customer satisfaction illustrates the spirit of the marketing concept. Later, this very client came to Lyons for information in selecting a new plant site.

The primary function of brokers is to bring buyers and sellers together. However, the knowledge and experience of brokers can benefit a client in many ways. (*Source: Based on Ron Stevens, "Above and Beyond the Call of Duty,"* Quick Frozen Foods, *Dec. 1983, pp. 18–19. Used by permission of Harcourt Brace Jovanovich, Inc.*)

Many warehouses order, deliver, collect accounts, and maintain display rooms where potential buyers can inspect products. A producer can place products in a bonded warehouse and use them as collateral for a loan.

Finance Companies

Products can be owned by a finance company or a bank while wholesalers or retailers maintain physical possession. Automobile dealers often call this form of financing "floor planning"; it allows them to maintain a large inventory of cars to give customers greater selection and increase sales.

Transportation Companies

Rail, truck, air, and other carriers help manufacturers and retailers transport products without the aid of middlemen. For example, freight forwarders combine less-than-full shipments into full loads at a savings to customers—perhaps at a carload rate rather than a less-than-carload rate. United Parcel Service is an example of a freight forwarder that provides door-to-door service for small containers and packages.

Trade Shows and Trade Marts

Trade shows and trade marts allow manufacturers or wholesalers to exhibit products to potential buyers and, therefore, assist in the selling and buying functions. *Trade shows* offer both selling and nonselling benefits. On the selling side, they allow vendors to identify prospects; gain access to key decision

Figure 10.5

Advertisement designed
to attract retailers to the
Chicago Apparel Mart
(Source: The Paristyle
Group, N.Y.C.)

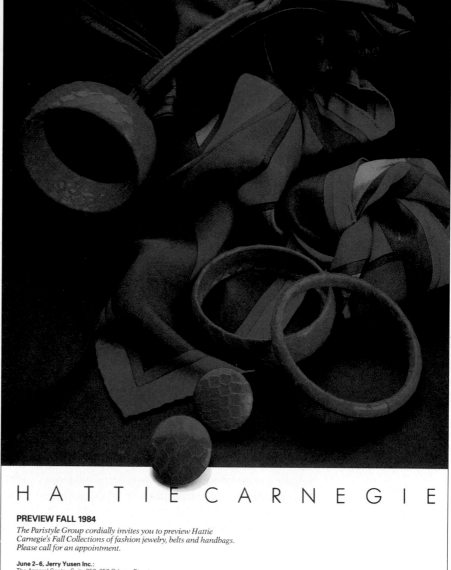

H A T T I E C A R N E G I E

PREVIEW FALL 1984

*The Paristyle Group cordially invites you to preview Hattie
Carnegie's Fall Collections of fashion jewelry, belts and handbags.
Please call for an appointment.*

June 2–6, Jerry Yusen Inc.:
The Apparel Center, Suite 953, 350 Orleans Street,
Chicago, IL 60654 (312) 222-0363

makers in current or potential customer companies; disseminate facts about
their products, services, and personnel; and actually sell products and service
current accounts through contacts at the show. The nonselling benefits include
opportunities to maintain the company image with competitors, customers,
and the industry and to gather information on competitors' products and prices.
Other important marketing variables on which trade shows have a positive
influence include maintaining or enhancing company morale, product testing,
and product evaluation.[15]

15. Thomas V. Bonoma, "Get More Out of Your Trade Shows," *Harvard Business Review,* Jan.–
Feb. 1983, pp. 75–83.

Trade shows can permit direct buyer-seller interaction and may eliminate the need for agents. For example, more than 35,000 graphic arts company owners and managers convene every fall in Chicago to attend the McCormick Place Graphic Expo.[16] Companies exhibit at trade shows because of a high concentration of prospective buyers for their products. Studies show that it takes an average of 5.1 sales calls to close an industrial sale but less than one sales call (0.8) to close a trade-show lead. The explanation for the latter figure is that more than half of the customers who purchase a product based on information gained at a trade show obtain it by mail or a phone order after the show. These more impersonal attempts by customers to gather information eliminate the need for major sales calls to provide such information.[17]

Trade marts are relatively permanent facilities that firms can rent to exhibit products year round. In Dallas, the Dallas Market Center, the Dallas Trade Mart, the Homefurnishing Mart, the World Trade Center, the Decorative Center, Market Hall, and the Apparel Mart are housed in six buildings specifically designed for the convenience of professional buyers. The advertisement shown in Figure 10.5 is intended to attract retailers to the Chicago Apparel Mart. Trade marts are located in several major cities besides Dallas, including New York, Chicago, Atlanta, and Los Angeles. At these marts, such products as furniture, home decorating supplies, toys, clothing, and gift items are sold to wholesalers and retailers.

Changing Patterns in Wholesaling

The distinction between wholesaling activities that can be performed by any business and the traditional wholesaling establishment is somewhat blurred. Manufacturers, retailers, and facilitating organizations perform wholesaling functions to bridge the gap between manufacturers and consumers. As has been pointed out, wholesaling functions can be shifted or shared, but not eliminated. They have to be performed by someone or by some institution.

Wholesalers Gain More Power

New marketing methods that offer more service, lower prices, or both have triggered a move away from traditional retail or wholesale establishments. New stores such as discount warehouses and superstores are flourishing. As a result, in the food industry the lines of demarcation between wholesalers and retailers are not as sharp as they once were. Several large grocery wholesalers are now operating or planning large retail outlets. Super Valu, Wetterau, and Fleming are examples of large wholesalers expanding into the retail store business.[18] This trend has sparked a controversy about wholesalers positioning themselves in direct competition with their retail customers.[19] Wholesalers argue that their

16. *Official Show Directory,* Graph Expo 81, Sept. 1981, p. 9.
17. Richard K. Swandby and Jonathan M. Cox, "Trade Show Trends: Exhibiting Growth Paces Economic Strengths," *Business Marketing,* May 1985, p. 50.
18. Patricia Natschke, "Not Meant as Threat to Any Independent," *Supermarket News,* Sept. 24, 1984, p. 1.
19. Ted C. Wetterau, "A Case for Consolidation," *Progressive Grocer,* March 1985, p. 17.

retail stores are not intended to break independent retailers but that they are a means of increasing volume.

The wholesale industry, like most major industries, including retailing, is also experiencing a great number of mergers. The underlying forces influencing firms to consolidate or combine at the wholesale level seem to be economic conditions that create price-sensitive buyers and new advances in materials handling and communication technology.[20] Many retailers consequently have fewer supply choices. It is claimed that conflict of interest occurs when wholesalers become dominant in a market through mergers with other wholesalers and purchases or openings of retail outlets. Nevertheless, the trend toward more mergers and consolidations in wholesaling appears to be advancing.[21]

New Types of Wholesalers

The nature of future types of wholesaling establishments will depend on the changing mix of activities that retailers and producers perform and on the innovative efforts of wholesalers to develop efficiency in the marketing channel.[22] The trend toward larger retailers—superstores and the like—will provide opportunities as well as threats to wholesaling establishments. Opportunities will develop from the expanded product lines of these mass merchandisers. A merchant wholesaler of groceries, for instance, may want to add other low-cost, high-volume products that are sold in superstores. On the other hand, some limited-function merchant wholesalers may not be needed. The volume of sales may eliminate the need for rack jobbers, for example, who usually handle slow-moving products that are purchased in limited quantities. The future of independent wholesalers, agents, and brokers depends on their ability to delineate markets and provide desired services.

Summary

Wholesaling includes all marketing transactions in which purchases are intended for resale or are used in making other products. Wholesaling functions can be shifted to or assumed by any marketing channel member, but those functions cannot be eliminated. They must be performed by someone—either by producers, retailers, or consumers, if not by wholesalers.

There are over 337,000 wholesaling establishments in the United States, and their sales volume is significantly higher than that of retail establishments. This high sales volume results from counting multiple transactions as products move through the marketing channel.

Wholesalers' major activities include wholesaling management, planning, and negotiating supplies, promotion, warehousing and product handling, transportation, inventory control and data processing, security, pricing, financing and budgeting, and management and merchandising assistance to clients.

A diversity of wholesalers exists to serve the requirements of different market segments. The three general categories of wholesalers are merchant

20. "Trends Are Changing Grocery Wholesaling," *Supermarket News,* March 18, 1985, pp. 1, 24.
21. David Merrefield, "Says Wholesaler Mergers Harm Independents," *Supermarket News,* August 27, 1984, p. 1.
22. Bruce Mallen, "Functional Spin-off: A Key to Anticipating Change in Distribution Structure," *Journal of Marketing,* July 1973, p. 22.

wholesalers, brokers and agents, and manufacturers' sales branches and offices. Merchant wholesalers take title to products and usually are involved in buying, physically handling, and reselling them. Brokers and agents are functional middlemen because they specialize in a limited number of marketing activities, primarily buying and selling. Manufacturers' sales branches and offices are vertically integrated units owned by manufacturers.

Facilitating organizations that perform wholesaling functions include public warehouses, finance companies, transportation companies, and trade shows and trade marts. In some instances, these organizations eliminate the need for a wholesaling establishment.

Important Terms

Wholesaling	Functional middlemen
Wholesalers	Brokers
Merchant wholesalers	Agents
Full-service wholesalers	Food brokers
Limited-service wholesalers	Real-estate brokers
General merchandise wholesalers	Manufacturers' agents
Limited-line wholesalers	Selling agents
Specialty-line wholesalers	Commission merchants
Cash-and-carry wholesalers	Sales branches
Truck wholesalers	Sales offices
Rack jobbers	Public warehouses
Drop shippers	Trade shows
Mail-order wholesalers	Trade marts

Discussion and Review Questions

1. Is there a distinction between wholesalers and wholesaling? If so, what is it?
2. Why do wholesaling establishments (excluding wholesaling activities of retailers) have a sales volume greater than retailers?
3. Why shouldn't retailers by-pass wholesalers? What major functions are performed by wholesalers?
4. Would it be appropriate for a wholesaler to stock both interior wall paint and office supplies? Under what circumstances would this product mix be logical?
5. Drop shippers take title to products but do not accept physical possession. Commission merchants take physical possession of products but do not accept title. Defend the logic of classifying drop shippers as wholesale merchants and commission merchants as agents.
6. What are the advantages of using agents to replace merchant wholesalers? What are the disadvantages?
7. What, if any, are the differences in marketing functions performed by manufacturers' agents and selling agents?
8. Why are manufacturers' sales offices and branches classified as wholesalers? Which independent wholesalers are replaced by manufacturers' sales branches? Which independent wholesalers are replaced by manufacturers' sales offices?

9. Why do you think merchant wholesalers have increased in number while manufacturers' sales branches have decreased?
10. "Public warehouses are really wholesale establishments." Comment on this statement.
11. Will efficient wholesaling help small independent retailers to survive?
12. Is there a trend toward by-passing wholesalers? What environmental variables favor direct distribution by manufacturers?
13. What are wholesalers doing to respond to changing economic conditions?

Cases

Case 10.1 Textron Outdoor Products Group[23]

TEXTRON

The Textron, Inc., Outdoor Products Group manufactures E-Z-Go, Homelite, and Jacobsen Turf outdoor equipment. Over the past decade, Textron has been revamping the division's distribution system to increase the exposure and overall availability of its products. The Homelite division phased out its direct sales method (see Channel E in Figure 9.3) and began selling equipment through wholesalers and industrial distributors who take title to the products. The following distribution methods are used for the Outdoor Products Group:

E-Z-Go: Three- and four-wheel gasoline and electric golf carts, as well as related parts and accessories, are sold through independent distributors and company outlets. E-Z-Go also produces utility vehicles for turf and industrial/commercial markets.

Homelite: Homelite makes gasoline and electric chain saws, string trimmers, pumps, generators, and leaf blowers. Lawn and garden equipment and snow throwers are marketed under the Jacobsen brand name. These products are sold through wholly owned branches and independent international distributors.

Jacobsen Turf: Jacobsen manufactures and markets turf maintenance machines and trucks suitable for use on large areas of turf grass, such as golf courses and municipal grounds. Its products include precision reel mowers, large and midsize turf tractors, rotary mowers, utility trucks, seeders, aerators, trimmers, edgers, and blowers. Jacobsen products are sold through independent distributors.

In 1984, its thirtieth year, E-Z-Go produced its best sales and income record to date; in 1985 it bettered these revenues. Widespread distribution has made E-Z-Go a leader in the electric and gas golf-car markets. Product expansion in existing lines and product development of new accessories have helped increase

23. Facts are from Textron's *1982, 1984,* and *1985 Annual Reports.*

its share of the turf utility vehicle market. By acquiring assets of Eagle Vehicle, a maker of industrial and commercial vehicles, and introducing new vehicles, E-Z-Go has also garnered a bigger share of the industrial/commercial market.

Homelite experienced sales and income declines in all areas except construction equipment. The increase in the construction area resulted from a surge in building activity in the United States and Canada. The decline elsewhere was primarily due to foreign competition and a previous lull in new-product developments. In the past several years, Textron has taken several steps to bolster the ailing Homelite line. The Homelite division has improved or redesigned existing products, introduced new ones, added whole new lines of equipment, and undergone a management overhaul. Consolidation of Homelite's Jacobsen (as distinct from Jacobsen Turf) lawn and garden equipment manufacturing into a single facility has created efficiencies. Expenses were cut further by closing several marginal service centers. Homelite also discontinued about thirty products, which represented nearly 20 percent of the entire Homelite line but accounted for less than 2 percent of sales.

In the Jacobsen Turf division, a strong promotional campaign boosted sales of mowers in 1985. Models and accessories for the HF-5 tractor/mower and Turfcat lines accounted for 30 percent of Jacobsen's sales, and golf-course maintenance equipment brought in over 50 percent. Jacobsen is now targeting its energies at a new market—landscape maintenance.

The creative use of wholesalers and industrial distributors has allowed Textron's Outdoor Products Group to maintain profits by getting maximum exposure for its product lines. By discontinuing marginally profitable Homelite products and adding Jacobsen products that can be sold through existing distributors, the company recorded a higher overall operating profit.

Questions for Discussion

1. Why did the shift from direct sales to industrial distributors and wholesalers maintain profits for the Outdoor Products Group in the face of both declining overall market potential and economic uncertainty?
2. Are there any opportunities for the E-Z-Go division to engage in joint distribution with Homelite or Jacobsen?
3. How has the use of wholesalers and industrial distributors affected the marketing strategies of the Outdoor Products Group?

Case 10.2 Ralston Purina[24]

Ralston Purina Company, headquartered in St. Louis and founded in 1894, is the world's largest producer of dry dog and dry and soft-moist cat foods and of commercial feed for livestock and poultry. The company also has acquired the largest wholesale baker of fresh bakery products in the United States. Other consumer products include cereal and canned seafood, and Purina is a major producer of isolated soy protein.

The Grocery Product Group includes pet and consumer foods. Pet foods account for approximately two-thirds of total grocery sales. They include the

24. Facts based on Ralston Purina Company *1983, 1984,* and *1985 Annual Reports.*

Purina Dog Chow, Chuck Wagon, Butcher's Blend, Purina Cat Chow, Tender Vittles, Happy Cat, Puppy Chow, Happy Kitten, Happy Dog, and *Hearty Chews* brands. As a component of its grocery product group, Ralston Purina also manufactures and sells Chex cereals, as well as specialty foods including crackers and cookies. Grocery products are marketed primarily in the United States, through direct sales forces, to grocery chains, wholesalers, industrial buyers, and other retailers. As pointed out in this chapter manufacturers' sales branches resemble merchant wholesalers in their operation. The firm may offer credit, give promotional assistance, and provide other services. Purina's principal competitors are national and regional manufacturers whose products compete with those of the company for shelf space and consumer acceptance.

Another product within the grocery category is *Chicken of the Sea* tuna. This product is sold primarily to grocery stores in the United States through a network of independent food brokers. Brokers specialize in a particular commodity and give their customers the benefit of established contacts. Food brokers sell tuna and other grocery products to retailer-owned and merchant wholesalers, grocery chains, and institutional buyers.

Continental Baking Company, acquired in October 1984, is the largest wholesale baker of fresh bakery products in the United States. Through an extensive distribution system, it operates fifty-two bakeries nationwide and delivers fresh products to major retailers daily on more than seven thousand individual routes. These routes are part of the vertically integrated distribution channel of Continental, which owns and controls sales branches or offices.

Continental Baking's bread products include *Wonder* and *Home Pride* breads, *Beefsteak* rye breads, English muffins, Italian breads, and dinner rolls. The *Breakfast Bake Shop* line encompasses a wide range of sweet rolls and donuts, and the *Hostess* line of snack cakes includes *Twinkies, Ding Dongs, Sno Balls, Suzy Q,* and *Choco-diles* brands, as well as cupcakes and fruit pies.

As the world's largest producer of commercial feed for livestock and poultry, Ralston Purina has for over ninety years been the industry leader in producing widely recognized, high-quality feeds for swine, poultry, dairy and beef cattle, horses, and other animals. It owns or operates facilities in thirty-two states nationwide. International operations in agricultural products include 126 feed-manufacturing and other facilities in twelve countries around the world.

Other agricultural products are soybean meal and oil, poultry products, animal health products, and breeding hogs. Feed products are distributed primarily through a network of approximately 5,500 domestic independent dealers and more than 3,200 dealers outside the United States. The dealers act as industrial distributors, taking title to products, assuming risk, and directing local marketing efforts aimed at agricultural buyers. The company competes with other large feed manufacturers, with cooperatives and single-owner establishments, and in international markets, with government feed companies.

Food protein and industrial polymer products are marketed in the United States primarily through direct sales forces and internationally through brokers and distributors. This dual distribution approach illustrates the necessity to change the marketing channel to match the environment. Ralston Purina has expertise and direct access to the United States market. Therefore a direct vertically integrated marketing channel is most effective. International markets need the expertise and local contacts that brokers and other intermediaries provide.

Questions for Discussion

1. Why does Ralston Purina use so many diverse marketing intermediaries in the distribution of its many products?
2. Why is a direct sales force used for most grocery products, while food brokers are used for tuna products?
3. How does Continental Baking's vertically integrated distribution system differ from other distribution networks at Ralston Purina?

11 / Retailing

Objectives

- To understand the purpose and function of retailers in the marketing channel.

- To examine how the environment of a retail store is developed.

- To classify retail stores.

- To understand nonstore retailing, franchising, and planned shopping centers.

- To learn about the wheel of retailing hypothesis, which attempts to explain the evolution and development of retail stores.

- To examine retail strategy development.

Figure 11.1

The Limited is adjusting its strategies to meet the changing desires of consumers (Source: Courtesy of The Limited)

The Limited Stores, Inc., a national clothing retailer, has demonstrated the flexibility needed to reposition itself in response to market trends. In the 1960s, The Limited was a trendy, junior-oriented business focusing on the females of the baby-boom generation. While still targeting the baby-boom generation The Limited more recently has muted its trendy image, grown with its target market, and become one of the largest women's apparel specialty retailers in the world (see Figure 11.1). In addition to its flagship stores, which carry the company's name, The Limited has a portfolio of stores with expertise in other profitable markets—Limited Express (junior wear), Lane Bryant (special sizes), Sizes Unlimited (off-price), Brylane (mail order), Victoria's Secret (lingerie), and most recently, Lerner's (budget women's apparel). As a whole, The Limited has identified profitable markets and has developed strategies that reflect how customers in those markets want to live and buy.[1]

1. Max L. Densmore and Sylvia Kaufman, "How Leading Retailers Stay on Top," *Business,* April–June 1985, pp. 28–35.

Marketing methods that satisfy consumers serve well as the guiding philosophy of retailing. Retailers are an important link in the marketing channel because they are both marketers and customers for producers and wholesalers. They perform many marketing activities such as buying, selling, grading, risk taking, and developing information about customers' wants. Of all marketers, retailers are the most visible to ultimate consumers. They are in a strategic position to gain feedback from consumers and to pass ideas along to producers and to intermediaries in the marketing channel.

Retailing is an extraordinarily dynamic area of marketing. In this chapter, we examine the nature of retailing, major types of retail stores, nonstore retailers, the "wheel of retailing" hypothesis, and the development of a retailing strategy.

The Nature of Retailing

It is fairly common knowledge that retailing is important to the national economy. The *Statistical Abstract of the United States* indicates that approximately 1,330,000 retailers are operating in the United States.[2] While this number has been relatively constant over the past twenty years, sales volume has increased over four times, implying that the average size of stores has increased. Most personal income is spent in retail stores, and nearly one out of every seven persons employed in the United States works in a retail store.

Retailing focuses on the activities required to facilitate exchanges with ultimate consumers. By definition, retail exchanges are entered into for personal, family, or household purposes. (Although most retailers' sales are to consumers, some nonretail transactions do occur with other businesses.) Retailing activities usually take place in a store or in a service establishment, but telephone selling, vending machines, and mail-order catalogs allow retail exchanges outside of stores.

By providing assortments of products that match consumers' wants, retailers create place, time, and possession utilities. They move products from wholesalers or producers to the location of demand (place utility). They make inventories or product stocks available when consumers want them (time utility). And they assume risk through ownership and financing of inventories (possession utility).

In the case of service products like hair styling, dry cleaning, and automotive repair, retailers themselves develop most of the product utilities. The services of such retailers provide aspects of form utility that are associated with the production process. Retailers of service products usually have more direct contact with consumers and more opportunity to alter the product in the marketing mix. Compared with physical goods, the unique aspect of services relates to (1) their intangible nature, which makes consumers' choices more difficult; (2) the fact that the retailer and the product are inseparable, which tends to localize service retailing and to give consumers fewer choices; (3) the perishability of services, which prevents storage and increases the risk associated with the retail operation; and (4) the heterogeneity of the delivery process, which makes delivery hard to standardize and quality control difficult.[3] (See Chapter 21 for more detail about services.)

2. *Statistical Abstract of the United States,* 1986, p. 778.
3. A. Parasuraman, Valarie A. Zeithaml, Leonard L. Berry, "A Conceptual Model of Service Quality and Its Implications for Future Research," *Journal of Marketing,* Fall 1985, p. 42.

The production process cannot be performed uniformly for each transaction in service retailing. For example, each cavity that a dentist fills requires a minor adjustment in approach, and every haircut requires a personal touch. A pleasant, trusting relationship between customer and retailer is necessary to overcome the customer's anxiety regarding the lack of uniform standards and, thus, to maintain the customer's confidence. Personal trust and mutual respect appear to be critical to success, in providing retail services.[4]

Retailers are positioned in the marketing channel between producers and consumers. As indicated in Chapter 10, retailer leadership in the marketing channel depends on the role and power relationships within the channel. Retailers stand closest to consumers in the channel, but most of what they sell is developed through the initiative of producers.[5] When producers conduct marketing research and develop products, they are designing products to match consumers' wants. Those producers often coordinate the marketing strategy for products sold at the retail level.

Most retailers develop **product assortments.** That is, they collect a variety of products from several competing producers and wholesalers. This is not always the case, however. A specialty store may provide a narrow selection of products—just women's shoes, for example—and some vertically integrated marketing channels carry only one producer's products. For example, Godiva chocolate stores and Fannie May Candy Shops carry only their own products. Retailers try to provide product assortments that allow consumers to compare, shop, and make purchasing decisions.

As Figure 11.2 illustrates, specialty stores have fewer product lines but more depth in the lines they do carry. In contrast, discount stores may have a wide product mix (such as housewares, automobile services, apparel, and food). Department stores may have a wide product mix with different product line depths. Nevertheless, it is usually difficult to maintain a wide and deep product mix because of the inventories required. In addition, some producers prefer to distribute through retailers who offer less variety so that their products get more exposure and less of an impact from competitors' influence.

A retailer's product assortment can be evaluated in terms of (1) purpose, (2) status, and (3) completeness.[6] *Purpose* relates to how well an assortment satisfies consumers and, at the same time, furthers the goals of the retailer. *Status* identifies by rank the relative importance of each product in an assortment. For example, phonograph records would have low status in a store that sells convenience foods. An assortment is *complete* when it includes the products necessary to satisfy a store's customers; it is incomplete when some products are missing. For example, an assortment of convenience foods must include milk to be complete. Most consumers expect to be able to purchase milk when purchasing other food products.

Consumers with different tastes, and with the ability and willingness to purchase, support a variety of retail establishments. The American retail market is splintered, forcing companies to target their products to many market segments, both established and new.[7] It is up to the retailer to determine what makes

4. Kathleen A. Krentler and Joseph P. Guiltinan, "Strategies for Tangibilizing Retail Services: An Assessment," *Journal of the Academy of Marketing Science,* Fall 1984, pp. 89–90.
5. Wroe Alderson, *Marketing Behavior and Executive Action* (Homewood, Ill.: Irwin, 1957), pp. 333–334.
6. C. Glenn Walters, *Marketing Channels,* 2nd ed. (Santa Monica, Calif.: Goodyear, 1977), p. 220.
7. "Marketing: The New Priority," *Business Week,* Nov. 21, 1983, p. 96.

Discount store

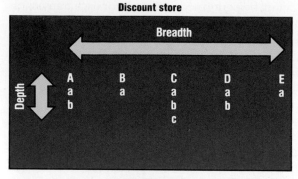

Department store

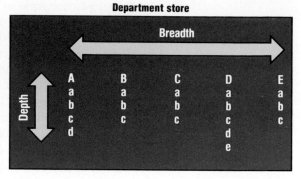

Specialty store

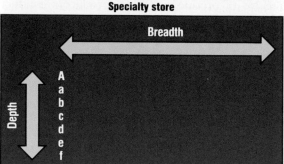

With the capital letters representing number or breadth of product lines, and the small letters depicting the choices in any one product line, it can be seen that discount stores are wide and shallow in merchandise assortment. Specialty stores, at the other extreme, have few product lines, but much more depth in the few they carry. The typical department store falls between these two extremes, having a broad assortment with many merchandise lines and medium depth in each line.

Figure 11.2   *Relationship between merchandise breadth and depth for a typical discount store, department store, and specialty store (Source: Robert F. Hartley,* Retailing: Challenge and Opportunity, *3rd ed., p. 118. Copyright © 1984 by Houghton Mifflin Company. Used by permission)*

target consumers shop in one store rather than another. J. C. Penney is an excellent example of a store that has been very active in using marketing research to plan and position itself as a leading retailer. Marketing research helps J. C. Penney determine its overall image, decide which magazines to advertise in, and learn which items in a department will sell.[8] The effectiveness and efficiency of the marketing channel depends on the ability of retailers to provide the right product assortments for specific target markets.

Developing Retail Store Image and Atmosphere

The ultimate purpose of a retail purchase is sometimes vague to buyers. We discuss the psychological factors and social influences relating to consumer behavior in Chapter 3. It is appropriate to apply some of these concepts as we examine reasons for consumer patronage. For many consumers, purchasing is an end in itself. Shopping trips can be used to escape boredom, to occupy time, or to learn about something new. Because a consumer does not always have a specific reason for going to a retail store, retailers must develop a stimulating and interesting environment for shopping.

8. "Retailers Taking a Closer Look at Customers," *Chain Store Age Executive,* Oct. 1984, p. 21.

For example, Wall Drug Store in South Dakota has created a retail experience that shoppers drive from all over the country to see. Wall Drug, a general store with an Old West environment, provides a nostalgic view of the past and in so doing draws over twenty thousand customers per day in the summer. The store has 50,000 square feet of unique and diverse high-quality merchandise ranging from leather products and gift items to five restaurants. A one-of-a-kind store specializing in excellence, Wall Drug is promoted on billboards all over the world. It is also an enormous success; sales were approximately $5.5 million in 1985. Wall Drug is an example of a store that has created an environment people will seek out for its entertainment value and novelty.[9]

Most industrial purchases are based on economic planning and necessity. Consumer products, on the other hand, are often purchased because of social influences and psychological factors. Consumers usually make a decision to go to one or more of several possible retail stores, most of which have fixed locations, when they search for products. Thus, retailers' marketing efforts are directed toward making desired products available and toward developing a marketing strategy that increases patronage. These goals demand attention to a retail store's image and atmosphere.

The Store's Image

A retail store must create an image that is acceptable to its target market. Social class and self-concept can be major determinants of patronage. Consumers in lower social classes tend to patronize small, high-margin, high-service food stores—and to prefer small, friendly, high-interest loan companies to the more impersonal banks. Saks Fifth Avenue appeals to consumers who are looking for a more distinctive store and a prestige label. For example, in Figure 11.3, Nino Cerruti suits, available at exclusive, high-quality establishments such as Saks, attract wealthy patrons. Harry Winston, Inc., also appeals to the upper social class. Winston's reputation is based on providing some of the most exquisite, unique, and expensive jewels in the world (see Figure 11.4). The Fifth Avenue store has a chandeliered salon done in black and gray. Jewels are brought out upon request. No item is priced less than $20,000, and the average Winston sale exceeds $100,000.[10]

With such varying preferences among consumers, it follows that "different marketing strategies may be required for increasing sales to existing customers and attracting new customers."[11] In other words, customers develop store images based on different characteristics. For example, one study found that the management of Sears should pay attention to "difficulty in finding items" and "friendliness" when trying to get low-frequency shoppers to shop more often. On the other hand, when Sears attempts to gain patronage from K mart customers, honesty and the old-fashioned attributes of K mart seem to affect comparisons between the two. The study found that "high-frequency, low-frequency and non-customers each have different . . . perceptions" of Sears.[12]

---

9. Constance Mitchell, "Some Stores Branch Out By Staying Put," *USA Today,* Feb. 26, 1985, pp. 1 and 2B.
10. Judith Dobrzynski, "The Jeweler to the Super-Rich Opens Its Doors a Crack," *Business Week,* Dec. 16, 1985, p. 81.
11. Gerald Albaum, Roger Best, and Del Hawkins, "Retailing Strategy for Customer Growth and New Customer Attraction," *Journal of Business Research,* March 1980, p. 7.
12. Ibid.

Figure 11.3

Nino Cerruti suits—available at select locations, such as Saks Fifth Avenue—complement the line's progressive, high-quality image (Source: Intercontinental Branded Apparel, a Hartmark Company)

ACCOMPLISHED

A virtuoso as only true artists are, Nino Cerruti engenders Italian styling of international distinction. Featuring pure wool, his Rue Royale Collection offers enduring style with a contemporary appeal.

NINO CERRUTI
RUE ROYALE

INTERCONTINENTAL BRANDED APPAREL

PURE WOOL

For the name of your nearest dealer, write Intercontinental Branded Apparel, 2020 Elmwood Ave., Buffalo, NY 14207.

To understand a store's image, both shopper characteristics and store characteristics must be understood. Shopper characteristics include demographics, lifestyle, perceptions, and behavior. Store characteristics include clientele, location, promotional emphasis, integrity, convenience, economy, and the clarity and strength of the existing store image.[13] Management must recognize that these various characteristics interact in forming store image. For example, a study involving the repositioning of store image revealed that changes in policies not related to price affect consumers' perceptions of other attributes. For example, changes in credit policy were perceived as influencing price.[14]

Figure 11.5 was constructed from 237 personal interviews in four large metropolitan areas. Respondents were a convenience sample of individuals

13. Edgar R. Pessemier, "Store Image and Positioning," *Journal of Retailing,* Spring 1980, pp. 96–97.
14. Philip E. Downs and Joel B. Haynes, "Examining Retail Image Before and After a Repositioning Strategy," *Journal of the Academy of Marketing Science,* Fall 1984, pp. 1–24.

Figure 11.4
Harry Winston's prestige image that appeals to the upper social class (Source: Courtesy of Harry Winston, Inc.)

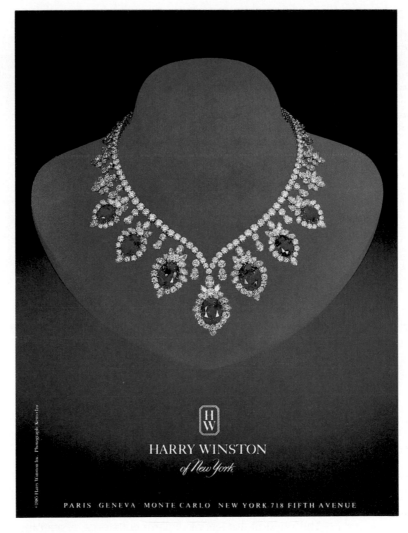

staying at both conventional and discount motels.[15] Discount motels such as Motel 6, Days Inn, Scottish Inns, and Family World have slightly smaller rooms, no elaborate lobbies, and no facilities for conventions and meetings. They also charge up to 50 percent less than conventional motels, such as Holiday Inn and Howard Johnson's. As Figure 11.5 illustrates, perceptions of eight of the characteristics of discount and conventional motels differ significantly, making it possible for a motel to develop an image that appeals to different kinds of customers. A motel with a vague or hazy image may have difficulty attracting consumers. Similarly, it seems reasonable that consumers' store preferences tend to be functions of the degree of "match" between their perceptions of the store's characteristics and of their own characteristics. Plainly, then, retailers must monitor a store's image in the minds of consumers.

15. Ronald F. Bush and Joseph F. Hair, Jr., "Consumer Patronage Determinants of Discount Versus Conventional Motels," *Journal of Retailing,* Summer 1976, p. 45.

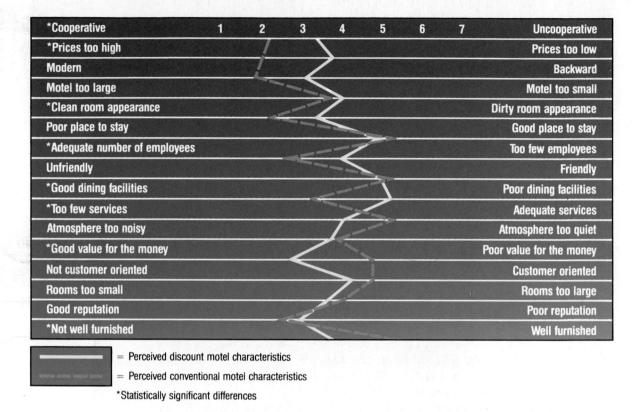

*Cooperative	1	2	3	4	5	6	7	Uncooperative
*Prices too high								Prices too low
Modern								Backward
Motel too large								Motel too small
*Clean room appearance								Dirty room appearance
Poor place to stay								Good place to stay
*Adequate number of employees								Too few employees
Unfriendly								Friendly
*Good dining facilities								Poor dining facilities
*Too few services								Adequate services
Atmosphere too noisy								Atmosphere too quiet
*Good value for the money								Poor value for the money
Not customer oriented								Customer oriented
Rooms too small								Rooms too large
Good reputation								Poor reputation
*Not well furnished								Well furnished

═══ = Perceived discount motel characteristics

╌╌╌ = Perceived conventional motel characteristics

*Statistically significant differences

Figure 11.5   *Perceived characteristics (image) of discount versus conventional motels* (Source: Ronald F. Bush and Joseph F. Hair, Jr., "Consumer Patronage Determinants, Discount Versus Conventional Motels," Journal of Retailing, *Summer 1976, p. 45*)

The Store's Atmosphere

The term **atmospherics** describes the conscious designing of a store's space to create emotional effects that enhance the probability that consumers will buy.[16] The physical aspects of department stores, restaurants, hotels, service stations, and shops create an atmosphere that might be perceived as warm, fresh, colorful, or depressing. Figure 11.6 shows an exclusive lodge that provides the ultimate in interior design and atmosphere.

A study has indicated that color can physically attract shoppers toward a retail display and provide certain perceptual qualities that affect the image of both the store and the merchandise. The study showed that subjects in a furniture store may be physically drawn to warm colors such as yellow or red and may sit closer to walls with those colors, which are considered bright and colorful. But they considered these warm colors less attractive and less pleasant than cool colors such as blue and green. Therefore, a good color configuration may be warm colors for a store's exterior or for display cases, with cool colors creating a pleasant environment near product displays.[17] Customers are also affected by a store's interior design and layout.

16. Phillip Kotler, "Atmospherics as a Marketing Tool," *Journal of Retailing,* Winter 1973–1974, p. 50.
17. Joseph A. Bellizzi and Ayn E. Crowley, "The Effects of Color in Store Design," *Journal of Retailing,* Spring 1983, pp. 21–25.

Figure 11.6

Atmospherics that contribute to an image of uniqueness and exclusivity at the Crowther of Lyon Lodge (Source: Crowther of Lyon Lodge, London)

A George II period pine panelled Library with finely carved chimneypiece, overdoors and coffered ceiling.

Period panelled rooms, Antique Fireplaces Wrought iron entrance gates, Classical statuary, garden temples, vases, seats, fountains, etc.

Interior designers welcome

Crowther of Syon Lodge LONDON

Other atmospheric considerations relate to sound, characterized by silence or soft music or even a noisy environment. Scent may be relevant as well. Stores that have a distinctive odor of perfume or of prepared food provide a unique atmosphere. Crowding in retail stores is another important part of the environmental psychology. It consists of two components: physical density and perceived crowding.[18] A crowded store may restrict exploratory shopping, impede mobility, and decrease shopping efficiency. In such a setting, buyers may rely more on familiar brands and disregard low-priority items.[19]

Retailers must determine what the target market seeks and then encourage the desired awareness and action in consumers through atmospheric variables.[20] Discount department stores must not seem too exclusive and expensive; high-fashion boutiques might well strive to attain an atmosphere of luxury and

18. Gilbert D. Harrell and Michael D. Hutt, "Crowding in Retail Stores," *MSU Business Topics,* Winter 1976, p. 34.
19. Ibid.
20. Kotler, "Atmospherics as a Marketing Tool," p. 62.

novelty. To appeal to multiple market segments, a store may create more than one atmosphere within its departments. The discount basement, the sports department, and the women's shoe department may all have unique atmospheres.

Major Types of Retail Stores

Retail stores provide assortments to match the shopping preferences of consumers. Figure 11.1 illustrates how the width of product mix and the depth of product line create different types of stores. These factors are important in classifying different types of stores, yet there is generally much variation among stores of a particular type. In this section, we examine the types of retail stores that account for most retail sales.

Department Stores

Department stores can be characterized as having a wide product mix; the depth of the product mix may vary, depending on the store. Today, the conventional department stores—Macy's, Hudson's, Bloomingdale's, Marshall Field, Bullock's, and others like them—obtain 75 percent of their sales from apparel and cosmetics.[21] Table 11.1 lists the top ten department stores that focus mainly on apparel and cosmetics ranked by sales volume. General merchandise department stores not reported in Table 11.1—J. C. Penney, Sears, and Montgomery Ward—carry virtually all merchandise lines. These three corporate chain department stores have many more store units and far greater sales volume than certain conventional department store units that usually operate on a regional basis.

Department stores are organized into separate departments—cosmetics, housewares, apparel, home furnishings, and appliances are examples—to facilitate marketing efforts and internal management. Recently, many general merchandise stores have added departments for automotive, recreational, and sports equipment, as well as services such as insurance, travel advice, and income tax preparation.

Department stores are distinctly service oriented. Their total product includes credit, delivery, personal assistance, merchandise returns, and a pleasant atmosphere. They are, for the most part, shopping stores—consumers compare the price, quality, and service for one store's products with those of competing stores.

Corporate chain department stores generate tremendous sales volume, which gives them considerable control over a wide range of the products they sell. For example, Sears has been very successful both in integrating marketing activities and in owning or controlling production. Consumers' loyalty and trusted private store brands make Sears extremely powerful in terms of channel leadership and competitive status.

Mass Merchandisers

Supermarkets and discount stores are mass merchandisers. **Mass merchandisers** tend to offer fewer customer services than department stores and to focus their attention on lower prices, high turnover, and large sales volumes. They generally have a wider—and shallower—product mix than department stores. Mass merchandisers appeal to large heterogeneous target markets. An image of efficiency and economy distinguishes these stores.

21. "The Future of Retailing," *Retailweek*, March 1, 1981, p. 27.

Table 11.1 Top ten U.S. department stores focusing on apparel and cosmetics, ranked by sales

Rank	Chain	1985 Sales[a] (millions)
1	Federated	$10,300
2	Dayton-Hudson	8,925
3	May Department Stores	5,200
4	Associated Dry Goods	4,500
5	R.H. Macy	4,368
6	Allied	4,250
7	Carter Hawley Hale	4,080
8	Mercantile	1,870
9	Dillard	1,600
10	Carson Pirie Scott	1,320

[a]Estimated for retail year ending January 31, 1986.
Source: Reprinted by permission from *The Value Line Investment* Survey.

Discount Stores

Discount stores are self-service, general merchandise outlets such as K mart, Wal-Mart, and Target. Table 11.2 lists the top ten discount stores. Note that K mart has a commanding lead over second-place Wal-Mart. Many of the discounters, including Wal-Mart, are regional. They carry a wide assortment of products, from appliances and housewares to clothing. Toys, automotive services, garden supplies, and sports equipment are also found in major discount establishments. Often, a food supermarket is operated as a department within a discount store.

In the face of increased competition, discounters have generally improved store services, atmosphere, and location, boosting prices and blurring the distinction between some discount houses and department stores. For example, K mart has developed a new program for handling customer complaints at the store level. Research has shown that more than half of all complaints handled to the customer's satisfaction result in strong customer loyalty. K mart hopes to improve customer relations and strengthen its image in the market through greater emphasis on service and customer satisfaction.[22]

In contrast Revco, an Ohio-based discount drug chain with 1,630 stores, focuses on price alone, trying to maintain consistently low prices and never running sales. "Everything we do is to try and reinforce the Revco name and reputation as a leading discount drug chain. We established our reputation as a discount outlet from the beginning, and we've attracted numbers by sticking to that image," stated a company spokesman.[23] The application on page 327 provides a closer look at another discount organization, 47th Street Photo, which competes on price alone. In general, however, many better-known discount houses have assumed the characteristics of department stores.

22. Molly Brauer, "K mart Shapes Policy to Settle Complaints," *Houston Chronicle,* Oct. 21, 1985, p. F1.
23. "Revco Focuses on Discounts," *Product Marketing,* April 1983, p. 32.

Table 11.2 Top ten discount stores (by retail sales)

Rank	Chain	Projected Sales for Current Fiscal year (millions)
1	K mart	$21,040
2	Wal-Mart	6,268
3	Target	3,550
4	Best Products	2,253
5	Zayre	2,195
6	T.G.&Y.	2,020
7	Toys Я Us	1,704
8	Service Merchandise	1,607
9	Bradlees	1,404
10	Gemco.	1,247

Source: Reprinted by permission from *Discount Store News,* September 19, 1983. Copyright © Lebhar-Friedman, Inc., 425 Park Avenue, New York, N.Y. 10022.

Warehouse Showrooms

The **warehouse showroom** is a retail facility with five basic characteristics: (1) a large, low-cost building, (2) use of warehouse materials-handling technology, (3) use of vertical merchandise display space, (4) a large on-premises inventory, and (5) minimum services. Most of the popular showrooms are operated by large furniture retailers. Wickes Furniture and Levitz Furniture Corporation have brought sophisticated mass merchandising to the highly fragmented furniture industry. These high-volume, low-overhead operations have reduced personnel and services. Lower costs are effected by shifting some marketing functions to consumers, who must transport, finance, and perhaps store merchandise. Most consumers carry away their purchases in the manufacturer's carton.

Catalog showrooms are another form of warehouse showroom. Consumers select products from a catalog they receive in the mail; they buy at a warehouse where all products are stored out of the buyer's reach. A clerk fills orders from the warehouse, and products are presented in the manufacturer's carton. Operating costs are low because closed inventory rooms reduce shoplifting and display expenses. Catalog showrooms usually sell established brands and models that have little risk of being discontinued. Such showrooms appear to be one of the fastest-growing areas of retailing.

Supermarkets

Supermarkets are large, self-service stores that carry a broad and complete line of food products and usually some nonfood products as well. They have central checkout facilities. Large grocery supermarkets were the first mass merchandisers. They developed over fifty years ago, but now their total share of the food market is declining. The top ten food chains, including nonsupermarket chains, are listed in Table 11.3.

Supermarkets sell a wide variety of products and feature lower prices than smaller neighborhood grocery stores, which offer convenient locations, personal services, or quality images. One consumer study found that the major reasons for shopping at a particular supermarket were low prices, wide variety, a good

A discount retailer of electronic products, 47th Street Photo, sells personal computers, calculators, typewriters, videotape players, and photographic equipment (although photographic equipment accounts for only 30 percent of sales). This retailer competes not on the basis of service or atmospherics, but strictly on the basis of price. In just fifteen years, 47th Street has achieved an estimated $100 million in annual sales, half from retail store sales and half from catalog sales. Yet the firm has only two stores, the main store on West 47th in Manhattan and the computer outlet two blocks away. A third location handles the mail-order business.

The stores are small, overcrowded, and almost dingy, offering very limited customer service. The store would rather have customers take merchandise home for a thorough inspection than linger to examine it on the premises—in a low-margin, high-volume operation, nothing is more important than turnover. When questioned about the store's low-budget interior decor, Marketing Manager Joseph Greenfeld replied, "We don't want the consumer to have to subsidize our inefficiency."

Although 47th Street tightly controls labor and design costs, perhaps its biggest price advantage is volume. It may sell a new camera at a rate of one hundred per day. In just a few months, it sold ten thousand Texas Instruments 994 home computers. This level of volume requires huge purchases and substantial inventory. For example, 47th Street buys hundreds of videotape players and ten thousand blank videotapes in a single order. Such purchases typically result in price breaks from manufacturers. The retailer's huge inventory consists of nearly twenty-five thousand products stocked in depth.

Although 47th Street is located in New York, the store has gained national visibility. It advertises in the *New York Times,* the *Wall Street Journal,* and *U.S. News and World Report.* Approximately 25 percent of the firm's weekly *New York Times* ads are underwritten by manufacturers. Catalogs make 47th Street products and prices available to consumers across the country. Perhaps more importantly, word of mouth communications carry credible news about low prices and extensive inventories. (*Source: John Merwin, "The Source,"* Forbes, *April 9, 1984, pp. 74–78.*)

selection of quality produce, and convenience of location.[24] Many supermarkets stock such products as cosmetics and nonprescription drugs and provide such services as check cashing. Supermarkets must be operated efficiently because net profits after taxes are usually less than 1 percent of sales.

Superstores

Superstores combine features of discount houses and supermarkets. These giant stores carry not only all food and nonfood products ordinarily found in supermarkets, but also most products normally purchased on a routine basis. Such product lines as housewares, hardware, personal care products, garden products, tires, and automotive services complement a complete food line. Consumers are most attracted to superstores by lower prices.

24. Jacquelyn Bivens, "Checking Our Consumer Response," *Chain Store Age Executive,* Aug. 1983, p. 19.

Table 11.3 Top ten food chains (ranked by sales volume)

Company	1984 Sales
1. Safeway Stores, Inc.	$19,642,201,000
2. The Kroger Co.	15,922,891,000
3. American Stores Co.	12,118,793,000
4. The Southland Corp.	12,105,001,000
5. Lucky Stores, Inc.	9,236,529,000
6. Winn-Dixie Stores, Inc.	7,774,480,000
7. The Great Atlantic and Pacific Tea Company (A & P)	5,878,286,000
8. Albertson's, Inc.	4,735,724,000
9. Supermarkets General Corporation	4,346,680,000
10. The Stop & Shop Companies, Inc.	3,247,298,000

Source: "Sales and Net Income of Top Publicly Owned Food Chains," *Supermarket Business,* Oct. 1985, p. 21. Used by permission.

Superstores use advanced technology and operating techniques to cut costs and increase sales volume. They often use tall, visible shelving and display entire assortments of products to reduce handling costs. Supermarkets' market share is declining because superstores are high-volume, low-margin, low-price stores. Consumers are increasingly concerned with prices, and economic uncertainty makes it difficult for supermarkets to compete as effectively as superstores.

Specialty Retailers

Specialty retailers are stores carrying a narrow product mix with deep product lines. The Gap, The Limited, County Seat, The Foot Locker, and The Athlete's Foot offer limited product lines but great depth. The Foot Locker, owned by Kinney Shoe Corp., specializes in running, tennis, and other types of athletic shoes. Florists, bakery shops, and book stores are usually small, independent specialty retailers that appeal to local target markets, although they can, of course, be owned and managed by large corporations. Even if this kind of retailer adds a few supporting product lines, the store may still be classified as a specialty store. Usually, such a store is distinguished by its small size and great variety in a few product lines.

Specialty stores attempt to provide a unique store image. A strategically positioned retailer may find it easier to compete on the basis of image than on the basis of price. The small specialty shop may be unable to compete directly with the prices of large retailers.[25] However, factors relating to fashion, service, personnel, physical characteristics, location, and social class can distinguish small retailers and contribute to favorable consumer attitudes toward them. For instance, Fila boutiques carry expensive, high-quality sportswear for tennis, golf, and skiing. Specialty stores give the small business owner an opportunity to provide unique services to match the varied desires of consumers. For consumers dissatisfied with the impersonal nature of large retailers, the opportunity for close, personal contact in a small specialty store can be a welcome change.

25. Leonard Berry, "Retail Positioning Strategies for the 1980s," *Business Horizons,* Nov.–Dec. 1982, p. 45.

Nonstore Retailing

Nonstore retailing takes place without consumers visiting a store. It includes personal sales such as in-home and telephone retailing and nonpersonal sales such as mail-order, vending, and catalog retailing. Nonstore retailing accounts for an increasing percentage of retail sales.

Personal Sales

In-home Retailing

In-home retailing involves personal contacts with consumers. Organizations such as Avon, Electrolux, and Fuller Brush Company send representatives to the homes of preselected prospects. Products such as *World Book Encyclopedia,* Kirby vacuum cleaners, and Avon and Mary Kay cosmetics are sold to consumers in their homes. Traditionally, in-home retailing relied on a random door-to-door approach. Companies such as World Book and Kirby (both divisions of Scott & Fetzer Co.) now employ a more efficient approach. Prospects are first reached by phone or intercepted in shopping malls or at fairs. These initial contacts are limited to a brief introduction and the setting of appointments. Salespeople then go to the customer's home to make their sales presentation.[26] However, some in-home selling still is undertaken without information about sales prospects. In-home selling of rugs, draperies, and home improvements is helpful to consumers since these products need to be blended carefully with the existing interior of a house.

Door-to-door selling without a prearranged appointment represents a tiny proportion of total retail sales—probably less than 1 percent. Because it has so often been associated with unscrupulous and fraudulent techniques, door-to-door selling is illegal in some communities. In general, this technique is regarded unfavorably because so many door-to-door salespersons are undertrained and poorly supervised. A big disadvantage of door-to-door selling is the large expenditure, effort, and time it demands. Sales commissions are usually 25 to 50 percent, or more, of the retail price; and consumers often pay more than a product is worth as a result. Door-to-door selling is used most often when a product is unsought and consumers will not make a special effort to go to a store to purchase it. Many encyclopedias are sold in this way. Avon and Fuller Brush, two successful and respected companies, have used door-to-door selling very effectively.

One variation of in-home retailing is the home demonstration or party, a method that is gaining popularity. One consumer acts as host and invites a number of friends to view merchandise at his or her home.

Telephone Retailing

Telephone retailing can be based on a cold canvass of the telephone directory, or prospective clients can be screened before calling. (In some areas, telephone numbers may be listed with an asterisk to indicate those people who consider

---

26. Bill Saporito, "A Door-to-Door Bell Ringer," *Fortune,* Dec. 10, 1984, pp. 83–84 and 88.

sales solicitations a nuisance.) Another tactic is to use advertising that encourages consumers to initiate a call or to request information about placing an order. Although this type of retailing represents a small part of total retail sales, its use is growing. According to AT&T, U.S. companies spent $13.6 billion in a recent year on telemarketing phone calls and equipment—phones, lines, and computers. Telephone Marketing Resources, a telemarketing firm, estimates telephone sales of goods and services at $75 billion annually (the figure includes business-to-consumer sales *and* business-to-business sales).[27] Among the many companies using telemarketing are IBM, Merrill Lynch, Allstate, Avis, Ford, Quaker Oats, Time, and American Express.

Nonpersonal Sales

Automatic Vending

Automatic vending makes use of machines and accounts for less than 2 percent of all retail sales. Approximately six million vending units generate about $15 billion in retail sales annually. It is significant that while vending retail sales increased rapidly in the 1970s, the sales trend in the 1980s has been relatively flat. Vending items that show a slight decline include milk, bottled cold drinks, cigarettes, cigars, ice cream, and canned hot foods. On the other hand, canned cold drinks and some nonfood items have increased in sales volume.[28]

Vending machine locations and the percentage of sales each generates are as follows:[29]

Plants and factories	36.4	Government facilities	6.5
Public locations (e.g., stores)	20.2	Hospitals and nursing homes	5.4
Offices	10.0	Primary and secondary schools	4.2
Colleges and universities	8.2	Others	9.4

Video game machines provide an entertainment service, and many banks now offer machines that dispense cash or offer other services, but these uses of vending machines are not reported in total vending sales volume.

Automatic vending is one of the most impersonal forms of retailing. Small, standardized, routinely purchased products (chewing gum, soft drinks, coffee) can be sold in machines because consumers usually purchase them at the nearest available location. Machines in areas of heavy traffic provide efficient and continuous services to consumers. The elimination of sales personnel and the small amount of space necessary for vending machines give this retailing method some advantages over stores. The advantages are partly offset by the expense of the frequent servicing and repair needed.

Mail-order Retailing

Mail-order retailing is a form of selling by description since buyers usually do not see the actual product until it arrives in the mail. Sellers contact buyers through direct mail, catalogs, television, radio, magazines, and newspapers. A wide assortment of products such as records, books, clothing, and household items are sold to consumers through the mail. Placement of mail orders by telephone is increasingly common. The advantages of mail-order selling include

27. Joel Dreyfuss, "Reach Out and Sell Something," *Fortune,* Nov. 26, 1984, pp. 127–128, 130, and 132.
28. *Vending Times,* "V/T Census of the Industry," July 1984, pp. 216 and 244.
29. Ibid.

efficiency and convenience. Mail-order houses can be located in remote lower-cost areas and can forego the expenses of store fixtures. Eliminating personal selling efforts and store operations may result in tremendous savings that can be passed along to consumers in the form of lower prices. On the other hand, mail-order retailing is inflexible, provides limited service, and is more appropriate for specialty products than for convenience products.

Catalog retailing is a specific type of direct marketing conducted by retailers. Orders may be delivered by mail, or customers may pick them up. Although in-store visits result in some catalog orders, most are placed by mail or telephone. Figure 11.7 illustrates catalog retailing at Spiegel.

General Foods has created Thomas Garroway, Ltd., a mail-order service providing gourmet pasta, cheese, coffee, and similar items. General Foods chose the fictitious British name to give the company a classier image. Other packaged-goods manufacturers involved in catalog retailing are Procter & Gamble, Hanes, Nestlé, Thomas J. Lipton, Sunkist, R.J. Reynolds, and Whitman Chocolates, to name a few.[30] These catalog retailers are able to reach many two-income families who have more money and less time for special shopping. Catalog sales have

---

30. Ronald Alsop, "Food Giants Take to Mails to Push Fancy Product Lines," *Wall Street Journal,* Feb. 28, 1985, p. 85.

Figure 11.8

Baskin-Robbins' promotion of strong company support and individual assistance for franchisees (Source: Baskin-Robbins, Inc.)

Over 40 years of successful operation has made Baskin-Robbins America's favorite ice cream store. We continue to lead the industry with over 3,000 stores in 37 countries, and an additional 100 opening every year.

All franchisees in the Baskin-Robbins system receive individual attention and assistance in order to meet their specific store requirements. In addition, their efforts are supported with national, regional and local advertising.

franchising opportunities to Jim Earnhardt, Vice President, Operations, Baskin-Robbins Ice Cream Company, 31 Baskin-Robbins Place, Glendale, California 91201. Send your inquiries regarding

BASKIN 31 ROBBINS

The sweet taste of success.

been growing 50 to 100 percent faster than annual retail sales over the past five years. There are approximately four thousand catalogs in circulation. Industry estimates place direct-mail sales of general merchandise and related goods at $30 billion and total catalog sales at around $40 billion.[31]

Franchising

Franchising is an arrangement in which a supplier, or franchisor, grants a dealer, or franchisee, the right to sell products in exchange for some type of consideration. For example, the franchisor may receive some percentage of total sales in exchange for furnishing equipment, buildings, management know-how, and marketing assistance to the franchisee. For instance, Baskin-Robbins (see Figure 11.8) promotes the individual attention and advertising support it gives to franchisees. The franchisee, in turn, must agree to operate according to the rules of the franchisor.

Franchised health clubs, exterminators, restaurants, and campgrounds abound. There are also franchised tax preparers and travel agencies. The real estate industry is experiencing rapid growth in franchising. Also expected to join the franchising ranks in large numbers are hair salons, tanning salons, and professionals such as dentists and lawyers.[32] In fact, franchising has been one of retailing's major growth areas over the past twenty years. During this period,

31. "The Sale Is in the Mail," *Chain Store Age Executive,* March 1984, pp. 44, 49, 51, 54.
32. Franchising types and examples are adapted from Robert F. Hartley, *Retailing: Challenge and Opportunity,* 3rd ed. Copyright © 1984 Houghton Mifflin Company. Adapted with permission.

Table 11.4 *Largest franchising sectors, ranked by sales*

	Sales (millions of dollars)	% of Total Franchise Sales
Automobile and truck dealers	$132,171	53.4
Gasoline service stations	52,409	21.2
Fast-food restaurants	17,075	6.9
Soft-drink bottlers	11,044	4.5
Retailing (nonfood)	10,883	4.4
Automotive products and services[a]	6,202	2.5
Other	17,791	7.1
Total	274,575	100.0

[a]Includes tires.
Source: Franchising in the Economy, 1976–1978, U.S. Department of Commerce (Washington, D.C.: U.S. Government Printing Office, 1978), pp. 1–2. Based on 1977 sales.

organizations such as McDonald's Corporation, Holiday Inns, Inc., Kentucky Fried Chicken, and Pizza Hut restaurants have emerged as major competitive forces in their respective industries.

Three basic types of franchising arrangements have been developed.[33] A producer may franchise a number of stores to sell a particular brand of product. One of the oldest franchising arrangements, this method prevails in the areas of passenger cars and trucks, farm equipment, shoes, paint, earth-moving equipment, and petroleum. Virtually all new cars and trucks are sold through franchised dealers, while an estimated 90 percent of all gasoline is sold through franchised independent retail service stations. Table 11.4 illustrates the largest franchising sectors, ranked by sales.

A producer may franchise wholesalers to sell to retailers. This arrangement is most common in the soft-drink industry. Most national producers of soft-drink syrups—Coca-Cola, Dr Pepper, Pepsi-Cola, 7UP, Royal Crown—franchise independent bottlers who then serve retailers.

Sometimes, rather than franchising a complete product, a franchisor provides brand names, techniques, procedures, or other services. While the franchisor may perform some manufacturing and wholesaling functions, its major contribution is a carefully developed, and controlled, marketing strategy. This is the most common type of franchise today. Examples are many, including Holiday Inn, Maaco, McDonald's, Dairy Queen, Avis, Hertz, Kentucky Fried Chicken, and H & R Block.

Franchising continues to grow at a rapid rate. The Department of Commerce indicates that franchise establishments were doing about $116 billion in sales in 1969. By 1980 sales had increased to approximately $338 billion. The number of new franchises or new businesses that entered the franchising arena is increasing by about 9 percent each year. The current trends of franchising growth will probably continue at approximately the same rate.

The expansion of the franchise system to many industries highlights the benefits of central management control and coordinated marketing efforts for

33. "Franchising—Opening the Doors to Expansion," *Retailweek,* Feb. 1, 1981, p. 29.

franchise members. The advantages for franchisees are tremendous. They are entrepreneurs who invest their own money and must perform at a high level to protect their investment. But unlike most entrepreneurs, they go into business under the protective wing of a company with a proven track record. Still, like all businesses, franchising does pose risks. Many franchisees have gone out of business as a result of poor management, minimal marketing research, poor marketing planning, or overexpansion.

Planned Shopping Centers

"Today the shopping center is replacing the central business district as a place for shopping, cultural, or recreational opportunities. This is particularly true with enclosed malls that attract large numbers of people for purposes other than shopping."[34] The planned shopping center is constructed by private owners to contain a complementary mix of stores that provides one-shop shopping for family and household needs. Although shopping centers may vary, the principle of a coordinated, complementary mix of stores that generates consumer traffic is a key factor.

Shopping centers are planned, coordinated, and promoted to appeal to heterogeneous groups of consumers. The shopping-center management ensures an environment that is comfortable and conveniently set up to serve consumers with a variety of needs. Parking facilities, landscaping, and special events create an overall atmosphere that attracts consumers.

Neighborhood Shopping Centers

Neighborhood shopping centers usually consist of several small convenience and specialty stores such as small grocery stores, drugstores, gas stations, and fast-food restaurants. They serve consumers who live less than ten minutes' driving time from the center. Many of these retailers consider their target markets to be consumers who live within a two- to three-mile radius of their stores. Since most purchases are based on convenience or personal contact, the coordination of selling efforts within a neighborhood shopping center usually is limited. Product mixes are usually held to essential products, and the depth of the product lines tends to be limited. Convenience stores are most successful when they are closer to the consumer than, for example, supermarkets. The best strategy for neighborhood centers is to locate along travel patterns that allow the center to intercept the greatest number of potential consumers before they reach a regional shopping center.[35]

Community Shopping Centers

Community shopping centers include one or two department stores and some specialty stores, as well as convenience stores. They serve a larger geographic area and draw consumers who are looking for shopping and specialty products that are not available in neighborhood shopping centers. Consumers drive longer distances to community shopping centers than to neighborhood shopping

34. Joseph Barry Mason, "First, Fifth and Fourteenth Amendment Rights: The Shopping Center as a Public Forum," *Journal of Retailing,* Summer 1975, p. 21.
35. Franklin S. Houston and John Stanton, "Evaluating Retail Trade Areas for Convenience Stores," *Journal of Retailing,* Spring 1984, p. 135.

centers. The community shopping center is carefully planned and coordinated to attract shoppers. Special events such as art exhibits, automobile shows, and sidewalk sales are used to stimulate traffic. The overall management of a community shopping center looks for tenants that complement the center's total assortment of products. There are wide product mixes and deep product lines.

Regional Shopping Centers

Regional shopping centers usually have the largest department stores, the widest product mix, and the deepest product lines of all shopping centers. They carry most products found in a downtown shopping district. The success of regional shopping centers has led to defensive measures by downtown retailers, who have modernized their stores and increased parking facilities. Intracity expressways and improved public transportation have helped many downtown shopping districts to remain competitive.

With 150,000 or more consumers in their target market, regional shopping centers must have well-coordinated management and marketing activities. Because of the expense of leasing space in regional shopping centers, their tenants are more likely to be national chain stores than small independents. These large centers usually advertise, have special events, furnish transportation to some consumer groups, and carefully select the mix of stores. West Edmonton Mall in Edmonton, Canada, is the largest shopping mall in the world with 828 stores, including 50 shoe stores, 8 department stores, and 135 eating places. The shopping center features a 438-foot-long lake with submarines, dolphins, and a Spanish galleon. The mall also features a 12-story roller coaster and a large skating rink.[36]

Intermarket patronage, or "outshopping," is important to regional shopping centers. Outshoppers are those who will forgo the convenience of hometown shopping and travel to out-of-town markets to purchase products. Studies indicate that frequent outshoppers have higher incomes and education, are more likely to own a home, have a negative attitude toward local shopping conditions, are shopping innovators, use more credit, shop less by catalog, and are more physically fit than those who shop locally.[37]

Nontraditional Shopping Centers

Two new types of discount malls or shopping centers are emerging that differ significantly from traditional shopping centers. The factory outlet mall features discount and factory outlet stores carrying traditional manufacturer brands, such as Van Heusen, Levi Strauss, International Silver, Munsingwear, Health-tex, and Wrangler. Manufacturers own these stores and must exert particular effort to avoid conflicting with traditional retailers of their products. Manufacturers claim that their stores are in noncompetitive locations, and indeed most factory outlet malls are located outside metropolitan areas. Not all factory outlets stock closeouts and irregulars, but almost all seek to avoid comparison with discount houses. The factory outlet mall attracts customers because of lower prices for quality and major brand names.

The factory outlet mall operates in much the same way as the regional shopping center and probably draws traffic from a larger shopping radius.

36. Lou Ziegler, "Canadian Mall: Wonder Under a Roof," *USA Today,* Jan. 3, 1986, p. 1.
37. Jon M. Hawes and James R. Lumpkin, "Understanding the Outshopper," *Journal of the Academy of Marketing Science,* Fall 1984, pp. 200–217.

Figure 11.9

The wheel of retailing, which explains the origin and evolution of new types of retail stores (Source: Adapted from Robert F. Hartley, Retailing: Challenge and Opportunity, 3rd ed. [Boston: Houghton Mifflin, 1984], p. 42)

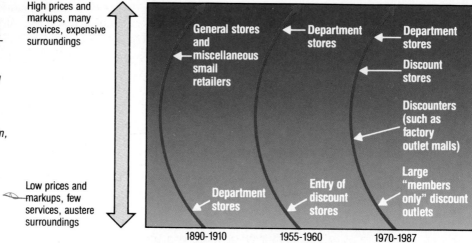

High prices and markups, many services, expensive surroundings

Low prices and markups, few services, austere surroundings

General stores and miscellaneous small retailers ← Department stores ← Department stores

Discount stores

Discounters (such as factory outlet malls)

Large "members only" discount outlets

Department stores

Entry of discount stores

1890-1910   1955-1960   1970-1987

If the "wheel" is considered to be turning slowly in the direction of the arrow, then the department stores around 1900 and the discounters later can be viewed as coming on the scene at the low end of the wheel. As it turns slowly, they move with it, becoming higher-price operations, and at the same time leaving room for lower-price firms to gain entry at the low end of the wheel.

Promotional activity is at the heart of these new shopping centers. Craft shows, contests, and special events attract a great deal of traffic.

Another nontraditional shopping center is the miniwarehouse mall. These loosely planned centers sell space to retailers, who operate what are essentially retail stores out of warehouse bays. The developers of the miniwarehouse mall may also sell space to wholesalers or even to light manufacturers who maintain a retail facility in their warehouse bay. Some of these miniwarehouses are located in high-traffic areas and provide ample customer parking, as well as display windows that can be seen from the street. Home improvement materials, specialty foods, pet supplies, and garden and yard supplies are often sold in these malls.

Unlike the traditional shopping center, the miniwarehouse mall usually does not have a coordinated promotional program and store mix. These nontraditional shopping centers come closest to a neighborhood or community shopping center.

The Wheel of Retailing

When new types of retail businesses develop, they hope to find a niche in the dynamic environment of retailing. One hypothesis attempts to account for the evolution of and future opportunities for new types of retail stores. The **wheel of retailing** hypothesis holds that "new types of retailers usually enter the market as low-status, low-margin, low-price operators. Gradually, they acquire more elaborate establishments and facilities, with both increased investments and higher operating costs. Finally, they mature as high-cost, high-price merchants, vulnerable to newer types who, in turn, go through the same pattern."[38]

38. Stanley C. Hollander, "The Wheel of Retailing," *Journal of Marketing,* July 1960, p. 37.

Table 11.5 *The marketing concept as applied to retailing*

The marketing concept in retailing has come to mean an understanding of the consumer's wants, needs, and desires so that the store, through its management and its marketing and merchandising plans, is better equipped to serve and satisfy those wants, needs, and desires.

The marketing concept means that merchandise and services that can be profitably offered are selected on the basis of perceived customer and consumer wants, needs, and desires.

The marketing concept means that these wants, needs, and desires must be ascertained before goods and services are offered for sale.

The marketing concept means that recognition of changing customer and consumer needs is paramount if the firm selling the goods and services is to survive, grow, and prosper.

Source: Promotion Exchange, National Retail Merchants Association, in New York, Aug. 1979. Used by permission.

For example, supermarkets have undergone many changes since their introduction in 1921. Initially, they provided limited services in exchange for lower food prices. However, over time they developed a variety of new services, including delicatessens, free coffee, gourmet food sections, and children's areas with cartoon films.

Superstores now are challenging supermarkets. As discussed earlier, superstores are huge mass merchandisers who operate on a low cost, self-service basis and carry most routinely purchased goods as well as groceries. Superstores have increased product choices over the original supermarket offerings and have undercut supermarket prices.

Figure 11.9 illustrates the wheel of retailing for department stores and discount houses. Department stores such as Sears developed as high-volume, low-cost merchants to compete with general stores and other small retailers. Discount houses developed in response to the rising expenses of services in department stores. Many discount houses now appear to be following the wheel of retailing by offering more services, better locations, quality inventories, and, therefore, higher prices. In some cases, it is hard to distinguish discount houses from department stores. The wheel of retailing, like most hypotheses, may not apply to all developments in its field. A major weakness is that the hypothesis does not predict what retailing innovations will develop or when. Still, the hypothesis works reasonably well in industrialized, expanding economies.

Retail Strategy Development

From a managerial point of view, retailing is the attempt to manage exchange at the point of ultimate consumption for the benefit of the organization and society.[39] Table 11.5 summarizes our central managerial philosophy—the marketing concept—as it applies to retailers in the 1980s. A marketing strategy for a retailer is the posture or central scheme assumed by management as it

39. Joseph Barry Mason and Morris Lehman Mayer, *Modern Retailing,* rev. ed. (Plano, Tex.: Business Publications, 1981), p. 18.

Figure 11.10

Retailing mix (Source: Adapted from Louis W. Stern and Adel I. El-Ansary, Marketing Channels, 1977, p. 61. Reprinted by permission of Prentice-Hall, Inc., Englewood Cliffs, New Jersey)

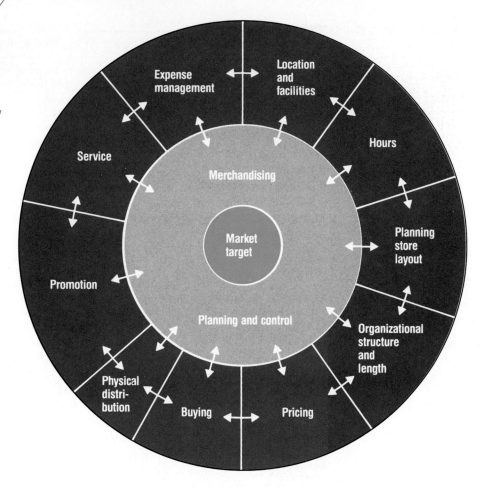

attempts to accomplish its objectives. Defining a target market and developing the retailing mix are critical concerns.

Developing a marketing strategy for a retailer involves five basic steps:

1. Segmenting the market for the type of product or service offering
2. Identifying competitive organizations that handle this class of products and assessing their strengths and advantages
3. Assessing the resources of the organization
4. Defining the specific market target
5. Developing the retailing mix[40]

Variables to monitor in the retail environment include unit sales growth, gross margin performance, and the ratio of operating expenses to sales. Problems in the business environment could be business cycles, inflation, and changing demographic trends. Once changes are detected, the firm must decide whether to make the necessary investment and changes to adapt to its changing environment. When Woolworth liquidated its Woolco discount division it made a decision that continuing the division would require greater risk and resources than the firm wanted to invest.[41]

40. Based on Louis W. Stern and Adel I. El-Ansary, *Marketing Channels,* © 1977, p. 60.
41. Joseph V. Rizzi, "Prospering in a Changing Retail Environment," *Retail Control,* March 1983, p. 13.

Application

Department Stores Answer Discounters with Private-label Brands

Name-brand clothing is a big business in America. Unfortunately for many retailers, name-brand clothes are now being distributed through discounters, and profit margins are suffering. Given the choice of buying Calvin Klein clothing at a department store or at a nearby discounter, consumers will generally opt for the lower-priced alternative. This competition has forced retailers to slash prices to move their name-brand inventory.

In an attempt to protect their margins and offer goods that buyers cannot find elsewhere, retail chains are now developing their own distinctive private-label lines, ranging from clothing to linens. But, unlike private-label goods of the past—which were often second-rate, cheaply manufactured items with department-store labels slapped on—this merchandise is created by designers, targeted at specific customers, and made to have a clearly identifiable look and image. Thus, retailers can sell these private-label goods exclusively, free from the cost competition they must face from brand-name items sold by other department stores.

Retailers are putting so much research and style into these private labels that they may even become preferred. Among the successful, high-quality private labels are Stuart Reed offered by Sakowitz, Allen Solly by Federated Department Stores, and Classis by Carter Hawley Hale Stores. The Gap, J. C. Penney, Dayton Hudson, and R. H. Macy are other retailers with popular private labels. Dayton Hudson introduced Boundary Waters, a casual line sporting a duck named "Matthew Mallard" over three years ago; within two years, the new line had produced sales of $40 million, and it is now being expanded to include 200 items. Another private-label line of apparel called Hunter's Run, sold by Limited and Casual Corner stores, has done so well that it has achieved the recognition of a name-brand product. Such private labels are the sword with which merchants are hoping to combat the off-price retailing of discounters and other department stores. (*Sources: "J. C. Penney Shops for a Trendier Image,"* Business Week, *Feb. 6, 1984, p. 58; Hank Gilman, "Retailers Bet Their Designer Wear Can Lure You Past Calvin Klein,"* Wall Street Journal, *Feb. 1, 1985, p. 23; and Amy Dunkin, "How Department Stores Plan to Get the Registers Ringing Again,"* Business Week, *Nov. 18, 1985, pp. 66–67.*)

The retailing mix is a specific application of the marketing mix concept. It includes location, hours, facilities, organizational structure and strength, merchandise planning and control, pricing, buying, promotion, service, and expense management. As Figure 11.10 indicates, merchandising is the main element of the mix. **Merchandising** involves selling the right products in the right quantities, at the right place, at the right time, and at the right price. Merchandise management involves planning and control of a merchandise inventory to serve target consumers and achieve the profit goals of the retailer. The application on this page shows how department stores are managing their merchandise assortment to deal with discount outlets more effectively.

Scrambled merchandising consists of adding unrelated products and product lines to the existing product mix. Retailers have adopted the practice in hopes of (1) converting a store into a one-stop shopping center, (2) generating more traffic, (3) realizing higher profit margins, and/or (4) increasing impulse purchases. Although there are benefits to be gained from scrambling merchandise, there are also limitations. The latter include dealing with diverse marketing channels—

and thus lowering the retailer's expertise in buying, selling, and servicing—and the possibility of creating a fuzzy store image in the minds of consumers.

A study of sales, contribution to income, and return on assets in a chain of retail stores showed that the level of inventory had a strong impact on each store's performance. Management needs to insure that individual store units stock an adequate product assortment, that inventory shortages are minimized, and that any unbalanced inventory situations are handled as quickly as possible. Check-out systems capable of automatic inventory maintenance are helpful in overcoming these problems.[42]

Failure to create a distinctive retailing mix makes it more difficult for a retailer to compete. In today's highly competitive, saturated markets, retailers must differentiate themselves by carefully selecting their market segments and projecting merchandising images designed to attract specific and well-differentiated markets.[43]

Summary

Retailing focuses on activities required to facilitate exchanges with ultimate consumers. Retailers are an important link in the marketing channel. They perform many marketing activities and add value to final consumer products. In addition, retailers are customers for wholesalers and producers. Retail institutions provide place, time, possession, and in some cases form utilities.

Manufacturers often develop the marketing strategy for a product, whereas retailers offer an assortment of products from competing manufacturers. The marketing functions that retailers perform depend on the role relationships and the division of labor within the marketing channel.

The environment of a retail store includes the store's image and its atmosphere. In planning these characteristics, retailers must consider the consumers' self-concepts and desires. To create an effective atmosphere, a store's space should be designed to develop an emotional effect that enhances the probability that consumers will buy.

The major types of retail stores are department stores, mass merchandisers (discount stores, warehouse showrooms, supermarkets, and superstores), and specialty stores. Types of nonstore retailing are in-home selling, telephone selling, automatic vending, and mail-order selling. Franchising is an arrangement in which a supplier grants a dealer the right to sell products in exchange for some type of consideration. Planned shopping centers provide an environment for a complementary mix of retail stores. They include neighborhood, community, regional, and nontraditional shopping centers.

The wheel of retailing hypothesis holds that new retail institutions develop as low-status, low-margin, low-price operators. As they increase service and prices, they become vulnerable to newer institutions, which enter and repeat the cycle. However, like most hypotheses, the wheel of retailing may not apply in every case.

42. Richard Hise, J. Patrick Kelly, Myron Gable, and James B. McDonald, "Factors Affecting the Performance of Individual Chain Store Units: An Empirical Analysis," *Journal of Retailing*, Summer 1983, p. 37.
43. Arthur I. Cohen and Ana Loud Jones, "Brand Marketing in the New Retail Environment," *Harvard Business Review*, Sept.–Oct. 1978, p. 142.

There are five basic steps to developing an overall marketing strategy for a retailer. The last two involve defining the target market and developing a retailing mix. The retailing mix consists of location, hours, facilities, organizational structure and strength, merchandise planning and control, pricing, buying, promotion, service, and expense management. Merchandising involves selling the right products in the right quantities, at the right place, at the right time, and at the right price. Scrambled merchandising is the addition of unrelated products and product lines to the existing product mix to create one-stop shopping, to generate greater traffic, to increase profits, and to spur impulse sales.

Important Terms

Retailing
Product assortments
Atmospherics
Department stores
Mass merchandisers
Discount stores
Warehouse showrooms
Catalog showrooms
Supermarkets
Superstores
Specialty retailers
Nonstore retailing

In-home retailing
Telephone retailing
Automatic vending
Mail-order retailing
Catalog retailing
Franchising
Neighborhood shopping centers
Community shopping centers
Regional shopping centers
Wheel of retailing
Merchandising
Scrambled merchandising

Discussion and Review Questions

1. Retailers develop product assortments to make final exchanges with ultimate consumers. What marketing activities must be performed to develop product assortments?
2. Retailers develop assortments from several competing manufacturers and serve consumers' interests. What do manufacturers do to ensure that their products are selected at the retail level?
3. How does the retail marketing of professional services differ from traditional retail marketing of goods?
4. Is it possible for a single retail store to have an overall image that appeals to sophisticated shoppers, extravagant ones, and bargain hunters? Why or why not?
5. How does atmosphere add value to products sold in a store? How important is atmospherics for convenience stores?
6. How should one determine the best retail store atmosphere?
7. What are the major differences between discount houses and department stores?
8. Furniture warehouse showrooms developed as a new kind of mass merchandiser in the late 1960s and 1970s. List other major shopping products that could be sold using the showroom method.
9. What do specialty retailers have in common? Do they compete with department stores?
10. Why is door-to-door selling a form of retailing? Some consumers feel that direct mail-orders skip the retailer. Is this true?

11. What management assistance does the typical franchisee gain from the franchisor? What are some reasons why many franchisees have gone out of business?
12. What is the "wheel of retailing" hypothesis?
13. What impact could the rising cost of gasoline have on the wheel of retailing?
14. Without a distinctive retailing mix it is difficult for a retailer to compete. Do you agree or disagree with this statement? Why?

Cases

Case 11.1 7-Eleven Stores[44]

THE SOUTHLAND CORPORATION

Of the roughly 57,000 convenience stores in the United States, the Southland Corporation dominates, operating over 7,760 7-Eleven retail convenience stores in forty-one states, the District of Columbia, and five provinces of Canada. Eight million customers a day shop at their neighborhood 7-Eleven stores; over half the U.S. population live within 2 miles of a 7-Eleven. 7-Eleven is the country's largest retailer of items such as tobacco products, magazines, beer, and coffee-to-go. 7-Eleven used to be a leader in sales of adult magazines such as *Forum, Penthouse,* and *Playboy,* but these products were deleted in 1986. This decision resulted in a loss of $13.5 to $15.5 million in sales. In addition, Southland is the largest independent retailer of gasoline in the United States. Self-serve gasoline is available at slightly less than half of the 7-Eleven locations.

Southland opened roughly 3,000 new 7-Eleven stores between 1978 and 1985. However, the corporation is strongly committed to what it considers its "real growth"—that is, increasing sales and earnings in all of its units. Its plan for increasing store productivity concentrates on product mix, personnel, operational efficiency, store location, and advertising and promotion.

The idea that store productivity is closely linked to the number and types of products offered has prompted the constant search for successful new products. 7-Eleven continually monitors its product line in terms of overall attractiveness and profit. Over the past several years, 7-Eleven has introduced Danish pastries, fountain soft drinks, burritos, juices, deli sandwiches, baked goods, and video games, all of which have been very successful. At the same time, it is continuing to promote established products with good sales potential. Its "Slurpee" frozen carbonated drink is an example of a product that found renewed success due to an effective promotional program.

The most recent addition to 7-Eleven's product mix is a line of customer services. Southland was one of the first retailers to test automatic teller machines (ATMs) and now has agreements for the installation of ATMs in 3,800 convenience stores. Other new services include video player and cassette rentals and credit and debit card programs. These new services are designed to increase store traffic and to attract new customers.

44. Facts are from the Southland Corporation *1982, 1984,* and *1985 Annual Reports;* Nov. 4, 1983, Marketing Presentation handout from Southland Corporation; Anne Reifenberg, "Citgo Pursues Aggressive Strategy," *Dallas Morning News,* April 6, 1986, pp. H-1, 5; "No More Adults," *Time,* April 21, 1986, p. 62; and *1985 Moody's Industrial Manual,* vol. 2, pp. 3544–3556.

Southland is committed to developing highly motivated personnel to manage and operate its stores. It has found that high-quality store managers, franchise owners, and sales personnel have greatly contributed to individual store productivity. For this reason, Southland has launched extensive training programs and offered improved compensation packages.

Southland has also increased productivity by improving store efficiency. This has involved careful attention to product placement and merchandising. Store layout and design have been improved to achieve a clean and modern look, to control customer traffic, and to make products more accessible and easily visible. Equally important to productivity and efficiency is the management of information. Accurate and timely information is critical. Management needs to know which merchandise is good, when inventory levels are lean, and which stores are operating at maximum efficiency. In an attempt to increase the speed and reliability of data transmission, Southland is outfitting itself with two-way transmission networks.

A greater emphasis on store location has led to the acquisition of corner sites for 90 percent of the stores established within the past five years. Although expensive, these corner sites are a key to greater productivity because they are more accessible and visible. They are also more suitable for selling gasoline, which is responsible for substantial increases in sales and profits. In addition to this emphasis on location, every store is measured against higher sales and earnings standards each year. This means that stores in marginal locations or lacking in market potential are closed down, leaving a base of competitive, productive stores.

Southland bought Citgo Petroleum Corporation in 1983. Only recently has Southland put its Citgo brand name on the gasoline sold at more than 3,000 7-Eleven outlets. Previously, 7-Eleven sold unbranded gasoline. Citgo President Ronald E. Hall stated, "We want to move off in time from having to sell an unbranded product—which would necessitate us always selling at the lowest price in order to do the volume we want. We think that with the brand, and with the credit card supporting that, we'll be able to extract some type of a premium for brand over and above our cost and get the same volume, but not have to be so super-competitive." When oil prices fluctuate, 7-Eleven has difficulty making its petroleum operations profitable. But when prices are stable, gasoline sales and adjacent, in-store purchases are profitable. 7-Eleven has, for the past decade, maintained a strong upward trend in gasoline sales, steadily increasing its market share during a time when total U.S. consumption remained relatively flat. It is hoped the Citgo brand identification will spur gasoline sales.

Another area that has contributed to increased productivity for 7-Eleven stores is advertising and promotion that emphasizes the convenience of shopping at 7-Eleven. The advertising theme "No One Keeps You Revvin' Like 7-Eleven" has been publicized in television and radio spots and in print advertising. But Southland spokesman Doug Reed said, "'Revvin' does not relate to every product we sell. It connotes speed, whereas freshness and convenience are more appropriate to selling sandwiches and numerous other food items." Reed went on to say, "Fast foods are the highest gross margin products in the store and fast foods draw people just as gasoline draws people. Quality-wise, the convenience store industry can compete with the fast-food industry."

Southland's plans for the future include a commitment to finding products that appeal to impulse, can be bought with cash, are convenience items, do not require much storage or display space, guarantee an adequate profit per square foot used, can be carried home, require a minimum of employee support, and are preferably, but not necessarily, male-oriented.

Questions for Discussion

1. Customers are not aware of the differences between 7-Eleven and other convenience outlets, even though 7-Elevens carry more products, are cleaner, and have proprietary products. Suggest a solution to this problem.
2. Consumers are unaware of 7-Eleven's competitive pricing on many major product segments: case beer, gallons of milk, carton cigarettes, gasoline. Suggest solutions to this problem.
3. The grocery business is low-profit and highly competitive. What new products and service lines must 7-Eleven look to for future growth?

Case 11.2   The Home Depot, Inc.[45]

The Home Depot, Inc., operates retail warehouse stores, selling a wide assortment of building materials and home improvement products primarily to the "do-it-yourself" and home remodeling markets. Stores are located in Atlanta, Jacksonville, Orlando, Tampa and southern Florida, New Orleans, Phoenix, Dallas, Houston, Tucson, Baton Rouge, Shreveport, Mobile, Detroit, Los Angeles, San Diego, and northern California.

Home Depot's extraordinary success in its first six years has been due to innovative merchandising concepts, unique commitment to training store personnel, and broad inventory selection. The extensive use of marketing research helps determine which markets to enter and where to locate stores within those markets. While all these factors are important, Home Depot also steadfastly educates customers in how to "do it yourself" and motivates the sales staff to serve customers well. This dedication is the key to making Home Depot the fastest-growing home improvement store in the United States. For example, in the period 1983–1985 Home Depot tripled its number of stores, and its revenues increased 740 percent. In fiscal 1985, Home Depot opened twenty new stores in both new and existing markets. By late 1986 the total number of stores was approximately sixty-four. Earnings per share have dropped somewhat because of interest expense and other expenses associated with rapid new-store development.

The idea for a chain of do-it-yourself warehouse home improvement stores was developed by Bernard Marcus and Arthur Blank, who were CEO and chief financial officer, respectively, of Handy Dan, another home improvement company. After leaving Handy Dan, Marcus and Blank used their managerial experience in home improvement retailing as the essential ingredient in putting together financing and then opening Home Depot stores.

The do-it-yourself home improvement market is one in which every homeowner potentially belongs, regardless of age, background, economic status, or geographic location. Home Depot's very broad inventory permits the do-it-yourselfer to design and gain assistance in planning a project such as home

45. Philip Bolton, "Building Growth in the South: The Home Depot Story," *The Southern Banker,* Jan. 1986, pp. 24–27; and Home Depot *1983, 1984,* and *1985 Annual Reports.*

improvement or renovation. The core strategy for attracting customers is the assertion that with proper guidance and instruction, any homeowner can learn to do his or her own projects and repairs, no matter how large the task may be. Home Depot creates new customers by motivating them to become dedicated do-it-yourselfers.

Each Home Depot store ranges from 60,000 to over 100,000 square feet of enclosed selling space with an additional 10,000 to 40,000 square feet of outdoor space filled with a complete line of homebuilding merchandise—enough to build an entire house from scratch and to fully landscape its grounds. Home Depot also sells all the tools necessary for the job and typically leads the industry in offering merchandise at the lowest possible prices.

The sales force is very knowledgeable and highly trained to provide expert advice on how to complete a project, including which tools and materials to buy. The company offers clinics in projects such as wallpapering, electrical wiring, cabinetry, and plumbing. The salespeople are always ready to respond to any questions customers may have at any point in their project's progress—not only at the moment of sale. The staff's greatest satisfaction comes when customers say, "I learned to do it at Home Depot, and I did it myself."

Home Depot's long-term strategy is twofold: to further penetrate the markets where its reputation is established and its stores are operating at capacity, and to become a national chain by forging into new markets, like Detroit, its first cold-weather location. When feasible, its expansion will mean acquiring existing stores and converting them, rather than starting from scratch. Home Depot's challenge is to continue to meet the expanding needs of its current customers and to develop and attract new ones. Since its first store opened in 1979, Home Depot has mostly had its markets to itself. However, now that other corporate chains have opened imitator stores in the markets it helped to expand, Home Depot has found that it must respond to retail trends and cost competition that were formerly nonexistent. But the experienced management team that made Home Depot the leading do-it-yourself retailer feels it has positioned the company to meet this competition head-on. It has computerized its stores with equipment that can help provide more efficient service, track sales, control inventory, and reduce operating costs; it has trained a new corps of personnel to keep pace with store expansion; and it is altering merchandizing and operations when environmental forces in its markets call for such flexibility. By adding these pluses to an already strong customer base, high visibility, excellent reputation, and sound financial position, Home Depot feels ready to take on all comers.

Questions for Discussion

1. What type of image and position does Home Depot have in the retail marketplace?
2. How should Home Depot compete with emerging imitators that now challenge the company in some markets?
3. What can Home Depot do to continue its relationship with its customers, once they have learned how to do home do-it-yourself projects? What should Home Depot do if competitors offer limited service at lower prices?
4. Should Home Depot continue store expansion at its current rate?

12 / Physical Distribution

Objectives

■ To understand how physical distribution activities are integrated in marketing channels and in overall marketing strategies.

■ To become aware of how inventory planning and control are conducted to develop and maintain adequate assortments of products for target markets.

■ To gain insight into the selection and coordination of transportation modes to bridge the producer-customer gap.

■ To learn how warehousing facilitates the storage and movement functions in physical distribution.

■ To illustrate how materials handling is a part of physical distribution activities.

■ To review the role of communications and data processing in physical distribution.

Figure 12.1
Price Slasher Warehouse Supermarket's Food Barn uses the most efficient inventory handling to ensure low prices (Source: Printed with permission of Safeway Stores, Incorporated © 1986)

Price Slasher Warehouse Supermarket, in the state of Virginia, is helping customers get away with their purchases quickly. High-tech spectro-physic scanners that can be pointed at the package rather than at the United Price Code provide quick check-out. The supermarket is designed with warehouse-style racks up toward the ceiling but has standard supermarket shelving within the shopper's reach. The store offers one-stop shopping at low prices because it utilizes the latest technology in inventory control, transportation, warehousing, materials handling, and communications.[1] See Figure 12.1.

1. Kenneth Wylie, "Warehouses Stock Up on Speed, Style, Sections," *Ad Age*, April 18, 1985, pp. 28, 30.

The concept of physical distribution deals with the integration of the movement and handling of goods and the processing of orders. These activities are necessary to provide a level of service that will satisfy customers. As implied in Chapter 9, the physical movement of products is costly. Physical distribution creates time and place utility, which maximizes the value of products by delivering them when and where they are wanted.

This chapter describes how marketing decisions are related to physical distribution. The major decisions discussed involve inventory planning and control, transportation, warehousing, materials handling, and communications. When reading this chapter, keep in mind both the importance of customer service considerations in physical distribution and the relationship of physical distribution to marketing channels. Figure 12.2 provides an overview of the major physical distribution activities discussed here. Closest to the center of the figure are the two major decision areas—physical movement and inventory holding. Arranged around these major decision areas are the specific activities that accomplish them. Before examining these activities in detail, however, we must consider some basic concepts related to physical distribution.

The Importance of Physical Distribution

Physical distribution is an integrated set of activities that deal with managing the movement of products within firms and through marketing channels.[2] Planning an effective physical distribution system can be a significant decision point in developing an overall marketing strategy. A company that places the right goods in the right place, at the right time, in the right quantity, and with the right support services is able to sell more than competitors who fail to accomplish these goals.[3] Physical distribution is an important variable in a marketing strategy because it can decrease costs and increase customer satisfaction. In fact, speed of delivery, along with services and dependability, is often as important to buyers as cost.

Physical distribution activities should be integrated with marketing channel decisions. The marketing channel is a group of interrelated organizations that direct products to customers; physical distribution deals with physical movement and inventory holding (storing and tracking inventory until it is needed) both within and among intermediaries. Often, one channel member will arrange the movement of goods for all channel members involved in exchanges. For example, a packing company ships fresh California cherries and strawberries (often by air) to remote markets on a routine basis. Frequently, buyers are found while the fruit is in transit.

The physical distribution system is often adjusted to meet the unique needs of a channel member. For example, a dealer of construction equipment who keeps a low inventory of replacement parts will require the fastest and most dependable service when the need arises for parts that are not in stock. In such a case, the physical distribution cost may be a minor consideration when compared with service, dependability, and timeliness.

2. Adapted from E. Jerome McCarthy and William D. Perreault, *Basic Marketing: A Managerial Approach,* 8th ed. (Homewood, Ill.: Irwin, 1984), p. 439.
3. Thomas Foster, "Bowing Down to the Beancounters," *Distribution,* Sept. 1983, p. 5.

Figure 12.2

Overview of major
physical distribution
activities

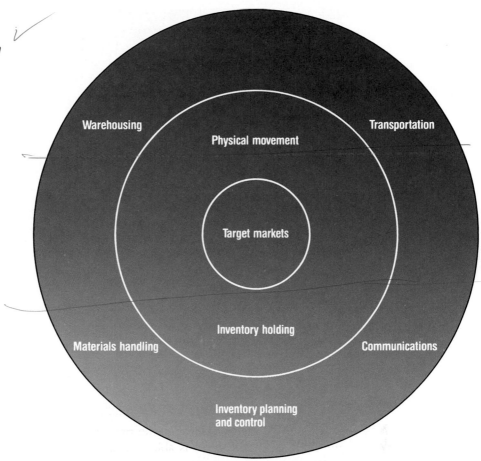

For most firms, physical distribution accounts for about one-fifth of a product's retail price. Of these costs, about one-third goes for movement of products and two-thirds for inventory holding. Specifically, 35 percent of the total physical distribution cost is incurred for transportation, 30 percent for inventory carrying, 20 percent for warehousing, and 10 percent for order processing and customer service. (The remaining 5 percent is attributable to various other distribution-related activities.)[4]

Inventory Planning and Control

Inventory planning and control are physical distribution activities that aid in developing and maintaining adequate assortments of products for the target markets. It is necessary to control the costs of obtaining and maintaining inventory in order to achieve profit goals. For example, it may be an unprofitable

4. Cynthia Milsap, "Distribution Costs Fall—Rules Off," *Business Marketing,* Feb. 1985. Reporting study conducted for the National Council of Physical Distribution Management.

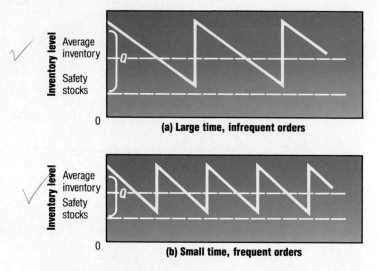

use of shelf space to store products that have a slow turnover. On the other hand, **stockouts** (running out of a product) reduce sales and lose customers.

An inventory system should, first of all, be planned so that the number of products sold and the number of products in stock can be determined at certain checkpoints. The control may be as simple as tearing off a code number from each product sold so that the correct sizes, colors, and models can be tabulated and reordered. In many larger stores, cash registers are connected to central computer systems to provide instantaneous updating of inventory and sales records. For continuous, automatic updating of inventory records, some firms use pressure-sensitive circuits installed under ordinary industrial shelving to weigh inventory, convert the weight to units, and display any inventory change on a video screen or computer print-out.

A most significant inventory control decision—in terms of customers and costs—is the average number of units maintained in inventory. If they are to eliminate shortages and avoid having too much capital tied up in inventory, firms must have a systematic method for determining efficient reorder points. The longer a product remains in stock, the greater the probability of obsolescence, pilferage, or damage. Yet inventory-carrying costs must be balanced against the probability of stockouts. The size of the inventory needed to prevent stockouts is independent of the size that should be reordered for efficient order processing and transportation. The overall **safety stock,** or inventory needed to prevent a stockout, depends on the general level of demand. Individual reorders depend on the trade-off between the cost of carrying larger average inventory (infrequent orders) and the cost of processing small orders (frequent orders).[5] Figure 12.3

5. J. Taylor Sims, J. Robert Foster, and Arch G. Woodside, *Marketing Channels: Systems and Strategies* (New York: Harper & Row, 1977), pp. 316–317.

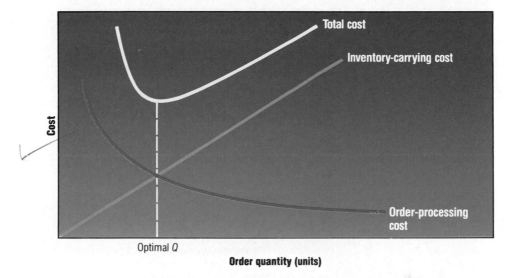

Figure 12.4 *Economic order quantity model (Source:* Marketing Channels: Systems and Strategies, *by J. Taylor Sims, J. Robert Foster, and Arch G. Woodside. Copyright © 1977 by J. Taylor Sims, J. Robert Foster, and Arch G. Woodside. Reprinted by permission of Harper & Row, Publishers, Inc.)*

illustrates two order systems involving different order quantities but the same level of safety stocks. Figure 12.3(a) indicates inventory levels for a given demand of infrequent orders; Figure 12.3(b) illustrates levels needed to fill frequent orders at the same demand.

Given the trade-off between the cost of carrying a larger average inventory with infrequent orders and the cost of processing many small orders, a model for an **economic order quantity (EOQ)** was developed. Figure 12.4 illustrates the EOQ as the order size that minimizes the total cost of ordering and carrying inventory.[6] The EOQ model is accepted widely, and the fundamental relationships that underlie it are the basis of many inventory control systems. Keep in mind, however, that the objective of minimum total inventory cost must be balanced against a customer-service level necessary to maximize profits. Therefore, since increased inventory-carrying costs are usually associated with a higher level of customer service, the order quantity often will lie to the right of the optimal point in the figure, resulting in a higher total cost of ordering and carrying inventory.

In the 1970s, rising selling prices of inventories tended to offset the cost of financing inventories (financing costs were less than 10 percent). Because interest rates have exceeded the rate of inflation in the 1980s, inventories have become the most volatile element in the cost of doing business.[7] The Federal Trade Commission estimates that a 50-percent reduction in a typical manufacturer's

6. The EOQ formula for the optimal order quantity is EOQ $= \sqrt{2DR/I}$, where EOQ = optimum average order size, D = total demand, R = cost of processing an order, and I = cost of maintaining one unit of inventory per year. See Frank S. McLaughlin and Robert C. Pickhardt, *Quantitative Techniques for Management Decisions* (Boston: Houghton Mifflin, 1978), pp. 104–119, for a more complete description of EOQ methods and terminology.
7. Lewis Beman, "A Big Payoff From Inventory Controls," *Fortune,* July 27, 1981, p. 77.

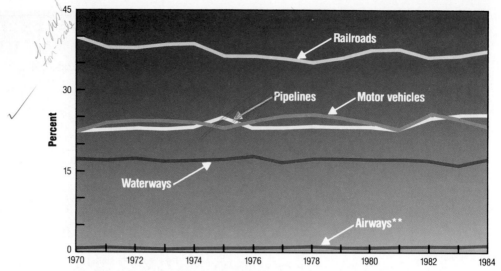

*A ton-mile is the movement of 1 ton (2,000 pounds) of freight for the distance of 1 mile.
**Airways represent less than 1% intercity traffic.

Figure 12.5 *Ton-miles* of domestic intercity freight traffic—percent distribution by type of transportation: 1970 to 1984 (Source: Statistical Abstract of the United States, 1986, p. 588)*

average inventory would increase operating income by about 11 percent. U.S. firms have increased the annual rate of inventory turnover by 20 percent in the past decade.[8]

Many companies have reduced inventories to save inventory-carrying costs. In addition to trying to reduce inventory, a company must monitor its inventory's performance. Some warning signals indicate that inventory is not in control: inventory growing at a faster rate than sales; surplus or obsolete inventory; customer deliveries that are consistently late or lead times that are too long; inventory growing as a percentage of assets; and large inventory adjustments or write-offs.[9]

It is important to try to properly balance all the conflicting objectives when establishing an inventory system. Inventory management requires a well-tuned communication system and a coordinated effort to make sure that the inventory control system supports the overall objectives of marketing and physical distribution. Inventory decisions have a strong impact on physical distribution costs—and on the level of customer service provided.

Transportation

Transportation is an essential and obvious physical distribution activity. As mentioned earlier, transportation represents one-third of all physical distribution costs. As Figure 12.5 indicates, there are five major **transportation modes** for

8. Ibid., p. 80.
9. "Watch for These Red Flags," *Traffic Management,* Jan. 1983, p. 8.

Part III / Distribution Decisions

Table 12.1 *Typical transportation modes for various products*

Railways	Motor Vehicles	Waterways	Pipelines	Airways
Coal	Clothing	Petroleum	Oil	Flowers
Grain	Paper goods	Chemicals	Processed	Perishable
Chemicals	Computers	Iron ore	coal	food
Lumber	Books	Bauxite	Natural gas	Instruments
Automobiles	Fresh fruit	Grain	Water	Emergency
Iron, steel	Livestock		Chemicals	parts
				Overnight
				mail

moving goods between cities in the United States: railways, pipelines, motor vehicles, inland waterways, and airways. Transportation technology takes advantage of each mode's strength by adopting physical handling procedures that permit the most effective transfers among different types of carriers.

Since the deregulation of transportation, marketers have been able to cut expenses and increase efficiency. Railroads, airlines, trucks, barges, and pipeline companies have all become more competitive and more responsive to customers' needs.[10] Surveys reveal that in recent years transportation costs as a percentage of sales and per hundredweight shipped have declined. Transportation costs average $33.45 per hundredweight or 7.5 percent of sales.[11] But this figure varies by industry; for example, electrical machinery, textiles, and instruments have transportation costs of only 3 or 4 percent of sales, while lumber products, chemicals, and food have transportation costs close to 15 percent of sales.[12]

Cost and capability (the ability to handle various products) are not the only considerations in choosing a transportation mode. Reliability and availability are also important. Although a truck can carry a replacement part for a computer system at low cost, air freight may provide more dependable delivery and get the part to the customer in less time. The nature of a product and the needs of its market also determine the type of carrier selected. Table 12.1 illustrates some typical transportation modes for various products.

Transportation creates time and place utility for a firm's products. Management must make many transportation decisions during the production, storage, and delivery stages of operation. The transportation system links the flow of products among various stages of operation and has a direct impact on the availability of the product. The choice of a transportation mode affects all elements of the physical distribution system, and the marketing strategy itself can be based on a unique transportation system. A transportation survey by the U.S. Census indicates that service, especially on-time delivery, is a major factor in a firm's decision to develop its own transportation system. A firm's ability to provide on-time deliveries is part of the total package of benefits that customers want and could be a key differentiating variable in a marketing strategy.

10. Lewis M. Schneider, "New Era in Transportation Strategy," *Harvard Business Review,* March–April, 1985, p. 118.
11. Milsap, "Distribution Costs Fall," p. 9.
12. Ibid.

A growing trend in the transportation industry is the development of "mega-carriers." A **megacarrier** is a freight transportation company like the CF Company shown in Figure 12.6 that provides many methods of shipment such as rail, truck, and air service. This trend has caused many railroads to acquire truck and barge lines and air carriers to increase their ground transportation services. The increased variety in transportation offerings has also spawned a greater service orientation; for example, many megacarriers offer warehousing, consulting, and personal leasing services.[13]

Transport Selection Criteria[14]

Marketers select a transportation mode on the basis of cost, transit time (speed), reliability, capability, accessibility, and security.

Cost

Marketers must determine whether the benefits provided by one transportation mode are worth higher costs compared with alternative modes. As long as

13. Joseph Barks, "Do Megacarriers Have You Covered—Or Smothered?" *Distribution,* March 1984, p. 10.
14. Some ideas in this section are based on John J. Coyle and Edward Bardi, *The Management of Business Logistics* (St. Paul, Minn.: West, 1976), pp. 150–153.

Figure 12.7

The Union Pacific rail system's special chemical handling capability (Source: Union Pacific Railroad)

service is similar, cost differences are an important criterion in selecting a transportation mode. For example, bicycles are often shipped by rail because an unassembled bicycle can be shipped more than a thousand miles that way for as little as $3.60. Therefore, bicycle wholesalers plan their purchases far enough in advance to be able to capitalize on this cost advantage.

Transit Time

The total time that a carrier possesses goods is called **transit time;** it includes the time required for pickup and delivery, for handling, and for movement between the points of origin and destination. Transit time obviously affects a marketer's ability to provide service, but there are some less obvious implications as well.

Transit time allows the shipper to process orders for goods enroute. This capability is especially important to agricultural and raw materials shippers. In addition, some railroads allow carloads already in transit to be redirected. A carload of peaches may be shipped to a closer destination if there is a danger that the fruit will ripen too quickly.

Reliability

The dependability and consistency of the service provided by a transportation mode make up its total reliability. Transit time and reliability affect a marketer's inventory costs, including sales lost when merchandise is not available. Unreliable transportation makes it necessary to maintain higher inventory levels to avoid stockouts. Marketers must be able to count on their carriers to deliver goods in an acceptable condition and when specified.

Capability

Capability refers to the ability of a transportation mode to provide the appropriate equipment and conditions for moving specific kinds of goods. Figure 12.7 illustrates Union Pacific's chemical-handling capabilities. Many products must be shipped under controlled conditions in terms of temperature or humidity.

Others—such as liquids or gases—require special equipment or facilities for shipment. Fifty percent of crude oil production is moved in vessels especially designed for large-volume transport of bulk commodities. These special bulk vessels are the only means of seaborne movement for crude petroleum production.[15]

Accessibility

The ability of a carrier to move goods over a specific route or network (rail lines, waterways, or truck routes) is the measure of its accessibility. Thus, the inability of a water-borne carrier to serve Great Falls, Montana, would eliminate it from consideration as a possible transportation mode to or from that city. Since Great Falls *is* accessible by rail line, truck routes, and scheduled airline service, those transportation modes are available to marketers there.

Some carriers differentiate themselves by servicing areas not accessed by competitors. For example, GETS—Guaranteed Emergency Transportation Service—is a motor carrier that serves 20,000 points not served by air carriers.[16]

Security

Whether or not goods arrive in the same condition in which they were shipped defines the security of a transportation mode. Since the common carrier is held liable for all loss and damage (with limited exceptions), the firm does not incur direct costs when goods are lost or delivered in a damaged condition. Nevertheless, unsafe service and poor security lead to increased costs for the firm as well as to foregone profits since damaged or lost goods are not available for immediate sale or use.

Security problems vary considerably among transportation companies and geographic regions. In the Northeast, for instance, truck hijacking is a rapidly growing crime. According to the FBI, approximately 19,000 truck tractors and 47,000 trailers are listed as stolen each year.[17] However, all transportation modes have security problems. Marketers must determine the relative risk associated with each mode in making a final selection. The application on page 359 discusses some approaches to protecting goods from theft.

Table 12.2 illustrates some of the cost and performance considerations that affect decisions concerning transportation modes. Keep in mind that these relationships are a general approximation and that they do vary. There are many trade-offs in the final selection of a transportation mode.

Traceability

Whether a shipment can be located and transferred, or found if lost, determines its traceability. Quick traceability is a convenience feature that some firms value highly. Roadway and many other carriers have introduced services called "QuikTrak." Shippers have learned that such customized services, consisting of prompt invoicing, tracing of shipments, and processing of claims, have increased customer loyalty and their image in the marketplace.[18]

15. *Overseas Shipholding Group, Inc. Annual Report, 1980,* pp. 8, 17.
16. Bruce Heydt, "Overnight Over the Road," *Distribution,* Sept. 1983, pp. 101, 102.
17. "Stop Thief," *Traffic Management,* June 1983, p. 84.
18. Thomas A. Foster and Joseph V. Barks, "Here Comes the Best," *Distribution,* Sept. 1984, p. 25.

Table 12.2 *Ranking of transportation modes by selection criteria, highest to lowest*

Cost	Transit Time	Reliability	Capability	Accessibility	Security	Traceability
Air	Water	Pipeline	Water	Truck	Pipeline	Air
Truck	Rail	Truck	Rail	Rail	Water	Truck
Rail	Pipeline	Rail	Truck	Air	Rail	Rail
Pipeline	Truck	Air	Air	Water	Air	Water
Water	Air	Water	Pipeline	Pipeline	Truck	Pipeline

Source: Some of this information has been adapted from J. L. Heskett, Robert Ivie, and J. Nicholas Glaskowsky, *Business Logistics* (New York: Ronald Press, 1973). Used by permission.

Coordinating Transportation Services

Because individual transportation companies often specialize in one mode of transportation, marketers must sometimes coordinate and integrate various modes. This task can be handled by the firm or by special transportation agencies. For example, **freight forwarders** consolidate shipments from several organizations into efficient lot sizes. The use of a freight forwarder usually increases transit time and sometimes lowers shipping costs.

Since costs for small shipments (under 500 pounds) are sharply higher than costs for full loads in railroad cars and trucks, consolidated shipments with firms sharing costs and services is possible. For example, United Parcel Service is a specialized transportation agency that efficiently combines shipments and uses various transportation methods.

The practice of consolidating many items into one container, sealed at the point of origin and opened at the destination, is generally referred to as **containerization.** Containerization adds great efficiency to shipping since individual items are not handled in transit. Another of its advantages is increased security.

Piggyback, fishyback, and *birdyback* describe different kinds of containerized shipping. Containerized shipping via railway flatcar or motor vehicle is piggyback, via water carriers is fishyback, and via air and motor vehicle is birdyback. Figure 12.8 illustrates one of CSX Corporation's intermodal facilities for loading containerized piggyback shipments. The number of railway flatcars carrying piggyback shipments has grown steadily over the years. Piggyback loadings constitute 12 to 13 percent of all rail business. Truck-rail shipments have been estimated to cost from 25 to 40 percent less than an all-highway move.[19] (Other aspects of containers are discussed in the section "Materials Handling" later in this chapter.) The use of containers and coordinated transportation systems is becoming more popular as transportation costs increase.

Warehousing

Designing and operating facilities to store and move goods are other important physical distribution activities. The essential processing functions performed by a warehouse are as follows:

19. "Intermodalism: It's Your Move," *Inbound Traffic,* April 1985, pp. 16–22.

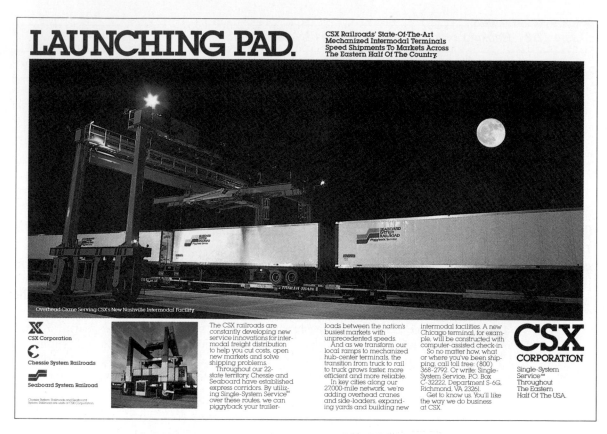

Figure 12.8 *An intermodal piggyback terminal of the CSX Corporation (Source: CSX Corporation)*

1. *Receives goods.* The warehouse accepts merchandise, delivered from outside transportation or from an attached factory, and is responsible for it.
2. *Identifies goods.* The appropriate stockkeeping units must be recorded, and a record made of the quantity of each item received. It may be necessary to mark the item with a physical code, tag, or other means. The item may be identified by an item code (a code on the carrier or container) or by physical properties.
3. *Sorts goods.* The warehouse may sort merchandise to the appropriate storage areas.
4. *Dispatches goods to storage.* The merchandise must be put away where it can be found later.
5. *Holds goods.* The merchandise is kept in storage under proper protection until needed.
6. *Recalls, selects, or picks goods.* Items ordered by customers, for example, must be efficiently selected from storage and grouped in a manner useful for the next step.
7. *Marshals the shipment.* The items making up a single shipment must be brought together and checked for completeness or for explainable omissions. Order records must be prepared or modified as necessary.

Theft is inevitable whenever resalable merchandise is distributed. What is surprising is that approximately 85 percent of all cargo thefts are committed by employees during regular working hours.

Most thefts can be prevented if companies give proper attention to packaging, personnel procedures, and warehouse security equipment. In terms of packaging measures, companies can avoid description labeling, consolidate packages into the largest unit possible, construct packages so that tampering can be recognized, and pick up deliveries promptly. Personnel procedures should be designed to minimize access opportunities, screen out dishonest employees, and thoroughly investigate thefts when they occur. The presence of uniformed guards is a psychological deterrent to theft and vandalism. Finally, security equipment, from simple locks to electronic surveillance devices, can help to secure warehouses. Proper fencing, lighting, and closed-circuit television and alarm systems can also prevent theft. (*Source: Betsy Haggerty, "To Stop a Thief: A Guide to Cargo Crime Prevention,"* Inbound Logistics, Oct. 1985, pp. 32–34.)

8. *Dispatches the shipment.* The consolidated order must be packaged suitably and directed to the right transport vehicle. Necessary shipping and accounting documents must be prepared.[20]

The expense of maintaining or renting warehouse facilities is a considerable cost of physical distribution. **Private warehouses** are owned and operated by a company for the purpose of distributing its own products. These warehouses may be a distinct and separate operation of the firm or they may be integrated with other activities. The largest user of private warehouses is retail chain stores.[21] As Figure 12.9 illustrates, ADM Corn Sweeteners has forty warehouse terminals nationwide to make corn sweeteners available to soft-drink bottlers.

Public warehouses are business organizations whose primary activity is to provide storage and related physical distribution facilities on a rental basis to other firms.[22] Public warehouses may provide such services as reshipping, filling orders, financing, displaying products, and coordinating shipments. In addition, many of them offer services such as providing security for products that are being used as collateral for loans. This service can be provided at a public warehouse or at the site of the owner's inventory. A **field warehouse** is a temporary warehouse established by a public warehouse at the owner's inventory location. The warehouser becomes the custodian of the products and issues a receipt that can be used as collateral for a loan. Also, public warehouses can provide **bonded storage.** In this case, products are not released unless U.S. custom duties, taxes, or other fees are paid by the owners of the products.[23]

20. Adapted from *Physical Distribution Systems* by John F. Magee. Copyright © 1967 McGraw-Hill, Inc. Used with permission of McGraw-Hill Book Company.
21. James C. Johnson and Donald F. Wood, *Contemporary Physical Distribution & Logistics,* 2nd ed. (Tulsa, Okla.: Penwell Publishing Company, 1982), p. 356.
22. Theodore N. Beckman, William R. Davidson, and W. Wayne Talarzyk, *Marketing,* 9th ed. (New York: Ronald Press, 1973), pp. 488–489.
23. Johnson and Wood, *Contemporary Physical Distribution,* p. 355.

Figure 12.9 *ADM Corn Sweeteners' promotion of its forty private warehouses nationwide* (Source: Archer Daniels)

Current trends in warehousing seem to indicate a shift from providing space for the storage of goods to offering services for the distribution of goods. A result of the new emphasis on services is the restructuring of prices. Additionally, public warehouses are tending toward customization by serving specific market segments rather than several different industries.[24] Efficiency in materials-handling techniques, better use of space, computer systems, and the holding of large inventories improve warehousing services.

Whether private or public, warehouse facilities represent a cost to the marketer or shipper. With a public warehouse, the cost is variable, since more space has to be rented as the volume of goods increases. Private warehouses entail fixed costs such as insurance, taxes, and debt expense. Of course, there also are noncost considerations, for instance, a firm's resources and the role of the warehouse in the overall marketing strategy.

Private warehouses usually are leased or purchased when a firm believes its warehouse needs are so stable that it can make a long-term commitment to fixed facilities. Retailers like Sears, Radio Shack, and even Burger King often find it economical to integrate the warehousing function with purchasing and distribution to retail outlets. When sales volumes are fairly stable, the ownership and control of a private warehouse may provide several gains, including financial ones such as property appreciation and tax shelters realized through depreciation of the facility.

24. "Warehousing Trends: Service Moves to Center Stage," *Traffic Management*, Oct. 1984, pp. 88–90.

For many firms, the best approach may be a combination of private and public warehousing. A minimum storage area might be committed to private warehousing, while overflow inventories could be placed in public warehousing. In such a case, a firm might lease or buy private facilities on a long-term basis and then use a nearby public warehouse for seasonal or overflow inventories.

Materials Handling

Materials handling, or physical handling of products, is important in efficient warehouse operations, as well as in transportation from points of production to points of consumption. The characteristics of the product itself often determine how it will be handled. For example, bulk liquids and gases have unique characteristics that determine how they can be moved and stored. On the other hand, handling processes may alter a product's characteristics or qualities.[25]

Materials-handling procedures and techniques should increase the usable capacity of a warehouse, reduce the number of times a good is handled, and improve service to customers and increase their satisfaction with the product. Packaging, loading, and movement systems must be coordinated to maximize cost reduction and customer satisfaction. The application on page 362 shows how a food wholesaler has improved its margins by using materials-handling technology.

Chapter 7 notes that the protective functions of packaging are important considerations in product development. Good decisions about packaging materials and methods make possible the most efficient physical handling. Most companies use packaging consultants or specialists to accomplish this important task.

Materials-handling equipment is used in the design of handling systems. **Unit loading** is the grouping of one or more boxes on a pallet or skid and permits movement of efficient loads by mechanical means such as forklifts, trucks, or conveyor systems. The next-sized load in materials handling is the container, discussed earlier. Containers are usually 8 feet wide, 8 feet high, and 10, 20, 25, or 40 feet long. Containerization has revolutionized physical distribution by broadening the capabilities of our transportation system, enabling shippers to transport a wider range of cargoes with speed, reliability, and stable costs. Not only is containerization energy efficient, but it also decreases the need for elaborate security measures and cuts down on losses and damage.

Communications and Data Processing

An information system for physical distribution should link producers, intermediaries, and customers. Computers, memory systems, display equipment, and other communications technology facilitate the flow of information among channel members. Crown Zellerback Corporation, a paper and container company headquartered in San Francisco, was selected as the "Official Supplier of Distribution Services" for the 1984 Summer Olympics in Los Angeles. Zellerback's

25. Johnson and Wood, *Contemporary Physical Distribution,* p. 322.

Wholesale margins in the food industry are thinner than the notoriously thin supermarket margins. Overall food sales are growing only 1 percent yearly. Despite these unimpressive figures, Fleming, the nation's second largest food wholesaler, has posted an average annual increase in earnings per share of 16.3 percent.

Committed to improving productivity and efficiency, Fleming designed a $5-million computerized system to cut fractions of cents off each dollar of shipping costs. For example, an IBM computer is used to sort orders from several super-markets. Orders are sorted into product categories such as breakfast cereal or canned beans. Rather than going to the cereal shelves for each order, workers can fill many orders in one trip. Employees place product cartons on a conveyor belt that moves past a laser scanner. The scanner directs each carton to the appropriate loading dock. The new system has helped boost productivity an average of 11 percent. (*Source: Brian Dumaine, "Fleming's Fast Rise in Whole-sale Foods,"* Fortune, *Jan. 21, 1985, p. 54.*)

---

main distribution center consisted of 350,000 square feet in downtown Los Angeles. Materials reaching Zellerback's facilities were disbursed to seven other facilities throughout the area after proper identification, scheduling, and packaging. A sophisticated computer system was developed to help with inventory control, purchasing, and warehousing. The system was able to automatically generate thousands of purchase orders at a time, taking into account delivery times, cash flow, and holding costs. The system handled an estimated half million data transactions.[26]

The three most frequently computerized functions are order entry, invoicing, and freight bill payment. The least computerized functions include rail costing, site location, private fleet management, and freight budgeting, which are accomplished mostly through planning.[27] Field sales order entry is especially important for companies that have many widely dispersed salespeople taking orders in their respective territories. The order entry system can include software, hardware, and networking technology. Besides recording orders, the system can provide salespeople with recommended substitutions for out-of-stock items, status of the last order, and shipping and credit information. The system can also list products that have the largest profit margins or commission incentives and therefore are most advantageous for salespeople to sell.[28]

The level of sophistication varies among the retail merchandise information systems that are in general use. By definition, an **electronic cash register (ECR)** depends on electronics for its logic and arithmetic functions. A **basic ECR (BECR)** is a stand-alone cash register that does not have the capacity for additional totals, features, and so forth. A **sophisticated ECR (SECR)** does not accumulate detailed transaction data but may be integrated with any number of peripherals. **POS** describes a retailer's **point-of-sale terminal,** which works like an ECR but is connected to a computer or some other device for detailed collection of data for subsequent processing, whether or not it is a stand-alone terminal

---

26. Nancy Eutwisle, "Everything But the Soviets . . ." *Distribution,* June 1984, p. 37.
27. Tom Foster, "Computerization: Where Are We?" *Distribution,* Sept. 1983, p. 86.
28. James L. Locke, "How to Automate Field Sales Order Entry," *Business Marketing,* June 1984, p. 88.

and regardless of the number of totals it accumulates. An ECR can become a POS terminal when it is so connected.

Universal vendor marking (UVM) is a coding system in which a vendor marks merchandise for individual retailers with a machine-readable code containing such information as department class, size, and color. It is the most common marking code in general merchandise retailing. The **universal product code (UPC)** is the standard source-symbol marking in the food industry. Finally, **electronic funds transfer (EFT)** systems allow electronic transfers of funds between the retailer and financial institutions. They also allow other functions such as credit and check authorization.[29]

The application of advanced computer hardware with appropriate software (computer programs) has greatly increased productivity in retail communications. These technologies have manifested themselves in many ways among typical vendors. Automated check-out systems in supermarkets utilize a fixed or hand-held optical scanner, an electronic cash register, and an in-store minicomputer to increase efficiency. When a product is packaged at the factory, it is marked with a symbol that can be read by the optical scanner. The symbol identifies the item down to the level of the individual stockkeeping unit. When it is received at the store, the item is put on a price-marked shelf, but it is not priced individually. The memory bank of the store's minicomputer contains the current price for each unit. As clerks check out shoppers' purchases, the scanner reads each item's product code into the computer, the computer finds the price in its memory files, and the electronic terminal tabulates and prints details of the item. At the same time, the computer uses each item's code to update inventory records. There is no need for the clerk to punch individual prices into a cash register.

Other applications of computers in physical distribution are increasing rapidly, in part because of the declining cost of computer power. For example, a trade journal, *Traffic Management*, published a guide to computer software and services for the transportation and distribution industry. The guide contained some two hundred listings classified under nine major headings—order processing, inventory management, distribution center/warehouse management, transportation analysis, fleet management, freight-rate maintenance/auditing, distribution system modeling, distribution requirements planning, and services.[30] There will be even more computer applications in the future. Figure 12.10 illustrates that DHL uses computers and other electronic technology to assist in communications and the delivery of cargo throughout the world.

Marketing Strategy Considerations in Physical Distribution

Changes in customers or technology may profoundly affect the place of physical distribution in the marketing strategy. Pressures to change service functions or reduce costs can bring about a total restructuring of marketing channel relationships. For example, the desire to reduce transportation costs in recent

29. J. Barry Mason and Morris L. Mayer, "Retail Merchandise Systems for the 1980s," *Journal of Retailing,* Spring 1980, p. 58.
30. Lisa H. Harrington, "Distribution Software Floods the Market," *Traffic Management,* Jan. 1985, pp. 70–81.

Figure 12.10 *DHL's cargo delivery system incorporating advanced communications technology (Source: DHL)*

years has brought about a careful evaluation of ways to increase efficiency. In some cases, combining orders and exerting centralized control over the physical movement of products has increased channel productivity. Independent wholesale distributors, too, can achieve improved productivity because they usually have a large potential customer base and standardized product lines. They can therefore provide small-quantity unit inventory to customers who require rapid delivery and service.[31]

Physical distribution should meet the requirements of an organization's marketing strategy. Marketers should accept a substantial responsibility for the design and control of the physical distribution system. While accounting and financial managers may concentrate on minimizing costs, marketers must relate costs to customer satisfaction. Speed of delivery, reliability, and economy of service are marketing considerations that define the total product in customers' eyes.

Changes in transportation, warehousing, materials handling, and inventory may increase or decrease services such as speed of delivery. Decreasing costs while increasing service should be the main objective in physical distribution. Consumer-oriented marketers analyze the characteristics of the target market and then design a system to provide products at acceptable costs.

31. James D. Hlavacek and Tommy J. McCuiston, "Industrial Distributors—When, Who and Why?" *Harvard Business Review,* March–April 1983, pp. 96–101.

Summary

Physical distribution is an integrated set of activities that deal with managing the movement of products within firms and through marketing channels. Physical distribution creates time and place utility by the performance of activities to store, transport, handle, and process orders for products. From a marketing standpoint, physical distribution focuses on integrating the activities of storage, transport, handling, and processing orders for products to minimize costs and provide the level of service desired by customers. Physical distribution is important in an overall marketing strategy; it can be the decision most visible in the marketing mix. But whatever the role of physical distribution in the marketing strategy, distribution decisions must be made for the physical movement of goods. The essential physical distribution activities are inventory planning and control, transportation, warehousing, materials handling, and communications and data processing.

Inventory planning and control require a systematic approach to determine efficient order points that on the one hand minimize the possibility of stockouts and on the other avoid having too much capital tied up in inventory. Although there are trade-offs between the costs of carrying larger average inventories and the costs of frequent orders, this problem can be alleviated by finding an optimal economic order quantity (EOQ).

Various transportation decisions are required during the production, storage, and delivery stages of operation. The five major modes of transporting goods between cities in the United States are railways, pipelines, motor vehicles, inland waterways, and airways. The selection of a transportation mode is based on cost, transit time (speed), reliability, capability, accessibility, security, and traceability. Because there are many trade-offs in the final selection of a transportation mode, a firm must coordinate its overall transportation process as goods move from production points to customers.

Warehousing involves designing and operating facilities to store and move goods. Private warehouses are owned and operated by a company for the purpose of distributing its own products. Public warehouses are business organizations that provide storage and related physical distribution facilities on a rental basis to other firms. While the variable cost per unit is less for a private warehouse than for a public one, a combination of private and public warehouses can provide a flexible approach to warehousing.

Materials handling, or the physical handling of products, is an important element of physical distribution. Packaging, loading, and movement systems must be coordinated to take into account both cost reduction and customer requirements. Basic handling systems are unit loading on pallets or skids, movement by mechanical devices, and containerization.

The crucial role of communications and data processing in physical distribution is as an information system linking producers, intermediaries, and customers. Instantaneous inventory updating and stockkeeping, transportation coordination, and forecasting are made possible through computer systems. The trend is toward more computer applications in physical distribution because of the availability of low-cost minicomputers and decentralized computer systems within firms.

Important Terms

Physical distribution	Public warehouses
Inventory planning and control	Field warehouse
Stockouts	Bonded storage
Safety stock	Materials handling
Economic order quantity (EOQ)	Unit loading
Transportation modes	Electronic cash register (ECR)
Megacarrier	Basic ECR (BECR)
Transit time	Sophisticated ECR (SECR)
Freight forwarders	Point-of-sale terminal (POS)
Containerization	Universal vendor marking (UVM)
Private warehouses	Universal product code (UPC)
	Electronic funds transfer (EFT)

Discussion and Review Questions

1. For what two main reasons is physical distribution sometimes a key variable in marketing strategy?
2. Why should physical distribution decisions be integrated with marketing channel decisions?
3. "Like other marketing tasks, physical distribution should be guided by what buyers want." Give some examples to support this statement.
4. What major tasks are involved in inventory planning and control?
5. List several important considerations in a firm's decision to develop its own transportation system.
6. Compare the five major transportation modes in terms of cost, transit time, reliability, capability, accessibility, security, and traceability.
7. Under what circumstances should a firm use a private warehouse instead of a public one?
8. In Chapter 11, we discuss miniwarehouses. Think about them in the context of this chapter and suggest some applications that could be discussed.
9. Do you see any conflicts between protective packaging decisions and promotional packaging decisions?
10. What types of products are unsuitable for containerization?
11. What is the likely impact on physical distribution of decentralizing computer systems within firms?
12. Discuss the cost and service trade-offs in developing a physical distribution system.

Cases

Case 12.1 Wal-Mart Stores, Inc.[32]

WAL-MART

Wal-Mart Stores, Inc., is a chain of 745 discount department stores and 11 Sam's Wholesale Clubs. These stores are located in twenty states in the Midwest and South. The first Wal-Mart store was opened over twenty years ago in Rogers,

32. Facts are from *1983* and *1985* Wal-Mart *Annual Reports;* "Wal-Mart 'Going for It,'" *Discount Merchandiser,* Aug. 1985, p. 12; "Wal-Mart To Almost Double Sam's in 1986," *Discount Merchandiser,* March 1986, p. 8; "Wal-Mart Savors Its Record Results," *Discount Merchandiser,* June 1984, pp. 73–74; and "David Glass Discusses Sam's Wholesale Clubs," *Discount Merchandiser,* April 1984, pp. 8, 10.

Arkansas. Dedicated to a philosophy of continuing, controlled, and profitable growth, Wal-Mart has experienced an annual growth rate over the past ten years of 38.5 percent in sales and 42.5 percent in profitability. Annual sales exceed $6.4 billion, producing profits of $271 million. Wal-Mart is the nation's second largest discounter and the fastest growing major retailer in the United States. But throughout Wal-Mart's phenomenal expansion and success, the company has remained true to its original business philosophy of providing low prices and guaranteed customer satisfaction.

The Wal-Mart stores range in size from 30,000 square feet to 80,000 square feet. They are located primarily in towns having populations of 5,000 to 25,000, although an increasing number of stores are located in and around the metropolitan areas within the chain's regional trade territory. The trading market for most stores covers large rural areas, and Wal-Mart stores are designed to be one-stop shopping centers. Now Wal-Mart plans to open small prototype stores of 25,000–30,000 square feet in communities smaller than typical Wal-Mart towns.

Sam's Wholesale Clubs and Wal-Mart's discount retail stores do not compete with each other because their customer bases differ. Wal-Mart stores sell to retail customers; Sam's stores are open to wholesale members only, 12 percent of whom are businessmen who make smaller, more frequent purchases than normal wholesale customers. Sam's sells 4,000 items at 10-percent gross margin. At least half of the items are stocked regularly; the other portion varies according to availability and price. At the end of 1985, Sam's had sales of $775 million, which were expected to reach $1.4 billion by 1986. The number of units was expected to double in the same period.

Sam's Wholesale Clubs have been successful because they've chosen the right items and made them available at the right price. Merchandise is moved efficiently, handled as economically as possible, and displayed properly. Atmospherics and ambience are not concerns when developing and designing a Wholesale Club; instead functionalism and efficiency are the keys to success.

Each standard-format Wal-Mart retail store offers a wide variety of quality merchandise at low everyday retail prices to satisfy most of the clothing, home, recreational, and personal needs of the families in the store's community (see Table 12.3). Regardless of store size, there are thirty-six full-line merchandise departments in each store. Nationally advertised merchandise accounts for the majority of sales; private-label goods are offered only when they provide exceptional value. Wal-Mart offers conveniences for its customers that range from extended shopping hours to free parking, quick check-out lanes, layaway and credit card purchases, and customer check-cashing courtesy cards.

To assure a constant flow of inventory to its stores, Wal-Mart operates seven distribution centers. About 77 percent of the merchandise sold in the stores is processed through these warehouses. Merchandise flows from the manufacturer to the company's distribution centers via a trucking network that includes company-owned trucks. The mechanized distribution facilities efficiently sort the large quantities received into outbound shipments to each store. Deliveries are made on Wal-Mart trucks, which backhaul inbound merchandise to the distribution centers, eliminating as many miles traveled with empty trailers as possible. Figure 12.11 illustrates the Wal-Mart service area and the locations of the seven distribution centers. Three distribution centers are in Bentonville, Arkansas.

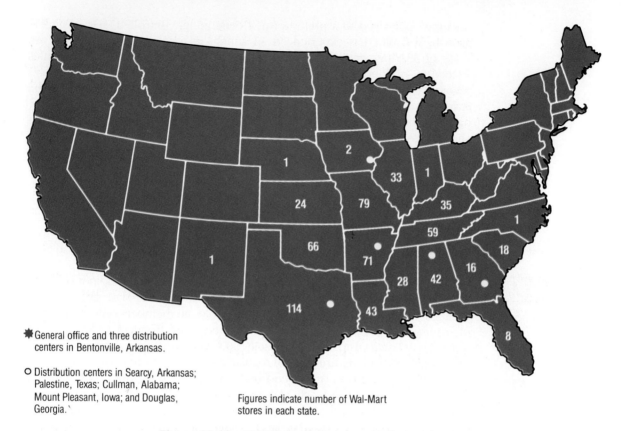

General office and three distribution centers in Bentonville, Arkansas.

○ Distribution centers in Searcy, Arkansas; Palestine, Texas; Cullman, Alabama; Mount Pleasant, Iowa; and Douglas, Georgia.

Figures indicate number of Wal-Mart stores in each state.

Figure 12.11 Wal-Mart's service area and distribution centers (Source: 1983, 1985 Wal-Mart Annual Report)

Table 12.3 Wal-Mart sales by product category, including licensed departments

Category	Percentage of Sales
Softgoods	30%
Hardgoods (hardware, housewares, auto supplies, and small appliances)	28
Sporting goods and toys	10
Stationery and candy	11
Health and beauty aids	9
Gifts, records, and electronics	5
Shoes*	3
Jewelry	2
Pharmaceutical*	2
	100%

*Sales in these categories are a combination of owned and licensed departments. While these percentages include sales of licensed departments, the Company records as revenues only rentals received from such departments.

Source: "Wal-Mart Savors Its Record Results," *Discount Merchandiser,* June 1984, p. 33. Used by permission.

Approximately 81,000 full- and part-time Wal-Mart employees have the responsibility of meeting the needs of millions of customers. Each employee is made knowledgeable about events throughout the company through training programs, an in-house newspaper, and many programs designed to communicate and recognize individual accomplishments. Wal-Mart's employees are called associates and partners. The company seeks out the best college graduates it can find for management, and Wal-Mart provides great recognition of its employees through their creed "Our people make the difference."

Questions for Discussion

1. Discuss the location and operation of the Wal-Mart distribution centers. Where should the next distribution center be constructed if growth patterns continue?
2. What impact does Wal-Mart's physical distribution system have on customers and profits?
3. Based on the facts presented in this case, does Wal-Mart integrate physical distribution decisions into its overall marketing strategy? Discuss.

Case 12.2 Air Cargo Deliveries: Federal Express and Its Competition[33]

Today all types of freight, from overnight letters to automobiles, arrive within three days, or two or even one, after they are shipped. The packages travel by truck, bus, air, or rail—any means that can deliver the goods in the necessary time frame. Different levels and rates of service are available, and they're being used by different types of customers, from corporate transportation managers to department heads and company presidents. The demand for expedited delivery services crosses all industry lines as well.

Managers spend $6.4 billion annually on domestically originated air cargo. Usually when the decision is not air delivery service, managers choose highway carriers that take slightly longer but usually charge cheaper rates for many products. Even Amtrak reported a 45-percent increase in rail express cargo revenue between 1984 and 1985. Small-package delivery services are usually fairly expensive. For example, it costs $15.50 to receive a 5-pound package overnight via United Parcel Service Red Label. The same package delivered in two days costs $6.50, yet overnight services attract physical distribution managers for several reasons:

Less handling: Freight that moves quickly is subject to less handling and therefore less chance for damage or theft.

Reduced inventory cost: Repair parts or other inventory needs may be received overnight, decreasing the need for costly warehouse stockpiling.

Quality service: Because companies know they can count on fast delivery, they are not willing to take a chance with some other delivery method.

33. Felecia Stratton, "Yes, There Is Life Beyond Federal Express," *Inbound Logistics,* Jan. 1986, pp. 11–13; Betsy Haggerty, "A Smart Shopper's Guide to Expedited Delivery Services," *Inbound Logistics,* Jan. 1986, pp. 15–16; and Jim Curley, "Long Night's Journey into Day: How Your Package Gets from There to Here," *Inbound Logistics,* Jan. 1986, pp. 19–23.

Figure 12.12 *Federal Express provides overnight air shipments for packages of all sizes (Source: Ad is used pursuant to a license agreement with Federal Express Corporation, the owner of all rights to the advertisement)*

The success of overnight mail—a twelve-year-old business with a 25-percent annual growth rate since 1981—is due in part to Federal Express. Only when that firm began tapping the office market, switching its hard sell from traffic managers to administrators, did competitors begin to offer overnight services. The market has been expanding ever since, boosted by the slowness and unreliability of the U.S. Postal Service.

The market leaders in the domestic air cargo market account for 80.9 percent of total domestic air shipments. Table 12.4 lists the leaders in domestic air cargo shipments. Federal Express outdistanced all other carriers in the number of shipments, as shown in the table, and also in domestic air cargo revenue. The air cargo increase has increased combined truck and air operations for all major competitors who provide those services. For a small item, such as a document, a machine repair part, or even Vermont-made ice cream, the options available for the professional buyer of delivery services are staggering. A physical distribution manager must set delivery priorities, study rates and routes carefully, and closely monitor service and performance to make sure that the right buying decision is made. In line with this chapter, it is obvious that cost is a consideration but quick and dependable availability is sometimes more important than price. In fact, reliability is found most often to be the

Table 12.4 *Domestic air cargo shipments 1975–1984 (thousands of shipments)*

Market Leaders	1975	1983	1984	Percent Change '83/'84
Federal Express	2,920	59,259	95,782	+61.6
Emery Worldwide	3,365	6,989	8,360	+19.6
Airborne Freight Corp.	1,691	9,551	13,056	+36.7
Purolator Courier	136	8,096	10,699	+32.2
UPS Air	25,203	41,400	55,600	+34.3
Burlington Northern Air Freight	722	2,936	3,160	+ 7.6
CF AirFreight	252	1,584	1,890	+19.3
Market Leaders' Total	34,289	129,815	188,547	+45.2
Other Forwarders	5,419	25,442	30,818	+21.1
Airlines Direct	14,133	13,073	13,753	+ 5.2
Total Market	53,841	168,330	233,118	+38.5

The market leaders in the domestic air cargo market accounted for 80.9 percent of total 1984 domestic air shipments, up from 77.1 percent of total 1983 domestic shipments. The market leaders handled 45.2 percent more shipments in 1984 than in 1983, compared to a 38.5 percent increase for the total market.

Source: The Colography Group Inc. © 1985 by Inbound Logistics. Used by permission.

most important variable in the final decision. Physical distribution managers find the best way to determine a carrier's performance is to test it out with noncritical deliveries. In addition, air cargo delivery carriers often offer special services to preferred customers, and these can have a major impact on the final decision. For example, some firms have on-site computer package tracing and offer automatic labeling devices to loyal patrons. Most air cargo companies offer volume discounts.

A company must determine what its needs are and how air cargo delivery may relate to implementation of its marketing strategies. Then it should seek to negotiate a delivery program that satisfies company requirements. Most companies find it beneficial to select two or three carriers. Often selection is made on a case by case basis.

Inbound Logistics, a magazine for transportation and purchasing professionals, called sixteen small-package delivery carriers and told representatives that they wanted to have a 10-pound package of printing material delivered to their offices at 1 Penn Plaza, New York City, from the Sears Tower, in downtown Chicago. Table 12.5 shows the rates quoted based on mileage (approximately 800 miles), weight, and delivery time. The discussion questions that follow relate to making this physical distribution decision.

Questions for Discussion

1. Discuss the criteria that you would use for making your decision for selecting a carrier for the 10-pound package of printing materials.
2. Which of the carriers in Table 12.5 would you select to deliver the 10-pound package of printing material from the Sears Tower to 1 Penn Plaza?

Table 12.5 A buyer's guide to expedited deliveries

| | Rates** | | | |
Carrier	Overnight	2nd Day	Other	Service Notes
Airborne	$48.00	N/A	N/A	—Door-to-door —Delivery by 10:30 a.m.

Air Express International
  (AEI)
	55.00	$40.00	N/A	—Door-to-door
				—Delivery between 9 a.m. and
				  5 p.m.

Amtrak	N/A	16.00	N/A	—No guaranteed time-definite
				  service, except as noted in
				  train schedule
				—No pickup or delivery service

Associated Air Freight	48.00	38.00	N/A	—Door-to-door —Noon delivery on overnight service

Burlington Northern
  Air Freight
	44.00	44.00	N/A	—Door-to-door
				—a.m. delivery usual, but not
				  guaranteed

CF AirFreight	40.66 38.63 (by noon) (by 5 p.m.)	N/A	24.40 (3 days)	—Door-to-door
DHL	49.00	N/A	N/A	—Door-to-door —Delivery by noon
Emery Worldwide	48.00 45.00 (before (p.m.) 10 a.m.)	22.00	N/A	—Door-to-door —2nd day delivery before 5 p.m.

Federal Express	45.00	20.50	N/A	—Door-to-door
				—Overnight delivery by
				  10:30 a.m.
				—2nd day delivery before
				  5 p.m.

3. Assume that the 10-pound package was not needed until the second day. Defend your choice of a carrier for this service. Assume that the 10-pound package of printing materials is absolutely necessary and highly critical for a meeting in four days. Which service would you select? Defend your selection.

Table 12.5 (continued)

Carrier	Rates**			Service Notes
	Overnight	2nd Day	Other	
Greyhound	N/A	26.90*	13.45 (2–3 day)	—Terminal-to-terminal —Door-to-door extra charge —Bus takes less than 24 hours
Pilot Air Freight	40.00	35.00	62.79 (5 day LTL)	—Door-to-door —Overnight and 2nd day deliveries before 5 p.m. —LTL is minimum rate
Purolator Courier	45.00	20.00	N/A	—Door-to-door —Overnight delivery before noon —2nd day delivery by 5 p.m.
Roadway	N/A	N/A	3.44 (3 days)	—Door-to-door —Deliveries for regular customers only, therefore exact rate not available —Base rate same as UPS
Trailways	N/A	11.10	N/A	—Terminal-to-terminal —Door-to-door extra charge
United Parcel Service	21.00	11.50	3.44 (3–4 days)	—Door-to-door —Delivery before 5 p.m.
U.S. Postal Service Express Mail	13.15	N/A	N/A	—Door-to-door —Delivery before 5 p.m.

**Rates based on a 10-lb. package, delivered approximately 800 miles
*Must pay higher rate for time-definite 2nd day service
Source: Betsy Haggerty, "A Smart Shopper's Guide to Expedited Delivery Services," *Inbound Logistics,* Jan. 1986, p. 18.

Part IV
Promotion Decisions

Part IV deals with communicating with target market members. A specific marketing mix cannot satisfy people in a particular target market unless they are aware of the product and where to find it. Some promotion decisions and activities are related to a specific marketing mix, while others, broader in scope, focus on the promotion of the whole organization. Chapter 13 presents an overview of promotion. We describe the communication process and the major promotion methods that can be included in promotion mixes. In Chapter 14, we analyze the major steps required to develop an advertising campaign, and we explain what publicity is and how it can be used. Chapter 15 deals with the management of personal selling and the role it can play in a firm's promotion mix. This chapter also explores the general characteristics of sales promotion and sales promotion techniques.

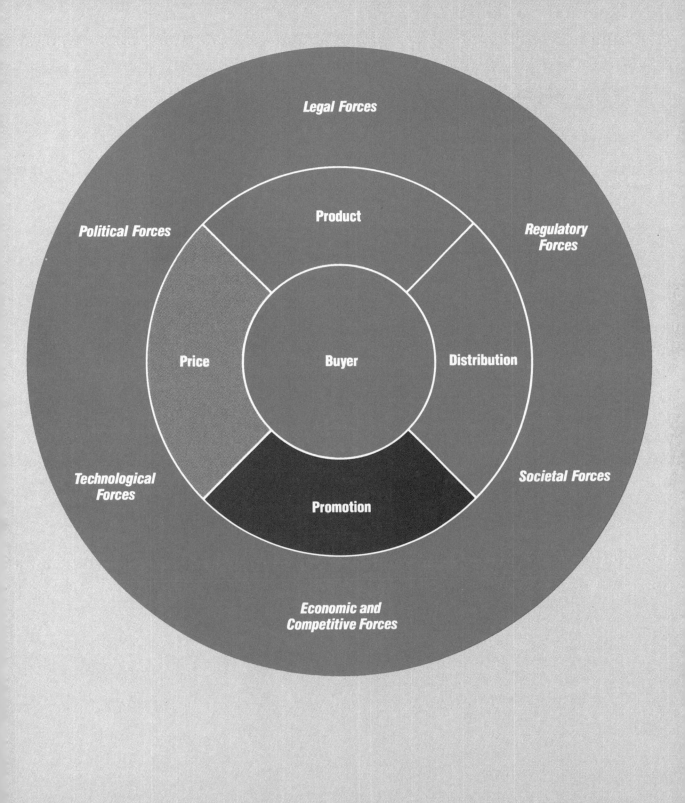

13 / Promotion: An Overview

Objectives

■ To understand the role of promotion in the marketing mix.

■ To examine the process of communication.

■ To understand the product adoption process and its implications for promotional efforts.

■ To gain an understanding of the promotion mix.

■ To acquire an overview of the major promotional methods that make up promotion mixes.

■ To explore factors that affect the choice of promotional methods.

Figure 13.1

Sugar-Free Dr Pepper's name changed to Diet Dr Pepper (Source: Dr Pepper Company)

Recently Dr Pepper Company decided to change the name of Sugar-Free Dr Pepper to Diet Dr Pepper. Consumer research showed that a majority of consumers and retailers already referred to Sugar-Free Dr Pepper as Diet Dr Pepper. Also, other soft-drink companies had educated consumers and bottlers by including the word diet *in their soft-drink brand names. Finally, the word* sugar-free *means diet. Use of the term* diet *in a brand name reinforces the rationale for people using a low-calorie soft drink.*

Dr Pepper Company employed a variety of promotional methods to introduce the name change and to create a new identity for the drink. The company instituted a large sampling program under which it offered a free can of Diet Dr Pepper to every household in specifically targeted markets. John Albers, president of Dr Pepper Company, appeared in television commercials to make this offer.

Through two-page Diet Dr Pepper advertisements in fifteen different magazines, Dr Pepper Company reached 40 million consumers with coupons. These coupons provided buyers the opportunity to acquire Diet Dr Pepper at a reduced price. The company offered its bottlers colorful, attractive, point-of-purchase displays promoting sweepstakes and prizes. Several sweepstakes were planned for the year in which the new name was launched.

Diet Dr Pepper advertising employed television, radio, magazines, and billboards. The theme for these advertisements was "Diet Dr Pepper: The Taste for Out of the Ordinary Bodies" (see Figure 13.1). Three Diet Dr Pepper television commercials were entitled "Stargazers," "Godzilla II," and "Droids." The commercials reinforced brand awareness. Radio commercials featured Dr. Ruth ("Good Sex") Westheimer and had a question-and-answer format in which Dr. Ruth was asked by callers about out of the ordinary problems that they had regarding soft drinks. She provided advice on "Good Soda." The billboards employed Godzilla II to promote Diet Dr Pepper. Dr Pepper Company also proposed that bottlers use a new truck design that would turn trucks into attractive, eye-catching advertisements. The magazine advertisements focused primarily on the coupon ads mentioned earlier.

Dr Pepper Company spent considerable amounts of time developing these promotional plans. The company did not use a single promotional effort but a mix of promotional activities. This mix was crucial to the effective promotion of Diet Dr Pepper.[1]

This chapter looks at the general dimensions of promotion. Initially, we consider the role of promotion. Then, to understand how promotion works, we analyze the meaning and process of communication and the product adoption process. The remainder of the chapter discusses the major types of promotional methods and the factors that influence an organization's decision to use specific methods.

The Role of Promotion

When people think about promotion, they frequently take one of two extreme positions. They may believe that the field of marketing consists entirely of promotional activities such as advertising and personal selling because those marketing activities are such a highly visible part of our everyday lives. People who take the other extreme see promotional activities as unnecessary and thus

1. *The Clock Dial*, Oct. 1985, pp. 8–12. Used with the permission of Dr Pepper Company.

Figure 13.2 Advertisements fostering a harmonious relationship between sponsors and society (Source: Ad on left courtesy of Stroh Brewery Company. Ad on right courtesy of Sun Company)

wasteful. They perceive that promotion costs (especially advertising) are high—sometimes excessively so—and believe these costs drive prices higher. Neither opinion is correct.

The role of **promotion** is to communicate with individuals, groups, or organizations to directly or indirectly facilitate exchanges by informing and persuading one or more of the audiences to accept an organization's products. To facilitate exchanges directly, marketers communicate with selected audiences about a firm and/or its goods, services, and ideas. Marketers indirectly facilitate exchanges by focusing communication about company activities and products on interest groups (such as environmental and consumer groups), current and potential investors, regulatory agencies, and society in general. (Consider the promotional role of Nike's athletic endorsers in the application on page 380.)

Viewed from this wider perspective, promotion can play a comprehensive communication role. Some promotional activities can be directed toward helping a company to justify its existence and to maintain positive, healthy relationships between itself and various groups in the marketing environment. The advertisements in Figure 13.2 for example, are not aimed directly at selling goods and services. They are designed to improve the relationship between the sponsors and society.

The running boom is over, but the fitness boom continues apace. Nike, a company that made its mark as a running-shoe marketer, suffered a severe 25.7-percent slump in running-shoe sales last year. But for the same period, basketball-shoe sales rose by 14.8 percent. Nike was for the first time experiencing a serious shift in the marketplace, one that required an equally dramatic change in marketing strategy.

Given these marketplace realities, Nike's planned promotion of its lines centered on well-publicized athletes. Tennis pro John McEnroe was signed to promote a tennis apparel line, while marathon runner Joan Benoit was recruited to endorse Nike's more traditional running lines. The most controversial of the promotional attempts featured basketball player Michael Jordan of the Chicago Bulls, who promoted the Air Jordan line.

Jordan, under a five-year contract with Nike, was supposed to earn his $2.5 million by playing in signature shoes bearing his name. The National Basketball Association objected, however. The NBA insisted Jordan follow its rule that players could not wear shoes which did not conform to a team's color scheme. The Chicago Bulls' scheme is red and white with black trim; Jordan's Nike shoe was black with a red Nike comet. Since Nike wanted Jordan to wear only its line, the shoemaker redesigned Air Jordan to fit the red-white-black Bull colors. Nike obtained marketing mileage from the NBA ruling by producing TV ads humorously pointing out that while the NBA tossed Nike out of a game, they couldn't prevent "you" from wearing Nike shoes. (*Sources: Jack Friedman, "Air Jordan Deal Scores for Nike,"* Advertising Age, *Feb. 28, 1985, p. 4; Ruth Stroud, "Nike Weighing Ad, Promo Budget Cuts,"* Advertising Age, *Jan. 21, 1985, p. 6; and "Nike Unit's Sole Goal Will Be New Products,"* Advertising Age, *Feb. 11, 1985, p. 86.*)

Although a firm can direct a single type of communication—such as an advertisement—toward numerous audiences, marketers often design a communication precisely for a specific audience. A firm frequently communicates several different messages concurrently, each to a different group. For example, a glass producer may direct one communication toward customers for double-paned windows, a second message toward investors about the firm's rapid growth, and a third communication toward society in general regarding what the company is doing to produce strong, safe glass.

To gain maximum benefit from promotional efforts, marketers must make every effort to be sure communications are properly planned, implemented, coordinated, and controlled. To develop and implement effective promotional activities, a firm must obtain and use information from the marketing environment (see Figure 13.3). How effectively marketers can use promotion to maintain positive relationships with environmental forces depends largely on the quantity and quality of information taken in by an organization. For example, marketers want to communicate effectively with customers to influence them to buy a particular product. To do so, they must have data about these customers and about the kinds of information these customers use in making purchase decisions for that type of product. Thus, to successfully communicate with selected audiences, marketers must collect and use information about these audiences.

Since the basic role of promotion is to communicate, we should analyze what communication is and how the communication process works.

Figure 13.3

*Information flows
into and out of an
organization*

| Information about customers and marketing environment forces | → | Organization | → | Promotion |

Promotion and the Communication Process

Communication can be viewed as the transmission of information. Information is form or pattern. Thus, the sending and receiving of form is communication. According to this description, we communicate with you when you perceive the following symbols:

在工廠吾人製造化粧品,在商店吾人銷售希望。[2]

We encounter a problem, however, because this view of communication does not consider the meaningfulness of the pattern that is transmitted.

For promotional purposes, a more useful approach is to define **communication** as a sharing of meaning.[3] Implicit in this definition is the notion of transmission of information because sharing necessitates transmission. More important, whatever is shared must, to some degree at least, have a common meaning for the individuals involved. Obviously, if we describe communication in these terms, we are not communicating with those who read English only when we transmit Chinese symbols, because these symbols are not meaningful to such readers. Since this second approach to understanding communication is more comprehensive and realistic, we shall view communication as a sharing of meaning.

As shown in Figure 13.4, communication begins with a source. A **source** is a person, group, or organization that has a meaning which it intends and attempts to share with a receiver or an audience. For example, a source could be a salesperson who wishes to communicate a sales message or an organization that wants to send a message to thousands of consumers through an advertisement.

To transmit meaning, a source must place the meaning into a series of signs that represent ideas. This is called the **coding process** or *encoding*. The coding process requires a source to convert the meaning into a series of signs that represent ideas or concepts. For example, in our attempt to communicate with you, we use the words on this page and the symbols in Figure 13.4 as signs that represent meanings we wish to share.

When coding meaning into a message, a source must take into account certain characteristics of the receiver or audience. First, to share meaning most easily, the source should use signs that are familiar to the receiver or audience. Marketers who understand this fact realize how important it is to know their target market and to make sure that an advertisement, for example, is written in language that the target market can understand. If the maker of Visine eye

2. In case you don't read Chinese, this says, "In the factory we make cosmetics, and in the drugstore we sell hope." Prepared by Chih Kang Wang.
3. Terence A. Shimp and M. Wayne Delozier, *Promotion Management and Marketing Communication* (Hinsdale, Ill.: Dryden, 1986), pp. 25–26.

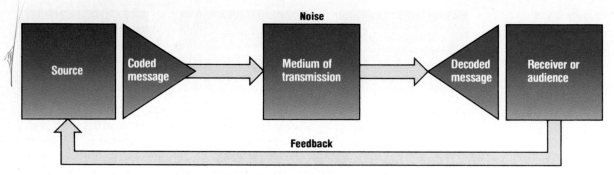

Figure 13.4 *The communication process*

freshener advertises to a general adult audience that the product contains tetrahydrocyline, the company may fail to share meaning. Most of the people in the audience are not likely to know what tetrahydrocyline will do for eyes. In fact, some adults may worry about using a potentially harmful chemical in their eyes. It is important that people understand the language in advertisements.

Second, when coding a meaning, a source should attempt to employ signs that the receiver or audience uses for referring to the concepts intended by the source. Marketers should generally avoid signs that can have several meanings for an audience. A national advertiser of soft drinks, for example, should avoid using the word *soda* as a general term for soft drinks. Although in some parts of the United States *soda* is taken to mean *soft drink,* in other regions it may evoke other concepts in receivers' minds—bicarbonate of soda, an ice-cream treat, or something that one mixes with Scotch whisky, for example.

To share a coded meaning with the receiver or audience, a source must select and use a medium of transmission. A **medium of transmission** carries the coded message from the source to the receiver or audience. Examples of transmission media include ink on paper, vibrations of air waves produced by vocal cords, chalk marks on a chalkboard, and electronically produced vibrations of air waves—in radio and television signals, for example.

When a source chooses an inappropriate medium of transmission, several problems may arise, and marketers should be especially alert to avoid them. A coded message may reach some receivers, but not the right ones. For example, suppose a community theater spends most of its advertising dollars on radio advertisements. If theatergoers depend mainly on newspapers for information about local drama, then the theater will not reach its intended target audience. Also, coded messages may reach intended receivers in an incomplete form because the intensity of the transmission is weak. For example, a marketer may choose a printing method that reproduces an advertisement so poorly that people cannot read it. If the advertisement is barely legible, the audience will form an impression of poor quality and may associate it with the product or company.

A **receiver,** or audience—another major component of the communication process—is the individual, group, or organization that decodes a coded message. An audience is two or more receivers who decode a message. In the **decoding process,** signs are converted into concepts and ideas.

Seldom does a receiver decode exactly the same meaning that a source coded. When the result of decoding is different from what was coded, **noise** exists. Noise has many sources and may affect any or all parts of the communication process. When a source selects a medium of transmission through which an audience does not expect to receive a message, noise is likely to occur. Noise sometimes arises within the medium of transmission itself. Radio static, faulty printing processes, and laryngitis are sources of noise. Interference on viewers' television sets during a commercial is noise and lessens the impact of the advertisement. Suppose the source uses a sign that is unfamiliar to the receiver or one that has a different meaning from the one that the source intended. In either case, noise will occur during decoding. Noise also may originate in the receiver. As discussed in Chapter 4, a receiver may be unaware of a coded message because it is blocked out by his or her perceptual processes.

The receiver's response to the decoded message is **feedback** to the source. The source usually expects and normally receives feedback, although it may not be immediate. During feedback, the receiver or audience is the source of a message that is directed toward the original source, which then becomes a receiver. Feedback is coded, sent through a medium of transmission, and is decoded by the receiver, the source of the original communication. It makes sense, then, to think about communication as a circular process.

During face-to-face communication, such as a personal selling situation, both verbal and nonverbal feedback can be immediate. This instant feedback allows communicators to adjust their messages quickly to improve the effectiveness of their communication. For example, when a salesperson realizes through feedback that a customer does not understand a sales presentation, the salesperson adapts the presentation to make it more meaningful to the customer. In inter-personal communication, feedback occurs through talking, touching, smiling, nodding, eye movements, and other body movements and postures.

When mass communication such as advertising is employed, feedback is often slow and difficult to recognize. For example, if a lawnmower manufacturer were to advertise the benefits of a steam-powered engine, it might be six to eighteen months before the firm could recognize the effects of such adver-tisements. It could easily take that long for the firm to detect an increase in sales or in customers' interest. Although it is harder to recognize, feedback does exist for mass communication. Advertisers, for example, obtain feedback in the form of changes in sales volume and in consumers' attitudes and product awareness levels.

Each communication channel has a limit regarding the volume of information it can handle effectively. This limit, called **channel capacity,** is determined by the least efficient component of the communication process. Think about com-munications that depend on vocal speech. An individual source can talk only so fast, and there is a limit to how much a receiver can take in aurally. Beyond that point additional coded messages cannot be decoded; thus meaning cannot be shared. Although a radio announcer can read several hundred words a minute, a one-minute advertising message should not exceed 150 words because most announcers cannot articulate the words into understandable messages at a rate beyond 150 words per minute. This figure is the limit for both source and receiver, and marketers should keep this in mind when developing radio commercials. At times, a firm creates a television advertisement that contains several types of visual materials and several forms of audio messages, all transmitted to viewers at the same time. Such communication may not be totally effective because receivers cannot decode all the messages concurrently.

Now that we have explored the basic communication process, let us consider more specifically just how promotion is used to influence individuals, groups, or organizations to accept or adopt a firm's products. Although we introduced the product adoption process in Chapter 8, we explore it more fully in the following section to gain a better understanding of the conditions under which promotion occurs.

Promotion and the Product Adoption Process

Marketers do not promote simply to inform, educate, and entertain. They communicate with individuals, groups, or organizations to facilitate exchanges. One long-run purpose of promotion is to influence and encourage buyers to accept or adopt goods, services, and ideas. At times, an advertisement may be informative or entertaining, yet it may fail to get the audience to purchase the product. For example, some Alka-Seltzer commercials have had this problem. The ultimate effectiveness of promotion is determined by the degree to which it affects product adoption among potential buyers.

To establish realistic expectations about what promotion can do, one should not view product adoption as a one-step process. Rarely can a single promotional activity cause an individual to buy a previously unfamiliar product. The acceptance of a product is a multistep process.

Although there are several ways to look at the **product adoption process,** one common approach is to view it as consisting of five stages: awareness, interest, evaluation, trial, and adoption.[4] In the awareness stage individuals become aware that the product exists, but they have little information about it and are not concerned about getting more. They enter the interest stage when they are motivated to get information about the product's features, uses, advantages, disadvantages, price, or location. During the evaluation stage individuals consider whether the product will satisfy certain criteria that are critical for meeting their specific needs. In the trial stage, they use or experience the product for the first time, possibly by purchasing a small quantity, by taking advantage of a free sample or demonstration, or by borrowing the product from someone. (The application on page 386 describes another type of product trial.) During this stage potential adopters determine the usefulness of the product under the specific conditions for which they need it. Individuals move into the adoption stage at the point when they choose that specific product when they need a product of that general type. Do not assume, however, that because a person enters the adoption process, he or she eventually will adopt the new product. Rejection may occur at any stage, including adoption. Both product adoption and product rejection can be temporary or permanent.

For the most part, people respond to different information sources at different stages of the adoption process. Mass communication sources are often effective for moving large numbers of people into the awareness stage. Producers of consumer goods commonly use massive advertising campaigns when introducing new products. They do so to create product awareness as quickly as

4. Many of the ideas in this section are drawn from Everett M. Rogers, *Diffusion of Innovations* (New York: Free Press, 1962), pp. 81–86 and 98–102.

Figure 13.5

Advertisement to generate product awareness (Source: Courtesy of Tomy® Corporation)

possible within a large portion of the target market. For example, through advertisements like the one in Figure 13.5, Tomy is trying to create awareness of one of its new products called Omnibot 2000.

Since people in the interest stage are seeking information, mass communications may also be effective then. During the evaluation stage, individuals often seek information, opinions, and reinforcement from personal sources—relatives, friends, and associates. In the trial stage, individuals depend on salespersons for information about how to use the product properly to get the most out of it. Friends and peers may also be important sources during the trial stage. By the time the adoption stage has been reached, both personal communication from sales personnel and mass communication through advertisements may be required. Even though the particular stage of the adoption process may influence the types of information sources consumers use, marketers must remember that other factors—such as the product's characteristics, price, uses, and the characteristics of customers—also affect the types of information sources that buyers seek out.

Because people in different stages of the adoption process often will require different types of information, marketers designing a promotional campaign must determine what stage of the adoption process a particular target audience is in before they can develop the message. Potential adopters in the interest stage will need different information than people who have already reached the trial stage.

Application

Trial Through Test
Drives

To move customers through the trial stage of the product adoption process, companies sometimes encourage them to test drive products. Test drives allow potential buyers to experience the product with very little economic risk. The experience of a test drive can be quite valuable in influencing customer perceptions of the product. Consider the following examples.

Harley-Davidson Motor Co., Inc. had experienced a sales slump for several years. In an attempt to reverse the trend, the company's marketers decided to take an innovative step in the motorcycle market—allowing potential customers to test drive Harley-Davidson motorcycles. Traditionally, motorcycle companies had not encouraged or promoted test drives because of the dangers of theft and accident liability. Harley-Davidson started slowly in promoting demonstration rides, introducing them nationwide over a three-year period. Last year Harley-Davidson's market share increased by 25 percent. Thus, promoting test rides was quite effective for that organization.

Apple Computer, Inc., designed a promotional campaign that invited customers to take a Macintosh personal computer for a "test drive." Any customer with good credit could walk out of a dealership with $2,000 worth of hardware and software and the assurance that within an hour or less he or she would be producing business graphics like pie charts and spreadsheets. Apple marketers knew that the strongest selling point of the Macintosh is its ease of use. They knew that it was so easy to use that many new customers would never bother to consult the manuals. Thus, Apple marketers made the decision to let the customers sell themselves in the comfort and convenience of the office or home. Dealers at the retail level strongly supported this effort. They found the test drive campaign to be very successful. (*Sources: Doris Walsh, "You Meet the Nicest People on a Harley,"* American Demographics, *July 1985, p. 18; William A. Robinson, "Apple Computer Drives the Point Home,"* Advertising Age, *Jan. 17, 1985, p. 30; and Thomas J. Murray, "Apple Is Back,"* Dun's Business Month, *June 1984, pp. 62–63.*)

When an organization introduces a new product, people do not all begin the adoption process at the same time, and they do not move through the process at the same speed. Of those who eventually adopt the product, some enter the adoption process rather quickly. Others start considerably later. (And, of course, for most products, there is a group of nonadopters who never begin the process.)

The amount of time people take to adopt a new product can be employed to classify them into adopter categories. The five major adopter categories are innovators, early adopters, early majority, late majority, and laggards.[5] Each adopter category, and the percentage of total adopters that it typically represents, is shown in Figure 13.6. **Innovators** are the first to adopt a new product. They enjoy trying new products and tend to be venturesome, rash, and daring. **Early adopters** choose new products carefully and are viewed as being "the people to check with" by persons in the remaining adopter categories. Individuals in the **early majority** adopt just prior to the average person; they are deliberate and cautious in trying new products. **Late majority** people, who are quite skeptical of new products, eventually adopt new products because of economic necessity

5. Rogers, *Diffusion of Innovations,* pp. 247–250.

Figure 13.6

Distribution of product adopter categories (Source: Reprinted with permission of Macmillan, Inc. From Diffusion of Innovations. *Third Edition,* by Everett M. Rogers. Copyright © 1983 by The Free Press, a Division of Macmillan, Inc.)

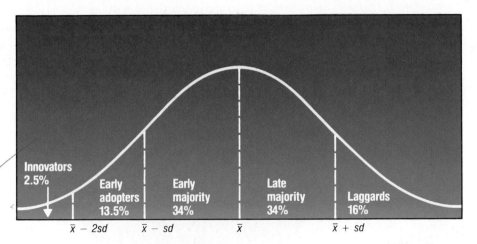

or social pressure. **Laggards,** the last to adopt a new product, are oriented toward the past. They are suspicious of new products, and when they finally have adopted the innovation, it already may have been replaced by a newer product. When developing promotional efforts, a marketer should bear in mind that persons in different adopter categories often need different forms of communication and different types of information.

Now, to gain a better understanding of how promotion is used to move people closer to the acceptance of goods, services, and ideas we will analyze the major promotional methods available to an organization.

The Promotion Mix

Several types of promotional methods can be used to communicate with individuals, groups, and organizations. When an organization combines specific ingredients to promote a particular product, that combination constitutes the promotion mix for that product. In this section, we analyze the major ingredients of a promotion mix. We also examine the primary factors that influence an organization to include specific ingredients in the promotion mix for a specific product.

Promotion Mix Ingredients

The four possible ingredients of a **promotion mix** are advertising, personal selling, publicity, and sales promotion (see Figure 13.7). For some products, firms employ all four ingredients. For other products, only two or three are necessary. At this point, we will consider some general characteristics of each promotion mix ingredient. In Chapters 14 and 15 we analyze the promotion mix in more detail.

Advertising

Advertising is a paid form of nonpersonal communication about an organization and/or its products that is transmitted to a target audience through a mass medium. Individuals and organizations use advertising to promote goods, services,

Figure 13.7

Possible ingredients
for an organization's
promotion mix

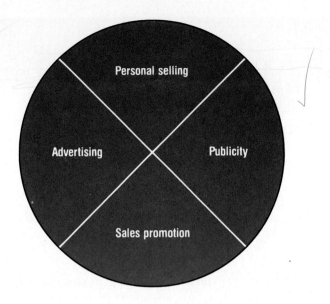

ideas, issues, and people. Some of the mass media commonly selected to transmit advertising are television, radio, newspapers, magazines, direct mail, mass transit vehicles, outdoor displays, handbills, catalogs, and directories. Being a highly flexible promotional method, advertising offers the options of reaching an extremely large target audience or of focusing on a small, precisely defined segment of the population. For example, Figure 13.8 is targeted at a very select, affluent segment of the antique market.

Advertising offers several benefits. It can be an extremely cost-efficient promotional method because it can reach a vast number of people at a low cost per person. For example, the cost of a black-and-white, one-page advertisement in *Time* magazine is $69,650. Because the magazine reaches 4.6 million subscribers, the cost of reaching 1,000 subscribers is only $15.14. Advertising allows the user to repeat the message a number of times. In addition, advertising a product in a certain way can add to its prestige. The visibility that an organization gains from advertising enhances the firm's public image.

Advertising also has several disadvantages. Even though its cost per person reached may be low, its absolute dollar outlay can be extremely high. The cost can limit, and sometimes preclude, its use in a promotion mix. Moreover, advertising rarely provides rapid feedback. Measuring its effect on sales is difficult, and it ordinarily has less persuasive impact on customers than personal selling.

Personal Selling

Personal selling is a process of informing customers and persuading them to purchase products through personal communication in an exchange situation. The phrase *purchase products* should be interpreted broadly to encompass the acceptance of ideas, issues, and political candidates.

Compared with advertising, personal selling has both advantages and limitations. While advertising is paid, nonpersonal communication aimed at a relatively large target audience, personal selling is aimed at one or several individuals. Reaching one person through personal selling costs considerably

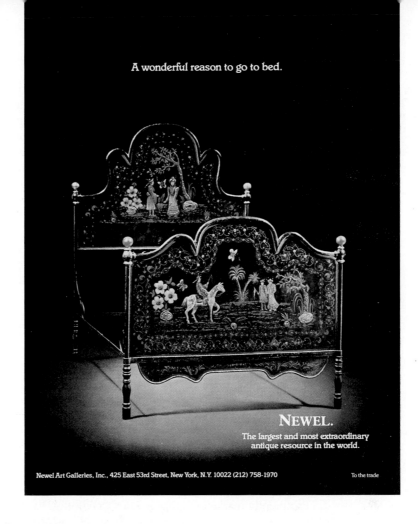

A wonderful reason to go to bed.

NEWEL.

The largest and most extraordinary antique resource in the world.

Newel Art Galleries, Inc., 425 East 53rd Street, New York, N.Y. 10022 (212) 758-1970   To the trade

more than it does through advertising, but personal selling efforts often have greater impact on customers. Remember, too, that personal selling provides immediate feedback, which allows marketers to adjust their message to improve communication. It also helps them to determine and respond to customers' needs for information.

When a salesperson and customer meet face to face, both individuals typically use several types of interpersonal communication. Obviously, the predominating communication form is language—both speech and writing. In addition, a salesperson and customer frequently use **kinesic communication,** or body language. They do this by moving their heads, eyes, arms, hands, legs, or torsos. Winking, head nodding, hand gestures, and arm motions are forms of kinesic communication. A good salesperson can often evaluate a prospect's interest in a product or presentation by watching for eye contact and head nodding. **Proxemic communication,** a less obvious form of communication used in personal selling situations, occurs when either party varies the physical distance that separates the two parties. When a customer backs away from a salesperson, for example, that individual may be saying that he or she is not interested in the product or may be expressing dislike for the salesperson. Touching, or **tactile communication,** can also be a form of communication, although it is not as popular in the United States as in many other countries. Handshaking is a common form of tactile communication in our country.

Publicity

Publicity is nonpersonal communication in news story form, regarding an organization and/or its products, that is transmitted through a mass medium at no charge. Examples of publicity include magazine, newspaper, radio, and television news stories about new retail stores, new products, or personnel changes in an organization. Although an organization does not pay for the mass medium, one should not view publicity as free communication. There are clear costs associated with preparing news releases and encouraging media personnel to broadcast or print them. A firm that uses publicity regularly must either have employees to perform these activities or must obtain the services of a public relations firm or an advertising agency. Either way, the firm bears the costs of the activities. Although both advertising and publicity are transmitted through mass communication, they differ in that the sponsor does not pay the media costs for publicity and is not identified. The communication is presented as a news story. Publicity must be planned and implemented so that it is compatible with, and supportive of, other elements in the promotion mix. Publicity cannot always be controlled to the extent that other elements of the promotion mix can be.

Sales Promotion

Sales promotion is an activity and/or material that acts as a direct inducement, offering added value or incentive for the product, to resellers, salespersons, or consumers.[6] Do not confuse the term *sales promotion* with *promotion;* sales promotion is but a part of the more comprehensive area of promotion. It encompasses efforts other than personal selling, advertising, and publicity. Currently, marketers spend about one and one-half times as much on sales promotion as they do on advertising.

Frequently marketers employ sales promotion to improve the eff ... eness of other promotion mix ingredients, especially advertising and personal selling. (Although such use is not common, sales promotion can be used as the primary promotion vehicle.) Marketers design sales promotion to produce immediate, short-run sales increases. If a company uses advertising or personal selling, it generally employs them on either a continuous or a cyclical basis. However, a marketer's use of sales promotion devices is usually irregular.

Sales promotion methods fall into one of two groups, depending on the intended audience. **Consumer sales promotion methods** are directed toward consumers; coupons, free samples, demonstrations, and contests are typical. Sales promotion methods that focus on wholesalers, retailers, and salespersons are called **trade sales promotion devices.** They are devised to encourage resellers to carry and aggressively market a specific product. Examples include sales contests, free merchandise, and displays.

Having discussed the basic components that can be included in an organization's promotion mix, we must now ask what factors and conditions affect the selection of the promotional methods that a specific organization uses in its promotion mix for a particular product.

---

6. This definition is adapted from John F. Luick and William L. Ziegler, *Sales Promotion and Modern Merchandising* (New York: McGraw-Hill, 1968), p. 4. Copyright © 1968 McGraw-Hill, Inc. Used with permission of McGraw-Hill Book Company.

Selecting Promotion Mix Ingredients

Marketers vary the composition of promotion mixes for many reasons. Although all four ingredients can be included in a promotion mix, frequently a marketer uses fewer than four. In addition, many firms that market multiple product lines use several promotion mixes simultaneously.

An organization's promotion mix (or mixes) is not an unchanging part of the marketing mix. Marketers can and do change the composition of their promotion mixes. The specific promotion mix ingredients employed and the intensity at which they are used depend on a variety of factors, including the following: the organization's promotional resources, objectives, and policies; the characteristics of the target market; the characteristics of the product; and the cost and availability of promotional methods.

Promotional Resources, Objectives, and Policies

The quality of an organization's promotional resources affects the number and relative intensity of promotional methods that can be included in a promotion mix. If a company's promotional budget is extremely limited, the firm is likely to rely on personal selling because it is easier to measure a salesperson's contribution to sales than to measure advertising's contribution. A business must have a sizable promotional budget if it is to employ regional or national advertising and sales promotion activities. Organizations with extensive promotional resources usually can include more ingredients in their promotion mixes. However, that they have more promotional dollars does not imply that they necessarily will use a greater number of promotional methods.

An organization's promotional objectives also influence the types of promotion employed. If a company's objective is to create mass awareness of a new convenience good, its promotion mix is likely to be heavily oriented toward advertising, sales promotion, and possibly publicity. If a company hopes to educate consumers about the features of durable goods such as home appliances, its promotion mix may consist of a moderate amount of advertising, possibly some sales promotion efforts designed to attract customers to retail stores, and a great deal of personal selling since this method is an excellent way to inform customers about these types of products. If a firm's objective is to produce immediate sales of consumer nondurables, the promotion mix probably will depend heavily on advertising and sales promotion efforts.

Another element that marketers should consider when they plan a promotion mix is whether to use a push policy or a pull policy. With a **push policy,** the producer promotes the product only to the next institution down the marketing channel. For instance, in a marketing channel with wholesalers and retailers, the producer promotes to the wholesaler since in this case the wholesaler is the channel member just below the producer (see Figure 13.9). Each channel member, in turn, promotes to the next channel member. A push policy usually relies heavily on personal selling. Sometimes, sales promotion and advertising are used in conjunction with personal selling to push the products down through the channel.

As shown in Figure 13.9, a firm that uses a **pull policy** promotes directly to consumers with the intention of developing a strong consumer demand for the products. Given strong consumer demand, consumers will seek the products in retail stores. Recognizing the demand, retailers will in turn go to wholesalers or the producer to buy the products. The policy is thus intended to "pull" the

Figure 13.9

Comparison of "push" and "pull" promotional policies

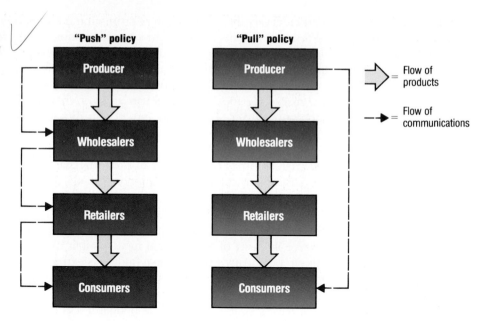

"Push" policy

- Producer
- Wholesalers
- Retailers
- Consumers

"Pull" policy

- Producer
- Wholesalers
- Retailers
- Consumers

⟹ = Flow of products

→ = Flow of communications

goods down through the channel by creating demand at the consumer level. To stimulate intensive consumer demand, an organization ordinarily must place a heavy emphasis on advertising and sometimes on sales promotion. When a major food company recently used a pull policy to introduce a new brand of flaked coffee, it advertised extensively and told consumers to ask for the product at their favorite stores.

Characteristics of the Target Market

The size, geographic distribution, and socioeconomic characteristics of an organization's target market also help dictate the ingredients included in the promotion mix for a product. Market size determines, to some degree, the promotion mix composition. If the size is quite limited, the promotion mix will probably emphasize personal selling, which can be quite effective for reaching small numbers of people. Organizations that sell to small industrial markets and firms that market their products through only a few wholesalers frequently emphasize personal selling as the major component of their promotion mixes. When markets for a product consist of millions of customers, organizations use advertising and sales promotion because these methods can reach masses of people at a low cost per person.

The geographic distribution of a firm's customers can affect the combination of promotional methods used. Personal selling is more feasible if a company's customers are concentrated in a small area than if they are dispersed across a vast geographic region. Advertising may be more practical when the company's customers are numerous and dispersed.

The distribution of a target market's socioeconomic characteristics, such as age, income, or education, may dictate the types of promotional techniques that a marketer selects. For example, personal selling may be much more successful than print advertisements for communicating with less-educated people.

Figure 13.10

Advertisement and sales promotion used by a toy company (Courtesy of Matchbox Toys (USA) Ltd.)

Characteristics of the Product

Generally, promotion mixes for industrial products concentrate heavily on personal selling. For promoting consumer goods, on the other hand, advertising plays a major role. Treat this generalization cautiously, however. Industrial goods producers do use some advertising to promote goods. Advertisements for computers, road building equipment, and aircraft are not altogether uncommon, and trade-type sales promotion occasionally is used to promote industrial goods. Personal selling is used extensively for consumer durables such as home appliances, automobiles, and houses, while consumer convenience items are promoted mainly through advertising and sales promotion. Publicity appears in promotion mixes both for industrial goods and for consumer goods.

Marketers of highly seasonal products are often forced to emphasize advertising, and possibly sales promotion, because off-season sales will not support an extensive year-round sales force. Although many toy producers have sales forces to sell to resellers, a number of these companies depend to a large extent on advertising to promote their products. Figure 13.10 illustrates Matchbox's use of advertising and sales promotion.

A product's price also influences the composition of the promotion mix. High-priced products call for more personal selling. Since consumers associate greater risk with the purchase of an expensive product, they usually want the advice of a salesperson. Few of us, for example, would be willing to purchase a major appliance such as a freezer from a self-service establishment. For low-priced convenience items, marketers use advertising rather than personal selling at the retail level. The profit margins on many of these items are too low to justify the use of salespersons, and most customers do not need advice from sales personnel when buying such products.

The stage of the product life cycle also enters into marketers' decisions regarding an effective promotion mix. In the introduction stage, considerable advertising may be necessary for both industrial and consumer products to produce widespread awareness among potential users. For many products, personal selling and sales promotion are also used during this stage. For consumer nondurables, the growth and maturity stages necessitate a heavy emphasis on advertising. Industrial products, on the other hand, often require a concentration of personal selling and some sales promotion efforts during these stages. In the decline stage, marketers usually decrease their promotional activities, especially advertising. Promotional efforts in the decline stage often center on personal selling and sales promotion efforts.

Another factor affecting the composition of the promotion mix is intensity of market coverage. When a product is marketed through intensive distribution, the firm depends strongly on advertising. Sales promotion can also play a major role in the promotion of such products. A number of convenience products such as lotions, cereals, cake mixes, and coffee are promoted through samples, coupons, and cash refunds.

Where marketers have opted for selective distribution, marketing mixes vary considerably in terms of type and amount of promotional methods. Items distributed through exclusive distribution frequently demand more personal selling and less advertising. Expensive watches, furs, and high-quality furniture are examples of products that are promoted heavily through personal selling.

How a product is used affects the combination of promotional methods. Manufacturers of highly personal products such as nonprescription contraceptives and hemorrhoid medications depend heavily on advertising for promotion because many users do not like to talk with salespersons about such products. The makers of the personal products in Figure 13.11, for instance, rely heavily on advertising as a promotional method. An organization attempting to promote such highly personal products through door-to-door selling would probably fail badly.

Cost and Availability of Promotional Methods

The costs of promotional methods are major factors to analyze when developing a promotion mix. National advertising and sales promotion efforts require large expenditures. However, if they are effective in reaching extremely large numbers of people, the cost per individual reached may be quite small, possibly a few pennies per person. Not all forms of advertising are expensive, however. Many small, local businesses advertise their products through local newspapers, magazines, radio and television stations, and outdoor displays.

Another consideration that marketers must explore when formulating a promotion mix is the availability of promotional techniques. Despite the tremendous number of media vehicles in the United States, a firm may find that no available advertising medium effectively reaches a certain market. For example,

"I don't take the pill anymore."

"Since I started using Encare, I see no reason to go back to the pill. I mean, Encare has no hormones and that's important because my doctor told me to get off the pill for a few months to give my body a rest. On top of that, Encare's 2-way protection makes me feel safe.

1. Encare Contraceptive Inserts give you a precise dose of the spermicide doctors recommend most.

2. Encare forms a foaming physical barrier against the cervix to help prevent pregnancy. I like that.

"Just remember, it's essential to insert Encare at least 10 minutes before intercourse and follow the package instructions. For your convenience, you can insert Encare up to 1 hour before intercourse if you choose. Some Encare users experience irritation. If you do, simply discontinue use.

"Encare is approximately as effective as vaginal foam contraceptives in actual use. It's not as effective as the pill, however no birth control method is 100% effective, so talk to your doctor. If he or she has told you not to become pregnant, ask which method including Encare is best for you and discover birth control you can trust."

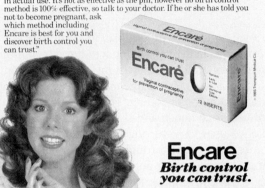

Encare
Birth control you can trust.

Am I pregnant?

New FIRST RESPONSE.: The truth in 20 minutes.

New FIRST RESPONSE™ Pregnancy Test is the most sensitive ever perfected. It's based on breakthrough technology from the maker of Tampax® tampons.

FIRST RESPONSE is as accurate as a lab test, without the weeks of waiting. It's three times more sensitive than any other home test. So you can use it as early as the day you're overdue—not 3 to 9 days later, as required by other tests. And get test results faster. With FIRST RESPONSE™, you'll know the truth in 20 minutes.

This test is simple to do and easy to read. You're pregnant if the liquid turns a distinct blue, and not pregnant if it remains clear. Results cannot be affected by vibration or movement as they can with ordinary tests. (If you have any questions, you can talk to a specially trained nurse at our toll-free number listed in the kit.)

New FIRST RESPONSE. Test earlier. Get results faster. You can always trust your FIRST RESPONSE™

a feed company may discover that no advertising media precisely reach the turkey growers of Oklahoma. The problem of media availability becomes even more pronounced when marketers try to advertise in foreign countries. Some media, such as television, simply may not be available. Other media that are available may not be open to certain types of advertisements. For example, in West Germany, advertisers are prohibited from making brand comparisons in television commercials. There are limits on other promotional methods as well. A firm may wish to increase the size of its sales force but be unable to find qualified personnel. In addition, some state laws prohibit the use of certain types of sales promotion activities such as contests. Those techniques are thus "unavailable" in those locales.

Summary

The primary role of promotion is to communicate with individuals, groups, or organizations in the environment to directly or indirectly facilitate exchanges.

Communication is a sharing of meaning. The communication process involves several steps. First, the source translates the meaning into code, a process known as coding or encoding. The source must use signs that are familiar to the receiver or audience and should attempt to employ signs that the receiver or audience uses for referring to the concepts or ideas being promoted. The coded message is sent through a medium of transmission to the receiver or audience. The receiver or audience then decodes the message, and usually the receiver supplies feedback to the source. When the decoded message differs from the message that was encoded, a condition called noise exists.

The long-run purpose of promotion is to influence and encourage customers to accept or adopt goods, services, and ideas. The product adoption process consists of five stages. The awareness stage exists when individuals become aware of the product. Next, people move into the interest stage when they seek more information about the product. In the evaluation stage, individuals decide whether the product will meet certain criteria that are critical for satisfying their needs. During the fourth stage, the trial stage, the individual actually tries the product. In the adoption stage, the individual decides to use the product on a regular basis. Rejection of the product may occur at any stage.

The promotion mix for a product may include four major promotional methods: advertising, personal selling, publicity, and sales promotion. Advertising is a paid form of nonpersonal communication about an organization and/or its products that is transmitted to a target audience through a mass medium. Personal selling is a process of informing customers and persuading them to purchase products through personal communication in an exchange situation. Publicity is nonpersonal communication in news story form, regarding an organization and/or its products, that is transmitted through a mass medium at no charge. Sales promotion is an activity and/or material that acts as a direct inducement, offering added value or incentive for the product, to resellers, salespersons, or consumers.

There are several major determinants of what promotional methods to include in a promotion mix for a product: the organization's promotional resources, objectives, and policies; the characteristics of the target market; the characteristics of the product; and the cost and availability of promotional methods.

Important Terms

Promotion
Communication
Source
Coding process
Medium of transmission
Receiver
Decoding process
Noise
Feedback
Channel capacity
Product adoption process
Innovators
Early adopters
Early majority
Late majority

Laggards
Promotion mix
Advertising
Personal selling
Kinesic communication
Proxemic communication
Tactile communication
Publicity
Sales promotion
Consumer sales promotion
    methods
Trade sales promotion devices
Push policy
Pull policy

Discussion and Review Questions

1. What is the major task of promotion? Do firms ever use promotion to accomplish this task and fail? If so, give several examples.
2. What is communication? Describe the communication process. Is it possible to communicate without using all the elements in the communication process? If so, which ones can be omitted?
3. Identify several causes of noise. How can a source reduce noise?
4. Describe the product adoption process. Under certain circumstances, is it possible for a person to omit one or more of the stages in adopting a new product? Explain your answer.
5. Describe a product that many persons are in the process of adopting. Have you begun the adoption process for this product? If so, what stage have you reached?
6. Identify and briefly describe the four major promotional methods that can be included in an organization's promotion mix. How does publicity differ from advertising?
7. What forms of interpersonal communication other than language can be used in personal selling?
8. Explain the difference between promotional efforts used with a pull policy and those used with a push policy. Under what conditions should each be used?
9. How do market characteristics determine the promotional methods to include in a promotion mix? Assume that a company is planning to promote a cereal to both adults and children. Along what major dimensions would these two promotional efforts have to be different?
10. How can a product's characteristics influence the composition of its promotion mix?
11. Evaluate the following statement: "Appropriate advertising media are always available if a company can afford them."

Cases

Case 13.1   New Coke and Coke Classic[7]

The Coca-Cola Company first considered changing to a new Coke five years ago when researchers, while developing Diet Coke, hit on a new cola formula. Secret taste tests at that time revealed that consumers preferred the new blend by 61 to 39 percent. Whether to proceed was a marketing decision, as the company's growth and old Coke's dominant position had eroded. At least some of this erosion could be attributed to Coke's chief competitor, Pepsi-Cola. In 1972, Pepsi began its Pepsi Challenge, which pitted the two colas against each other in blind taste testing. Pepsi sales and market share increased, while Coke's market share began a slow decline. More recently, Coke has been losing ground to Pepsi in the American supermarket, where 45 percent of all soft drinks are sold. Some industry watchers have said that in recent years Coca-Cola has neglected Coke in favor of diet drinks such as Tab, Fresca, and Diet Coke. This too, may have attributed to Coke's market share decline.

When the new Coke was discovered, Coca-Cola's president, Roberto C. Goizueta, perceived two options: "We could do nothing—put it on the shelf and forget we ever developed it. Or we could change the taste and give the world a new Coca-Cola."

Between 1981 and 1985, in twenty-five cities in the United States and Canada, Coke tested three or four new tastes on approximately 200,000 consumers. The new Coke flavors beat the old one by 55 to 45 percent when not identified and 61 to 39 percent when new and old Coke were identified. Also the results were positive when tested against Pepsi. Following these tests Coke began secret and serious preparations to introduce its new taste.

On April 23, 1985, the company announced the introduction of the new Coke with its new formula that would replace the old one. Coke brought back the "I'd Like To Buy the World a Coke" theme and produced a series of advertisements featuring Bill Cosby. Coke was going all out. Even though Pepsi claimed "The other guy blinked!", 150 million people tried the new Coke, which is more people than have tried any other new product in history. A large majority said that they would buy it again.

For several weeks following the introduction of new Coke, sales were excellent, even though complaints about the replacement of old Coke were immediate (this was not anticipated). Shipments to bottlers rose by the highest percentage in five years. Then—suddenly, according to the head of Coke's market research department—the mood of consumers changed. Bottlers, who are Coke's front-line contacts with consumers, were first to feel the heat. At a Dallas regional convention, they petitioned the Coca-Cola Company demanding a return to the old formula. Coke's Atlanta office was besieged with a steady 1,500 calls a day requesting a return to the old Coke. Consumer groups, too, sprang up around the country demanding a return to the old Coke. In many cases, they acted via boycotts, write-ins, and call-ins. Perhaps the most publicity was received by Seattle's Gay Mullins and his Old Cola Drinkers of America. He crusaded against the new Coke with T-shirts, protests, banners, and posters, and he even threatened a class-action lawsuit and a demonstration at Coke's

7. This case was contributed by James H. Kennedy, Navarro College.

stockholders' meeting. Others booed a new Coke advertisement flashed on the TV screen in Houston's Astrodome. People stockpiled the old Coke. Some sold it at premium prices. Consumers referred to the new Coke as furniture polish, sewer water, and two-day-old Pepsi. The popular consensus was that new Coke was sweeter and somewhat flatter. Coca-Cola officials began to feel the heat and finally began to consider what to do. With their minds virtually made-up, Coke officials had two important meetings—one with distributors/bottlers for five of their largest markets and another with distributors/bottlers in Atlanta. At both meetings the consensus was to bring back the old Coke.

On Wednesday, July 10, 1985, the Coca-Cola Company announced that it would bring back the old Coke under the new name of Coke Classic. The new Coke would still be available, and efforts would be made to maintain it as the company's flagship drink. Soft-drink fans across the nation rejoiced!

Coca-Cola Company officials would admit no failure, but President Goizueta did state, "We knew some people were going to be unhappy, but we could never have predicted the depth of their unhappiness. . . . you cannot quantify emotion." Another executive denied a widely held belief that the company brought out new Coke as part of a deliberate plot to create support for the older product and increase its sales. He admitted, "The passion for original Coke was something that just flat caught us by surprise. The simple fact is that all of the time and money and skill poured into consumer research on new Coke could not measure or reveal the depth of emotional attachment to the original Coke felt by so many people." He added, "Some critics will say Coca-Cola has made a marketing mistake. Some cynics say that we planned the whole thing. The truth is, we're not that dumb, and we're not that smart."

While admitting that eliminating the old Coke was a mistake, Coke officials began looking at the two-cola strategy in a positive manner. They could see the market as significantly larger for the combination of two cola brands than for either one alone. Those that tried new Coke in the first eleven weeks following its introduction amounted to more than double the number of usual Coke drinkers. And dedicated users of old Coke could be relied on as a significant source of business.

Prior to the introduction of the new Coke, the Coca-Cola Company spent less on advertising than Pepsi-Cola. Evidently, it also failed to budget for the additional advertising expenditures of bringing back the old Coke. Overall, the costs of advertising have created a substantial unplanned expense.

At the same time, though, the Coca-Cola Company and its old and new Cokes received immense publicity in many trade magazines and in mass media of all kinds. All this publicity was free. Coke is more of a household word than ever. Virtually everyone, and particularly those that drank Coke, talked about the new Coke, the old Coke's removal, and then the return of the old Coke.

Consumers were probably confused enough with the initial replacement of the original Coke with new Coke. Now they are confronted also with the return of the old Coke, complicated by its new name, Coke Classic. Some question the validity of the Coca-Cola Company's market research, which has been criticized as incomplete and less than thorough.

According to one advertising executive, "No one knows what Coke is now." Many marketers and even the general public view the entire incident as a mistake, a blunder, or worse. One marketing professional even cited it as smacking of amateurism. Pepsi-Cola Company and Royal Crown Company, among others, have seized this incident as an opportunity to attack Coke with creative and aggressive advertising.

Because of the recent addition of product lines, retailers already have limited soft-drink shelf space. Now they must try to accommodate two cokes with the premium space that the Coca-Cola Company and its bottlers prefer. Even a double display of Coke would not necessarily make up for the loss of sales on other, displaced soft drinks. In addition, many bottlers are equipped to bottle only one Coke syrup. To handle another increases costs, thus adding to the distribution problems fostered by retailers' limited shelf space.

Questions for Discussion

1. Assess Coca-Cola's use of information received from consumers both before and after the introduction of new Coke.
2. The decisions and behavior of Coca-Cola's management during the introduction of new Coke and the elimination and reintroduction of old Coke communicated several adverse perceptions associated with the Coca-Cola Company. Discuss these perceptions and why they were so widely disseminated.

Case 13.2   Promotion of Scripto's Disposable Lighters[8]

Three years ago there were three major sellers of disposable lighters in the United States. Bic had 53 percent of the market with sales of $175 million. Scripto had annual sales of $80 million, which represented approximately 24 percent of the market, and Gillette's Cricket had a 16-percent market share, which accounted for about $50 million in sales. Less than one year later, Gillette totally discontinued the Cricket lighter with its sales, at that point, of $42 million annually.

Recently, Scripto introduced a new "family of disposable lighters." The least expensive of the family is called Mighty Match—a clear plastic lighter that sells for 49 cents. Scripto's Ultra Lite model comes in silver and gold and sells for 69 cents. The top-of-the-line model is the 99-cent Electra, which features an electric ignition generated from a crystal instead of a flint. Scripto is owned by Tokai Seiki of Yokohama, Japan. This organization, the world's largest producer of disposable lighters, makes approximately 90 million of them a month.

Industry sales for disposable lighters are not increasing rapidly because consumers are smoking less cigarettes. However, because only about half of the Americans who do smoke regularly use lighters, industry executives believe the market for throwaway lighters has growth potential.

To capture its fair share of the market, Scripto is taking a very aggressive stance with price cuts, TV commercials, and store distribution. It is now selling a package of four lighters for a dollar and is distributing 20 million cents-off coupons. To garner the interest of impulse buyers, it is putting out thousands of eye-catching displays at check-out counters in supermarkets. To expand distribution of its products, Scripto has increased its sales force by 60 percent.

---

8. This case is based on Ronald Alsop, "Sparks Fly in Scripto's Battle to Dump Bic as Lighter King," *Wall Street Journal,* May 2, 1985, p. 33; "Extinguished," *Time,* Oct. 15, 1984, p. 93; and "Scripto Plans a Big Push for a New Lighter," *Business Week,* Aug. 6, 1984, p. 93.

In addition, 100 jobbers are being added to monitor and resupply store displays. Marketing executives at Scripto believe that having store displays and shelves well stocked is crucial to maintain sales of impulse purchases such as lighters.

A new $5-million advertising campaign has been launched by Scirpto to promote its new family of lighters. The last time this-size ad budget was used for disposable lighters was in the 1970s when Bic Corporation spent more than $6 million in one year. Scripto feels that this level of spending is necessary because the name of competitor Bic has become such a household word. In fact, "Bic" is used generically to mean disposable lighter—rather than asking for a lighter, a customer asks for a Bic. For its TV commercials, Scripto is using the comedy team of Jerry Stiller and Ann Meara.

Competitors vying for market share are coming up with their own gimmicks to rival Scripto's new disposables. Bic has developed a flashy, new lighter—the Bic 2000, a miniature model designed to appeal to women. Other specialized lighters hitting the market include a version that doubles as a breath-freshener dispenser and another that has a device to protect the flame in wind gusts of up to 40 miles per hour.

Questions for Discussion

1. Evaluate Scripto's decision to spend $5 million on an advertising campaign.
2. Do buyers move through a product adoption process when acquiring a new disposable lighter such as Scripto's Electra?
3. What main form of promotion is Scripto apparently using least?

14 / Advertising and Publicity

Objectives

- To explore the uses of advertising.
- To become aware of the major steps involved in developing an advertising campaign.
- To find out who is responsible for developing advertising campaigns.
- To gain an understanding of publicity.
- To analyze how publicity can be used.

Figure 14.1

Promotion of Federal Express and UPS services (Source: Ad on left is used pursuant to a license agreement with Federal Express Corporation, the owner of all rights to the advertisement. Ad on right courtesy of United Parcel Service)

In 1985 Federal Express and United Parcel Service (UPS) both stepped up their advertising campaigns to persuade customers to use their overnight delivery services (see Figure 14.1). Federal Express was trying to increase use of its drop-off service for overnight letters to reduce the manpower demands and operating expenses of its pickup service. A $3 discount was offered to customers who dropped off letters at retail centers or drop boxes. The discount resulted in an $11 charge, compared to the U.S. Postal Service's $10.75 charge for Express Mail. Federal Express claimed that, for an extra 25 cents, it was faster, more reliable, and reached more areas.

In seventeen different markets, Federal Express ran a $3-million campaign directly attacking the Postal Service's Express Mail. The private carrier used half-page newspaper ads and radio spots to inform customers about its drop-off discount. The newspaper ads pictured Express Mail and Federal Express packages and asked the question, "If money were no object, which would you use?" "Well it isn't," answered a fast-following ad that gave a comparison of the two prices offered. The radio spots emphasized the claim that Federal Express has faster delivery than Express Mail.

United Parcel Service joined the competition in the overnight package delivery business in 1982. More recently, the company introduced its overnight letter service. Filling customers' needs for reliable and low-cost letter service was a major reason for the move into the overnight delivery market.

403

UPS spent over $10 million in a recent year for TV commercials during prime time, late news, and sports programs. The TV commercials also were shown on cable networks. The ads stressed both the efficiency of UPS's operations and the shortcomings of its competitors'. The UPS motto "We run the tightest ship in the shipping business" was a predominant theme. One commercial was narrated by UPS founder Jim Casey, who shared his "Hustle where others dawdle" philosophy; another commercial promoted the overnight letter service offered by UPS.

The new advertising campaign was directed mainly at present UPS users. The company wanted to inform customers that UPS has more to offer than the traditional package delivery service. The new print ads carried in Time, Forbes, *and transportation trade magazines promoted the full spectrum of UPS services, including Next Day Air, 2nd Day Air, automatic daily pickups, and 48-state service.*

UPS and Federal Express also recently ventured into the international air-courier market, where four companies are already entrenched. In its advertising campaign, Federal Express claimed that, because it used its own air fleet, it was more efficient than services like UPS, which used commercial airlines. UPS ads, on the other hand, said that the company's longer track record in delivering items overseas, from Europe to the United States and within Europe itself, gave it a competitive edge over rival couriers.[1]

Often credited with being the savior of certain companies and the executioner of others, advertising is associated with numerous "success stories" like those of Federal Express and United Parcel Service and a multitude of less visible "failure stories." This chapter explores many dimensions of advertising and publicity. Our discussion initially focuses on how advertising is used; then we consider the major steps involved in developing an advertising campaign. Next, we describe who is responsible for developing advertising campaigns. As we analyze publicity, we compare its characteristics with those of advertising and explore the different forms it may take. Then we consider how publicity is used and what is required for an effective publicity program. Finally, we discuss negative publicity and some of the problems associated with the use of publicity.

The Nature of Advertising

Advertising permeates our daily lives. At times people view it positively; at other times they curse it. Some of it informs, persuades, or entertains us; some of it bores, insults, or deceives us.

1. "Federal Express Ads Ask 'Spare a Quarter?'" *Advertising Age,* Sept. 9, 1985, p. 6; "UPS Delivers Overnight Pitch," *Advertising Age,* Sept. 9, 1985, p. 128; and "Federal, UPS Take Battle to Foreign Soil," *Advertising Age,* Oct. 14, 1985. All by Brian Moran.

As defined in Chapter 13, **advertising** is a paid form of nonpersonal communication that is transmitted through mass media such as television, radio, newspapers, magazines, direct mail, mass transit vehicles, and outdoor displays. An organization can use advertising to reach a variety of audiences ranging from small, precise groups such as the paper weight collectors of Wyoming to extremely large audiences such as all gumchewers in the United States.

When they think of major advertisers, most people immediately mention business organizations. However, many types of organizations—including governments, churches, universities, civic groups, and charitable organizations—take advantage of advertising. In 1984, for example, the federal government was the twenty-sixth largest advertiser in the country, spending over $287 million.[2] So even though we analyze advertising in the context of business organizations here, remember that much of what we say applies to all types of organizations.

Marketers sometimes give advertising more credit than it deserves. This attitude causes them to use advertising when they should not. There are certain conditions under which advertising can work effectively for an organization. The questions in Table 14.1 raise some general points that a marketer should consider when trying to decide whether advertising could be an effective ingredient in a product's promotion mix. However, this list is certainly not all-inclusive. Numerous factors enter into deciding whether and how much advertising should be used.

The Uses of Advertising

Organizations employ advertising in a variety of ways and for many reasons. This section describes some of the ways that individuals and organizations use advertising.

To Promote Products and Organizations

Advertising is used to promote a great many things. For example, it is used to promote goods, services, images, issues, ideas, and people. Depending on what is being promoted, advertising can be classified as either institutional advertising or product advertising. **Institutional advertising** promotes organizational images, ideas, or political issues. **Product advertising** promotes goods and services. It is used by business, government, and private nonbusiness organizations to promote the uses, features, images, and benefits of their goods and services.

To Stimulate Primary and Selective Demand

Product advertising often serves to stimulate demand directly. When a specific firm is the first to introduce a revolutionary innovation, the marketer tries to stimulate primary demand through pioneer advertising. Primary demand is demand for the product category, not for a specific brand. **Pioneer advertising** informs people about a product: what it is, what it does, how it can be used, and where it can be purchased. Since pioneer advertising is used in the

---

2. "100 Leading National Advertisers by Rank," *Advertising Age,* Sept. 26, 1985, p. 1.

Table 14.1 *Some issues to consider when deciding whether to use advertising*

1. Does the product possess unique, important features?

Although homogeneous products such as cigarettes, gasoline, and beer have been advertised successfully, they usually require considerably more effort and expense than other products. On the other hand, products that are differentiated on physical, rather than psychological, dimensions are much easier to advertise. Even so, "being different" is rarely enough. The advertisability of product features is enhanced when buyers believe that those unique features are important and useful.

2. Are "hidden qualities" important to buyers?

If by viewing, feeling, tasting, or smelling the product buyers can learn all there is to know about the product and its benefits, advertising will have less chance of increasing demand. Conversely, if not all product benefits are apparent to consumers on inspection and use of the product, advertising has more of a story to tell, and the probability that it can be profitably employed increases. The "hidden quality" of vitamin C in oranges once helped to explain why Sunkist oranges could be advertised effectively while the advertising of lettuce has been a failure.

3. Is the general demand trend for the product favorable?

If the generic product category is experiencing a long-term decline, it is less likely that advertising can be used successfully for a particular brand within the category.

4. Is the market potential for the product adequate?

Advertising can be effective only when there are sufficient actual or prospective users of the brand in the target market.

5. Is the competitive environment favorable?

The size and marketing strength of competitors and their brand shares and loyalty will greatly affect the possible success of an advertising campaign. For example, a marketing effort to compete successfully against Kodak film, Morton salt, or Campbell's soups would demand much more than simply advertising.

6. Are general economic conditions favorable for marketing the product?

The effects of an advertising program and the sale of all products are influenced by the overall state of the economy and by specific business conditions. For example, it is much easier to advertise and sell luxury leisure products (stereos, sailboats, recreation vehicles) when disposable income is high.

7. Is the organization able and willing to spend the money required to launch an advertising campaign?

As a general rule, if the organization is unable or unwilling to undertake an advertising expenditure that, as a percentage of the total amount spent in the product category, is at least equal to the market share it desires, advertising is less likely to be effective.

8. Does the firm possess sufficient marketing expertise to market the product?

The successful marketing of any product involves a complex mixture of product and buyer research, product development, packaging, pricing, financial management, promotion, and distribution. Weakness in any area of marketing is an obstacle to the successful use of advertising.

Source: Adapted from Charles H. Patti, "Evaluating the Role of Advertising," *Journal of Advertising*, Fall 1977, pp. 32–33. Used by permission.

introductory stage of the product life cycle when there are no competitive brands, it neither emphasizes the brand name nor compares brands. The first company to introduce the home video recorder, for instance, initially tried to stimulate primary demand by emphasizing the benefits of the product in general rather than the benefits of its brand. Product advertising is also sometimes

Figure 14.2

Advertisement to stimu-
late primary demand
(Source: Beef Industry
Council)

employed to stimulate primary demand for an established product. At times, an industry trade group, rather than a single firm, sponsors advertisements to stimulate primary demand. In Figure 14.2, for example, the Beef Industry Council is trying to stimulate primary demand for beef.

An advertiser uses competitive advertising to build selective demand, which is demand for a specific brand. **Competitive advertising** points out a brand's uses, features, and advantages that benefit consumers and that may not be available in competing brands. Because a large number of producers currently sell color televisions, RCA promotes the features and advantages of RCA color television sets to encourage customers to select that specific brand. There is no longer any need to promote the advantages of color television itself.

An increasingly popular form of competitive advertising is **comparative adver-tising,** which compares two or more specified brands on the basis of one or more product attributes. Both the sponsored brand and one or more competitive brands are identified in a comparative advertisement. This type of advertising is prevalent among manufacturers of toothpastes, deodorants, tires, automobiles, and a multitude of other products (see Figure 14.3).

To Offset Competitors' Advertising

When marketers advertise to offset or lessen the effects of a competitor's promotional program, they are using **defensive advertising.** Although defensive advertising does not necessarily increase a company's sales or market share, it may prevent a loss in sales or market share. For example, Procter & Gamble,

Figure 14.3

A comparative adver-
tisement (Source: ©
1985 Hollywood Foods)

manufacturer of Crest toothpaste, tried to limit the impact of Lever Brothers'
direct-mail campaign for Aim toothpaste. Lever Brothers sent free samples to
households in many parts of the United States. Procter & Gamble countered
with television commercials emphasizing that there was no need even to try
the free sample of the new fluoride toothpaste since Crest was so effective.
Procter & Gamble used defensive advertising in an attempt to hold on to its
sizable share of the toothpaste market. Defensive advertising is employed most
often by firms in extremely competitive consumer product markets.

**To Make
Salespersons
More Effective**

Business organizations that allot a significant proportion of their promotional
effort to personal selling often use advertising to improve the effectiveness of
sales personnel. Advertising that is created specifically to support personal
selling activities tries to presell buyers by informing them about a product's
uses, features, and benefits and by encouraging them to contact local dealers
or sales representatives. This form of advertising helps salespeople to find good
sales prospects. Sometimes advertisements indicate that a person can get more
information (or even a free gift) by sending a letter or a completed information
blank to a certain address. Salespeople generally view the individuals who

send for more information as prospective buyers and contact them. Advertising is often designed to support personal selling efforts for industrial products, insurance, and consumer durables such as automobiles and major household appliances.

To Increase the Uses of a Product

The absolute demand for any product is limited. Persons in a market will consume only so much of a particular product. Because of the absolute limit on demand and because of competitive conditions, marketers can increase sales of a specific product in a defined geographic market only to a certain point. To increase sales beyond this point, they must either enlarge the geographic market and sell to more people or develop and promote a larger number of uses for the product. If a firm's advertising convinces buyers to use its products in more ways, then the sales of its products increase. For years, General Foods has advertised recipes that call for Jell-O brand products. Arm & Hammer has increased demand for its baking soda by promoting additional uses. When promoting new uses, an advertiser attempts to increase the demand for its own brand without increasing the demand for competing brands.

To Remind and Reinforce Customers

Marketers sometimes use **reminder advertising** to let consumers know that an established brand is still around and that it has certain uses, characteristics, and benefits. **Reinforcement advertising** tries to assure current users that they have made the right choice and tells them how to get the most satisfaction from the product. Both reminder and reinforcement advertising are used to prevent a loss in sales or market share.

To Reduce Sales Fluctuations

The demand for many products varies from one month to another because of such factors as climate, holidays, seasons, and customs. A business, however, cannot be operated at peak efficiency when sales fluctuate markedly. Changes in sales volume translate into changes in the production or inventory, personnel, and financial resources required. To the extent that marketers can generate sales during slow periods, they can smooth out the fluctuations. When advertising reduces fluctuations, a manager can use the firm's resources more efficiently.

Advertising is often designed to stimulate sales during sales slumps. For example, advertisements promoting price reductions of lawn-care equipment or air conditioners can increase sales during fall and winter months. On occasion, a business organization advertises that customers will get better service by coming in on certain days rather than others. For example, a firm in Texas advertised that customers could get better optical services Tuesdays through Fridays. During peak sales periods a marketer may refrain from advertising to prevent overstimulation of sales to the point that the firm cannot handle all the demand.

A firm's use of advertising depends on the firm's objectives and resources and on environmental forces. The degree to which advertising accomplishes the marketer's goals depends in large part on the advertising campaign.

Figure 14.4

General steps for developing and implementing an advertising campaign

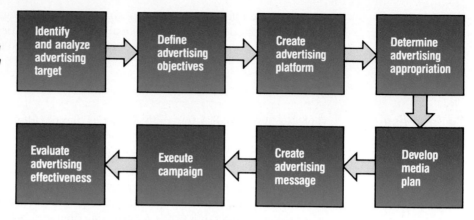

Developing an Advertising Campaign

Several steps are required to develop an advertising campaign. The number of steps and the exact order in which they are carried out may vary according to an organization's resources, the nature of its product, and the types of audiences to be reached. However, as indicated in Figure 14.4, the major steps in the creation of an advertising campaign are (1) identifying and analyzing the advertising target, (2) defining the advertising objectives, (3) creating the advertising platform, (4) determining the advertising appropriation, (5) developing the media plan, (6) creating the advertising message, (7) executing the campaign, and (8) evaluating the effectiveness of the advertising. These general guidelines for developing an advertising campaign are appropriate for all types of organizations.

Identifying and Analyzing the Advertising Target

A basic question that marketers must answer as they begin to develop an advertising campaign is: "Whom are we trying to reach with our message?" The **advertising target** is the group of people toward which advertisements are aimed. Identifying and analyzing the advertising target is critical because the other steps in developing the campaign are based on this. The advertising target often includes everyone in a firm's target market. Marketers may, however, seize some opportunities to slant a campaign at only a portion of the target market. For example, the maker of a brand of hair-care products may define the target market for a shampoo as being females, 12–49 years old. The company may nonetheless wish to aim a specific campaign at women in the 35–49 age range. For this campaign, the firm's advertising target would be women 35–49 years old, rather than females in the 12–49 age group.

Advertisers analyze advertising targets to develop an information base for a campaign. Information that is commonly needed includes the location and geographic distribution of the target group; the distribution of age, income, race, sex, and education; and consumer attitudes regarding the purchase and use both of the advertiser's products and of competing products. The exact kinds of information that an organization will find useful depend on the type of product being advertised, the characteristics of the advertising target, and the type and amount of competition.

Application

Chevrolet's Advertisements Focus More on Women

Chevrolet is decreasing spending on television commercials that air during sports programs and is increasing advertising efforts directed toward female audiences. Chevy is making this switch because women are making higher salaries and buying more cars than in the past. Besides TV, Chevy uses women's magazines, direct mail, and direct response print ads to reach this target market. Chevy also has organized a creative task force and a women's marketing committee to concentrate on the campaign.

In the area of network television, Chevy has planned to test production of its own daytime TV show on ABC. The company has shifted millions of advertising dollars from sports programs and has advertised more during popular prime-time programs. In 1985 Chevy dropped out of the Super Bowl; in 1986 it discontinued National Football League coverage and cut back advertising during college football games.

An eight-page insert appeared in a recent issue of *Cosmopolitan* magazine. The insert included an editorial section, a credit application from General Motors Acceptance Corporation, and print ads targeted at women. The editorial section highlighted different sports, and the ads pictured beautiful models in various sportswear. The magazine and television ads were designed to create a lifestyle image rather than a hard product sell.

Chevy is trying to appeal to career women not only by advertising in magazines they read, but also by offering a nationwide series of career conferences. Well-known women from several career fields were recruited to speak at the conferences. Each of the ten 2-day conferences was expected to draw six to ten thousand executive women. Promotion for the conferences was handled by direct-mail, print, and broadcast advertising.

Chevy's new commitment to the women's market seems to be paying off. Four out of the top ten cars sold to women last year were Chevrolet models— Cavalier, Celebrity, Camaro, and Chevette. According to Chevy's preliminary data, its new car models (Sprint, Spectrum, Nova, and Astro) are attracting more women buyers than ever before. (*Source: Verne Day and Paul L. Edwards, "Chevy Woos Women," Advertising Age, Sept. 9, 1985, pp. 1, 130. Reprinted from* Advertising Age, *Sept. 9, 1985. Copyright © 1985 Crain Communications Inc.*)

Generally, the more that advertisers know about the advertising target, the more able they are to develop an effective advertising campaign. When the advertising target is not precisely identified and properly analyzed, the campaign has less chance of success. (The application on this page deals with how Chevrolet has changed its advertising to focus more on women.)

Defining the Advertising Objectives

The advertiser's next step is to consider what the firm hopes to accomplish with the campaign. Since advertising objectives guide campaign development, advertisers should define their objectives carefully to make certain that the campaign will accomplish what they desire. Advertising campaigns based on poorly defined objectives are seldom successful.

Advertising objectives should be stated in clear, precise, and measurable terms. Precision and measurability allow advertisers to evaluate advertising success—to judge whether or how well the objectives have been accomplished after the campaign is completed. Imagine that an advertiser sets the following vague objective: "The objective of our campaign is to increase sales." If this advertiser's sales increase by one dollar, has the objective been achieved? Without a reference point, no one knows.

Advertising objectives should contain benchmarks giving the current condition or position of the firm. They also should indicate how far and in what direction an advertiser wishes to move from these benchmarks. In the above example, the advertiser should state the current sales level (the benchmark) and the amount of sales increase that is sought through advertising. Assuming that average monthly sales are $450,000, this advertiser might set the following objective: "Our primary advertising objective is to increase average monthly sales from $450,000 to $540,000."

Although this example may appear to be precise and clear, it is not. An advertising objective also should specify the time allotted for its achievement. By placing an objective into a time frame, advertisers know exactly how long they have to accomplish their objective. They also know when they should begin to evaluate the effectiveness of the campaign. To make our objective specific as to time, the advertiser could state, "Our primary advertising objective is to increase average monthly sales from $450,000 to $540,000 within twelve months."

Advertising objectives usually are stated in terms of either sales or communication. When an advertiser defines objectives in terms of sales, the objectives focus on raising absolute dollar sales, increasing sales by a certain percentage, or increasing the firm's market share.

Even though the long-run goal of an advertiser is to increase sales, not all campaigns are designed to produce immediate sales. Some campaigns are aimed at increasing product or brand awareness, at making consumers' attitudes more favorable, or at increasing consumers' knowledge of a product's features. These objectives are stated in terms of communication. When Apple, for example, introduced home computers, its initial campaign did not focus on sales, but instead created brand awareness and educated consumers about the features and uses of home computers. A specific communication objective might be to increase product feature awareness from 0 to 40 percent of the target market in the first six months.

Creating the Advertising Platform

Before launching a political campaign, party leaders meet and develop a political platform. The platform states the major issues on which the party will base its campaign. Like a political platform, an **advertising platform** consists of the basic issues or selling points that an advertiser wishes to include in the advertising campaign. For example, a motorcycle producer might wish to include economy, speed, ease of handling, and accessories in its advertising platform. A single advertisement in an advertising campaign may contain one or several issues in the platform. Although the platform contains the basic issues, it does not indicate how they should be presented.

A marketer's advertising platform should consist of issues that are important to consumers. One of the best ways to determine what those issues are is to survey consumers to learn what they consider most important in the selection and use of the product involved. The selling features must not only be important to consumers; if possible, they should also be features that competitive products do not have. The safety of their money is important to bank customers, yet they believe that virtually all banks are equally safe. Thus, the advertising platform for a specific bank should not emphasize safety. In this case, the marketer should look for other selling features that are important to bank customers and that are not available at competing banks.

Research—although it is the most effective method for determining the issues of an advertising platform—is expensive. As a result, the advertising platform is most commonly based on the opinions of personnel within the firm and of individuals in the advertising agency, if an agency is used. This trial-and-error approach generally leads to some successes and some failures.

Because the advertising platform provides a base on which to build the message, marketers should analyze this stage carefully. A campaign can be perfect in terms of the selection and analysis of its advertising target, the statement of its objectives, its media strategy, and the form of its message. But the campaign will still fail miserably if the advertisements communicate information that consumers do not consider important when they select and use the product.

Determining the Advertising Appropriation

The **advertising appropriation** is the total amount of money that a marketer allocates for advertising for a specific time period. It is hard to decide how much to spend on advertising for a month, three months, a year, or several years, because there is no way to measure what the precise effects of spending a certain amount of money on advertising will be.

Many factors affect a firm's decision about how much to appropriate for advertising. The geographic size of the market and the distribution of buyers within the market have a great bearing on this decision. As shown in Table 14.2, both the type of product advertised and a firm's sales volume relative to competitors' sales volumes also play a part in determining what proportion of a firm's revenue goes for advertising. Advertising appropriations for industrial products are usually quite small relative to the sales of the products. Consumer convenience items such as soft drinks, tobacco, soaps, drugs, and cosmetics generally have large advertising appropriations.

Of the many techniques used to determine the advertising appropriation, one of the most logical is the **objective and task approach.** Using this approach, marketers initially determine the objectives that a campaign is to achieve and then attempt to list the tasks required to accomplish them. Once the tasks have been identified, their costs are added to arrive at the amount of the total appropriation. This approach has one main problem: marketers usually find it hard to estimate the level of effort needed to achieve certain objectives. A coffee marketer, for example, might find it extremely difficult to determine how much to increase national television advertising to raise a brand's market share from 8 to 12 percent. Because of this problem, the objective and task approach is not used widely by advertisers.

A more widely used method is the **percent of sales approach.** To use this method, marketers simply multiply a firm's past sales, forecasted sales, or a combination of the two by a standard percentage that is based on both what the firm traditionally spends on advertising and what the industry averages. For example, from the data in Table 14.2 and from experience, a large food processing firm might determine its total advertising appropriation by multiplying the past year's sales by 6.5 percent (the average for the seventeen food processors shown in Table 14.2). This approach has one major disadvantage. It is based

Table 14.2 *Sales volume and advertising expenditures for the top 100 leading national advertisers (in millions of dollars)*

Primary Business	Rank	Company	Advertising Expenditures	Sales	Advertising as % of Sales
Airlines	59	UAL Inc.	$136,700	$ 6,967,599	2.0
	72	AMR Corp.	110,800	5,353,721	2.1
	95	Delta Air Lines	66,900	4,684,000	1.4
	96	Trans World Airlines	66,200	2,049,361	3.2
	99	Eastern Airlines	60,800	4,363,898	1.4
Automotive	2	General Motors Corp.	763,800	69,355,600	1.1
	8	Ford Motor Co.	559,400	36,788,000	1.5
	23	Chrysler Corp.	317,400	17,239,700	1.8
	47	Nissan Motor Corp.	164,200	N/A	N/A
	57	Toyota Motor Sales Co.	137,900	N/A	N/A
	60	American Honda Motor Co.	134,700	N/A	N/A
	68	American Motors Corp.	120,500	4,215,191	2.9
	75	Volkswagen of America	103,000	N/A	N/A
	92	Mazda Motor Corp.	71,797	N/A	N/A
	97	Goodyear Tire & Rubber Co.	64,700	7,091,500	0.9
Chemicals and petroleum	27	American Cyanamid	284,410	2,686,959	10.6
	42	Mobil Corp.	172,500	25,574,000	0.7
	78	Union Carbide Corp.	93,000	6,766,000	1.4
	79	E.I. du Pont de Nemours	91,000	24,486,000	0.4
Electronics and office equipment	18	International Business Machines	376,000	27,371,000	1.4
	24	Eastman Kodak Co.	301,000	7,118,000	4.2
	37	General Electric	202,400	25,968,000	0.8
	38	Tandy Corp.	190,000	2,344,527	8.1
	64	Xerox Corp.	127,583	5,584,800	2.3
	76	Canon Inc.	100,000	1,260,000	7.9
	77	Apple Computer	100,000	1,187,839	8.4
Entertainment and communications	33	RCA Corp.	239,400	9,164,000	2.6
	40	Warner Communications	181,749	1,726,784	10.5
	41	CBS Inc.	179,800	4,295,600	4.2
	50	Gulf & Western Industries	149,249	4,867,000	3.1
	61	Time Inc.	133,900	3,067,353	4.4
	89	MCA Inc.	77,058	1,381,170	5.6
	94	American Broadcasting Cos.	68,900	3,708,000	1.9

on the incorrect assumption that sales create advertising, rather than that advertising creates sales. A marketer who uses this approach and experiences declining sales will reduce the amount spent on advertising. The reduction may, in fact, cause a further decline in sales. Although illogical, this technique has widespread acceptance because it is easy to use and is less disruptive competitively. It stabilizes a firm's market share within an industry.

Marketers usually are concerned about the type and intensity of their competitors' advertising. Another way to arrive at the advertising appropriation is the **competition-matching approach.** Marketers who follow this approach try to match their major competitors' appropriations in terms of absolute dollars or

Table 14.2 (continued)

Primary Business	Rank	Company	Advertising Expenditures	Sales	Advertising as % of Sales
Food	4	Beatrice Cos.	680,000	9,832,000	6.9
	10	McDonald's Corp.	480,000	8,071,000	6.0
	12	General Foods Corp.	450,000	6,876,040	6.5
	14	Ralston Purina Co.	428,600	4,980,100	8.6
	21	Nabisco Brands	334,977	3,950,400	8.5
	22	Pillsbury Co.	318,473	4,344,500	7.3
	28	General Mills	283,400	5,094,500	5.6
	29	Dart & Kraft	269,200	7,129,000	3.8
	32	Sara Lee Corp.	258,362	6,631,000	3.9
	34	H.J. Heinz Co.	227,286	2,661,700	8.5
	35	Kellogg Co.	208,800	1,789,600	11.7
	39	Nestlé Enterprises	186,848	5,100,000	3.7
	49	Quaker Oats Co.	161,300	2,586,000	6.2
	53	Campbell Soup Co.	142,000	3,345,000	4.3
	65	IC Industries	127,289	3,874,900	3.3
	66	CPC International	123,500	1,815,300	6.8
	80	Wendy's International	90,833	944,768	9.6
Gum and candy	54	Mars Inc.	139,282	N/A	N/A
	88	Hershey Foods Corp.	79,200	1,892,506	4.2
	93	Wm. Wrigley Jr. Co.	70,400	417,206	16.9
Miscellaneous	26	U.S. Government	287,807	N/A	N/A
	43	American Express Co.	172,100	10,449,000	1.6
	86	Greyhound Corp.	80,200	2,757,000	2.9
	87	Kimberly-Clark Co.	80,000	2,655,400	3.0
Pharmaceuticals	13	Warner-Lambert Co.	440,000	1,910,000	23.0
	16	American Home Products	412,000	3,435,900	12.0
	25	Johnson & Johnson	300,000	3,735,900	8.0
	31	Bristol-Myers Co.	258,440	3,148,800	8.2
	45	Sterling Drug Co.	166,600	1,187,897	14.0
	48	Richardson-Vicks	163,500	N/A	N/A
	52	Schering-Plough Corp.	144,300	1,075,700	13.4
	74	Bayer AG	105,296	3,638,700	2.9
	83	Pfizer Inc.	86,400	2,150,200	4.0
Retail	3	Sears, Roebuck & Co.	746,937	35,885,000	2.1
	9	K mart Corp.	554,400	20,329,000	2.7

(continued next page)

to allocate the same percentage of sales for advertising as competitors do. Although a wise marketer should be cognizant of what competitors spend on advertising, this technique should not be used by itself because a firm's competitors probably have different advertising objectives and different resources available for advertising.

At times, marketers use the **arbitrary approach.** In using this method, a high-level executive in the firm states how much can be spent on advertising for a certain time period. The arbitrary approach often leads to underspending or overspending. Although it is not a scientific budgeting technique, it is expedient.

Table 14.2 (continued)

Primary Business	Rank	Company	Advertising Expenditures	Sales	Advertising as % of Sales
	11	J.C. Penney Co.	460,000	12,963,000	3.5
	67	Levi Strauss & Co.	122,000	1,912,417	6.4
	98	Cotter & Co.	63,900	1,653,199	3.9
Soaps and cleaners	1	Procter & Gamble Co.	872,000	10,240,000	8.5
	17	Unilever U.S.	395,700	3,606,000	11.0
	30	Colgate-Palmolive Co.	258,731	2,342,678	11.0
	73	Clorox Co.	109,600	N/A	N/A
	81	S.C. Johnson & Son	90,000	N/A	N/A
Soft drinks	15	PepsiCo Inc.	428,172	6,706,600	6.4
	20	Coca-Cola Co.	343,300	4,566,400	7.5
Telephone	7	American Telephone & Telegraph	563,200	N/A	N/A
	44	ITT Corp.	168,000	6,685,000	2.5
	82	GTE Corp.	89,775	13,421,882	0.7
Tobacco	5	R.J. Reynolds Industries	678,176	10,216,000	6.6
	6	Philip Morris Inc.	570,435	10,034,000	5.7
	56	Loews Corp.	137,900	5,603,354	2.5
	62	American Brands	133,000	3,064,900	4.3
	71	Batus Inc.	113,400	6,211,078	1.8
	90	Grand Metropolitan p.l.c.	76,200	2,040,000	3.7
Toiletries and cosmetics	36	Revlon Inc.	205,000	1,728,914	11.9
	46	Gillette Co.	165,673	1,102,400	15.0
	51	Chesebrough-Pond's	145,500	1,479,521	9.8
	58	Beecham Group p.l.c.	137,000	1,023,500	13.4
	69	Cosmair Inc.	119,500	N/A	N/A
	91	Noxell Corp.	74,200	N/A	N/A
Toys	63	Mattel Inc.	132,892	697,123	19.1
	85	Hasbro Inc.	83,691	560,787	14.9
Wine, beer, and liquor	19	Anheuser-Busch Cos.	364,401	6,501,200	5.6
	55	Adolph Coors Co.	138,700	1,262,903	11.0
	70	Jos E. Seagram & Sons	115,827	1,752,000	6.6
	84	Stroh Brewery Co.	85,200	1,600,000	5.3
	100	Van Munching & Co.	58,970	350,000	16.9
		Totals	22,504,512	508,670,720	4.4

Source: Adapted with permission from "100 Leading National Advertisers with U.S. Sales," *Advertising Age*, Sept. 26, 1985, p. 16. Reprinted with permission from *Advertising Age*, Sept. 26, 1985. Copyright © 1985 by Crain Communications Inc.

Establishing the advertising appropriation is critically important. If it is set too low, the campaign cannot achieve its full potential in terms of stimulating demand. When too much money is appropriated for advertising, overspending occurs, and financial resources are wasted.

Developing the Media Plan

As shown in Table 14.3, advertisers spend tremendous amounts of money on advertising media. These amounts have grown rapidly during the last forty years. To derive the maximum results from media expenditures, a marketer

Table 14.3 *Estimated annual advertising media expenditures for selected years (in millions of dollars)[a]*

Medium	1940 $	1940 %	1960 $	1960 %	1980 $	1980 %
Newspapers	815	38.6	3,681	30.8	15,615	28.5
Magazines	186	8.8	909	7.6	3,225	5.9
Farm publications	19	0.9	66	0.6	135	0.2
Television			1,627	13.6	11,330	20.7
Radio	215	10.2	693	5.8	3,690	6.7
Direct mail	334	15.8	1,830	15.3	7,655	14.0
Business papers	76	3.6	609	5.0	1,695	3.2
Outdoor	45	2.2	203	1.7	610	1.1
Miscellaneous	420	19.9	2,342	19.6	10,795	19.7
National total	1,190	56.3	7,305	61.0	30,435	55.6
Local total	920	43.7	4,655	39.0	24,315	44.4
Grand total	2,110		11,960		54,750	

[a]Figures not adjusted for inflation.
Source: Adapted from "Estimated Annual U.S. Ad Expenditures: 1935–1977," *Advertising Age*, Sept. 4, 1978, pp. 32–33; and from Robert J. Coen, "Ad Growth in 1981: Sluggish, Then Bullish," *Advertising Age*, Jan. 5, 1981, pp. 10, 56. Reprinted with permission from the September 1978 and January 1981 issues of *Advertising Age*. Copyright 1978, 1981 by Crain Communications, Inc.

must develop an effective media plan. A **media plan** sets forth the exact media vehicles to be used (specific magazines, television stations, newspapers, and so forth) and the dates and times that the advertisements will appear. To formulate a media plan, the planner selects the media for a campaign and draws up a time schedule for each medium. The media planner's primary goal is to reach the largest number of persons in the advertising target per dollar spent on media.

Media planners begin by making rather broad decisions; eventually, however, they must make very specific choices. A planner first must decide which kinds of media to use. The major kinds are radio, television, newspapers, magazines, direct mail, outdoor displays, and mass transit vehicles. After making the general media decision, the planner selects specific subclasses within each medium. A toothpaste marketer, for example, might decide to use television and magazines. The marketer then must consider whether to use children's, women's daytime, family, and/or late-night adult television programming and whether to use men's, women's, teen-agers', children's, and/or general-audience magazines. Finally, the planner must select the specific media vehicles. Having chosen family television programs and women's magazines, the toothpaste marketer must select the exact television programs and stations as well as the specific women's magazines to be used.

Media planners take many factors into account as they devise a media plan. They analyze the location and demographic characteristics of people in the advertising target, as the various media appeal to particular demographic groups in particular locations. For example, there are radio stations especially for teenagers, magazines for men in the 18–34 age group, and television programs aimed at adults. Media planners also should consider the sizes and types of

Figure 14.5 *Comparison of black and white and color advertisements (Source: Reprinted with permission of Campbell Soup Company)*

audiences reached by specific media. Several data services collect and periodically publish information about the circulations and audiences of various media.

The cost of media is an important but troublesome consideration. Planners try to obtain the best coverage possible for each dollar spent. Yet there is no accurate way of comparing the cost and impact of a television commercial with the cost and impact of a newspaper advertisement.

The content of the message sometimes affects the choice of media. Print media can be used more effectively than broadcast media to present many issues or numerous details. If an advertiser wants to promote beautiful colors, patterns, or textures, then media that offer high-quality color reproduction— magazines or television—should be used instead of newspapers. For example, food can look extremely appetizing and delicious in a full-color magazine advertisement, but it might look far less so in black and white. Compare the black and white and color versions of the advertisement in Figure 14.5.

The information in Table 14.3 indicates that media are used quite differently from one another and that the pattern of media usage has changed over the years. For example, the proportion of total media dollars spent on magazines has declined slowly but steadily since 1940. This variation in usage arises from the characteristics, advantages, and disadvantages (like the ones shown in Table 14.4) of the major mass media used for advertising. Given the variety of vehicles within each medium, media planners must deal with a vast number of alternatives; and the multitude of factors that affect media rates obviously add to the complexity of media planning. A **cost comparison indicator** allows an advertiser to compare the costs of several vehicles within a specific medium (such as two radio stations) in terms of the number of persons reached by each vehicle. For example, the "milline rate" is the cost comparison indicator for newspapers; it shows the cost of exposing a million persons to a space equal to one agate line.[3] A Houston advertiser that can afford to use only one local newspaper probably will compare the milline rates of the *Houston Post* and the *Houston Chronicle* to determine whether there are cost differences relative to their circulations.

The development of the media plan is another crucial step in the creation of an advertising campaign. The effectiveness of the plan determines the number of people in the advertising target who are exposed to the message. It also determines, to some degree, the effects of the message on those individuals. Media planning is a complex task that requires thorough analysis of the advertising target.

Creating the Advertising Message

The basic content and form of an advertising message are a function of several factors. The product's features, uses, and benefits affect the message's content. Characteristics of the people in the advertising target—their sex, age, education, race, income, occupation, and other attributes—influence both the content and form. When the American Cancer Society, for example, creates a message that informs fifth- and sixth-graders about smoking hazards, that message differs radically from messages aimed at adults. To communicate effectively, an advertiser must use words, symbols, and illustrations that are meaningful, familiar, and attractive to those persons who make up the advertising target.

The objectives and platform of an advertising campaign affect the content and form of its messages. If a firm's advertising objectives involve large sales increases, for example, the message demands hard-hitting, high-impact language and symbols. When campaign objectives aim at increasing brand awareness, the message may use much repetition of the brand name and words and illustrations associated with it. The advertising platform consists of the basic issues or selling features to be stressed in the campaign; it is the foundation on which campaign messages are built. A bank, for example, might build an advertising campaign on a platform of such features as convenient locations, "no-charge" checking accounts, twenty-four-hour service, and friendly personnel.

The choice of media obviously influences the content and form of the message. Effective outdoor displays and short broadcast spot announcements require concise, simple messages. Magazine and newspaper advertisements can include much detail and long explanations. Because several different kinds of media offer geographic selectivity, a precise message content can be tailored to a particular geographic section of the advertising target. Some magazine publishers produce **regional issues.** For a particular issue, the advertisements and editorial content of copies appearing in one geographic area differ from

---

3. An agate line is one column wide and the height of the smallest type normally used in classified newspaper advertisements. There are fourteen agate lines in one column inch.

Table 14.4 Characteristics, advantages, and disadvantages of major advertising media

Medium	Types	Unit of Sale	Factors Affecting Rates	Cost Comparison Indicator	Advantages	Disadvantages
Newspaper	Morning Evening Sunday Sunday supplement Weekly Special	Agate lines Column inches Counted words Printed lines	Volume and frequency discounts Number of colors Position charges for preferred and guaranteed positions Circulation level	Milline rate = cost per agate line × 1,000,000 divided by circulation	Almost everyone reads a newspaper; purchased to be read; national geographic flexibility; short lead time; frequent publication; favorable for cooperative advertising; merchandising services	Not selective for socioeconomic groups; short life; limited reproduction capabilities; large ad volume limits exposure to any one ad
Magazine	Consumer Farm Business	Pages Partial pages Column inches	Circulation level Cost of publishing Type of audience Volume discounts Frequency discounts Size of advertisement Position of advertisement (covers) Number of colors Regional issues	Cost per thousand (CPM) = cost per page × 1,000 divided by circulation	Socioeconomic selectivity; good reproduction; long life; prestige; geographic selectivity when regional issues are available; read in leisurely manner	High absolute dollar cost; long lead time
Direct mail	Letters Catalogs Price lists Calendars Brochures Coupons Circulars Newsletters Postcards Booklets Broadsides Samplers	Not applicable	Cost of mailing lists Postage Production costs	Cost per contact	Little wasted circulation; highly selective; circulation controlled by advertiser; few distractions; personal; stimulates actions; use of novelty; relatively easy to measure performance; hidden from competitors	Expensive; no editorial matter to attract readers; considered junk mail by many; criticized as invasion of privacy

Table 14.4 (continued)

Medium	Types	Unit of Sale	Factors Affecting Rates	Cost Comparison Indicator	Advantages	Disadvantages
Radio	AM FM	Programs: sole sponsor, cosponsor, participative sponsor Spots: 5, 10, 20, 30, 60 seconds	Time of day Audience size Length of spot or program Volume and frequency discounts	Cost per thousand (CPM) = cost per minute × 1,000 divided by audience size	Highly mobile; low-cost broadcast medium; message can be quickly changed; can reach a large audience; geographic selectivity; socioeconomic selectivity	Provides only audio message; has lost prestige; short life of message; listeners' attention limited because of other activities while listening
Television	Network Local CATV	Programs: sole sponsor, cosponsor, participative sponsor Spots: 5, 10, 15, 30, 60 seconds	Time of day Length of program Length of spot Volume and frequency discounts Audience size	Cost per thousand (CPM) = cost per minute × 1,000 divided by audience size	Reaches large audience; low cost per exposure; uses audio and video; highly visible; high prestige; geographic and socioeconomic selectivity	High-dollar costs; highly perishable message; size of audience not guaranteed; amount of prime time limited
Inside transit	Buses Subways	Full, half, and quarter showings are sold on a monthly basis	Number of riders Multiple-month discounts Production costs Position	Cost per thousand riders	Low cost; "captive" audience; geographic selectivity	Does not reach many professional persons; does not secure quick results
Outside transit	Buses Taxicabs	Full, half, and quarter showings; space also rented on per-unit basis	Number of advertisements Position Size	Cost per thousand exposures	Low cost; geographic selectivity; reaches broad, diverse audience	Lacks socioeconomic selectivity; does not have high impact on readers
Outdoor	Papered posters Painted displays Spectaculars	Papered posters: sold on monthly basis in multiples called "showings" Painted displays and spectaculars: sold on per-unit basis	Length of time purchased Land rental Cost of production Intensity of traffic Frequency and continuity discounts Location	No standard indicator	Allows for repetition; low cost; message can be placed close to the point of sale; geographic selectivity; operable 24 hours a day	Message must be short and simple; no socioeconomic selectivity; seldom attracts readers' full attention; criticized for being traffic hazard and blight on countryside

Sources: Some of the information in this table is from S. Watson Dunn and Arnold M. Barban, *Advertising: Its Role in Modern Marketing,* 6th ed. (Hinsdale, Ill.: Dryden, 1986); and Anthony F. McGann and J. Thomas Russell, *Advertising Media* (Homewood, Ill.: Irwin, 1981).

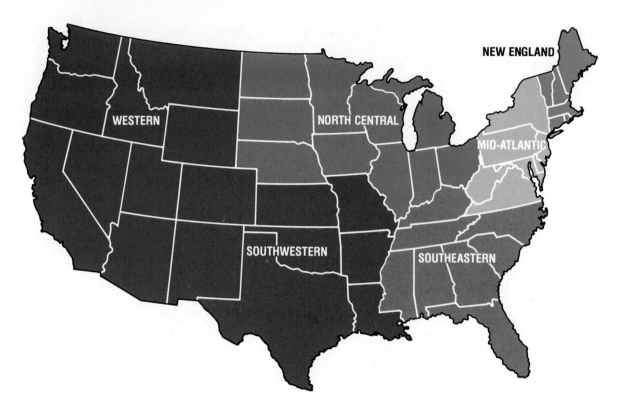

Figure 14.6 *Geographic divisions for* Playboy's *regional issues (Source: Reproduced by special permission of* Playboy *magazine; copyright © 1983 by* Playboy*)*

those appearing in other areas. As shown in Figure 14.6, *Playboy* publishes six regional issues. A clothing manufacturer that advertises in *Playboy* might decide to use one message in the western region and another in the rest of the nation. In addition, a company may choose to advertise in only a few regions. Such geographic selectivity allows a firm to use the same message in different regions at different times.

The basic components of a print advertising message are identified in Figure 14.7. The messages for most advertisements depend on the use of copy and artwork. Let us examine these two elements in more detail.

Copy

Copy is the verbal portion of an advertisement. It includes headlines, subheadlines, body copy, and the signature (see Figure 14.7). When preparing advertising copy, marketers attempt to move readers through a persuasive sequence called AIDA—attention, interest, desire, and action. Not all copy need be this extensive, however.

The headline is critical. It is often the only part of the copy that people read. It should attract readers' attention and create enough interest to make them want to read the body copy. The subheadline, if there is one, links the headline to the body copy. It sometimes aids in explaining the headline.

Body copy for most advertisements consists of an introductory statement or paragraph, several explanatory paragraphs, and a closing paragraph. Some

Figure 14.7

Basic components of a print advertisement (Source: Courtesy of American Medical International)

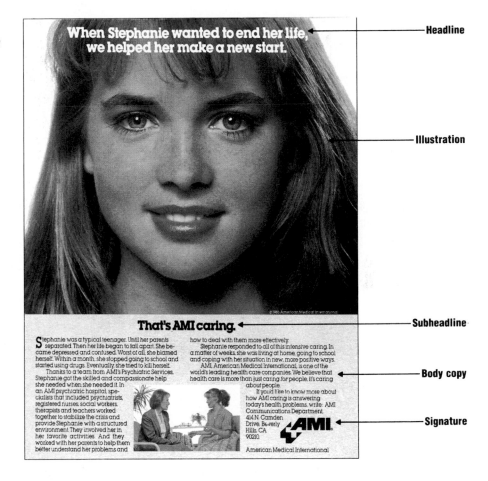

copywriters adopt a pattern or set of guidelines to develop body copy systematically: (1) identify a specific desire or problem of consumers, (2) suggest the good or service as the best way to satisfy that desire or solve that problem, (3) state the advantages and benefits of the product, (4) indicate why the advertised product is the best for the buyer's particular situation, (5) substantiate the claims and advantages, and (6) ask the buyer for action.[4]

The signature identifies the sponsor of the advertisement. It may contain several elements, including the firm's trademark, name, and address. The signature should be designed to be attractive, legible, distinctive, and easy to identify in a variety of sizes.

Since radio listeners often are mentally not fully "tuned in," radio copy should be informal and conversational to attract listeners' attention, resulting in greater impact. The radio message is highly perishable. Thus, radio copy should consist of short, familiar terms. Its length should not require a rate of speech exceeding approximately two and one-half words per second.

In television copy, the audio material must not overpower the visual material and vice versa. However, a television message should make optimal use of its

4. James E. Littlefield and C. A. Kirkpatrick, *Advertising: Mass Communication in Marketing* (Boston: Houghton Mifflin, 1970), p. 178.

DOYLE DANE BERNBACH ADVERTISING

RADIO • TELEVISION

client	HERSHEY CHOCOLATE CO.	air date	
product	KIT KAT	length	:30
		job no.	HSKK-55006
		code #	HUKK-5072
	AS RECORDED 8/22/85	title	"MOUNTAIN CLIMBER" Rev. 2

VIDEO	AUDIO
	(music throughout)
OPEN ON MAN CLIMBING UP MOUNTAIN. CAMERA ZOOMS IN FOR CU.	V/O: Only 3,000 feet to go.
CUT TO CU OF MOUNTAIN CLIMBER OPENING KIT KAT.	SFX: TEARING OF WRAPPER.
CUT TO CU OF TWO KIDS IN CLASS AS EXAM PAPERS ARE BEING HANDED OUT.	V/O: This exam should take you about 5 hours.
CUT TO XCU OF BOY OPENING KIT KAT.	SFX: TEARING OF WRAPPER.
CUT TO CU OF KIDS EATING KIT KAT.	ANNCR: When you get the urge for a delicious snack, have a Kit Kat.
CUT TO CU OF CHOCOLATE BEING POURED OVER KIT KAT WAFERS.	Light, crispy wafers with chocolatey cream smothered in rich, milk chocolate.
DISSOLVE TO KIT KAT WAFERS ON TOP OF WRAPPER.	Kit Kat's irresistible!
CUT TO ROAD SIGN SEEN FROM PASSENGER's VIEWPOINT. SIGN: NEXT FOOD STOP 400 MILES	
CUT TO CU OF WOMAN PASSENGER.	WOMAN: Food...400 miles off?
CUT TO XCU OF WOMAN OPENING KIT KAT.	SFX: TEARING OF WRAPPER.
CUT TO CU OF WOMAN EATING KIT KAT. CAMERA ZOOMS IN.	ANNCR: So when you get the urge... for a delicious snack,
CUT TO PRODUCT SHOT.	have a Kit Kat.
SUPER: The Irresistible Snack.	

visual portion. As illustrated in Figure 14.8, copy for a television commercial is initially written in parallel script form. The video is described in the left column and the audio in the right column. When the parallel script is approved, the copywriter and artist combine the copy with the visual material through use of a **storyboard** (see Figure 14.9), which depicts a series of miniature television screens to show the sequence of major scenes in the commercial. Beneath each screen is a description of the audio portion that is to be used with the video message shown. Technical personnel use the storyboard as a blueprint when they produce the commercial.

Artwork

Artwork consists of the illustration and layout of the advertisement (see Figure 14.7). Although **illustrations** are often photographs, they also can be drawings, graphs, charts, and tables. Illustrations are used to attract attention, to encourage

Figure 14.9 *Storyboard for a television commercial (Source: Doyle Dane Bernbach Advertising)*

the audience to read or listen to the copy, to communicate an idea quickly, or to communicate an idea that is difficult to put into words.[5] Advertisers use a variety of illustration techniques, which are identified and described in Table 14.5.

The **layout** of an advertisement is the physical arrangement of the illustration, headline, subheadline, body copy, and signature. The arrangement of these parts in Figure 14.8 is only one possible layout. These same elements could be positioned in many ways. The final layout is the end result of several stages of layout preparation. As it moves through these stages, the layout serves people involved in developing the advertising campaign by helping them to exchange ideas. It also provides instructions to production personnel.

5. S. Watson Dunn and Arnold M. Barban, *Advertising: Its Role in Modern Marketing,* 6th ed. (Hinsdale, Ill.: Dryden Press, 1986), p. 493.

Table 14.5 *Illustration techniques for advertisements*

Illustration Technique	Description
Product alone	Simplest method; advantageous when appearance is important, when identification is important, when trying to keep a brand name or package in the public eye, or when selling through mail order
Emphasis on special features	Shows and emphasizes special details or features as well as advantages; used when product is unique because of special features
Product in setting	Shows what can be done with product; people, surroundings, or environment hint at what product can do; often used in food advertisements
Product in use	Puts action into the advertisement; can remind readers of benefits gained from using product; must be careful not to make visual cliché; should not include anything in illustration that will divert attention from product; used to direct readers' eyes toward product
Product being tested	Uses test to dramatize product's uses and benefits versus competing products
Result of product's use	Emphasizes satisfaction from using product; can liven up dull product; useful when nothing new can be said
Dramatizing headline	Appeal of illustration dramatizes headline; can emphasize appeal, but dangerous to use illustrations that do not correlate with headlines
Dramatizing situation	Presents problem situation or shows situation in which problem has been resolved

Executing the Campaign

The execution of an advertising campaign requires an extensive amount of planning and coordination. Regardless of whether an organization uses an advertising agency, a large number of people and firms are involved in the execution of a campaign. Production companies, research organizations, media firms, printers, photoengravers, and commercial artists are just a few examples of the types of people and organizations that contribute to a campaign.

Implementation requires detailed schedules to insure that various phases of the work are done on time. Advertising management personnel must evaluate the quality of the work and take corrective action when necessary. In some instances, changes have to be made during the campaign to make it more effective in meeting campaign objectives.

Table 14.5 (continued)	
Illustration Technique	**Description**
Comparison	Compares product with "something" established; the "something" must be positive and familiar to audience
Contrast	Shows difference between two products or two ideas or differences in effects between use and nonuse; before-and-after format is a commonly used contrast technique
Diagrams, charts, and graphs	Used to communicate complex information quickly; may make presentations more interesting
Phantom effects	X-ray or internal view; can see inside product; helpful to explain concealed or internal mechanism
Symbolic	Symbols used to represent abstract ideas that are difficult to illustrate; effective if readers understand symbol; must be positive correlation between symbol and idea
Testimonials	Actually shows the testifier; should use famous person or someone to whom audience can relate

Sources: Dorothy Cohen, *Advertising* (New York: Wiley, 1972), pp. 458–464; and Dunn and Barban, *Advertising*, pp. 497–498.

Evaluating the Effectiveness of the Advertising

There are a variety of reasons for measuring the effectiveness of advertising. They include measuring achievement of advertising objectives; assessing the effectiveness of copy, illustrations, or layouts; or evaluating certain media.

Advertising can be evaluated before, during, and after the campaign. Evaluations performed before the campaign begins are called **pretests** and usually attempt to evaluate the effectiveness of one or more elements of the message. To pretest advertisements, marketers sometimes use a **consumer jury,** which consists of a number of persons who are actual or potential buyers of the advertised product. Jurors are asked to judge one or several dimensions of two or more advertisements. Such tests are based on the belief that consumers are more likely to know what will influence them than advertising experts are.

To measure advertising effectiveness during a campaign, marketers usually take advantage of "inquiries." In the initial stages of a campaign, an advertiser may use several advertisements simultaneously, each containing a coupon or a form requesting information. The advertiser records the number of coupons that are returned from each type of advertisement. If an advertiser receives 78,528 coupons from advertisement A, 37,072 coupons from advertisement B, and 47,932 coupons from advertisement C, advertisement A is judged superior to advertisements B and C.

Evaluation of advertising effectiveness after the campaign is called a posttest. Advertising objectives often indicate what kind of posttest will be appropriate. If an advertiser sets objectives in terms of communication—product awareness, brand awareness, or attitude change—then the posttest should measure changes in one or more of these dimensions. Advertisers sometimes use consumer surveys or experiments to evaluate a campaign based on communication objectives. These methods are costly, however.

For campaign objectives stated in terms of sales, advertisers should determine the change in sales or market share that can be attributed to the campaign. Unfortunately, changes in sales or market share that result from advertising cannot be measured precisely; many factors independent of advertisements affect a firm's sales and market share. Competitive actions, government actions, changes in economic conditions, consumer preferences, and weather are only a few factors that might enhance or diminish a company's sales or market share. However, by using data about past and current sales and advertising expenditures, an advertiser can make gross estimates of the effects of a campaign on sales or market share.

Because consumer surveys and experiments are so expensive, and because it is so difficult to determine the direct effects of advertising on sales, many advertisers evaluate print advertisements in terms of the degree to which consumers can remember them. The posttest methods based on memory include recognition and recall tests. Such tests usually are performed by research organizations through consumer surveys. If a **recognition test** is used, individual respondents are shown the actual advertisement and are asked whether they recognize it. If they do, the interviewer asks additional questions to determine how much of the advertisement was read by each respondent. When recall is evaluated, the respondents are not shown the actual advertisement but instead are asked about what they have seen or heard recently.

Recall can be measured either through unaided recall or through aided recall methods. In an **unaided recall test,** subjects are asked to identify advertisements that they have seen recently but are not shown any clues to stimulate their memory. A similar procedure is used with an **aided recall test,** except that respondents are shown a list of products, brands, company names, or trademarks to jog their memories. Several research organizations, including Daniel Starch and Gallup & Robinson, provide syndicated research services regarding recognition and recall of advertisements.

The major justification for using recognition and recall methods is that individuals are more likely to buy a product if they can remember an advertisement about it than if they cannot. That individuals remember an advertisement, however, does not mean they will actually buy the product or brand advertised.

Who Develops the Advertising Campaign?

An advertising campaign may be handled by (1) an individual or a few persons within the firm, (2) an advertising department within the organization, or (3) an advertising agency.

In very small firms one or two individuals are responsible for advertising (and many other activities as well). Usually these individuals depend heavily on personnel at local newspapers and broadcast stations for copywriting, artwork, and advice about scheduling media.

In certain types of large businesses—especially in larger retail organizations—advertising departments create and implement advertising campaigns. Depending on the size of the advertising program, an advertising department may consist of a few multiskilled persons or of a sizable number of specialists such as copywriters, artists, media buyers, and technical production coordinators. An advertising department sometimes obtains the services of independent research organizations and also hires free-lance specialists when they are needed for a particular project.

When an organization uses an advertising agency, the firm and the agency usually develop the advertising campaign jointly. How much each participates in the campaign's total development depends on the working relationship between the firm and the agency. Ordinarily a firm relies on the agency for copywriting, artwork, technical production, and formulation of the media plan.

An advertising agency can assist a business in several ways. An agency, especially a larger one, supplies the firm with the services of highly skilled specialists such as copywriters, artists, media experts, researchers, legal advisors, and production coordinators. Agency personnel often have had broad experience in advertising and are usually more objective about an organization's products than the firm's employees are.

A firm can obtain some agency services at a low or moderate cost because the agency traditionally receives most of its compensation from a 15-percent commission paid by the media. For example, if an agency contracts for $400,000 of television time for a firm, it receives a commission of $60,000 from the television station. Although the traditional compensation method for agencies is changing and now includes other factors, the media commission still offsets some costs of using an agency.

Now that we have explored advertising as a potential promotion mix ingredient, let us consider a related ingredient—publicity.

Publicity ✓

As indicated in Chapter 13, **publicity** is communication in news story form, regarding an organization and/or its products, that is transmitted through a mass medium at no charge. Publicity can be presented through a variety of vehicles, several of which we will examine in this section.

Within an organization, publicity is sometimes viewed as part of public relations—a larger, more comprehensive communication function. **Public relations** is a broad set of communication activities employed to create and maintain favorable relations between the organization and its publics—customers, employees, stockholders, government officials, and society in general.

Publicity and Advertising Compared

Although publicity and advertising both depend on mass media, they differ in several respects. Whereas advertising messages tend to be informative or persuasive, publicity is mainly just informative. Advertisements sometimes are designed to have an immediate impact on sales; publicity messages are more subdued. Publicity releases do not identify sponsors as their sources, while advertisements do.

When advertising is used, the sponsor pays for the media time or space. For publicity, an organization does not pay for the use of time or space; communications through publicity usually are included as part of a program or a print story. Advertisements usually are separated from the broadcast programs or editorial portions of print media so that the audience or readers can easily recognize (or ignore) them.

Publicity may have greater credibility than advertising among consumers since as a news story it may appear more objective. Whereas media personnel often provide assistance in preparing advertising messages, they are not as helpful in creating publicity releases. Finally, a firm can use advertising to repeat the same messages or issues as many times as desired; publicity is generally not subject to repetition.

Kinds of Publicity

There are several types of publicity mechanisms.[6] The most common is the **news release,** which is usually a single page of typewritten copy containing fewer than three hundred words. A news release also gives the firm's or agency's name, its address and phone number, and the contact person. Figure 14.10 is an example of a news release. A **feature article** is a longer manuscript (up to three thousand words) that usually is prepared for a specific publication. A **captioned photograph** is a photograph with a brief description that explains the picture's content. Captioned photographs are especially effective for illustrating a new or improved product with highly visible features.

There are several other kinds of publicity. A **press conference** is a meeting used to announce major news events. Media personnel are invited to a news conference and usually are supplied with written materials and photographs. In addition, letters to the editor and editorials sometimes are prepared and sent to newspapers and magazine publishers. However, newspaper editors frequently allocate space on their editorial pages to local writers and to national columnists. Finally, films and tapes may be distributed to broadcast stations in the hope that they will be aired.

A marketer's choice of specific types of publicity depends on considerations that include the type of information being transmitted, the characteristics of the target audience, the receptivity of media personnel, the importance of the item to the public, and the amount of information needing to be presented. (The application on page 433 focuses on how AT&T generates publicity.)

Sometimes, a marketer uses a single type of publicity in a promotion mix. In other cases, a marketer may employ a variety of publicity mechanisms, with publicity being the primary ingredient in the promotion mix.

Uses of Publicity

Publicity has a number of uses. It can be used to make people aware of a firm's products, brands, or activities; to maintain a certain level of positive public visibility; and to enhance a particular image, such as innovativeness or progressiveness. It also can be used to overcome negative images. Some firms

---

6. Richard E. Stanley, *Promotion* (Englewood Cliffs, N.J.: Prentice-Hall, 1982), pp. 245–246.

Figure 14.10

Example of a news release (Source: Adolph Coors Company)

News Release

Adolph Coors Company
Corporate Communications Department
Golden, Colorado 80401

Telephone:
(303) 279-6565, ext. 2555
(800) 332-3725 (Colo. only)
(800) 525-3786

CONTACT: Don Shook   FOR IMMEDIATE RELEASE
             Joe Fuentes   Feb. 10, 1986

GOLDEN, Colo.-- Beer sales aren't the only figures that went up at Coors during 1985. The number of visitors taking guided tours of the world's largest brewery increased by 2,781 to a total of 290,834 guests.

"We were extremely gratified to have such a large number of visitors," said Marvin D. "Swede" Johnson, vice president for public relations. "Coors has long been a showplace for modern brewing technology, and we're pleased that visitors to Golden and Colorado include us on their agenda."

Notable guests who toured Coors in 1985 include actor Ossie Davis and singer Harry Belafonte.

To date, more than 7.3 million individuals have visited Coors. They arrive from throughout the world and include students from Asia as well as brewers from Australia and Germany. The typical guest is the tourist visiting Colorado for the first time. Many visit with friends and relatives who already have experienced Coors hospitality.

General tour information may be obtained by calling (303) 277-BEER. Special tours are available for the hearing and mobility-impaired and foreign-speaking visitors. Special evening programs also are available. For more information, call 277-2552.

\#\#\#

use publicity for a single purpose, while others employ it for several purposes. Companies can include a multitude of specific issues in publicity releases; Table 14.6 lists some of them.

Requirements of a Publicity Program

For maximum benefit, a firm should create and maintain a systematic, continuous publicity program. A single individual or department—within the organization or from its advertising agency or public relations firm—should be responsible for managing the program.

It is important to establish and maintain good working relationships with media personnel. Personal contact with editors, reporters, and other news personnel is often necessary. Without their input, it is difficult to determine exactly how to design an organization's publicity program so as to facilitate the work of media news people.

Media personnel reject a great deal of publicity material because it is not newsworthy or because it is poorly written. If a firm hopes to have an effective publicity program, it must do its best to avoid these flaws. Guidelines and checklists are sometimes helpful in achieving these goals.

Table 14.6 Possible issues for publicity releases

Marketing developments	Reports on current developments
New products	Reports of experiments
New uses for old products	Reports on industry conditions
Research developments	Company progress reports
Changes of marketing personnel	Employment, production, and sales statistics
Large orders received	Reports on new discoveries
Successful bids	Tax reports
Awards of contracts	Speeches by principals
Special events	Analyses of economic conditions
Company policies	Employment gains
New guarantees	Financial statements
Changes in credit terms	Organization appointments
Changes in distribution policies	Opening of new markets
Changes in service policies	**Personalities—names are news**
Changes in prices	Visits by famous persons
News of general interest	Accomplishments of individuals
Annual election of officers	Winners of company contests
Meetings of the board of directors	Employees' and officers' advancements
Anniversaries of the organization	Interviews with company officials
Anniversaries of an invention	Company employees serving as judges for contests
Anniversaries of the senior officers	Interviews with employees
Holidays that can be tied to the organization's activities	**Slogans, symbols, endorsements**
Annual banquets and picnics	Company's slogan—its history and development
Special weeks, such as Clean-up Week	A tie-in of company activities with slogans
Founders' Day	Creation of a slogan
Conferences and special meetings	The company's trademark
Open house to the community	The company's name plate
Athletic events	Product endorsements
Awards of merit to employees	
Laying of cornerstone	
Opening of an exhibition	

Source: Albert Wesley Frey, ed., *Marketing Handbook,* 2nd ed. (New York: Ronald Press), pp. 19–35. Copyright © 1965. Reprinted by permission of John Wiley & Sons, Inc.

Finally, a firm has to evaluate its publicity efforts. Usually, the effectiveness of publicity is measured by the number of releases actually published or broadcast. To monitor print media and determine which releases are published and how often, an organization can hire a clipping service, a firm that clips and sends published news releases to client companies. No independent monitoring service is available to measure the effectiveness of broadcast news releases. A firm can enclose a card with its publicity releases and request that the station record its name and the dates when the news item is broadcast, but station personnel do not always comply.

Application
AT&T Reaches Out Through Publicity

AT&T knows the importance of publicity and has taken several creative steps to increase the company's visibility via that route. One such step is the financial backing of sporting events, theatrical productions, and art exhibitions. Sponsoring events is an effective technique for generating desirable media coverage. AT&T believes it is thus able to reach potential customers who are part of highly segmented markets. AT&T does not arbitrarily select events to sponsor: events with the greatest possibility for publicity are the ones chosen.

In the 1984 Summer Olympics, AT&T was able to demonstrate its technological sophistication by supplying the temporary telephone system used during the Games. In return, the company received much free publicity. AT&T Communications sponsored the Torch Relay, and in doing so pulled off a huge public relations success. In safely ushering the Olympic flame to its destination, AT&T also supported the Youth Legacy Kilometer program, a fund-raiser for youth sports programs. The goodwill generated from this in turn enhanced AT&T's new corporate image.

AT&T has set a goal to perpetuate artistic freedom, and has sponsored several controversial art exhibitions and theater productions. The company backed the summer festival at the Kennedy Center, which features a variety of presentations from the world of performing arts. The Live Aid concert and telethon, committed to raising money to aid African famine victims, would have been greatly handicapped without the network set up by AT&T to receive pledge calls. And AT&T donated the cost of using its corporate equipment to the relief effort.

Although AT&T's major goal is to increase visibility through publicity, society as a whole benefits from this sponsorship activity. Corporations that help to develop a community's cultural environment increase social and economic well-being which attracts and keeps employees. (*Source: Ed Sikov, "Brought to You By . . . ," AT&T Magazine, no. 3, 1985, pp. 30–33; "A Case of Mutual Back-Scratching," Computerworld, May 2, 1985, p. 54; and John A. Fransen and Charles L. Mitchell, Jr., "Public Relations Captures the Gold/Carrying the Torch," Public Relations Journal, vol. 40, no. 9, Sept. 1984, pp. 14–17.*)

Dealing with Unfavorable Publicity

Up to this point, we have discussed publicity as a planned promotion-mix ingredient. However, firms may have to deal with unfavorable publicity regarding an unsafe product, an accident, the actions of a dishonest employee, or some other negative event.

The negative impact of unfavorable publicity can be quick and dramatic. A single negative event that produces unfavorable publicity can wipe out a firm's favorable image and destroy consumer attitudes that took years to build through promotional efforts. To protect an organization's image, it is important to avoid unfavorable publicity or, at least, to lessen its effects. First and foremost, the organization can directly reduce negative incidents and events through safety programs, inspections, and effective quality control procedures. But since firms obviously cannot eliminate all negative occurrences, it is important that they establish policies and procedures for the news coverage of such events. These policies should be designated to lessen negative impact.

In most cases, organizations should expedite news coverage of negative events rather than trying to discourage or block it; the facts are more likely to be reported accurately. If news coverage is discouraged, there is a chance that rumors and misinformation will be passed along. An unfavorable event can easily balloon into a scandal or a tragedy. It could even result in public panic.

Six Flags Over Texas, a theme amusement park, has established a set of policies and procedures to be used when a negative event occurs. The policies are aimed at helping news personnel get into the park quickly and providing them with as much information as possible. Not only does this approach tend to lessen the effects of negative events; it also enables the organization to maintain positive relationships with media personnel. Such relationships are essential if news personnel are to cooperate with a firm and broadcast favorable news stories about an organization.

Limitations in Using Publicity

That media do not charge for transmitting publicity is a double-edged sword. Although it provides a financial advantage, it brings with it several limitations. Media personnel must believe that messages are newsworthy if they are to be published or broadcast. That means that messages must be timely, interesting, and accurate. Many communications simply do not qualify. Considerable time and effort may be necessary to convince media personnel of the news value of publicity releases.

Although marketers usually encourage media personnel to air a publicity release at a certain time, they control neither the content nor the timing of the communication. Media personnel alter the length and content of publicity releases to fit publishers' or broadcasters' requirements. They may delete the parts of the message that are most important—at least from the firm's perspective. Media personnel generally use publicity releases in time slots or positions that are most convenient for them; thus, the messages are frequently presented at times or in locations that do not effectively reach the audiences an organization hopes to reach. Despite its drawbacks, though, properly managed publicity offers significant benefits to an organization.

Summary

Advertising is a paid form of nonpersonal communication that is transmitted to consumers through mass media such as television, radio, newspapers, magazines, direct mail, mass transit vehicles, and outdoor displays. Both nonbusiness and business organizations employ advertising.

Organizations use advertising in many ways. Institutional advertising is employed to promote organizations' images and ideas as well as political issues and candidates. Product advertising focuses on uses, features, images, and benefits of goods and services. To make people aware of a new or innovative product's existence, uses, and benefits, marketers use pioneer advertising in the introductory stage to stimulate primary demand for a general product category. Marketers switch to competitive advertising to increase selective demand by promoting the uses, features, and advantages of a particular brand.

Advertising sometimes is used to lessen the impact of a competitor's promotional program. It is sometimes designed to make the sales force more effective. To increase market penetration, an advertiser sometimes focuses a campaign on promoting an increased number of uses for the product. Some advertisements for an established product remind consumers that the product is still around and that it has certain characteristics and uses. Marketers may try to assure users of a particular brand that they are using the best brand. Marketers also use advertising to smooth out fluctuations in sales.

Although marketers may vary in how they develop advertising campaigns, they should follow a general pattern. First, they must identify and analyze the advertising target. Second, they should establish what they want the campaign to accomplish by defining the advertising objectives. The next step is to create the advertising platform, which contains the basic issues to be presented in the campaign. Next, the advertiser must decide how much money is to be spent on the campaign. Fifth, the marketer must develop the media plan by selecting and scheduling the media to be used in the campaign. In the sixth stage, the advertiser uses copy and artwork to create the message. Finally, the advertiser must devise one or more methods for evaluating the effectiveness of the advertisements.

Advertising campaigns can be developed by personnel within the firm or in conjunction with advertising agencies. When a campaign is created by the firm's personnel, it may be developed by only a few people, or it may be the product of an advertising department within the firm. The use of an advertising agency may be advantageous to a firm because an agency can provide highly skilled, objective specialists with broad experience in the advertising field at low to moderate costs to the firm.

Publicity is communication in news story form, regarding an organization and/or its products, that is transmitted through a mass medium at no charge. Usually publicity is part of the larger, more comprehensive communication function of public relations. Publicity is mainly informative and usually is more subdued than advertising. There are many types of publicity, including news releases, feature articles, captioned photographs, press conferences, editorials, films, and tapes. Marketers can use one or more of these to achieve a variety of objectives. To have an effective publicity program, someone—either in the organization or in the firm's agency—must be responsible for creating and maintaining systematic and continuous publicity efforts.

An organization should avoid negative publicity by reducing the number of negative events that result in unfavorable publicity. To diminish the impact of unfavorable publicity, an organization should institute policies and procedures for properly handling news personnel when negative events do occur. Problems that surround the use of publicity include reluctance of media personnel to print or air releases and lack of control over the timing and content of messages.

Important Terms

Advertising	Comparative advertising
Institutional advertising	Defensive advertising
Product advertising	Reminder advertising
Pioneer advertising	Reinforcement advertising
Competitive advertising	Advertising target

Advertising platform
Advertising appropriation
Objective and task approach
Percent of sales approach
Competition-matching approach
Arbitrary approach
Media plan
Cost comparison indicator
Regional issues
Copy
Storyboard
Artwork
Illustration

Layout
Pretest
Consumer jury
Posttest
Recognition test
Unaided recall test
Aided recall test
Publicity
Public relations
News release
Feature article
Captioned photograph
Press conference

Discussion and Review Questions

1. What is the difference between institutional and product advertising?
2. When should advertising be used to stimulate primary demand? To stimulate selective demand?
3. How can advertising be used as a competitive tactic?
4. Describe the relationship between advertising and personal selling.
5. How does a marketer use advertising to promote year-round sales stability?
6. What are the major steps in creating an advertising campaign?
7. What is an advertising target? How does a marketer analyze the target audience after it has been identified?
8. Why is it necessary to define advertising objectives?
9. What is an advertising platform and how is it used?
10. What factors affect the size of an advertising budget? What techniques are used to determine this budget?
11. Describe the steps required in developing a media plan.
12. What is the role of copy in an advertising message?
13. How is artwork used in the development of a message?
14. What role does an advertising agency play in developing an advertising campaign?
15. Discuss some ways to posttest the effectiveness of advertising.
16. What is publicity? How does it differ from advertising?
17. Identify and describe the major types of publicity.
18. How is publicity used by organizations? Give several examples of publicity releases that you observed recently in local media.
19. How should an organization handle negative publicity? Identify a recent example of a firm that received negative publicity. Did the firm deal with it effectively?
20. Explain the problems and limitations associated with using publicity. How can some of these limitations be minimized?

Cases

Case 14.1 Burger King's "Herb" Advertising Campaign[7]

Pillsbury Corporation owns Burger King, the second-largest restaurant chain in the United States (McDonald's is number one, with 7,000 units). Of the 4,000 Burger Kings worldwide, approximately 14 percent are company-owned operations, while the remainder are owned and operated by individual franchisees. The annual sales volume for each restaurant averages $750,000. For these stores to sustain continued growth, it is crucial that Burger King be able to develop and implement effective advertising programs.

Burger King is shifting its advertising approach away from comparative advertising. In 1982, it took on McDonald's by launching a major comparative ad campaign. This "battle of the burgers" campaign claimed that Burger King's Whoppers had beaten McDonald's Big Mac in a national taste test. It also focused on Burger King's broiling of meat versus McDonald's frying. Though competitors Wendy's and McDonald's filed lawsuits contesting Burger King's claims, the campaign was very successful for Burger King. But top-level marketers determined that the approach had lost its ability to attract more customers. That summer, Burger King launched a $30-million advertising blitz to promote the "new" Whopper. As it turned out, though, Burger King executives felt that this campaign reached existing Whopper eaters but failed to convert many customers to the new Whopper.

Recently, Burger King launched a new $40-million advertising campaign featuring Herb, a lackluster fellow who has never tasted a Burger King burger. Burger King unveiled its new campaign in a sixty-second prime-time television commercial that aired on the three major networks. Shortly afterward, through a series of 2 × 2-inch newspaper advertisements, Burger King ran the statement "It's not too late, Herb." Burger King feels that Herb will allow its advertising to focus on food-quality attributes, as opposed to hammering away at McDonald's and Wendy's deficiencies. This advertising bent, away from comparisons that denigrate competitors, is the approach that McDonald's president has publicly espoused. In an industry conference he spoke out against comparative advertising, stating that it was detrimental to the industry as a whole because it gave "[nutritionalist] extremist groups, zealots, and the press" more reason to attack fast-food chains.

For the initial effort, Burger King's advertising agency prepared seven television commercials. Herb's parents, a former schoolteacher, and two friends were featured in some of the spots. The Herb promotional effort included such gimmicks as in-store signs for use in closed seating areas saying "Reserved for Herb." Then Burger King announced that it had found Herb.

7. Based on *Pillsbury Annual Report, 1984*; Brian Moran, "Herb Helped BK Visibility, But Little Else," *Advertising Age*, March 24, 1986, pp. 1, 120; "Herb Comes Out of Hiding," *Time*, Feb. 3, 1986, p. 59; "Burger King Takes the Bite Out of Its Ads," *Business Week*, Oct. 28, 1985, p. 38; Scott Hume, "Mac Chief Explodes 'Burger Wars,'" *Advertising Age*, April 14, 1986, pp. 3, 110; and Steve Raddock, "They Sizzle While the Competition Burns," *Marketing & Media Decisions*, Spring 1983, pp. 67–75.

Herb received a lot of publicity. He appeared on MTV, "Today," "PM Magazine," and "Entertainment Tonight." Herb was mentioned 5,000 times in newspaper headlines, and the Herb campaign generated more mail at Burger King headquarters than has any other campaign.

Burger King's Herb campaign experienced difficulty in achieving early success because of McDonald's enormous campaign for a new beef-lettuce-tomato sandwich called the McD.L.T. McDonald's was spending over $5 million a week on television commercials, which is about $2\frac{1}{2}$ times Burger King's media expenditures for Herb. In addition, McDonald's was offering coupons to customers for free McD.L.T.'s. Burger King executives indicated that they had never experienced such a high intensity of McDonald's advertising.

Burger King used two 30-second spots on NBC's Super Bowl coverage to announce a "Find Herb" manhunt. Burger King provided a description and offered $5,000 to customers who could track Herb down. The Herb advertising campaign ended several months later with a tie-in to a $1-million sweepstakes.

Initially, the Herb campaign's results were unimpressive. Consumer awareness of Burger King advertising actually went down, due partly to the McDonald's blitz. In the second month of the campaign, the advertisements gained considerably in consumer awareness. Still, sales were only 1 percent higher than for the same period the previous year. Some critics have questioned whether the Herb commercials generated an adequate level of consumer awareness. Others have pointed out that the commercials simply were not that interesting and that they failed to turn Herb into a cult phenomenon.

Questions for Discussion

1. In what ways did Burger King use Herb in its promotional efforts?
2. Do you feel that this campaign was effective?
3. Should Burger King have delayed the launch of the Herb campaign to avoid competing with the McDonald's McD.L.T. blitz?

Case 14.2 Dr Pepper Changes Its Advertising Campaign[8]

For some time, Dr Pepper used its "Be a Pepper" theme in an attempt to position its product as the soft drink for everyone. Over the last decade, Dr Pepper had used song-and-dance advertising that was later imitated by many competitors. Now the company has dropped its slogan, discarded its song-and-dance routine, and revamped its advertising strategy.

Dr Pepper's new advertising campaign focuses on the unique product attributes that made Dr Pepper a successful soft drink—its distinctive and unique taste. The 1984 campaign cost $35 million, a 25% increase in the budget compared to the previous year. This increase helped to support Dr Pepper's return to network commercials after a year of primarily locally funded television advertisements. Network spots were purchased for prime-time, day, special, and syndicated programs, as well as the MTV cable station.

8. This case is based on information found in Tom Bayer, "Dr Pepper Shucks Off P&G Philosophy," *Advertising Age*, Oct. 10, 1983, pp. 4, 79; Gary A. Hemphill, "Sales Up: Rejuvenated Dr Pepper Bounces Back," *Beverage Industry*, Dec. 1984, pp. 4, 21; and Fred Gardner, "Soft Drink Line Up," *Marketing & Media Decisions*, Feb. 1984, pp. 140–141.

The 12–34 age group was the target market for the TV commercials because the company expected this group to be less apt to have long-standing preferences in soft drinks and more apt to be flexible in trying new tastes. Dr Pepper's advertising target was to be reached during shows such as "Gimme a Break," "Hart to Hart," "The A-Team," "Facts of Life," and "Three's Company." Network specials such as the "Solid Gold Special"—a one-hour music program with high audience ratings—were to provide optimum exposure for Dr Pepper's new campaign, aiding in the rapid and firm establishment of the advertising messages.

According to the creative director who guided message development, the ad campaign's appeal was based on its originality and sparkle. The ads suggested that Dr Pepper's distinctive taste and personality appeal only to people who are ready to explore the unique aspects of life and who are inspired by the unusual. The tag line, "Hold out for the out of the ordinary," was simple and direct and was based on market research on the attributes of Dr Pepper and of the target audience. A study on values and lifestyles had noted that 30 percent of youths tend to be introspective; the company wanted to appeal to that inwardly directed, growing segment. The slogan was intended to develop strong brand identification for Dr Pepper in the soft-drink market.

The "Hold out for the out of the ordinary" campaign was included in seven television commercials. Three of the commercials supported Dr Pepper, two Pepper Free, and two Sugar Free Dr Pepper. The television commercials were loosely based on historical figures and sagas and enlivened with zany twists. They featured characters who resembled Tarzan, a hunchback bellringer, and Marie Antoinette, to name a few.

In addition to television commercials, Dr Pepper used radio, print, and outdoor media. The radio commercials included "out of the ordinary" personalities such as Irene Cara and Mickey Gilley. Irene Cara is well known for her title songs for the movies *Fame* and *Flashdance*. Mickey Gilley is famous for his club in Houston.

The commercials were successfully tested through comprehensive interviews with consumers. The tagline, "Hold out for the out of the ordinary" was found to be straightforward and distinct. The approach was considered appropriate for a product as unique as Dr Pepper. In addition, the commercials were highly rated for their originality in not following other soft drink advertisements that contain burly young men and bikini-clad women frolicking on the beach. The consumer interviews revealed that the Dr Pepper ads were simply enjoyable and would have strong appeal among persons in the targeted group.

Questions for Discussion

1. Based on the information in this case, assess whether Dr Pepper's advertising objectives were stated in terms of sales or in terms of communication.
2. What were the primary issues in Dr Pepper's advertising platform?
3. In general, do you believe that this campaign was successful?

15 / Personal Selling and Sales Promotion

Objectives

- To understand the major purposes of personal selling.

- To learn the basic steps in the personal selling process.

- To identify the types of sales force personnel.

- To gain insight into sales management decisions and activities such as setting objectives for the sales force and determining its size; recruiting, selecting, training, compensating, and motivating salespeople; creating sales territories; and routing, scheduling, and controlling sales personnel.

- To become aware of what sales promotion activities are and how they can be used.

- To become familiar with specific sales promotion methods used.

Figure 15.1

Promotion of both IBM computers and IBM people (Source: © Copyright IBM Corporation 1983)

Company reputation, claimed a recent survey, is the most important factor in running a quality selling operation in the precision instruments industry. That same survey gave Eastman Kodak the highest-ranking reputation of all the firms surveyed. At Kodak, policies, personnel, and operations reflect an emphasis on customer relations. Strong support from within—through initial training programs, refresher courses on products, and regular performance reviews—enables the sales force to carry out the corporate goal of backing quality products with quality service. Each and every customer, from independent store owners to mass merchandisers, receives high-caliber service from a sales force that works hard to resolve customers' problems without delay.

In the 1970s, when Marriott Hotels and Resorts was continually building new hotels, a sales position was considered a mere rung on the ladder to a managerial post. Since growth has slowed, the focus of upper-level management has switched from adding new properties to increasing the productivity of existing ones. In line with this corporate redirection, work in sales and marketing is now considered prestigious. People who prove themselves

in sales can make more money and receive better promotions, and they are being trained to sell to specific industries. To keep pace with Marriott's former growth, managers used to move to new locations on a regular basis. Now, however, managers are more stationary and are thus able to establish and nurture client relationships. Such relationships are the foundation of Marriott's repeat business, which is the key to its present sales growth.

IBM's sales success in the computer industry is attributed in part to the superior skills of its sales personnel in selling and in meeting the product application needs of individual customers and specific industries (see Figure 1.1). IBM sales recruits have technical backgrounds, good communication skills, and college grade averages of 3.5 or better. New sales reps are sent to a highly competitive training program where each helps to determine personal performance objectives. Other criteria are specified for them in such areas as customer satisfaction and territory and marketing management. Sales reps are trained to maintain and troubleshoot accounts, using every available company resource. The worst mistake a sales representative can make, says a former IBM salesman, is to lose an account to a competitor.[1]

Much of personal selling today requires highly trained individuals who are called on daily to help customers solve complex problems. Personal selling is becoming more professional and sophisticated as it leans further toward consulting with and advising customers. In a number of business organizations, sales personnel are among the highest-paid employees. As many salespeople become familiar with their firm's total marketing and company operations, they move up rapidly into managerial positions. Many of today's high-level executives, such as those at Kodak, Marriott, and IBM, began their careers in sales.

As indicated in Chapter 13, personal selling and sales promotion are two possible ingredients in a promotion mix. Personal selling is the most widely used. Sometimes, it is a company's sole promotional tool. Generally, it is used in conjunction with other promotion mix ingredients. Occasionally, personal selling plays only a minor role in an organization's total promotional activities.

This chapter focuses on personal selling and sales promotion. Our discussion considers the purposes of personal selling, its basic steps, the types of individuals who make up a sales force and how they are selected, and the major sales management decisions and activities. In our discussion, we also examine several characteristics of sales promotion efforts. Then we look at the reasons for using sales promotion and at the sales promotion methods available for use in a promotion mix.

1. "Kodak's Reputation Makes a Pretty Picture," *Sales and Marketing Management,* Dec. 3, 1984, p. 34; "Selling Becomes Chic at Marriott," *Sales and Marketing Management,* Dec. 3, 1984, p. 42; and "The IBM Salesperson Is King," *Sales and Marketing Management,* Dec. 3, 1984, p. 39.

The Nature of Personal Selling

Business organizations spend more money on personal selling than on any other promotion mix ingredient. Millions of people earn their livings through personal selling.

As defined earlier, **personal selling** is a process of informing customers and persuading them to purchase products through personal communication in an exchange situation. Personal selling gives marketers the greatest freedom to adjust a message to satisfy customers' information needs. In comparison with other promotion methods, personal selling is the most precise. It enables marketers to focus on the most promising sales prospects. Other promotion mix ingredients are aimed at groups of people, some of whom may not be prospective customers. A major disadvantage of personal selling is its cost. In fact, it generally is the most expensive ingredient in the promotion mix. The average industrial sales call, for example, costs about $230, and selling costs are increasing faster than advertising costs.[2]

Personal selling goals vary from one firm to another. However, they usually involve finding prospects, convincing prospects to buy, and keeping customers satisfied. Identifying potential buyers who are interested in an organization's products is critical. Later in this chapter, we discuss this issue in more detail.

Although finding prospects is important, it is pointless unless some of the prospects can be convinced to buy. Since most prospects seek certain types of information before they make a purchase decision, salespersons must ascertain prospects' informational needs and then provide the relevant information. To do so, sales personnel must be well trained regarding both their products and the selling process in general.

Few businesses survive solely on profits from one-sale customers. For long-run survival most marketers depend, to some degree, on repeat sales. A company has to keep its customers satisfied to obtain repeat purchases. Also, satisfied customers help to attract new ones by telling potential customers about the organization and its products.

Even though the whole organization is responsible for providing customer satisfaction, much of the burden falls on salespeople. They are almost always closer to customers than anyone else in the company. The sales force often provides buyers with information and service after the sale. Such activities allow a salesperson to generate additional sales while evaluating the strengths and weaknesses of the company's products and other marketing mix ingredients. These observations are helpful in developing and maintaining a marketing mix that better satisfies both customers and the firm.

A salesperson may be involved with achieving one or several of these general goals. In some organizations, there are individuals whose sole job is to find prospects. This information is relayed to salespeople, who contact the prospects. After the sale, these same salespeople may do the follow-up work, or a third group of employees may have the job of maintaining customer satisfaction. In many smaller organizations, a single person handles all of these functions. Regardless of how many groups are involved, several major sales tasks must be performed to achieve these general goals.

2. "Cost of Industrial Sales Call Increases to $229.70," Laboratory of Advertising Performance, McGraw-Hill Research Department, 1985.

Elements of the Personal Selling Process

The exact activities involved in the selling process vary among salespersons and differ for particular selling situations. No two salespersons use exactly the same selling methods. However, many salespersons—either consciously or unconsciously—move through a general selling process as they sell products. This process consists of seven elements, or steps: prospecting and evaluating, preparing, approaching the customer, making the presentation, overcoming objections, closing, and follow up.

Prospecting and Evaluating

Developing a list of potential customers is called **prospecting.** A salesperson seeks the names of prospects from such sources as the company's sales records, other customers, trade shows, newspaper announcements (of marriages, births, deaths, and the like), public records, telephone directories, trade association directories, and many others. Sales personnel also use responses from advertisements that encourage interested persons to send in an information request form (see the advertisements in Figure 15.2).

After developing the prospect list, a salesperson evaluates whether each prospect is able, willing, and authorized to buy the product. Based on this evaluation, some prospects may be deleted, while others are deemed acceptable and are ranked relative to their desirability or potential.

Preparing

Before contacting acceptable prospects, a salesperson should find and analyze information regarding each prospect's specific product needs, current use of brands, feelings about available brands, and personal characteristics. A salesperson uses this information when he or she selects an approach and puts together a sales presentation. A salesperson with more information about a prospect is better equipped to develop an approach and presentation that precisely communicates with the prospect.

Approaching the Customer

The **approach**—the manner in which a salesperson contacts a potential customer—is a critical step in the sales process. The prospect's first impression of the salesperson may be a lasting one, with long-run consequences.

One type of approach is based on referrals. The salesperson approaches the prospect and explains that an acquaintance, an associate, or a relative has suggested the call. The salesperson who uses the cold canvass method calls on potential customers without their prior consent. Repeat contact is another common approach; when making the contact, the salesperson mentions a prior meeting. The exact type of approach depends on the salesperson's preferences, the product being sold, the firm's resources, and the characteristics of the prospect.

Making the Presentation

During the sales presentation, the salesperson must attract and hold the prospect's attention in order to stimulate interest and stir up a desire for the product. The salesperson should have the prospect touch, hold, or actually use the product. If possible, the salesperson should demonstrate the product and get the prospect more involved with it to stimulate greater interest.

Figure 15.2 *Advertisements with information request forms to identify prospects (Source: Ad on left courtesy of State of Florida Department of Commerce. Ad on right courtesy of State Mutual Life Assurance Company of America)*

During the presentation, the salesperson must not only talk but also listen. The sales presentation provides the salesperson with the greatest opportunity to determine the prospect's specific needs by listening to questions and comments and by observing responses. Even though the salesperson has planned the presentation in advance, he or she must be able to adjust the message to meet the prospect's information needs.

Overcoming Objections

One of the best ways to overcome a prospect's objections is to anticipate and counter them before the prospect has an opportunity to raise them. However, this approach can be risky. The salesperson may mention some objections that the prospect would not have raised. If possible, the salesperson should handle objections when they arise. They also can be dealt with at the end of the presentation.

An effective salesperson usually seeks out a prospect's objections in order to answer them. If they are not apparent, the salesperson cannot deal with them, and they may keep the prospect from buying.

Closing

Closing is the element in the selling process in which the salesperson asks the prospect to buy the product or products. During the presentation, the salesperson may employ a "trial close" by asking questions that assume the prospect will buy the product. For example, the salesperson might ask the potential customer about financial terms, desired colors or sizes, delivery arrangements, or the quantity to be purchased. The reactions to such questions usually indicate how close the prospect is to buying. A trial close lets prospects indirectly respond that they will buy the product without having to say those sometimes difficult words, "I'll take it."

A salesperson should try to close at several points during the presentation because the prospect may be ready to buy. Often an attempt to close the sale will result in objections. Thus, closing can serve as an important stimulus that uncovers hidden objections.

Following Up

After a successful closing, the salesperson must follow up the sale. In the follow-up stage, the salesperson should determine whether the order was delivered on time and installed properly, if installation was required. The salesperson should contact the customer to learn what problems or questions have arisen regarding the product. The follow-up stage also can be used to determine customers' future product needs.

Types of Salespersons

To intelligently develop a sales force, a marketing manager must decide what kind of salesperson will sell the firm's products most effectively. Most business organizations use several different kinds of sales personnel. Based on the functions they perform, salespersons can be classified into three groups: order getters, order takers, and support personnel. One salesperson can, and often does, perform all three functions.

Order Getters

To obtain orders, a salesperson must inform prospects and persuade them to buy the product. The job of **order getters** is to increase the firm's sales by selling to new customers and by increasing sales to present customers. This task sometimes is called creative selling. It requires salespeople to recognize potential buyers' needs and then to provide them with the necessary information. Order-getting activities sometimes are divided into two categories: current customer sales and new-business sales.

Current Customer Sales

Sales personnel who concentrate on current customers call on people and organizations that have purchased products from the firm at least once. These salespeople seek more sales from existing customers by following up previous sales. Current customers can also be sources of leads for new prospects.

New-business Sales

Business organizations depend on sales to new customers, at least to some degree. New-business sales personnel locate prospects and convert them to buyers. Salespersons in many industries help to generate new business, but industries that depend in large part on new-customer sales are real estate, insurance, furniture, appliances, heavy industrial machinery, and automobiles.

Order Takers

Taking orders is a repetitive task that salespersons perform to perpetuate long-lasting, satisfying relationships with customers. **Order takers** seek repeat sales. One of their major objectives is to be absolutely certain that customers have sufficient product quantities where and when they are needed. Order takers can be categorized into two groups, inside order takers and field order takers.

Inside Order Takers

In many businesses, inside order takers, who work in sales offices, receive orders by mail and telephone. Certain producers, wholesalers, and even retailers have sales personnel who sell from within the firm rather than in the field. That does not mean that inside order takers never communicate with customers face to face. Salespeople in retail stores, for example, are classified as inside order takers.

Mid-Continent Bottlers, a Des Moines soft-drink distributor, traditionally sold beverages to retailers off its trucks. Sometimes, the brands needed by a retailer were not on the truck. The rising cost of fuel forced Mid-Continent to switch to inside order takers. Today, the bottler telephones 75 percent of its accounts to determine what the retailers need; then the beverages are loaded and delivered. The use of inside order takers has helped Mid-Continent significantly reduce costs.[3]

Field Order Takers

Salespersons who travel to customers are referred to as "outside," or "field," order takers. Often a customer and a field order taker develop an interdependent relationship. The buyer depends on the salesperson to take orders periodically (and sometimes to deliver them), and the salesperson counts on the buyer to purchase a certain quantity of products periodically.

Field or inside order takers should not be thought of as passive functionaries who simply record orders in a machinelike manner. Order takers generate the bulk of many organizations' total sales.

Support Personnel

Support personnel facilitate the selling function but usually are not involved only with making sales. They are engaged primarily in marketing industrial products. They are active in locating prospects, educating customers, building goodwill, and providing service after the sale. Although there are many kinds of sales support personnel, the three most common are missionary, trade, and technical.

Missionary Salespersons

Missionary salespersons, who usually are employed by manufacturers, assist the producer's customers in selling to their own customers. A missionary salesperson may call on retailers to inform and persuade them to buy the manufacturer's

3. "Mid-Continent Keeps Costs Bottled Up," *Sales and Marketing Management Portfolio,* 1982, p. 7.

products. If the call is successful, the retailers purchase the products from wholesalers, who are the producer's customers. Manufacturers of medical supplies and pharmaceutical products often use missionary salespersons to promote their products to physicians, hospitals, and retail druggists.

Trade Salespersons

Trade salespersons are not strictly support personnel because they usually perform the order-taking function as well. However, they direct much of their efforts toward helping customers, especially retail stores, promote the product. They are likely to restock shelves, obtain more shelf space, set up displays, provide in-store demonstrations, and distribute samples to store customers. Food producers and processors commonly employ trade salespersons.

Technical Salespersons

Technical salespersons provide technical assistance to the organization's current customers. They advise customers on product characteristics and applications, system designs, and installation procedures. Since this job is often highly technical, the salesperson usually needs to have formal training in one of the physical sciences or in engineering. Technical sales personnel often sell technical industrial products such as computers, heavy equipment, steel, and chemicals.

When hiring sales personnel, marketers seldom restrict themselves to a single category because most firms require different types. Several factors dictate how many of each type of salesperson a particular firm should have. A product's uses, characteristics, complexity, and price influence the kind of sales personnel used, as do the number of customers and their characteristics. The kinds of marketing channels and the intensity and type of advertising also have an impact on the selection of sales personnel.

Management of the Sales Force

The sales force is directly responsible for generating an organization's primary input—sales revenue. Thus, in many cases, the effectiveness of sales-force management determines a firm's success. Without adequate sales revenue, a business cannot survive long.

Our discussion of sales management explores nine general areas, each of which requires numerous decisions and activities. The specific areas analyzed are (1) establishing sales-force objectives, (2) determining sales-force size, (3) recruiting and selecting salespeople, (4) training sales personnel, (5) compensating salespeople, (6) motivating salespeople, (7) creating sales territories, (8) routing and scheduling salespeople, and (9) controlling and evaluating the sales force.

Establishing Sales-force Objectives

To manage a sales force effectively, a sales manager must develop sales objectives. Sales objectives should be stated in precise, measurable terms and should specify the time period and the geographic areas involved.

Sales objectives usually state goals both for the total sales force and for each salesperson. Objectives for the entire force are normally stated in terms of sales volume, market share, or profit. Volume objectives refer to a quantity of dollars or sales units. For example, the objective for an electric-drill producer's sales force might be to sell $10 million worth of drills annually or 600,000 drills annually. When sales goals are stated in terms of market share, they ordinarily call for an increase in the proportion of the firm's sales relative to the total number of products sold by all businesses in that particular industry. When sales objectives are based on profit, they are usually stated in terms of dollar amounts or return on investment.

Sales objectives for individual salespersons commonly are stated in terms of dollar or unit sales volume. Other bases used for individual sales objectives include average order size, average number of calls per time period, and the ratio of orders to calls.

Sales objectives tell salespersons what they are expected to accomplish during a specified time period. They give the sales force direction and purpose. They also serve as performance standards for the evaluation and control of sales personnel.

Determining Sales-force Size

Deciding how many salespersons to use is important because it influences the company's ability to generate sales and profits. In addition, the size of the sales force affects the compensation methods used, salespersons' morale, and overall sales-force management. Sales-force size must be adjusted from time to time. A firm's marketing plans change, as do markets and forces in the marketing environment. There are several methods for determining the optimal size of the sales force. Two analytical techniques are the equalized workload method and the incremental productivity method.

Equalized Workload Method[4]

The **equalized workload method** allows a marketing manager to base the sales-force size on the condition that every salesperson is assigned a roughly equal set of accounts in terms of the total amount of sales time and effort needed. Marketers must answer several questions if they are considering this method. First, can the manager divide the customers into groups based on size of purchases? Second, is it possible to determine the number of sales calls required to service various account sizes adequately? Third, what is the annual average number of calls per salesperson?

To determine sales-force size through the equalized workload method, a marketing manager must (1) multiply the number of customers in each size group by the number of sales calls required annually to serve those groups effectively, (2) add the products, and (3) divide this sum by the average number of calls made annually by each salesperson.

As a hypothetical case, assume that a company divides its customers into two size groups. It has 300 Class A customers who each require 20 sales calls annually, and 900 Class B customers who require 12 sales calls annually. The firm's average salesperson makes 600 calls annually. In this case, sales-force size is determined as follows:

$$\frac{300\,(20) + 900\,(12)}{600} = 28$$

4. This method, developed by Walter J. Talley, is described in "How to Design Sales Territories," *Journal of Marketing,* Jan. 1961, pp. 7–13.

Table 15.1 Selling costs, sales, and operating margin information for incremental productivity analysis

Number of Salespersons	Total Selling Costs	Sales per Salesperson	Total Sales	Operating Margin
1	$ 25,000	$200,000	$200,000	$175,000
2	50,000	150,000	300,000	250,000
3	75,000	120,000	360,000	285,000
4	100,000	100,000	400,000	300,000
5	125,000	85,000	425,000	300,000
6	150,000	72,000	432,000	282,000

Several problems confront the manager who opts for this technique. Estimating the number of sales calls required to service an account is difficult because, regardless of their size, individual customers have different problems and different needs. Moreover, a salesperson's workload depends not only on the number of sales calls, but also on travel time between customers and on the amount of time spent with each account. Although these factors help to determine the average annual number of sales calls per salesperson, there may be marked variations between the average and the actual number of calls that a specific salesperson can make.

Incremental Productivity Method

As a firm adds salespersons within a geographic market, total sales normally increase. However, total selling costs increase as well. According to the **incremental productivity method,** a marketer should continue to increase the sales force as long as the additional sales increases are greater than the additional selling-cost increases. The optimal sales-force size allows the firm to obtain the greatest operating margin.[5]

The incremental productivity method is illustrated in Table 15.1. Notice that as each of the first four salespersons is added to the sales force, the company experiences increases in its operating margin, the difference between total sales and total selling costs. However, adding the fifth salesperson does not increase the firm's operating margin. Thus, the best sales-force size for this business is four.

The incremental productivity method has several limitations. Its users must be able to estimate accurately how much sales will rise when a salesperson is added. They must also estimate the incremental selling costs. This method's effectiveness depends on management's ability to develop accurate estimates.

Marketers seldom depend on one technique to determine sales-force size. While they may use one or several analytical methods, marketing managers usually temper their decisions with a good deal of subjective judgment.

Recruiting and Selecting Salespeople

To create and maintain an effective sales force, a sales manager must recruit the right type of salespeople. **Recruiting** is a process by which the sales manager develops a list of applicants for sales positions.

5. Walter J. Semlow developed this method and provides a more detailed analysis of it in "How Many Salesmen Do You Need?" *Harvard Business Review,* May–June 1959, pp. 126–132.

To ensure that the recruiting process produces a usable list, a sales manager should establish a set of required qualifications before beginning to recruit. Although for years marketers have attempted to enumerate a set of traits that characterize effective salespeople, there is currently no such set of generally accepted characteristics. Therefore, a sales manager must develop a set tailored to the sales tasks in a particular company. Two activities can help establish this set of requirements. The sales manager should prepare a job description that lists the specific tasks to be performed by salespersons. The manager also should analyze the characteristics of the firm's successful salespersons, as well as those of ineffective sales personnel. From the job description and the analysis of traits, the sales manager should be able to develop a set of specific requirements.

A sales manager usually recruits applicants from several sources: departments within the firm, other firms, employment agencies, educational institutions, respondents to advertisements, and individuals recommended by current employees. The specific sources a sales manager uses depend on the type of salesperson required and the manager's experiences with particular sources.

The process of hiring a sales force varies tremendously from one company to another. In some firms, the selection process consists of a single interview. In others the process may include an initial interview, a written application, a series of follow-up interviews, written and oral examinations, an evaluation of recommendations, and a physical examination. Sales management should design a selection procedure that specifically satisfies the company's needs. The process should include enough steps to yield the information that is needed to make accurate selection decisions. However, because each step incurs a certain expense, there should be no more steps than necessary. The stages of the selection process should be sequenced so that the more expensive steps, such as physical examination, are near the end. Fewer people will then move through the higher-cost stages.

Recruitment and selection of salespeople are not one-time decisions. The market and marketing environment change, as do an organization's objectives, resources, and marketing strategies. Maintaining the proper mix of salespeople thus requires continued decision making by the firm's sales management.

Recruitment should not be sporadic. It should be a continuous activity aimed at reaching the best applicants. The selection process should systematically and effectively match applicants' characteristics and needs with the requirements of specific selling tasks. Finally, the selection process should ensure that new sales personnel are available where and when they are needed.

Training Salespeople

Both new and experienced salespersons require sales training, even though the types of training may vary considerably. A good number of organizations have formal training programs, while others depend on on-the-job training. Some systematic training programs are quite extensive; others are rather short and rudimentary. Regardless of whether the training program is to be complex or simple, its developers must consider the following questions.

Who Should Be Trained and Who Does the Training?

Training programs can be aimed at newly hired salespeople, at experienced salespersons, or at both. Ordinarily, new sales personnel require comprehensive training, whereas experienced personnel need both refresher courses regarding

Figure 15.3 *Promotion of sales training program (Source: Learning International)*

established products and training that provides new-product information. Training programs can be directed at the entire sales force or at one segment of it.

Sales managers as well as other salespeople often get involved in giving sales training. Such training may occur daily, on the job, or periodically in sales meetings. Salespeople sometimes receive training from technical specialists within their own organizations. Also, there are a number of individuals and organizations that sell special sales training programs. Some of these programs consist of actual teaching sessions; others take the form of books and manuals or computerized instructional materials. As shown in Figure 15.3, Learning International (formerly Xerox Learning Systems) offers a variety of sales training programs.

Where and When Should the Training Occur?

Sales training may be performed in the field, at educational institutions, in company facilities, or in several of these locations. In some firms, new employees receive most of their training, or at least a substantial portion of it, before being assigned to a specific sales position. Other business organizations put new recruits into the field immediately. After a brief period, the new salespersons begin their formal training. Training programs for new personnel can be as short as several days or as long as three years or more.

Sales training for experienced personnel often is scheduled during a period when sales activities are not too demanding. It is not reasonable to interrupt sales efforts during peak selling periods. Usually, sales training meetings for experienced salespeople are short but intense training efforts. Depending on the size and geographic distribution of the sales force, the training may occur at a single national site or be done on a regional basis. Since training of experienced salespeople is commonly a recurring effort, a firm's sales management must determine the frequency, sequencing, and duration of these activities.

What Should Be Taught?

A sales training program can concentrate on the company (general background, plans, policies, and procedures), on products (features, uses, advantages, problem areas, parts, service, warranties, packaging, sales terms, promotion, and distribution), or on selling methods. Training programs often cover all three areas.

Training for experienced company salespersons usually emphasizes product information, although salespeople also must be informed about new selling techniques and any changes in company plans, policies, and procedures.

How Should the Information Be Taught?

Many teaching methods and materials are appropriate for sales training programs. Lectures, films, texts, manuals, simulation exercises, programmed learning devices, audio and video cassettes, demonstrations, cases, and on-the-job training can all be effective. The methods and materials employed in a particular sales training program depend on the type and number of trainees, the program's content and complexity, the length of the training program, the size of the training budget, the location, the number of teachers, and the teachers' preferences for methods and materials.

Compensating Salespeople

To develop and maintain a highly productive sales force, a business must formulate and administer a compensation plan that attracts, motivates, and holds the most effective individuals. A compensation plan should give sales management the desired level of control and provide sales personnel with an acceptable level of freedom, income, and incentive. The sales compensation program should be flexible, equitable, easy to administer, and easy to understand. Good compensation programs facilitate and encourage proper treatment of customers.

Even though these requirements appear to be logical and easily satisfied, it is actually quite difficult to incorporate all of them into a simple program. Some of them will be satisfied, and others will not. Therefore, in formulating a compensation plan, sales management must strive for a proper balance among these factors.

The developer of a compensation program must determine the general level of compensation required and the most desirable method of calculating it. In analyzing the required compensation level, sales management tries to ascertain a salesperson's value to the company on the basis of the tasks and responsibilities associated with the sales position. The sales manager may consider a number of factors, including salaries of other types of personnel in the firm, competitors' compensation plans, costs of sales-force turnover, and the size of nonsalary selling expenses.

Sales compensation programs usually reimburse salespersons for their selling expenses, provide a certain number of fringe benefits, and deliver the required compensation level. To do that, a firm may use one or more of three basic compensation methods: straight salary, straight commission, or a combination of salary and commission. In a **straight salary compensation plan,** salespeople are paid a specified amount per time period. This sum remains the same until they receive a pay increase or decrease. In a **straight commission compensation plan,** salespeople's compensation is determined solely by the amount of their sales for a given time period. A commission may be based on a single percentage of sales or on a sliding scale involving several sales levels and percentage rates. In a **combination compensation plan,** salespeople are paid a fixed salary and a commission based on sales volume. Some combination programs require a salesperson to exceed a certain sales level before earning a commission; other combination plans are designed so that a commission is paid for any level of sales.

Table 15.2 lists the major characteristics of each sales-force compensation method. Notice that the combination method is most popular. Some methods are especially well suited for certain selling situations. When selecting a compensation method, sales management weighs the advantages and disadvantages shown in Table 15.2.

Proper administration of the sales-force compensation program is crucial for developing high morale and productivity among sales personnel. To maintain an effective compensation program, sales management should periodically review and evaluate the plan and make necessary adjustments.

Motivating Salespeople

A sales manager should develop a systematic approach for motivating salespersons in order to obtain high productivity. Motivating should not be viewed as a sporadic activity reserved for periods of sales decline. Effective sales-force motivation is achieved through an organized set of activities performed continuously by the company's sales management.

Although financial compensation is important, a motivational program must also satisfy employees' nonfinancial needs. Sales personnel, like other people, join organizations to satisfy personal needs and to achieve personal goals. A sales manager must become aware of their motives and goals and then must attempt to create an organizational climate that allows sales personnel to satisfy their personal needs.

A sales manager can employ a variety of positive motivational incentives other than financial compensation. For example, enjoyable working conditions, power and authority, job security, and an opportunity to excel are effective motivators. Sales contests and other devices that provide an opportunity to earn additional rewards can be effective motivators as well. Consider Johnson and Johnson's recognition program discussed in the application on page 457. A firm can develop its own special incentive program, or it can purchase one—like the program advertised in Figure 15.4—from an incentive program supplier. Some organizations also employ negative motivational measures—financial penalties, demotions, even terminations.

Creating Sales Territories

The effectiveness of a sales force that must travel to its customers is influenced, to some degree, by sales management's decisions regarding sales territories. Sales managers deciding on territories must consider size, shape, routing, and scheduling.

Table 15.2   *Characteristics of sales-force compensation methods*

Compensation Method	Frequency of Use (percent)[a]	Especially Useful	Advantages	Disadvantages
Straight salary	17.4	When compensating new salespersons; when firm moves into new sales territories that require developmental work; when salespersons need to perform many nonselling activities	Provides salesperson with maximum amount of security; gives sales manager large amount of control over salespersons; easy to administer; yields more predictable selling expenses	Provides no incentive; necessitates closer supervision of salespersons' activities; during sales declines, selling expenses remain at same level
Straight commission	6.5	When highly aggressive selling is required; when nonselling tasks are minimized; when company cannot closely control salesforce activities	Provides maximum amount of incentive; by increasing commission rate, sales managers can encourage salespersons to sell certain items; selling expenses relate directly to sales resources	Salespersons have little financial security; sales manager has minimum control over sales force; may cause salespeople to provide inadequate service to smaller accounts; selling costs less predictable
Combination	76.1	When sales territories have relatively similar sales potentials; when firm wishes to provide incentive but still control salesforce activities	Provides certain level of financial security; provides some incentive; selling expenses fluctuate with sales revenue	Selling expenses less predictable; may be difficult to administer

[a]The figures in this column are computed from "Alternative Sales Compensation and Incentive Plans," *Sales and Marketing Management,* Feb. 17, 1986, p. 57. *Note:* The percentage for Combination includes compensation methods that involved any combination of salary, commission, or bonus. *Source:* Reprinted by permission of the *Harvard Business Review.* An exhibit from "How to Pay Your Sales Force" by John P. Steinbrink (July/August 1978). Copyright © 1978 by the President and Fellows of Harvard College; all rights reserved.

Size of Territory

Sales managers usually try to create territories that have similar sales potentials or that require about the same amount of work. If territories have equal sales potentials, they will almost always be unequal in geographic size. The salespersons who get the larger territories will have to work longer and harder to generate a certain sales volume. When a sales manager attempts to create territories that require equal amounts of work, sales potentials for those territories will often vary. If sales personnel are partially or fully compensated through commissions, they will have unequal income potentials. Rather than relying on a

Figure 15.4

Promotion of an incentive program (Source: Princess Cruises, Pacific Princess)

Finally.
An incentive worth working for.

Travel has always been an irresistible incentive. And there's nothing in the world of travel like a Princess Cruise. Because only Princess promises the best of everything cruising has to offer. Magnificent ships. Charming British crew. Attentive Italian dining staff. Exquisite cuisine prepared by award-winning chefs. Dazzling Broadway-style entertainment. And the most wonderful destinations in the world.

Princess Cruises (famous as the Love Boat) journeys to the enchanting Mexican Riviera, the colorful Caribbean, majestic Alaska, the spectacular Panama Canal, and our newest destination – the historic Mediterranean.

Here's the best news of all. The price. You'll be delighted to learn how affordable a Princess incentive really is. In fact, you'll find our price comparable to the average 7-day travel incentive. And we offer a discount of up to 25% to groups of ten or more.

Our professional staff is eager to help you plan your program, or just answer questions. Call Rick James, Vice President, Group Sales, or Hilary Sullivan, National Group Sales Manager at (213) 553-1770. Or call your travel agent or local incentive house.

Join the growing list of companies that have had tremendous results using Princess as their incentive. Successful companies such as The Southland Corporation, Whirlpool Home Appliances, Toyota, and many more. See for yourself what a difference it makes when you give your people the incentive worth working for. Call now and step up to a Princess Cruise.

Step up to Princess Cruises

MEXICO • PANAMA CANAL • ALASKA
CARIBBEAN • MEDITERRANEAN
REGISTRY: BRITISH

single approach, many sales managers try to balance territorial workloads and earning potentials by employing differential commission rates. Although a sales manager seeks equity when developing and maintaining sales territories, some inequities will always prevail.

Shape of Territory

Several factors enter into designing the shape of sales territories. First, sales managers must construct the territories so that sales potentials can be measured. Thus, sales territories often consist of several geographic units for which market data are obtainable, such as census tracts, cities, counties, or states. Second, a territory's shape should help the sales force provide the best possible customer coverage. Third, the territories should be designed to minimize selling costs. Fourth, the territory shapes should take into account the density and distribution of customers. And finally, the territory shapes may have to reflect topographical features.

Sales territories seldom form symmetrical patterns. However, sales managers often use geometric shapes as general patterns for sales territories. Circles, rectangles, wedges, and cloverleaves are a few patterns used in designing sales territories.

Application

Sales Force Recognition at Johnson & Johnson

Johnson & Johnson established a sales force recognition program ten years ago. The same awards are offered annually so each year's recipients can experience the same level of recognition. However, the criteria for the awards may vary to support changing company goals and strategies.

The awards available to sales representatives are linked together by tiering, with each level of recognition more difficult to achieve than the previous level. Generally, 40 to 60 percent of the representatives achieve their annual sales forecasts and receive the first-level recognition award, the Sales Achievement Award. Recipients are given a personalized plaque and a cash award that is geometrically increased for consecutive year winners.

Recipients of the Sales Achievement Award are eligible for the Ring Club, which recognizes the top 20 percent of the sales force each year. To qualify, a representative must meet a number of other criteria besides the annual sales forecast. Qualifiers receive a gold ring, a personalized plaque, a compensation award, and stock shares. An Outstanding Sales Performance Award is given to individuals who are honored by the Ring Club for three consecutive years. The Ring Club is a highly sought-after award because of the long-lasting recognition it brings.

At Johnson & Johnson sales-force employees who achieve top recognition become candidates for the Ambassador Club. To be elected to the Ambassador Club, a representative must meet the Ring Club criteria and receive a unanimous vote from the selection committee. Winners of this award enjoy a luxury trip for two; they also receive cash, a plaque, and an oil portrait of themselves. The company believes trips are an excellent way to reward outstanding salespeople and to share the award with spouses.

Johnson & Johnson acknowledges the collective work of individuals by presenting the division with the best sales performance the Division of the Year Award and the President's Trophy. Competition for this award is shared by everyone throughout the year.

The company strives to motivate the most people possible and to recognize individuals with outstanding sales performances. Johnson & Johnson uses achievement awards as an effective tool for stimulating the sales force to meet annual sales goals. (*Source: William M. Mahar, "Johnson & Johnson's Rx for Recognition,"* Sales and Marketing Management, *June 3, 1985, pp. 94–100. Reprinted by permission of* Sales and Marketing Management.)

Routing and Scheduling

Someone must route and schedule sales calls in the field. That person must consider the sequence in which customers are called on, the specific roads or transportation schedules to be used, the number of calls to be made in a given period, and what time of day the calls will occur. In some firms, salespeople plan their own routes and schedules with little or no assistance from the sales manager. In other organizations, the sales manager draws up the routes and schedules. No matter who plans the routing and scheduling, the major goals should be to minimize salespersons' nonselling time (the time spent in traveling and waiting) and to maximize their selling time. The planners should try to achieve these goals in a way that also holds a salesperson's travel and lodging costs to a minimum.

The geographic size and shape of a sales territory are the most important factors affecting routing and scheduling. Next come the number and distribution of customers within the territory, followed by the frequency and duration of sales calls. Finally, the availability of roads and public transportation and the location of the salesperson's home base vis-à-vis customers' locations dictate possible routes and schedules.

Controlling and Evaluating Sales-force Performance

To control and evaluate sales-force activities properly, sales management first of all needs information. A sales manager cannot observe the field sales force on a daily basis. A manager therefore relies upon call reports, customer feedback, and invoices. Call reports identify the customers called on and present detailed information about interaction with those clients. Traveling sales personnel often must file work schedules indicating where they plan to be during specific future time periods.

The dimensions used to measure a salesperson's performance are determined largely by sales objectives. These objectives are normally set by the sales manager. If an individual's sales objective is stated in terms of sales volume, then that person should be evaluated on the basis of sales volume generated. Even though a salesperson may be assigned a major objective, he or she ordinarily is expected to achieve several related objectives as well. Thus, salespeople often are judged along several dimensions. Sales managers evaluate many performance indicators, including average number of calls per day, average sales per customer, actual sales relative to sales potential, number of new-customer orders, average cost per call, and average gross profit per customer.

To evaluate a salesperson, a sales manager may compare one or more of these dimensions with a predetermined performance standard. However, sales management commonly compares one salesperson's performance with the performance of other employees operating under similar selling conditions or compares current performance with past performance. Sometimes, management judges factors that have less direct bearing on sales performance, such as personal appearance, verbal skills, aggressiveness, cooperativeness, and knowledge of the product, company, market, and competitors.

After evaluating salespeople, sales managers must take any needed corrective action, for it is their job to improve the performance of the sales force. They may have to adjust performance standards, provide additional sales training, or try other motivational methods. Corrective action may demand comprehensive changes in the sales force.

Obviously, effective management of sales activities is crucial to an organization's survival. These activities help to generate the revenues that a firm uses to acquire its resources.

The Nature of Sales Promotion

As defined earlier, **sales promotion** is an activity and/or material that acts as a direct inducement, offering added value or incentive for the product, to resellers, salespersons, or consumers.[6] It encompasses all promotional activities and

6. John F. Luick and William L. Ziegler, *Sales Promotion and Modern Merchandising* (New York: McGraw-Hill, 1968); and Dan E. Schultz and William A. Robinson, *Sales Promotion Management* (Chicago: Crain Books, 1982).

materials other than personal selling, advertising, and publicity. Many sales promotion activities are noncyclical and are designed to produce immediate, short-run effects. For example, cents-off coupons and consumer contests have relatively short deadlines so that consumers must act quickly.

An organization often uses sales promotion activities in concert with other promotional efforts to facilitate personal selling, advertising, or both. For example, people may have to go to a store to enter a consumer contest. This facilitates personal selling by drawing people into the establishment. To improve the effectiveness of advertisements, point-of-purchase displays often are designed to include pictures, symbols, and messages that appear in advertisements.

Sales promotion efforts are not always secondary to other promotion mix ingredients. Companies sometimes employ advertising and personal selling to support sales promotion activities. For example, marketers frequently use advertising to promote trading stamps, cents-off offers, contests, free samples, and premiums. Manufacturers' sales personnel occasionally administer sales contests for wholesale or retail salespersons. In any case, the most effective sales promotion efforts are highly interrelated with other promotional activities. Decisions regarding sales promotion therefore often affect advertising and personal selling decisions, and vice versa.

Sales Promotion Objectives

Marketers utilize sales promotion for a variety of reasons. A single sales promotion activity may be employed to achieve one or several objectives, or several sales promotion activities may be required to accomplish a single goal or set of goals. Marketers use sales promotion to achieve the following objectives:

1. To identify and attract new customers
2. To introduce a new product
3. To increase the total number of users for an established brand
4. To encourage greater usage among current customers
5. To educate consumers regarding product improvements
6. To bring more customers into retail stores
7. To stabilize a fluctuating sales pattern
8. To increase reseller inventories
9. To combat or offset competitors' marketing efforts
10. To obtain more and better shelf space and displays[7]

Some of these objectives are designed specifically to stimulate resellers' demand and effectiveness; some are directed at increasing consumer demand; and others focus on both resellers and consumers. Sales promotion is effective for both offensive and defensive purposes. Whatever its use, the marketer should be certain that the sales promotion objectives are consistent with the organization's overall objectives, as well as its marketing and promotion objectives. (The application on page 460 discusses some problems with using price-oriented sales promotion efforts.)

---

7. Richard E. Stanley, *Promotion: Advertising, Publicity, Personal Selling, and Sales Promotion* (Englewood Cliffs, N.J.: Prentice-Hall, 1982), pp. 304–305.

A General Foods executive recently discussed a promotion trap having to do with the steady increase in expenditures for trade deals and consumer coupons and a reduction in advertising expenditures. He felt that this trade-off is great for improving short-term sales volume, but may be damaging to long-run company image and profitability. The problem is widespread and growing.

Manufacturers give trade deals to retailers. In return, retailers are expected to perform certain marketing activities, for instance, providing the manufacturer with more shelf space, aisle displays, or product appearances in local weekly specials featured by the recipient stores. These trade deals are very popular because they offer sales managers a way to increase their monthly case shipments rather easily. They have special appeal for young managers, who often are just out of school and anxious to impress the boss.

Trade allowances got started in the early 1970s when inflation was high. Fearing that government price controls were on the horizon, marketers raised their prices to high levels to protect their profit margins. To help reduce the sudden impact of the price increases, special discounts were provided that became known as trade allowances. These discounts were supposed to be withdrawn as inflation receded but instead have lingered.

As a result, the purchasing habits of many retailers have changed substantially. In the past retailers were labeled as "passive distributors." Today, they have grown much more powerful and sophisticated and are able to influence manufacturers' pricing policies. The problem is compounded by the manufacturers themselves. Their sales managers are often rewarded for how much they can sell, regardless of how it affects future profitability. And many companies have found that when advertising does not work, sales promotion methods are effective.

Perhaps the biggest problem that has arisen from the heavy emphasis on sales promotion is that strong price competition tarnishes the product's image. Also, price competition that entails substantial price cuts can drastically reduce profit margins on heavily advertised items.

Like retailers, the consumer has been conditioned by sales promotion and price deals. Coupons intended to introduce customers to new products at special prices are used by consumers who have already tried the product. The combination of the coupons and the special prices has turned the consumer into a bargain hunter stalking the aisles for low prices instead of favorite products. Discounting has thus encouraged bargain preference instead of brand preference. (*Source: William Meyers, "Trying to Get Out of the Discounting Box,"* Adweek, *Nov. 11, 1985, pp. 2–4. Reprinted with the permission of* Adweek.)

Sales Promotion Methods

Most sales promotion methods can be grouped into two categories: consumer sales promotion and trade sales promotion. **Consumer sales promotion techniques** encourage or stimulate consumers to patronize a specific retail store or to try and/or purchase a particular product. Consumer sales promotion techniques can be used to draw people into particular retail stores, to introduce new products, or to promote established products. **Trade sales promotion methods** stimulate wholesalers and retailers to carry a producer's products and to market these products aggressively. Most trade sales promotion techniques provide incentives—money, merchandise, gifts, or promotional assistance—to resellers who purchase products or perform certain activities.

Marketers consider a number of factors before deciding which sales promotion method or methods to use. The objectives of the effort are of primary concern. Marketers must weigh product characteristics—size, weight, costs, durability, uses, features, and hazards—and target market characteristics—age, sex, income, location, density, usage rate, and shopping patterns—before choosing a sales promotion method. How the product is distributed and the number and types of resellers may determine the type of method used. Finally, the competitive environment and legal forces influence the selection of sales promotion methods.

To understand sales promotion, we need to examine several sales promotion techniques. Our analysis divides the major sales promotion methods into four categories: (1) sales promotion methods used by retailers, (2) new-product sales promotion techniques, (3) sales promotion methods for established products, and (4) sales promotion methods aimed at resellers.[8]

Sales Promotion Methods Used by Retailers

The variety of sales promotion methods that retailers use fall into four broad categories: retailer coupons, demonstrations, trading stamps, and point-of-purchase displays.

Retailer Coupons

Retailer coupons usually take the form of "cents-off" coupons distributed through advertisements or handouts and redeemable only at specific stores. They are especially useful when price is a primary motivation for consumers' purchasing behavior. For example, a discount supermarket might distribute retailer coupons that allows 30 cents off the price of a specific brand of bread.

Retailer coupons bring customers into a particular store and build sales volume for a specific brand. Competitive counteroffers can significantly reduce the effectiveness of retailer coupons, however. Given their emphasis on price, coupons may undercut customer loyalty to a retailer.

Demonstrations

Demonstrations are excellent attention getters. They are often used by manufacturers on a temporary basis either to encourage trial use and purchase of the product or to actually show how the product works. Because labor costs can be extremely high, demonstrations are not used widely. They can, however, be highly effective for promoting certain types of products, such as appliances. Recent demonstrations have included those for extrusion pasta machines and microconvection ovens.

Trading Stamps

Trading stamps are dispensed in proportion to the amount of a consumer's purchase and can be accumulated and redeemed for goods. Retailers use trading stamps to attract consumers to specific stores. In addition, they can increase sales of specific items by giving extra stamps to purchasers of those

---

8. Much of the information in the descriptions of the sales promotion techniques is from *Sales Promotion and Modern Merchandising*, by John F. Luick and William L. Ziegler. Copyright © 1968 by McGraw-Hill, Inc. Used with permission of McGraw-Hill Book Company.

items. Stamps are attractive to consumers as long as they do not drive up the price of goods. They are effective for many types of retailers.

Point-of-purchase Displays

Point-of-purchase materials include such items as outside signs, window displays, counter pieces, display racks, and self-service cartons. These items, which are frequently provided by producers, attract attention, inform customers, and encourage retailers to carry particular products. A retailer is likely to use point-of-purchase materials if they are attractive, informative, well-constructed, and in harmony with the store.

New-product Sales Promotion Techniques

Several sales promotion methods can be used to promote new products. Three of the most common techniques are free samples, coupons, and money refunds.

Free Samples

Marketers use **free samples** for several reasons: to stimulate trial of a product, to increase sales volume in early stages of the product's life cycle, or to obtain desirable distribution. When Shulton introduced Blue Stratos cologne, for example, 10 million men in the 18–34 target market received samples in the mail just before Father's Day to encourage product trial immediately prior to that heavy gift-giving period.[9]

In designing a free sample, marketers should consider certain factors such as the seasonality of the product, the characteristics of the market, and prior advertising. Free samples are not appropriate for mature products and slow-turnover products.

Sampling is the most expensive of all sales promotion methods. Production and distribution through such channels as mail delivery, door-to-door delivery, in-store distribution, and on-package distribution entail very high costs.

Coupons

Coupons are used to stimulate trial of a new or established product, to increase sales volume quickly, to attract repeat purchasers, or to introduce new package sizes or features (see Figure 15.5). Coupons usually reduce the purchase price of an item. For example, a cereal manufacturer might use a 20-cent coupon to promote a new type of cereal. The savings may be deducted from the purchase price or offered as cash. For best results, coupons should be easy to recognize and should state the offer clearly. The nature of the product (seasonality, maturity, frequency of purchase, and the like) is the prime consideration in setting up a coupon promotion. Coupons have two disadvantages: fraud or misredemption is possible, and the redemption period can be quite lengthy.

An increasing number of households are redeeming coupons. A Nielsen survey in 1971 indicated that 58 percent of all households were using coupons, while a recent similar study revealed that over 76 percent of all households use them.[10]

9. Steven G. Rothschild, "Hang Gliding Theme Used to Unveil New Fragrance," *Marketing Times,* July–Aug. 1981, p. 32.
10. Mary M. English, "Like 'Em or Not, Coupons Surely Are Here to Stay," *Advertising Age,* Aug. 22, 1983, p. M-26.

Figure 15.5

Promotion of a
coupon offer (Source:
Kingsford Company)

Money Refunds

With **money refunds,** consumers submit proof of purchase and are mailed a specific amount of money. Usually, manufacturers demand multiple purchases of the product before a consumer can qualify for a refund. For example, a money refund may require a consumer to mail in five box tops. This method, used primarily to promote trial use of a product, is relatively low in cost. Nevertheless, because money refunds sometimes generate a low response rate, they have limited impact on sales.

Sales Promotion Devices for Established Products

Sales promotion devices for established products are usually aimed at providing additional value for the customer who purchases the item. Four methods commonly used to promote sales of established products are premiums, cents-off offers, consumer contests, and consumer sweepstakes.

Premiums

Premiums are items offered free or at a minimum cost as a bonus for purchasing a product. They can attract competitors' customers, introduce different sizes of established products, add variety to other promotional efforts, and stimulate loyalty. To be effective, premiums must be easily recognizable and desirable. Premiums usually are distributed through retail outlets or through the mail, but they may also be placed on or in packages.

Cents-off Offers

When a **cents-off offer** is used, buyers receive a certain amount off the regular price shown on the label or package. This method can provide a strong incentive for trying the product, stimulate product sales, yield short-lived sales increases, and promote products in off-seasons. It is an easy method to control and is used frequently. However, it reduces the price to customers who would buy at the regular price, and frequent use of cents-off offers may cheapen a product's image. In addition, the method often requires special handling by retailers.

Consumer Contests

In **consumer contests** individuals compete for prizes based on their analytical or creative skill. This method generates traffic at the retail level. Contestants are usually more involved in consumer contests than they are in sweepstakes (discussed next), even though the total participation may be lower. Contests may be used in conjunction with other sales promotion methods such as coupons.

Consumer Sweepstakes

The entrants in a **consumer sweepstakes** submit their names for inclusion in a drawing for prizes. Sweepstakes are employed to stimulate sales and, like contests, are sometimes teamed with other sales promotion methods. Sweepstakes are used more often than consumer contests, and they tend to attract a greater number of participants. The cost of a sweepstakes (about $3 per 1,000 entrants) is considerably less than the cost of a contest.[11]

Successful sweepstakes can generate widespread interest and short-term increases in sales or market share. For example, Levi Strauss attracted 1.75 million entries in a two-week sweepstakes; the Benson & Hedges sweepstakes generated 5 million participants; and Cracker Jacks sponsored a $6-million sweepstakes that helped the firm increase sales by 25 percent in one year.[12] Sweepstakes are, however, prohibited in some states.

Sales Promotion Methods Aimed at Resellers

Producers use sales promotion methods to encourage resellers to carry their products and promote them effectively. The methods include buy-back allowances, buying allowances, counts and recounts, free merchandise, merchandise allowances, cooperative advertising, dealer listings, premium or push money, sales contests, and dealer loaders.

Buy-back Allowances

A **buy-back allowance** is a certain sum of money that is given to a purchaser for each unit bought after an initial deal is over. This method is a secondary incentive in which the total amount of money that buyers can receive is proportional to their purchases during an initial trade deal such as a coupon offer. Buy-back allowances encourage cooperation during an initial sales promotion effort and stimulate repurchase afterwards. The main drawback of this method is its expense.

---

11. Eileen Norris, "Everyone Will Grab at a Chance to Win," *Advertising Age,* Aug. 22, 1983, p. M-10.
12. Franklynn Peterson and Judi Kesselman-Turkel, "Catching Customers with Sweepstakes," *Fortune,* Feb. 8, 1982, pp. 84–87.

Buying Allowances

A **buying allowance** is a temporary price reduction to resellers for purchasing specified quantities of a product. A soap producer, for example, might give retailers $1 for each case of soap purchased. Such offers may provide an incentive to handle a new product, achieve a temporary price reduction, or stimulate the purchase of an item in larger than normal quantities. The buying allowance, which takes the form of money, yields profits to resellers and is simple and straightforward to use. There are no restrictions on how resellers use the money, and this fact increases the method's effectiveness.

Count and Recount

The **count and recount** promotion method is based on the payment of a specific amount of money for each product unit moved from a reseller's warehouse in a given time period. Units of a product are counted at the start of the promotion and again at the end to determine how many have moved from the warehouse. This method can reduce retail stockouts by moving inventory out of warehouses and can also clear distribution channels of obsolete products or packages and reduce warehouse inventories.

The count and recount method might benefit a producer by reducing resellers' inventories, making resellers more likely to place new orders. However, this method is often difficult to administer and may not appeal to resellers who have small warehouses.

Free Merchandise

Free merchandise is sometimes offered to resellers who purchase a stated quantity of the same or different products. Occasionally, free merchandise is used as payment for allowances provided through other sales promotion methods. To avoid handling and bookkeeping problems, the giving of free merchandise usually is accomplished by reducing the invoice.

Merchandise Allowances

A **merchandise allowance** consists of a manufacturer's agreement to pay resellers certain amounts of money for providing special promotional efforts such as advertising or displays. Before paying retailers, manufacturers usually verify their performance. Manufacturers hope that the retailers' additional promotional efforts will yield substantial sales increases.

This method is best suited to high-volume, high-profit, easily handled products. One major problem with using merchandise allowances is that some retailers perform their activities at a minimally acceptable level simply to obtain the allowances.

Cooperative Advertising

Cooperative advertising is an arrangement in which a manufacturer agrees to pay a certain amount of a retailer's media costs for advertising the manufacturer's products. The amount allowed usually is based on the quantities purchased. Before payment is made, a retailer must show proof that advertisements did appear. These payments provide additional funds to retailers for advertising. They can, however, put a severe burden on the producer's advertising budget. Some retailers exploit cooperative advertising programs by crowding too many products into one advertisement. Surprisingly, though, not all available cooperative advertising dollars are used. Some retailers cannot afford to advertise. Others can afford it but do not want to advertise. Still others actually do advertising that qualifies for an allowance but are not willing to do the paperwork necessary to receive reimbursement from producers.[13]

Dealer Listings

A **dealer listing** is an advertisement that promotes a product and identifies the names of participating retailers who sell the product. Dealer listings can influence retailers to carry the product, build traffic at the retail level, and encourage consumers to buy the product at participating dealers.

Premium or Push Money

Premium or **push money** is used to push a line of goods by providing additional compensation to salespeople. It is appropriate when personal selling is an important part of the marketing effort; it is not effective for promoting products that are sold through self-service. This method helps a manufacturer obtain commitment from the sales force, but it can be very expensive.

Sales Contests

A **sales contest** is designed to motivate distributors, retailers, and sales personnel by recognizing outstanding achievements. To be effective, this method must be equitable for all salespersons involved. One advantage to this method is that it can achieve participation at all levels of distribution. However, results are temporary, and prizes are usually expensive.

Dealer Loaders

A **dealer loader** is a gift that is given to a retailer who purchases a specified quantity of merchandise. Often, dealer loaders are used in an attempt to obtain special display efforts from retailers by offering essential display parts as premiums. A manufacturer, for example, might design a display that includes a sterling silver tray as a major component and give the tray to the retailer. Marketers use dealer loaders to obtain new distributors and to push larger quantities of goods.

Summary

Personal selling is the process of informing customers and persuading them to purchase products through personal communication in an exchange situation. The three general purposes of personal selling are finding prospects, convincing them to buy, and keeping customers satisfied. The selling process consists of prospecting and evaluating potential customers, preparing and approaching the customer, making the presentation, overcoming objections, closing, and following up.

In developing a sales force, marketing managers must consider which types of salespersons will sell the firm's products most effectively. The three classifications of salespersons are order getters, order takers, and support personnel. Order getters inform prospects and persuade them to buy. Order-getting activities

13. Ed Crimmins, "A Co-op Myth: It Is a Tragedy That Stores Don't Spend All Their Accruals," *Sales and Marketing Management,* Feb. 7, 1983, pp. 72–73.

can be divided into two categories: those aimed at current customer sales and those aimed at new-business sales. Order takers seek repeat sales and are divided into two categories: inside order takers and field order takers. Sales support personnel facilitate the selling function, but their duties usually extend beyond making sales. The three types of support personnel are missionary, trade, and technical salespersons.

The effectiveness of sales-force management is an important determinant of a firm's success because the sales force is directly responsible for generating an organization's primary input—sales revenue. Major decision areas and activities on which sales managers focus are establishing sales objectives, determining sales-force size, recruiting and selecting salespeople, training sales personnel, compensating salespeople, motivating salespeople, creating sales territories, routing and scheduling salespeople, and controlling and evaluating the sales force.

Sales objectives should be stated in precise, measurable terms and should specify the time period and the geographic areas involved. The size of the sales force must be adjusted from time to time because a firm's marketing plans change, as do markets and forces in the marketing environment. Two techniques that sometimes are used to determine the size of the sales force are the equalized workload method and the incremental productivity method.

Recruiting and selecting salespeople involves attracting and choosing the right type of salesperson to maintain an effective sales force. When developing a training program, one must consider a variety of dimensions, such as who should be trained, where and when the training should occur, what should be taught, and how the information should be presented. Compensation of salespeople involves formulation and administration of a compensation plan that attracts, motivates, and holds the right types of salesperson for the firm. Motivation of salespeople should allow the firm to attain high productivity. Creating sales territories, another aspect of sales-force management, focuses on such factors as size, shape, routing, and scheduling. To control and evaluate sales-force performance, the sales manager must use information obtained through salespersons' call reports, customer feedback, and invoices.

Sales promotion is an activity and/or material that acts as a direct inducement, offering added value or incentive for the product, to resellers, salespersons, or consumers. Marketers use sales promotion to identify and attract new customers, to introduce a new product, and to increase reseller inventories. Sales promotion techniques can be divided into two general categories: consumer and trade. Consumer sales promotion methods encourage consumers to trade at specific stores or to try and/or buy a specific product. Trade sales promotion techniques stimulate resellers to handle a manufacturer's products and to market these products aggressively.

Important Terms

Personal selling
Prospecting
Approach
Closing
Order getters
Order takers
Support personnel

Missionary salespersons
Trade salespersons
Technical salespersons
Equalized workload method
Incremental productivity method
Recruiting
Straight salary compensation plan

Straight commission
  compensation plan
Combination compensation plan
Sales promotion
Consumer sales promotion
  techniques
Trade sales promotion methods
Retailer coupons
Demonstrations
Trading stamps
Point-of-purchase materials
Free samples
Coupons
Money refunds

Premiums
Cents-off offer
Consumer contests
Consumer sweepstakes
Buy-back allowance
Buying allowance
Count and recount
Free merchandise
Merchandise allowance
Cooperative advertising
Dealer listing
Premium or push money
Sales contest
Dealer loader

Discussion and Review Questions

1. What is personal selling? How does personal selling differ from other types of promotional activities?
2. What are the primary purposes of personal selling?
3. Identify the elements of the personal selling process. Must a salesperson include all these elements when selling a product to a customer? Why or why not?
4. How does a salesperson find and evaluate prospects? Do you consider any of these methods to be questionable ethically?
5. Are order getters more aggressive or creative than order takers? Why or why not?
6. What are the similarities and differences between the equalized workload method and the incremental productivity method for determining sales-force size? Can marketers in a new firm use either of these methods to determine the size of the initial sales force? Why or why not?
7. Identify several characteristics of effective sales objectives.
8. How should a sales manager establish criteria for selecting sales personnel? What are the general characteristics of a good salesperson?
9. What major issues or questions should be considered when developing a training program for the sales force?
10. Explain the major advantages and disadvantages of the three basic methods of compensating sales personnel. In general, which method do you most prefer? Why?
11. What major factors should be taken into account in designing the shape of a sales territory?
12. How does a sales manager—who cannot be with each salesperson in the field on a daily basis—control the performance of sales personnel?
13. What is sales promotion? Why is it used?
14. For each of the following, identify and describe three techniques and give some examples: (a) sales promotion methods for retail establishments, (b) new-product sales promotion techniques, (c) sales promotion devices for established products, and (d) sales promotion methods aimed at resellers.
15. What types of sales promotion methods have you observed or experienced recently?

Cases

Case 15.1 Sanders Cutlery Company

Every six months Betty Laven, the sales manager for Sanders Cutlery Company, evaluates the size of the sales force for each of ten geographic areas in which the company's industrial product line is marketed. Currently, Laven is concerned with the number of order getters and support personnel in area C. There are 10 order getters and 28 support salespersons in area C. (The size of the order-taker sales force is not of concern now, as this function is mainly handled internally through telephone contacts.)

Sanders' products are not distributed through the usual wholesaler-retailer channels. The company produces a large assortment of high-quality knives that provide unique benefits to several different target markets, each of which is serviced directly by the company's sales force. The three principal markets are butcher shops, cafeterias and restaurants, and hospitals.

Laven's staff members have compiled information that they think is needed in order for her to make a decision about the size of the sales force. This information is shown in Tables 15.3 and 15.4.

Table 15.3 Estimated total sales and selling costs for the range of 10–18 salespersons

Number of Salespersons	Total Sales	Total Selling Costs
10	$1,500,000	$550,000
11	1,580,000	580,000
12	1,650,000	610,000
13	1,700,000	640,000
14	1,750,000	670,000
15	1,790,000	700,000
16	1,830,000	730,000
17	1,850,000	760,000
18	1,870,000	790,000

Table 15.4 Optimum call frequency and number of customers in each market segment for industrial knife product line

Market Segment	Annual Sales Calls Required	Number of Customers
Butcher shops	2	3,000
Restaurants and cafeterias	3	4,800
Hospitals	1	600

Note: Each salesperson should make an average of 1,200 calls a year.

Questions for Discussion

1. Determine the optimum size of the sales force.
2. What additional information do you think the sales force should provide?
3. What methods of salesperson compensation do you think are appropriate for Sanders? Why?

Case 15.2 Avon Products' Sales Organization[14]

With approximately a 15-percent market share, Avon Products Incorporated is the largest producer and distributor of fragrances, cosmetics, and fashion jewelry in the United States. D. H. McConnell, the founder of Avon, took a very bold and radical step when he introduced local women as sales representatives in 1886. These women were the first "Avon ladies." Today, there are 425,000 Avon representatives visiting a total of 21 million homes every two weeks and leaving brochures that describe Avon products. Avon's catalog reaches more households than does *Reader's Digest* or *TV Guide.*

Avon's sales force relies on an aggressive product development program, which introduces numerous new products annually and drops items that aren't selling. An extensive multimillion-dollar advertising campaign helps to support sales reps' efforts.

Currently, however, Avon's direct selling sales force is experiencing several problems. Because many women now work outside the home during the day, Avon's customer base is diminishing and its sales are decreasing. To compound the problem, Avon is facing new competition from mass merchandisers who are upgrading their cosmetics offerings. And even stiffer market rivalry is coming from direct-mail catalogs replete with designer selections. Avon's sales force is also experiencing problems from within. Avon's compensation program for reps has not been competitive with other direct-sales marketers, and job opportunities for women have improved. As a result, the firm is finding it difficult to attract and keep effective sales representatives.

To reach working women and increase the number of customers it serves, Avon is testing the use of direct mail. Accordingly, women receive the Avon catalog and also order products from the catalog. Sales representatives make deliveries, demonstrate products, and take additional orders. Deliveries are made at night and on weekends. Direct mail also could be employed for sampling Avon products. Thus, if Avon decides to use direct mail on a large scale, these efforts would augment but not replace sales reps' activities.

To maintain and increase its sales force, Avon is improving its compensation program. First, Avon is now paying a 5-percent bonus on new representatives' sales to the reps who brought the new recruits into the organization. Second, each sales group leader receives an additional 3-percent bonus on all first-year sales by new Avon recruits. Third, Avon has instituted a new 35-to-50-percent commission scale, tied to sales performance, to replace the flat rate of 40 percent.

14. This case is based on information from JoAn Paganetti, "An American Best Seller's Story Is Still Direct," *Advertising Age,* March 19, 1984, pp. M4, M5, M44; Pat Sloan, "Avon Comes Back in Force, Plans Doubled Ad Budget," *Advertising Age,* Jan. 31, 1983, pp. 1, 51; and Pat Sloan, "Avon Ladies to Toughen Up Sales Pitch," *Advertising Age,* March 12, 1984, p. 12.

Questions for Discussion

1. What type of compensation method is Avon using?
2. Evaluate Avon's efforts to improve its sales-force compensation program.
3. Besides direct mail, what other methods could Avon use to reach women who work outside the home?

Part V
Pricing Decisions

Obviously, for an organization to provide a satisfying marketing mix, the price must be considered, at least, to be acceptable by target market members. Pricing decisions can have numerous effects on other parts of the marketing mix. For example, a product's price can influence how customers perceive it, what types of marketing institutions are used in distributing the product, and how the product is promoted. In Chapter 16, we discuss the importance of price and look at some of the characteristics of price and nonprice competition. Then we examine the major factors that affect marketers' pricing decisions. Eight major stages used by marketers in establishing prices are discussed in Chapter 17.

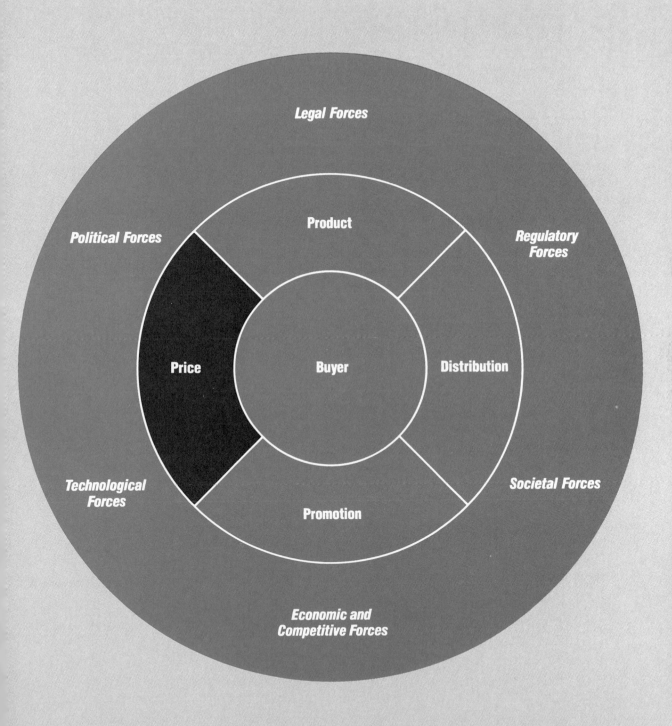

16 / Pricing Concepts

Objectives

■ To understand the nature and importance of price.

■ To be aware of characteristics of both price and nonprice competition.

■ To examine various pricing objectives.

■ To explore several key factors that may influence marketers' pricing decisions.

■ To consider issues bearing on the pricing of products for industrial markets.

Figure 16.1

Dessert section of
The Elms Inn's Menu
(Source: The Elms Inn)

Changing consumer tastes and tougher drunk driving laws have caused a decline in liquor consumption in restaurants. Alcoholic beverage sales in restaurants have dropped approximately 10 percent over the last two years. To recover lost revenue, restaurants have had to increase entrée prices as well as the prices of desserts (see Figure 16.1).

Bennigan's Restaurants have raised their prices slightly overall. However, they have taken steps to introduce several higher-priced desserts. One dessert named "Death by Chocolate" sells for $2.95. Franco's Hidden Harbor in Seattle has added ten new chocolate desserts, some priced as high as $4.50. Nikolaisens' Restaurant in St. Louis increased many of its prices by 20 percent. The restaurant has been remodeled from a dark heavy-drinking atmosphere to a lighter atmosphere with arched windows, brass chandeliers, and mirrors. New brass stoves have been installed so that meals can be prepared at patrons' tables, and new desserts have been introduced to increase profit levels. A single scoop of ice cream previously sold for $1.25 at Nikolaisens'; with the addition of nuts and a touch of liqueur, it now sells for $3.75.[1]

DESSERTS

Pastries from the Cart	3.75	Cherries Jubilée	5.25
Cheese from the Board	3.50	Coupes Marrons	4.25
Black and White Parfait	3.25	Eclair Maison	3.75
Peach Flambé Au Brandy	5.25	Peach Melba	3.75
Cherry Herring Parfait	4.25	Zabaglione	3.75
Various Ice Creams	3.00		

Crepes Suzettes for Two	10.00	Baked Alaska for Two	12.00

Pot of Coffee	1.25	Pot of Tea	1.25	Irish Coffee	4.25
Espresso	2.50	Sanka	1.25	Herb Tea	1.25
		Viennese Iced Coffee	3.75		

1. John Curley, "With Liquor Sales Slipping, Restaurants Try Fancier Desserts and Higher Prices," *Wall Street Journal,* June 14, 1985, p. 23. Reprinted by permission of *Wall Street Journal,* © Dow Jones & Company, Inc., 1985. All Rights Reserved.

These are just a few examples of how various restaurants are adjusting prices to improve their profit positions. Pricing is a crucial element in an organization's total marketing mix. In this chapter we initially focus on the nature of price and its importance to marketers. Then we consider some of the characteristics of price and nonprice competition. Next we explore the various types of pricing objectives that marketers may establish, and we examine in some detail the numerous factors that can influence pricing decisions. Finally, we discuss selected issues related to the pricing of products for industrial markets.

The Nature of Price

Price is probably the most flexible variable in the marketing mix. Marketers can usually adjust their prices more easily and more quickly than they can change any other marketing mix variable. Bear in mind, however, that under certain circumstances, the price variable may be relatively inflexible.

To a buyer, **price** is the value placed on what is exchanged. Something of value—usually purchasing power—is exchanged for satisfaction or utility. **Purchasing power** depends on a buyer's income, credit, and wealth. It is a mistake to believe that price is always money paid or some other financial consideration. In fact, trading of products—**barter**—is the oldest form of exchange. Money may or may not be involved.

Buyers' concern for and interest in price is related to their expectations about the satisfaction or utility associated with a product. To illustrate, one study indicates that 25 percent of all meat purchase decisions are based primarily on price.[2] Since buyers have limited resources, they must allocate their purchasing power to obtain the most desired products. Buyers must decide whether the utility gained in an exchange is worth the purchasing power sacrificed.

Almost anything of value—ideas, services, rights, and goods—can be assessed by a price because in our society the financial price is the measurement of value commonly used in exchanges. Thus, a painting by Picasso may be valued, or priced, at $500,000. Financial price, then, quantifies value. It is the basis of most market exchanges.

Terms Used to Describe Price

Price is expressed in different terms for different exchanges. For instance, auto insurance companies charge a *premium* for protection from the cost of injuries or repairs stemming from an automobile accident. An officer who stops you for speeding writes a ticket that requires you to pay a *fine*. If a lawyer defends you, a *fee* is charged, and if you use a railway or taxi, a *fare* is charged. A *toll* is charged for the use of bridges or turnpikes.

Rent is paid for the use of equipment or an apartment. A *commission* is remitted to an agent for the sale of real estate. *Dues* are paid to allow membership in a club or group. A *deposit* can be made to hold or lay away merchandise. A *tip* helps pay waitresses or waiters for their services. *Interest* is charged for the loan that you obtain, and *taxes* are paid for government services. The value

---

2. "Yankelovich Says Effort to Up Consumption of Meat Must Focus on Life-Style Changes," *Frozen Food Age,* Nov. 1983, p. 20.

of many products is of course called *price*. Although price may be expressed in many different ways, it is important to remember that the purpose of this concept is to quantify and express the value of the items in a market exchange.

The Importance of Price to Marketers

As pointed out in Chapter 8, it can take a long time to develop a product. It takes time to plan promotion and to communicate benefits. Distribution usually requires a long-term commitment to dealers who will handle the product. Often, the only thing a marketer can change quickly to respond to changes in demand or to the actions of competitors is price.

Price is also a key element in the marketing mix because it relates directly to the generation of total revenue. The equation shown below is an important one for the entire organization.

$$\text{Profits} = \text{Total Revenues} - \text{Total Costs}$$
$$\text{or}$$
$$\text{Profits} = (\text{Prices} \times \text{Quantities Sold}) - \text{Total Costs}$$

Prices affect an organization's profits, which are its lifeblood for long-term survival. Price affects the profit equation in several ways. It directly influences the equation because it is a major component. It has an indirect impact because it can be a major determinant of the quantities sold. Even more indirectly, price influences total costs through its impact on quantities sold.

Because price has a psychological impact on customers, marketers can use it symbolically. By raising a price, they can emphasize the quality of a product and try to increase the status associated with its ownership. By lowering a price, they can emphasize a bargain and attract customers who go out of their way—spending extra time and effort—to save a small amount. Price can have a strong effect on sales.

Price and Nonprice Competition

A product offering can compete on a price or nonprice basis. The choice will affect not only pricing decisions and activities but also those associated with other marketing mix decision variables.

Price Competition

When **price competition** is employed, a marketer emphasizes price as an issue and matches or beats the prices of competitors who are also emphasizing low prices (see the advertisements in Figure 16.2). A seller who competes based on price may change prices frequently or at least must be willing and able to do so. Whenever competitors change their prices, the seller must respond quickly and aggressively.

Price competition provides a marketer with flexibility. Prices can be altered to account for changes in the firm's costs or in demand for the product. If competitors try to gain market share by cutting prices, an organization competing on a price basis can react quickly to such competitive efforts. However, a major disadvantage of price competition is that competitors also have the flexibility

Figure 16.2   *Companies competing through price competition (Source: Ad on left courtesy of The Hertz Corporation. Ad on right copyright Budget Rent a Car Corporation, 1985)*

to adjust their prices. Thus, they can quickly match or beat an organization's price cuts. Furthermore, if a user of price competition is forced to raise prices, competing firms that are not under the same pressures may decide not to raise their prices. (The application on page 479 focuses on an industry that shows signs of shifting toward price competition.)

Nonprice Competition

Nonprice competition occurs when a seller elects not to focus on price, and instead emphasizes distinctive product features, service, product quality, promotion, packaging, or other factors in order to distinguish its product from competing brands. Thus, nonprice competition is based on factors other than price. It affords an organization the opportunity to increase its brand's unit sales through means other than changing the brand's price. One major advantage of nonprice competition is that by using factors other than price, a firm can build customer loyalty to its brand. If customers prefer a brand because of nonprice issues, they may not easily be lured away by competing firms and brands. But when price is the primary reason why customers buy a particular brand, the competition can attract such customers through price cuts.

Nonprice competition is workable under the right conditions. A company must be able to distinguish its brand through unique product features, higher product quality, customer service, promotion, packaging, and the like. Buyers not only must be able to perceive these distinguishing characteristics but also

Lowering prices to stimulate sales is a common retailer practice. However, until recently bookstores usually sold books at suggested publishers' prices. B. Dalton bookstores and a few publishers have been experimenting with marked-down prices for recently released books. If price cutting becomes a popular practice, the book-selling industry could undergo quite a change in pricing practices.

In some early trials the B. Dalton bookstore chain found that markdowns helped cut inventories and the number of returns. (Bookstores return unsold books to their publishers, a practice that involves significant costs for shipping, storage, and recordkeeping.) Other markdown experiments by a large publisher, Simon and Schuster, resulted in a decrease of 15 to 25 percent in the return rate.

Markdowns also allow full-price bookstores to challenge discount chains. In the past, retailers had to absorb the loss of profits from markdowns, but in the experiments now being conducted the publishers share in the price reductions. When a publisher decides to mark down a book, the reduction will not be kept a secret. There will be a promotional program with posters indicating the discount offer.

It is not known if the markdown programs are here to stay. Some publishers are wary of the risks involved in discounting books. There are already customers who say they'll wait a year until a book is available in paperback before buying it. Publishers now worry that other customers will anticipate sales and will wait to buy until hardcover prices are lowered. Publishers are also concerned that consumers will expect markdowns on all new releases. In spite of these concerns, Random House and Houghton Mifflin are planning to mark down a number of newly published books. (*Source: Steve Weiher, "Booksellers and Publishers Try Markdowns in Face of Competition and Fickle Readers,"* Wall Street Journal, *June 5, 1985, p. 37. Reprinted by permission of* Wall Street Journal, © *Dow Jones & Company, Inc., 1985. All Rights Reserved.*)

must view them as desirable. The distinguishing features that set a particular brand apart from its competitors should be difficult, if not impossible, for competitors to imitate. Finally, the organization must be able to promote extensively the distinguishing characteristics of the brand to establish its superiority and to set it apart from competitors in the minds of buyers.

A marketer attempting to compete on a nonprice basis cannot ignore competitors' prices, however. The firm must be aware of competitors' prices and will probably price its brand near or slightly above competing brands. Price thus remains a crucial marketing mix component in situations that call for nonprice competition.

Pricing Objectives

Pricing objectives are overall goals that describe what the firm wants to achieve through its pricing efforts. Since pricing objectives influence decisions in most functional areas—including finance, accounting, and production—the objectives must be consistent with the organization's overall mission and purpose. Because of the many areas involved, a marketer often uses multiple pricing objectives.

In this section, we look at a few of the typical pricing objectives that firms might set for themselves.

Survival

A fundamental pricing objective is to survive. Most organizations will tolerate short-run losses, internal upheaval, and almost any other difficulties if they are necessary for survival. Since price is such a flexible and convenient variable to adjust, it sometimes is used to increase sales volume to levels that match the organization's expenses. For example, Continental Airlines, when faced with severe price competition and bankruptcy, was forced to offer discount fares that were significantly below competitors'. This tactic was designed to generate revenue and permit short-term survival. Passenger traffic increased dramatically, and the chance of organizational survival improved.

Profit

Although businesses sometimes claim that their objective is to maximize profits for their owners, the objective of profit maximization is rarely operational, since its achievement is difficult to measure. Apple Computer, for instance, is more concerned with long-range survival in the computer industry than with maximizing profits in the short run. The chairman at Apple claims that building good computers is the most important objective at the company.[3] As a result of the difficulty in measurement, profit objectives tend to be set at levels that the owners and top-level decision makers view as "satisfactory." Specific profit objectives may be stated in terms of actual dollar amounts or in terms of percentage change relative to the profits of a previous period.

Return on Investment

Pricing to attain a specified rate of return on the company's investment is a profit-related pricing objective. Although General Motors prices for profit objectives, actual earnings have fluctuated dramatically between 1980 and 1985. Most pricing objectives based on return on investment (ROI) are achieved by trial and error because not all cost and revenue data needed to project the return on investment are available when prices are set.

Market Share

Market share, which is a firm's sales in relation to total industry sales, is a very meaningful benchmark of success.[4] Many firms establish pricing objectives to maintain or increase market share. For example, a company's pricing objective might be to increase its market share from 22 to 28 percent within the next twelve months. (The organizations discussed in the application on page 481 are trying to increase market share through pricing.)

Maintaining or increasing market share need not depend upon growth in industry sales. Remember that an organization can increase its market share even though sales for the total industry are decreasing. For example, in recent years Philip Morris has focused all marketing strategies on increasing its market share in the cigarette industry. With increased awareness of the negative health

---

3. Peter Nulty, "Apple's Bid to Stay in the Big Time," *Fortune,* Feb. 7, 1983, p. 36.
4. Martin L. Bell, *Marketing: Concepts and Strategy,* 3rd ed. (Boston: Houghton Mifflin, 1979), p. 398.

Part V / Pricing Decisions

The last three years have been difficult for many cable television operators. Competition has been increasing sharply as VCR prices have fallen drastically to within the range of many consumers' budgets. Purchase of a VCR has played a major role in the decision of many subscribers to disconnect from cable. However, many cable companies are fighting back with attractive package deals for current and potential subscribers.

One cable company, Daniels & Associates of Denver, is offering four pay-TV channels for a monthly fee of only $15.95. The package includes Cinemax, American Movie Classics, Bravo, and a choice of the Disney or the Playboy Channel. As an extra, the company is offering HBO as a substitution for Cinemax for $5.00 more. To purchase each channel separately would normally cost as much as $9.95 each. This new plan is expected to bring in about 5,000 subscriptions from current cable subscribers and new subscribers.

The vice president of marketing for Daniels & Associates stated that even if the firm loses some of its present HBO subscribers to the new package, its profits will still be strong. For HBO-only subscribers, Daniels nets $5.75, but on the new package plan, called Showcase, the net is around $10.00. Either plan is profitable for Daniels. Many other cable companies appear to be carefully watching the results of Daniels' package pricing experiment.

While some companies are waiting, some are acting. American Television & Communications is planning a similar package plan, and Continental Cablevision of Boston has offered a free pay-TV service when two are purchased. Still other companies are offering special bonus features to new subscribers such as free remote control or free installation. Whether they offer a special package deal or a free channel, cable companies are finding new ways to compete with the VCR by offering more for less. (*Source:* Susan Spillman, "Cable Operators Discount Multi-Channel Packages," Advertising Age, *Feb. 4, 1985, p. 44. Reprinted from* Advertising Age, *Feb. 4, 1985. Copyright © 1985 Crain Communications Inc.*)

consequences of smoking, there is the potential for declining sales in the industry as a whole.[5] On the other hand, an organization's sales volume may, in fact, increase while its market share within the industry decreases, assuming that the overall market is growing.

Cash Flow

Some organizations set prices to recover cash as fast as possible. Financial managers are understandably interested in quickly recovering capital spent to develop products. This objective may have the support of the marketing manager who anticipates a short product life cycle.

While it may be acceptable in some situations, the use of cash flow and recovery as an objective oversimplifies the value of price in contributing to profits. A disadvantage of this pricing objective could be high prices, which might allow competitors with lower prices to gain a large share of the market.

Status Quo

In some instances, an organization may be in a favorable position and, desiring nothing more, may set an objective of status quo. Status quo objectives can

5. "Why Cigarette Makers Are So Nervous," *Business Week,* Dec. 20, 1982, p. 55.

Figure 16.3

Promotion of high-
quality product (Source:
BMW of North America,
Inc.)

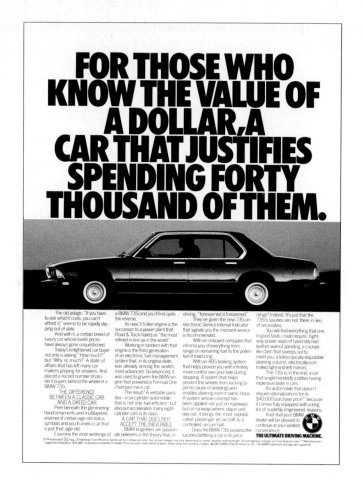

focus on several dimensions—maintaining a certain market share, meeting (but not beating) competitors' prices, achieving price stability, or maintaining a favorable public image. A status quo pricing objective can reduce a firm's risks by helping to stabilize demand for its products. The use of status quo pricing objectives sometimes deemphasizes price as a competitive tool, which can lead to a climate of nonprice competition in an industry.

Product Quality

A company might have the objective of product quality leadership in the market. This goal normally dictates a high price to cover the high product quality and the high cost of research and development. For instance, BMW positions its cars as expensive but high-quality automobiles, as shown in Figure 16.3.

Factors Affecting Pricing Decisions

Pricing decisions can be complex because of the number of details that must be considered. In addition, there frequently is considerable uncertainty regarding the reaction of buyers, channel members, competitors, and others. Most price-

Figure 16.4

Factors that affect
pricing decisions

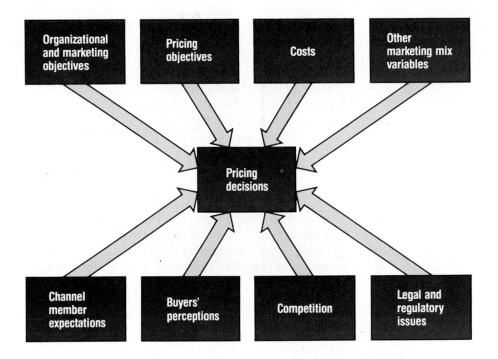

decision factors can be grouped into one of the eight categories shown in Figure 16.4. In this section we will explore how each of these eight groups of factors enters into price decision making.

Organizational and Marketing Objectives

Marketers should set prices that are consistent with the goals and mission of the organization. For example, a retailer trying to position itself as value oriented—meaning that for the prices charged, its products are above average in quality—may wish to set prices that are quite reasonable relative to product quality. In this case, a marketer would not want to set premium prices on products but instead would strive to price products in line with this overall organizational goal.

The firm's marketing objectives must also be considered. Decision makers should make pricing decisions that are compatible with the organization's marketing objectives. Say, for instance, that one of a producer's marketing objectives is to increase unit sales by 12 percent by the end of the next year. Assuming that buyers are price sensitive, a price increase or setting a price above the average market price would not be in line with the firm's sales objective.

Types of Pricing Objectives

The type of pricing objectives used by a marketer should have considerable bearing on the determination of prices. An objective of a certain target return on investment (such as the 20 percent ROI after taxes set by General Motors) requires that prices be set at a level that will generate a high enough sales volume to yield the specified target. A market-share pricing objective usually causes a firm to price a product below competing brands of similar quality to attract competitors' customers to the company's brand. This type of pricing can lead to lower profits. A marketer sometimes uses temporary price reductions with the hope of gaining market share. A cash-flow pricing objective may cause an organization to set a relatively high price, which can place the product at a competitive disadvantage. On the other hand, a cash-flow pricing objective sometimes results in a long, sustained low price. However, this type of objective is more likely to be addressed by using temporary price reductions such as sales, rebates, and special discounts.

Costs

Obviously, costs must be an issue when establishing price. A firm may temporarily sell products below cost to match competition, to generate cash flow, or even to increase market share, but in the long run it cannot survive by selling its products below cost. Even when a firm has a high-volume business, it absolutely cannot survive if each item is sold slightly below what it costs. A marketer should be careful to analyze all costs so that they can be included in the total cost associated with a product. Most marketers view a product's cost as a minimum or floor below which the product cannot be priced. We discuss cost analysis in more detail in the next chapter and in Chapter 19.

Other Marketing Mix Variables

All marketing mix variables are highly interrelated. Pricing decisions can influence decisions and activities associated with product, distribution, and promotion variables. A product's price frequently affects the demand for the item. A high price, for instance, may result in low unit sales, which in turn may lead to higher production costs per unit. Conversely, lower per unit production costs may result from a low price. For many products, buyers associate better product quality with a high price and lower product quality with a low price. This perceived price-quality relationship influences the overall image customers have of products or brands. The price sometimes determines the degree of status associated with ownership of the product.

Pricing decisions can influence the number of competing brands in a product category. When a firm introduces a new product, sets a relatively high price, and achieves high unit sales, competitors may be attracted to this product category. If a firm uses a low price, the low profit margin may be unattractive to potential competition.

The price of a product is linked to several dimensions of its distribution. Premium-priced products often are marketed through selective or exclusive distribution, while lower-priced products in the same product category may be sold through intensive distribution. For example, Cross pens are distributed through selective distribution and Bic pens through intensive distribution. The manner in which a product is stored and transported may also be associated with its price. When a producer is developing the price of a product, the profit margins of marketing channel members such as wholesalers and retailers must be considered. Channel members must be adequately compensated for the functions they perform. Inadequately compensated channel members will withdraw from a marketing channel.

The way a product is promoted can be affected by its price. Bargain prices often are included in advertisements while premium prices are less likely to appear in advertising messages. Compare the advertisements in Figure 16.2

with those in Figure 17.4. The issue of a premium price is sometimes included in advertisements for upscale items such as luxury cars (see Figure 16.3) or fine jewelry. Higher-priced products are more likely to require personal selling efforts than are lower-priced ones. For example, a customer may be willing to purchase an inexpensive watch in a self-service environment; yet, that same person would hesitate to buy an expensive watch if it was available in the same store.

The price structure can affect a salesperson's relationship with his or her customers. A complex pricing structure takes longer to explain to customers, is more likely to confuse the buyer, and may engender misunderstandings that result in long-term customer dissatisfaction. For example, the pricing structures of many airlines are complex and frequently confuse ticket sales agents and travelers alike.

Price is an important consideration in marketing planning, market analysis, and sales forecasting. It also is a major issue when assessing a brand's position relative to competing brands.

Channel Member Expectations

When making price decisions, a producer must consider what distribution channel members (such as wholesalers and retailers) expect. A channel member certainly expects to receive a profit for the functions it performs. The amount of profit expected depends on what the intermediary could make if it were handling a competing product instead. Also, the amount of time and the resources required to carry the product influence the expectations of intermediaries.

Channel members often expect producers to provide discounts for large orders and quick payment. (Discounts are discussed later in this chapter.) At times, resellers expect producers to provide several support activities such as sales training, service training, repair advisory service, cooperative advertising, sales promotions, and perhaps a program for returning unsold merchandise to the producer. These support activities clearly have costs associated with them. A producer must be sure to consider these costs when determining prices. Failure to price the product so that the producer can provide some of these support activities may cause the product to be viewed less favorably by resellers.

Buyers' Perceptions

One important question that marketers should assess when making price decisions is "How important is the price to people in the target market?" The importance of price is not absolute; it can vary from market to market and from market segment to market segment. However, for a particular product, some buyers perceive the price to be more important than do other buyers. Members of one market segment may be more price sensitive than members in a different target market. Also, the importance of price to buyers will vary across different product categories. For example, price may be a more important factor in the purchase of gasoline than in the purchase of a pair of jeans, because buyers may be more price sensitive to gasoline than they are to jeans.

For numerous products, buyers have a range of acceptable prices. In some cases this range is fairly narrow, while for other product categories a wider range exists. A marketer should become aware of the acceptable range of prices in the relevant product category. (This issue and related ones are discussed in more detail in the next chapter.)

Buyers' perceptions of a product relative to competing products may allow or encourage a firm to price the item at a price significantly different from those of competing products. If the product is viewed as being superior to most of the competition, a premium price may be feasible. Strong brand loyalty sometimes provides the opportunity to charge a premium price. When buyers have an unfavorable view of the product (assuming that they are not extremely negative), a lower price may be required to generate sales.

Competition

A marketer needs to remain aware of the prices charged by competitors. This information helps the firm adjust its prices relative to competitors' prices. This does not mean that a marketer necessarily will keep the price the same as competitors' prices. Marketers may set a price above or below that of most competitors. Thus, knowledge of the prices charged for competing brands is one important factor among several.

When adjusting prices, a marketer must assess how competitors will respond. Will competitors change their prices (some, in fact, may not), and if so, will they move their prices up or down? In Chapter 2 we describe several types of competitive market structures. The structure that characterizes the industry in which a firm participates affects flexibility of price setting. When an organization operates under conditions of a monopoly and is unregulated, the firm can set prices at whatever the traffic will bear. However, an organization may choose not to price the product at the highest possible level for fear of inviting government regulation or because the company desires to penetrate a market by using a lower price. If the monopoly is regulated, pricing flexibility normally is reduced, with the regulatory body allowing the organization to set prices that generate a reasonable, but definitely not excessive, return. A government-owned monopoly may price products below cost to make them accessible to people who otherwise could not afford them. Transit systems, for example, are sometimes operated in this way. However, government-owned monopolies sometimes charge higher prices to control demand. In states with state-owned liquor stores, the price of liquor tends to be significantly higher than in states where liquor stores are not owned by a government body.

In an oligopoly there are high barriers to competitive entry into the industry, meaning that there are only a few sellers in that industry. Examples of oligopolistic industries are automobiles, mainframe computers, and steel. A firm in such industries can raise its price hoping that its competitors will do the same. When an organization cuts its price to gain a competitive edge, other firms also are likely to cut theirs, which means that very little is gained through price cuts in an oligopolistic market structure. Marketers obviously must remain aware of the competition's prices to be able to keep their prices in line.

There are numerous sellers with differentiated product offerings in a market structure characterized by monopolistic competition. The products are differentiated on the basis of physical characteristics, features, quality, and brand images. An organization may be able to use a price that differs from those of competitors because of its product's distinguishing characteristics. Nevertheless, firms engaged in a monopolistic competitive market structure are likely to practice nonprice competition, which was discussed earlier in this chapter.

Under conditions of perfect competition there are many sellers. Buyers view all sellers' products to be the same. All firms sell their products at the going market price, and buyers will not pay more than that. Thus, for this type of market structure a marketer has no flexibility in setting prices.

Legal and Regulatory Issues

Government action at times strongly influences marketers' pricing decisions. In an attempt to curb inflation, the federal government may invoke price controls, "freeze" prices at certain levels, or determine the rates at which prices can be increased. In some states, regulatory agencies set the prices of such products as insurance, liquor, dairy goods, and electricity.

Many regulations and laws have an effect on pricing decisions and activities. The Sherman Act prohibits conspiracies to control prices, and court interpretations of the act have ruled that price fixing among firms in an industry is illegal per se. Marketers not only must refrain from fixing prices, but also must develop independent pricing policies and set prices in ways that do not even suggest collusion. Both the Federal Trade Commission Act and the Wheeler-Lea Act prohibit deceptive pricing. In establishing prices, marketers must not deceive customers.

The Robinson-Patman Act has had a strong impact on pricing decisions. For various reasons, marketers may wish to sell the same type of product at different prices. Provisions in the Robinson-Patman Act, as well as those in the Clayton Act, limit the use of such price differentials. If price differentials tend to lessen or injure competition, they are considered discriminatory and are prohibited. Not all price differentials, however, are discriminatory. Marketers can employ them for a product if any one of the following conditions is satisfied:

1. The price differentials do not injure or lessen competition.
2. The price differentials result from differences in the costs of selling to various customers.
3. The customers are not competitors.
4. The price differentials arise because the firm has had to cut its price to a particular buyer to meet competitors' prices.

Until 1975, manufacturers of consumer goods could set and enforce minimum retail prices for their products in some states. Now the Consumer Goods Pricing Act prohibits the use of price maintenance agreements among producers and resellers involved in interstate commerce.

Retailers and wholesalers in states that have effective unfair trade practices acts are limited in their use of pricing as a competitive tool. Since such acts place a "floor" under prices that retailers and wholesalers can regularly charge, marketers who compete on the basis of price must be cognizant of legal constraints on their competitors' pricing policies.

Pricing for Industrial Markets

Industrial or organizational markets consist of individuals and organizations that purchase products for resale, for use in their own operations or for producing other products. Quoting prices to this category of buyers is sometimes different from setting prices for consumers.

Differences in the size of purchases, geographic factors, and transportation considerations require sellers to make adjustments in prices. Also, the rational purchase motives of industrial customers may limit the use of psychological and some promotional pricing policies.

Price Discounting

Producers commonly provide intermediaries with discounts off list prices. Although there are many types of discounts, they usually fall into one of five categories: trade, quantity, cash, seasonal discounts, and allowances.

Trade Discounts

A reduction off the list price given to a middleman by a producer for performing certain functions is called a **trade,** or **functional discount.** A trade discount usually is stated in terms of a percentage or series of percentages off the list price. Middlemen are given trade discounts to compensate them for performing such functions as selling, transporting, storing, final processing, and perhaps providing credit services. Although certain trade discounts are often a standard practice within an industry, discounts do vary considerably among industries.

Quantity Discounts

Deductions from list price that reflect the economies of purchasing in large quantities are called **quantity discounts.** Some of the fixed costs of serving a customer, such as billing and sales contacts, may remain the same—or even go down—as the size of an order increases. A large purchase also reduces per-unit selling costs and may shift some of the storage, finance, and risk-taking functions to the buyer. Thus, quantity discounts usually reflect legitimate reductions in costs.

Quantity discounts can be either cumulative or noncumulative. **Cumulative discounts** are quantity discounts aggregated over a stated period of time. Purchases of $10,000 in a three-month period, for example, might entitle the buyer to a 5-percent, or $500, rebate. Such discounts are supposed to reflect economies in selling and encourage the buyer to purchase from one seller. **Noncumulative discounts** are one-time reductions in prices based on the number of units purchased, the dollar size of the order, or the product mix purchased. Like cumulative discounts, these discounts should reflect some economies in selling or trade functions.

Cash Discounts

A **cash discount** exists when prompt payment or cash payment results in a price reduction to the buyer. Accounts receivable are an expense and a collection problem for many organizations. A policy to encourage prompt payment is a popular practice and sometimes a major concern in setting prices.

Discounts are based on cash payments or cash paid within a stated period of time. For example, "2/10 net 30" means that a 2-percent discount will be allowed if the account is paid within 10 days and that the balance is due within 30 days without a discount. If the account is not paid within 30 days, interest may be charged.

Seasonal Discounts

A price reduction to buyers who buy goods or services out of season is a **seasonal discount.** These discounts allow the seller to maintain steadier production during the year. For example, automobile rental agencies offer seasonal discounts in winter and early spring to encourage firms to use automobiles during the slow months of the automobile rental business.

Allowances

Another type of reduction from the list price is an **allowance**—a concession in price to achieve a desired goal. Trade-in allowances, for example, are price reductions given for turning in a used item when purchasing a new one. Allowances help to give the buyer the ability to make the new purchase. This type of discount is popular in the aircraft industry. Another example is promotional allowances, which are price reductions granted to dealers for participating in advertising and sales support programs intended to increase sales of a particular item.

For example, because supermarkets focus on major brands first, in their own price discount promotions, consumers often find that Dr Pepper is priced higher than Coke or Pepsi. This price disadvantage has hurt Dr Pepper's attempts to increase the market share of its noncola in a nation of heavy cola drinkers. To overcome this price disadvantage, Dr Pepper is urging bottlers and retailers to establish new lower prices for its six-packs of 10-ounce bottles. The company offers a promotional allowance so that retailers and bottlers can retain their usual profit margins.[6]

Geographic Pricing

Geographic pricing involves reductions for transportation costs or other costs associated with the physical distance between the buyer and the seller. Prices may be quoted as being **F.O.B. (free-on-board) factory,** which is a price that excludes transportation charges and indicates a shipping point. F.O.B. factory indicates the price of the merchandise at the factory, before it is loaded onto the carrier vehicle. The buyer must pay for shipping. Although this is an easy way to price products, it is sometimes difficult for marketers to administer, especially when a firm has a wide product mix or when customers are dispersed widely. Since customers will want to know about the most economical method of shipping, the seller must keep posted on shipping rates.

To avoid the problems involved with charging different prices to each customer, **uniform geographic pricing,** sometimes called postage-stamp pricing, may be used. This type of pricing results in a fixed average cost of transportation. Gasoline, paper products, and office equipment often are priced on a uniform basis.

Zone prices are regional prices that take advantage of a uniform pricing system; prices are adjusted for major geographic zones as the transportation costs increase. For example, a Florida manufacturer's prices may be higher for buyers on the Pacific Coast and in Canada than for buyers in Georgia.

Base-point pricing is a geographic pricing policy that includes the price at the factory plus freight charges from the base point nearest the buyer. This approach to pricing has been abandoned, as its legal status has been questioned. The policy resulted in all buyers paying freight charges from one location, say Detroit or Pittsburgh, regardless of where the product was manufactured.

6. Al Urbanski, "Dr Pepper Heals Itself," *Sales and Marketing Management,* March 14, 1983, pp. 33–36.

When the seller absorbs all or part of the actual freight costs, **freight absorption pricing** is being used. The seller might employ this method because it wishes to do business with a particular customer or to get more business; more business will cause the average cost to fall and counterbalance the extra freight cost. This strategy is used to improve market penetration and to retain a hold in an increasingly competitive market.

Transfer Pricing

When one unit in a company sells a product to another unit, **transfer pricing** is used. The price is determined by one of the following methods:

Actual full cost: calculated by dividing all fixed and variable expenses for a period into the number of units produced

Standard full cost: calculated on what it would cost to produce the goods at full plant capacity

Cost plus investment: calculated as full cost plus the cost of a portion of the selling unit's assets used for internal needs

Market-based cost: calculated at the market price less a small discount to reflect the lack of sales effort and other expenses.

The choice of a method of transfer pricing depends upon management strategy for the company and the nature of the units' interaction. The company might initially choose to determine price by the actual full cost method and later change to a market-based method or whatever method the management of the company decides is best suited for the company's changed business situation.[7]

Price Discrimination

A policy of **price discrimination** results in different prices being charged to give a group of buyers a competitive advantage. Price differentiation becomes discriminatory when a seller gives one reseller or industrial buyer an advantage over competitors by providing products at a price lower than other similar customers can obtain. If customers are not in competition with each other, different prices may be charged legally.

Price differentials are legal when they can be justified on the basis of cost savings, when they are used to meet competition in good faith, or when they do not damage competition. The Robinson-Patman Act prohibits price discrimination that lessens competition among wholesalers and retailers, and it prohibits producers from giving disproportionate services to large buyers.

Table 16.1 shows the principal forms of price discrimination. For price discrimination to work, the following conditions are necessary: (1) the market must be segmentable; (2) the cost of segmenting should not exceed the extra revenue from price discrimination; (3) the practice should not breed customer ill will; (4) competition should not be able to steal the segment that is charged the higher price; and (5) the practice should not violate any applicable laws.

---

7. Robert G. Eccles, "Control with Fairness in Transfer Pricing," *Harvard Business Review,* Nov.–Dec. 1983, pp. 149–161.

Table 16.1 Principal forms of price discrimination

Main Classes	Bases of Discrimination	Examples
Personal	Incomes of buyers	Income-based sliding scale for doctors' fees
	Earning power of buyers	Royalties paid for use of patented machines and processes
Group	Buyers' socioeconomic characteristics such as age or sex	Children's haircuts, lower admission charges for individuals in uniform, senior citizen rates
	Location of buyers	Zone prices, in-state vs. out-of-state tuition, lower export prices (dumping)
	Status of buyers	Lower prices to new customers, quantity discounts to big buyers
	Use of product	Railroad rates, public utility rates
Product	Qualities of products	Relatively higher prices for deluxe models
	Labels on products	Lower prices of unbranded products
	Sizes of products	Relatively lower prices for larger sizes (the "giant economy" size)
	Peak and off-peak services	Lower prices for off-peak services; excursion rates in transportation, off-season rates at resorts, holiday and evening telephone rates.

Summary

Price is the value placed on what is exchanged. The buyer exchanges purchasing power—which depends on the buyer's income, credit, and wealth—for satisfaction or utility. Price is not always money paid; barter—trading of products—is the oldest form of exchange. Various terms are used to describe price such as *premium, tip, taxes, dues,* and *interest.* Price is a key element in the marketing mix because it relates directly to the generation of total revenue. The profit factor can be determined mathematically by multiplying price times quantity sold and then subtracting total costs from total revenues. Price is the only variable in the marketing mix that can quickly and easily be adjusted to respond to changes in the external environment.

A product offering can compete either on a price or nonprice basis. Price competition emphasizes price as the product differential. Prices fluctuate frequently, and price competition among sellers is aggressive. Price competition can be effective when products in a market are standardized and undifferentiated and demand is elastic. Nonprice competition emphasizes product differentiation through distinctive features, services, product quality, or other factors. Establishing brand loyalty by employing nonprice competition works best when the product can be physically differentiated and these distinguishing characteristics can be recognized by the customer.

Pricing objectives are overall goals that describe the role of price in an organization's long-range plans. The broadest and most fundamental pricing objective is survival. Price is easily adjusted to increase sales volume or to combat competition so that the organization can stay alive. Profit objectives, which usually are stated in terms of sales dollar volume or percentage change, are normally set at a satisfactory level rather than at a level designed for profit maximization. A sales growth objective focuses on increasing the profit base by increasing sales volume. Pricing for return on investment (ROI) has a specified profit as its objective. A pricing objective to maintain or increase market share implies that market position is linked to success. Other types of pricing objectives include cash flow and recovery, status quo, and product quality.

A diverse group of eight factors enters into price decision making. The eight factors are organizational and marketing objectives, pricing objectives, costs, other marketing mix variables, channel member expectations, buyer perceptions, competition, and legal and regulatory issues. When setting prices, marketers should make decisions that are consistent with the goals and mission of the organization. Pricing objectives (for example, an ROI target) heavily influence price-setting decisions. Most marketers view a product's cost as the floor below which a product cannot be priced. Due to the interrelation of the marketing mix variables, price can affect product, promotion, and distribution decisions. The revenue that channel members expect for the functions they perform must also be considered when making price decisions.

Buyers' perceptions of price vary. While some consumer segments are price sensitive, others may not be; thus, before determining price a marketer needs to be aware of its importance to the target market. Knowledge of the prices charged for competing brands is essential in order for the firm to adjust its prices relative to those of competitors. Government regulations and legislation also strongly influence pricing decisions. Several acts have been passed by Congress to enhance perfect competition in the marketplace. Moreover, the government has the power to invoke price controls to curb inflation.

Unlike consumers, industrial buyers purchase products for the purpose of using them in their own operations or for producing other products. When adjusting prices, industrial sellers take into consideration the size of the purchase, geographic factors, and transportation requirements. Producers commonly provide discounts off list prices to intermediaries. The categories of discounts include trade, quantity, cash, or seasonal discounts, and allowances. A trade discount is a price reduction for performing such functions as storing, transporting, final processing, or providing credit services. If a middleman purchases in large enough quantities, a quantity discount is given by the producer. Quantity discounts can be either cumulative or noncumulative. A cash discount is a price reduction resulting from prompt payment or payment in cash. Buyers who buy goods or services out of season may be granted a seasonal discount. These discounts help the seller to maintain a more consistent production schedule throughout the year. A final type of reduction from the list price is an allowance. An example is a trade-in allowance.

Geographic pricing involves reductions for transportation costs or other costs associated with the physical distance between the buyer and the seller. A price quoted as F.O.B. factory means the buyer pays for shipping. This is the easiest way to price products, but it can be difficult for marketers to administer. When the seller charges a fixed average cost for transportation, this is known as uniform geographic pricing. Zone prices take advantage of a uniform pricing system adjusted for major geographic zones as the transportation costs increase. Base-point pricing is similar to zone pricing; prices are adjusted for shipping expenses incurred by the seller from the base point nearest the buyer. A seller who absorbs all or part of the freight costs is employing freight absorption pricing.

Price discrimination is a policy that results in different prices being charged to give a group of buyers a competitive advantage. Price differentials are legal only when they can be justified on the basis of cost savings, when they meet competition in good faith, or when they do not attempt to damage competition.

Important Terms

Price
Purchasing power
Barter
Price competition
Nonprice competition
Pricing objectives
Trade or functional discount
Quantity discounts
Cumulative discounts
Noncumulative discounts
Cash discount

Seasonal discount
Allowance
Geographic pricing
F.O.B. factory
Uniform geographic pricing
Zone prices
Base-point pricing
Freight absorption pricing
Transfer pricing
Price discrimination

Discussion and Review Questions

1. Why are pricing decisions so important to an organization?
2. Compare and contrast price and nonprice competition. Describe the conditions under which each one works best.
3. How does a pricing objective of sales growth and expansion differ from an objective to increase market share?
4. Why is it crucial that marketing objectives and pricing objectives be considered when making pricing decisions?
5. In what ways do other marketing mix variables affect pricing decisions?
6. What types of expectations may channel members have about producers' prices, and how do these expectations affect pricing decisions?
7. How do legal and regulatory forces influence pricing decisions?
8. Compare and contrast a trade discount and a quantity discount.
9. What is the purpose of using the term *F.O.B.*?
10. What is the difference between a price discount and price discrimination?

Cases

 Pricing at People Express Airlines[8]

People Express Airlines made its first scheduled commercial flight in April 1981. In 1986, with the purchase of a second airline, it became the fifth-largest U.S. passenger carrier. People Express differs from other major airlines in two fundamental ways. First, it has a simpler, three-tier structure of management: managing officers, general managers, and everyone else—maintenance, flight, and customer service personnel. Employees have wide-ranging responsibilities and often rotate jobs; no one, not even the CEO, has a secretary. Telephone work, aircraft maintenance, and baggage handling are farmed out to independent vendors. The airline's other unique feature is that all its employees own stock in the company and are paid lower salaries than their counterparts at other airlines. By purchasing planes at low prices, paying less in wages, using outside vendors, and charging extra for the conveniences that other, full-service airlines include in the cost of the ticket, no-frills People Express runs a very cost-efficient operation.

Compared to those of other major airlines, People Express prices are lower. While some airlines have special fares for a certain number of seats and the fares are available only with numerous restrictions, People Express has no restrictions on its fares. Peak fares are 45–65 percent of standard coach fares and off-peak prices are 25–30 percent of a standard coach ticket. The ticket fare includes transportation only. It does not include meals, coffee, soft drinks, or baggage check. All of these services are available for an extra charge. Coffee is 50 cents a cup.

The low fares provided by People Express allow a wide variety of passengers to travel by air. While many airlines depend heavily on the business traveler, People Express attracts tourists, students, the elderly, and a number of people who would not ordinarily fly because of high air fares. Such passengers are willing to put up with the inconvenience of traveling on People Express. Frequently, they must stand in line to buy tickets. It is difficult to make a reservation by telephone. Although People Express does attract some business travelers, other businesspeople prefer to use airlines that have frequent-flier programs. To lure business travelers, People Express has started advertising in a few business publications, as well as in the *New Yorker.* In 1987, the airline will move into a new terminal in Newark that will reduce check-in delays and help attract the business traveler.

To combat People Express' low fares, competitors are making their ticket prices come close to or meet People's head-on. When this happens, travelers choose the other, full-service airlines, and the percent of People's seats filled falls short of what the no-frills carrier needs to operate in the black. As a result, People Express has had to reduce the number of flights and use smaller planes on certain routes—those to Minneapolis, Chicago, Denver, and Detroit. The other major airlines have also begun to squeeze People Express on its California flights by reducing the booking requirements for discount fares from, say, one month to three days.

8. Based on John A. Byrne, "Up, Up, and Away?" *Business Week,* Nov. 25, 1985, pp. 80–94; Howard Banks, "Now Everybody's Doing It," *Forbes,* May 6, 1985, pp. 32–33; Chuck Hawkins and Aaron Bernstein, "Frank Lorenzo, High Flier," *Business Week,* March 10, 1986, pp. 104–110.

Questions for Discussion

1. How does People Express' pricing differ from that used by other airlines?
2. What are the major advantages and disadvantages of People Express' approach to pricing?
3. Should People Express introduce a frequent-flier program to attract more business travelers?

Case 16.2 Toys 'Я' Us Competes Through Price[9]

The first Toys 'Я' Us store opened in 1957. Today Toys 'Я' Us has approximately 230 stores, each with about 46,000 square feet. Each store's 18,000 products are arranged the same. Annually, management assesses whether changes need to be made in store arrangement. If a decision is made to rearrange, then all of the stores are rearranged in the same way. This toy chain has a 15-percent share of the U.S. toy market.

Toys 'Я' Us is highly computerized. When a sale is made at any store, information about that sale travels to a central processing operation at the company's headquarters in Rochelle Park, New Jersey. Such information is used by top management to track sales and respond to market trends, to control inventory, and to stock merchandise at different stores.

Toys 'Я' Us offers a broad range of products from an ample inventory. The retailer has strived to develop and keep a low-price image by selling popular items, such as Cabbage Patch dolls, at little or no profit. At times of short supply and large demand, the chain does not waver from its commitment to maintain everyday low prices. Toys 'Я' Us does not operate like most retailers, who base the retail price of an item on its wholesale price. Instead, Toys 'Я' Us decides what volume of an item can be sold at what price; then its management decides at what price it wants to buy the item and drives a hard bargain with the manufacturer, from whom it buys in volume, to get that price.

The top priority of the firm is to increase market share, and it is willing to offer low prices to do so. It does not hold sales. The average price per item is $5, and the average customer spends $50 per transaction. Prices range from 10 cents for a party favor up to $600 for a swimming pool. Overall, toys are priced 20–50 percent below those of retail specialty and department stores.

The success of Toys 'Я' Us is quite evident, and its pricing strategy has been a key factor. The company has increased its profits 35 percent annually since 1978 and has enough working capital to finance the construction of thirty new stores a year. Toys 'Я' Us promotes only from within, lets all full-time employees take part in a stock option plan, and rewards successful executives well.

Questions for Discussion

1. What are the major pricing objectives of Toys 'Я' Us?
2. Assess the practice at Toys 'Я' Us of not raising prices of products that are scarce and in high demand.
3. A major disadvantage of using price competition is that competitors can match prices. Evaluate this potential problem for Toys 'Я' Us.

9. Based on Angela Cuccio, "The Super Marketer of Toys," *Women's Wear Daily,* July 29, 1985, p. 22; Hank Gilman, "Founder Lazarus Is a Reason Toys 'Я' Us Dominates Its Industry," *Wall Street Journal,* Nov. 21, 1985, pp. 1, 27; "Toys 'Я' Us: King of the Hill," *Dun's Business Month,* Dec. 1985, pp. 40–41.

17 / Setting Prices

Objectives

■ To understand eight major stages that can be used to establish prices.

■ To explore issues connected with selecting pricing objectives.

■ To realize the importance of identifying the target market's evaluation of price.

■ To gain insight into demand curves and the elasticity of demand.

■ To examine the relationships among demand, costs, and profits.

■ To gain some insights into analyzing competitive prices.

■ To learn about different types of pricing policies.

■ To examine the major kinds of pricing methods.

Figure 17.1

Promotion of a compact disc player (Sony Corporation of America)

As prices for the compact disc player and the compact disc itself fall, the new technology is gradually making its way toward the throne of the audio industry. Price appears to be the only reason for slow sales when one considers the technological superiority of the disc and disc player.

A compact disc is a piece of plastic, 4.7 inches wide by ⅛ inch thick, with a quarter-sized hole in the center. It has a 3.3-mile-long spiral track that contains digital coding protected by a thin layer of plastic. A compact disc player spins the disc and uses a frictionless laser beam to read the encoded signals (see Figure 17.1). The signals are then amplified and transformed into music through a stereo system. The result is clean, clear music that closely resembles the quality of the original recording without the scratch of vinyl records or the hiss of tape.

Together, the compact disk and disk player offer many advantages when compared to the record and turntable. Compact disks can store up to seventy-five minutes of music. The disk produces a wider sound range and is much less susceptible to damage or deterioration than its vinyl counterpart. Compact disk players offer such luxuries as music scan and program selection, which allow the listener, at the touch of a button, to rearrange the order of the songs for playback. In short, the compact disk packs better sound, convenience, and durability than the traditional record album, and soon perhaps, these advantages will be available at a low price.

In 1985 the price of compact disk players dropped from $1,000 to under $300, with some approaching the $200 range. Prices of the disks themselves dropped from $22 to $14. It is projected that the prices of both will continue to decline. The price drop, as well as heavier advertising and a larger selection of disk recordings, were expected to triple sales volumes for 1986 over 1985 for both the disk and the disk player.

While the compact disk player continues to drop in price, the disk itself may linger at prices a few dollars above record albums. Production of the disks is limited to only twelve plants worldwide, only one of which is in the United States. Production costs are currently $3 per disk, as compared to about 80 cents for an album. The manufacturers, like Sony and CBS, feel that a prerecorded disk that is higher in quality and more durable should cost more. Therefore, disk manufacturers may hesitate to lower disk prices even if production costs become competitive with those of albums.[1]

Setting prices of products such as disks or disk players requires careful consideration of numerous issues. In this chapter we discuss eight stages of a process that marketers can use when setting prices. These stages should not be viewed as rigid steps that all marketers must employ. They are guidelines that provide a logical sequence for establishing prices. In some situations, there may be other stages that should be included in the price setting process; in other situations, some of the stages may not be necessary.

Figure 17.2 identifies the eight stages that marketers can use when establishing prices. The first stage is to develop a pricing objective that dovetails with the organization's overall objectives and its marketing objectives. Then in stage 2, an assessment is made of the target market's evaluation of price and its ability to purchase. Next, the nature and elasticity of demand should be examined (stage 3). Stage 4—analysis of demand, cost, and profit relationships—is necessary to estimate the economic feasibility of alternative prices. Evaluation of competitors'

1. Brian Dumaine, "The Compact Disk's Drive to Become the King of Audio," *Fortune,* July 8, 1985, pp. 104–107. © 1985 Time, Inc. All rights reserved.

Figure 17.2

Stages for establishing prices

prices (stage 5) is helpful in determining the role of price in the marketing strategy. Competitors' prices and the marketing mix variables that they emphasize in part determine how important price will be to customers. Stage 6 consists of selecting a pricing policy—the guidelines for using price in the marketing mix. In stage 7, a method for calculating the price charged to customers is selected. Stage 8, determination of the final price, depends on environmental forces and marketers' understanding and use of a systematic approach to establishing prices.

Selection of Pricing Objectives

In Chapter 16 we explore the various types of pricing objectives. Selection of pricing objectives is an important task because pricing objectives provide a foundation on which decisions related to other stages of pricing are based. Thus, pricing objectives must be explicitly stated. The statement of pricing objectives should include the time period over which the objectives are to be accomplished.

Marketers must be certain that the pricing objectives they set are consistent with the organization's overall objectives and with its marketing objectives. Inconsistent objectives result in internal conflicts and confusion and also can prevent the organization from achieving its overall goals. Furthermore, pricing objectives that are inconsistent with organizational and marketing objectives may cause marketers to make poor decisions associated with the other stages in the price-setting process.

Organizations normally have multiple pricing objectives, some short term and others long term. For example, the pricing objective of gaining market share is normally a short-term objective because it often requires the firm to price its product quite low relative to competitors' prices. For each product, an organization should have one or more pricing objectives. For the same product aimed at different market segments, marketers sometimes choose different pricing objectives. Over time, a marketer typically will alter pricing objectives.

Assessment of the Target Market's Evaluation of Price and Its Ability to Purchase

Although we generally assume that price is a significant issue for buyers, the importance of price depends on the type of product and the type of target market. For example, buyers, in general, are probably more sensitive to gasoline prices than to luggage prices. If we look specifically at gasoline as a product category, we find that some gasoline buyers are more price sensitive than others. Gasoline buyers who seek out independent service stations to pay lower prices are probably more price sensitive than those who use oil company credit cards to buy the higher-priced, major brands of gasoline. By assessing the target market's evaluation of price, a marketer is in a better position to know how much emphasis to place on price. Information about the target market's price evaluation may also aid a marketer in determining how far above the competition a firm can set its prices.

As pointed out in Chapter 3, the people who make up a market must have the ability to buy a product. Buyers must need a product, be willing to use their buying power, and have the authority (by law or social custom) to buy. Their ability to buy, like their evaluation of price, has direct consequences for marketers. The ability to purchase involves such resources as money, credit, wealth, and other products that could be traded in an exchange. Understanding the purchasing power of customers and knowing how important a product is to them in comparison with other products helps marketers to assess the target market's evaluation of price correctly.

Determination of Demand

Determining the demand for a product is the responsibility of marketing managers with the help of marketing researchers. Marketing research techniques yield estimates of sales potential or the quantity of a product that could be sold during a specific period. (Chapter 3 describes such techniques as surveys, time series analyses, correlation methods, and market tests.) These estimates are helpful in establishing the relationship between a product's price and the quantity demanded.

The Demand Curve

For most products, the quantity demanded goes up as the price goes down; and as price goes up, the quantity demanded goes down. Thus, there is an inverse relationship between price and quantity demanded. As long as the marketing environment and buyers' needs, ability (purchasing power), willingness, and authority to buy remain stable, this fundamental inverse relationship will continue.

Figure 17.3 illustrates the effect of one variable—price—on the quantity demanded. The classic **demand curve** (D_1) is a line sloping downward to the right, showing that as price falls, quantity demanded will increase. Demand also depends on other factors in the marketing mix, among them product quality, promotion, and distribution. An improvement in any of these factors

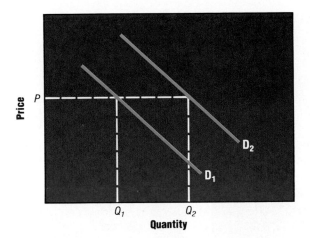

may cause a shift to, say, demand curve D_2. In such a case, an increased quantity (Q_2) will be sold at the same price (P).

There are many types of demand and not all conform to the classic demand curve shown in Figure 17.3. Prestige products such as selected perfumes, cosmetics, and jewelry seem to sell better at high prices than at low ones. For example, the jewelry and perfumes shown in Figure 17.4 are known to be expensive and thus have a prestigious image. In fact, these products are desirable partly because their expense makes their buyers feel elite. If the price fell drastically and many people owned them, they would lose some of their appeal.

The demand curve in Figure 17.5 shows the relationship between price and quantity for prestige products. Demand is greater, not less, at higher prices. For a certain price range—from P_1 to P_2—the quantity demanded (Q_1) goes up to Q_2. After a point, however, raising the price backfires. If the price of a product goes too high, the quantity demanded goes down. The figure shows that if the price is raised from P_2 to P_3, quantity demanded goes back down from Q_2 to Q_1.

Demand Fluctuations

Changes in buyers' attitudes, other components of the marketing mix, and uncontrollable environmental factors can influence demand. Although demand can fluctuate unpredictably, some organizations have been able to anticipate change in demand by correlating demand for a specific product to demand for the total industry or to some other economic variable. If a brand maintains a fairly constant market share, its sales can be estimated as a percentage of industry sales.

Determining Elasticity of Demand

To this point, we have discussed how marketers identify the target market's evaluation of price and its ability to purchase and examine demand to learn whether price is related to quantity inversely or directly. The next stage in the process is to determine elasticity of demand. **Elasticity of demand** (see Figure 17.6) is the relative responsiveness of changes in quantity demanded to changes in price. The percentage of change in quantity demanded caused by a percentage change in price is much greater for elastic demand than for inelastic demand.

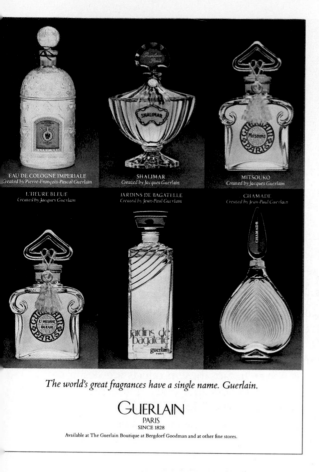

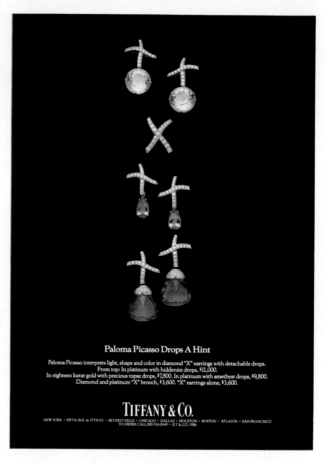

Figure 17.4 *Promotion of prestige products (Source: Ad on left courtesy of Guerlain, Inc. Ad on right © 1986 Tiffany & Co.)*

For a product such as electricity, demand is relatively inelastic. When its price is increased, say from P_1 to P_2, quantity demanded goes down only a little, from Q_1 to Q_2. For products such as recreational vehicles, demand is relatively elastic. When price rises sharply, from P'_1 to P'_2, quantity demanded goes down a great deal, from Q'_1 to Q'_2.

If marketers can determine **price elasticity,** then setting a price is much easier. By analyzing total revenues as prices change, marketers can determine whether a product is price elastic. Total revenue is price times quantity; thus, 10,000 rolls of wallpaper sold in one year at a price of $10 per roll equals $100,000 of total revenue. If demand is *elastic,* a change in price causes an opposite change in total revenue—an increase in price will decrease total revenue, and a decrease in price will increase total revenue. An *inelastic* demand results in a parallel change in total revenue—an increase in price will increase total revenue, and a decrease in price will decrease total revenue. The following formula gives the price elasticity of demand:

$$\text{Price elasticity of demand} = \frac{\% \text{ change in quantity demanded}}{\% \text{ change in price}}$$

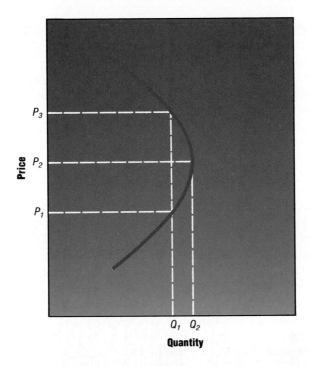

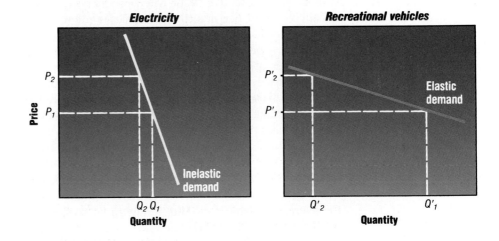

For example, if demand falls by 8 percent when a seller raises the price by 2 percent, the price elasticity of demand is -4 (the negative sign indicating the inverse relationship between price and demand). If demand falls by 2 percent when price is increased by 4 percent, then elasticity is $-\frac{1}{2}$. The less elastic the demand, the more beneficial it is for the seller to raise the price. Products without available substitutes and for which there is a strong need perceived by consumers usually have inelastic demand.

Marketers cannot base prices solely on elasticity considerations. They must also examine the costs associated with different volumes and see what happens to profits.

Analysis of Demand, Cost, and Profit Relationships

Having looked at the role demand plays in setting prices and at various costs and their relationships, we will go on to examine the relationships among demand, cost, and profit. To stay in business, a company has to set prices that cover all its costs. To help set prices, there are two approaches to understanding demand, cost, and profit relationships: marginal analysis and breakeven analysis. Before exploring these two approaches, we will identify several different types of costs.

Types of Costs

Costs are associated with the production of any good or service. To determine the costs of production, it is necessary to distinguish fixed costs from variable costs. **Fixed costs** do not vary with changes in the number of units produced or sold. The cost of renting a factory, for example, does not change because production increases from one shift to two shifts a day or because twice as much wallpaper is sold. Rent may go up, but not because the factory has doubled production or revenue. **Average fixed cost** is the fixed cost per unit produced. It is calculated by dividing the fixed costs by the number of units produced.

Variable costs do vary directly with changes in the number of units produced or sold. The wages for a second shift and the cost of twice as much paper and dye are extra costs that occur when production is doubled. Variable costs are usually constant per unit; that is, twice as many workers and twice as much material produces twice as many rolls of wallpaper. **Average variable cost,** the variable cost per unit produced, is calculated by dividing the variable costs by the number of units produced.

Total cost is the sum of fixed costs and variable costs times the quantity produced. **Marginal cost (MC)** is the extra cost a firm incurs when it produces one more unit of a product. The **average total cost** is the sum of the average fixed cost and the average variable cost. Table 17.1 illustrates various costs and their relationships. Notice that the average fixed cost declines as the output increases. The average variable cost follows a U-shape, as does the average total cost. Since the average total cost continues to fall after the average variable cost begins to rise, its lowest point is at a higher level of output than that of the average variable cost. The average total cost is lowest at 5 units at a cost of $22, whereas the average variable cost is lowest at 3 units at a cost of $11.67. Marginal cost equals average total cost at the latter's lowest level, between 5 and 6 units of production. Average total cost decreases as long as the marginal cost is less than the average total cost, and it increases when marginal cost rises above average total cost.

Marginal Analysis

Marginal analysis involves examining what happens when something is changed by one unit. **Marginal revenue (MR),** therefore, is the change in total revenue that occurs when a firm sells an additional unit of a product. Marginal revenue is depicted in Figure 17.7. The relationship between marginal cost and average cost is shown in Figure 17.8.

The vast majority of firms in the United States face downward sloping demand curves for their products. In other words, they must lower their prices

Table 17.1 Costs and their relationships

(1) Quantity	(2) Fixed Cost	(3) Average Fixed Cost (2) ÷ (1)	(4) Average Variable Cost	(5) Average Total Cost (3 + 4)	(6) Total Cost (5) × (1)	(7) Marginal Cost
1	$40	$40.00	$20.00	$60.00	$ 60	
						$10
2	40	20.00	15.00	35.00	70	
						5
3	40	13.33	11.67	25.00	75	
						15
4	40	10.00	12.50	22.50	90	
						20
5	40	8.00	14.00	22.00	110	
						30
6	40	6.67	16.67	23.33	140	
						40
7	40	5.71	20.00	25.71	180	

Figure 17.7

Typical marginal revenue and average revenue relationships

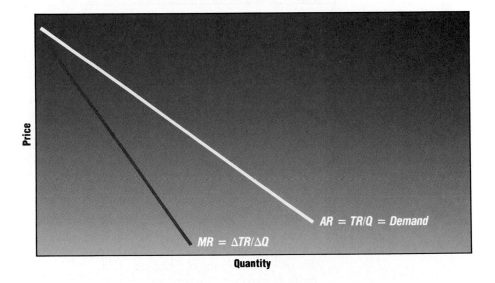

to sell additional units. This situation means that each additional product sold will provide less revenue to the firm than did the previous unit sold. MR would then be less than average revenue, as shown in Figure 17.7. Eventually, MR will reach zero and the sale of additional units would merely hurt the firm.

Before the firm can determine if a unit makes a profit, though, it must know its cost as well as its revenue, since profit equals revenue minus cost. If MR is a unit's addition to revenue and MC is a unit's addition to cost, then MR minus MC tells us whether the unit is profitable or not. Table 17.2 illustrates the relationships between price, quantity sold, total revenue, marginal revenue,

Figure 17.8

Typical marginal cost
and average cost
relationships

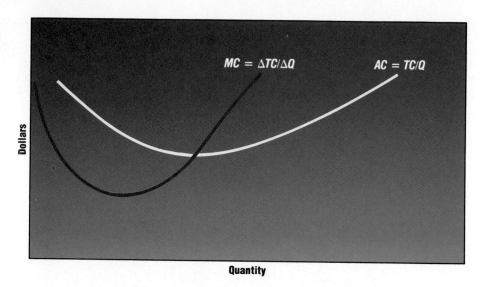

Table 17.2   Marginal analysis: method of obtaining maximum
profit-producing price

(1)	(2)	(3)	(4)	(5)	(6)	(7)
Price	Quantity Sold	Total Revenue (1) × (2)	Marginal Revenue	Marginal Cost	Total Cost	Profit (3) − (6)
$57.00	1	$ 57	$57	$—	$ 60	− $ 3
55.00	2	110	53	10	70	40
40.00	3	120	10	5	75	45
37.50*	**4**	**150**	**15**	**15**	**90**	**60**
32.40	5	162	12	20	110	52
27.80	6	167	5	30	140	37
23.40	7	164	−3	40	180	24

*Boldface indicates best price-profit combination.

marginal cost, and total cost. It indicates where maximum profits are possible
at various combinations of price and cost.

Profit is maximized where MC = MR (see Table 17.2). In this table MC =
MR at 4 units. The best price is $37.50 and the profit is $60. Up to this point,
the additional revenue generated from an extra unit of sale exceeds the additional
total cost. Beyond this point, the additional cost of another unit sold exceeds
the additional revenue generated, and profits decrease. If the price were based
on minimum average total cost—$22 (Table 17.1)—it would result in less
profit: only $52 (Table 17.2) for 5 units at a price of $32.40, versus $60 for 4
units at a price of $37.50.

Graphically combining Figures 17.7 and 17.8 into Figure 17.9 shows that
any unit for which MR exceeds MC is adding to a firm's profits, while any unit
for which MC exceeds MR is subtracting from a firm's profits. The firm should

Figure 17.9

Combining the marginal cost and marginal revenue concepts for optimum profit

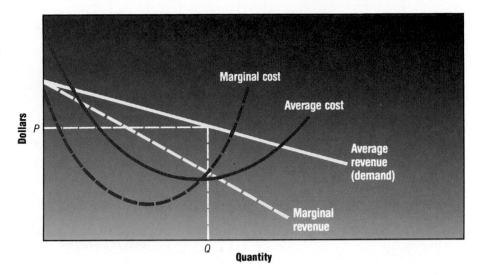

therefore produce at the point where MR equals MC because this is the most profitable level of production.

This economic concept gives the false impression that pricing can be highly precise. If revenue (demand) and cost (supply) remained constant, then prices could be set for maximum profits. In practice, however, cost and revenue are constantly changing.

Recently, Japanese manufacturers of motorcycles such as Honda and Yamaha overestimated U.S. demand for their products. As a result, they found themselves with a twelve- to eighteen-month inventory. Price cutting by dealers and manufacturer rebates to both dealers and consumers were used to decrease the supply. Imports also were reduced dramatically. The massive inventories and discount prices threatened to destroy the one remaining American motorcycle manufacturer, Harley-Davidson. Acting on a recommendation of the U.S. International Trade Commission, the president increased tariffs on imported heavyweight motorcycles (directly competitive with Harley-Davidson). The tariff resulted in a 25-percent increase in the prices of larger motorcycles in an already glutted market. All of these events clogged the inventory pipeline in a market where supply, demand, and price were not properly coordinated.[2]

The competitive tactics of other firms or government action, as in the case of the motorcycle industry, can quickly undermine a firm's expectations of revenue. Thus, the economic concept we have discussed here is only a model from which to work. It offers little help in pricing new products before costs and revenues are established. On the other hand, in setting prices of existing products—especially in competitive situations—most marketers can benefit by understanding the relationship between marginal cost and marginal revenue.

Breakeven Analysis

The point at which costs of producing a product equal revenue made from selling the product is the **breakeven point.** If a wallpaper manufacturer has total annual costs of $100,000 and the same year it sells $100,000 worth of wallpaper, then the company has broken even.

2. Bob Woods, "Wheeling and Dealing," *Sales and Marketing Management*, May 16, 1983, pp. 43–50.

Figure 17.10

Determining the
breakeven point

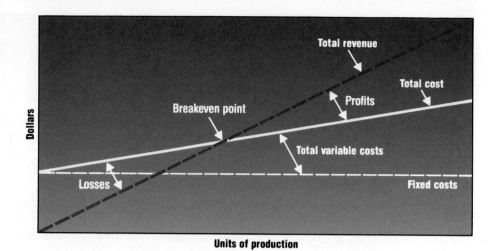

Figure 17.10 illustrates the relationships of costs, revenue, profits, and losses involved in determining the breakeven point. Knowing the number of units necessary to break even is important in setting the price. If a product priced at $100 per unit has an average variable cost of $60 per unit, then the contribution to fixed costs is $40. If total fixed costs are $120,000, here is the way to determine the breakeven point in units:

$$\text{Breakeven point} = \frac{\text{fixed costs}}{\text{per unit contribution to fixed costs}}$$

$$= \frac{\text{fixed costs}}{\text{price} - \text{variable costs}}$$

$$= \frac{\$120,000}{\$40}$$

$$= 3,000 \text{ units}$$

To calculate the breakeven point in terms of dollar sales volume, all one need do is multiply the breakeven point in units by the price per unit. In the example above, the breakeven point in terms of dollar sales volume would be 3,000 (units) times $100, or $300,000.

To use breakeven analysis effectively, a marketer should determine the breakeven point for each of several alternative prices. This determination allows the marketer to compare the effects on total revenue, total costs, and the breakeven point for each price under consideration. Although this comparative analysis may not tell the marketer exactly what price to charge, it will identify highly undesirable price alternatives that should definitely be avoided.

Breakeven analysis is simple and straightforward. It does assume, however, that the quantity demanded is basically fixed (inelastic) and that the major task in setting prices is to recover costs. This analysis focuses more on how to break even than on how to achieve a pricing objective such as percentage of market share or return on investment. Marketing managers can use this concept to determine more accurately whether a product will achieve at least a breakeven volume. In other words, it is easier to answer the question "Will we sell at least the minimum volume necessary to break even?" than to answer the question "What volume of sales will we expect to sell?"

Evaluation of Competitors' Prices

In most cases, a marketer is in a better position to establish prices when he or she knows the prices charged for competing brands. Learning competitors' prices may be a regular function of marketing research. Some grocery and department stores, for example, have full-time comparative shoppers who systematically collect data on prices. Companies may also purchase price lists, sometimes weekly, from syndicated marketing research services.

Becoming aware of competitors' prices is not always easy, especially in producer and reseller markets. Competitors' price lists are often closely guarded. Even if a marketer has access to price lists, they may not reflect the actual prices at which competitive products are sold. The actual prices may be established through negotiation.

Awareness of the prices charged for competing brands can be very important for a marketer. Marketers in an industry in which nonprice competition prevails need competitive price information to ensure that their organization's prices are the same as competitors' prices. In some instances, an organization's prices are designed to be slightly above competitors' prices to give its products an exclusive image. Another company may employ price as a competitive tool and attempt to price its brand below competing brands. (See the application on page 510 for related issues.)

Selection of a Pricing Policy

A **pricing policy** is a guiding philosophy or course of action designed to influence and determine pricing decisions. Pricing policies set guidelines for achieving pricing objectives. They are an important component of an overall marketing strategy. In general, pricing policies should answer this recurring question: How will price be used as a variable in the marketing mix? This question may relate to (1) introduction of new products, (2) competitive situations, (3) government pricing regulations, (4) economic conditions, or (5) implementation of pricing objectives. Pricing policies help marketers solve the practical problems of establishing prices. Let us examine some of the most common pricing policies.

Pioneer Pricing Policies

Pioneer pricing—setting the base price for a new product—is a necessary part of formulating a marketing strategy. The base price is easily adjusted (in the absence of government price controls), and its establishment is one of the most fundamental decisions in the marketing mix. The base price can be set high to recover development costs quickly or to provide a reference point for developing discount prices to different market segments.

When they set base prices, marketers also consider how quickly competitors will enter the market, whether they will mount a very strong campaign upon

Commodore International faced an unanticipated problem. Its strength had been in home computer systems priced under $500. In 1983 Commodore held 35 percent of the home computer market. But more recent figures indicated that consumers wanted more efficient and powerful models selling for $500 to $1,000, as shown in Figure 17.11.

The shift in preference occurred when educational and business computers fell under $1,000. Two computers in this category are the IBM PC*jr* (which has been discontinued) and the Apple IIc. The fully equipped Commodore was selling for $600 to $800, but customers found the features of competing brands to be more attractive relative to the price than those of the Commodore.

Coleco Industries suffered the same fate as Commodore. Its Adam computer never reached company sales goals even though Coleco cut its price and offered a $500 scholarship with each sale. Coleco developed a high-end home computer, but it still could not compete with the Apple or IBM units.

Although unit sales are expected to increase for computers selling for less than $500, Commodore and Coleco are not capturing the fastest-growing and most profitable segment of the home computer market. Computers selling for less than $500 will account for only 23 percent of total home computer revenue, as compared with 51 percent three years ago. Commodore and Coleco need to be aware of consumer sensitivity to quality and price and must direct their pricing strategies and new-product introductions to match customer demand. The success or failure of most domestic microcomputer brands depends largely on how they are positioned relative to IBM's microcomputers. (*Source: Geoff Lewis, "It's Anybody's Race Now in Home Computers,"* Business Week, *Jan. 21, 1985, p. 32; "Computers,"* Forbes, *Jan. 14, 1985, pp. 122–124; and* International Business Machines 1984 Annual Report.)

entry, and the effect of their entry on the development of primary demand. If competitors will enter quickly, with considerable marketing force and with limited effect on the primary demand, then a firm may wish to adopt a base price that will discourage their entry.

Price Skimming

This pioneer approach provides the most flexible introductory base price. Demand tends to be inelastic in the introductory stage of the product life cycle. **Price skimming** is charging the highest possible price that buyers who most desire the product will pay.

Price skimming can provide several benefits, especially when a product is in the introductory stage of its life cycle. A skimming policy can generate much-needed initial cash flows to help offset sizable developmental costs. Kodak, for example, used a skimming introductory price for its disk camera to help defray large development costs. Price skimming protects the marketer from problems that arise when the price is set too low to cover costs. When a firm introduces a product, its production capacity may be limited. A skimming price can help to keep demand consistent with a firm's production capabilities.

Penetration Price

A **penetration price** is a price that is below the prices of competing brands and is designed to penetrate a market and produce a larger unit sales volume.

Figure 17.11

The shift in home computer sales (Source: Courtesy of Business Week)

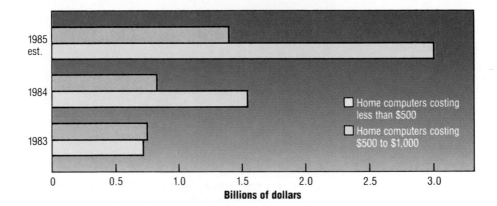

When introducing a product, a marketer sometimes uses a penetration price to gain a large market share quickly. This approach places the marketer in a less flexible position than price skimming because it is more difficult to raise a penetration price than to lower or discount a skimming price. It is not unusual for a firm to use a penetration price after having skimmed the market with a higher price.

Penetration pricing can be especially beneficial when marketers suspect that competitors could enter the market easily. First, if the penetration price allows one marketer to gain a large market share quickly, competitors might be discouraged from entering the market. Second, entering the market may be less attractive to competitors when a penetration price is used since the lower per-unit price results in lower per-unit profit; this may cause competitors to view the market as not being especially lucrative. Honda may have used one or both of these justifications when establishing a penetration price for its Rebel motorcycle, shown in Figure 17.12.

In contrast, environmental conditions can cause a penetration price to become less attractive to consumers. Private-label and generic-brand food products are promoted primarily on the basis of a penetration price advantage. However, their market share has been declining in recent years. An improving economy and an easing of food price increases are two main reasons given for the decrease in the share of these lower-priced products. This example illustrates that penetration policy is not always effective in a dynamic environment.[3]

A penetration price is particularly appropriate when demand is highly elastic, meaning that target market members would purchase the product if it were priced at the penetration level, but few would buy the item if it were priced higher. A marketer should consider using a penetration price when a lower price would result in longer production runs, increasing production significantly and reducing the firm's per-unit production costs.

Psychological Pricing

Psychological pricing is designed to encourage purchases that are based on emotional reactions rather than on rational responses. It is used most often at the retail level. Psychological pricing has limited use in pricing industrial products.

3. *Frozen Food Age,* Nov. 1983, pp. 1, 32.

Chapter 17 / Setting Prices   **511**

Odd-even Pricing

Odd-even pricing attempts to influence buyers' perceptions of the price or the product by ending the price with certain numbers. Odd pricing assumes that more of a product will be sold at $99.95 than at $100.00. Supposedly, customers will think, or at least tell friends, that the product is a bargain—not $100, mind you, but $99 plus a few insignificant pennies. Also, customers are supposed to think that the store could have charged $100 but instead cut the price to the last cent, to $99.95. Some claim, too, that certain types of customers are more attracted by odd prices than by even ones. Odd prices seem to have little genuine effect on sales, except that they do force the cashier to use the cash register to make change. There are no substantial research findings that support the notion that odd prices produce greater sales. The daily newspaper is full of examples of odd prices. In fact, even prices are far more unusual today than odd prices.

Even prices are used to give a product an exclusive or upscale image. An even price supposedly will influence a customer to view the product as being a high-quality, premium brand. A shirt maker, for example, may print on a premium shirt package a suggested retail price of $32.00 instead of $31.95. The even price of the shirt is utilized to enhance its upscale image.

Customary Pricing

In **customary pricing**, certain goods are priced primarily on the basis of tradition. Recent economic uncertainties have made most prices fluctuate fairly widely,

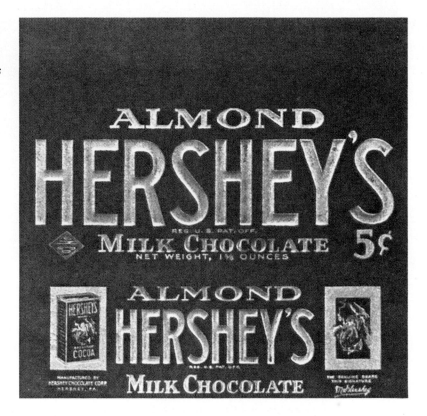

but the classic example of the customary or traditional price is the candy bar. For scores of years, the price of a candy bar was 5 cents, as shown in Figure 17.13. A new candy bar would have had to be something very special to sell for more than a nickel. This price was so sacred that rather than change it, manufacturers increased or decreased the size of the candy bar itself as chocolate prices fluctuated. Now, of course, the nickel candy bar has disappeared, probably forever. Yet, most candy bars still sell at the same price. Thus, customary pricing remains the standard for this market.

Prestige Pricing

In **prestige pricing,** prices are set at an artificially high level to provide prestige or a quality image. Pharmacists report that some consumers complain if a prescription does not cost enough. Apparently, some consumers associate a drug's price with its potency. Consumers may also associate quality in beer with high price.

Prestige pricing is used especially when buyers associate a higher price with higher quality. Typical product categories in which selected products are prestige priced include perfumes, automobiles, liquor, and jewelry. If producers that use prestige pricing lowered their prices dramatically, it would be inconsistent with the perceived images of such products.

Price Lining

When an organization sets a limited number of prices for selected groups or lines of merchandise, it is using a form of psychological pricing called **price**

Figure 17.14

Price lining

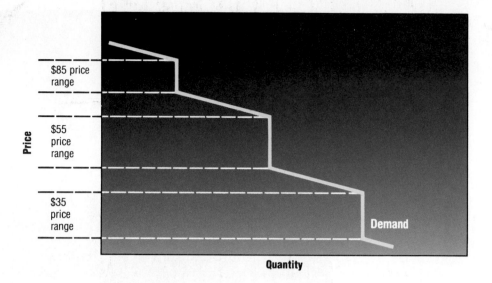

lining. A retailer may have various styles and brands of men's shirts that sell for $15. Another line of shirts may sell for $22. Price lining simplifies consumers' decision making by holding constant one key variable in the final selection of style and brand within a line.

The basic assumption in price lining is that the demand is inelastic for various groups or sets of products. If the prices are attractive, customers will concentrate their purchases without responding to slight changes in price. Thus, if a women's dress shop carries dresses priced at $85, $55, and $35, the store's management is indicating its belief that these are "good" prices and that a drop to, say, $83, $53, and $34 would not attract many more sales. The "space" between the prices of $55 and $35, however, can stir change in consumer response. With price lining, the demand curve looks like a series of steps, as shown in Figure 17.14.

Professional Pricing

Professional pricing is used by persons who have great skill or experience in a particular field or activity. Some professionals who provide such products as medical services feel that their fees (prices) should not relate directly to the time and involvement in specific cases; rather, a standard fee is charged regardless of the problems involved in performing the job. Some doctors' and lawyers' fees are prime examples: $35 for a checkup, $400 for an appendectomy, and $199 for a divorce. Other professionals set prices in other ways. (See related issues in the application on page 515.)

The concept of professional pricing carries with it the idea that professionals have an "ethical" responsibility not to overcharge unknowing customers. In some situations a seller can charge customers a high price and continue to sell many units of the product. Medicine offers several examples. If a diabetic requires one insulin treatment per day to survive, the individual will buy that treatment whether its price is $1 or $10. In fact, the patient surely would purchase the treatment even if the price went higher. In these situations sellers could charge exorbitant fees. Drug companies claim that despite their positions

Application

Pricing Legal
Services

The American Bar Association (ABA) sets quite flexible ground rules for the methods and standards lawyers should use in billing clients. The ABA basically states that lawyers should not charge blatantly excessive or unreasonable fees. The ABA has also established three factors that a lawyer should consider in setting a fee for a case: the amount of time the lawyer and his or her support staff spend on the case, the fee that lawyers in the same geographic region charge for a similar case, and whether the case was won or lost.

The vagueness of the ABA's ground rules has contributed to the wide variations in the methods lawyers use to set their fees. Some lawyers charge by the hour, while others establish in advance a flat fee for which they will work on a case. A flat fee set in advance is called a negotiated fee. A negotiated fee can be either a specific dollar amount or a percentage of the award that the client receives. Discount law firms publish schedules of the flat fees they charge for common types of cases such as divorce proceedings (see Figure 17.15). Various branch offices of one discount law firm list fees varying from $100 to $400 for the same type of divorce case. The variation is due to differences in court costs and paperwork requirements among the regions in which the branches are located.

Lawyers also differ in the services for which they bill clients. Some lawyers bill for every action that can be viewed as a service, even advice given over the telephone; other lawyers bill more selectively. For instance, one lawyer charges for the initial meeting with a client only if that client decides to hire him. Another attorney does not charge widows for advice on personal problems such as disputes with servants. (*Source: Sonja Steptoe, "Not All Lawyers Charge a Pound of Flesh, But Arcane Billing Makes It Hard to Tell,"* Wall Street Journal, *Nov. 26, 1985, p. 31. Reprinted by permission from* Wall Street Journal, *© Dow Jones & Company, Inc. 1985. All Rights Reserved.*)

of strength in this regard, they charge "ethical" prices rather than what the traffic will bear.

Promotional Pricing

Price is an ingredient in the marketing mix, and it often is coordinated with promotion. The two variables sometimes are so interrelated that the pricing policy is promotion oriented.

Price Leaders

Sometimes a firm prices a few products below the usual markup or below cost. If some products are sold at less than cost, they are **price leaders;** management hopes that sales of regularly purchased merchandise will rise and increase sales volume and profits. This type of pricing is used most often in supermarkets and department stores to attract consumers by giving them an impression of low prices.

Special-event Pricing

To increase sales volume, many organizations coordinate price with advertising for seasonal or special situations. **Special-event pricing** involves advertised sales or price cutting to increase revenue or lower costs. If the pricing objective is survival, then special sales events may be designed to generate the necessary operating capital. Special-event pricing also entails coordination of production,

Figure 17.15

Promotion of legal services (Source: Clovermill Associates, Inc., Forest Hills, NY)

scheduling, storage, and physical distribution. Whenever there is a sales lag, a special sales event may be launched.

Superficial Discounting

Superficial discounting, sometimes called "Was-Is pricing" in the trade, is fictitious comparative pricing. "Was $259, Is $199" is an example. The Federal Trade Commission and the Better Business Bureau discourage these deceptive mark-downs. Legitimate discounts are not questioned, of course, but when a pricing policy gives only the illusion of a discount, it is unethical and, in some states, illegal.

Superficial discounting is typified by one large retailer that sells 93 percent of its power tools on sale with discounts ranging from 10 to 40 percent. The retailers' frequent special events or sales mean that the tools are sold at sale prices most of the year. To combat such superficial discounting, Canada now requires retailers to post a base price for at least six months before discounting a product.

Experience Curve Pricing

In **experience curve pricing,** a company fixes a low price that high-cost competitors cannot match and thus expands its market share. This practice is possible when a firm gains cumulative production experience and is able to reduce its manufacturing costs at a predictable rate through improved methods, materials, skills, and machinery. Texas Instruments used this strategy in marketing both its computers and its calculators. The experience curve depicts the inverse relationship between production costs per unit and cumulative production quantity. To take advantage of the experience curve, a company must gain a dominant market share early in a product's life cycle. An early market share lead, with the greater cumulative production experience that it implies, will place a company farther down the experience curve than its competitors. To avoid antitrust problems, companies must objectively examine the competitive structure of the market before and after implementing the experience curve strategy. The strategy should not be anticompetitive, and the company must have specific and accurate data that will be unshakable in a court of law. Under the proper conditions—a high probability of success, suitable precaution, sound legal counsel—the method is perfectly acceptable as a primary policy.[4]

Development of a Pricing Method

After selecting a pricing policy, a marketer must choose a **pricing method,** a mechanical procedure for setting prices on a regular basis. The pricing method structures the calculation of the actual price. The nature of a product, its sales volume, or the amount of product carried by the organization will determine how prices are calculated. For example, a procedure for pricing the thousands of products in a supermarket must be more direct and simple than that for calculating the price of a new earth-moving machine manufactured by Caterpillar. Here we examine three types of market-oriented pricing methods: cost-oriented pricing, demand-oriented pricing, and competition-oriented pricing.

Cost-oriented Pricing

Cost-oriented pricing determines price by adding a dollar amount or percentage to the cost of a product. The method thus involves calculations of desired margins or profit margins. Cost-oriented pricing methods do not necessarily take into account the economic aspects of supply and demand, nor do they necessarily relate to a specific pricing policy or ensure the attainment of pricing objectives. They are, however, simple and easy to implement. Two common cost-oriented pricing methods are cost-plus and markup pricing.

Cost-plus Pricing

Cost-plus pricing is a pricing method in which the seller's costs are determined (usually during or after a project is completed) and then a specified dollar amount or percentage of the cost is added to the seller's cost to set the price. When production costs are unpredictable or production takes a long time, cost-plus pricing is appropriate. Custom-made equipment and commercial construction projects often are priced by this method. The government frequently uses such cost-oriented pricing in granting defense contracts. One pitfall for the buyer is that the seller may increase costs to establish a larger profit base. Also, some costs, such as overhead, may be difficult to determine.

In periods of rapid inflation, cost-plus pricing is popular, especially when the producer must use raw materials that are fluctuating in price. For industries in which cost-plus pricing is common and sellers have similar costs, price competition may not be especially intense.

---

4. Alan R. Beckenstein and H. Landis Gabel, "Experience Curve Pricing Strategy: The Next Target of Antitrust?" *Business Horizons*, Sept.–Oct. 1982, pp. 71–77.

Markup Pricing

A common pricing method among retailers is **markup pricing.** A product's price is derived by adding a predetermined percentage of the cost, called *markup,* to the cost of the product. Although the percentage markup in a retail store varies from one category of goods to another (35 percent of cost for hardware and 100 percent of cost for greeting cards, for example), the same percentage often is used to determine the price on items within a single product category, and the same or similar percentage markup may be standardized across an industry at the retail level. Using a rigid percentage markup for a specific product category reduces pricing to a routine task that can be performed quickly.

Markup can be stated as a percentage of the cost or as a percentage of the selling price. The following example illustrates how percentage markups are determined and points out the differences in the two methods. Assume that a retailer purchases a can of tuna at 45 cents, adds 15 cents to the cost, and then prices the tuna at 60 cents. Here are the figures:

$$\text{Markup as a percentage of cost} = \frac{\text{amount added to cost}}{\text{cost}}$$

$$= \frac{15}{45}$$

$$= 33.3\%$$

$$\text{Markup as a percentage of selling price} = \frac{\text{amount added to cost}}{\text{selling price}}$$

$$= \frac{15}{60}$$

$$= 25.0\%$$

Obviously, when discussing a percentage markup, it is important to know whether the markup is based on cost or on selling price.

Markups usually reflect expectations about operating costs, risks, and stock turnovers. Wholesalers and manufacturers often suggest standard retail markups that are considered to be profitable. An average percentage markup on selling price may be as high as 75 percent or more for jewelry or as low as 20 percent for the textbook you are reading. To the extent that retailers use similar markups for the same product category, price competition is reduced. In addition, the use of rigid markups is convenient, which is the major reason that retailers—who face numerous pricing decisions—employ this method.

Demand-oriented Pricing

Rather than basing the price of a product on its cost, marketers sometimes employ a pricing method based on the level of demand for the product—**demand-oriented pricing.** This method results in a high price when demand for the product is strong and a low price when demand is weak. To use this method, a marketer must be able to estimate the amounts of a product that consumers will demand at different prices. The marketer then chooses the price that generates the highest total revenue. Obviously, the effectiveness of this method depends on the marketer's ability to estimate demand accurately. Phone companies have done an excellent job of estimating market response to various long distance rates at different times of the day (see Figure 17.16).

Figure 17.16

*AT&T's promotion of
demand-oriented pricing
(Source: AT&T)*

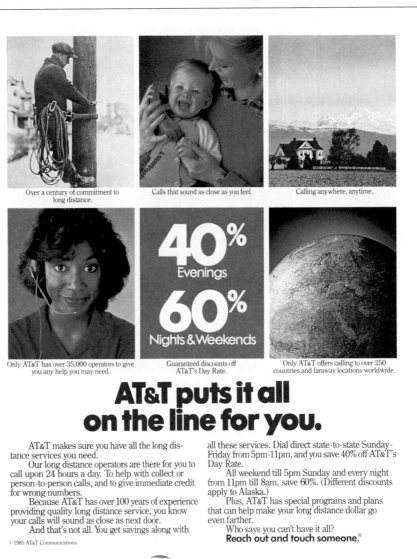

A marketer sometimes uses a demand-oriented pricing method called **price differentiation** when the firm wants to use more than one price in the marketing of a specific product. Price differentiation can be based on such considerations as type of customer, type of distribution channel used, or the time of the purchase.

Here are some examples. A 12-ounce canned soft drink costs less from a supermarket than from a vending machine. Florida hotel accommodations are more expensive in the winter than in the summer. A homeowner pays more for air-conditioner filters than does an apartment complex owner who purchases the same size filters in greater quantity. Christmas tree ornaments are usually cheaper on December 26 than on December 16.

For price differentiation to work properly, the marketer must be able to segment a market on the basis of different strengths of demand and then keep the segments separate enough so that segment members who buy at lower prices cannot then sell to buyers in segments that are charged a higher price. This isolation could be accomplished, for example, by selling to geographically separated segments.

Also, price differentiation can be based on employment in a public service position. For example, USAIR, Inc., as well as most other airlines, permits 50 percent off each regular one-way or round-trip fare for all U.S. military personnel on active duty, leave furlough, or a pass.

Compared with cost-oriented pricing, demand-oriented pricing places a firm in a better position to reach higher profit levels, assuming that buyers value the product at levels sufficiently above the product's cost. To use demand-oriented pricing, however, a marketer must be able to estimate demand at different price levels, which is frequently difficult to do accurately.

Competition-oriented Pricing

In using **competition-oriented pricing,** an organization considers costs and revenue secondary to competitors' prices. The importance of this method increases if competing products are almost homogeneous and the organization is serving markets in which price is the key variable of the marketing strategy.

One leading discount retail chain that has stores in the Midwest and South uses a competitive pricing method. Stores price products slightly below other discount outlets in the immediate area. The assistant manager of one Louisiana store goes to competing stores and records the prices of routinely purchased merchandise; this store's prices then are set 1 cent below competitors'. This pricing method is easy to use, and the resulting prices increase store traffic.

Competition-oriented pricing should help attain a pricing objective to increase sales or market share. Competition-oriented pricing methods may be combined with cost approaches to arrive at price levels necessary for a profit.

Determination of a Specific Price

Pricing policies and methods should direct and structure the selection of a final price. If they are to do so, it is important for marketers to establish pricing objectives, to know something about the target market, and to determine demand, price elasticity, costs, and competitive factors. In addition to those economic factors, the role of price in the marketing mix will affect the final price.

Although we suggest a systematic approach to pricing, in practice prices often are finalized after only limited planning. Trial and error, rather than planning, may be used to set a price; then marketers determine whether revenue minus costs yields a profit. This approach to pricing is not recommended because it makes it much harder to discover pricing errors.

In the absence of government price control, pricing remains a flexible and convenient way to adjust the marketing mix. In most situations, prices can be adjusted quickly—in a matter of minutes or over a few days. This flexibility and freedom do not characterize the other components of the marketing mix. Since so many complex issues are involved in establishing the right price, pricing is indeed as much an art as a science.

Summary

There are eight stages in the process of establishing prices. They are (1) selection of pricing objectives; (2) assessment of the target market's evaluation of price and its ability to purchase; (3) determination of demand; (4) analysis of demand, cost, and profit relationships; (5) analysis of competitors' prices; (6) selection of a pricing policy; (7) development of a pricing method; and (8) determination of a specific price.

The first stage, setting pricing objectives, is critical because the objectives provide a foundation on which the decisions of subsequent stages are based. Organizations may employ numerous pricing objectives. Some are short term; others are long term. Different objectives are used for different products and market segments.

The second stage in establishing prices is an assessment of the target market's evaluation of price and its ability to purchase. This stage tells a marketer how much emphasis to place on price and may aid the marketer in determining how far above the competition the firm can set its prices. Understanding the purchasing power of customers and knowing how important a product is to them in comparison with other products helps marketers correctly assess the target market's evaluation of price.

In the third stage of setting prices, the organization must determine the demand for its product. The classic demand schedule shows an inverse relationship between price and quantity demanded; as the price of the product decreases, the demand increases, and vice versa. However, there is sometimes a direct positive relationship between price and quantity demanded, as in the case of prestige products, where demand increases as price increases. In setting prices, the organization must learn whether price is related to quantity inversely or directly. Next, elasticity of demand—the relative responsiveness of changes in quantity demanded to changes in price—must be determined. The percentage of change in quantity demanded caused by a percentage change in price is much greater for products with elastic demand than for products with inelastic demand. If demand is elastic, a change in price causes an opposite change in total revenue. Inelastic demand results in a parallel change in total revenue when a product's price is changed.

The production of any product results in cost. Average fixed cost is the fixed cost per unit produced. Average variable cost is the variable cost per unit produced. Average total cost is the sum of average fixed cost and average variable cost times the quantity produced.

Analysis of demand, cost, and profit relationships, the fourth stage of the process, can be accomplished through marginal analysis or breakeven analysis. Marginal analysis combines the demand schedule with a firm's costs to develop an optimum price for maximum profit. This optimum price is the point at which marginal cost—the cost associated with producing one more unit of the product—equals marginal revenue. Marginal revenue is the change in total revenue that occurs when one additional unit of the product is sold. In reality, an organization's cost and revenue relationships are difficult to determine. Therefore, marginal analysis serves only as a model. It offers little help in pricing new products before costs and revenues are established.

The point at which the costs of producing a product equal the revenue made from selling the product is the breakeven point. Knowing the number of units necessary to break even is important in setting the price. To use breakeven analysis effectively, a marketer should determine the breakeven point for each of several alternative prices. This determination makes it possible to compare the effects on total revenue, total costs, and the breakeven point for each price under consideration. Breakeven analysis identifies undesirable price alternatives that should definitely be avoided. This approach assumes, however, that the quantity demanded is basically fixed and that the major task is to set prices to recover costs.

A marketer needs to be aware of the prices charged for comparing brands. This allows a firm to keep its prices the same as competitors' prices when nonprice competition is used. If a company employs price as a competitive tool, it can price its brand below competing brands.

A pricing policy is a guiding philosophy or course of action designed to influence and determine pricing decisions. Pricing policies help marketers to solve the practical problems of establishing prices. Two types of pioneer pricing policies are price skimming and penetration pricing. Price skimming means that an organization charges the highest possible price that buyers who most desire the product will pay. This policy provides several benefits, especially when a product is in the introductory stage of its life cycle. Generating much-needed initial cash flows to help offset sizable development costs is one of the most important benefits. A penetration price is a lower price designed to penetrate the market and produce a larger unit sales volume.

Psychological pricing, another pricing policy, encourages purchases that are based on emotional reactions rather than on rational responses. It includes odd-even pricing, customary pricing, prestige pricing, and price lining. A third pricing policy, professional pricing, is used by persons who have great skill or experience in a particular field. Promotional pricing, in which price is coordinated with promotion, is another type of pricing policy. Price leaders, special-event pricing, and superficial discounting are examples of promotional pricing. Experience curve pricing fixes a low price that high-cost competitors cannot match. Experience curve pricing is possible when experience reduces manufacturing costs at a predictable rate.

A pricing method is a mechanical procedure for assigning prices to specific products on a regular basis. Three types of pricing methods are cost-oriented pricing, demand-oriented pricing, and competition-oriented pricing. In using cost-oriented pricing, a firm determines price by adding a dollar amount or percentage to the cost of the product. Two common cost-oriented pricing methods are cost-plus and markup pricing. Demand-oriented pricing is based on the level of demand for the product. To use this method, a marketer must be able to estimate the amounts of a product that buyers will demand at different prices. Demand-oriented pricing results in a high price when demand for a product is strong and a low price when demand is weak. In the case of competition-oriented pricing, costs and revenues are secondary to competitors' prices. Competition oriented pricing and cost approaches may be combined to arrive at price levels necessary for a profit.

Important Terms

Demand curve
Elasticity of demand
Price elasticity
Fixed costs
Average fixed cost
Variable costs
Average variable cost
Total cost
Marginal cost (MC)
Average total cost
Marginal revenue (MR)
Breakeven point
Pricing policy
Price skimming
Penetration price
Psychological pricing
Odd-even pricing

Customary pricing
Prestige pricing
Price lining
Professional pricing
Price leaders
Special-event pricing
Superficial discounting
Experience curve pricing
Pricing method
Cost-oriented pricing
Cost-plus pricing
Markup pricing
Demand-oriented pricing
Price differentiation
Competition-oriented pricing

Discussion and Review Questions

1. Identify the eight stages that make up the process of establishing prices.
2. Why do most demand curves demonstrate an inverse relationship between price and quantity?
3. List the characteristics of products that have inelastic demand. Give several examples of such products.
4. Explain why optimum profits should occur when marginal cost equals marginal revenue.
5. The Chambers Company has just gathered estimates for doing a breakeven analysis for a new product. Variable costs are $7 a unit. Additional plant will cost $48,000. The new product will be charged $18,000 a year for its share of general overhead. Advertising expenditures will be $80,000, and $55,000 will be spent on distribution. If the product sells for $12, what is the breakeven point in units? What is the breakeven point in dollar sales volume?
6. Why should a marketer be aware of competitors' prices?
7. For what type of products would a pioneer price-skimming policy be most appropriate? For what type of products would penetration pricing be more effective?
8. Why do consumers associate price with quality? When should prestige pricing be used?
9. Are price leaders a realistic approach to pricing?
10. What are the benefits of cost-oriented pricing?
11. Under what conditions is cost-plus pricing most appropriate?
12. If a retailer purchases a can of soup for 24 cents and sells it for 36 cents, what is the percentage markup on selling price?

Figure 17.17

Percentages of shoppers who use lists to avoid salt/sodium (Source: A.C. Nielsen, 1983 Nielsen Review of Retail Grocery Store Trends, from survey sponsored by the FDA)

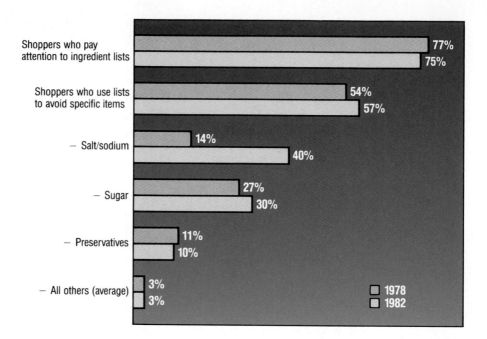

Shoppers who pay attention to ingredient lists — 77% / 75%

Shoppers who use lists to avoid specific items — 54% / 57%

— Salt/sodium — 14% / 40%

— Sugar — 27% / 30%

— Preservatives — 11% / 10%

— All others (average) — 3% / 3%

☐ 1978
☐ 1982

Cases

Case 17.1 Parsley Patch, Inc.[5]

Parsley Patch, Inc., was founded in Santa Rosa, California, by two women who were looking for money to pay for graduate school. From spices, herbs, and dried vegetables, one of the founders had concocted salt-free seasonings that delighted their friends. So the two partners decided to bring this nutritional alchemy to the retail consumer market. They positioned their products as offering high price and high quality for the affluent gourmet.

About this time, many people were becoming sodium conscious and began to use salt substitutes (see Figure 17.17). Medical studies have identified salt, or sodium chloride, as a contributing factor to high blood pressure. Dietary guidelines issued by many organizations, including the American Medical Association, advocate that all Americans should moderate their sodium intake. This sodium consciousness led to the introduction of many new brands of salt substitutes in a variety of grocery items (see Figure 17.18).

At the right time, in April 1981, Parsley Patch introduced its six spice blends at a gourmet food show in San Francisco and obtained several thousand dollars' worth of orders. Soon, the founders and their families were working six days a week to manufacture and ship the spices. Five employees were hired and operations expanded to a rented warehouse. The spices met with success in hundreds of gourmet shops and department stores.

5. The facts in this case are from Sanford L. Jacobs, "A Dash of Cost-Control Savvy Helps Turn Spice Firm Around," *Wall Street Journal*, March 26, 1984, p. 25; "Salt and High Blood Pressure," *Consumer Reports*, Jan. 1984, pp. 17, 21; and "Progressive Grocer's Guide to Usage of Supermarket Products," *Progressive Grocer*, July 1983, pp. 39–41; "California Herb Growers Face Rising Tide of Import Pressure," *Chemical Marketing Reporter*, Sept. 26, 1983, pp. 45, 48.

Figure 17.18

Low or no sodium new product introductions (Source: A.C. Nielsen Company, 1983 Nielsen Review of Retail Grocery Store Trends)

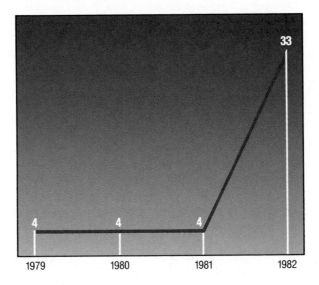

The retail price of Parsley Patch spices was $4.15 per 5-ounce jar, almost double that of rival products. The wholesale price was $2.75. Pricing had become a crucial marketing mix variable as customers began to mention that the products were good but too expensive. The prices of other spices were getting cheaper because domestic growers were facing intense market competition from foreign sources. The founders had not paid much attention to costs and pricing. They now began an inquiry into their products' cost components. They had been buying 5-ounce jars at 70 cents apiece, and they found that this variable cost could be reduced by using alternative 4-ounce jars priced at 17 cents each. They also found that ordering ingredients less frequently and in larger quantities reduced the variable costs even further. The women then set a target gross margin (sales minus cost of goods sold) of 60 percent.

Parsley Patch began sales forecasting and breakeven analysis. After considering all the costs and pricing objectives, final prices were set. The wholesale price was fixed at $1.50 per 4-ounce jar; with a markup, the retail price became a competitive $2.25. This lower price stimulated sales in health-food stores and facilitated the products' entry into supermarkets. In supermarkets, spices and seasonings are ranked eleventh among food items in terms of frequency of use by consumers. Parsley Patch's sales climbed to $700,000 a year, and the company posted a profit.

Questions for Discussion

1. Is the demand for this product elastic or inelastic? Explain.
2. If Parsley Patch had total variable costs of $1.03 per 4-ounce jar and annual fixed costs of $200,000, what would be the breakeven point in units? In dollar sales volume?
3. If variable costs went up to $1.25 per 4-ounce jar and annual fixed costs remained at $200,000, what would be the total costs per annum, assuming sales of 500,000 units? Should prices be raised?

Case 17.2   How Domestic Compact Cars Are Priced[6]

The U.S. automobile industry has been combating increased competition from foreign auto makers. A full 35 percent of the cars sold in the United States are imported compacts, and the number of imports sold has comprised as much as 45 percent of the U.S. compact market. Japanese cars make up almost 80 percent of these imports. The 1983 Customer Satisfaction Index indicated that the overall gap between domestic and imported cars had not changed for two consecutive years. Imports continued to account for over 85 percent of the above-average index rankings, while domestic cars received nearly 67 percent of the below-average ratings.

Pricing competition is fierce in the automotive industry. U.S. auto makers cannot compete with their Japanese counterparts. To bring a small car to the U.S. market costs the Japanese auto maker $1,700 less, even after paying $500 for shipping and tariffs. Part of this price differential can be attributed to the $80-billion retooling effort—to switch to front-wheel drives and small-car designs—that U.S. auto makers have to pay for. Also, when U.S. auto makers put a new small car into production, at a cost of almost $2 billion, they attempt to break even within four to five years, whereas the Japanese stretch their payback period to eight years. So, to compete with the Japanese, U.S. car makers have to cut production costs drastically. They have been trying, by reducing overhead and negotiating concessions from the labor unions. But the higher costs of American manufacturing, labor, and raw materials, plus inflation and the difference between the two countries' tax structures, means Detroit cannot match the Japanese cost advantage.

Rather than basing the price of a car on true production costs and then adjusting that price to stay competitive in the marketplace, Detroit fixes on the sticker price of a car five years in advance. The auto maker conducts intensive market research of the niche the car is intended to fill, determines what features will be included, and settles on a price that allows for inflation. Car makers look for at least 10-percent profit on the sale of a car, but that margin depends on variables that are hypothetical at the point of price formulation: production costs, sales volume, and price competition.

Table 17.3 illustrates how the price of a car increases as it moves from the assembly line to the dealer's showroom. The total cost of the car includes both fixed and variable costs incurred through the manufacturing process. The sticker price covers the total cost plus a profit markup by the manufacturer and another profit markup by the dealer.

Since domestic car makers cannot beat their foreign competitors, they are looking to join them in a variety of ways. U.S. manufacturers are using more raw materials produced overseas and cheaper, foreign-made components. Analysts predict that foreign-made auto parts, which accounted for 6 percent of the U.S. market in 1980, will climb to 15 percent by 1990, becoming a $4-billion-a-year business. To produce a competitive subcompact, General Motors has replaced the assembly line with modular construction and is using intelligent robots to

---

6. The facts in this case are from "The All-American Small Car Is Fading," *Business Week*, March 12, 1984, pp. 88–95; "Why Detroit Can't Cut Prices," *Business Week*, March 1, 1982, pp. 110–111; and Amal Nag, "To Build a Small Car, GM Tries to Redesign Its Production System," *Wall Street Journal*, May 14, 1984, pp. 1, 12.

Table 17.3 How a small car's price increases from assembly line to showroom

Manufacturing		Overhead		Marketing	
Body	$ 688	Fixed Costs	$ 992	Dealer markup	$1,156
Transmission	112	Profit target	248		
Vehicle assembly	667	R&D special			
Engine	387	tooling	1,537		
Chassis	626				
Total	$2,480	Total	$2,777		
		Overall total	$5,257	Overall total	$6,413

Source: Adapted from data of Rath & Strong, Inc. Used by permission.

reduce labor costs. The effort was named "Project Saturn" after the program that was developed to overcome the Russians' early lead in space exploration.

Another strategy American car manufacturers have adopted is to buy their compact cars from Japanese producers or build them in this country using designs and major components supplied by foreign partners. American Motors, for example, through a joint venture with Renault, produced the Alliance. American Motors invested $200 million, a tenth of the cost of producing the car on its own. Such compact car ventures appeal to foreign manufacturers, who increasingly fear legislative measures that might affect their imports into the United States. Some manufacturers, such as Honda and Nissan of Japan, have set up U.S. manufacturing facilities. Others have set up joint ventures with American manufacturers, as Toyota has with General Motors.

Questions for Discussion

1. Price alterations are frequently the easiest changes in the marketing mix for competitors to match. Is this a problem for domestic compact cars? Why or why not?
2. Should U.S. auto makers increase their payback period to eight years to match what Japanese manufacturers have been doing? How would this affect the breakeven point of U.S. auto makers?
3. What pricing objectives should domestic compact auto makers utilize?

Part VI
Marketing Management

We have divided marketing into several sets of variables and have discussed the decisions and activities associated with each variable. By now, you should understand (1) how to analyze marketing opportunities, and (2) the components of the marketing mix. It is time to put all these components together in our discussion of marketing management issues. In Chapter 18 we discuss strategic market planning. Specifically, we focus on the planning process, the setting of marketing objectives, the assessment of opportunities and resources, and specific product/market matching approaches to strategic market planning. Chapter 19 deals with other marketing management issues including organization, implementation, and control. Approaches to organizing a marketing unit, issues regarding strategy implementation, and techniques for controlling marketing strategies are explored in this chapter.

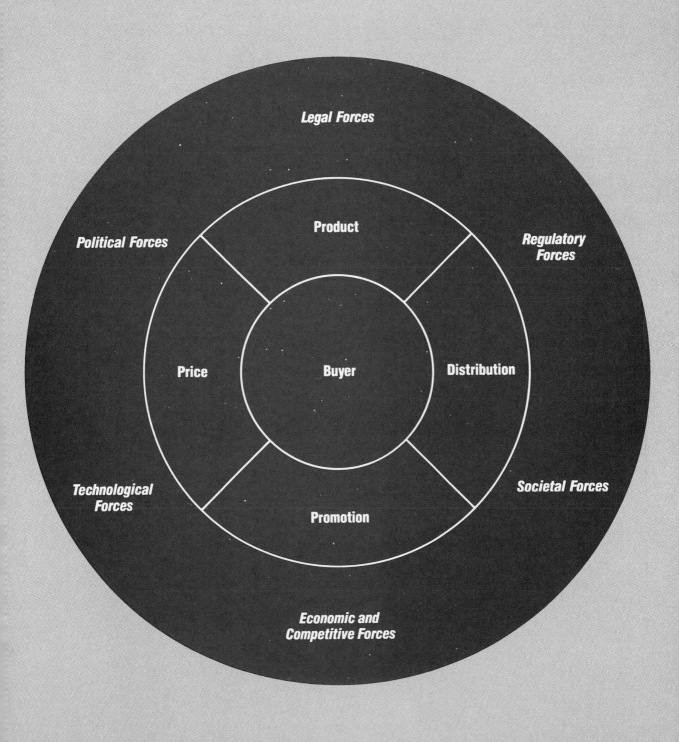

18 / Strategic Market Planning

Objectives

- To provide an overview of the strategic market planning process.

- To define marketing planning and differentiate it from strategic market planning.

- To describe three major approaches to strategic market planning including product-portfolio analysis, the market attractiveness/business position model, and PIMS (Profit Impact on Marketing Strategy).

- To evaluate strategic market planning and relate it to the development of functional marketing strategies and activities.

Figure 18.1

Parfums de Coeur's unique strategy—marketing imposter brands of leading perfumes (Source: Courtesy of Parfums de Coeur)

Parfums de Coeur (Perfumes of the Heart) was founded on an unusual corporate and marketing strategy. After Mark Laracy had invested fifteen years of his professional life working on leading perfume brands (Opium, Cachet, Aviance, and Enjoli), he was fired from Charles of the Ritz. Rather than take a job with another fragrance firm, he decided to use his knowledge about the business to develop a new company based on a unique strategy. Laracy developed a product line of six so-called impostures (imitations of well-known brands), beginning with Ninja, an Opium substitute that Laracy claims is even better than the original. His product line of designer knockoffs includes Lindsay (a Ralph Lauren imposter), Fairchild (Oscar De Laurenta and Amy Vanderbilt), Hampton (Halston), Smoldering Musk (Jovan), and Primo (Giorgio) (see Figure 18.1). In all, more than 9 million bottles of imposter products were sold in 1985, yielding Laracy $25 million in sales.

Each imposter brand has a chemical composition similar to the designer brand it imitates. Even lab tests indicate that the imposter and the original brand have similar cromatograms that indicate a similar fragrance. Instead of selling image, Parfums de Coeur sells price. And instead of distributing through upscale department stores, Parfums de Coeur markets its products through K mart, Wal-Mart, and other discount stores. Parfums de Coeur promotes its fragrances by blatantly comparing them to the competition in ads, at the point of sale, and even on the packaging. In addition, Parfums de Coeur advertises in People, Cosmopolitan, Play Girl, Ebony, *and other similar magazines. At a time when perfume sales have gone flat, Parfums de Coeur has appealed to middle- and lower-middle-income women who do not have the resources or inclination to spend $32.50 on a bottle of Opium. The company has found that consumers are willing to spend $7.50 for Ninja, and sales results indicate that the strategy is working. The founder of Parfums de Coeur credits sound strategic planning and management with much of his success. A good idea that was properly implemented led to market success. Now managing growth and planning future marketing strategies is as great a challenge as getting the business started was.*[1]

Strategic planning requires a general management orientation, rather than a narrow functional orientation. Nevertheless, with market analysis becoming more important, the lead responsibility for formulating corporate strategy is increasingly being entrusted to the marketing department in many companies. The **corporate strategy** determines the means for utilizing resources in the areas of production, finance, research and development, personnel, and marketing to reach the organization's goals. Corporate strategy addresses the composition of the firm's distinct business operations and how the firm should divide business activities into manageable units.[2]

Corporate strategy planners are concerned with issues such as diversification, competition, differentiation, interrelationships among business units, and environmental issues. Diversity can be a key idea in a corporate strategy. For example, McDonald's corporate strategy has been to concentrate on being the world's largest hamburger chain, while Burger King has sought the acquisition of other restaurants, and Wendy's is experimenting with a chicken restaurant chain. Obviously, Wendy's and Burger King are using a different corporate strategy than McDonald's.[3]

1. Kevin T. Higgins, "By Any Other Name Would Smell As Sweet—Imposture Line from Parfums de Coeur Striving to Knock Off Designer Brands, Literally and Figuratively," *Marketing News,* Jan. 17, 1986, pp. 1, 12. Reprinted from *Marketing News,* published by the American Marketing Association.
2. Michael E. Porter, *Competitive Advantage* (New York: Free Press, 1985), p. 317.
3. Monci Jo Williams, "McDonald's Refuses to Plateau," *Fortune,* Nov. 12, 1984, p. 34.

Corporate strategic planning focuses on the decision-making process that governs the overall direction of the corporation, including many marketing considerations. As we state in Chapter 1, a **marketing strategy** encompasses selecting and analyzing a target market and creating and maintaining an appropriate marketing mix. Unfortunately, the marketing concept and concerns such as segmentation, product positioning, and marketing research have sometimes been ignored by corporate strategic planners.[4]

This chapter looks closely at one portion of marketing management—planning. More specifically, we provide a general overview of planning activities and approaches to strategic market planning. First, we provide an overview of the strategic market planning process, including the development of organizational goals, corporate strategy, and marketing objectives and strategy. We also examine organizational opportunities and resources as they relate to planning. We then look at approaches or methods used in product-portfolio analysis, the market attractiveness/business position model, and Profit Impact on Marketing Strategy (PIMS). We conclude the chapter by examining competitive strategies for marketing.

Strategic market planning should guide marketing strategy and marketing planning. Planning of marketing activities strongly affects the overall success of marketing efforts. Other aspects of the marketing management process—organizing, implementing, and controlling—are covered in Chapter 19.

Strategic Market Planning Defined

A **strategic market plan** takes into account not only marketing but all other functional areas of a business unit that must be coordinated, such as production, finance, and personnel, as well as concern about the environment. The concept of the strategic business unit is used to define areas for consideration in a specific strategic market plan. Each **strategic business unit (SBU)** is a division, product line, or other profit center within the parent company. Each sells a distinct set of products and/or services to an identifiable group of customers, and each is in competition with a well-defined set of competitors. In the context of the parent company, meaningful separation can be made of an SBU's revenues, operating costs, investments, and strategic plans.

How a company conceives of its SBUs can have a direct impact on the nature of the strategic market plans. If management fails to define the SBUs correctly, the best planning available cannot undo the damage. Unfortunately, some firms use familiar rationales for SBU boundaries, such as geography, old acquisition deals, and so on, that turn out to be very poor for strategic market planning purposes. For example, a manufacturer of plastic control devices had vaguely defined one SBU as a product supplier rather than as a unit that treated the precision-molding process control problems of manufacturers in general.[5] By properly defining each SBU, planning and strategy development can be improved.

4. Yoram Wind, "Marketing and Corporate Strategy," *The Wharton Magazine,* Summer 1982, p. 38.
5. Daniel H. Gray, "Uses and Misuses of Strategic Planning," *Harvard Business Review,* Jan.–Feb. 1986, p. 92.

Figure 18.2

Components of strategic
market planning

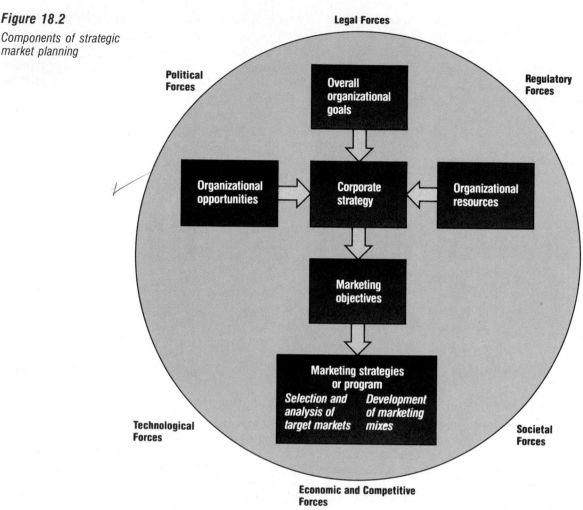

A strategic market plan is *not* the same, therefore, as a marketing plan; it
is a plan of *all* aspects of an organization's strategy in the marketplace. A
marketing plan, in contrast, deals primarily with implementing the market
strategy as it relates to target markets and the marketing mix.[6]

The process of **strategic market planning** yields a marketing strategy that is
the framework for a marketing plan. Through this process, an organization can
develop marketing strategies that, when properly implemented and controlled,
will contribute to achieving the organization's overall goals. To develop a
marketing strategy, all aspects of an organization that interface with the marketplace
must be considered.

The components of strategic market planning are shown in Figure 18.2.
The process is based on the establishment of an organization's overall goals,
and it must stay within the bounds of the organization's opportunities and
resources. When the firm has determined its overall goals and identified its
resources, it can then assess its opportunities and develop corporate strategy.

6. Derek F. Abell and John S. Hammond, *Strategic Market Planning* (Englewood Cliffs, N.J.: Prentice-
Hall, 1979), p. 10.

TreeSweet Products Company, a regional producer of citrus juice beverages, is currently changing its corporate strategy to become a recognizable national company and join the ranks with the top three juice producers, Minute Maid, Tropicana, and Citrus Hill.

To achieve this long-term goal, TreeSweet has developed a multitiered corporate strategy. First, its product line will be expanded to offer the now popular blended fruit drinks, a variety of other fruit juices, and juice-added soft drinks. TreeSweet has already purchased the country's leading breakfast beverage, Awake (orange flavored, no juice content) and Orange Plus (10-percent juice) from General Foods. It intends to bring other proven products, from smaller regional labels to major brands, under its TreeSweet name. The company also plans to expand its distribution channels, formerly limited to six states, to include half the country.

TreeSweet is changing many components of its marketing strategy. Its fifty-one-year-old logo and package design have been altered to convey a higher-quality image. The new package, which emphasizes the TreeSweet company name, displays fruit hanging from the tree, a departure from the smiling oranges that covered TreeSweet packages for many decades. To support all of these changes, an aggressive advertising and promotional program has also been developed. The new campaign's theme is "TreeSweet. You know a good name when you taste it." And finally, TreeSweet has aggressively pursued major price cuts that it feels have had a direct impact on the national brands. Other orange juice manufacturers have matched and sometimes exceeded TreeSweet's price cuts on frozen concentrate. To sum up, TreeSweet has evaluated each element of its marketing strategy and made adjustments to achieve the marketing objective of gaining national distribution, awareness, and sales (*Sources: Tom Bayer, "TreeSweet Jumps Into '86 Ripe for Growth,"* Advertising Age, *Feb. 3, 1986, p. 58; Jon Berry, "TreeSweet Branches Out,"* Adweek, *Dec. 16, 1985, pp. 1, 50; and Judith Crown, "TreeSweet Bets Future on Aggressive Marketing Tactics,"* Houston Chronicle, *Jan. 12, 1986, p. 5-1.*)

Thereafter, marketing objectives must be designed so that their achievement will contribute to the corporate strategy and so that they can be accomplished through efficient use of the organization's resources.

To reach its marketing objectives, an organization must develop a marketing strategy, or a set of marketing strategies, as shown in Figure 18.2. Usually, several marketing strategies are used simultaneously in an effort to achieve the firm's marketing objectives. The set of marketing strategies that are implemented and used at the same time is referred to as the organization's **marketing program.**

As we have mentioned before, to formulate a marketing strategy, the marketer identifies and analyzes the target market and develops a marketing mix to satisfy individuals in that market. *Marketing strategy is best formulated when it reflects the overall direction of the organization and is coordinated with all of the firm's functional areas.* (The application on this page illustrates a change in both corporate and marketing strategy at TreeSweet Products Company.)

Table 18.1 *Some typical business goals*

| Possible Attributes | Possible Indices | Targets and Time Frame | | |
		Year One	Year Two	Year Three
Growth	$ sales	$100 million	$120 million	$140 million
	Unit sales	x units	$1.10x$ units	$1.20x$ units
Efficiency	$ profits	$10 million	$12 million	$15 million
	Profits/sales	.10	.10	.11
Utilization of	ROI	.15	.15	.16
resources	ROE	.25	.26	.27
Contribution to	Dividends	$1.00/share	$1.10/share	$1.30/share
owners	Earnings per share	$2.00/share	$2.40/share	$2.80/share
Contribution to	Price	Equal to or	Equal to or	Equal to or
customers	Quality	better than	better than	better than
	Reliability	competition	competition	competition
Contributions to	Wage rate	$3.50/hour	$3.75/hour	$4.00/hour
employees	Employment stability	<5% turnover	<4% turnover	<4% turnover
Contributions to	Taxes paid	$10 million	$12 million	$16 million
society	Scholarships awarded	$100,000	$120,000	$120,000

Source: Adapted from C. W. Hofer, "A Conceptual Scheme for Formulating a Total Business Strategy," Case 9-378-726 (Boston: HBS Case Services 9-378-726, 1976), p. 2. Used by permission of the author.

As indicated in Figure 18.2, the strategic market planning process is based on an analysis of the environment, by which it is very much affected. Environmental forces can place constraints on an organization and possibly influence its overall goals. The amount and type of resources that a firm can acquire are also affected by forces in the environment. However, such forces do not always constrain or work against the firm; they can also create favorable opportunities that can be translated into overall organizational goals and marketing objectives. For example, in the mid-eighties oil prices plummeted, causing many small refineries and exploration companies to go out of business. This situation created an opportunity for the larger, better-leveraged oil companies to acquire oil rigs and drilling equipment at a fraction of original cost. The environmental situation of decreased oil prices created an opportunity for select large oil companies to pick up valuable equipment at little expense, relatively speaking.

Environmental variables have an impact on the creation of a marketing strategy in several ways. When environmental variables affect an organization's overall goals, resources, opportunities, or marketing objectives, they also affect the firm's marketing strategies, which are based on these factors. More directly, environmental forces influence the development of a marketing strategy through their impact on consumers' needs and desires. In addition, marketing mix decisions are influenced by a variety of forces in the environment.

Competition, for instance, has an important impact on marketing mix decisions. The organization must diagnose the marketing mix activities it performs, taking into consideration competitors' marketing mix decisions, and develop some competitive advantage to support a strategy. For example, Federated, a discount consumer electronics superstore, has examined its competitors and developed a strategy that has produced 41-percent sales growth annually over the past

Figure 18.3

Hilton's goal—to become the number-one business hotel (Source: Hilton Hotels Corporation)

AMBITION

It's the will to win.
It makes Hilton America's Business Address.®

HILTON
AMERICA'S BUSINESS ADDRESS

five years. Federated sells fast moving items such as TVs, VCRs, and compact disc players at close to cost. These items represent approximately 40 percent of Federated's inventory and generate just 20 percent of its income. The sale of the remaining 60 percent of Federated's inventory has a larger margin and therefore contributes 80 percent of their income. This strategy effectively reinforces the retailer's low-price image and increases repeat business for all of its product offerings.[7]

In the next several sections, we discuss the major components of strategic market planning.

Establishing Organizational Goals

A firm's organizational goals should direct its planning efforts. Table 18.1 illustrates some typical business goals. A company's overall goals may focus on one or several business activities. Goals specify ends or results that are sought. For example, a firm that is in serious financial trouble may be concerned solely with short-run results needed to stay in business. There always seems to be an airline or major retailer taking drastic action to stay in business due to cash shortages. On the other hand, the central goal of Hilton, as shown in Figure 18.3, is to be a winner. This means Hilton wants to be the number-one

7. Scott Ticer, "Federated Is Taking Its 'Show' on the Road," *Business Week,* June 24, 1985, p. 85.

business hotel. A successful company, however, may want to sacrifice this year's profits for the long run and at the same time pursue other goals, such as finding new customers. For example, Coca-Cola believed that its soft-drink profits could not be pushed to grow any faster than 10 percent per year. To realize faster growth in profits, the company purchased Columbia Pictures Industries, Inc. Coca-Cola hopes to make profits at Columbia increase 20 percent per year.[8]

Organizational Opportunities and Resources

There are three major considerations in assessing opportunities and resources: market opportunity must be evaluated; environmental forces (discussed in Chapter 2) must be monitored; and the firm's capabilities should be understood. For example, Eastman Kodak Co. earns a 55 percent pretax profit margin from film, and the company controls as much as 85 percent of the U.S. market in color film.[9] In the large amateur photography market, Kodak historically has competed successfully against Japanese competitors. But more recently, Kodak has failed to identify opportunities properly. Over the past several years, Kodak has lacked new product development, while competitors have run away with the markets for instant photography, 35 mm cameras, and video-cassette recorders. Kodak's recent response represents their immense capabilities. Kodak has commissioned a Japanese manufacturer to produce a 35 mm camera under the Kodak brand name. This step was taken to secure a share of the market while development continues on Kodak's own version of the 35 mm camera. Other new product developments include electronic publishing systems for corporate documents and automated microfilm-imaging systems.[10] Kodak is striving to carefully assess the opportunities and apply their resources to develop objectives and revise marketing strategies. All these activities are a part of strategic market planning.

Market Opportunity

A **market opportunity** arises when the right combination of circumstances occurs at the right time to allow an organization to take action toward reaching a target market. An opportunity provides a favorable chance or opening for the firm to generate sales from identifiable markets. The term *strategic window* has been used to describe what are often only limited periods of optimum fit between the key requirements of a market and the particular capabilities of a firm competing in that market.[11]

For example, The Gap has for years been positioned as a youth-oriented store for popularly priced blue jeans and limited casual wear. Despite changes in consumer tastes, The Gap maintained its image—until slumping profitability

8. Myron Magnet, "Coke Tries Selling Movies Like Pop," *Fortune,* Dec. 26, 1983, p. 119.
9. Alex Taylor III, "Kodak Scrambles to Refocus," *Fortune,* March 3, 1986, p. 36.
10. Barbara Buell and Alex Beam, "Kodak Just Can't Get Its Giant Feet Moving Fast Enough," *Business Week,* Feb. 24, 1986, pp. 37–38.
11. Derek F. Abell, "Strategic Windows," *Journal of Marketing,* July 1978, p. 21.

caused a major strategy reorientation. The Gap today reflects an entirely new image. Stores have been remodeled, apparel has been imported, and a complete line of classic, high-quality, private-label merchandise has been developed. According to The Gap's marketing vice-president, "Historically, we had no character or point of view other than Levi's. But now, like other great specialty stores—Brooks Brothers, Laura Ashley, or Ann Taylor, for example—we stand for something. We're bringing quality, taste, and style to a wide public at the same time."[12] This example illustrates that understanding the environment as well as the firm's ability to respond to a market opportunity are important considerations in strategic market planning.

Determinants of the attractiveness of market opportunity include market factors such as size and growth rate and other factors such as competition, financial and economic factors, technological factors, and social, legal, and political factors.[13] Since each industry and product is somewhat different, the factors that determine attractiveness tend to vary. For example, Japan's Shiseido Company, Ltd., has historically been known as a worldwide cosmetic producer. Operating 25,000 franchised stores, Shiseido specializes in providing personalized service and consulting. In the United States, its cosmetics are distributed through exclusive department stores such as Bloomingdale's and Macy's (both of New York) and Emporium Capwell (Los Angeles). Operations are being expanded to include many unrelated products and services, with the hope that customers will associate the Shiseido name with quality and accept its diversifications. Shiseido shops can now carry fashion clothing, household products, and health foods. Other developments include sports clubs, restaurants, and boutiques. Shiseido sees new market opportunities and is attempting to respond by using its available resources to fill existing needs.[14]

Market requirements relate to the customers' needs or desired benefits. The market requirement is satisfied by components of the marketing mix that provide these benefits to buyers. Of course, buyers' perceptions of what requirements fill their needs and provide the desired benefits determine the success of any marketing effort. Marketers must devise strategies to outperform the competition by determining product attributes that buyers use to select products. An attribute must be important and differentiating if it is to be useful in strategy development. Therefore, understanding buyer perceptions is the key to building a strategy based on important and differentiating attributes. For instance, Hershey's (see Figure 18.4) has developed products emphasizing different attributes that appeal to varying consumer groups.[15]

As we mention in Chapter 2, market requirements often change as competition offers new benefits to consumers. For example, Kentucky Fried Chicken added nuggets in response to McDonald's highly successful Chicken McNuggets. Kentucky Fried Chicken hopes that their image in the market as chicken experts will give them a competitive advantage even though they were not the first producer of nuggets.

---

12. William Meyers, "Giving The Gap a New Niche," *Adweek,* Dec. 16, 1985, p. RR 12.
13. Abell and Hammond, *Strategic Market Planning,* p. 213.
14. Andrew Tanzer, "Is Beauty More Than Skin Deep?" *Forbes,* Dec. 16, 1985, pp. 147–150.
15. Behram J. Hansotia, Muzaffar A. Shaikh, and Jagdish N. Sheth, "The Strategic Determinancy Approach to Brand Management," *Business Marketing,* Feb. 1985, p. 66.

Figure 18.4

Hershey's new-product developments created to appeal to different consumer groups (Source: Hershey Foods Corporation)

Environmental Monitoring

Environmental monitoring is the process that seeks information about events and relationships in a company's outside environment, knowledge of which assists marketers in identifying opportunities and planning.

Some corporations have derived substantial benefits from establishing an "environmental scanning (or monitoring) unit" within the strategic planning group or from including line management in teams or committees to conduct environmental analysis.[16] Management is thus integrally involved in the process of environmental forecasting, and the likelihood of successfully integrating forecasting efforts into strategic market planning is considerably enhanced.[17] Results of forecasting research show that even simple quantitative forecasting techniques outperform the unstructured intuitive assessments of experts.[18]

Monitoring change in the environment is extremely important if a firm is to avoid crisis management. The Nestlé Company tried ignoring protestors and

16. Liam Fahey, William K. King, Vodake K. Naraganan, "Environmental Scanning and Forecasting in Strategic Planning—The State of the Art," *Long Range Planning,* Feb. 1981, p. 38.
17. Ibid.
18. David M. Georgaff and Robert G. Mundick, "Managers Guide to Forecasting," *Harvard Business Review,* Jan.–Feb. 1986, p. 120.

took activists who questioned the firm's promotion of its infant formulas to court. The controversy involved the marketing of a product that promoted bottle feeding over breast feeding. Allegations were made that babies in less-developed countries suffered from diarrhea and malnutrition when fed this product. To deal with this problem, Nestlé has formed an audit commission to review complaints and has taken its defense directly to the news media.[19]

An environmental change can suddenly alter a firm's opportunities or resources. Reformulated, more effective strategies may then be needed to guide marketing efforts. An environmental force such as technology can have far-reaching impact on diverse businesses. Since nearly every firm, including service firms, uses technology to provide benefits to buyers, it is imperative that organizations integrate technology considerations into their strategy. Companies do not have to be technology developers or leaders to benefit from technology change. Thus, organizations must understand the position and role of technology in their strategy. This, however, does not necessarily mean that an organization should instantly respond to each technological development. Sometimes a firm is wise not to implement technological change too quickly if it leads to a competitive disadvantage. General Motors' decision to launch diesel engines in its automobiles before they were mechanically ready for the market turned out to be a costly mistake.[20] The technologically inferior domestically produced diesel engine has been the result of customer dissatisfaction and caused General Motors great expense in terms of loss of customer loyalty. The engines were converted gas engines—not "ground up" diesel engines. The stress associated with the extra compression in a diesel engine caused these engines mechanical difficulties, especially over 60,000 miles. Environmental monitoring should identify new developments and determine the nature and rate of change.

Capabilities and Resources of the Firm

A firm's capabilities relate to distinctive competencies that it has developed to do something well and efficiently. For example, Popingo Video is a franchised VCR and tape rental company. Popingo's strategy is to locate in small cities where the competition is minimal or nonexistent, a strategy pioneered by Wal-Mart, the fastest growing discount retailer in the United States. Popingo provides a wide assortment of merchandise that competitors often do not carry. Items available at many outlets include video cassettes, video player/recorders, blank tapes, computer software, cable TV service, satellite dishes, and even a crunchy cookie snack. As a retail video establishment, Popingo's distinct capability is in providing a variety of products to small, previously untapped markets. Cooperative buying through the franchise agreement makes the products available at a fair price. Popingo's marketing strategy has reached a target market that many larger competitors have ignored.[21]

A company is likely to enjoy a differential advantage in an area where its competencies outmatch those of its potential competition.[22] Often a company

19. Kevin Higgins, "Instant Formula Protest Teaches Nestlé a Tactical Lesson," *Marketing News,* June 10, 1983, p. 1.
20. Alan L. Frohman, "Putting Technology Into Strategy," *Journal of Business Strategy,* Spring 1985, p. 54.
21. Alex Ben Block, "I've Put Everything on the Line," *Forbes,* Dec. 16, 1985, pp. 69, 70.
22. Philip Kotler, "Strategic Planning and the Marketing Process," *Business,* May–June 1980, pp. 6–7.

Figure 18.5

Herlin Press's promotion of its capabilities as a high-quality graphic arts company (Source: Herlin Press, Inc.)

may possess manufacturing or technical skills that are valuable in areas outside of its traditional industry. Film-producing companies, for example, apply coatings to webs as a part of the film-manufacturing process. This technological skill is possessed by only a few companies and can be applied to a number of nonfilm products. This example demonstrates that a firm's distinctive competencies may not always be obvious.[23] Herlin Press, Inc., illustrates its superior graphic reproduction capabilities in Figure 18.5. Herlin stresses that its quality, service, and dependability set it apart from other printers.

Today marketing planners are especially concerned with resource constraints. Due to shortages in energy and other scarce economic resources, strategic planning options are often limited. On the other hand, planning to avoid shortages can backfire. For example, early in the 1980s 7-Eleven's parent company, The Southland Corporation, purchased Citgo Petroleum Corp. Southland's strategy was to become more vertically integrated and avoid gasoline shortages. But Southland's marketing research and environmental monitoring did not reveal that overcapacity and falling demand would cause an oversupply and that the

23. Alan L. Frohman, "Putting Technology Into Strategic Planning," *California Management Review,* Winter 1985, pp. 48–59.

Table 18.2 *A framework for viewing resource constraints and opportunities in different planning periods*

Present (few or no resource constraints)	Short/Intermediate-Range Horizon (increasingly severe resource and social-governmental constraints)
Current products (*benefits*) produced and supplied at currently feasible[a] technology/resource combinations (*costs*)	Somewhat modified products (*benefits*) that will be demanded at *costs* based on feasible[a] extensions of current technology/resource combinations
Intermediate/Long-Range Horizon (extremely severe resource and social-governmental constraints)	**Long-Range Horizon (resource constraints disappearing, continuing severe social-governmental constraints)**
Extensively modified products (*benefits*) that will be demanded at *costs* based on feasible[a] major modifications of current resource/technology combinations	Products (*benefits*) that will be demanded at *costs* based on feasible[a] new resources/new technology combinations

[a]Most advantageous to the corporation in terms of its long-run organizational goals.

Source: Reprinted by permission from *Business* magazine. "Strategic Planning Under Resource Constraints," by Jacob Naor, Sept.–Oct. 1981, p. 18. Copyright © 1981 by the College of Business Administration, Georgia State University, Atlanta.

price of gasoline would drop dramatically. The result was that Southland could have purchased gasoline more cheaply on the spot market than refine it through Citgo. Yet the firm's strategy has not been a complete failure. The purchase of Citgo has increased 7-Eleven's gasoline sales, which in turn has drawn more customers into the stores, increasing total sales and profits. Also, if there is ever again a gasoline shortage, Southland will be prepared to weather the crisis.[24]

Table 18.2 provides a framework for viewing opportunities and resources in different planning periods. This framework suggests that individual firms face four distinct planning horizons, each constrained to a different degree in regard to resources, social concerns, and government regulations.[25] These constraints increase from the present to the intermediate long-range period, with resource constraints possibly declining thereafter as radically new technologies and resource applications become commercially available. Crucial to the usefulness of this framework is the ability to predict future technological developments or at least the likely direction of future breakthroughs. For example, the projected direction of technological innovation could, in effect, suggest the strategic horizons facing firms and industries. In that case, technological forecasting could be a crucial element in the strategic-planning process.

Costs (resulting from various technology/resource combinations) and benefits must go through a series of modifications or extensions as constraints become more severe. As we have already pointed out, scarce resources are not always constraints; they may provide the impetus a firm needs to provide benefits at the most desirable cost. For example, Transamerica Corporation attempts to

24. Steve Klinkerman, "Why Southland Won't Unload Its Albatross," *Business Week,* July 1, 1985, p. 71.
25. This section is reprinted by permission from *Business* magazine. "Strategic Planning Under Resource Constraints," by Jacob Naor, Sept.–Oct. 1981, p. 17. Copyright © 1981 by the College of Business Administration, Georgia State University, Atlanta.

be a low-cost marketer by reducing costs because its products are closely related and because of operating efficiencies between complementary businesses the firm owns. Transamerica seeks to maximize the benefits of diversification and maintain a compatible mix of companies. This strategy permits the company to provide products (benefits) at resource/technology combinations (costs) to achieve industry leadership in service, reputation, innovation, and overall efficiency.

Corporate Strategy

Corporate strategy defines the means and direction of reaching organizational goals. The resources of the corporation are matched with the opportunities and risks in the environment. Corporate strategy attempts to define the scope and role of the strategic business units of the firm that are coordinated to reach the ends that are desired. Xerox, for example, focuses on reprographics (photocopying, electronic printers), office systems, and work stations. The acquisition of Crum & Forster, a leading property and liability insurance company, represented a major change in the direction of Xerox and provided new opportunities and risks. Xerox does not engage in businesses to produce robots, automobiles, or earth-moving equipment because they do not fit into the corporate strategy.

A corporate strategy determines not only the scope of the business, but also its resource deployment, competitive advantages, and overall coordination of production, finance, marketing, and other functional areas. For example, Black & Decker's traditional corporate strategy has been to provide customized power tools for specialized markets. But many Japanese manufacturers are providing standardized products worldwide, taking a significant portion of Black & Decker's former market share. Black & Decker has responded by developing a global manufacturing and marketing strategy that has cut the number of production centers from eight to two and produces fewer specialized professional power tools. Black & Decker also acquired General Electric small appliances and is now producing these home appliances under its own name. The firm hopes the diversification will compensate for the temporary flattening in the professional power tool market.[26] Competition, diversification, and the interrelationships between marketing, manufacturing, and financial considerations are corporate strategy concerns.

Marketing Objective

A **marketing objective** is a statement of what is to be accomplished through marketing activities. It specifies the results expected from marketing efforts. It should be expressed in clear, simple terms so that all marketing personnel understand exactly what they are to try to achieve. It should be written in such a way that its accomplishment can be measured accurately. If a company has

26. Christopher S. Eklund, "Why Black & Decker Is Cutting Itself Down to Size," *Business Week*, Nov. 25, 1985, pp. 42, 44.

an objective of increasing its market share by 12 percent, the firm should be able to measure changes in its market share accurately. A marketing objective should also indicate the time frame for accomplishing the objective. For example, a firm that sets an objective of introducing three new products should state the time period in which this is to be done.

A marketing manager who fails to set marketing objectives that are consistent with the firm's general goals not only will be less likely to accomplish the marketing objectives, but also may work against the achievement of the firm's overall goals. Suppose a marketing manager sets an objective that requires greater use of consumer credit, but an overall goal of the firm is to reduce bad-debt loss. The two objectives probably will conflict.

Consider the corporate strategy of Transamerica Corporation: Transamerica should focus on key market segments related to primary businesses including insurance and financial services, travel services, and the manufacturing of precision engineered products used in industry. "A key dimension of Transamerica is the value added to our operating companies from being part of a larger corporation."[27] This is obviously a corporate strategy because it indicates the overall thrust of the corporation. Now take a look at a marketing objective of the same corporation:

Achieve a significant market share in each segment of our businesses.[28]

It is evident that achieving a significant market share is a statement of what is to be accomplished through marketing activities. This marketing objective is clear and can be measured accurately once it is quantified. For example, to achieve a 25-percent market share in each segment of Transamerica's businesses in the next three years would explain exactly what is to be accomplished and when it is to be done. Also note that the corporate strategy and the marketing objective are consistent. Transamerica Corporation maintains a staff group to focus on strategic planning. Besides setting corporate goals, corporate strategy, and marketing objectives, the planning actions of Transamerica encompass all of the strategic market planning activities described in this chapter.

Marketing Strategy and Marketing Planning

Marketing strategy focuses on defining a target market and developing a marketing mix to gain long-run competitive and consumer advantages. The application on page 546 illustrates the impact of marketing strategies on the mail-order catalog business. Therefore, a degree of overlap exists between corporate strategy and marketing strategy. Marketing strategy is unique in that it has the responsibility to assess buyer needs and the firm's potential for gaining competitive advantage, both of which ultimately must guide the corporate mission.[29] In other words, marketing strategy guides the firm's direction in relationships between customers and competitors. The bottom line is that a marketing strategy must be consistent with consumer needs, perceptions, and beliefs. From the

27. Transamerica *1982 Annual Report*. Published in 1983, p. 5.
28. Ibid.
29. Yoram Wind and Thomas S. Robertson, "Marketing Strategy: New Directions for Theory and Research," *Journal of Marketing,* Spring 1983, p. 12.

Application

Marketing Strategies in the Mail-order Catalog Business

New marketing strategies have helped the mail-order catalog business grow from approximately $4 billion in 1978 to $10 billion in 1985, more than doubling in just seven years (see Figure 18.6). The majority of this growth has come from new entrants that use new and innovative strategies to enter the catalog merchandising field. There are now more mail-order catalogs than ever before, and the competition for sales and survival is fierce, so fierce that the oldest U.S. catalog recently ended its distribution after 113 years. Montgomery Ward could not maintain profitability in its mail-order catalog division and it was, therefore, abandoned. The retailer had maintained its traditional strategy of a general catalog instead of developing specific catalogs to cover a narrower range of items.

To survive, many companies have had to assess their catalog division's strategies and adapt them to maintain profitability. For example, Sears (with annual catalog sales of $3.9 billion) has shifted much of its emphasis away from its mainstay general merchandise catalog. Sears is instead focusing on its much smaller specialty catalogs. In the twenty-two "specialogues," Sears features everything from petite clothing to power tools to toys. Spiegel is echoing Sears' market segmentation strategy and now has thirty different catalogs. Since adoption of the new multicatalog strategy, Spiegel's catalog sales have risen over 10 percent. Industry analysts believe that Montgomery Ward's failure to adopt a similar catalog strategy resulted in its failure.

Another strategy used by catalog merchandisers is to secure mailing lists from alternate sources. Most catalogs use the same basic mailing lists, thereby bombarding the mass market. Alternate lists can provide untapped customer bases. For example, Nature Company, which sells science-oriented toys, obtained its mailing list from natural history museums.

Catalog companies are also reaching new customers through their retail locations. For example, Banana Republic, originally a catalog business, has been so successful as a retailer that it has expanded from two retail outlets to thirty-five in seven years. Founders Mel and Pat Ziegler believe their business is "driven by catalogs." Mel Ziegler, the company president, continued, "We're a catalog business with two means of distribution—mail and stores."

Advertising is another strategy catalog retailers are adopting. Selling advertising space within the catalog helps offset printing and distribution costs. For example, The Sharper Image accepts full-page color advertising at a cost of $45,000 per page. The Sharper Image has developed a magazine appearance that appeals to a large segment of its target market.

The field of catalog retailing has become so fiercely competitive that entrants must evaluate, monitor, and reevaluate their marketing strategies frequently to assure survival. Smaller competitors have taken market share from the former catalog giants by employing unique mail-order marketing strategies. (*Source: William Bulkeley, "Catalog Merchants Try New Strategies as the Field Crowds with Companies,"* Wall Street Journal, *Jan. 20, 1986, p. 17. Reprinted by permission from* Wall Street Journal, © *Dow Jones & Company, Inc. 1986. All Rights Reserved.*)

perspective of marketing strategy development, there must be actual assessment of buyer responses to strategic options. Marketing management, on the other hand, is more directly concerned with design and implementation of the marketing strategy.[30] Managing the sales force is a marketing management concern.

30. Ibid.

Figure 18.6

Mail-order catalog sales increase in billions, 1978–1985 (Source: Reprinted by permission from William Bulkely, "Catalog Merchants Try New Strategies as the Field Crowds with Companies," Wall Street Journal, Jan. 20, 1986, p. 17. © Dow Jones & Company, Inc., 1986. All Rights Reserved)

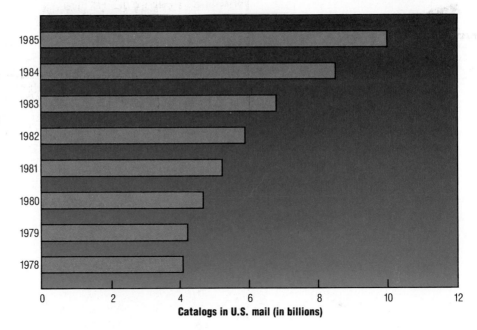

Catalogs in U.S. mail (in billions)

Marketing management is a process of planning, organizing, implementing, and controlling marketing activities in order to facilitate and expedite exchanges effectively and efficiently. "Effectively," an important dimension of our definition, refers to the degree to which an exchange furthers an organization's objectives. "Efficiently" refers to the minimization of the resources that an organization must expend to achieve a specific level of desirable exchanges. Thus, the purpose of the marketing management process is to facilitate highly desirable exchanges and to minimize as much as possible the costs of doing so.

As we noted at the start, this chapter deals with the planning part of the marketing management definition. So far, we have discussed strategic market planning. In this section, we describe how the strategic plan is implemented. **Marketing planning** is a systematic process that involves the assessment of marketing opportunities and resources, the determination of marketing objectives, and the development of a plan for implementation and control. A **marketing plan** includes the framework and entire set of activities to be performed; it is the written document or blueprint for implementing and controlling an organization's marketing activities. A firm should have a plan for each marketing strategy it develops. Since a firm's plans must be changed as forces in the firm and the environment change, marketing planning is a continuous process.

Because most organizations have existing plans and are engaged in ongoing activities, marketing managers must start with an organization's current situation and performance and then assess future marketing opportunities and constraints. The planning process calls for information about the difference, if any, between objectives and current performance. Probable performance in the future should be assessed; then the current marketing strategy can be altered or objectives changed if forecasted performance does not meet desired objectives in the next planning period. Figure 18.7 illustrates the **marketing planning cycle.** Note that marketing planning is a circular process. As the dotted feedback lines in

Figure 18.7

The marketing planning cycle

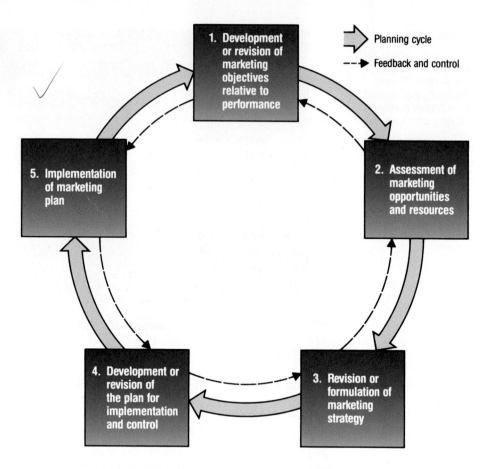

the figure indicate, planning is not unidirectional. Feedback is used to coordinate and synchronize all stages of the planning cycle.

When formulating a marketing plan, a new enterprise or a firm with a new product does not have current performance to evaluate or an existing plan to revise. Therefore, its marketing planning centers on analyzing available resources and options to assess opportunities. Managers can then develop marketing objectives and a strategy. In addition, many firms recognize the need to include information systems in their plans so that they can have continuous feedback and keep their marketing activities oriented toward objectives. (Information systems are discussed in Chapter 6.)

To illustrate the marketing planning process, consider the decisions that went into the planning of the introduction of a national newspaper—*USA Today*. Table 18.3 lists some of the more important marketing decisions. Of course, to reach the objective, a detailed course of action was communicated throughout the organization. In short, specific marketing plans should do the following:

1. Specify expected results so that the organization can anticipate what its situation will be at the end of the current planning period.
2. Identify the resources needed to carry out the planned activities so that a budget can be developed.

Table 18.3 *Planning for the introduction of a national newspaper: USA Today*

Objective: Achieve 1 million in circulation by reaching an upscale market, primarily of males who hold professional and managerial positions and who made at least one trip of 200 miles or more within the last year.

Opportunity: Paper tends to be a second newspaper purchase for readers. *USA Today* is not in competition directly with local papers, and it is not positioned against other national newspapers/magazines.

Market: Circulation within a 200-mile radius of 15 major markets, representing 54% of the U.S. population, including such cities as Chicago, Houston, New York, Los Angeles, and Denver.

Product: Superior graphic quality; appeal to the TV generation through short stories, a color weather map, and other contemporary features.

Price: Competitive.

Promotion: Pedestal-like vending machines with attention-grabbing design and a higher position than competitors to differentiate the paper and bring it closer to eye level. Outdoor advertising and some print advertising promotes the paper.

Distribution: Newsstand, vending machines in high-traffic locations, and direct mail.

Implementation and Control: Personnel with experience in the newspaper business who can assist in developing a systematic approach for implementing the marketing strategy and design as well as an information system to monitor and control the results.

Source: Kevin Higgins, "*USA Today* Nears Million Reader Mark," *Marketing News,* April 15, 1983, pp. 1, 5. Reprinted by permission of the American Marketing Association.

3. Describe the activities that are to take place in sufficient detail so that responsibilities for implementation can be assigned.
4. Provide for the monitoring of activities and results so that control can be exerted.[31]

The duration of marketing plans varies. Plans that cover a period of one year or less are called **short-range plans. Medium-range plans** usually encompass two to five years. Marketing plans that extend for more than five years are generally viewed as **long-range plans.** These plans can sometimes cover a period as long as twenty years. Marketing managers may have short-, medium-, and long-range plans all at the same time. Long-range plans are relatively rare. However, as the marketing environment continues to change and business decisions grow in complexity, profitability and survival will be more and more dependent upon the development of long-range plans.[32]

The extent to which marketing managers develop and use plans also varies. Although planning provides numerous benefits, some managers do not use formal marketing plans because they spend almost all their time dealing with

31. David J. Luck and O. C. Ferrell, *Marketing Strategy and Plans,* 2nd ed. © 1985. Adapted by permission of Prentice-Hall, Inc., Englewood Cliffs, N.J.
32. Ronald D. Michman, "Linking Futuristics with Marketing Planning, Forecasting, and Strategy," *Journal of Consumer Marketing,* Summer 1984, pp. 17–23.

daily problems—many of which would be eliminated by adequate planning. However, planning is becoming more important to marketing managers. They realize that planning is necessary to develop, coordinate, and control marketing activities effectively and efficiently.

Approaches to Strategic Market Planning

In recent years, marketing managers have developed target market/marketing mixes, sometimes called product/market matching approaches to strategic market planning. Because these approaches to planning are widely used today, let us focus briefly on three approaches that can be useful in structuring the overall strategic market plan. The Boston Consulting Group (BCG) product-portfolio analysis and the market attractiveness/business position model are popular approaches to strategic planning. The Profit Impact on Marketing Strategy (PIMS) project provides data to help direct strategic market planning efforts.

The Boston Consulting Group (BCG) Product-portfolio Analysis

Product-portfolio analysis, the BCG approach, is based on the philosophy that a product's market growth rate and its relative market share are important considerations in determining its marketing strategy. All the firm's products should be integrated into a single, overall matrix and evaluated to determine appropriate strategies for individual SBUs and the overall portfolio strategies. Just as financial investors have different investments with varying risks and rates of return, firms have a range of products characterized by different market growth rates and relative market shares. However, a balanced product-portfolio matrix is the end result of a number of actions, not the result of the analysis alone. Portfolio models can be created based on present and projected market growth rate and proposed market share strategies (build share, maintain share, harvest share, or divest business). Managers can use these models to determine and classify each product's expected future cash contributions and future cash requirements.

In general, managers who use a portfolio model must examine the competitive position of a product (or product line) and the opportunities for improving that product's contribution to profitability and cash flow.[33] The BCG analytical approach is more of a diagnostic tool than a guide for making strategy prescriptions.

Figure 18.8, which is based on work by the Boston Consulting Group, enables the marketing manager to classify a firm's products into four basic types: stars, cash cows, dogs, and problem children.[34] Stars are products with a dominant share of the market and good prospects for growth; they generally generate a lot of cash, but it is used to finance growth, add capacity, and increase market share. Cash cows have a dominant share of the market but low prospects for growth; typically they generate more cash than is required to maintain market share. Dogs have a subordinate share of the market and low prospects for growth; these products are often found in mature markets.

33. Joseph P. Guiltinan and Gordon W. Paul, *Marketing Management: Strategies and Programs* (New York: McGraw-Hill, 1982), p. 31.
34. George S. Day, "Diagnosing the Product Portfolio," *Journal of Marketing* (American Marketing Association), April 1977, pp. 30–31.

Figure 18.8

Illustrative growth-share matrix developed by the Boston Consulting Group (Source: Adapted from "The Product Portfolio," Perspectives No. 66, The Boston Consulting Group, Inc., 1970. See also George Day, "Diagnosing the Product Portfolio," Journal of Marketing, April 1977, pp. 29–38)

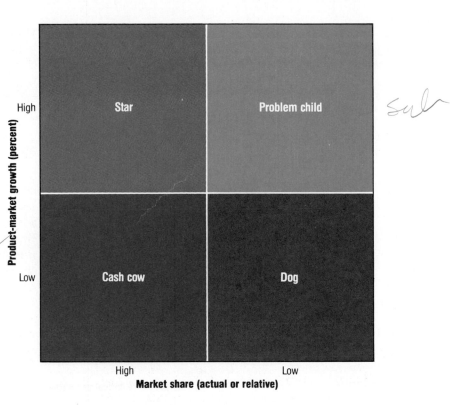

Problem children have a subordinate share of a growing market and generally require a large amount of cash to build share.

The growth-share matrix in Figure 18.8 can be expanded as in Figure 18.9 to show a firm's whole portfolio by providing for each product (1) its dollar sales volume, illustrated by the size of a circle on the matrix; (2) its market share relative to competition, represented by the horizontal position of the product on the matrix, and (3) the growth rate of the market, indicated by the position of the product in the vertical direction. Figure 18.9 illustrates the growth-share matrix for a cigarette company. Although total unit sales of cigarettes have been almost constant in recent years, firms that have introduced low-tar and, more recently, ultra-low-tar brands have obtained a larger share of the total cigarette market. In other words, some market segments have been growth areas while others have declined in growth. Brown & Williamson, for example, has extended its product line, anchored by the cash cow Kool Filter Kings, to include Kool Lights, a low-tar menthol cigarette, and Kool Ultra, an ultra-low-tar product. Figure 18.10 suggests marketing strategies appropriate for each of the four basic types of products: cash cows, stars, dogs, and problem children.

The long-run health of the corporation depends on having some products that generate cash (and provide acceptable reported profits) and others that use cash to support growth. Among the indicators of overall health are the size and vulnerability of the cash cows, the prospects for the stars, if any, and the number of problem children and dogs. Particular attention must be paid to those products with large cash appetites. Unless the company has an abundant cash flow, it cannot afford to sponsor many such products at one time. If

Figure 18.9

Illustrative growth-share matrix for a cigarette company

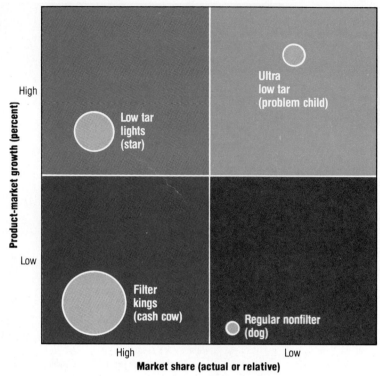

The area of each circle represents dollar sales of the product on the matrix.

resources, including debt capacity, are spread too thin, the company simply will wind up with too many marginal products and suffer a reduced capacity to finance promising new product entries or acquisitions in the future. For many years, Zenith was known as a one-product company (television sets). Zenith's acquisition of Heath Company has led to parlaying a hobby computer into an excellent personal computer. Zenith has achieved a leadership position with machines powerful enough to handle software written for IBM personal computers. Today Zenith Data Systems represents over 12 percent of Zenith's total sales, and this SBU is one of the fastest-growth areas in the company. More than 275 universities have chosen Zenith for teaching, research, and administrative purposes. In addition, Zenith has become the leading seller of video monitors for the computer industry.[35]

Market Attractiveness/ Business Position Model

The **market attractiveness/business position model,** illustrated in Figure 18.11, is a two-dimensional matrix. The vertical dimension, *market attractiveness,* includes all strengths and resources that relate to the market, such as seasonality, economies of scale, competitive intensity, industry sales, and the overall cost and feasibility of entering the market. The horizontal axis, *business position,* is a composite of factors such as sales, relative market share, research and development, price competitiveness, product quality, and market knowledge as they relate to the product in building market share. A slight variation of this matrix is called General Electric's Strategic Business Planning Grid because General Electric is

35. "Zenith: The Surprise in Personal Computers," *Business Week,* Dec. 12, 1983, p. 102.

Figure 18.10

Characteristics and strategies for the four basic product types in the growth share matrix (Source: Concepts in this figure adapted from George S. Day, "Diagnosing the Product Portfolio," Journal of Marketing, April 1977, pp. 30–31)

	Stars	**Problem children**
High	**Characteristics** *Market leaders* *Fast growing* *Substantial profits* *Require large investment to finance growth* **Strategies** *Protect existing share* *Reinvest earnings in the form of price reductions, product improvements, providing better market coverage, production efficiency* *Obtain a large share of the new users*	**Characteristics** *Rapid growth* *Poor profit margins* *Enormous demand for cash* **Strategies** *Invest heavily to get a disproportionate share of new sales* *Buy existing market shares by acquiring competitors* *Divestment (see below)* *Harvesting (see below)* *Abandonment (see below)* *Focus on a definable niche where dominance can be achieved*
	Cash cows	**Dogs**
Low	**Characteristics** *Profitable products* *Generate more cash than needed to maintain market share* **Strategies** *Maintain market dominance* *Invest in process improvements and technological leadership* *Maintain price leadership* *Use excess cash to support research and growth elsewhere in the company*	**Characteristics** *Greatest number of products fall in this category* *Operate at a cost disadvantage* *Few opportunities for growth at a reasonable cost* *Markets are not growing; therefore, little new business* **Strategies** *Focus on a specialized segment of the market that can be dominated and protected from competitive inroads* *Harvesting—cut back all support costs to a minimum level that supports cash flow over the product's remaining life* *Divestment—sale of the product to another firm* *Abandonment—deletion from the product line*

Product-market growth (vertical axis: High / Low)

Market share (horizontal axis: High / Low)

credited for extending the product-portfolio planning tool to examine market attractiveness and business strength. The best situation is for a firm to have a strong business position in an attractive market.

The upper left area in Figure 18.11 represents the opportunity for an invest/grow strategy, but the matrix does not indicate how to implement this strategy. The purpose of the model is to serve as a diagnostic tool to highlight SBUs that have an opportunity to grow or that should be divested or approached

Figure 18.11

Market attractive-ness/business position matrix (Source: Adapted from Derek F. Abell and John S. Hammond, Strategic Market Planning: Problems and Analytical Approaches, © 1979, p. 213. Reprinted by permission of Prentice-Hall, Inc., Englewood Cliffs, N.J.)

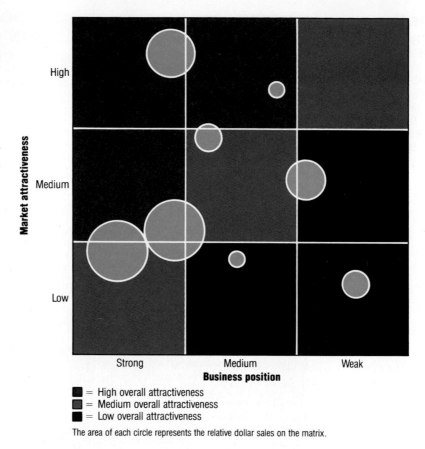

= High overall attractiveness
= Medium overall attractiveness
= Low overall attractiveness

The area of each circle represents the relative dollar sales on the matrix.

selectively. SBUs that occupy the invest/grow position can lose their position through faulty marketing strategies.

Decisions on resource allocation in regard to SBUs characterized by medium overall attractiveness should be arrived at on a basis relative to other SBUs that are either more attractive or less attractive. The lower right area of the matrix is a low-growth harvest/divest area. Harvesting is a gradual withdrawal of marketing resources on the assumption that sales will decline at a slow rate but profits will still be significant at a lower sales volume. Harvesting and divesting may be appropriate strategies for SBUs characterized by low overall attractiveness. For example, Westinghouse has decided to place less emphasis (harvest) on medium- and low-attractiveness sectors in utility businesses in favor of sectors with high overall attractiveness, such as services, cable television, robotics, and defense electronics.[36]

PIMS (Profit Impact on Marketing Strategy)

The Strategic Planning Institute (SPI) has developed a data bank of information on over 1,700 products that members provide for the **PIMS (Profit Impact on Marketing Strategy)** research program. Over two hundred member firms of the institute provide confidential information on successes, failures, and marginal

36. "Operation Turnaround," *Business Week,* Dec. 5, 1983, p. 124.

Figure 18.12

Sample page from PIMS data forms (Source: PIMS Data Form 1 reproduced by permission of the Strategic Planning Institute [PIMS Program], Cambridge, Massachusetts, 1979)

103: "LIFE CYCLE" STAGE OF PRODUCT CATEGORY

How would you describe the stage of development of the types of products or services sold by this business during the last three years? *(Check one)*

. . . Introductory Stage: Primary demand for product just starting to grow; products or services still unfamiliar to many potential users ☐ 1

. . . Growth Stage: Demand growing at 10% or more annually in real terms; technology or competitive structure still changing ☐ 2

. . . Maturity Stage: Products or services familiar to vast majority of prospective users; technology and competitive structure reasonably stable ☐ 3

. . . Decline Stage: Products viewed as commodities; weaker competitors beginning to exit ☐ 4

104: What was this business's first year of commercial sales? *(Check one)*

Prior to 1930	1930-1949	1950-1954	1955-1959	1960-1964	1965-1969	1970-1974	1975-
☐ 0	☐ 1	☐ 2	☐ 3	☐ 4	☐ 5	☐ 6	☐ 7

105: At the time this business first entered the market, was it . . . *(Check one)*

. . . One of the pioneers in first developing such products or services? ☐ 1

. . . An early follower of the pioneer(s) in a still growing, dynamic market? ☐ 2

. . . A later entrant into a more established market situation? ☐ 3

106-107: PATENTS AND TRADE SECRETS

Does this business benefit *to a significant degree* from patents, trade secrets, or other proprietary methods of production or operation . . .

106: Pertaining to products or services? NO ☐ 0 YES ☐ 1

107: Pertaining to processes? NO ☐ 0 YES ☐ 1

108: STANDARDIZATION OF PRODUCTS OR SERVICES

Are the products or services of this business . . . *(Check one)*

. . . More or less standardized for all customers? ☐ 0

. . . Designed or produced to order for individual customers? ☐ 1

109: FREQUENCY OF PRODUCT CHANGES

Is it typical practice for the business and its major competitors to change all or part of the line of products or services offered . . . *(Check one)*

. . . Annually (for example, annual model changes)? ☐ 1

. . . Seasonally? ☐ 2

. . . Periodically, but at intervals longer than one year? ☐ 3

. . . No regular, periodic pattern of change? ☐ 4

110: TECHNOLOGICAL CHANGE

Have there been *major* technological changes in the products offered by the business or its major competitors, or in methods of production, during the last 8 years? *(If in doubt about whether a change was "major," answer NO.)* NO ☐ 0 YES ☐ 1

products. Figure 18.12 shows a PIMS data form. The data are analyzed to provide reports for members on strategy.

Table 18.4 shows the types of information provided on each business in the PIMS data base. The results of PIMS include both diagnostic and prescriptive information to assist in analyzing marketing performance and formulating marketing strategies. The analysis focuses on options, problems, resources, and opportunities. The unit of observation in PIMS is an SBU.

The data on member firms' experiences have proved useful for evaluating current marketing strategies and examining alternatives. The following nine major strategic influences on profitability and net cash flow have been identified:

1. Investment intensity. *Technology and the chosen way of doing business govern how much fixed capital and working capital are required to produce a dollar of sales or a dollar of value added in the business. Investment intensity generally produces a negative impact on percentage measures of*

Table 18.4 *Types of information provided on each business in the PIMS data base*

Characteristics of the business environment
Long-run growth rate of the market
Short-run growth rate of the market
Rate of inflation of selling price levels
Number and size of customers
Purchase frequency and magnitude

Competitive position of the business
Share of the served market
Share relative to largest competitors
Product quality relative to competitors
Prices relative to competitors
Pay scales relative to competitors
Marketing efforts relative to competitors
Pattern of market segmentation
Rate of new product introductions

Structure of the production process
Capital intensity (degree of automation, etc.)
Degree of vertical integration
Capacity utilization
Productivity of capital equipment
Productivity of people
Inventory levels

Discretionary budget allocations
R&D budgets
Advertising and promotion budgets
Sales force expenditures

Strategic moves
Patterns of change in the controllable elements
  above

Operating results
Profitability results
Cash flow results
Growth results

Source: Reproduced by permission of the Strategic Planning Institute (PIMS Program), Cambridge, Mass.

profitability or net cash flow; i.e., businesses that are mechanized or automated or inventory-intensive generally show lower returns on investment and sales than businesses that are not.

2. Productivity. *Businesses producing high value added per employee are more profitable than those with low value added per employee. (Definition: "value added" is the amount by which the firm increases the market value of raw materials and components it buys.)*

3. Market position. *A business's share of its served market (both absolute and relative to its three largest competitors) has a positive impact on its profit and net cash flow. (The "served market" is the specific segment of the total potential market—defined in terms of products, customers, or areas—in which the business actually competes.)*

4. Growth of the served market. *Growth is generally favorable to dollar measures of profit, indifferent to percent measures of profit, and negative to all measures of net cash flow.*

5. Quality of the products and/or services offered. *Quality, defined as the customers' evaluation of the business's product/service package as compared to that of competitors, has a generally favorable impact on all measures of financial performance.*

6. Innovation/differentiation. *Extensive actions taken by a business in the areas of new product introduction, R&D, marketing effort, and so on, generally produce a positive effect on its performance if that business has strong market position to begin with. Otherwise usually not.*

7. Vertical integration. *For businesses located in mature and stable markets, vertical integration (i.e., make rather than buy) generally impacts favorably on performance. In markets that are rapidly growing, declining, or otherwise changing, the opposite is true.*

8. *Cost push. The rates of increase of wages, salaries, and raw material prices, and the presence of a labor union, have complex impacts on profit and cash flow, depending on how the business is positioned to pass along the increase to its customers and/or absorb the higher costs internally.*

9. Current strategic effort. *The current direction of change of any of the above factors has effects on profit and cash flow that are frequently opposite to that of the factor itself. For example, having strong market share tends to increase net cash flow, but getting share drains cash while the business is making that effort.*

Additionally, there is such a thing as being a good or a poor "operator." A good operator can improve the profitability of a strong strategic position or minimize the damage of a weak one; a poor operator does the opposite. The presence of a management team that functions as a good operator is therefore a favorable element of a business and produces a financial result greater than one would expect from the strategic position of the business alone.[37]

Significance of Strategic Market Planning Approaches

The Boston Consulting Group's portfolio analysis, the market attractiveness/ business position model, and the Profit Impact on Marketing Strategy (PIMS) studies of the Strategic Planning Institute are planning tools only. They should not be viewed as strategic solutions but as diagnostic aids, which is all they are intended to be. The emphasis should be on making sound decisions using these analytical tools.[38]

The key to understanding the approaches to strategic market planning described in this chapter is recognition that strategic market planning takes into account all aspects of an organization's strategy in the marketplace. Whereas most of this book is about functional decisions and strategies of marketing as a part of business, this chapter focuses on the recognition that all functional strategies, including marketing, production, and finance, must be coordinated to reach organizational goals. Results of a survey, sponsored by the *Harvard Business Review,* of top industrial firms indicate that portfolio planning and other depersonalized planning techniques help managers strengthen their planning process and solve the problems of managing diversified industrial companies. However, the results also indicate that analytical techniques alone do not result in success. Management must blend this analysis with managerial judgment to deal with the reality of the existing situation.

One word of caution in regard to the use of portfolio approaches is necessary. The classification of SBUs into a specific portfolio position is dependent upon four factors: (1) the operational definition of the matrix dimensions; (2) the rules used to divide a dimension into high and low categories; (3) the weighting of the variables used in composite dimensions, if composite dimensions are used; and (4) the specific model used.[39] In other words, changes in any of these four factors may well result in different classification for a single SBU.

37. *The PIMS Letter on Business Strategy No. 1* (Cambridge, Mass.: The Strategic Planning Institute, 1977), pp. 3–5. Reproduced by permission of the Strategic Planning Institute (PIMS Program), Cambridge, Massachusetts.
38. David W. Cravens, "Strategic Marketing's New Challenge," *Business Horizons,* March–April 1983, p. 19.
39. Yoram Wind, Vijay Mahajan, and Donald J. Swire, "An Empirical Comparison of Standardized Portfolio Models," *Journal of Marketing,* Spring 1983, pp. 89–99.

There are other approaches to strategic market planning besides those discussed here. For example, marketing planners have for many years used the product life cycle that is discussed in Chapters 7 and 8. Many firms have their own approaches to planning that incorporate, to varying degrees, some of the approaches that we have discussed. All strategic planning approaches have some similarity in that some of the components of strategic market planning outlined in Figure 18.2 (especially market/product relationships) are related to a plan of action for reaching objectives. The PIMS project makes a major contribution by providing data gathered from a broad range of companies to draw conclusions about strategic market planning.

The approaches presented here should provide you with an overview of the most popular analytical methods used in strategic market planning. These approaches are meant to be supplements to, not substitutes for, the marketing manager's own judgment. The real test of each approach, or any integrated approach, is how well it assists management in diagnosing the firm's strengths and weaknesses and prescribing strategic actions for maintaining or improving performance. At many companies, management has moved strategic market planning to the top of its list of corporate priorities for the 1980s. The issues of product/market-share definition, strategic information procurement, and organizational change will inevitably grow in importance as a result of increased use of strategic market planning concepts.[40]

Competitive Strategies for Marketing

After evaluating business operations and business performance, the next step in strategic planning is to determine future business directions and to develop marketing strategies. A business may choose competitive strategies. Figure 18.13 shows competitive strategy on a product-market matrix. This matrix can be helpful in determining growth that can be implemented through marketing strategies.

Intense Growth

Intense growth can take place when current products and current markets have the potential for increasing sales. There are three main strategies for intense growth: market penetration, market development, and product development.

Market penetration is a strategy of increasing sales in current markets with current products. A fast-food chain, for instance, would probably attempt to increase its market share by increasing its advertising budget and the size of its marketing staff.

Market development is a strategy of increasing sales of current products in new markets. For example, a European aircraft manufacturer was able to enter the U.S. market by offering financing to Eastern Airlines that Boeing could not match.

Product development is a strategy of increasing sales by improving present products or developing new products for current markets. To remain competitive, Apple Computer has developed a product development strategy. To promote

40. Ben M. Enis, "GE, PIMS, BCG and the PLC," *Business,* May–June 1980, pp. 17–18.

Figure 18.13

Competitive strategies (Adapted from Corporate Strategy *by H. I. Ansoff, p. 109. Copyright © 1965 by McGraw-Hill. Used with permission of McGraw-Hill Book Company)*

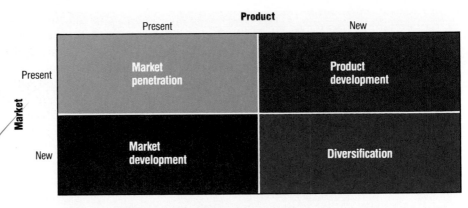

growth, Apple introduced an improved MacIntosh and Laser Writer printer. One of Apple's strengths is its ability to maintain a strong hold on the educational market (grade school to college). To maintain and grow in this market segment, Apple will allow schools to trade in any of their computers (Apple or otherwise) for a credit toward any Apple computer. The company believes this effort will encourage schools with older computer equipment (IBM, Radio Shack, and the like) to consider Apple when making additions or replacements. A similar offer has also been made to businesses and schools that purchased the early Lisa and MacIntosh XL. These models, which Apple feels were deficient, can be traded in on the new MacIntosh Plus for a total cost of $1,500. Apple is showing a strong consumer commitment in hopes of increasing sales in its educational and business market segments. This illustrates the strategy of improving present products or developing new products to increase sales in existing markets.[41]

Diversified Growth

Diversified growth occurs in three ways, depending on the technology of the new products and the nature of the new markets the firm enters. The three forms of diversification are horizontal, concentric, and conglomerate.

When new products that are not technologically related to current products are introduced to current markets, horizontal diversification occurs. An airline might diversify horizontally by starting or acquiring a chain of hotels at the destinations it serves.

In concentric diversification, the marketing and technology of new products are related to current products, but the new ones are introduced into new markets. For example, the advertisement in Figure 18.14 describes how Bell Atlantic is introducing its complex technologies into new markets. The advertisement stresses one case in which the company's technology was used to make access to a whole university practical.

Conglomerate diversification occurs when new products are unrelated to current technology, products, or markets and are introduced to markets new to the firm. If an electronics company were to start a car-rental business, the move would represent conglomerate diversification.

41. Steve Wilstein, "Apple Rebounds with Products, Promises," *Houston Chronicle,* Jan. 18, 1986, sec. 2, p. 1.

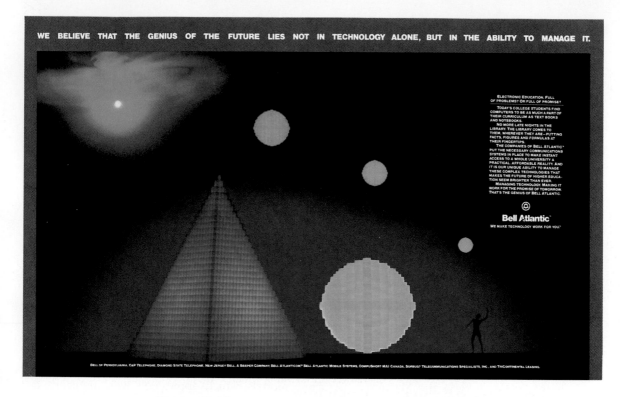

Figure 18.14 *Bell Atlantic's concentric diversification—reaching out to new markets* (Source: Bell Atlantic, Pete Turner Photography, Ketchum Advertising)

Integrated Growth

Integrated growth can occur in the same industry that the firm is in and in three possible directions: forward, backward, and horizontally.

A firm growing through forward integration takes ownership or increased control of its distribution system. For example, a shoe manufacturer might start selling its products through wholly owned retail outlets.

In backward integration, a firm takes ownership or increased control of its supply systems. A newspaper company that buys a paper mill is integrating backward.

Horizontal integration occurs when a firm takes ownership or control of some of its competitors. A hotel chain integrating horizontally might purchase a competing motel chain.

Summary

Strategic planning requires a general management orientation, rather than a narrow functional orientation. Corporate strategy determines the means for utilizing resources in the areas of production, finance, research and development, personnel, and marketing to reach the organization's goals. The concept of a strategic business unit (SBU) is used to define areas for consideration in a specific strategic market plan. Each SBU is a division, product line, or other profit center within its parent company. Each sells a distinct set of products and/or services to an identifiable group of customers, and each is in competition with a well-defined set of competitors. In the context of the parent company, meaningful separation can be made of an SBU's revenues, operating costs, investments, and strategic plans. This chapter deals with strategic market planning and planning processes in marketing management.

When a marketing strategy—which is developed through strategic market planning—is implemented properly, it achieves the organization's marketing objectives; these, in turn, contribute to accomplishing the organization's overall goals. Environmental forces are an important consideration in the strategic market planning process and very much affect it. These forces imply opportunities and threats that influence the overall goals of an organization. The amount and type of resources that a firm can acquire are also affected by forces in the environment. However, such forces need not constrain or work against the firm. They may also create favorable opportunities that can be translated into overall organizational goals.

There are three major considerations in assessing opportunities and resources: market opportunity must be evaluated; environmental forces must be monitored; and the firm's capabilities should be understood. A market opportunity arises when the right combination of circumstances occurs at the right time to allow an organization to take action toward a target market. An opportunity provides a favorable chance or opening for the firm to generate sales from markets. Determinants of market opportunity include market size, market requirements, and the actions of other firms.

Environmental monitoring is the process that seeks information about events and relationships in a company's outside environment, the knowledge of which assists marketers in planning. A firm's capabilities relate to distinctive competencies that it has developed to do something well and efficiently. A company is likely to enjoy a differential advantage in an area where its competencies outmatch those of its potential competition.

Corporate strategy defines the means and direction of reaching organizational goals. Marketing objectives are statements of what is to be accomplished through marketing activities. They should be expressed in clear, understandable, and measurable terms, and they must be consistent with an organization's overall goals. Marketing management is the process of planning, organizing, implementing, and controlling marketing activities in order to facilitate and expedite exchanges effectively and efficiently.

Marketing planning is a systematic process that involves the assessment of opportunities and resources, the determination of marketing objectives, the development of a marketing strategy, and the development of plans for implementation and control. A well-written plan clearly specifies when, how, and who is to perform marketing activities. Plans that cover one year or less are called short-range plans. Medium-range plans usually encompass two to five years, and plans that last for more than five years are long-range plans. Marketing planning has several benefits. Planning forces marketing managers to think ahead, to establish objectives, and to consider future marketing activities. Effective planning also reduces or eliminates daily crises.

In recent years, marketing managers have developed target market/marketing mixes, sometimes referred to as product/market matching approaches to strategic market planning. These approaches to planning are widely used today to structure the overall strategic market planning process. The Boston Consulting Group (BCG) product-portfolio analysis, the market attractiveness/business position model, and PIMS (Profit Impact on Marketing Strategy) are popular approaches to strategic planning.

The BCG approach is based on the philosophy that a product's market growth rate and its market share are key factors influencing marketing strategy. All of the firm's products should be integrated into a balanced product portfolio. Just as financial investors hold investments with varying risks and rates of return, firms have a variety of products. Managers can use portfolio models to classify products to determine each product's expected future cash contributions and future cash requirements. In general, managers who use a portfolio model must examine the competitive position of a product (or product line) and the opportunities for improving that product's contribution to profitability and cash flow.

The market attractiveness/business position model is a two-dimensional matrix. The vertical dimension, *market attractiveness,* includes all the sources of strength and resources that relate to the market; competition, industry sales, and the cost of competing are among them. The horizontal axis, *business position,* measures sales, relative market share, research and development, and other factors that relate to building a market share for a product.

The Strategic Planning Institute (SPI) has developed a data bank of information on over 1,700 products that members report on for the PIMS (Profit Impact on Marketing Strategy) research program. Over two hundred members of the institute provide confidential information on successes, failures, and marginal products. The data are analyzed to provide reports for member firms on strategy. The results of PIMS include diagnostic and prescriptive information to assist in analyzing marketing performance and formulating marketing strategies. The analysis focuses on options, problems, resources, and opportunities. The unit of observation in PIMS is an SBU.

The real test of strategic planning is how well it helps in diagnosing a firm's strengths and weaknesses and improving performance. The approaches to strategic market planning covered in this chapter are meant to be supplements to, not substitutes for, the marketing manager's own judgment.

Competitive strategies that can be implemented through marketing include intense growth, diversified growth, and integrated growth. Intense growth includes market penetration, market development, or product development. Diversified growth includes horizontal, concentric, and conglomerate diversification. Integrated growth includes forward, backward, and horizontal integration.

Important Terms

Corporate strategy	Environmental monitoring
Marketing strategy	Marketing objective
Strategic market plan	Marketing management
Strategic business unit (SBU)	Marketing planning
Strategic market planning	Marketing plan
Marketing program	Marketing planning cycle
Market opportunity	Short-range plans
Market requirements	Medium-range plans

Long-range plans
Product-portfolio analysis
Market attractiveness/business
  position model
PIMS (Profit Impact on
  Marketing Strategy)

Intense growth
Diversified growth
Integrated growth

Discussion and Review Questions

1. Why should an organization develop a marketing strategy? What is the difference between strategic market planning and the strategy itself?
2. Identify the major components of strategic market planning, and explain how they are interrelated.
3. In what ways do environmental forces affect strategic market planning? Give specific examples.
4. Why is price flexibility important in implementing the marketing strategy?
5. What are some of the issues that must be considered in analyzing a firm's opportunities and resources? How do these issues affect marketing objectives and market strategy?
6. Why is market opportunity analysis necessary? What are determinants of market opportunity?
7. In relation to resource constraints, how can environmental monitoring affect a firm's long-term strategic market planning? Consider product costs and benefits affected by the environment.
8. What is marketing management, and why is it important to the survival of business organizations?
9. What benefits do marketing managers gain from planning? Is planning necessary for long-run survival? Why or why not?
10. How should an organization establish marketing objectives?
11. What are the major considerations in developing the product-portfolio grid? Define and explain the four basic types of products suggested by the Boston Consulting Group.
12. When should marketers consider using PIMS for strategic market planning?

Cases

Case 18.1 Campbell Soup Company's Strategic Business Units

Campbell Soup Company

Campbell Soup Company is a diverse consumer goods firm composed of fifty-two separate business units. An average business unit produces $35 million in sales per year.[42] Campbell's flagship product is, of course, soup. But with changing demographic patterns, family structures, and family eating patterns, Campbell's has been forced to continuously monitor and evaluate its long- and short-term strategies and plans, as reflected in the diversity of products offered. Campbell's diverse product lines include Pepperidge Farm, Swanson, Franco-American, Godiva, and Mrs. Paul's.

42. James R. Russo, "Campbell Soup Company: 'Souperstar' of Innovation," *Packaging,* Nov. 1985, p. 34.

Campbell's products were initially grouped into two basic business categories—canned foods and frozen foods—based upon how the product was manufactured.[43] Campbell's current president, Gordon McGovern, came into the organization and recognized that the dual categorization was a major problem. At that point, he determined to transform Campbell from a production orientation to a consumer orientation. In the past, Campbell's new-product development efforts had been restricted by what the production system could produce, not determined by what the consumer really wanted. According to Albert A. Austin, vice president of containers, "For years, the packaging function was a metal can function. We are a self-manufacturer of cans, producing over 5 billion cans per year. Obviously, we know cans best and in the past we tended to go with cans as the package for new products. However, Campbell's is not a can-making company; we're a food company. We have to find out what the consumer wants, then fulfill that need."[44] Campbell's current strategic business units reflect the company's commitment to understanding market requirements and opportunities. These corporate changes can basically be attributed to Gordon McGovern, who has been known to hold board meetings in supermarkets where members can ask consumers what they think about Campbell's products. In addition, McGovern sends company executives to women's kitchens to see how meals are prepared.[45]

Of Campbell's major strategic business units, Campbell's soup division provides one-fourth of the company's sales. The newest products in this line include Creamy Natural Soups, Chunky Fisherman's Chowder, an expanded line of Home Style Soups and Campbell's Quality Soup and Recipe Mix lines (both dry soups). Experimentation is also occurring with frozen soup. The frozen soup would be packaged in different-type plastic bowls that could go from the microwave to the table. Research and development is concentrating on validating the form of packages (various bowls, for instance) and the essence of products (fresh taste, gourmet entrees, and so on). Understanding consumers' eating habits, lifestyles, and convenience needs is therefore a focus of the market research. Management is more concerned with performance than with cost because it is far-sighted enough to understand that, as the technology for its new packages and products matures and as sales increase, mass-volume production will lower its costs. The former corporate policy was that a product must have a projected profit in one year or be dropped. With a longer payout, many more new-product/package developments, such as soup in a cup, are possible. Environmental monitoring has revealed that snacking habits are continuing but that consumers are trying to make more healthy choices. Soup as a snack could be perceived as very nutritious and convenient.[46] Campbell's promotional and TV campaigns stress the company's commitment to quality and the nutritional value of its soup: "Soup is good food."

Campbell's frozen foods group consists of LeMenu, Great Start Breakfasts, and the Swanson product line. This business unit has grown based on consumers' continued interest in frozen convenience foods. LeMenu dinners have been a phenomenal success. The dinners are positioned as much more upscale than Swanson's and are packaged in a round thermoset plastic plate with a plastic

43. Aimée Stern, "The New ... Souped Up Campbell," *Marketing Communications,* Feb. 1984, p. 34.
44. Russo, " 'Souperstar'," p. 29.
45. Christopher S. Eklund, "Campbell Soup's Recipe for Growth: Offering Something for Every Palate," *Business Week,* Dec. 24, 1984, pp. 66–77.
46. Russo, " 'Souperstar'," p. 32.

dome lid. McGovern has commented, "It's very important to us that we have table-presentable packages that don't have institutional connotations. We don't want the package to cause the consumer to have any negative perceptions about our food."[47] Packaging has been a problem for the Swanson dinners. Swanson sales have been dropping, and the company blames its thirty-year-old aluminum tray, which is being replaced with a microwavable version.[48]

Pepperidge Farm, Campbell's second largest division, has been successful recently because of its overall strategy of allocating resources to its profitable segments and divesting or harvesting its unprofitable businesses and products. Pepperidge Farm's basic strategy is to return to the traditional product lines and quality standards that initially established its success.[49] Products such as Deep Dish Danish, some varieties of Deli's, and the Snack Bar products have been discontinued. The Vegetables in a Pastry (VIP) line was overhauled with quality improvements and expanded diversity in the product line. Pepperidge Farm's apple juice operations were shifted to Campbell's beverage group, and a number of unrelated businesses such as Lexington Gardens, a garden-center chain, were divested.

Mrs. Paul's Kitchens is the market leader in the production of prepared seafood. Mrs. Paul's responds to consumer preferences for convenient seafood products that are nutritious, low in calories, microwavable, and relatively low in cost. Campbell's has recently strived to boost Mrs. Paul's image. A new product line called Light Seafood Entrees was intended to establish Mrs. Paul's as an upscale label with such items as Fish Dijon, Fish Florentine, Scallops Mediterranean, Shrimp Primavera, Seafood Newburg, and Fish Mornay. All forms of advertising and promotion support this quality image with the tag line "It tastes good because it is good." The newest product developments stress unbreaded fish, and Mrs. Paul's is successfully moving the bulk of its product line sales from heavier fried seafood to lighter, broiled products—taking advantage of shifting consumer preferences.

Vlasic foods is Campbell's third-largest division. Vlasic pickles hold the number-one position in the pickle market. Future plans include the development of new products and line extensions, improving product quality, and increasing category and brand store growth through greater marketing spending. Part of this marketing effort has been used to promote Vlasic's new color-coded labels, which help consumers quickly select their favorite products. New products take advantage of consumers' interest in flavor variation in their pickles. Zesty Pickles and Bread and Butter Whole Pickles represent new product lines for Vlasic.

Campbell's short-term plans—to achieve a 5-percent annual sales increase per annual product line—will be a difficult task. But Campbell's new-product developments and older-product renovations indicate an astute understanding and awareness of the consumer's wants and needs. Campbell's basic strategy is to target specific market niches and refine products for their respective consumers. "Companies that go with a product in search of a market or one that has no fit with their existing businesses are doomed to a bloody nose."[50]

47. Ibid., p. 29.
48. *1985 Campbell Soup Company Annual Report,* p. 10.
49. *1984 and 1985 Campbell Soup Company Annual Reports.*
50. "Campbell Soup: Cooking Up a Separate Dish for Each Consumer Group," *Business Week,* Nov. 21, 1983, pp. 102–103.

Questions for Discussion

1. Identify several market opportunities of which Campbell's has taken advantage. Consider current market and consumer developments and identify new opportunities you see for Campbell.
2. Consider various products in Campbell Soup Company's strategic business units and attempt to place them in a growth-share matrix to provide portfolio analysis.
3. Identify and evaluate the marketing strategies for each Campbell strategic business unit presented in this case.
4. Should Campbell consider harvesting the Swanson product line and reintroducing it under a new name with new packaging? Evaluate the pros and cons of this decision.
5. Should Campbell create more market identity between its corporate name and the product lines of its strategic business units, as other companies such as Beatrice and Ralston Purina have done? Consider the quality theme that is pervasive in all Campbell product lines.

Case 18.2   Strategic Market Planning of Sigma Marketing Concepts[51]

During the summer of 1986, Sigma Marketing Concepts was reviewing its recent organizational changes and past performance and was developing a new long-range plan and necessary marketing strategies. It had started fourteen years earlier as a small commercial printer, Sigma Press, Inc. When it moved its plant to new facilities at the intersection of two important interstate highways in Illinois, the prestigious location, with its high visibility, created a then-unwarranted image of success. Don Sapit, the president of Sigma, was a mechanical engineer with an MBA from the University of Chicago. It seemed to him that Sigma should try to capitalize on its high visibility to change the emphasis of the business and, he hoped, improve its record of growth and profit. Over the next few years, the marketing strategy of the company was oriented toward building a reputation for producing the most creative and highest-quality printing in its service area, which had a thirty-five- to forty-mile radius. The firm took a calculated risk. Sapit anticipated that this new direction would give his firm a solid reputation as an expensive quality printer—but one that justified the prices it charged. The strategy paid off, and sales volume increased by 220 percent by 1976.

One of the factors that had prompted the 1972 move was a perceived market for a specialized advertising desk-pad calendar. The calendar, sold to businesses for distribution as a free marketing tool, kept an advertising message on customers' desks at all times (see Figure 18.15). Sales of the calendar had increased slowly but steadily. Management wanted growth, but it wanted it in an orderly and manageable manner, and it wanted it to be more profitable than the industry average of approximately 5 percent on sales. It was becoming obvious that to be successful in the printing business, one had to specialize. After long and deliberate discussion and investigation in 1976, the company management wrote a three-year corporate plan.

51. Contributed by Donald Sapit, President, Sigma Marketing Concepts, 8845 San Jose Blvd., Jacksonville, Florida 32217.

Figure 18.15 *Sigma's desk-top calendar (Source: Courtesy of Sigma Marketing Concepts and Amstar Sugar Corporation)*

The corporate plan emphasized marketing, which was unique for a small commercial printer. The marketing plan focused a major share of the sales and marketing effort on building a market for the Salesbuilder desk calendar. The target market consisted primarily of larger corporate accounts. The marketing mix emphasized product and promotion. Space advertising in sales and marketing-oriented publications created large numbers of inquiries, but sales levels did not follow. Direct mail, primarily to manufacturers, produced a much higher return on investment. Sigma had created a unique product that was very flexible in terms of unusual designs, advertising messages, photographic techniques, and other special requirements.

Within the next few calendar seasons, prime accounts such as Federal Express, Serta Mattress, Archway Cookies Inc., Borden Inc., and other blue-chip companies were added to the list of satisfied customers. Reorder rates were very high, usually in the 88- to 90-percent range. Quantities ordered by individual companies tended to increase annually for three or four years and then level off. Total calendar sales had increased at a rate of approximately 40 percent per year during the 1976–1980 period, during which commercial printing sales increased at a much lower rate.

Because of the success of the marketing plan, production capacity was being taxed. In 1979–1980 major capital commitments were made to add a new high-speed two-color press and to purchase, redesign, and rebuild a specialized collating machine to further automate calendar assembly. This opened the way to mass marketing of the Salesbuilder calendar line. Direct mail techniques were improved to allow selection of prospects by S.I.C. number and sales volume. A toll-free phone line encouraged direct response by interested parties. Whenever possible, the company responded to inquiries by sending a sample calendar that contained advertising ideas related to the respondent's line of business. This sample would be followed up with personal phone calls within two to three weeks. Calendar sales continued to improve until, by 1983, they represented 40 percent of total sales and approximately 75 percent of net profit.

In spite of the success of the calendar marketing programs, Sapit was disturbed by trends in the printing industry that pointed toward a diminishing market and increased competition for the commercial segment particularly in Sigma's local area of the Rust Belt. Sigma's management had for some time been considering selling the commercial portion of its business in favor of becoming an exclusive marketer of custom-designed calendar products. Through its connection with the Printing Industry of Illinois, a buyer was found for the plant, equipment, and the goodwill of the commercial portion of the business. The buyer agreed to enter into a long-term contract to handle all calendar production for Sigma, using the same plant and staff that had been handling the production for the previous six or seven years.

Sigma's management now found itself free of the daily problems of production and plant management and able to commit all of its efforts to creating and marketing new calendar products. Sapit had a long-standing personal desire to move the business to the Sun Belt for the better weather and, more important, for the better business climate. In May of 1985 the corporate offices were moved to Jacksonville, Florida. Concurrently, Sapit was joined in the business by his son Mike, a graduate in graphic arts of Illinois State University.

The new organization's first actions were to expand its product line to include several additional products, all designed to be highly personalized, and to develop a much more aggressive marketing program.

Test advertisements for custom-designed calendars were run in *Advertising Age* and in several marketing journals. These advertisements appealed to larger corporate accounts. In addition, the sales staff became much more aggressive in searching out individual accounts that appeared to have a high potential as quality-calendar customers. These accounts were then researched and contacted by phone and mail, requesting an opportunity to provide the customers with samples and with detailed comprehensive layouts suggesting possible designs.

The goal was to establish Sigma Marketing Concepts as a publisher of high-quality, creatively designed custom calendars. Initial response to the new marketing strategy was good, with indications that the blue chip companies could, in fact, be reached through this approach.

To reach its growth goals, Sigma must be successful in this marketing strategy. Since this type of highly customized product design is very demanding on the creative staff, it is important that their efforts be spent on the high-potential accounts.

Questions for Discussion

1. Compare and contrast the need for long-range versus short-range marketing planning at Sigma Press.
2. Compare the changes in Sigma's marketing strategy from 1972 to 1986. What were the primary considerations for marketing strategy changes?
3. If you were Sigma's marketing consultant, what recommendation would you make for future strategic market planning?

19 / Organization, Implementation, and Control

Objectives

- To become aware of how the marketing unit fits in a firm's organizational structure.

- To become familiar with the ways of organizing a marketing unit.

- To examine several issues relating to the implementation of marketing strategies.

- To understand the control processes used in managing marketing strategies.

- To be aware of how cost and sales analyses can be employed to evaluate the performance of marketing strategies.

Figure 19.1

An advertisement for Mattel's Masters of the Universe toys (Source: Mattel Toys)

Masters of the Universe! Rainbow Brite! Mattel created these toy lines, hoping they would win the hearts of America's children (see Figure 19.1). And if sales of these product lines are any indication, Mattel has succeeded.

A year before it introduced the toy lines, Mattel faced near bankruptcy with a $420-million loss due primarily to a failed electronics division. The home video game market was oversupplied, and the result was disastrous price cutting by competitors. To combat imminent disaster, Mattel initiated an intensive marketing research program to help anticipate consumer demand in the toy market. This research amounted to more than five hundred studies in which more than sixty thousand children and parents were interviewed. Out of this research came the Masters of the Universe line, featuring heroic figures locked in deadly combat with formidable villains, all in a high-tech, science fiction environment. In addition, Mattel created the Rainbow Brite line, made up of the kind of soft, cuddly dolls and accessories that appeal to today's consumers.

The most popular of the Masters of the Universe line, He-Man, totaled almost $500 million in sales in its third year. The Rainbow Brite line of dolls totaled $110 million in sales. Mattel's net income rose 160 percent to $44 million.[1]

This chapter focuses first on the marketing unit's position in the organization and the ways in which the unit itself can be organized. Then we examine several issues regarding the implementation of marketing strategies. Next, we consider the basic components of the process of control and discuss the use of cost and sales analyses to evaluate the effectiveness of marketing strategies. Finally, we describe a marketing audit.

Organizing Marketing Activities

The structure and relationships of a marketing unit, including lines of authority and responsibility that connect and coordinate individuals, strongly affect marketing activities. This section first looks at the place of marketing within an organization and examines the major alternatives available for organizing a marketing unit. Next it shows how marketing activities can be structured to fit into an organization so as to contribute to the accomplishment of overall objectives.

Marketing's Place in an Organization

Marketing's place within a company is determined largely by whether the firm is production, sales, or marketing oriented. A **production-oriented organization** concentrates either on improving production efficiency or on producing high-quality, technically improved products; it has little regard for customers' desires. In a **sales-oriented organization,** there is a general belief that personal selling and advertising are primarily responsible for generating profits and that regardless of consumers' needs, most products can be sold if the right quantity and quality of personal selling and advertising are employed. Thus, sales and advertising managers are at the same level in the company's hierarchy as are production, financial, and personnel managers, and all participate in top-level management. Upper-echelon sales and advertising executives, along with other executives at the same level, are involved in setting the company's overall objectives and policies. In a **marketing-oriented organization,** the focus is on finding out what buyers want and providing it in a manner that allows the organization to achieve its objectives. As Figure 19.2 shows, the marketing manager in a marketing-oriented organization has a position equal to that of the financial, production, and personnel managers. This structure permits the marketing manager to participate in top-level decision making. Note, too, that the marketing manager is responsible for a variety of activities, several of which (sales forecasting and supervision and product planning) are under the jurisdiction of other functional managers in production- or sales-oriented firms.

Both the relationships between marketing and other functional areas (such as production, finance, and personnel) and marketing's importance to management depend heavily on the firm's basic orientation. Marketing encompasses the greatest number of business functions and occupies an important position when

1. "... New Lines Revive Mattel," *Advertising Age,* March 4, 1985, p. 94; Mattel *Annual Report, 1984, 1985.*

Figure 19.2

Organizational chart of a
marketing-oriented firm

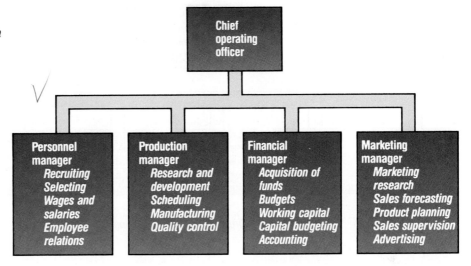

a firm is marketing oriented; it has a minimal role when the firm is production oriented. However, a marketing-oriented organization does not make a firm marketing oriented. The marketing orientation is not achieved simply by redrawing the organizational chart; management must also adopt and use the marketing orientation as a management philosophy.

Major Alternatives for Organizing the Marketing Unit

How effectively a firm's marketing management can plan and implement marketing strategies depends on how the marketing unit is organized. The organizational structure of a marketing department establishes the authority relationships among marketing personnel and specifies who is responsible for making certain decisions and performing particular activities. This internal structure provides the vehicle for directing marketing activities.

In organizing a marketing unit, managers divide the work into specific activities and delegate responsibility and authority for those activities to persons in various positions within the marketing unit. These positions include, for example, the sales manager, the research manager, and the advertising manager.

No single approach to organizing a marketing unit works equally well in all businesses. A marketing unit can be organized according to (1) functions, (2) products, (3) regions, or (4) types of customers. The best approach or approaches depend on the number and diversity of the firm's products, the characteristics and needs of the people in the target market, and other factors. Let us consider each organizational approach in detail.

Organizing by Functions

Some marketing departments are organized by general marketing functions such as marketing research, product development, distribution, sales, advertising, and customer relations. As shown in Figure 19.3, the personnel who direct these functions report directly to the top-level marketing executive. This structure is fairly common because it works well for small businesses with centralized marketing operations. In large firms, which tend to have decentralized marketing

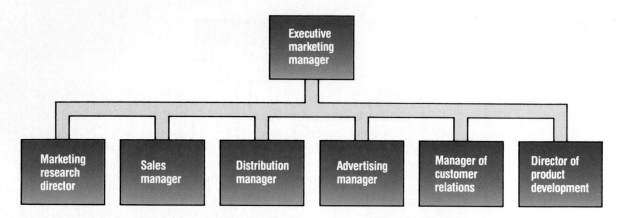

Figure 19.3 *Organization of a marketing unit by functions*

operations, functional organization can raise severe coordination problems. The functional approach may, however, suit a large centralized company whose products and customers are neither numerous nor diverse.

Organizing by Products

An organization that produces and markets diverse products may find the functional approach inadequate. The decisions and problems related to a single marketing function for one product may be quite different from those related to the same marketing function for another product. As a result, businesses that produce diverse products sometimes organize their marketing units according to product groups. In this type of organization, a product manager takes full responsibility for the marketing of a product or product group. As Figure 19.4 shows, the product manager for product group C has authority over the functional managers who are lower in the organizational hierarchy. The product manager may also draw upon the resources of specialized staff in the company. Organizing by product groups gives a firm the flexibility to develop special marketing mixes for different products. The firm may, for example, hire specialists to market specific types of products.

One disadvantage of organizing by products is that some marketing activities may be duplicated by the different product groups. For example, salespersons from three product groups may call on the same customer in a single day. (This form of internal organization is discussed in more detail in Chapter 8.)

Organizing by Regions

A large company that markets products nationally (or internationally) may organize its marketing activities by geographic regions (see Figure 19.5). All the regional marketing managers report directly to the executive marketing manager. Managers of marketing functions for each region report to their regional marketing manager, as shown in Figure 19.5 for region 2. This form of organization is especially effective for a firm whose customers' characteristics and needs vary greatly from one region to another.

Figure 19.4

*Organization of a
marketing unit by
product group*

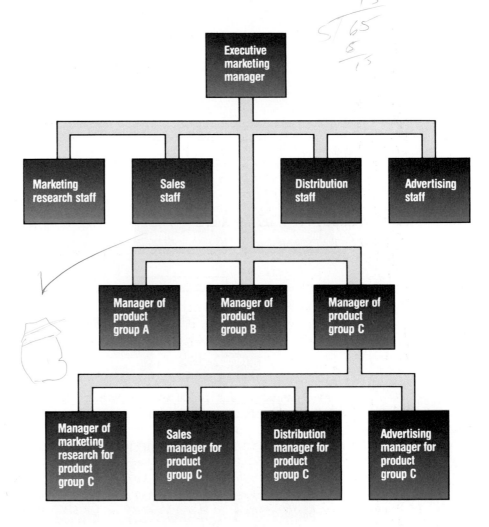

The company depicted in Figure 19.5 has a complete marketing staff at its headquarters to provide assistance and guidance to regional marketing managers. However, not all firms organized by regions maintain a full marketing staff at their home offices. Companies that try to penetrate the national market intensively sometimes divide regions into subregions.

Organizing by Types of Customers

Sometimes the marketing unit is organized according to types of customers, as shown in Figure 19.6. This form of internal organization works well for a firm that has several groups of customers whose needs and problems differ significantly. For example, an appliance manufacturer may sell to large retail stores, wholesalers, and institutions. Retailers may want more rapid delivery of small shipments and more personal selling by the producer than do either wholesalers or institutional buyers. Because the marketing decisions and activities required for these three groups of customers differ considerably, the company may find it efficient to organize its marketing unit by types of customers.

As Figure 19.6 shows, the marketing manager for each customer group reports to the top-level marketing executive and directs most marketing activities

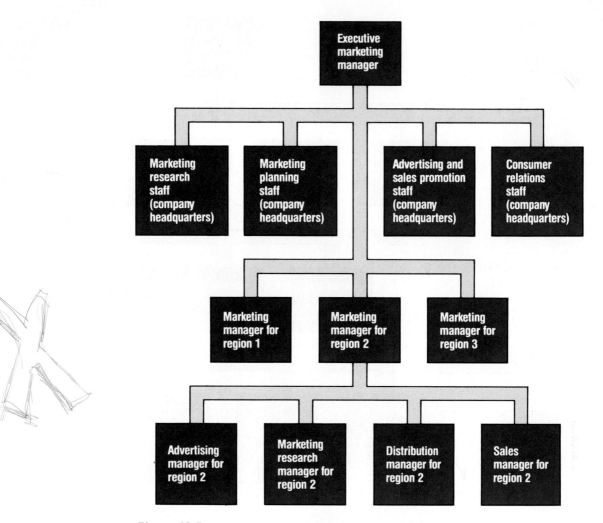

Figure 19.5 *Organization of a marketing unit by regions*

for that group. The figure also shows that a marketing manager directs all activities needed to market products to a specific customer group.

Using Several Forms of Organization

You may have noticed that Figures 19.4, 19.5, and 19.6 each involve more than one type of organization. The marketing unit in Figure 19.4 is organized by products, but each product manager has authority over functional managers within the product groups. The marketing units organized by regions and types of customers show a similar combination of forms.

Firms often use some combination of organization by functions, products, regions, or customer types. Product features may dictate that the marketing unit be structured by products, while customers' characteristics require that it be organized by geographic region or by types of customers. By using more than one type of organization, a flexible marketing unit can develop and implement marketing plans to match customers' needs precisely.

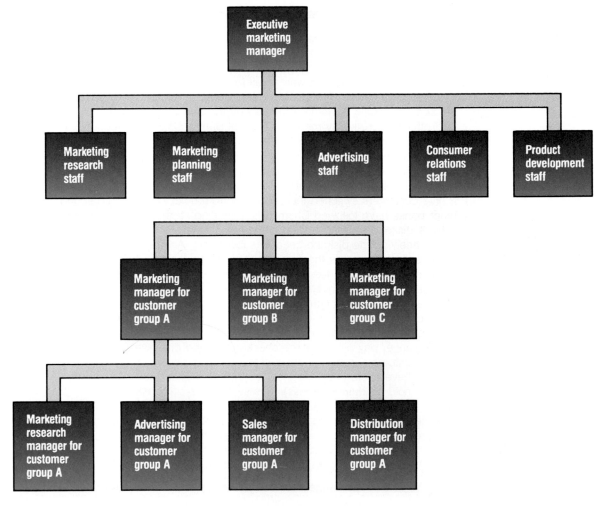

Figure 19.6 *Organization of a marketing unit by types of customers*

(handwritten note) internal market — management action neccause to make organyat to accept their role in the market

Implementing Marketing Activities

The planning and organizing functions provide purpose, direction, and structure for marketing activities. However, until marketing managers implement the marketing plan, exchanges cannot occur. Proper implementation of a marketing plan depends on the coordination of marketing activities, the motivation of personnel who perform those activities, and effective communication within the marketing unit. (See the application on page 578.) We will examine these three aspects of implementing the marketing plan.

Coordinating Marketing Activities

Because of job specialization and differences related to marketing activities, marketing managers must synchronize individuals' actions to achieve marketing objectives. In addition, they must work closely with managers in research and development, production, finance, accounting, and personnel to see that marketing

Chapter 19 / Organization, Implementation, and Control

Application

Chemical Bank Implements Pronto Strategy

Is banking at home a mass market? If not, what sort of customer would prefer to bank at home? With the introduction of Pronto, an electronic banking information service, into the New York City market, Chemical Bank found that although the answer to the first question was a definite no, the answer to the second was resoundingly positive. The customer who preferred home banking was precisely the sort of upscale customer preferred by the banks.

In the New York City market, Chemical Bank's $20-million technological investment paid off handsomely. With eighteen thousand subscribers, growing at the rate of one thousand a month, Chemical's Pronto was the first to offer home banking. Being first, Chemical lured prime, upscale customers from other New York banks. Two measures of Pronto's success are, first, that 17 percent of Pronto customers switched their accounts from other banks and, second, that other banks have followed Chemical's marketing strategy. Chemical mailed a sample diskette allowing people to experiment with Pronto. Twenty percent of those receiving the diskette became subscribers. Another highly effective promotional technique was the demonstration of the system at Chemical's branch locations; seven out of ten Pronto customers reported that they signed up because they had seen it demonstrated.

The Pronto system, compatible with Apple, Atari, Commodore, and IBM personal computers, appeals especially to customers who want the convenience of not having to visit a bank. Customers who use Pronto can transfer funds, check their balance, pay bills, balance checkbooks, and organize home budgets, all at home. Customers in this segment of the banking population are primarily under age 49, have average annual incomes of $50,000, and are highly educated (39 percent hold graduate degrees). This segment is composed mainly of professionals and managers. Chemical found that the penetration of home computers in a metropolitan area must be at least 10 percent of the households for a system like Pronto to pay off, and that demographically upscale people usually own personal computers. (*Source: Based on Cheryl Russell, "At Home with Chemical Bank," American Demographics, April 1985, pp. 20, 51.*)

---

activities mesh with other functions of the firm. Marketing managers must not only coordinate the activities of marketing staff within the firm but also integrate those activities with the marketing efforts of external organizations—advertising agencies, resellers (wholesalers and retailers), researchers, and shippers, among others. Marketing managers can improve coordination by making each employee aware of how one job relates to others and of how each person's actions contribute to the achievement of marketing plans.

Motivating Marketing Personnel

An important element in implementing the marketing plan is motivating marketing personnel to perform effectively. People work to satisfy physical, psychological, and social needs. To motivate marketing personnel, managers must therefore discover their employees' needs and then base their motivation methods on those needs.

To put this another way, managers must base their motivational efforts on the value systems of individuals within a specific organization. Various studies have shown that the income, power, and prestige that accompany a high position in the organization are often motivators.[2] Marketing managers can motivate marketing personnel to perform at a high level if they identify employees' goals and provide rewards and some means of goal attainment. It is most important that the plan to motivate personnel be fair, that it provide incentives, and that it be understood by employees. Also keep in mind that what is a minor reward or accomplishment for one employee may be the ultimate fulfillment for someone else. Obviously, the degree to which a manager can motivate personnel has a major impact on the success of all marketing efforts.

Communicating Within the Marketing Unit

Without good communication, marketing managers cannot motivate personnel or coordinate their efforts. Marketing managers must be able to communicate with the firm's high-level management to ensure that marketing activities are consistent with the overall goals of the company. Communication with top-level executives keeps marketing managers aware of the company's overall plans and achievements. It also guides what the marketing unit is to do and how its activities are to be integrated with those of other departments—such as finance, production, or personnel—with whose management the marketing manager must also communicate to coordinate marketing efforts. Marketing personnel must work with the production staff, for example, to help design products that customer groups want. To direct marketing activities, marketing managers must communicate with marketing personnel at the operations level, such as sales and advertising personnel, researchers, wholesalers, retailers, and package designers.

To facilitate communication, marketing managers should establish an information system within the marketing unit. The information system should allow for easy communication among marketing managers, sales managers, and sales personnel. Marketers need an information system to support a variety of activities such as planning, budgeting, sales analyses, performance evaluations, and the preparation of reports. An information system should also expedite communications with other departments in the organization and minimize destructive competition among departments for organizational resources.[3]

Controlling Marketing Activities

To achieve marketing objectives, as well as general organizational objectives, it is imperative for marketing managers to effectively control marketing efforts. The **marketing control process** consists of establishing performance standards, evaluating actual performance by comparing it with established standards, and reducing the differences between desired and actual performance. Figure 19.7 illustrates the process. We will discuss these steps in the control process and look at the major problems they involve.

2. E. Frank Harrison, *Management and Organizations* (Boston: Houghton Mifflin, 1978), p. 28.
3. Robert E. Sweeney and Dan A. Boswell, "Obey 10 Commandments When Designing Marketing Info System," *Marketing News*, April 16, 1982, p. 16.

Figure 19.7
The marketing control
process

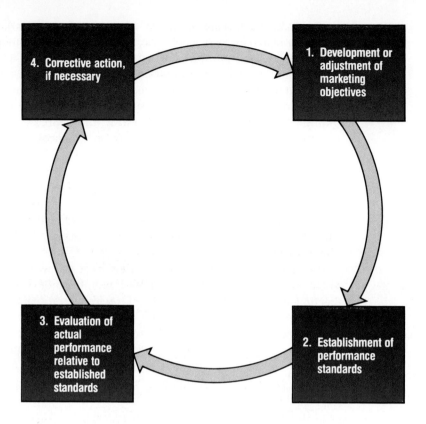

1. Development or adjustment of marketing objectives

2. Establishment of performance standards

3. Evaluation of actual performance relative to established standards

4. Corrective action, if necessary

Establishing Performance Standards

Planning and controlling are closely interrelated because plans include statements about what is to be accomplished. For purposes of control, these statements function as performance standards. A **performance standard** is an expected level of performance against which actual performance can be compared. Examples of performance standards might be the reduction of customers' complaints by 20 percent, a monthly sales quota of $150,000, or a 10-percent increase per month in new customer accounts. Performance standards are also given in the form of budget accounts; that is, marketers are expected to achieve a certain objective without spending more than a given amount of resources.

Evaluating Actual Performance

To compare actual performance with performance standards, marketing managers must both know what marketers within the company are doing and have information about the activities of external organizations that provide the firm with marketing assistance. (We will talk about specific methods for assessing actual performance later in this chapter.) Information is required about the activities of marketing personnel at the operations level and at various marketing management levels. Most businesses obtain marketing assistance from one or more external individuals or organizations, such as advertising agencies, middlemen, marketing research firms, and consultants. To maximize benefits from external sources, a firm's marketing control process must monitor their activities. Although it may be difficult to obtain the necessary information, it is impossible to measure actual performance without it.

Records of actual performance are compared with performance standards to determine whether and how much of a discrepancy exists. For example, a salesperson's actual sales are compared with his or her sales quota (performance standard). If a significant negative discrepancy exists, the marketing manager takes corrective action.

In some organizations, electronic data processing equipment enhances a marketing manager's ability to evaluate actual performance. For example, L'eggs hosiery is sold mainly through self-service displays in supermarkets and drugstores. The displays are replenished and cleaned by traveling representatives who drive vans containing inventories of L'eggs products. Drivers pick up the inventories from a local branch warehouse. A local branch manager supervises the warehouse operations and the sales activities of the L'eggs representatives. When servicing a display, the representative records on a special sales form the amount of various products that have been sold and the types of products that are sold out. This information goes to a centralized data processing center in Atlanta, where it is assembled weekly by display, by account, by route, and by branch warehouse. The company uses these weekly reports not only for billing purposes but also for analyzing the performance of marketing activities from the mill right down to individual display units.[4]

Taking Corrective Action

Marketing managers have several options for reducing a discrepancy between established performance standards and actual performance. They can take steps to improve actual performance, can reduce or totally change the performance standard, or do both. Changes in actual performance may require the marketing manager to use better methods of motivating marketing personnel or to employ more effective techniques for coordinating marketing efforts.

Sometimes, performance standards are unrealistic when they are written. In other cases, changes in the marketing environment make them unrealistic. For example, a firm's annual sales goal may become unrealistic if several aggressive competitors enter the firm's market. In fact, changes in the marketing environment may force managers to change their marketing objectives completely.

Requirements for an Effective Control Process

A marketing manager should consider several requirements in creating and maintaining effective control processes.[5] Effective control depends heavily on the quantity and quality of information available to the marketing manager and the speed at which it is received. The control process should be designed so that the flow of information is rapid enough to allow the marketing manager to detect quickly differences between actual and planned levels of performance. A single control procedure is not suitable for all types of marketing activities, and internal and environmental changes affect an organization's activities, so control procedures should be flexible enough to adjust to both varied activities and changes in the organization's situation. For the control process to be usable, its costs must be low relative to the costs that would arise if there were no controls. Finally, the control process should be designed so that both managers and subordinates can understand it.

4. David T. Harrold, "L'eggs Revisited," Point of Purchase Advertising Institute Workshop, Atlanta, Ga., March 24, 1971.
5. See Theo Haimann, William G. Scott, and Patrick E. Connor, *Management*, 5th ed. (Boston: Houghton Mifflin, 1985), pp. 478–492.

Problems in Controlling Marketing Activities

When marketing managers attempt to control marketing activities, they frequently run into several problems. Often, the information required to control marketing activities is unavailable or is only available at a high cost. Even though marketing controls should be flexible enough to allow for environmental changes, the frequency, intensity, and unpredictability of such changes may hamper effective control. In addition, the time lag between marketing activities and their effects limits a marketing manager's ability to measure the effectiveness of marketing activities.

Consider the problem of an electric utility company that wanted to build a nuclear power plant. Faced with public concern about nuclear safety and increasingly well-organized antinuclear activists, the company mounted a rather expensive advertising campaign to swing public opinion to the side of nuclear energy. The utility company emphasized nuclear safety and independence from foreign energy sources. Three years after the campaign was launched, public attitudes were indeed slightly more favorable toward nuclear energy and toward the utility. How much of this change could the company attribute to its own marketing efforts and how much to extraneous factors—magazine articles on energy resources, high unemployment in the area, and the high costs and technical difficulties of some solar installations? How could the utility measure the impact of each factor?

Since marketing and other business activities often overlap, marketing managers cannot determine the precise cost of marketing activities. Without an accurate measure of marketing costs, it is difficult to know if the effects of marketing activities are worth their expense. Finally, marketing control may be difficult because it is very hard to develop exact performance standards for marketing personnel.

Methods of Evaluating Performance

Specific methods exist for assessing and improving the effectiveness of a marketing strategy. A marketer should state, through plans and objectives, what a marketing strategy is supposed to accomplish. These statements should set forth performance standards, which usually are stated in terms of profits, sales, or costs. Actual performance must be measured in similar terms so that comparisons are possible. This section describes sales analysis and cost analysis—two general ways of evaluating the actual performance of marketing strategies. The application on page 583 summarizes strategy changes at Big Boy restaurants resulting from sales and cost analyses.

Sales Analysis

Sales analysis uses sales figures to evaluate a firm's current performance. It is probably the most common method of evaluation because sales data partially reflect the target market's reactions to a marketing mix and often are readily available, at least in aggregate form.

Marketers use current sales data to monitor the impact of current marketing efforts. However, that information alone is not enough. To provide useful analyses, current sales data must be compared with forecasted sales, with industry sales, with specific competitors' sales, or with the costs incurred to

A significant benefit of sales and cost analyses is their ability to determine when and in what ways marketing strategies need to be altered. For instance, Marriott Corporation, through strategic control, recognized the need to change marketing strategies at its Big Boy restaurants.

Remember the smiling pudgy boy dressed in checked overalls holding the tasty looking hamburger platter overhead? Marriott, owner of 850 Big Boy restaurants, planned to scrap the entire Big Boy image. Company marketers were beginning to think that the Big Boy was outdated. One marketing director even referred to the Big Boy as a nerd. But rather than drop the Big Boy immediately, Marriott surveyed consumer opinion. Surprisingly, the findings showed that respondents favored the Big Boy by six to one. The Big Boy seemed to be viewed as a piece of art and culture, not a nerd. This amazing show of popularity changed the minds of Marriott marketers.

That the Big Boy will stay the same does not mean that everything else will. Big Boy restaurants have been instituting changes to provide the menu and decor for the diverse crowds that its popular restaurants appeal to. Big Boy restaurants are moving away from red meats and fried foods by adding more fish, chicken, and salad bars. Many have also added garden rooms to please their customers. These additions, along with the traditional favorites—big burgers and thick shakes—will provide the diversity that Big Boy fans desire. (*Source: Brad Edmondson, "Big Boy Bounces Back,"* American Demographics, *Sept. 1985, p. 18. Used by permission.*)

achieve the sales volume. For example, knowing that a variety store achieved a $600,000 sales volume this year does not tell management whether or not the marketing strategy has been successful. However, if managers know that expected sales were $550,000, then they are in a better position to determine the effectiveness of the firm's marketing efforts. In addition, if they know that the marketing costs needed to achieve the $600,000 volume were 12 percent less than budgeted, they are in an even better position to analyze their marketing strategy precisely.

Types of Sales Measurements

Although sales may be measured in several ways, the fundamental unit of measurement is the sales transaction. A sales transaction results in a customer order for a specified quantity of an organization's product sold under specified terms by a particular salesperson or sales group on a certain date. Many organizations record these bits of information about their transactions. With such a record, a company can analyze sales in terms of dollar volume or market share.

Firms frequently use dollar volume sales analysis because the dollar is a common denominator of sales, costs, and profits. However, price increases and decreases affect total sales figures. For example, if a firm increased its prices by 10 percent this year and its sales volume is 10 percent greater than last year, it has not experienced any increase in unit sales. A marketing manager who uses dollar volume analysis should factor out the effects of price changes.

A firm's market share is the firm's sales of a product stated as a percentage of industry sales of that product. For example, Coca-Cola at one time sold 38 percent of all the cola sold annually in this country and thus had a market share of 38 percent. Market share analysis allows a firm to compare its marketing strategy with the strategies of competitors.

The primary reason for using market share analysis is to estimate whether sales changes have resulted from the firm's marketing strategy or from uncontrollable environmental forces. When a company's sales volume declines but its share of the market stays the same, the marketer can assume that industry sales declined (because of some uncontrollable factors) and that this decline was reflected in the firm's sales. However, if the firm experiences a decline in both sales and market share, it should consider the possibility that its marketing strategy is not effective.

Even though market share analysis can be helpful in evaluating the performance of a marketing strategy, the user must interpret results cautiously. When attributing a sales decline to uncontrollable factors, a marketer must keep in mind that such factors do not affect all firms in the industry equally. Not all firms in an industry have the same objectives, and some firms change objectives from one year to the next. Changes in the objectives of one firm can affect the market shares of one or all firms in that industry. For example, if a competitor significantly increases promotional efforts or drastically reduces prices to increase market share, then a company could lose market share despite a well-designed marketing strategy. Within an industry, the entrance of new firms or the demise of established ones also affects a specific firm's market share, and market share analysts should attempt to account for these effects.

Bases for Sales Analysis

Whether it is based on sales volume or market share, sales analysis can be performed on aggregate sales figures or on disaggregated data. Aggregate sales analysis provides an overview of current sales. Although helpful, aggregate sales analysis is often insufficient, because it doesn't bring to light sales variations within the aggregate. It is not uncommon for a marketer to find that a large proportion of aggregate sales comes from a small number of products, geographic areas, or customers. (This is sometimes called the "iceberg principle" because only a small part of an iceberg is visible above the water.) To find such disparities, total sales figures usually are broken down by geographic unit, salesperson, product, customer type, or a combination of these categories.

In sales analysis by geographic unit, sales data can be classified by city, county, district, state, country, or any other geographic designation for which a marketer collects sales information. Actual sales in a geographic unit can be compared with sales in a similar geographic unit, with last year's sales, or with an estimated market potential for the area. For example, if a firm finds that 18 percent of its sales are coming from an area that represents only 8 percent of the potential sales for the product, then it can be assumed that the marketing strategy is successful in that geographic unit.

Because of the cost associated with hiring and maintaining a sales force, businesses commonly analyze sales by salesperson to determine the contribution each makes. Performance standards for each salesperson often are set in terms of sales quotas for a given time period. Evaluation of actual performance is accomplished by comparing a salesperson's current sales to a preestablished quota or some other standard, such as last period's sales. If actual sales meet or exceed the standard and the sales representative has not incurred costs above those budgeted, that person's efforts are acceptable.

Sales analysis is often performed according to product group or specific product item. Marketers break down their aggregate sales figures by product to determine the proportion that each contributed to total sales. A firm usually sets a sales volume objective—and sometimes a market share objective—for each product item or product group, and sales analysis by product is the only way to measure such objectives. A marketer can compare the breakdown of current sales by product with those of previous years. In addition, within industries for which sales data by product are available, a firm's sales by product type can be compared with industry averages. To gain an accurate picture of where sales of specific products are occurring, marketers sometimes combine sales analysis by product with sales analysis by geographic area or salesperson.

Analyses based on customers are usually broken down by types of customers. Customers can be classified by the way they use a firm's products, by their distribution level (producer, wholesaler, retailer), by their size, by the size of orders, or by other characteristics. Sales analysis by customer type allows a firm to ascertain whether its marketing resources are allocated in a way that achieves the greatest productivity. For example, sales analysis by type of customer may reveal that a large group of customers served by 60 percent of the sales force actually accounts for only 15 percent of total sales.

A considerable amount of information is needed for sales analyses, especially if disaggregated analyses are desired. The marketer must develop an operational system for collecting sales information; obviously, the effectiveness of the system for collecting sales information largely determines a firm's ability to develop useful sales analyses.

Marketing Cost Analysis

Although sales analysis is critical for evaluating the effectiveness of a marketing strategy, it gives only part of the picture. A marketing strategy that successfully generates sales may also be extremely costly. To get a complete picture, a firm must know the marketing costs associated with using a given strategy to achieve a certain sales level.

Marketing cost analysis breaks down and classifies costs to determine which are associated with specific marketing activities. By comparing costs of previous marketing activities with results generated, a marketer can better allocate the firm's marketing resources in the future. Marketing cost analysis allows a firm to evaluate the effectiveness of an ongoing or recent marketing strategy by comparing sales achieved and costs incurred. By pinpointing exactly where a firm is experiencing high costs, this form of analysis can help to isolate profitable or unprofitable customer segments, products, or geographic areas. In some organizations, personnel in other functional areas—such as production or accounting—think that marketers are primarily concerned with generating sales regardless of the costs incurred. By conducting cost analyses, marketers can undercut this criticism and put themselves in a better position to demonstrate how marketing activities contribute to generating profits.

Determining Marketing Costs

Frequently, the task of determining marketing costs turns out to be complex and difficult. Simply ascertaining the costs associated with marketing a product is rarely adequate. Marketers must usually determine the marketing costs of serving specific geographic areas, market segments, or even specific customers.

A first step in determining the costs is to examine accounting records. Most accounting systems classify costs into accounts such as rent, salaries, office supplies, utilities, and so on, that are based on how the money was actually spent. Unfortunately, many of these accounts, called **natural accounts,** do not help to explain what functions were performed through the expenditure of those funds. It does little good, for example, to know that $80,000 is spent for rent each year. The analyst has no way of knowing whether the money is spent for the rental of production, storage, or sales facilities. Therefore, marketing cost analysis usually requires that some of the costs in natural accounts be reclassified into **marketing function accounts.** Common marketing function accounts are transportation, storage, order processing, selling, advertising, sales promotion, marketing research, and customer credit.

In some instances a specific marketing cost is incurred to perform several functions. A packaging cost, for example, could be considered a production function, a distribution function, a promotional function, or all three. The marketing cost analyst must reclassify such costs across multiple functions.

Three broad categories are used in marketing cost anaylsis: direct costs, traceable common costs, and nontraceable common costs. **Direct costs** are directly attributable to the performance of marketing functions. For example, sales force salaries might be allocated to the cost of selling a specific product item, selling in a specific geographic area, or selling to a particular customer. **Traceable common costs** can be allocated indirectly, using one or several criteria, to the functions that they support. For example, if the firm spends $80,000 annually to rent space for production, storage, and selling, the rental costs of storage could be determined on the basis of cost per square foot used for storage. **Nontraceable common costs** cannot be assigned according to any logical criteria and thus are assignable only on an arbitrary basis. Interest, taxes, and the salaries of top management are viewed as nontraceable common costs.

The manner of dealing with these three categories of costs depends on whether the analyst uses a full-cost or a direct-cost approach. When a **full-cost approach** is used, cost analysis includes direct costs, traceable common costs, and nontraceable common costs. Proponents of this approach claim that if an accurate profit picture is desired, all costs must be included in the analysis. However, opponents point out that full costing does not yield actual costs because nontraceable common costs are determined by arbitrary criteria. With different criteria, the full-costing approach yields different results. A cost-conscious operating unit can be discouraged if numerous costs are assigned to it arbitrarily. To eliminate such problems, the **direct-cost approach** is used. It includes direct costs and traceable common costs but does not include nontraceable common costs. Opponents say that this approach is not accurate because it omits one cost category.

Methods of Marketing Cost Analysis

Marketers can use several methods to analyze costs. The methods vary in their precision. This section examines three cost analysis methods, beginning with the least precise.

Table 19.1 Reclassification of natural accounts into functional accounts

Profit and Loss Statement		Functional Accounts					
Sales	$250,000						
Cost of Goods Sold	45,000						
Gross	205,000						
Expenses (natural accounts)		Advertising	Personal Selling	Transportation	Storage	Marketing Research	Non-marketing
Rent	$ 14,000		$ 7,000		$6,000		$ 1,000
Salaries	72,000	$12,000	32,000	$7,000		$1,000	20,000
Supplies	4,000	1,500	1,000			1,000	500
Advertising	16,000	16,000					
Freight	4,000			2,000			2,000
Taxes	2,000				200		1,800
Insurance	1,000				600		400
Interest	3,000						3,000
Bad debts	6,000						6,000
Total	$122,000	$29,500	$40,000	$9,000	$6,800	$2,000	$34,700
Net Profit	$ 83,000						

Analysis of natural accounts   Marketers sometimes can perform a cost analysis by studying a firm's accounting records, or natural accounts. The precision of this method depends heavily on how detailed the firm's accounts are. For example, if accounting records contain separate accounts for production wages, sales-force wages, and executive salaries, the analysis can be more precise than if all wages and salaries are lumped into a single account. An analysis of natural accounts is more meaningful, and thus more useful, when current cost data can be compared with those of previous periods or with average cost figures for the entire industry. Cost analysis of natural accounts frequently treats costs as percentages of sales. The periodic use of cost-to-sales ratios allows a marketer to ascertain cost fluctuations quickly.

Analysis of functional accounts   As indicated earlier, the analysis of natural accounts may not shed much light on the cost of marketing activities. In such cases, natural accounts must be reclassified into marketing function accounts, as shown in the simplified example in Table 19.1. Note that a few natural accounts, such as advertising, can be reclassified easily into functional accounts because they do not have to be split across several accounts. For most of the natural accounts, however, marketers must develop criteria for assigning them to the various functional accounts. For example, the number of square feet of floor space used was the criterion for dividing the rental costs in Table 19.1 into functional accounts. Whether or not certain natural accounts are reclassified into functional accounts, and the criteria used to reclassify them, depend to some degree on whether the analyst is using direct costing or full costing. After natural accounts have been reclassified into functional accounts, the cost

Table 19.2 *Functional accounts divided into product group costs*

Functional Accounts		Product Groups		
		A	B	C
Advertising	$29,500	$14,000	$ 8000	$ 7,500
Personal selling	40,000	18,000	10,000	12,000
Transportation	9,000	5,000	2,000	2,000
Storage	6,800	1,800	2,000	3,000
Marketing research	2,000		1,000	1,000
Total	**$87,300**	**$38,800**	**$23,000**	**$25,500**

of each function is determined by summing the costs in each functional account. Thus, Table 19.1 shows that the firm's cost of personal selling was $40,000.

Once the costs of these marketing functions have been determined, the analyst is ready to compare the resulting figures with budgeted costs, with sales analysis data, with cost data from earlier operating periods, or perhaps with average industry cost figures, if available.

Cost analysis by product, geographic area, or customer   Although marketers ordinarily get a more detailed picture of marketing costs by analyzing functional accounts than by analyzing natural accounts, some firms need an even more precise cost analysis. The need is especially great if the firms sell several types of products, sell in multiple geographic areas, or sell to a wide variety of customers. Activities vary in marketing different products in specific geographic locations to certain customer groups. Therefore, the costs of these activities also vary. By allocating the functional costs to specific product groups, geographic areas, or customer groups, a marketer can find out which of these marketing entities are the most cost effective to serve. In Table 19.2, the functional costs derived in Table 19.1 are allocated to specific product categories. A similar type of analysis could be performed for geographic areas or for specific customer groups. The criteria employed to allocate the functional accounts must be developed so as to yield results that are as accurate as possible. Use of faulty criteria is likely to yield inaccurate cost estimates which, in turn, lead to less effective control of marketing strategies. Marketers determine the marketing costs for various product categories, geographic areas, or customer groups and then compare them to sales. This analysis allows them to evaluate the effectiveness of the firm's marketing strategy or strategies.

The Marketing Audit

A **marketing audit** is a systematic examination of the marketing unit's objectives, strategies, organization, and performance. It is the intelligence system used to gather the information needed to determine whether the marketing strategy is working. A marketing audit identifies what the marketing unit is doing and how it is performing these activities, evaluates the effectiveness of these activities in terms of the organization's objectives and resources, and recommends future marketing activities.[6] Like an accounting or financial audit, a marketing audit should be conducted regularly. The marketing audit is not a control process to be used only during a crisis, although a business in trouble may use it to isolate problems and generate solutions.

A marketing audit may be specific and focus on one or a few marketing activities, or it may be comprehensive and encompass all of a company's marketing activities. Table 19.3 lists many possible dimensions of a marketing audit. An audit might deal with only a few of these areas, or it might include all of them. Its scope depends on the costs involved, the target markets served, the structure of the marketing mix, and environmental conditions. The results of the audit can be used to reallocate marketing effort and to reexamine marketing opportunities.

The marketing audit should aid evaluation by doing the following:

1. Describe current activities and results related to sales, costs, prices, profits, and other performance feedback
2. Gather information about customers, competition, and environmental developments that may affect the marketing strategy
3. Explore opportunities and alternatives for improving the marketing strategy
4. Provide an overall data base to be used in evaluating the attainment of organizational goals and marketing objectives

Marketing audits can be performed by people within a company or outside it. An internal auditor may be a top-level marketing executive, a company-wide auditing committee, or a manager from another office or of another function. Although it is more expensive, an audit by outside consultants is usually more effective because external auditors have more objectivity, more time for the audit, and greater experience.

There is no single set of procedures for all marketing audits. Firms should adhere to several general guidelines. Audits are often based on a series of questionnaires that are administered to the firm's personnel. These questionnaires should be developed carefully to ensure that the audit focuses on the right issues. Auditors should develop and follow a step-by-step plan to guarantee that the audit is systematic. When interviewing company personnel, the auditors should strive to talk with a diverse group of people from many parts of the company. To achieve adequate support, the auditors normally focus on the firm's top management initially and then move down through the organizational hierarchy. The results of the audit should be set forth in a comprehensive written document.[7]

The marketing audit allows an organization to change tactics or alter day-to-day activities as problems arise. For example, a regular audit of a U.S. women's apparel firm operating in South Africa uncovered a counterproductive failure in a sales incentive program. The firm's salesclerks were supposed to receive one free brassiere for every ten sold, but the local warehouse failed to send salesclerks the incentive products they had earned. Although the mistake

6. Abe Schuchman, "The Marketing Audit: Its Nature, Purposes, and Problems," in *Analyzing and Improving Marketing Performance,* Report No. 32 (New York: American Management Association, 1959), pp. 16–17.
7. Martin L. Bell, *Marketing: Concepts and Strategies,* 3rd ed. (Boston: Houghton Mifflin, 1979), p. 472.

Table 19.3 *Examples of dimensions to include in a marketing audit*

Part I. The Marketing Environment Audit

Macroenvironment

A. Economic-Demographic

1. What does the company expect in the way of inflation, material shortages, unemployment, and credit availability in the short run, intermediate run, and long run?
2. What effect will forecasted trends in the size, age distribution, and regional distribution of population have on the business?

B. Technology

1. What major changes are occurring in product technology? In process technology?
2. What are the major generic substitutes that might replace this product?

C. Political-Legal

1. What laws are being proposed that may affect marketing strategy and tactics?
2. What federal, state, and local agency actions should be watched? What is happening with pollution control, equal employment opportunity, product safety, advertising, price control, etc., that is relevant to marketing planning?

D. Social-Cultural

1. What attitude is the public taking toward business and toward the types of products produced by the company?
2. What changes in consumer life styles and values have a bearing on the company's target markets and marketing methods?

Task Environment

A. Markets

1. What is happening to market size, growth, geographical distribution, and profits?
2. What are the major market segments and their expected rates of growth? Which are high opportunity and low opportunity segments?

B. Customers

1. How do current customers and prospects rate the company and its competitors on reputation, product quality, service, sales force, and price?
2. How do different classes of customers make their buying decisions?
3. What are the evolving needs and satisfactions being sought by the buyers in this market?

C. Competitors

1. Who are the major competitors? What are the objectives and strategy of each major competitor? What are their strengths and weaknesses? What are the sizes and trends in market shares?
2. What trends can be foreseen in future competition and substitutes for this product?

D. Distribution and Dealers

1. What are the main trade channels bringing products to customers?
2. What are the efficiency levels and growth potentials of the different trade channels?

E. Suppliers

1. What is the outlook for the availability of key resources used in production?
2. What trends are occurring among suppliers in their pattern of selling?

F. Facilitators

1. What is the outlook for the cost and availability of transportation services?
2. What is the outlook for the cost and availability of warehousing facilities?
3. What is the outlook for the cost and availability of financial resources?
4. How effectively is the advertising agency performing? What trends are occurring in advertising agency services?

Part II. Marketing Strategy Audit

A. Marketing Objectives

1. Are the corporate objectives clearly stated? Do they lead logically to the marketing objectives?
2. Are the marketing objectives stated clearly enough to guide marketing planning and subsequent performance measurement?
3. Are the marketing objectives appropriate, given the company's competitive position, resources, and opportunities? Is the appropriate strategic objective to build, hold, harvest, or terminate this business?

B. Strategy

1. What is the core marketing strategy for achieving the objectives? Is it sound?
2. Are the resources budgeted to accomplish the marketing objectives inadequate, adequate, or excessive?

Table 19.3   (continued)

3. Are the marketing resources allocated optimally to prime market segments, territories, and products?
4. Are the marketing resources allocated optimally to the major elements of the marketing mix, i.e., product quality, service, sales force, advertising, promotion, and distribution?

Part III. Marketing Organization Audit

A. Formal Structure

1. Is there a high-level marketing officer with adequate authority and responsibility over those company activities that affect customer satisfaction?
2. Are the marketing responsibilities optimally structured along functional, product, end user, and territorial lines?

B. Functional Efficiency

1. Are there good communication and working relations between marketing and sales?
2. Is the product-management system working effectively? Are the product managers able to plan profits or only sales volume?
3. Are there any groups in marketing that need more training, motivation, supervision, or evaluation?

C. Interface Efficiency

1. Are there any problems between marketing and manufacturing that need attention?
2. Are there any problems between marketing and other units—R&D, finance, purchasing?

Part IV. Marketing Systems Audit

A. Marketing Information System

1. Is the marketing intelligence system producing accurate, sufficient, and timely information about developments in the marketplace?
2. Is marketing research being adequately used by company decision makers?

B. Marketing-Planning System

1. Is the marketing-planning system well conceived and effective?
2. Is sales forecasting and market-potential measurement soundly carried out?
3. Are sales quotas set on a proper basis?

C. Marketing Control System

1. Are the control procedures (monthly, quarterly, etc.) adequate to insure that the annual-plan objectives are being achieved?
2. Is provision made to analyze periodically the profitability of different products, markets, territories, and channels of distribution?
3. Is provision made to examine and validate periodically various marketing costs?

D. New-Product Development System

1. Is the company well organized to gather, generate, and screen new product ideas?
2. Does the company do adequate concept research and business analysis before investing heavily in a new idea?
3. Does the company carry out adequate product and market testing before launching a new product?

Part V. Marketing Productivity Audit

A. Profitability Analysis

1. What is the profitability of the company's different products, served markets, territories, and channels of distribution?
2. Should the company enter, expand, contract, or withdraw from any business segments, and what would be the short- and long-run profit consequences?

B. Cost-Effectiveness Analysis

1. Do any marketing activities seem to have excessive costs? Are these costs valid? Can cost-reducing steps be taken?

Part VI. Marketing Function Audits

A. Products

1. What are the product line objectives? Are these objectives sound? Is the current product line meeting these objectives?
2. Are there particular products that should be phased out?
3. Are there new products that are worth adding?
4. Are any products able to benefit from quality, feature, or style improvements?

B. Price

1. What are the pricing objectives, policies, strategies, and procedures? Are prices set on sound cost, demand, and competitive criteria?

(continued next page)

Table 19.3 *(continued)*

2. Do the customers see the company's prices as being in line or out of line with the perceived value of its products?
3. Does the company use price promotions effectively?

C. Distribution
1. What are the distribution objectives and strategies?
2. Is there adequate market coverage and service?
3. Should the company consider changing its degree of reliance on distributors, sales reps, and direct selling?

D. Sales Force
1. What are the organization's sales force objectives?
2. Is the sales force large enough to accomplish the company's objectives?
3. Is the sales force organized along the proper principle(s) of specialization (territory, market, product)?

4. Does the sales force show high morale, ability, and effort? Are they sufficiently trained and are there sufficient incentives?
5. Are the procedures for setting quotas and evaluating performances adequate?
6. How is the company's sales force perceived in relation to competitors' sales forces?

E. Advertising, Sales Promotion, and Publicity
1. What are the organization's advertising objectives? Are they sound?
2. Is the right amount being spent on advertising? How is the budget determined?
3. Are the ad themes and copy effective? What do customers and the public think about the advertising?
4. Are the advertising media well chosen?
5. Is sales promotion used effectively?
6. Is there a well-conceived publicity program?

Source: Philip Kotler, *Marketing Management: Analysis, Planning, and Control,* 5th ed. © 1984, pp. 767–770. Adapted by permission of Prentice-Hall, Inc., Englewood Cliffs, N.J.

was an oversight by those in charge of physical distribution, it created negative feelings toward the company. By promptly sending the salesclerks the brassieres they had earned, the company made its sales incentive program function properly.

The concept of auditing implies an official examination of marketing activities. Many organizations audit their marketing activities informally. Any attempt to verify operating results and to compare them with standards can be considered an auditing activity. Many smaller firms probably would not use the word *audit,* but they do perform auditing activities.

Several problems may arise in an audit of marketing activities. Marketing audits can be expensive in time and money. Selecting the auditors may be difficult because objective, qualified personnel may not be available. Marketing audits can also be extremely disruptive because employees sometimes fear comprehensive evaluations, especially by outsiders.

Summary

The organization of marketing activities involves the development of an internal structure for the marketing unit. The internal structure is the key to directing marketing activities. The marketing unit can be organized by (1) functions, (2) products, (3) regions, or (4) types of customers. An organization may use only one approach or a combination.

Implementation is an important part of the marketing management process. Proper implementation of marketing plans depends on the coordination of marketing activities, the motivation of marketing personnel, and effective communication within the unit. Marketing managers must coordinate the activities of marketing personnel and integrate these activities both with those in other areas of the firm and with the marketing efforts of personnel in external organizations. Marketing managers also must motivate marketing personnel. The communication system of an organization must allow the marketing manager to communicate with high-level management, with managers of other functional areas in the firm, and with personnel involved in marketing activities both inside and outside the organization.

The marketing control process consists of establishing performance standards, evaluating actual performance by comparing it with established standards, and reducing the difference between desired and actual performance. A performance standard is an expected level of performance against which actual performance can be compared. Performance standards are established in the planning process. In evaluating actual performance, marketing managers must know what marketers within the firm are doing and must have information about the activities of external organizations that provide the firm with marketing assistance. Then actual performance is compared with performance standards. Marketers must decide whether a discrepancy exists and, if so, whether it requires corrective action such as changing the performance standards or improving actual performance.

An effective control process has several requirements. First, it should be designed so that the flow of information is rapid enough to allow the marketing manager to quickly detect differences between actual and planned levels of performance. Second, a variety of control procedures must accurately monitor different kinds of activities. Third, control procedures should be flexible enough to accommodate changes. Fourth, the control process must be economical so that its costs are low relative to the costs that would arise if there were no controls. Fifth, the control process should be designed so that both managers and subordinates are able to understand it.

To maintain effective marketing control, an organization needs to develop a comprehensive control process that evaluates its marketing operations at a given time. The control of marketing activities is not a simple task. Problems encountered include environmental changes that hamper effective control, time lags between marketing activities and their effects, and problems in determining the costs of marketing activities. In addition, it may be difficult to develop performance standards.

Control of marketing strategy can be achieved through sales and cost analyses. For purposes of analysis, sales usually are measured in terms of either dollar volume or market share. For a sales analysis to be effective, it must compare current sales performance with forecasted company sales, with industry sales, with specific competitor's sales, or with the costs incurred to generate the current sales volume. A sales analysis can be performed on the firm's total sales, or the total sales can be disaggregated and analyzed by product, geographic area, or customer group.

Marketing cost analysis involves an examination of accounting records and frequently a reclassification of natural accounts into marketing function accounts. Such an analysis is often difficult because there may be no logical, clear-cut way to allocate natural accounts into functional accounts. The analyst may choose either direct costing or full costing. Cost analysis can focus on (1) an aggregate cost analysis of natural accounts or functional accounts or (2) an analysis of functional accounts for products, geographic areas, or customer groups.

To control marketing strategies, it is sometimes necessary to audit marketing activities. Auditing is a systematic appraisal and review of activities in relation to objectives. A marketing audit attempts to identify what a marketing unit is doing, to evaluate the effectiveness of these activities, and to recommend future marketing activities.

Important Terms

Production-oriented organization
Sales-oriented organization
Marketing-oriented organization
Marketing control process
Performance standard
Sales analysis
Marketing cost analysis
Natural accounts

Marketing function accounts
Direct costs
Traceable common costs
Nontraceable common costs
Full-cost approach
Direct-cost approach
Marketing audit

Discussion and Review Questions

1. What determines marketing's place within an organization? Which type of organization is best suited to the marketing concept? Why?
2. What factors can be used to organize the internal aspects of a marketing unit? Discuss the benefits of each type of organization.
3. Why might an organization use multiple bases for organizing its marketing unit?
4. How does communication help in implementing marketing plans?
5. Why is motivation of marketing personnel important in implementing marketing plans?
6. What are the major steps of the marketing control process?
7. List and discuss the five requirements for an effective control process.
8. Discuss the major problems in controlling marketing activities.
9. What is a sales analysis? What makes it an effective control tool?
10. Identify and describe three cost analysis methods. Compare and contrast direct costing and full costing.
11. How is the marketing audit used to control marketing program performance?

Cases

Case 19.1 The "New" Beatrice[8]

"Our goal is to become a united, directed marketing company, with real power in the markets we serve, and with the skills needed to enter new markets successfully." This statement regarding long-range goals was made by the president

8. Based on *Organizing Corporate Marketing* (New York: Conference Board, 1984), pp. 44–45; *Beatrice Annual Report, 1985*; Alan Karo, "Developing Corporate Identity," *Marketing & Media Decisions*, April 1984, pp. 98, 100, 102; and Laura Konrad Jereski, "Beatrice Make-Over," *Marketing & Media Decisions*, May 1984, pp. 74–77.

of Beatrice several years ago. It represented a total refocusing of the company's growth—from its historical strategy of acquisition to a cohesive marketing-driven orientation. Only four years ago the giant food company had 435 profit centers in 54 groups. Some 9,000 products, sporting several hundred brand names, were sitting on retail shelves with less promotional backup than competitors' offerings and no long-term strategy to chart their future. The corporate marketing function was nonexistent.

Soon thereafter, though, Beatrice went through an extensive reorganization to change Beatrice from a loose aggregation of profit centers into the unified, directed marketing company described by the president. It established its first-ever corporate marketing department to oversee the planning and implementation of marketing efforts throughout the company. The company business units were divided into six operating groups. The heads of these six groups were to perform the functions, which traditionally had been performed by the company's president, in developing and implementing marketing plans and programs. The six group heads were to be advocates of better marketing performance. They would report directly to the CEO.

While in the past, Beatrice had had a large number of small regional profit centers, management realized that to be competitive, the corporation needed broad product lines with national advertising and nationally coordinated distribution systems. The new organization, with a smaller number of larger business units, has put Beatrice in position to implement national distribution and national advertising. A further reorganization of the company last year reduced the six divisions to four operating divisions: U.S. Food, Consumer Products, International Foods, and Avis/Other Operations.

The U.S. Food division has more than 150 brands in 90 product categories and is viewed as the cornerstone of Beatrice's business. It is the largest segment of the company's operations and represents the broadest base of national food and beverage brands in the industry. The U.S. Food division has major operations in grocery products, soft drinks, bottled water, warehousing, food service, dairy products, meats, cheeses, and fruit juices.

The Consumer Products division consists of consumer durables and personal products. Its major operations are in water treatment, luggage, intimate apparel, active wear, health and beauty aids, and fragrances. Popular brand names include Playtex, Samsonite, Max Factor, Stiffel Lamps, Almay and Halston.

The International Foods division has operations in over thirty countries. This division's major product categories include dairy, processed meats, snacks and confectionery goods, beverages and fruit juices, and grocery products.

The fourth major division is called Avis/Other Operations. Avis is the second-largest U.S. car rental agency. It operates in over 100 countries from 3,500 locations including 1,200 airports. Avis has a commitment to speedy, reliable service and state-of-the-art communication capabilities.

The reorganization has vastly increased Beatrice's marketing clout. Today Beatrice is the third largest advertiser in the United States, having spent approximately $680 million on advertising and sales promotion last year, which is a dramatic increase over its historical spending patterns in this area. Beatrice undertook this level of spending to develop and maintain a leadership position in today's highly competitive marketplace. Prior to the promotional campaign, Beatrice was hardly a household word. Though many Beatrice brands and products—such as Tropicana orange juice, Cutty Sark whiskey, La Choy Chinese food, and Samsonite luggage—had widespread national recognition, and many more enjoyed regional popularity, the Beatrice name had no corporate identity. The results of these investments have been impressive. For example, in the past year, consumer awareness of the Beatrice name has tripled and consumers have come to associate that name with quality and value. Beatrice has also attempted to improve consumer awareness through a corporate-identity program used in packaging, advertising campaigns, and branding.

Questions for Discussion

1. On what basis has Beatrice reorganized its divisions?
2. Why did Beatrice management reorganize?
3. Although the overall long-term effects of Beatrice's strategy may be quite favorable, the company may face some adverse short-term effects. What are they?

Case 19.2 Shoreline Seafood Corporation

The Shoreline Seafood Corporation is a small seafood processor that currently produces three products. Marketers at Shoreline are concerned about whether their marketing strategies for their three products are effective.

Shoreline marketers have decided to analyze the sales and costs of marketing the three products to provide information for assessing their marketing strategies. The income statement for Shoreline Seafood Corporation for last year is shown in Table 19.4.

Table 19.4 Income statement for Shoreline Seafood Corporation

	Total	Product A	Product B	Product C
Sales	$520,000	$120,000	$150,000	$250,000
Costs of goods sold	250,000	55,000	70,000	125,000
Gross profit on sales	270,000			
Marketing costs				
Salespeople's salaries	24,500	8,000	7,000	9,500
Salespeople's commissions	27,500	11,000	6,000	10,500
Advertising	65,000	13,000	13,000	39,000
Transportation and delivery	8,400	2,310	2,520	3,750
Warehouse	4,500	1,500	1,500	1,500
Sales office expenses	14,800	4,900	4,900	5,000
Nonmarketing costs	19,110			
General and administrative costs	41,250			
Total costs	$205,060			
Net profit	$ 64,940			

Questions for Discussion

1. What type of sales measurement and bases for sales analysis are used in this case?
2. What types of costs appear on the income statement?
3. What are the implications of the data on the income statement for products A, B, and C?

Part VII
Selected Applications

The remaining chapters in this book deal with strategic applications in industrial, services and nonbusiness, and international marketing. Emphasis is placed on the features and issues that are unique to each of these selected areas of marketing when formulating and implementing marketing strategies. Chapter 20 analyzes industrial marketing strategy development and discusses the decisions and activities that characterize industrial marketing. Chapter 21 explores selected aspects of services and nonbusiness marketing strategies. In Chapter 22, we focus on the development and implementation of marketing strategies for foreign markets.

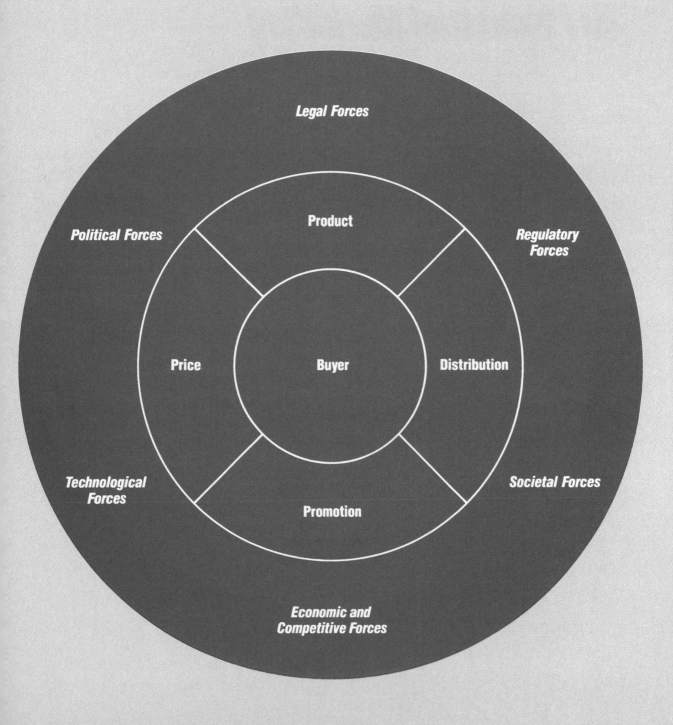

20 / Industrial Marketing

Objectives

- To understand some unique characteristics of industrial marketing.

- To see how the demand for industrial products differs from the demand for consumer products.

- To learn how to select and analyze industrial target markets.

- To find out how industrial marketing mix components differ from the components in consumer product marketing mixes.

Figure 20.1

A Mack truck provides unique customer benefits (Source: Courtesy of Mack Truck Company)

The basic mission of the Mack Truck Company is to build and service trucks for worldwide businesses that range from logging to construction companies. Mack's strength is understanding industrial customers' needs and providing the product options and prices that influence purchase decisions. The company is known for quality service and innovative design, engineering, and manufacturing.

Mack is unique as a manufacturer of trucks in that it makes many of its own power-train components, diesel engines, transmissions, and rear axle carriers. (A Mack truck is shown in Figure 20.1.) To streamline production, however, the firm is now buying some parts from companies like Rockwell International, when such "outsourcing" does not compromise quality, and it is using computer-aided design to create products that are easier to manufacture. To stay competitive, Mack is also introducing new truck designs and technically trying to reduce the operating costs of its vehicles. Since deregulation has forced truckers to cut their rates, the efficiency and durability of their vehicles have become increasingly important to them.

Mack's marketing strategy is to emphasize particular segments of the industrial truck market and develop the proper marketing mix. Serving the truck customer means tailoring the product to meet a specific need, actually customizing the vehicle for the purchaser. It also means making twenty-one different types of truck. The company is working hard to convince owner operators (independent truckers) to make Mack their choice. Independents typically select large, powerful, well-equipped trucks. The Mack Ultra-Liner, a new high-cab-over-engine model, is making considerable progress in this segment.

Mack also attempts to understand the needs of fleet owners. Its R-model has gained the largest share of the conventional-cab heavy-duty truck market in North America. Mack creates value for fleet customers by providing the expertise necessary to analyze applications and engineer productive solutions that contribute to fleet profitability. United Parcel Service, one of Mack's largest customers, has been purchasing trucks from Mack for twenty-five years; before making a purchase, UPS provides suggested modifications and specifications. Mack also has a wholly owned subsidiary in Canada that provides the same products and services that the truck maker does in the United States.

Mack has a far-reaching U.S. network of company-owned branches, independent distributors, and service dealers. The Mack field organization helps the company understand its customers and fulfill presale expectations through continuous after-sale service. For example, a product council, composed of representatives of key distributors, periodically joins the Mack corporate engineering staff to help determine the character of future products. Mack's confidence in its product is demonstrated by its warranty covering major power-train components. The terms—three years or 300,000 miles and 100 percent of parts and labor—are the best in the industry.[1]

Industrial marketers experience some problems similar to those of consumer product marketers and rely on basic marketing concepts and decisions. However, those concepts and decisions are applied in unique ways that take into account the nature of industrial markets and products.

Industrial marketing is a set of activities directed toward facilitating and expediting exchanges involving industrial products and customers in industrial markets. As discussed in Chapter 2, an **industrial market** consists of individuals, groups, or organizations that purchase a specific kind of product for direct use in producing other products or for use in day-to-day operations. Industrial

1. Mack Trucks, Inc., *Annual Reports, 1984 and 1985*; "Mack Is Back," *Barron's*, March 5, 1984, pp. 20, 21, 42; and Clem Morgello, "Curcio: A New Age of Innovation," *Dun's Business Month*, November 1985, pp. 53-54.

markets are made up of numerous types of customers including commercial producers, governments, and institutions.

This chapter focuses on dimensions that are unique to the marketing of industrial products. Initially, we examine the major characteristics of industrial marketing. Then we focus on the development of industrial marketing strategies, discussing the selection and analysis of industrial target markets and the distinctive features of industrial marketing mixes.

The Nature of Industrial Marketing

As pointed out in Chapter 5, an **industrial product** differs from a consumer product in that it is purchased to be used directly or indirectly to produce other products or to be used in the operations of an organization. Industrial products fall into seven categories:

1. *Raw materials* actually become a part of a physical product. They are the basic materials provided from mines, farms, forests, oceans, and recycled solid wastes.
2. *Major equipment* includes large tools and machines used for production.
3. Though it does not become a part of the product, *accessory equipment* consists of standardized items used in production and office activities.
4. *Component parts* become part of the physical product and are either finished items ready for assembly or products that need little processing before assembly.
5. *Process materials* are used directly in production but, unlike component parts, are not readily identifiable.
6. *Supplies* facilitate a firm's production and operations but do not become an actual part of the finished product.
7. *Services* are the intangible products that organizations use in their operations.

In addition to product differences, industrial marketing is considered unique for the following reasons: (1) the buyer's decision-making process, (2) characteristics of the product market, and (3) the nature of environmental influences.[2] Chapter 5 discusses organizational buying behavior and environmental influences, while Chapter 1 discusses the characteristics of the products. These differences create a need to adjust and fine-tune industrial marketing activities.

Selection and Analysis of Industrial Target Markets

Marketing research is becoming more important in industrial marketing. Most of the marketing research techniques that we discuss in Chapter 6 can be applied to industrial marketing. As Figure 20.2 indicates, Haworth, a maker of office furniture systems, concerns itself with its customers' needs. Here we will focus on some important and unique approaches to selecting and analyzing industrial target markets.

2. Edward F. Fern and James R. Brown, "The Industrial/Consumer Marketing Dichotomy: A Case of Insufficient Justification," *Journal of Marketing*, Spring 1984, pp. 168–77.

Figure 20.2

Haworth's primary marketing objective of understanding the needs of its target market (Source: Materials are reproduced courtesy of Haworth, Inc.)

Industrial marketers have considerable information about potential customers, much of which appears in government and industry publications; comparable data are not available regarding ultimate consumers. Even though industrial marketers may use different procedures to isolate and analyze target markets, most follow a similar pattern of (1) determining who potential customers are and how many there are, (2) locating where they are, and (3) estimating their purchase potential.[3]

Determining Who Potential Customers Are and How Many There Are

A lot of information about industrial customers is based on the **Standard Industrial Classification (SIC) system,** which was developed by the federal government to classify selected economic characteristics of industrial, commercial, financial, and service organizations. This system is administered by the Statistical Policy

3. Robert W. Haas, *Industrial Marketing Management* (New York: Petrocelli Charter, 1976), pp. 37–48.

Table 20.1 *Example of product classification in the Standard Industrial Classification system*

Level	SIC Code	Description
Division	D	Manufacturing
Major group	22	Textile mill products
Industry subgroup	225	Knitting mills
Detailed industry	2251	Women's full-length and knee-length hosiery
Product category	22513	Women's finished seamless hosiery
Product item	2251311	Misses' finished knee-length socks

Sources: 1972 Standard Industrial Classification Manual, Office of Management and Budget; and *Census of Manufacturers 1972,* Bureau of the Census.

Table 20.2 *Types of government information available about industrial markets (based on SIC categories)*

Value of industry shipments
Number of establishments
Number of employees
Exports as a percentage of shipments
Imports as a percentage of apparent consumption
Compound annual average rate of growth
Major producing areas

Division of the Office of Management and Budget. Table 20.1 shows how the SIC system can be used to categorize products. Various types of business activities are separated into lettered divisions, and each division is divided into numbered, two-digit major groups. For example, major group 22 includes all firms that manufacture textile mill products. Each major group is divided into three-digit-coded subgroups, and each subgroup is separated into detailed industry categories that are coded with four-digit numbers. In the most recent SIC Manual, there are 84 major groups, 596 subgroups, and 976 detailed industry categories.[4] To categorize manufacturers in more detail, the *Census of Manufacturers* further subdivides manufacturers (Division D) into five- and seven-digit-coded groups. The fifth digit denotes the product class, and the sixth and seventh digits designate the specific product.

A large amount of data is available for each SIC category through various government publications, such as *Census of Business, Census of Manufacturers*, and *County Business Patterns*. Table 20.2 shows some types of information that can be obtained through government sources. Some data are available by state, county, and metropolitan area. Industrial market data also appear in such nongovernment sources as Dun & Bradstreet's *Market Identifiers, Sales and*

4. *1972 Standard Industrial Classification Manual,* Office of Management and Budget.

Marketing Management's Survey of Industrial Purchasing Power, and other trade publications.

The SIC system is a ready-made tool that allows industrial marketers to divide industrial firms into market segments based mainly on the types of products produced or handled. Although the SIC system provides a vehicle for segmentation, it must be used in conjunction with other types of data to allow a specific industrial marketer to determine exactly which customers it is possible to reach and their number.

In conjunction with the SIC system, input-output analysis can be used effectively. It is based on the assumption that the output or sales of one industry are the input or purchases of other industries. **Input-output data** report which types of industries purchase the products of a particular industry. A major source of national input-output data is the *Survey of Current Business*, published by the Office of Business Economics, U.S. Department of Commerce. These data are presented in matrix form with 83 industries listed horizontally across the top of the table. To determine which industries purchase the output of a specified industry, one simply reads down the left column to the specified industry and then reads across the horizontal row, which shows how much each of the 83 industries spends on the output of the specified industry. For example, 62 of the 83 industries purchase paints and allied products (industry number 30). However, the purchases of three industries (new construction, maintenance and repair construction, and motor vehicles and equipment) account for 54 percent of the total purchases of paint and allied products. Each of the remaining 54 industries buys less than 4.7 percent of the total.

After finding out which industries purchase the major portion of an industry's output, the next step is to determine the SIC numbers for those industries. Because firms are grouped differently in the input-output tables and the SIC system, ascertaining SIC numbers can be difficult. However, the Office of Business Economics does provide some limited conversion tables with the input-output data. These tables can assist industrial marketers in assigning SIC numbers to the industry categories used in the input-output analysis. For example, the motor vehicle and equipment industry, an industry that buys significant quantities of paint and allied products, can be converted into SIC categories 3711 and 3715.

After determining the SIC numbers of the industries that buy the firm's output, an industrial marketer is in a position to ascertain the number of firms that are potential buyers nationally, by state, and by county. Government publications such as the *Census of Business*, the *Census of Manufacturers*, and *County Business Patterns* report the number of establishments within SIC classifications, along with other types of data such as those shown in Table 20.2. For manufacturing industries, *Sales and Marketing Management's Survey of Industrial Purchasing Power* contains state and county SIC information regarding the number and size of plants and shipment sizes. The *Survey of Industrial Purchasing Power*, unlike most government sources, is updated annually.

Locating Industrial Customers

At this point, an industrial marketer knows what types of industries purchase the kinds of products his or her firm produces, as well as the number of establishments in those industries and certain other information. However, that marketer has still to find out the names and addresses of potential customers.

One approach to identifying and locating potential customers is to use state or commercial industrial directories such as *Standard & Poor's Register* and Dun & Bradstreet's *Middle Market Directory* or *Million Dollar Directory*. These sources contain such information about a firm as its name, SIC number, address, phone number, and annual sales. By referring to one or more of these sources, an industrial marketer can isolate industrial customers that have SIC numbers, determine their locations, and thus develop lists of potential customers by city, county, and state.

A second approach, more expedient but also more expensive, is to use a commercial data company. Dun & Bradstreet, for example, can provide a list of firms that fall into a particular four-digit SIC group. For each firm on the list, Dun & Bradstreet identifies the name, location, sales volume, number of employees, type of products handled, names of chief executives, and other information.

Either approach can effectively identify and locate a group of potential industrial customers. However, an industrial marketer probably cannot pursue all firms on the list. Since some firms have a greater purchase potential than others, the marketer must determine which segment or segments to pursue.

In industrial marketing, situation-specific variables are usually more relevant in segmenting markets than general customer characteristics. Industrial customers concentrate on benefits sought; therefore, understanding end use of the product is more important than the psychology of decisions or socioeconomic characteristics. Segmenting by benefits rather than customer characteristics can provide insight into the structure of the market and opportunities for new customers.[5] Figure 20.3 shows that Texaco Chemical Company has found that selling the benefits of its surfactants as emulsifiers, wetting agents, and dispersants is more important than segmenting by customer characteristics.

Estimating Purchase Potential

To estimate the purchase potential of industrial customers or groups of customers, an industrial marketer must find a relationship between the size of potential customers' purchases and a variable available in SIC data, such as number of employees. For example, a paint manufacturer might attempt to determine the average number of gallons purchased by a specific type of potential industrial customer relative to the number of persons employed. If the industrial marketer has no previous experience in this market segment, it will probably be necessary to survey a random sample of potential customers to establish a relationship between purchase sizes and numbers of persons employed. Once this relationship has been established, the relationship can be applied to potential customer segments to estimate their purchases. After deriving these estimates, the industrial marketer selects the customers to be included in the target market.

Despite their usefulness in isolating and analyzing industrial target markets, SIC data pose several problems for users. First, a few industries do not have specific SIC designations. Second, because a transfer of products from one establishment to another is counted as a part of total shipments, double counting may occur when products are shipped between two establishments within the same firm. Third, since the census bureau is prohibited from publishing data that would identify a specific business organization, some data—such as value

5. Peter Doyle and John Saunders, "Market Segmentation and Positioning in Specialized Industrial Markets," *Journal of Marketing*, Spring 1985, p. 25.

of total shipments—may be understated. Finally, since SIC data are provided by government agencies, there is usually a significant lag between the time the data are collected and when that information becomes available.

Characteristics of Industrial Marketing Mixes

After selecting and analyzing a target market, an industrial marketer must create a marketing mix that will satisfy the customers in that target market. In many respects, the general concepts and methods involved in developing an industrial marketing mix are similar to those used in consumer product marketing. Let us focus here on the features of industrial marketing mixes that differ from the marketing mixes for consumer products. We will examine each of the four components in an industrial marketing mix: product, distribution, promotion, and price.

Product

After selecting a target market, management has to decide how to compete. Production-oriented managers fail to understand the need to develop a distinct appeal for their product to give it a competitive advantage. Positioning the

W.W. Grainger sells industrial products such as air compressors, spraying equipment, and power and hand tools, some of which it manufactures. The firm sells over 12,500 items and has 180 sales branches throughout the United States.

Grainger regards service as the way to increase sales. The size of branch showrooms has been increased to provide more display space and to improve the likelihood of on-the-spot purchases. The company encourages cash-and-carry purchases and also guarantees next-day delivery of products. Grainger has found that industrial buyers will often buy drills and smaller equipment on the spot if they see something they like. More important, the company makes sure that all of its products are available in each of its sales regions. Branches are tracked by a computerized inventory control system so that the company can provide next-day delivery of orders. The firm has found that one out of three customers will not place an order if the item is not in stock.

Grainger believes that service is being able to say yes. Often, services or availability of products can be more important to industrial purchasers than price. The lost revenues caused by not having the right products can be more costly than paying a few extra dollars for improved service. W.W. Grainger's efforts to improve service have paid off: in each of the last five years, the company has broken its sales record. (*Source: "Grainger Sells Service,"* Sales and Marketing Management, *June 3, 1985, pp. 26–27. Reprinted by permission of* Sales and Marketing Management.)

product (discussed in Chapter 8) is necessary to successfully serve a market, whether consumer or industrial.[6]

Compared with consumer marketing mixes, the product ingredients of industrial marketing mixes often include a greater emphasis on services, both before and after sales. W.W. Grainger, the subject of the application on this page, is a good example of this service emphasis. Services including on-time delivery, quality control, custom design, and a nationwide parts distribution system may be important components of the product.

Before making a sale, industrial marketers provide potential customers with technical advice regarding product specifications, installation, and application. Many industrial marketers depend heavily on long-term customer relationships that perpetuate sizable repeat purchases. Therefore, industrial marketers also make a considerable effort to provide services after the sale. Because industrial customers depend heavily on having products available when needed, on-time delivery is another service included in the product component of many industrial marketing mixes. An industrial marketer who is unable to provide on-time delivery cannot expect the marketing mix to satisfy industrial customers. Availability of parts must also be included in the product mixes of many industrial marketers because a lack of parts can result in costly production delays. The industrial marketer who includes availability of parts within the product component has a competitive advantage over a marketer who fails to offer this service. Customers whose average purchases are large often desire credit; thus, some industrial marketers include credit services in their product mixes.

6. Ibid., p. 25.

When planning and developing an industrial product mix, an industrial marketer of component parts and semifinished products must realize that a customer may decide to make the items instead of buying them. In some cases, then, industrial marketers compete not only with each other but also with their own potential customers.

Industrial products frequently must conform to standard technical specifications desired by industrial customers. Thus, industrial marketers tend to concentrate on product research that is directed at functional features rather than on marketing research.[7] This focus has led to some less than successful marketing mixes. For example, Steel Company of Canada (Stelco) sold trainloads of common nails to a market it did not really know. Its marketers did not know who bought Stelco nails; nor did they know for what applications the nails were used. Stelco introduced a revolutionary nail, an inexpensive spiral-threaded nail that is stronger than common nails, has more holding power, and is easier to drive. However, the new nails have not sold as well as management expected.[8] The primary reason is that Stelco's research focused on nails rather than on the needs of customers.

Since industrial products often are sold on the basis of specifications and are rarely sold through self-service, the major consideration in package design is protection. Less emphasis is placed on the package as a promotional device.

Research on industrial customer complaints indicates that industrial buyers usually complain when problems are encountered with product quality or delivery time. Consumers, on the other hand, exhibit more varying complaint behavior. This type of feedback from buyers allows industrial marketers to gauge marketing performance and to provide satisfaction where possible. It is important that industrial marketers respond to valid complaints, since the success of most industrial products depends on repeat purchases. Because buyer complaints serve a useful purpose, many industrial firms facilitate this feedback by providing customer service departments.[9]

If an industrial marketer is in a mature market, growth can come from attracting share from another industrial marketer; or a firm can look at new applications or uses of its products. Wescon Products of Wichita, Kansas, is a maker of handtrucks and other handling devices, mainly for heavy industrial customers. In recent years, prospects for sales growth have been quite limited because heavy manufacturing has been on the decline in the United States. To compensate, the company developed a gadabout, a stylish handtruck that is useful in offices, and thereby made further growth possible in its handtruck business.[10]

Distribution

The distribution ingredient in industrial marketing mixes differs from that of consumer products with respect to the types of channels used; the kinds of intermediaries available; and the transportation, storage, and inventory policies in effect.

7. Jon G. Udell, *Successful Marketing Strategies in American Industries* (Madison, Wis.: Mimir, 1972), pp. 48–49.
8. Peter M. Banting, "Unsuccessful Innovation in the Industrial Market," *Journal of Marketing*, Jan. 1978, p. 100.
9. Hiram C. Barksdale, Jr., Terry E. Powell, and Earnestine Hargrove, "Complaint Voicing by Industrial Buyers," *Industrial Marketing Management*, May 1984, pp. 93–99.
10. "Consider: Industrial Marketers Entering the Consumer Zone," *Marketing News*, Aug. 30, 1985, p. 1.

Figure 20.4

Four major types of
industrial marketing
channels

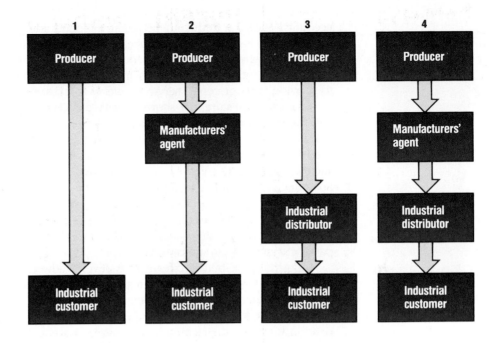

Distribution channels tend to be shorter for industrial products than for many consumer products. Four commonly used industrial channels are shown in Figure 20.4. Other, less popular channels also may be available. Although **direct distribution channels,** those in which products are sold directly from producers to users (see channel 1, Figure 20.4), are not employed frequently in the distribution of consumer products, they are the most widely used channels for industrial products. Over half of all industrial products are sold through direct channels. Industrial buyers like to communicate directly with producers, especially when expensive or technically complex products are involved. In these circumstances, an industrial customer wants the technical assistance and personal assurances that only a producer can provide.

In channel 2 (Figure 20.4), a manufacturers' agent is employed. As described in Chapter 10, a **manufacturers' agent** or representative is an independent business person who sells complementary products of several producers in assigned territories and is compensated through commissions. A manufacturers' agent does not acquire title to the products and usually does not take possession. Acting as a salesperson on behalf of the producers, a manufacturers' agent has no latitude, or very little, in negotiating prices or sales terms.

Using manufacturers' agents can benefit an industrial marketer. These agents usually possess considerable technical and market information and have an established set of customers. For an industrial seller with highly seasonal demand, a manufacturers' agent can be an asset because the seller does not have to support a year-round sales force. That manufacturers' agents are paid on a commission basis also may present an economical alternative for a firm that has highly limited resources and cannot afford a full-time sales force.

Certainly, the use of manufacturers' agents is not free of problems. Even though straight commissions may be cheaper for an industrial seller, the seller may have little control over manufacturers' agents. Because of the compensation method, manufacturers' agents usually want to concentrate on their larger accounts. They are frequently reluctant to spend adequate time following up sales, to put forth special selling efforts, or to provide sellers with market information when such activities reduce the amount of productive selling time. As they rarely maintain inventories, manufacturers' agents have a limited ability to provide parts or repair services quickly to customers.

Channel 3 in Figure 20.4 shows an **industrial distributor** between the producer and the customer. Like manufacturers' agents, industrial distributors are independent business organizations. However, they do take title to products, and they do carry inventories. Industrial distributors usually sell standardized items such as maintenance supplies, production tools, and small operating equipment. Some industrial distributors carry a wide variety of product lines; others specialize in one or a small number of lines. Industrial distributors can be most effectively used when a product has broad market appeal, is easily stocked and serviced, is sold in small quantities, and is needed rapidly to avoid high losses (as is a part for a machine in an assembly line).[11]

Industrial distributors offer sellers several advantages. They can perform the needed selling activities in local markets at relatively low cost to a manufacturer. They can reduce a producer's financial burden by providing credit services to their customers. And because industrial distributors usually maintain close relationships with their customers, they are aware of local needs and can pass on market information to producers. By holding adequate inventories in their local markets, industrial distributors reduce the producers' capital requirements.

Clark Equipment Company has successfully turned its industrial distributors into a mass marketing organization to reach smaller industrial concerns. The first step was to downsize its material-handling-systems products to fit anyone's needs. Next, distributors were trained to sell automated systems to smaller firms. To participate in the program, industrial distributors had to invest from $150,000 to $200,000 in stock and send sales and service people for intensive training. Clark is relying on its industrial distributors to get closer to smaller customers so as to boost sales.[12]

There are, though, several disadvantages to using industrial distributors. Like manufacturers' agents, industrial distributors may be difficult to control since they are independent firms. They frequently stock competing brands, so an industrial seller cannot depend on them to sell a specific brand aggressively. Since industrial distributors maintain inventories—for which they sustain numerous expenses—they are less likely to handle items that are bulky, that are slow sellers relative to profit margin, that need specialized facilities, or that require extraordinary selling efforts. In some cases, industrial distributors lack the technical knowledge necessary to sell and service certain industrial items.

As shown in Figure 20.4, channel 4 has both a manufacturers' agent and an industrial distributor between the producer and the industrial customer. This channel may be appropriate when the industrial marketer wishes to cover a large geographic area but maintains no sales force because of highly seasonal demand or because the firm cannot afford a sales force. This type of channel

11. James D. Hlavacek and Tommy J. McCuistion, "Industrial Distributors: When, Who, and How?" *Harvard Business Review*, March–April 1983, p. 97.
12. "Clark 'Retails' Plant Automation Systems," *Sales and Marketing Management*, April 1, 1985, p. 16.

Figure 20.5

Monfort precooked pas-
trami—a new product to
satisfy changing market
requirements (Source:
Monfort Annual Report)

also can be useful for an industrial marketer that wants to enter a new geographic market without expanding the firm's existing sales force.

Selecting an industrial channel or channels requires careful analysis along several dimensions. So far, our discussion has perhaps implied that all channels are equally available and that an industrial producer can select the most desirable option. However, in a number of cases, only one or perhaps two channels are available for the distribution of certain types of products.

An important issue in channel selection is the manner in which particular products are normally purchased. If customers ordinarily buy certain types of products directly from producers, it is unlikely that channels with intermediaries will be effective. Other dimensions one should consider are the cost and physical characteristics of the product, the costs of using various channels, the amount of technical assistance needed by customers, and the size of product and parts inventory needed in local markets. The application on page 614 illustrates how Monfort has changed distribution to keep pace with changes in the way products are purchased. Figure 20.5 illustrates a new pastrami product that Monfort produced for retail customers.

Physical distribution decisions regarding transportation, storage, and inventory control are especially important for industrial marketers. The continuity of most industrial buyer-seller relationships depends on the seller's having the right products available when and where the customer needs them. This requirement is so important that industrial marketers must sometimes make a considerable investment in order-processing systems, materials handling equipment, warehousing facilities, and inventory control systems. Like marketers of consumer products, industrial marketers try to use the proper mix of these resources to minimize total physical distribution costs while maintaining a satisfactory level of service.

Application

The Changing Channel Relationships of Monfort

Monfort is engaged in a vertically integrated line of businesses: the production, transportation, physical distribution, and sale of beef and lamb products. Historically, Monfort has been a buyer and seller of commodities. The company buys feeder cattle, lambs, corn, cattle feed, protein feeds, and many other commodity items. It sells lambs, beef carcasses, beef chucks, tenderloins, hides, and a host of other commodity items. Through nationwide sales offices, the company has marketed its products to hotels, restaurants, and institutions, as well as to wholesale distributors.

A few years ago most retailers wanted to do their own packaging and promotion of fresh meat items. More recently, the marketplace changed. Customers such as large retailers demanded that their products be processed into steaks and roasts and other prepackaged, prelabeled, and prepriced products that can be placed directly into the meat case. Many customers even wanted the Monfort name on those labeled products.

With so many of its industrial customers wanting the products further processed, Monfort had to become a marketer of meat products rather than simply a buyer and seller of commodities. As a result, Monfort must think in terms of new products and services. American eating habits are changing, and families no longer sit down to big dinners featuring chuck roast or pork loins each night. New products, such as precooked pastrami or ground-beef patties with bran added, will be required to satisfy new consumer preferences. Monfort is now committed to finding out how it can best sell lamb and beef in a changing marketplace. To do this, the company must understand the changing desires and tastes of the consumer at the end of the marketing channel, as well as the requirements of its direct customers in the channel.

This application illustrates that an industrial marketer must change the way it relates to its channel members as changes occur in the consumption of products by the final consumer. Physical distribution and all aspects of channel management must be adjusted to meet new requirements. In this case, Monfort is beginning to recognize that it is as much a marketer of meat products as it is a producer and physical distributor of commodities. (*Source: Monfort* 1985 Annual Report, *published 1986, pp. 2, 8. Used by permission.*)

Promotion

The combination of promotional efforts used in industrial marketing mixes generally differs considerably from those used for consumer products, especially convenience goods. The differences are evident both in the emphasis placed on various promotion mix ingredients and in the activities performed in connection with each promotion mix ingredient.

For several reasons, most industrial marketers rely on personal selling to a much greater extent than do consumer product marketers (except, perhaps, marketers of consumer durables). Since an industrial seller often has fewer customers, personal contact with each customer is more feasible. Some industrial products have technical features that are too numerous or too complex to explain through nonpersonal forms of promotion. Because industrial purchases frequently are high in dollar value and must be suited to the job and available where and when needed, industrial buyers want reinforcement and personal assurances from industrial sales personnel. Since industrial marketers depend on repeat purchases, sales personnel must follow up sales to make certain that

Figure 20.6

Hammermill's advertise-
ment soliciting direct-
mail responses from
potential customers
(Source: Reprinted with
permission of Hammermill
Papers Group, Division of
Hammermill Paper
Company)

advertising messages that present numerous details and complex product information (which are frequently the type of messages that industrial advertisers
wish to get across).

Compared with consumer product advertisements, industrial advertisements
are usually less persuasive in nature and are more likely to contain a large
amount of copy and to set forth numerous details. In contrast, marketers that
advertise to reach ultimate consumers sometimes avoid extensive advertising
copy because consumers are reluctant to read it. Industrial advertisers, however,
believe that industrial purchasers who have any interest in their product will
search for information and read long messages. Industrial advertisers do not
rely heavily on comparative advertising. Despite a 1972 Federal Trade Commission
memo advocating comparative advertising to provide industrial purchasers with
more complete information, its use for industrial products has decreased significantly. Even when this type of advertising is used, the comparisons are

rarely explicit and pointed but rather are implied. Furthermore, comparisons tend to stress product features over price, distribution, or promotion.[19]

Sales promotion activities can play a significant role in industrial promotion mixes and include such efforts as catalogs, trade shows, and trade-type sales promotion methods like merchandise allowances, buy-back allowances, displays, sales contests, and other methods discussed in Chapter 15. Industrial marketers go to considerable effort and expense to provide catalogs that describe their products to customers. Customers refer to various sellers' catalogs to determine specifications, terms of sale, delivery times, and other information about products. Catalogs thus assist buyers in deciding which suppliers to contact.

Trade shows can be effective vehicles for making many customer contacts in a short time. Although trade shows can be expensive, industrial marketers can use them for various purposes: to show and demonstrate new products, to find new customers, to take orders, to develop mailing lists, to promote the company image, and to find out what competitors are doing. Before exhibiting at trade shows, a firm must clearly specify its objectives. These objectives will influence the firm's choice of trade shows and the content of its exhibits.[20]

The manner in which industrial marketers use publicity in their promotion mixes may not be much different from the way that marketers of consumer products use it.

Price

Compared with consumer product marketers, industrial marketers face many more price constraints from legal and economic forces. As indicated in Chapter 2, the Robinson-Patman Act significantly influences the pricing practices of producers and wholesalers by regulating price differentials and the use of discounts. When the federal government invokes price controls, the effect ordinarily is to regulate industrial marketers' prices directly and to a greater extent than consumer product prices. With respect to economic forces, an individual industrial firm's demand is often highly elastic, requiring the firm's price to approximate competitors' prices. This condition often results in nonprice competition and in a considerable amount of price stability.

Today's route to sustainable competitive advantage lies in offering the customer better value, even at a slightly higher price.[21] Customers are used to buying on the basis of price, which is visible and measurable, and producers are used to competing on the same basis; but a strategic advantage based on the total value delivered is far less easily duplicated by competitors.[22] Companies like Caterpillar and Hewlett-Packard have shown that a value-based strategy can effectively garner a commanding lead over competition. Both firms emphasize the highest-quality products at slightly higher prices.

Although there are a variety of ways for determining prices of industrial products, the three most common are administered pricing, bid pricing, and negotiated pricing. With **administered pricing,** the seller determines the price (or series of prices) for a product, and the customer pays that specified price.

19. Thomas H. Stevenson and Linda E. Swayne, "Comparative Industrial Advertising: The Content and Frequency," *Industrial Marketing Management,* May 1984, pp. 133–138.
20. Joseph A. Bellizzi and Delilah J. Lipps, "Managerial Guidelines for Trade Show Effectiveness," *Industrial Marketing Management,* Feb. 1984, pp. 49–52.
21. John L. Forbis and Nitin T. Mehta, "Value-Based Strategies for Industrial Products," *Business Horizons,* May–June 1981, p. 32.
22. Ibid.

Marketers who use this approach may employ a one-price policy in which all buyers pay the same price, or they may set a series of prices that are determined by one or more discounts. In some cases, list prices are posted on a price sheet or in a catalog. The list price acts as a beginning point from which trade, quantity, and cash discounts are deducted. Thus, the actual (net) price paid by an industrial customer is the list price less the discount(s). When a list price is used, an industrial marketer sometimes specifies the price in terms of list price times a multiplier. For example, the price of an item might be quoted as "list price × .78," which means the seller is discounting the item so that the buyer can purchase the product at 78 percent of the list price. Simply changing the multiplier allows the seller to revise prices without having to issue new catalogs or price sheets.

With **bid pricing,** prices are determined through sealed bids or open bids. When a buyer uses sealed bids, sellers are notified that they are to submit their bids by a certain date. Usually, the lowest bidder is awarded the contract, providing the buyer believes the firm is capable of supplying the specified products when and where needed. Under an open bidding approach, several but not all sellers are asked to submit bids. This differs from sealed bidding in that the amounts of the bids are not made public. Finally, an industrial purchaser sometimes uses negotiated bids. Under this arrangement, the customer seeks bids from a number of sellers, screens the bids, and then negotiates the price and terms of sale with the most favorable bidders until a final transaction is consummated or until negotiations are terminated with all sellers.

Sometimes, a buyer will be seeking either component parts to be used in production for several years or custom-built equipment to be purchased currently and through future contracts. In such a circumstance, an industrial seller may submit an initial, less profitable bid to win "follow-on" (subsequent) contracts. The seller that wins the initial contract is often substantially favored in the competition for follow-on contracts. In such a bidding situation, an industrial marketer must determine how low the initial bid should be, the probability of winning a follow-on contract, and the combination of bid prices on both the initial and the follow-on contract that will yield an acceptable profit.[23]

For certain types of industrial markets, a seller's pricing component may have to allow for **negotiated pricing.** That is, even when there are stated list prices and discount structures, negotiations may determine the actual price paid by an industrial customer. Negotiated pricing can benefit seller and buyer because price negotiations frequently lead to discussions of product specifications, applications, and perhaps product substitutions. Such negotiations may give the seller an opportunity to provide technical assistance to the customer and perhaps sell a product that better fits the customer's requirements; the final product choice might also be more profitable for the seller. The buyer benefits by gaining more information about the array of products and terms of sale available and may acquire a more suitable product at a lower price.

Some industrial marketers sell in markets in which only one of these general pricing approaches prevails. Such marketers can simplify the price components of their marketing mixes. However, a number of industrial marketers sell to a wide variety of industrial customers and must maintain considerable flexibility

23. Douglas G. Brooks, "Bidding for the Sake of Follow-on Contracts," *Journal of Marketing*, Jan. 1978, p. 35.

in pricing practices. For example, 3M maintains flexibility by selling a variety of tape dispensers at prices that match product benefits (see Figure 20.7).

Summary

Industrial marketing is a set of activities directed at facilitating and expediting exchanges involving industrial products and customers in industrial markets. Industrial markets consist of producers, governments, or institutions that purchase a specific kind of product for direct use in producing other products or for use in day-to-day operations.

Industrial marketers have a considerable amount of information available to them for use in planning their marketing strategies. Much of the available information is based on the Standard Industrial Classification (SIC) system developed by the federal government. This system categorizes businesses into major industry groups, industry subgroups, and detailed industry categories. The SIC system provides industrial marketers with information needed to identify market segments. It can best be used for this purpose in conjunction with other information, such as input-output data. After identifying target industries, the marketer can locate potential customers by using state or commercial industrial directories or by employing a commercial data company. The marketer then must estimate the potential purchases of industrial customers by finding a relationship between a potential customer's purchases and a variable available in published sources.

Like marketers of consumer products, an industrial marketer must develop a marketing mix that satisfies the needs of customers in the industrial target market. The product component frequently emphasizes services since they are often of primary interest to industrial customers. The marketer also must consider that the customer may elect to make the product rather than buy it. Industrial products must meet certain standard specifications desired by industrial users.

The distribution of industrial products differs from that of consumer products in the types of channels used; the kinds of intermediaries available; and transportation, storage, and inventory policies. A direct distribution channel is common in industrial marketing. Industrial marketers also use channels containing manufacturers' agents, industrial distributors, or both. Channels are chosen on the basis of availability, the typical mode of purchase for a product, and several other variables. The primary objective of the physical distribution of industrial products is to ensure that the right products are available when and where needed.

Personal selling is a primary ingredient of the promotional component in industrial marketing mixes. Sales personnel often act as technical advisors both before and after a sale. Advertising sometimes is used to supplement personal selling efforts. Industrial marketers generally use print advertisements containing a larger amount of information but less persuasive content than consumer advertisements. Other promotional activities include catalogs, trade shows, and trade-type sales promotion methods.

The price component for industrial marketing mixes is influenced by legal and economic forces to a greater extent than it is for consumer marketing mixes. Pricing may be affected by competitors' prices as well as by the type of customer who buys the product.

Important Terms

Industrial marketing
Industrial market
Industrial product
Standard Industrial Classification
  (SIC) system
Input-output data

Direct distribution channels
Manufacturers' agent
Industrial distributor
Administered pricing
Bid pricing
Negotiated pricing

Discussion and Review Questions

1. How do industrial products differ from consumer products?
2. What function does the SIC system perform for industrial marketers?
3. List some sources that an industrial marketer can use to determine the names and addresses of potential customers.

4. How do industrial marketing mixes differ from those of consumer products?
5. What are the major advantages and disadvantages of using industrial distributors?
6. Why do industrial marketers rely on personal selling more than consumer products marketers?
7. Why would an industrial marketer spend resources on advertising aimed at stimulating consumer demand?
8. Compare and contrast three methods for determining the price of industrial products.

Cases

Case 20.1 Caterpillar Tractor Company[24]

Caterpillar Tractor Company designs and manufactures products multinationally in two product categories:

Earth moving, construction, and materials handling machinery: track and wheel tractors, track and wheel loaders, lift trucks, pipe layers, motor graders, asphalt and soil compactors, wheel tractor-scrapers, track and wheel excavators, backhoe loaders, track and wheel skidders, log loaders, tree harvesters, off-highway trucks, asphalt and concrete paving machines, asphalt plants, pavement profilers, and related parts and equipment.

Engines: for earth moving and construction machines; on-highway trucks; locomotives, marine, petroleum, agricultural, industrial, and other applications; electric power generation systems; and related parts.

Figure 20.8 shows Caterpillar's worldwide sales broken down by end-use.

After several unprofitable years, Caterpillar has recently been making money. The return to profitability was spurred by higher sales, continued cost reductions, lower nonrecurring charges, greater benefit from inventory reductions, currency exchange gains, and a gain on the sale of one of the company's divisions, Solar's Turbomach. Caterpillar's profit, though, has been a result more of international than domestic success.

In the United States, Caterpillar has been negatively affected by the slowdowns in the oil, natural gas, metals, and agricultural industries. Since industrial demand is derived from the demand for consumer products, decreases in consumer buying in these areas has decreased industrial sales. Growth in the United States has occurred in the construction market. Increased highway spending, more commercial and industrial construction, and continued strength in home building have accounted for this growth. Caterpillar's domestic strategy has been to provide the industrial buyer with a quality product and superior service at a price slightly higher than the competition's. Caterpillar emphasizes the quality of its higher-priced products by focusing on long-term cost effectiveness. This strategy has been helpful in distinguishing Caterpillar from the competition. More recently, however, problems have arisen as Japanese competitors have greatly discounted their prices while at the same time broadening their product

24. Facts are from Caterpillar *1984 and 1985 Annual Reports*; and Michael Rogers, "Updating the Diesel Locomotive," *Fortune*, March 3, 1986, p. 52.

Figure 20.8

Worticwide dealer sales of Caterpillar machines and engines by major end use (*Source: Caterpillar 1985 Annual Report*)

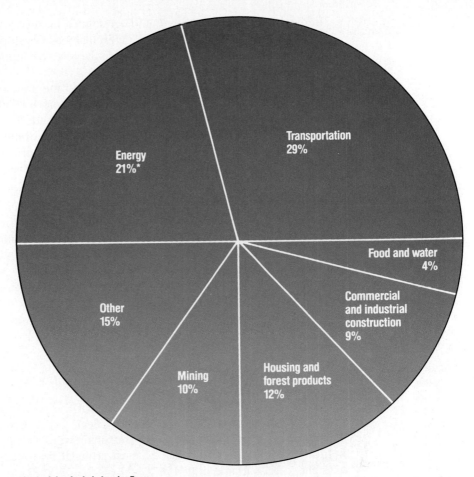

Transportation
29%

Energy
21%*

Food and water
4%

Commercial
and industrial
construction
9%

Other
15%

Housing and
forest products
12%

Mining
10%

*Coal mining included under Energy.

line. Since many industrial contracts are negotiated based on bid pricing, the foreign competition has been able to offer lower bids than Caterpillar could.

Internationally, Caterpillar has opened markets in Turkey, China, and Russia while increasing sales in existing markets—Canada, Australia, Italy, the United Kingdom, and France. In the oil-producing developing countries of the Middle East, once-large sales have declined because of lower oil prices. As a result of loss in government revenues due to the oil industry recession, many developmental construction projects were dropped from Middle Eastern budgets. Industrial sales in South Africa, also, have fallen sharply as a result of the oil recession, high interest rates, and social unrest. In Australia, industrial sales rose as a result of accelerated economic growth and government support of developmental projects. In Canada, sales increased as a result of strong economic growth and improved government attitudes toward business. Canadian industrial sales were especially strong in the areas of housing and highway construction.

One of Caterpillar's most extensively developed industrial sales networks is in China. Sales in China have been increasing as a result of looser restrictions on the import of U.S. goods. Caterpillar China Limited, located in Hong Kong, provides direct sales to industrial buyers and product support to end-users. With the increasing modernization of China, sales of equipment in transportation, mining, energy development, and agriculture have increased dramatically. To show its support for these sales, Caterpillar has developed an on-site service facility in China for one of the world's largest coal mines, where more than eighty Caterpillar machines are working.

Because of moderate industry growth and the availability of new products and marketing strategies designed to capture more of the available business, Caterpillar expects to continue its upward sales trends. In developing its product mix, Caterpillar has continued to place a strong emphasis on high product quality and diverse customer services. As it has historically, this strong service orientation still helps to differentiate Caterpillar from its competitors.

Questions for Discussion

1. Specify some characteristics of the industrial demand for Caterpillar products?
2. With increased competition from low-cost foreign competitors, what strategy would you recommend to Caterpillar for maintenance or growth of their market share?
3. Describe Caterpillar's strengths or particular competencies as an industrial product manufacturer.
4. Would you suggest that Caterpillar harvest or divest any specific business categories? Evaluate international trends.

Case 20.2   NutraSweet[25]

NutraSweet is G.D. Searle's brand name for the new sweetener aspartame. It is an artificial sweetener produced by Searle, a pharmaceutical company. It tastes like sugar, looks like sugar, contains fewer calories than sugar, but does not have the bitter aftertaste of most artificial sweeteners. Searle has patent rights on aspartame until 1987.

NutraSweet is made from a combination of two amino acids. It is a highly concentrated sweetener—200 times sweeter than sugar and 6 times sweeter than cyclamate. NutraSweet contains no sodium, and it is not a carbohydrate. It can easily be used by diabetics, and it can also be used safely by pregnant women. Although it is a sweetener, it does not promote tooth decay. Compared with sugar, NutraSweet's only shortcomings are that it does not hold together under high heat and cannot be used as a thickening agent the way sugar can.

Approved by the FDA in 1981, NutraSweet is an industrial product found in a variety of food products normally containing sugar or sugar substitutes. Products using NutraSweet can be reduced in calories by about 95 percent. Moreover, the sweetener can extend a product's shelf life and enhance certain fruit flavors. NutraSweet currently is found in the following product categories:

Beverages: Diet Pepsi, Diet Coke, Hires Root Beer, Orange Crush, Diet 7Up, Diet Squirt, RC Cola, Dad's Root Beer, Sugar Free Dr Pepper
Beverage Mixes: Lipton's Ice Tea Mix, Swiss Miss and Carnation cocoa mixes, Ovaltine, Alba, Kool-Aid, Crystal Light, Wyler's Drink Mix

25. The information in this case is from Gene Bylinski, "The Battle for America's Sweet Tooth," *Fortune,* July 26, 1982, pp. 28–32; "NutraSweet Fact Sheet," *Advertising Age,* May 9, 1983, p. M-21; "NutraSweet: What It Is and What It Isn't," Searle Food Resources, Inc., 1983; Jayne Pearly, "Technology," *Forbes,* Nov. 7, 1983, pp. 256–258; and "It's Sugar, Alright, But It's Not Fattening," *Fortune,* Dec. 9, 1985, p. 117.

Candies: Wrigley's peppermint gum, Wrigley's spearmint gum
Cereal: Halfsies
Desserts: Whipped toppings, Shimmer, D-Zerta gelatin mix

All products that contain aspartame must display the NutraSweet name and logo.

Thus far, Searle's marketing efforts have been effective. The firm promoted NutraSweet, an industrial product, to a consumer market. Searle spent $1 million on consumer advertising using the theme, "Introducing NutraSweet— You can't buy it, but you're gonna love it." Searle advertised both on TV and in magazines. To demonstrate the excellent taste of NutraSweet, the company used direct mail to provide free samples of gumdrops sweetened with NutraSweet to a large number of consumers. Trial of the gumdrops was encouraged through television commercials.

Searle sells NutraSweet for $90 a pound, which is more than 20 times the price of saccharine. The price is expected to decline, perhaps to as low as $40 a pound by 1990. Despite NutraSweet's high price, it is faring quite well in the market. Searle's biggest challenge so far has been how to meet the rising demand for the product.

Searle is not the only firm committing itself to the industrial artificial sweetener market. Research and development are still the key for success in this highly competitive market. For example, Biospherics has completed testing a product called L-Sugars that resembles regular sugar in almost every way, especially taste, but cannot be metabolized and has no calories. Taste tests at Purdue University indicate that L-Sugars is indistinguishable from regular sugar. Unlike aspartame and saccharine, L-Sugars looks, handles, and cooks like regular sugar and browns naturally when baked. Biospherics must perform large-scale tests for FDA approval and carry out multigeneration tests of animals to prove that L-Sugars does not cause cancer, birth defects, or other problems. If the product works out, Biospherics will be able to tap into the $900-million a year diet sweetener market, selling its product to companies that produce chewing gum, baking products, drugs, cereals, and soft drinks.

Questions for Discussion

1. Why is NutraSweet considered to be an industrial product? What type of industrial product is NutraSweet?
2. Why did Searle promote NutraSweet to consumers when the average consumer cannot buy even a pound of NutraSweet?
3. Why is Searle able to charge a price that appears to be so much higher than the prices for competing products?
4. How should Searle deal with future competitive products such as L-Sugars?

21 / Services and Nonbusiness Marketing

Objectives

- To understand the nature and characteristics of services.

- To classify services.

- To understand the development of strategies for services.

- To explore the concept of marketing in nonbusiness situations.

- To understand the development of marketing strategies in nonbusiness organizations.

- To describe methods for controlling nonbusiness marketing activities.

Figure 21.1

A U.S. Postal Service advertisement for its Express Mail service (Source: Reprinted with the permission of the United States Postal Service)

The United States Postal Service is a nonprofit service organization with 740,000 employees. In 1985 it delivered 140 billion pieces of mail, a volume that increases by an annual 6.5 percent. Labor costs average $19 per worker and take an 83-cent bite out of every revenue dollar.[1] Besides a mounting workload and labor costs, the organization must respond to changes in the marketplace, such as setting up new mail carriers for routes that commercial airlines dropped after deregulation or handling a new deluge of mail after newspapers and magazines were injected into the first-class mail stream. Moreover, the nation's mail-delivery system must counter fierce competition from private carriers of packages, letters, and electronic mail.

In face of these pressures, the quality of service and market share of the Postal Service has eroded. Its next-day-delivery Express Mail letters (illustrated in Figure 21.1) have only a 90-percent on-time arrival rate, com-

1. "New Broom for Postal Service Cobwebs," *U.S. News and World Report*, Jan. 20, 1986, p. 8.

pared to the 99-percent rate of some private companies.[2]
Customers opting for the most reliable carrier are ship-
ping 70 percent of their parcels by United Parcel Service
and 40 percent of their overnight letters via Federal
Express.

   The effectiveness of the Postal Service has been
impeded by deep-seated bureaucracy, inefficient opera-
tions, short-sighted management that has been too
sluggish in automating mail-sorting and other tasks, and
an inability to stem the stamp and money-order tamper-
ing that results in heavy annual losses.

   Marketing strategies could be helpful in improving
the productivity of the Postal Service. For example, a new
strategy could be developed for handling first- and third-
class mail, which carry different price tags, meet the
needs of different target markets, and yet move through
the system at almost the same rate. Marketing could also
be the answer to revamping the tarnished image of the
Postal Service by touting such lesser-known offerings as
Stamps by Mail—the free delivery of rolls or books of
stamps as well as stamped envelopes.[3]

This chapter presents concepts that apply to marketing in organizations dealing primarily with services and nonbusiness activities. These two areas overlap in that most nonprofit marketing is concerned with services such as education, health care, and government. On the other hand, services marketing also involves for-profit areas like finance, personal services, and professional services.

   The chapter first discusses the growing importance of service industries in our economy. Second, it addresses the unique characteristics of services and the problems they present to marketers. Next, various classification schemes are presented that can help service marketers develop marketing strategy. Additionally, a variety of marketing mix considerations are discussed. Next, the chapter discusses nonbusiness marketing. We define nonbusiness marketing and then examine the development of nonbusiness marketing strategies and the control of nonbusiness marketing activities.

The Nature and Characteristics of Services

The product concept refers to a physical good, a service, an idea, or any combination of these three. As mentioned in Chapter 7, all products, whether they are goods or not, possess a certain amount of intangibility. Goods are those tangible products that consumers can physically possess. A service is the result of applying human or mechanical efforts to people or objects. Services are intangible products involving a deed, a performance, or an effort that cannot

---

2. "Can U.S. Postal Service Lick Its Troubles?" *U.S. News and World Report*, Dec. 16, 1985, p. 54.
3. "Order Stamps by Mail," *U.S. News and World Report*, Dec. 23, 1985, p. 61.

Goods (tangible) — Flour, Jewelry, Clothing, Automobiles/Maintenance, Fast Food Restaurants, Airlines, Financial Services, Health Care, Telephone Services, Education — Services (intangible)

Figure 21.2 A continuum of product tangibility and intangibility

be physically possessed.[4] We should note that few products can be classified as a pure good or a pure service. Consider, for example, an automobile. When consumers purchase a car, they take ownership of a physical item that provides transportation, but the warranty associated with the purchase is a service. When consumers rent a car, they purchase a transportation service that is provided through temporary use of an automobile. Most products, like automobiles and automobile rentals, contain both tangible and intangible components. One component, however, will dominate. It is this dominant component that leads to the classification of goods, services, and ideas.

Figure 21.2 illustrates the tangibility concept by placing a variety of products on a continuum of tangibility and intangibility. Tangible-dominant products are typically classified as goods, while intangible-dominant products are typically considered services. Thus, **services** are defined as intangible-dominant products that cannot be physically possessed.

Growth and Importance of Services

The increasing importance of services in the U.S. economy has led many to call this country the world's first service economy. Today, service industries account for approximately 60 percent of our gross national product, almost 50 percent of U.S. consumer expenditures, and two-thirds of private sector employment.[5] An audit of *Forbes* 500 largest companies reveals that 150 are service organizations. Many of the other 350 largest firms derive substantial resources from subsidiaries in service industries.[6] Comparing *Fortune*'s top 500 service firms to the top 500 industrial firms reveals that net income for the service firms is greater than net income for the industrial firms.[7] Projections through 1990 predict that services will continue to grow in terms of consumer expenditures and employment. Companies in service industries are struggling to fill entry-level jobs. The supply of workers is shrinking as the demand for new employees increases.[8]

One major catalyst to the growth in consumer services has been the general economic prosperity of the United States. This prosperity has led to a growth in financial services, travel, entertainment, and personal care. Lifestyle changes

4. Leonard L. Berry, "Services Marketing Is Different," *Business Horizons*, May–June 1980, pp. 24–29.
5. Bureau of Economic Analysis, U.S. Commerce Department, 1982.
6. Gregory D. Upah, "The Explosion and Interest in Services Marketing," *Services Marketing Newsletter*, American Marketing Association, Fall 1984, p. 1.
7. "The Fortune Service 500," *Fortune*, June 10, 1985, pp. 166–196; and "The Fortune 500," *Fortune*, April 29, 1985, pp. 252–286.
8. Sylvia Nasav, "Jobs Go Begging at the Bottom," *Fortune*, March 17, 1986, p. 33.

have likewise encouraged expansion of the service sector. In the last thirty-five years, the number of women in the work force has more than doubled. With approximately 68 percent of the women between the ages of eighteen and thirty-four now working, the need for child care, domestic services, and other time-saving services has increased. Consumers want to avoid tasks like house cleaning, home maintenance, and tax preparation. Therefore, franchise operations like Merry Maid, Chemlawn, and H & R Block have experienced rapid growth. Americans are becoming more fitness and recreation oriented. Thus, the demand for fitness and recreational facilities has escalated. In terms of demographics, the U.S. population is growing older. This change has promoted tremendous expansion of health-care services. Finally, the number and complexity of goods needing servicing have increased demand for repair services.

Not only have consumer services grown in our economy; business services have prospered as well. Business or industrial services include repairs and maintenance, consulting, installation, equipment leasing, marketing research, advertising, temporary office personnel, overnight mail service, and janitorial services, to name a few. It is believed that expenditures for business and industrial services have grown even faster than consumer services. This growth has been attributed to the increasingly complex, specialized, and competitive business environment.

Characteristics of Services

The problems of service marketing are not the same as those of goods marketing. To understand these unique problems, it is first necessary to understand the distinguishing characteristics of services. Services have four basic characteristics: (1) intangibility, (2) inseparability of production and consumption, (3) perishability, and (4) heterogeneity.[9] These characteristics and the marketing problems they entail are summarized in Table 21.1.

Intangibility stems from the fact that services are performances. They cannot be seen, touched, tasted, or smelled, nor can they be possessed. Intangibility also relates to the difficulty that consumers may have in understanding service offerings.[10] Services have few tangible attributes, called **search qualities,** that can be viewed prior to purchase. When consumers cannot view a product in advance and examine its properties, they may not understand exactly what is being offered. And even when consumers gain sufficient knowledge about service offerings, they may not be able to evaluate the possible alternatives. On the other hand, services are rich in experience and credence qualities. **Experience qualities** are those qualities that can be assessed only after purchase and consumption (satisfaction, courtesy, and the like). **Credence qualities** are those qualities that cannot be assessed even after purchase and consumption.[11] An appendix operation is an example of a service high in credence qualities. How many consumers are knowledgeable enough to assess the quality of an

9. Valarie A. Zeithaml, A. Parasuraman, and Leonard L. Berry, "Problems and Strategies in Services Marketing," *Journal of Marketing*, Spring 1985, pp. 33–46.
10. John E. G. Bateson, "Why We Need Service Marketing," in *Conceptual and Theoretical Developments in Marketing*, eds. O. C. Ferrell, S. W. Brown, and C. W. Lamb, Jr. (Chicago: American Marketing Association, 1979), pp. 131–146.
11. Valarie A. Zeithaml, "How Consumer Evaluation Processes Differ between Goods and Services," in *Marketing of Services*, eds. James H. Donnelly and William R. George (Chicago: American Marketing Association, 1981), pp. 186–190.

Table 21.1 *Service characteristics and marketing problems*

Unique Service Features	Resulting Marketing Problems
Intangibility	Cannot be stored
	Cannot be protected through patents
	Cannot be readily displayed or communicated
	Prices are difficult to set
Inseparability	Consumer is involved in production
	Other consumers are involved in production
	Centralized mass production is difficult
Perishability	Services cannot be inventoried
Heterogeneity	Standardization and quality are difficult to control

Source: Valarie A. Zeithaml, A. Parasuraman, Leonard L. Berry, "Problems and Strategies in Services Marketing," *Journal of Marketing,* Spring 1985, pp. 33–46. Used by permission of the American Marketing Association.

appendectomy, even after it has been performed? In summary, it is difficult to go into a store, examine a service, purchase it, and take it home with you.

Related to intangibility is **inseparability** of production and consumption. Services are normally produced at the same time they are consumed. A medical examination is an example of concurrent production and consumption. In fact, the doctor cannot possibly perform the service without the patient's presence, and the consumer is actually involved in the production process. With other services, such as air travel, many consumers are simultaneously involved in production. Due to high consumer involvement in most services, standardization and control are difficult to maintain.

Because production and consumption are simultaneous, services are also characterized by **perishability.** In other words, unused capacity in one time period cannot be stockpiled or inventoried for future time periods. Consider medical examinations again. A doctor may have eight hours per day to see patients. On Monday the doctor may see only two patients for thirty minutes each, leaving seven hours of unused capacity. On Tuesday, the doctor has twenty patients requesting his or her services, each requiring thirty minutes. Since the doctor can see only sixteen patients per day, Tuesday's demand exceeds the doctor's capacity. Unfortunately, the seven hours of excess time on Monday cannot be stockpiled for use on Tuesday when demand is high. This illustrates how service perishability presents problems very different from the supply and demand problems encountered in the marketing of goods.[12]

12. Leonard L. Berry, Valarie A. Zeithaml, and A. Parasuraman, "Responding to Demand Fluctuations: Key Challenge for Service Businesses," in *AMA Educators Proceedings*, eds. Russell Belk, et al. (Chicago: American Marketing Association, 1984), pp. 231–234.

One airline offers a higher level of service, even on the ground.

See your Travel Agent.

Lufthansa
German Airlines

Finally, because most services are labor intensive, they are susceptible to **heterogeneity.** People typically perform services, and people are not always consistent in their performance. There may be variation from one service to another within the same organization or variation in the service provided by a single individual from day to day and from customer to customer. Thus, standardization and quality are extremely difficult to control.

Classification of Services

There is a general body of knowledge concerning the marketing of all products—the marketing concept, target markets, the four marketing mix components, and marketing strategy. This general knowledge, however, must be adjusted in strategy development to the very wide diversity and the unique nature of products. Thus, product classification schemes have been developed to help marketers in the development of a specific marketing strategy. All products, including services, can be classified as consumer or industrial; durables or nondurables; and convenience, shopping, or specialty products.

Services are a very diverse group of products, and an organization may provide more than one kind. For example, in Figure 21.3, Lufthansa, a German airline, promotes not only airline service but also a ground service. Services

Table 21.2 *Classification of services*

Category	Examples
Type of Market	
Consumer	Repairs, child care, legal counsel
Industrial	Consulting, lawn care, installation
Degree of Labor Intensiveness	
Labor based	Repairs, education, hair cuts
Equipment based	Telecommunications, health spas, public transportation
Degree of Customer Contact	
High contact	Health care, hotels, air travel
Low contact	Repairs, dry cleaning, postal service
Skill of the Service Provider	
Professional	Legal counsel, health care, accounting services
Nonprofessional	Air travel, dry cleaning, public transportation
Goal of the Service Provider	
Profit	Financial services, insurance, health care
Nonprofit	Health care, education, government

encompass such industries as car rentals, repairs, health care, barber shops, health spas, amusement parks, day care, domestic services, legal counsel, banking, insurance, air travel, education, business consulting, dry cleaning, and accounting. Nevertheless, services can be meaningfully analyzed by means of a five-category classification scheme. The five categories are (1) type of market, (2) degree of labor intensiveness, (3) degree of customer contact, (4) skill of the service provider, and (5) goal of the service provider. This scheme is summarized in Table 21.2.

Services can be viewed in terms of the market or type of customer they serve—consumer or industrial. The implications of this distinction are very similar to those for all products and will not be discussed here. A second way to classify services is by degree of labor intensiveness. Many services such as repairs, education, and hair care rely heavily upon human labor. Others such as telecommunications, health spas, and public transportation are more equipment intensive. The mutual-fund industry relies on computer technologies to facilitate handling daily transactions. Use of computer technologies has enabled mutual-fund companies to improve service and expand offerings. For example, Fidelity Investments has $40 billion in assets, 2 million customers, and offers twenty-four-hour service. Customers can call anytime to check fund prices or to move money between funds. The firm logs an average of 1,700 calls a night between midnight and 4:00 A.M.[13] For many mutual-fund customers, the service they receive is just as important as the performance of their funds.

13. "The People's Choice: Mutual Funds," *Business Week*, Feb. 24, 1986, p. 56.

Labor, or people-based services are more susceptible to heterogeneity than are most equipment-based services. Marketers of people-based services must recognize that the service providers are often viewed as the service itself. Therefore, strategies relating to selecting, training, motivating, and controlling employees are extremely important.

The third way in which services can be classified is in terms of customer contact. High-contact services include health care, hotels, real estate agencies, and restaurants. Low-contact services include repairs, movie theaters, dry cleaning, and spectator sports.[14] Note that high-contact services generally involve actions directed toward individuals. Since these services are directed at people, the consumer must be present during production. Although it is sometimes possible for the service provider to go to the consumer, high-contact services typically require the consumer to go to the production facility. Thus, the physical appearance of the facility may be a major component of the consumer's overall evaluation of the service. Since the consumer must be present during production of high-contact service, the process of production may be just as important as the final outcome of the production process. Low-contact service commonly involves actions directed at things. Consequently, the consumer is usually not required to be present during service delivery. The consumer's presence, however, may be required to initiate or terminate the service. The appearance of the production facilities and the interpersonal skills of actual service providers are thus not as critical in low-contact services as they are in high-contact services.[15]

Skill of the service provider is a fourth way to classify services. Professional services tend to be more complex and more highly regulated than nonprofessional services. In the case of legal counsel, for example, consumers often do not know what the actual service will involve or its cost until the service is completed. This is true because the final product is very situation specific. Additionally, attorneys are regulated by both the law and by professional associations.

Finally, services can be classified according to the goal of the service provider—profit or nonprofit. The second half of this chapter examines nonbusiness marketing. Most nonbusiness organizations provide services rather than goods.

Developing Marketing Strategies for Services

Before we discuss the development of a marketing mix for service firms, one major point needs to be made: the marketing concept is equally applicable to goods, services, and ideas. Thus, service marketers, like goods marketers, must strive to provide a bundle of benefits that satisfies the needs of consumers.[16] Table 21.3 illustrates alternative benefits derived from services grouped according to process and results.

14. Christopher H. Lovelock, "Classifying Services to Gain Strategic Marketing Insights," *Journal of Marketing*, Summer 1983, p. 15.
15. Christopher H. Lovelock, *Services Marketing* (Englewood Cliffs, N.J.: Prentice-Hall, 1984), pp. 49–64.
16. Ben M. Enis and Kenneth J. Roering, "Services Marketing: Different Products, Similar Strategy," in *Marketing of Services*, eds. J. H. Donnelly and W. R. George (Chicago: American Marketing Association, 1981), pp. 1–4.

Table 21.3 *Alternative benefits derived from services*

Type of Benefit	Example
Process Benefits	
Related to personal interaction	Loans and counseling
	Relaxation and pleasure
	Expert advice
Related to facilities, operations	Easy access
	Speed of service
	Care and attention
Results Benefits	Improved appearance
	Ease of care
	Convenience

Source: Kathleen A. Krentler and Joseph P. Guiltinan, "Strategies for Tangibilizing Retail Services: An Assessment," *Journal of the Academy of Marketing Science,* Fall 1984, p. 80. Used by permission.

The development phase, including defining target markets and finalizing a marketing mix, is a basic requirement of any marketing strategy. The application on page 636 illustrates some creative ideas that can be used in the development of a marketing strategy. In the following sections we discuss some of the unique requirements for finalizing a services marketing strategy.

Product

Goods can be defined in terms of their physical attributes, but services cannot be because they are intangible. As we point out earlier in the chapter, it is often difficult for consumers to understand service offerings and to evaluate possible service alternatives. For example, in the health-care industry, companies that can standardize a service and market it more effectively than other providers are most successful. With Medicare putting a limit on what it will pay for specific illnesses, health-care providers also have to maintain cost control to provide service at a profitable level. Therefore, health-care providers must understand their target markets and provide services that are needed and cost effective.[17]

There may also, though, be tangibles (such as facilities, employees, or communications) associated with a service. These tangible elements help to form a part of the product and are often the only aspects of a service that can be viewed prior to purchase. For this reason, marketers must pay close attention to associated tangibles and make sure that they are consistent with the selected image of the service product.[18]

The service product is often equated with the service provider. Thus, for example, does the teller or the beautician become the service provided by a bank or a beauty parlor. Because consumers tend to view services in terms of the service personnel and because personnel are inconsistent in their behavior,

17. Ann B. Fisher, "Who Prospers Next in Health Care," *Fortune,* Feb. 17, 1986, pp. 105–106.
18. G. Lynn Shostack, "Breaking Free from Product Marketing," *Journal of Marketing,* April 1977, pp. 73–80.

Application

Seven Ideas for Service Marketing Success

According to Leonard Berry, American Marketing Association president and Foley's Federated Professor of Retailing and Marketing Studies at Texas A&M University, service marketers can be more effective if they pay attention to seven anchor ideas.

1. Distinguish between the marketing department and the marketing function. The marketing department in a service organization should not be isolated. Everyone in the organization should be practicing marketing. Employees should be educated about the concept, purposes, and applications of marketing; it is up to the marketing department to push marketing responsibility down into the organization.

2. Leverage the freedom factor. Giving customers what they want is marketing's oldest and most important tenet, but unfortunately service organizations often maintain strict sets of rules concerning the handling of specific transactions, making the service too inflexible. A service organization's management has to examine to what extent policies and procedures tie the hands of contact personnel. Firms should also look at symbolic messages that govern the behavior of customers and employees. For example, at Disney theme parks customers are called "guests" and employees "hosts."

3. Market to employees. Service firms must first satisfy the wants and needs of their internal customers, that is, their employees. Employees can make or break the service organization. Firms can use marketing research to better understand internal customers, just as they use it to understand external customers. They can segment employee markets just as they do consumer or business markets, and they can use advertising campaigns to involve, teach, and inspire internal audiences.

4. Market to existing customers. This builds sales volume and prevents a loss of customers. Good services marketing requires selling after customers become customers, not just before. Companies should stay in touch with customers, periodically thank them for their business, reward their best customers with price discounts and service extras, and be responsive when customers have special needs.

5. Be skillful at problem resolution. Service firms that solve problems quickly and competently are more likely to repair damage to their reputation than firms that take a casual, "we'll do it when we can" attitude.

6. Think high tech and high touch. High technology can lower service delivery costs, speed up delivery, control quality, and free up personnel to provide more and better services. High-touch capabilities can mean more-customized service, superior problem resolution, effective selling, and greater confidence in technology.

7. Be a power brander. Power branders have four characteristics. The company brands are distinctive, communicate the company's reason for being, evoke concrete vision, and are tightly linked to the services provided and to the overall company brand. For example, packaged-goods consumers buy Tide rather than Procter & Gamble. Service customers, on the other hand, often buy H & R Block or Merrill Lynch rather than a specific brand of service. This is why power branding is so important for service organizations. (*Source: Leonard Berry, "Services Marketers Can Find Success in 7 Ideas,"* Marketing News, *Dec. 6, 1985, pp. 1, 8. Reprinted from* Marketing News, *published by the American Marketing Association.*)

Figure 21.4

Complexity/variability grid for medical services (Source: Adapted from Lynn Shostack, 1985. American Marketing Association Faculty Consortium on Services Marketing, Texas A&M University, July 7–11)

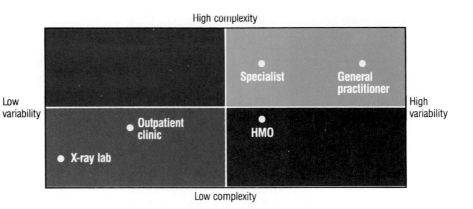

it is imperative that marketers effectively select, train, motivate, and control contact people. Service marketers are selling long-term relationships as well as performance.

After testing many variables, the Strategic Planning Institute (SPI), in Cambridge, Massachusetts, has developed an extensive data base on the impact of various business strategies on profits. The institute has found that "relative perceived product quality" is the single most important factor in determining long-term profitability. The strength or weakness of service provided often impacts upon consumers' perceptions of product quality. Of the companies in the SPI data base, businesses that rate low on service lose market share at the rate of 2 percent a year and average a 1-percent return on sales. Companies that score high on service gain market share at the rate of 6 percent a year, average a 12-percent return on sales, and charge a significantly higher price.[19] This indicates that firms having service-dominant products must score high on service quality.

Other product concepts discussed in Chapters 7 and 8 are also relevant here. Management must make decisions regarding the product mix, positioning, branding, and new-product development. Marketers can make better decisions if they analyze their service products in terms of complexity and variability. Complexity is determined by the number of steps required to perform the service, and variability is determined by the number of decisions required of service workers or the ability to customize.[20] An examination of the complete service delivery process, including the number of steps and the number of decisions, will allow marketers to plot their service product on a complexity/variability grid like that shown in Figure 21.4. The position of a service on the grid will have implications for its positioning in the market. Furthermore, any alterations in the service delivery process that shift the position of the service on the complexity/variability grid will have an impact on the positioning of the service in the marketplace. The effects of such changes are detailed in Table 21.4. When structuring the service delivery system, marketers should explicitly consider the firm's marketing goals and target market.

19. Tom Peters, "More Expensive, But Worth It," *U.S. News and World Report*, Feb. 3, 1986, p. 54.
20. G. Lynn Shostack, 1985 American Marketing Association Faculty Consortium on Services Marketing, Texas A&M University, July 7–11.

Table 21.4 *Effects of shifting positions on the complexity/variability grid*

Downshifting Complexity/Variability	Upshifting Complexity/Variability
Standardizes the service	Increases costs
Requires strict operating controls	Indicates higher-margin/lower-volume strategy
Generally widens potential market	Personalizes the service
Lowers costs	Generally narrows potential market
Indicates lower-margin/higher-volume strategy	Makes quality more difficult to control
Can alienate existing markets	

Source: Adapted from G. Lynn Shostack, 1985 American Marketing Association Faculty Consortium on Services Marketing, Texas A&M University, July 7–11.

Promotion

As intangible-dominant products, services are not easily advertised. The intangible is difficult to depict in advertising, whether the medium is print, television, or radio. Service advertising should thus emphasize tangible cues that will help consumers understand and evaluate the service. The cues may be the physical facilities in which the service is performed or some relevant tangible object that symbolizes the service itself.[21] For example, restaurants may stress their physical facilities—clean, elegant, casual, and so on—to provide cues as to the quality or nature of the service. Insurance firms such as Allstate and Travelers employ objects as symbols to help consumers understand their service. Outstretched hands ("You're in good hands with Allstate") symbolize security, while the "Travelers Umbrella" suggests the protection provided by Travelers' insurance plans. Citibank, as illustrated in Figure 21.5, parallels the freshness of strawberries with the timeliness and fullness of its financial information and services.

Customer contact personnel are an important secondary audience for service advertising. We have seen that variability in service quality, which arises from the labor-intensive nature of many services, is a problem for service marketers. We have also seen that consumers often associate the service with the service provider. Advertising can have a positive effect on customer contact personnel. It can shape employees' perceptions of the company, their job, and how management expects them to perform, and it can be a tool for motivating, educating, and communicating with employees.[22]

Personal selling is potentially powerful in services since this form of promotion allows consumers and salespeople to interact. When consumers enter into a service transaction, they must, as a general rule, interact with service firm employees. Customer contact personnel can be trained to use this opportunity to reduce customer uncertainty, give reassurance, reduce dissonance, and promote the reputation of the organization.[23] Once again, this emphasizes the importance of properly managing contact personnel.

21. William R. George and Leonard L. Berry, "Guidelines for the Advertising of Services," *Business Horizons*, July–Aug. 1981, pp. 52–56.
22. George and Berry, "Guidelines," pp. 55–70.
23. William R. George and J. Patrick Kelly, "The Promotion and Selling of Services," *Business*, July–Sept. 1983, pp. 14–20.

Fresh daily.

Timely information.
Lets you study your options
and get into markets earlier.

100% early notification.
Know your company's cash position
by 11 A.M. Eastern Time.

Controlled disbursement.
Lets you pinpoint your exact
cash outlays every day.

Zero-balance account.
No idle or excess balances.

Flexible options.
Notification by phone or terminal,
on-line stops, float summary reports,
automatic funding, sub-accounts and more.

Citibank's commitment.
Our $12 million facility
in Delaware is devoted exclusively
to corporate cash management
banking services.

Personal service.
Your own Citibank customer
service representative.

More information.
Contact your local Citibanker.

With CitiDisbursement, you can put
your company's cash into action with the freshest
information in controlled disbursement.

CITIBANK◆CITICORP®
Cash management information
and the power to act on it.

Although consumer service firms have the opportunity to interact with actual customers and those potential customers who contact them, they have little opportunity to go out into the field and solicit business from all potential consumers. The very large number of potential customers and the high cost per sales call rules out such efforts. On the other hand, marketers of industrial services, like the marketers of industrial goods, are dealing with a much more limited target market and may find personal selling to be the most effective way of reaching customers.

Sales promotions, such as contests, are feasible for service firms, but other types of promotions are more difficult to implement. How do you display a service? How do you give a free sample without giving away the whole service? Possibly a visit to a health club or a free skiing lesson could be considered a free sample.

Although the role of publicity and the implementation of a publicity campaign do not differ significantly in the goods and services sectors, service marketers appear to rely on publicity much more than goods marketers do.[24] Consider, for example, the use of publicity by the provider of a "Fun in the Sun" cruise to Mexico or Jamaica. The provider could use senior citizen groups to get the word out about the tour. Hospitals and other health-care providers use consumer education programs and health fairs as a major component in their promotion mix. In fact, certain segments of the service sector have made publicity the single communications medium.[25]

Consumers tend to value word-of-mouth communications more than company-sponsored communications. This preference is probably true for all products but is especially true for services since they are experiential in nature. For this reason, service firms should attempt to stimulate and to simulate word-of-mouth communications.[26] Word-of-mouth can be stimulated by encouraging consumers to tell their friends about satisfactory performance. Many firms, for instance, prominently display signs urging customers to tell their friends if they like the service and to tell the firm if they don't. Word-of-mouth can be simulated through communications messages that use a testimonial type of format, for example, television advertisements featuring consumers who vouch for the benefits of a service offered by a particular firm.

One final note should be made in regard to service promotion. The promotional activities of most professional service providers such as doctors, lawyers, and CPAs are severely restricted. Until recently, all of these professionals were prohibited by law from advertising. Although restrictions have now been lifted, there are still many obstacles to be overcome. Not used to seeing professionals advertise, consumers may reject advertisements for those who do. Furthermore, professionals are not familiar with advertising and consequently do not always develop advertisements appropriate for their services. Finally, the professions themselves exert pressure on their members not to advertise or promote, since such activities are still viewed as highly unprofessional.

Price

Price plays both an economic and a psychological role in the service sector, just as it does with physical goods. However, the psychological role of price in respect to services is magnified somewhat because consumers must rely on price as the sole indicator of service quality when other quality indicators are absent. In its economic role, price determines revenue and influences profits.

As noted in Table 21.1, service intangibility may complicate the setting of prices. When pricing physical goods, management can look to the cost of production (direct and indirect materials, direct and indirect labor, and overhead) as an indicator of price. It is often difficult, however, to determine the cost of service provision and thus to identify a minimum price. Price competition is severe in many service areas characterized by standardization. Usually price is not a key variable when marketing is first implemented in an organization. Once market segmentation and specialized services are directed to specific

24. John M. Rathmell, *Marketing in the Services Sector* (Cambridge, Mass.: Winthrop, 1974), p. 100.
25. Ibid.
26. George and Kelly, "Promotion and Selling," pp. 14–20; and George and Berry, "Guidelines," pp. 55–70.

markets, specialized prices are set. Next comes comparative pricing as the service becomes fairly standardized. Price competition is quite common in legal services related to divorce and bankruptcy, in long-distance phone service, and in airline transportation.[27]

Many services, especially professional services, are very situation specific. Thus, neither the service firm nor the consumer knows the extent of the service prior to production and consumption. Once again, since cost is not known beforehand, price is difficult to set. Despite the difficulties in determining cost, many service firms use cost-plus pricing. Others set prices according to the competition or based on market demand. For example, Curtis Mathes Corporation sells televisions and video recorders at up to a 30-percent price premium. Curtis Mathes is growing fast and its franchisees are highly profitable because the company stands behind its products. Service before and after the sale is the key to the success of the Curtis Mathes pricing policy.[28]

Pricing of services can also help to smooth fluctuations in demand. Given the perishability of service products, this is an important function. A higher price may be used to deter demand during peak periods, while a lower price may be used to stimulate demand during slack periods. Airlines rely heavily on price to help smooth their demand, as do many bars, movie theaters, and hotels.

Distribution

Almost by definition, service industries are limited to direct channels of distribution. Many services are produced and consumed simultaneously; for high-contact services in particular, service providers and consumers cannot be separated. With low-contact services, however, service facilities and service providers may be separated from retail outlets.[29] Dry cleaners, for example, generally maintain strategically located retail stores. These stores, which may be independent or corporate owned, are simply drop-off centers. Consumers go to the retail store to initiate and terminate service, while the actual service is performed at a different location. The separation is possible because the service is directed toward the consumer's physical possessions and because the consumer is not required to be present during service delivery.

Other service industries are developing unique ways to distribute their services. Airlines, car rental companies, and hotels have long used intermediaries to make it more convenient for consumers to obtain their services. The intermediaries are the travel agencies who handle reservations. Automated teller machines (ATMs) have provided a new electronic means of distribution for financial services. Consumers no longer must go to their bank for routine transactions but can now receive service from the closest ATM. Bank credit cards have enabled banks to extend their credit services to consumers over widely dispersed geographic areas through a nationwide network of intermediaries, namely, the retail merchants who assist consumers in applying for and using the cards.

27. Stephen W. Brown, "New Patterns Are Emerging in Service Marketing Sector," *Marketing News*, June 7, 1985, p. 2.
28. Peters, "More Expensive," p. 54.
29. Richard B. Chase, "Where Does the Customer Fit in a Service Operation?" *Harvard Business Review*, Nov.–Dec. 1978, pp. 137–142.

In the service context, *distribution* refers to making services available to prospective users. *Marketing intermediary* refers to the entities between the actual service provider and the consumer that make the service more available and more convenient to use.[30] The distribution of services is very closely related to product development. Indirect distribution of services may be made possible by a tangible representation or a facilitating good (for example, a bank credit card).[31]

Strategic Considerations

The basic concept of services marketing—identical to that of any type of marketing—is to provide customers with benefits that satisfy their needs. In other words, the marketer must develop the right service for the right people at the right price and at the right place. The marketer must also communicate with consumers so that they are aware of the need-satisfying services available to them. Nevertheless, the unique characteristic of services create special problems for a marketing strategy.

One of the unique challenges service marketers face is matching supply and demand. We have seen that price can be used to help smooth demand for a service. There are other ways, too, that marketers can alter the marketing mix to deal with the problem of fluctuating demand. Through price incentives, advertising, and other promotional efforts, marketers can remind consumers of busy times and encourage them to come for service during slack periods. Additionally, the product itself can be altered to cope with fluctuating demand. Restaurants, for example, may change their menus, vary their lighting and decor, open or close the bar, and add or delete entertainment. A ski resort may install an Alpine slide to attract customers during summer months. Finally, distribution can be modified to reflect changes in demand. Theaters have traditionally offered matinees over the weekend when demand is greater, and some libraries have mobile units that travel to different locations during slack periods.[32]

Before understanding such strategies, service marketers must first understand the pattern and determinants of demand. Does the level of demand follow a cycle? What are the causes of this cycle? Are the changes random?[33] The need to answer such questions is best illustrated through an example. Consider, for instance, an attempt to use price decreases to shift demand for public transportation to off-peak periods. Such an attempt would likely fail because of the cause of the cyclical demand for public transportation—employment hours. Employees have little control over working hours and are therefore unable to take advantage of pricing incentives.

Table 21.5 summarizes ways in which service firms may deal with the problem of fluctuating demand. Note that the strategies fall into two categories, marketing strategies and nonmarketing strategies. Nonmarketing strategies essentially involve internal, employee-related actions.[34] They may be the only available alternative when fluctuations in demand are random. For example, a strike may cause fluctuations in consumer demand for public transportation.

---

30. James H. Donnelly, Jr., "Marketing Intermediaries in Channels of Distribution for Services," *Journal of Marketing*, Jan. 1976, pp. 55–70.
31. Ibid.
32. Lovelock, "Classifying Services," pp. 279–289.
33. Ibid.
34. Berry, Zeithaml, and Parasuraman, "Responding to Demand Fluctuations."

Table 21.5 *Strategies for coping with fluctuations in demand for services*

Marketing Strategies	Nonmarketing Strategies
Use differential pricing	Hire extra help/lay off employees
Alter product	Work employees overtime/part-time
Change distribution	Cross-train employees
Use promotional efforts	Use employees to perform nonvital tasks during slack times
	Subcontract work/seek subcontract work
	Slow the pace of work
	Turn away business

Nonbusiness Marketing

Nonbusiness marketing includes marketing activities conducted by individuals and organizations to achieve some goal other than ordinary business goals such as profit, market share, or return on investment. Remember that we broadly defined marketing as a set of individual and organizational activities aimed at facilitating and expediting satisfying exchanges in a dynamic environment through the creation, distribution, promotion, and pricing of goods, services, and ideas. Although most examples used in this text involve business enterprises, this section examines the unique aspects of marketing in nonbusiness situations. Most of the previously discussed concepts and approaches to managing marketing activities apply to nonbusiness situations. Of special relevance is the material offered in the first half of this chapter, since many nonbusiness organizations provide services.

As discussed in Chapter 1, an exchange situation exists when individuals, groups, or organizations possess something that they are willing to give up in an exchange. In nonbusiness marketing, obligations or rewards often are not clearly specified in advance. Also, the objects of the exchange may not be specified in financial terms. Usually, such exchanges are facilitated through **negotiation** (mutual discussion or communication of terms and methods) and **persuasion** (convincing and prevailing upon by argument). Acceptance of nonbusiness products is attained through constant efforts to further an organization's goals. Often negotiation and persuasion are conducted without reference to or awareness of the role that marketing plays in transactions. We are concerned with nonbusiness performance of marketing activities, whether or not the exchange is consummated.

Why Is Nonbusiness Marketing Different?

In this section we first examine the concept of nonbusiness marketing and see how organizational and individual goals determine whether an organization is a business or a nonbusiness. Next, we explore the overall objectives of nonbusiness organizations, their marketing objectives, and the development of their marketing strategies. Finally, we illustrate how an audit of marketing activities can promote marketing awareness in a nonbusiness organization.

Traditionally and mistakenly, people have not thought of nonbusiness exchange activities as marketing. Only organizations that attempt to make a profit— including those such as mutual insurance companies that seek profits by marketing services—have been viewed as the type that must perform marketing activities. But consider the following example. The University of Minnesota has developed a comprehensive marketing program to fill the stands at women's basketball games. An essential feature of the plan is awareness-building advertisements to put people in the stands. The university depends on voluntary professional services and donated media time and space to reach the Minneapolis market. Viewing women's athletics as a viable form of family entertainment, the university is building a market by entering the competition for the entertainment dollar. Promotions have helped Minnesota boost average attendance at women's basketball games to about one thousand, but more than just advertising will be necessary to realize the goal of five thousand fans per game. The creator of the program hopes to develop a marketing campaign that can be applied generically to women's sports across the nation.[35]

Profit is a variable that only indirectly changes the nature of marketing activities. Many nonbusiness organizations strive for effective marketing activities. Charitable organizations and supporters of social causes are major nonbusiness marketers in this country. Political parties, unions, religious sects, and fraternal organizations also perform marketing activities; yet they are not considered businesses. Whereas the chief beneficiary of a business enterprise is whoever owns or holds stock in it, in theory the only beneficiaries of a nonbusiness organization are its clients, its members, or the public at large.

Nonbusinesses have a greater opportunity for creativity than most business organizations, but they are generally less productive and efficient because of less direct accountability to an owner or ownership group. For example, trustees or board members of nonbusinesses are likely to have trouble judging performance when services can be provided only by trained professionals. It is harder for administrators to evaluate the performance of doctors, professors, or social workers than it is for sales managers to evaluate the performance of salespersons.

Nonbusinesses May Be Controversial

Nonbusiness organizations may have goals that are not accepted by some members of society. Opposing organizations may spring up to combat the success of a movement or social cause with which individuals disagree. Nonprofit groups such as Common Cause, the American Postal Workers Union, and Gun Owners of America spend lavishly on lobbying efforts to persuade Congress, the White House, and even the courts to support their interests, in part because acceptance of their aims is far from guaranteed.[36] Few people, however, oppose the basic goals of the American Cancer Society (to prevent cancer and treat victims) or of the March of Dimes (to prevent birth defects).

The professional who manages marketing activities that promote the cause of a controversial group must make more value judgments about marketing their cause or organization than do marketers in most business enterprises.

35. Kevin T. Higgins, "Gopher the Goal: Minnesota Marketers Dominate Services, Media to Aid Women's Sports Program," *Marketing News*, Feb. 14, 1986, p. 1.
36. "Lobbyists: Washington's 'Hidden Persuaders,'" *U.S. News and World Report*, Sept. 19, 1983, p. 63.

Figure 21.6

A vivid direct-mail piece used to stimulate sub- scription memberships in the Houston Sym- phony Orchestra
(Source: Houston Sym- phony Orchestra)

A new Pops season has just hatched.

The Houston Symphony-Exxon Pops Series
The 1985/86 Season

Also, the use of marketing by controversial groups may be called into question by various members of society.

Marketing as a field of study does not attempt to state what an organization's goals should be or to debate the issue of nonbusiness versus business goals. Marketing only attempts to provide a body of knowledge and concepts to help further an organization's goals. Individuals must decide whether they approve or disapprove of a particular organization's goal orientation. Most marketers would agree that profit and consumer satisfaction are appropriate goals for business enterprises, but there probably would be considerable disagreement about the goals of a controversial nonbusiness organization.

Nonbusiness Marketing Objectives

The basic aim of nonbusiness organizations is to obtain a desired response from a target market (public). The response could be a change in values, a financial contribution, the donation of services, or some other type of exchange. In Figure 21.6, the Houston Symphony promotes a concert series to increase membership. This flamboyant direct mail piece resulted in a 300-percent increase

Figure 21.7

Examples of marketing objectives for different types of exchanges (Source: Philip Kotler, Marketing for Nonprofit Organizations, 2nd ed., © 1982, p. 38. Adapted by permission of Prentice-Hall, Inc., Englewood Cliffs, N.J.)

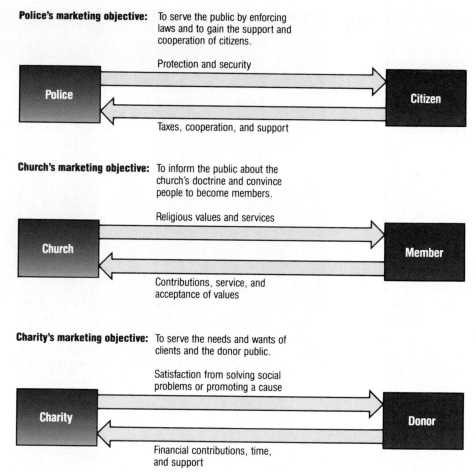

Police's marketing objective: To serve the public by enforcing laws and to gain the support and cooperation of citizens.

Police — Protection and security → Citizen
Police ← Taxes, cooperation, and support — Citizen

Church's marketing objective: To inform the public about the church's doctrine and convince people to become members.

Church — Religious values and services → Member
Church ← Contributions, service, and acceptance of values — Member

Charity's marketing objective: To serve the needs and wants of clients and the donor public.

Charity — Satisfaction from solving social problems or promoting a cause → Donor
Charity ← Financial contributions, time, and support — Donor

in subscriptions over the previous year. Nonbusiness marketing objectives are shaped by the nature of the exchange and the goals of the organization. Figure 21.7 illustrates how the exchange transactions and the purpose of the organization can influence marketing objectives. (These objectives are used as examples and may or may not apply to specific organizations.)

Nonbusiness marketing objectives should state the rationale for an organization's existence. An organization that defines its marketing objective as providing a product can be left without a purpose if the product becomes obsolete. However, serving and adapting to the perceived needs and wants of a target public, or market, enhances an organization's chance to survive and to achieve its goals.

Developing Nonbusiness Marketing Strategies

A marketing strategy encompasses (1) defining and analyzing a target market and (2) creating and maintaining a marketing mix. A nonbusiness organization may not think in terms of the needs, perceptions, or preferences of its market

Application

Economic Development Managers Need to Know More About Marketing

Economic development authorities across the country spend millions on marketing campaigns to lure new plants and corporate offices to their areas. Unfortunately, many government officials lack the marketing background to conduct research and plan a strategy capable of attracting new industry. Economic development efforts often amount to nothing more than placing advertisements in trade publications. Officials may be confused about what constitutes a target market and may lack an understanding of the marketing mix elements that must be considered. As marketers, these officials must set goals and objectives, develop an overall organizational strategy, and then develop marketing strategies for each subsegment of business that they are trying to attract.

Economic developers probably focus too much on high-tech or auto assembly plants and ignore the hard realities of the benefits and deficiencies of their respective areas. It is a mistake to think that a few tax breaks and other economic incentives will continue to lure high-tech corporations. On the other hand, many observers believe that Tennessee's aggressive efforts to attract industry resulted in obtaining General Motors' widely publicized $3.5-billion Saturn plant.

The biggest problem in economic development efforts is the belief that throwing money into blind advertising will provide results. One questionable program was the Illinois Department of Commerce's attempt to use comparative advertising to attract or retain industry. The department bought $245,000 worth of time on Illinois radio stations for advertisements that made disparaging comments about companies that had moved to Indiana, Rhode Island, and Florida and had then gone out of business. That campaign was followed by $100,000 in newspaper advertisements slighting Illinois companies that had moved to Texas. While comparative advertising may work with consumer products, it is more likely to tarnish the image of a state using it for economic development. One expert labeled the Illinois campaign as strategically off base and offensive to the target market. (*Source: Kevin T. Higgins, "True Marketing Absent in Economic Development Efforts,"* Marketing News, *Oct. 11, 1985, pp. 1, 16. Reprinted from* Marketing News, *published by the American Marketing Association.*)

or public. It is very easy for an organization to assume that it knows what the public needs or wants. For example, an interest group may assume that it is only right to protect animals such as coyotes. But a group that is also concerned with the environment, ranchers, may view coyotes as a threat to their livestock and thus to their livelihood. Similarly, people who work for hospitals, welfare organizations, municipal transportation systems, and the like often assume that they have the technical competence to decide what services the public needs. However, hospitals often offend or frighten patients by failing to explain procedures; welfare organizations are sometimes patronizing; and city buses can be dirty and overcrowded. The application on this page discusses misdirected marketing efforts by government economic development authorities. From such examples, it is clear that an organization's strategy failures often can be traced to its neglect of the basic desires and concerns of target markets.

Target Markets

We must revise the concept of target markets slightly to apply it to nonbusiness organizations. Whereas a business is supposed to have target groups that are potential purchasers of its product, a nonbusiness organization may attempt

Table 21.6 *Art-form audience segments*

Market Segment	Type of Performance Attended	Type of Performance Not Attended
Classical	Symphony Chamber music Opera Ballet	Experimental theater Rock Comedians
Country/folk	Country-western Folk/bluegrass Rock	Musicals Plays Symphony
Theater	Musicals Traditional plays Experimental theater	Rock Chamber music
Pop	Jazz Big bands Pop vocalist/group	Gospel
Recital	Instrumental recitals Solo vocal recitals	Musicals Pop

Source: John R. Nevin and S. Tamer Cavusgil, "Audience Segments for the Performing Arts," *Marketing of Services,* eds. James H. Donnelly and William R. George (Chicago: American Marketing Association, 1981), p. 127. Reprinted with permission of the publisher.

to serve many diverse groups. For our purposes, **target public** is broadly defined as a collective of individuals who have an interest in or concern about an organization, a product, or a social cause. It follows that the terms *target market* and *target public* are difficult to distinguish for many nonbusiness organizations. Once an organization is concerned about exchanging values or obtaining a response from the public, it views the public as a market.[37]

In nonbusiness organizations, direct consumers of the product are called **client publics,** and indirect consumers are called **general publics.**[38] For example, the client public for a university is its student body, while its general public includes parents, alumni, and trustees. The client public usually receives most of the attention when an organization develops a marketing strategy. Techniques and approaches to segmenting and defining target markets are discussed in Chapter 3. These techniques apply also to nonbusiness target markets.

Table 21.6 exemplifies behavioral segmentation of the performing-arts market in a large urban area. By delineating markets for classical, country/folk, theater, pop, and recital art forms, arts administrators can provide more and better performances for defined audiences and develop new programs for unique market segments.[39] Notice that Table 21.6 indicates not only the types of performances attended, but also the types of performances that particular market

37. Philip Kotler, *Marketing for Nonprofit Organizations* (Englewood Cliffs, N.J.: Prentice-Hall, 1982), p. 37.
38. Ibid.
39. John R. Nevin and S. Tamer Cavusgil, "Audience Segments for the Performing Arts," *Marketing of Services,* eds. James H. Donnelly and William R. George (Chicago: American Marketing Association, 1981), p. 128.

segments are more likely not to attend. Arts administrators know, therefore, that the country/folk market segment is unlikely to attend musicals, plays, or symphonies.

Developing a Marketing Mix

A marketing mix strategy limits alternatives and directs marketing activities toward achieving organizational goals. The strategy should outline or develop a blueprint for making decisions about product, distribution, promotion, and price. These decision variables should be blended to serve the target market.

A successful strategy requires careful delineation of a target market through marketing research and the development of a complete marketing mix. For example, many states have established agencies that use promotional methods to attract foreign investment for continued economic growth of the state. Some concrete examples include the following methods:

1. Personal selling—U.S. or foreign-based individuals directly contact potential investors.
2. Sales promotion—direct investment is encouraged through seminars and investment missions.
3. Advertising—printed and audiovisual promotional materials are utilized in foreign countries, along with advertisements in newspapers and magazines.
4. Publicity—the press is utilized systematically.

An examination of attempts by various southeastern states to attract foreign investment found that none of the states determined the wants and needs of potential investors. Instead, their selection of target markets was based on such factors as past investment levels and the feelings of state agency representatives. Another major problem was the agencies' failure to evaluate feedback from foreign investors regarding their states' promotional programs. Also, product was not emphasized as much as the promotion variable.[40]

The level of application for any given marketing mix variable may range from low to high (see Table 21.7), depending on the needs of the nonbusiness industry.[41] As Table 21.7 indicates, however, a marketing mix should always involve some decision about each of the four major elements—product, distribution, price, and promotion. For example, ethical and legal considerations tend to limit the use of promotional tools in the health-care industry. Keep in mind that Table 21.7 is based on a survey of nonbusiness organizations in one city. The marketing mix emphasis of similar organizations elsewhere can vary.

Product

Nonbusiness organizations deal more often with ideas and services than with goods. Problems in developing a product configuration evolve when an organization fails to define what is being provided. What product does the Peace Corps provide? Its services include vocational training, health services, nutritional

40. Spero C. Peppas, "An Application of Marketing Theory to the Attraction of Foreign Investment," *A Spectrum of Contemporary Marketing Ideas,* eds. John H. Summey, Blaise J. Bergiel, and Carol H. Anderson (Carbondale, Ill.: Southern Marketing Association, 1982), pp. 204–208.
41. Philip D. Cooper and George E. McIlvain, "Factors Influencing Marketing's Ability to Assist Non-Profit Organizations," *Evolving Marketing Thought for 1980, Proceedings of the Southern Marketing Association,* eds. John H. Summey and Ronald D. Taylor (Nov. 19–22, 1980), p. 316.

Table 21.7 Marketing mix emphasis of nonbusinesses in a major Midwest city

Nonbusiness Industry	Level of Application			
	Product	Distribution	Price	Promotion
Health care organizations	High	Medium-High	Low-Medium	Low-Medium
Educational facilities	High	Medium	Low-Medium	High
Political organizations	High	Medium	Low-Medium	High
Cultural organizations	Medium	Low-Medium	High	Medium-High
Public service agencies	Medium-High	High	Low	Low-Medium
Professional organizations	High	Low	Medium	Low-Medium
Religious organizations	High	Medium	Low-Medium	Low
Human services organizations	High	Low-Medium	Low	Medium-High

Source: Philip D. Cooper and George E. McIlvain, "Factors Influencing Marketing's Ability to Assist Non-Profit Organizations," *Evolving Marketing Thought for 1980, Proceedings of the Southern Marketing Association,* eds. John H. Summey and Ronald D. Taylor (Nov. 19–22, 1980), p. 317. Used by permission.

assistance, and community development. Ideas include international cooperation and the implementation of U.S. foreign policy. The Peace Corps product is more difficult to define than the average business product. As indicated in the first part of this chapter, services are intangible and therefore need special marketing efforts. The marketing of ideas and concepts is likewise more abstract than the marketing of tangibles, and it requires much effort to present benefits.

Distribution

Nonbusiness products must be available before an exchange can take place. Marketers usually analyze distribution as it relates to decisions about product and promotion. Since most nonbusiness products are ideas and services, distribution decisions relate to how these ideas and services will be made available to clients. If the product is an idea, selecting the right media (the promotional strategy) to communicate the idea will facilitate distribution. The availability of services is closely related to product decisions. By nature, services consist of assistance, convenience, and availability. Availability is part of the total service (product). For example, making a product such as health services available calls for knowledge of such retailing concepts as site-location analysis.

Most nonbusiness organizations in capitalist nations do not get involved in the physical distribution of goods. If goods must be moved, a facilitating agency such as the Postal Service or United Parcel Service may carry out the task. One

Figure 21.8 *An effective billboard advertising Chicago's Brookfield Zoo (Source: Brookfield Zoo)*

exception is the U.S. Geological Survey, which arranges for sporting-goods stores and other commercial outlets to sell its maps. Also, the Geological Survey has joined with another government office to sell colorful satellite images of the globe.[42]

Developing a channel of distribution to coordinate and facilitate the flow of nonbusiness products to clients is a necessary task, but in a nonbusiness setting the traditional concept of the marketing channel may need to be reviewed. The independent wholesalers available to a business enterprise do not exist in most nonbusiness situations. Instead, a very short channel—nonbusiness organization to client—is prevalent because production and consumption of ideas and services are often simultaneous.

Promotion

Making promotional decisions may be the first sign that nonbusiness organizations are performing marketing activities. Nonbusiness organizations use advertising and publicity to communicate with clients and the public, as Figure 21.8 illustrates for Chicago's Brookfield Zoo. Although personal selling may be called something else, it too is used by many nonbusiness organizations. Churches and charities rely on personal selling when they send volunteers to recruit new members or request donations. The U.S. Army uses personal selling when its recruiting

42. Paul Harris, "Uncle Sam Discovers Marketing," *Sales and Marketing Management*, March 14, 1983, p. 50.

Chapter 21 / Services and Nonbusiness Marketing

officers attempt to convince men and women to enlist. Special events to obtain funds, communicate ideas, or provide services are sales promotion activities. Contests, entertainment, and prices offered to attract donations resemble the sales promotion activities of business enterprises.

Religious advertising has changed drastically in recent years. For televison, religious advertisers increasingly are injecting "slice of life" themes into commercials that might be confused with advertisements for Kodak, Pepsi, or Coke. In one advertisement for the Mormon Church, three muddy farm kids are having a water fight when their parents pull up in a truck. Instead of reprimanding the children, the father takes out his camera and snaps their picture. The commercial is capped by the message, "Don't let the magic pass you by." Most Mormon advertisements deal with family values; the church's name, in fact, is revealed only in the final three seconds. The Episcopal Church has run an advertisement featuring the line, "In the church started by a man who had six wives, forgiveness goes without saying." Behind the engaging attempt at humor, the real message emphasized that the Episcopal Church is concerned about forgiveness. While some churches believe that personal contact is the best marketing tool, advertising seems to have helped many churches achieve their goals.[43]

Price

The broadest definition of price (valuation) must be used to develop nonbusiness marketing strategy. Financial price, an exact dollar value, may or may not be charged for a nonbusiness product. Economists recognize the giving up of alternatives as a cost. **Opportunity cost** is the value of the benefit that is given up by selecting one alternative rather than another. This traditional economic view of price means that if a nonbusiness organization can convince someone to donate time to a cause or to change his or her behavior, then the alternatives given up are a cost to (or a price paid by) the individual.

This concept of price can be used to determine what price a new recruit pays to join the all-volunteer armed forces. The price is giving up both personal freedom (by submitting to military rules and regulations) and earning potential, if any, outside the armed service. In the marketing strategy of the armed forces, price is not viewed as a major controllable aspect of the marketing mix, although a consideration of what the new recruit is giving up is programmed into product and promotion decisions. To counter the sacrifice, recruiting promotions stress military service as a challenging opportunity by which dedicated men and women can broaden their horizons and improve their prospects.

For other nonbusiness organizations, financial price is an important part of the marketing mix. Nonbusiness organizations today are raising money by upping the prices of their services or starting to charge for services if they have not done so before. They are using marketing research to determine what kinds of products people will pay for.[44] Pricing strategies of nonbusiness organizations often stress public and client welfare over equalization of costs and revenues. If additional funds are needed to cover costs, then donations, contributions, or grants may be solicited.

43. Ronald Alsop, "Advertisers Promote Religion in a Splashy . . . Style," *Wall Street Journal*, Nov. 21, 1985, p. 31.
44. Kelly Walker, "Not-for-Profit Profits," *Forbes*, Sept. 10, 1984, p. 165.

Table 21.8 Examples of data useful in controlling nonbusiness marketing activities

1. Product mix offerings
  A. Types of product or services
  B. Number of organizations
      offering the product or service
2. Financial resources
  A. Types of funding used
    1. Local grants
    2. State grants
    3. Federal grants
    4. Foundations
    5. Public solicitation
    6. Fees charged
  B. Number using each type of
     funding
  C. Number using combinations of
     funding sources
3. Size
  A. Budget (cash flows)
	B. Number of employees
	  1. By organization
	  2. Total industrywide
	C. Number of volunteers
	  1. By organization
	  2. Total industrywide
	D. Number of customers serviced
	  1. By type of service
	  2. By organization
	  3. Total industrywide
	4. Facilities
	  A. Number and type
	    1. By organization
	    2. Total industrywide
	  B. Location
	    1. By address
	    2. Zip code
	    3. Census tract

Source: Adapted from Philip D. Cooper and George E. McIlvain, "Factors Influencing Marketing's Ability to Assist Non-Profit Organizations," *Evolving Marketing Thought for 1980, Proceedings of the Southern Marketing Association,* eds. John H. Summey and Ronald D. Taylor (Nov. 19–22, 1980), p. 315. Used by permission.

Controlling Nonbusiness Marketing Activities

To control marketing activities in nonbusiness organizations, managers use information obtained in the marketing audit to make sure that goals are achieved. Table 21.8 lists several helpful summary statistics. It should be obvious that the data in Table 21.8 are useful for both planning and control. Control is designed to identify what activities have occurred in conformity with the marketing strategy and to take corrective action where any deviations are found. The purpose of control is not only to point out errors and mistakes, but also to revise organizational goals and marketing objectives as necessary. For example, universities view alumni as one of their most important markets. In most cases, little is known about former students' motivation to provide assistance to their alma mater. In one study, it was learned that graduates with applied majors, such as agriculture, and those who participated in university activities are more likely to provide long-term continuing support to their universities. These results indicate that universities might be able to gain more long-run support from alumni by encouraging student participation in activities.[45]

To control nonbusiness marketing activities, managers must make a proper inventory of activities performed and prepare to adjust or correct deviations

45. Steven W. Hartley and Eric N. Berkowitz, "Identifying Membership Strategies: An Investigation of University Alumni," *1983 Educators' Proceedings,* eds. Patrick E. Murphy et al. (Chicago: American Marketing Association, 1983), p. 352.

from standards. Knowing where and how to look for deviations and knowing what types of deviations to expect are especially important in nonbusiness situations. Since nonbusiness marketing activities may not be perceived as marketing, managers must clearly define what activity is being examined and how it should function.

It may be difficult to control nonbusiness marketing activities because it is often hard to determine whether goals are being achieved. A mental health center that wants to inform community members of its services may not be able to determine whether it is communicating with persons who need assistance. A growing case load does not guarantee that all needs have been met. Surveying to determine the percentage of the population that is aware of a mental health program can show whether or not the awareness objective has been achieved; but it fails to indicate what percentage of the persons with mental health problems has been assisted. The detection and correction of deviations from standards is certainly a major purpose of control, but standards must support the organization's overall goals. Managers can refine goals by examining the results that are being achieved and by analyzing the ramifications of those results.

Techniques for controlling overall marketing performance must be compatible with the nature of an organization's operations. Obviously, it is necessary to control the marketing budget in most nonbusiness organizations, but budgetary control is not tied to profit-and-loss standards. Responsible management of funds is the objective. Nonbusiness organizations have diverse missions; there is no hard-and-fast formula to determine what control techniques are appropriate or how to use them.

Central control responsibility can facilitate orderly, efficient administration and planning. For example, Illinois Wesleyan University evaluates graduating students' progress in order to control and improve the quality of the educational product. The audit phase relies on questionnaires sent to students and their employers after graduation. The employer completes a questionnaire to indicate the student's progress; the student completes a questionnaire to indicate which additional concepts or skills were needed to perform duties. In addition, a number of faculty members interview certain employers and students to obtain information for control purposes. Results of the audit are used to develop corrective action if university standards have not been met. Corrective action might include an evaluation of the deficiency and a revision of the curriculum.

Summary

Services are intangible-dominant products that cannot be physically possessed—the result of applying human or mechanical efforts to people or objects. Services are a growing part of our economy. They now account for approximately 60 percent of our gross national product and almost 50 percent of consumer expenditures.

Services have four distinguishing characteristics: (1) intangibility, (2) inseparability of production and consumption, (3) perishability, and (4) heterogeneity. Because services include a diverse group of industries, classification schemes are used to help marketers analyze their products and develop the most appropriate marketing mix. Services can be viewed in terms of (1) the type of market, (2) degree of labor intensiveness, (3) degree of customer contact, (4) skill of the service provider, and (5) goal of the service provider.

When developing a marketing mix for services, several aspects deserve special consideration. In terms of product, service offerings are often difficult for consumers to understand and evaluate. The tangibles associated with a service may be the only visible aspect of the service, and marketers must manage these scarce tangibles with care. Since services are often viewed in terms of the providers, service firms must carefully select, train, motivate, and control employees.

Advertising services is problematic because of their intangibility. Advertising should stress the tangibles associated with the service or should use some relevant tangible object. Customer contact personnel should be considered an important secondary audience for advertising. Personal selling is very powerful in service firms since customers must interact with personnel. Some forms of sales promotion, such as displays and free samples, are difficult to implement with services. The final component of the promotion mix, publicity, is vital to many service firms. Since customers value word-of-mouth communications, messages should attempt to stimulate or simulate word-of-mouth. Many professional service providers, however, are severely restricted in their use of promotional activities.

Price plays three major roles in service firms. It plays a psychological role by indicating quality and an economic role by determining revenues. Price is also a way to help smooth fluctuations in demand.

Service distribution channels are typically direct due to simultaneous production and consumption. However, innovative approaches such as drop-off centers, intermediaries, and electronic distribution are being developed.

Fluctuating demand is a major problem for most service firms. Marketing strategies (product, price, promotion, and distribution), as well as nonmarketing strategies (primarily internal, employee-based actions), can be used to deal with the problem. Before attempting to undertake any such strategies, however, service marketers must understand the patterns and determinants of demand.

Nonbusiness marketing includes marketing activities conducted by individuals and organizations to achieve some goal other than normal business goals. Nonbusiness marketing uses most concepts and approaches that are applied to business situations. An exchange situation exists when individuals, groups, or organizations possess something that they are willing to give up in an exchange.

While the chief beneficiary of a business enterprise is whoever owns or holds stock in it, the beneficiary of a nonbusiness enterprise should be its clients, its members, or its public at large. The goals of a nonbusiness organization reflect its unique philosophy or mission. Some nonbusiness organizations have very controversial goals, but many organizations exist to further generally accepted social causes.

The marketing objective of nonbusiness organizations is to obtain a desired response from a target market. Developing a nonbusiness marketing strategy consists of defining and analyzing a target market and creating and maintaining a marketing mix. In nonbusiness marketing the product is usually an idea or service. Distribution is not involved as much with the movement of goods as with the communication of ideas and the delivery of services, which results in a very short marketing channel. Promotion is very important in nonbusiness marketing; personal selling, sales promotion, advertising, and publicity are all used to communicate ideas and inform people about services. Price is more difficult to define in nonbusiness marketing because of opportunity costs and the difficulty of quantifying values exchanged.

It is important to control nonbusiness marketing strategies. Control is designed to identify what activities have occurred in conformity with marketing strategy and to take corrective actions where any deviations are found. The standards against which deviations are measured must support the overall goals of the nonbusiness organization.

Important Terms

Service	Nonbusiness marketing
Intangibility	Negotiation
Search qualities	Persuasion
Experience qualities	Target public
Credence qualities	Client publics
Inseparability	General publics
Perishability	Opportunity cost
Heterogeneity	

Discussion and Review Questions

1. Identify and discuss the distinguishing characteristics of services. What problems do these characteristics present to marketers?
2. What is the significance of "tangibles" in service industries?
3. Analyze a housecleaning service in terms of the five classification schemes, and discuss the implications for marketing mix development.
4. How do search, experience, and credence properties impact on the way consumers view and evaluate services?
5. Discuss the role of promotion in services marketing.
6. Analyze the demand for dry cleaning, and discuss ways to cope with fluctuating demand.
7. Compare and contrast the controversial aspects of nonbusiness versus business marketing.
8. Relate the concepts of product, distribution, promotion, and price to a marketing strategy aimed at preventing drug abuse.
9. What are the differences among clients, publics, and consumers? What is the difference between a target public and a target market?
10. What is the function of control in a nonbusiness marketing strategy?
11. Discuss the development of a marketing strategy for a university. What marketing decisions should be made in developing strategy?

Cases

Case 21.1   BellSouth Corporation[46]

BellSouth Corporation, a regional holding company created as a result of the breakup of American Telephone and Telegraph Company, is one of the largest corporations in the United States. As a holding company, BellSouth's major

46. Facts are from *BellSouth—The Right Company in the Right Place at the Right Time;* and BellSouth Corporation *1984* and *1985 Annual Reports.*

role is to handle financial matters and long-range planning for its subsidiaries—South Central Bell, Southern Bell, BellSouth Services Incorporated, BellSouth Advertising and Publishing Corporation (providing specialized directories and directory services to other telephone companies), and BellSouth Mobility Inc. (providing cellular phones). BellSouth's corporate mission is to provide an attractive return for shareholders, high-quality service to customers, and good employment opportunities. BellSouth's primary orientation is to be service driven. At the same time, the company realizes that to prosper in the long run it must diversify, seeking new markets for its many products and services. The breakup of AT&T has increased the number of competitors in the marketplace and caused a struggle among long-distance services trying to secure customer commitments.

The breakup has had a significant impact on BellSouth. Before, BellSouth made a large amount of revenue from the rental of customer-premises equipment (phones, answering machines, and the like) to AT&T. This revenue source has declined as most customers have started buying such equipment directly from various manufacturers. BellSouth's revenues also declined as a result of the loss of interstate toll business, which fell by approximately 52 percent in the first year after the breakup. BellSouth has been forced to transform itself from a company that provides local and long-distance telephone service into a company fervently attempting to differentiate itself from the competition by providing new and relevant services.

BellSouth's telephone companies offer services in two broad areas: local access—local telephone service is their strength and their major source of revenue—and transport areas, providing local and long-distance service. BellSouth's local service includes dial tone from the central office, an access line connecting the customer's equipment to the central office, repair service for the access line and dial tone, and listings in the phone book for businesses and individuals. BellSouth offers either premium flat-rate service with unlimited calling or, in some areas, budget-measured service. Custom calling services, business network services, Touch-Tone service, inside wiring, directory assistance, and calling cards are some additional services offered by BellSouth's telephone companies.

One of BellSouth's greatest concerns is the threat of "bypass," which refers to the use of alternative local-exchange communications techniques. In essence, customers who bypass do not use their local telephone company's facilities. This technique has been practiced mostly by large corporations that have historically generated a disproportionate share of BellSouth's revenues. To cope with the problem, BellSouth plans to aggressively pursue high-technology applications, effective marketing, and expense reduction. The company plans to move very quickly toward cost-based pricing in place of the subsidized pricing used in the past. The industry's previous system attached a premium price to certain services, and these revenues in turn subsidized basic phone service. Individual services must now begin to pay their way; long-distance revenues will no longer support other services. Therefore, services must be priced more closely to costs, and rates for local service—which have traditionally been priced below cost—will have to rise.

BellSouth Services Incorporated is jointly owned by South Central Bell and Southern Bell. It represents BellSouth's commitment to the telecommunications industry servicing its own subsidiaries and helps provide services that differentiate

South Central Bell and Southern Bell from their competitors. BellSouth Services also helps the larger corporation maintain low costs so that telephone service can be offered at an affordable price. Its objective is to deliver cost-effective, professional services to its owners and other members of its corporation. Services are provided in the following areas:

1. Information System Services plans and develops computer-based systems and maintains data bases.

2. Personnel provides management with salary, job evaluations, and employee assessment; develops and delivers training programs.

3. Marketing conducts feasibility studies on new lines of business, formulates long-range plans, provides strategic technical support, and devises compensation plans.

4. Corporate support provides centralized procurement of products and services and other support operations, including automotive and aviation services, building and real estate management, and administrative and corporate communications.

5. Network Strategic Planning handles network architectural planning, helps maintain technical procedures and standards, and provides procurement support through product evaluation.

BellSouth Services Incorporated provides an important operational efficiency for the corporation. It enables member companies to avoid duplication of common services or functions, which reduces costs, makes more efficient use of resources, and encourages common operating procedures.

BellSouth Corporation plans to grow based on the development and promotion of new services. For example, Prestige is an advanced system providing three-way conferencing and intercom services previously available only to large corporations. Another system, Touchstar, will provide automatic call back and recall, selective call forwarding, and nuisance-call rejection. Bell Communications research continues to provide member companies with information regarding changing consumer wants and needs. BellSouth Corporation must provide excellence in its service and product offering if it is to maintain customers and enlarge its market share. With the increased threat of bypass and the growth in competition, phone service suppliers will have to do more than simply provide local and long-distance services. BellSouth's success depends on its ability to identify customer needs and provide the right services to fill those needs.

Questions for Discussion

1. Does BellSouth hold a monopoly in some of its offered services? What impact does this have on marketing strategy?
2. What new services should BellSouth consider offering to maintain future growth?
3. What areas of services marketing discussed in this chapter are most important for BellSouth's success?

Case 21.2 Developing a New Poison Prevention Program[47]

It is a sad fact that in the United States over 700,000 children each year are the victims of accidental poisoning. The most tragic aspect of this situation is that 95 percent of the children poisoned are under adult supervision at the time, and so most incidents could be averted if the parents of the victims took ordinary safety precautions.

These statistics have prompted the development of poison control centers based in hospitals throughout the country. Brokaw Hospital's Poison Control Center in Normal, Illinois, is typical of many of these facilities; it is coordinated through the hospital's pharmacy department. Brokaw Hospital's pharmacy staff decided they had an obligation to do more than merely be efficient in treating poisonings as they occurred. They felt that active attempts had to be made to lower the number of accidental poisonings within the community. This resolution among the pharmacy staff initiated a movement to investigate the basic problem and implement an effective marketing strategy to prevent poisonings.

Through marketing research, it became apparent to the staff members that children will eat or drink just about anything. It found that most poisoning agents are located in and around the house. The most commonly ingested substances were plants, household cleaning products, aspirin, vitamins, and cold medicines—in that order. Four basic factors were identified as leading to childhood poisonings: (1) accessibility of toxic agents, (2) the inquisitive nature of children, (3) the limited environment of a small house or apartment, which causes children to play near poisonous products (as in the kitchen or basement), and (4) the problems of communicating with children who are too young to understand the dangers of toxic products. The communications aspect was seen as the most crucial factor in establishing an effective poison prevention program.

Presented with these facts, Terry Trudeau, director of the Poison Control Center, set about the task of developing an educational program that would teach children to avoid poisons and would instruct teachers and parents in the basics of poison prevention. This year-round program drew on existing ideas concerning poison prevention, and innovation was provided by staff members and professionals within the community.

A key aspect of poison prevention is the use of an easily recognized symbol. The traditional symbol for poison has been the skull and cross-bones, but research shows that children often are attracted to this symbol because it suggests "playing pirate for fun" rather than danger and death. Symbols developed by other poison control centers in the United States also were ruled out, since none had sufficient impact to inspire a year-round poison prevention effort. It was decided to develop a new poison symbol that would be easily recognized yet repellent to all age groups.

Designed with the help of the Illinois State University art staff, the symbol shown in Figure 21.9 has proven effective in tests with preschool and kindergarten children. Named "SIOP," the symbol is a stylized green snake against a bright orange, circular background. The symbol is effective both because of its colors

47. The material in this case was contributed by Terry Trudeau, Associate Professor, Department of Pharmacy Practice, Howard University College of Pharmacy and Pharmacal Sciences, Washington, D.C. Reprinted by permission of the author.

Figure 21.9

Educational pamphlet with the SIOP symbol (Source: Terry Trudeau, R.Ph., M.B.A., Associate Professor, Department of Pharmacy Practice, Howard University College of Pharmacy and Pharmacal Sciences, Washington, D.C.)

A PARENT AND TEACHER'S INTRODUCTION TO THE

SIOP

POISON PREVENTION PROGRAM

(green has proved to be repellent, and orange is among the hues that are first recognized) and because of its shape (the circle is the first shape children recognize and remember). The SIOP symbol comes with an adhesive band that is long enough to fit around most household products. The band is also orange, a color not frequently used in commercial packaging, thus increasing the visibility of the symbol from all angles.

SIOP was designed to be as frightening to children as possible. This improves the chances that children will stay away from the symbol, even though they might not know what it stands for. However, the key to making the SIOP symbol an effective deterrent to all children was the creation of an educational program that conditions children to stay away from SIOP. Whenever and wherever children see the fanged green snake, they are taught to say, "No! SIOP!" (which

Figure 21.10

Educational pamphlet with the ''Happy'' symbol (Source: Terry Trudeau, R.Ph., M.B.A., Associate Professor, Department of Pharmacy Practice, Howard University College of Pharmacy and Pharmacal Sciences, Washington, D.C.)

is *poison* spelled backward). In addition, ''Happy,'' the Poison Prevention Dog (see Figure 21.10), was developed to serve as a foil to SIOP and teach children to avoid poisons. Happy barks whenever SIOP is near. This theme of good versus bad is carried throughout the program.

A wide range of materials was developed for the prevention program. For children, the program includes a story pamphlet, Happy's song, Happy's activity book, Happy and SIOP puppets, and Happy buttons, Frisbees, balloons, iron-on decals, and posters. For teachers and parents there are pamphlets about poison-proofing the home, poisonous plants, the use of Ipecac syrup, a SIOP poison first-aid chart, and SIOP poison prevention rules. Audio-visual shows, educational lesson plans, and SIOP stickers have also been developed.

The launching of the SIOP program coincided with the beginning of the National Poison Prevention Week. Much publicity was used in the area, including newspaper, television, and radio coverage of the new poison symbol. Distribution of the first SIOP symbols was accomplished by using the telephone company's mailing list to send SIOP stickers and a guide to poison prevention to each family in the county. Educational materials were delivered to all kindergartens, nursery schools, and day-care centers. Teachers received a packet of materials containing instructions for using the program year round. Each child received an activity book, a story pamphlet, a poison prevention guide, and a button. Additional materials were supplied on request.

Today, when new residents arrive in the community, they are sent SIOP stickers and pamphlets. The materials are also distributed in the school system. Natural childbirth classes, the public health department, and Brokaw's pediatrics ward help perpetuate the program by distributing SIOP materials. Grants from such organizations as the Jaycees and the Brokaw Hospital Service have enabled free distribution of the materials. Many pharmacists serve on a speaker's bureau to present educational programs to schools and PTA groups.

Terry Trudeau and others involved in developing the SIOP program feel greatly rewarded since the program's inception. Among the many awards received is a federal grant from the Consumer Product Safety commission for continued service in poison prevention. Most important has been the decrease in the number of calls made to the center. And the severity of reported poisonings has diminished to an appreciable extent.

New ways are constantly sought to improve and spread the SIOP program and materials. The program is now becoming a national effort; Texas and Louisiana have adopted it, and other areas are in the process of doing so. Worldwide recognition is extending the program, with inquiries coming from as far as Australia and France. New ideas about distribution and target markets (such as industrial chemicals) are being explored in an effort to develop a single, comprehensive poison prevention program for the country. While accidental poisonings will always be a problem, the SIOP program is taking positive steps to prevent them.

Questions for Discussion

1. Describe the basic elements of the marketing strategy used in the SIOP program.
2. Terry Trudeau took several university courses in marketing while obtaining his master's degree and developing the SIOP program. How do you think these marketing courses helped Trudeau in developing SIOP?
3. How could the SIOP symbol be promoted successfully as the national symbol for poison prevention?

22 / International Marketing

Objectives

- To define the nature of international marketing.

- To describe the use of international marketing intelligence in understanding foreign markets and environments.

- To examine the potential of marketing mix standardization among nations.

- To describe adaptation of the international marketing mix when standardization is impossible.

- To look at ways to become involved in international marketing activities.

Figure 22.1

The Made in America label, emphasizing the quality of U.S. products (Source: "American Made" designed and manufactured by Graph Mark, Inc., Superior, Wisconsin)

With the U.S. trade deficit reaching almost $150 billion in 1985, pressure is building from business, labor, and Congress to do something to increase U.S. exports. More than four hundred trade bills have been introduced in Congress in the last few years to protect specific industries and to curb the exports of other countries. For example, one bill asked the president to restrict imports from Japan unless the Japanese allowed foreign producers wider access to their markets.[1] In contrast to the large American trade deficit, Japan has close to a $40-billion trade surplus with the United States.

Competition between American and Japanese companies in the United States has become severe. Motorola, a U.S. maker of semiconductors and transistors, was a shoo-in to lead the U.S. cellular phone market. But when the firm was experiencing problems in manufacturing and distribution, the Japanese stepped in to capture a large share of the market with cutthroat pricing. The U.S. Commerce Department has since judged eight Japanese companies guilty of dumping (selling products below cost) and penalized them with special import duties. The Japanese, however, are regrouping by transferring production to American locations.[2] In the U.S. auto industry, where import quotas have been lifted, the Japanese have also grabbed a big share of the market with aggressive prices. Detroit cannot match them and is violently opposed to the end of quotas.

American companies face similarly stiff competition from Korean firms. Automobiles, personal computers, video-cassette recorders, televisions, and microwaves made in Korea are offering high quality at prices even lower than those of Japanese products. Hyundai's Excel subcompact automobile, with four doors, a hatchback, and a radio, sells for $5,500. In Canada it has supplanted the Honda as the top-selling imported car.[3]

1. Sylvia Nasar, "America's War on Imports," *Fortune,* Aug. 19, 1986, pp. 26–28.
2. Ford S. Worthy, "A Phone War That Jolted Motorola," *Fortune,* Jan. 20, 1986, pp. 45–46.
3. "The Koreans Are Coming," *Business Week,* Dec. 23, 1985, pp. 46–47.

In industry after industry, the United States seems to be losing its advantage, and manufacturing is shifting to other countries. For example, microwave cooking technology was developed by Raytheon Company in Massachusetts, but the last U.S.-manufactured magnetron tube, the heart of the microwave product, was produced in 1977. Today companies such as General Electric and Tappan have phased out their U.S. production and buy the microwave ovens they sell under their own names from Japanese and South Korean companies.

In efforts to revitalize America's competitiveness in its home markets and abroad, marketing will play a key role at several levels. First, marketing will be important to understanding needs and benefits desired in both domestic and international markets. Second, marketing will be important in stressing the traditional quality and reliability of American products. An example is the use of Made in America labels on products (see Figure 22.1).[4] Companies such as Chrysler, Motorola, and Remington have probably benefited from the strong Made in America themes used in their marketing communications in the United States.

Management of international marketing activities requires an understanding of marketing variables and a grasp of the environmental complexities of foreign countries. In many cases, serving a foreign target market requires more than minor adjustments of marketing strategies. There may also be many submarkets within a particular market that reflect different lifestyles and consumption behaviors. For example, significant differences in consumption behaviors, media usage, and durable goods ownership have been found among French-speaking, bilingual, and English-speaking Canadian families.[5]

International marketing is marketing activities performed across national boundaries.[6] The planning and control of such marketing activities can differ significantly from marketing within national boundaries. This chapter looks closely at the unique features of international marketing and at the marketing mix adjustments businesses make when they cross national boundaries.

We begin by examining American firms' levels of commitment to and degree of involvement in international marketing. Then we analyze several examples to see why international marketing intelligence is necessary when a firm is moving beyond its domestic market. Next, we analyze marketing mix standardization and adaptation. Finally, we describe a number of ways of getting involved in international marketing.

4. Bernie Whalen, "National Campaign Promotes American Made Theme Product Emblem as Marketing Strategy," *Marketing News,* March 16, 1985, sec. 2, p. P1.
5. Charles M. Schaninger, Jacques C. Bourgeois, W. Christian Buss, "French-English Canadian Subcultural Consumption Differences," *Journal of Marketing,* Spring 1985, p. 82.
6. Vern Terpstra, *International Marketing,* 3rd ed. (Hinsdale, Ill.: Dryden, 1983), p. 4.

Table 22.1 Revenues and profits of the ten largest U.S. multinationals (in millions)

Company	Foreign Revenue	Total Revenue	Foreign as % of Total	Foreign Operating Profit	Total Operating Profit	Foreign as % of Total
Exxon	$63,042	$90,854	69.4%	$3,082	$5,561	55.4%
Mobil	31,900	57,029	55.9%	990	1,268	78.1%
Texaco	23,729	47,334	50.1%	787	1,709	46.1%
Chevron	20,964	53,903	38.9%	892	1,534	58.1%
IBM	18,536	45,937	40.4%	2,592	6,582	39.4%
Phibro-Salomon	17,300	28,911	59.8%	233	212	109.9%
Ford Motor	15,578	52,366	29.7%	516	2,907	17.8%
General Motors	14,534	83,890	17.3%	627	4,517	13.9%
E.I. du Pont de Nemours	11,429	35,764	32.0%	358	1,676	21.4%
Citicorp	10,200	20,494	49.8%	456	890	51.2%

Source: Forbes, July 29, 1985, p. 186.

International Marketing Involvement

Among the technological developments needed to support international marketing, worldwide transportation and communication systems are critical. Equally important is the ability to analyze different environments and determine market potentials in foreign countries. Before international marketing could achieve its current level of importance, enterprises with the necessary resources had to develop an interest in expanding their businesses beyond national boundaries. Global marketing strategies then developed to increase profits and to increase the size and influence of firms.

Multinational Involvement

The term **multinational enterprise** refers to the organizational aspects of firms that have operations or subsidiaries located in many countries to achieve a common goal. Often the parent firm is based in one country, and the multinational company is developed by cultivating production, management, and marketing activities in other countries. Such petroleum companies as Exxon, Shell, and Mobil are multinational companies that have worldwide operations. ITT Corporation (ITT) is a multinational giant with subsidiaries in many countries. ITT subsidiaries that operate on a multinational basis include its many telecommunications manufacturing units in various countries, Sheraton (an international hotel chain), and ITT World Communications (international communications services).

Table 22.1 lists ten U.S.-based multinationals that depend on foreign revenue for a significant proportion of their total operating profit. Look at the contribution of foreign profit as a percentage of total profit to see how important international

Figure 22.2 *Levels of involvement in international marketing (Source: Vern Terpstra, International Marketing, 3rd ed., copyright © 1983. Used by permission of CBS College Publishing)*

involvement can be. The table indicates that Exxon, for instance, earned nearly 56 percent of its 1984 profit from foreign operations. Many of these firms could not operate at an acceptable profit without their foreign operations.

The level of involvement in international marketing covers a wide spectrum (see Figure 22.2). "Casual or accidental exporting" represents the lowest level of commitment. "Active exporting" concentrates on selling activities to gain foreign market acceptance of existing products. "Full-scale international marketing involvement" means that top management recognizes the importance of developing international marketing strategies to achieve the firm's goals. "Globalization of markets" requires total commitment to international marketing; it embodies the view that the world is a single market.

Globalization Versus Customized Marketing Strategies

Only full-scale international marketing involvement and **globalization of markets** represent a full integration of international marketing into strategic market planning. Globalization of markets is to develop marketing strategies as if the entire world (or regions of it) were a single entity; standardized products are marketed the same way everywhere. Traditional full-scale international marketing involvement is based on products customized according to cultural, regional, and national differences. Marketing strategies are developed to serve specific target markets; from a practical standpoint, this means that to standardize the marketing mix, the strategy needs to group countries in terms of social, cultural, technological, political, and economic similarities. A multinational enterprise is thus diversified to correspond to market differences. For example, until a few years ago, Black & Decker customized lighter electric drills for Americans, while its German subsidiary made higher-powered heavy-duty drills for Germans.

Nevertheless, for many years firms have attempted to standardize the marketing mix as much as possible. The economic and competitive payoffs for standardized marketing strategies are great. Brand name, product characteristics, packaging, and labeling are among the easiest marketing mix variables to standardize. Media allocation, retail outlets, and price may be more difficult. In the end, the degree of similarity among environmental and market conditions determines the feasibility of standardization. For example, Kodak, using a customized marketing strategy, has been able to claim the number-three spot in the European copier-duplicator market (IBM and Xerox are number one and two, respectively). Kodak did not assemble and ship an unmodified American product. The product was revamped for the European market. One adaptation was alteration in language keys on the control panel, and variable reduction capabilities were added because offices, factories, and government agencies throughout Europe handle a variety of paper sizes.[7] Kodak also tailored the entire sales, advertising, and support effort to the target market.

Some companies have changed from customizing products or standardizing products for a region of the world to offering globally standardized products that are advanced, functional, reliable, and low priced.[8] A firm committed to the globalization of markets develops marketing strategies as if the entire world (or major regions of it) were a single entity; it sells the same things in the same way everywhere.[9] Examples of globalized products are electrical equipment, western American clothing, movies, soft drinks, rock music, and cosmetics. Sony televisions, Levi jeans, and American cigarette brands seem to make year-to-year gains in the world market. Even McDonald's seems to be widely accepted in markets throughout the world. Attempts are now being made to globalize industrial products such as computers, robots, and carbon filters and professional engineering products such as earth-moving equipment and communications equipment. But the question remains whether promotion, pricing, and distribution of these products can also be standardized. Nestlé has taken a global approach to new candy brands such as Alpine White with Almonds, illustrated in Figure 22.3. Only recently has the company identified itself as a Swiss firm.

Many leading marketers, including Philip Kotler of Northwestern University, believe that for international marketing, most products must vary in quality, packaging, promotion, and distribution. Kotler believes that McDonald's was not successful in Germany until it began offering beer, and the company itself has recognized that Germans feel McDonald's eating style is too "plastic." An advertising campaign in Germany pointed out that "every culture's eating style has its little tricks" but suggested that even gourmets don't eat at fancy restaurants every day. The ad offered McDonald's as an alternative to fine dining because the restaurant offers good food, inexpensive prices, and fast service. Thus McDonald's saw a need to reinforce a proper cultural image in the German environment.[10]

The debate will doubtless continue about which products, if any, can be standardized globally. As we point out, some firms, such as Black & Decker, have recently adopted globalized marketing strategies. For some products, such as soft drinks, a global marketing strategy, including advertising, seems to work well. For others, though, such as beer, strategies must incorporate local, regional, and national differences.[11]

7. Joseph A. Lawton, "Kodak Penetrates the European Copier Market with Customized Marketing Strategy and Product Changes," *Marketing News*, Aug. 3, 1984, p. 1.
8. Theodore Levitt, "The Globalization of Markets," *Harvard Business Review*, May–June 1983, p. 92.
9. Ibid., p. 93.
10. Dagmar Mussey, "McDonald's Image Gets Polished in German Ads," *Advertising Age*, July 8, 1985, p. 36.
11. "Global Brands Need Local Ad Flavor," *Advertising Age*, Sept. 3, 1984, p. 26.

Figure 22.3

Nestlé's global marketing approach for its new Alpine White candy bar (Source: Used with the permission of copyright owner, Nestlé Foods Corporation)

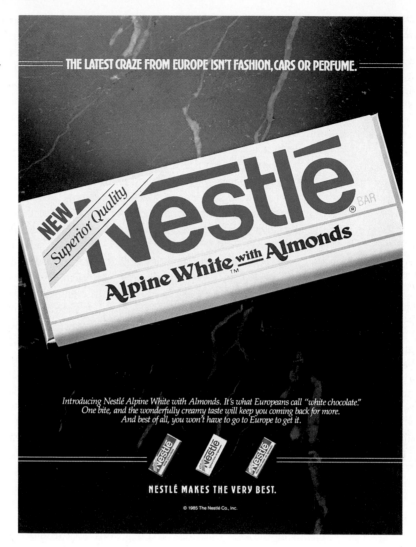

THE LATEST CRAZE FROM EUROPE ISN'T FASHION, CARS OR PERFUME.

NEW
Superior Quality
Nestlé® BAR
Alpine White™ with Almonds

Introducing Nestlé Alpine White with Almonds. It's what Europeans call "white chocolate."
One bite, and the wonderfully creamy taste will keep you coming back for more.
And best of all, you won't have to go to Europe to get it.

NESTLÉ MAKES THE VERY BEST.

© 1985 The Nestlé Co., Inc.

International Marketing Intelligence

Despite the debate over globalization of markets, most American firms perceive international markets as differing in some ways from domestic markets. International markets can be analyzed in terms of culture, institutions, and behavior of buyers. Table 22.2 lists types of statistical data that may help marketers to ascertain whether buyers are able, willing, and authorized to purchase products. To determine the willingness to buy, marketers must investigate buying behavior and environmental influences.

Gathering secondary data (see Table 22.2) should be the first step in analyzing a foreign market. Sources of statistical data include U.S. government publications, international organizations such as the United Nations, governments of foreign countries, and international trade organizations. Depending on the source, secondary data can be misleading, however. The reliability, validity, and comparability of data from some countries is often problematic.

Table 22.2 *Types of statistical data used to define international markets*

A. Cultural
1. Distribution of the population by educational levels
2. Distribution of the population by occupations
3. Distribution of the population by religions

B. Economic
1. Total personal income
2. Per capita income
3. Income distribution
4. Disposable income
5. Discretionary income
6. Distribution of wealth
7. Availability of consumer credit
8. Availability of capital
9. Rate of savings and capital formation

C. Demographic
1. Population size, persons and families
2. Age distribution
3. Regional distribution
4. Urban versus rural distribution
5. Marriage rate
6. Rate of family formation
7. Birth rate
8. Death rate
9. Distribution of families in various stages of the family life cycle

D. Geographic
1. Climate—temperate, jungle, arid
2. Elevation above sea level—lowlands, highlands
3. Access to transportation—seacoast, waterways, railroads, highways
4. Terrain—hilly, flat, rocky, grassland, forest

E. Technological
1. Advances in the physical sciences— applicable to agriculture, manufacturing, transportation, communication
2. Advances in the social sciences— applicable to governmental and political practices, business organization practices

F. Commercial (manufacturers, retailers, wholesalers, and service industries)
1. Number
2. Types
3. Location
4. Labor conditions
5. Employment record
6. Stage of technical advancement, especially mechanization, automation
7. Rate of growth
8. Management progressiveness

Source: Adapted from Gordon E. Miracle and Gerald S. Albaum, *International Marketing Management* (Homewood, Ill.: Irwin, 1970), pp. 190–191. © 1970 by Richard D. Irwin, Inc. Reprinted by permission of Gordon E. Miracle.

To overcome these shortcomings, marketers may need primary data to understand consumers' buying behavior in the country under investigation. After analyzing secondary and primary data, marketers should plan a marketing strategy. Finally, after market entry, review and control will result in decisions to withdraw from the foreign market, to continue to expand operations, or to consider additional foreign markets.

For foreign markets, marketers may need to adjust techniques of collecting primary data. Attitudes toward privacy, unwillingness to be interviewed, language differences, and low literacy rates can present serious research obstacles. In a bicultural country such as Canada, a national questionnaire that uses identical questions is impossible because of the cultural and language differences. In most areas of Africa, where the literacy rate is low, self-administered questionnaires would never work.

In many developing countries, purchasing behavior is based on unique symbols. It may be necessary to investigate basic patterns of social behavior, values, and attitudes to plan a final marketing strategy. Primary research should uncover significant cultural characteristics before a product is launched so that the marketing strategy is appropriate for the target market. Overall, the cost of obtaining international information may be higher than the cost of domestic research. This may occur because of the large number of foreign markets to be investigated, the distance between the marketer and the foreign market, unfamiliar cultural and marketing practices, language differences, or the scarcity and unreliability of published statistics.[12]

Environmental Forces in International Markets

A detailed analysis of the environment is an absolute necessity before a company enters foreign markets. If a marketing strategy is to be effective across national boundaries, the complexities of all the environments involved must be understood. In this section, we will see how the cultural, social, economic, technological, political, and legal forces in other countries differ from those found in the United States. The application on page 674, for instance, illustrates environmental differences in Latin American markets.

By moving from the analysis of individual behavior to the more abstract level of institutions, we can better understand foreign markets. Institutions serve as structures for achieving some necessary societal goals. For example, **social institutions** include family, education, religion, health, and recreational systems. **Economic institutions** are made up of producers, wholesalers, retailers, buyers, and other organizations that produce, distribute, and purchase products. **Political and legal institutions** include public agencies, laws, courts, legislatures, and government bureaus.

Cultural Forces

Concepts, values, and tangible items such as tools, buildings, and foods make up **culture.** Culture is passed on from one generation to another; in a way, it is the blueprint for acceptable behavior in a given society. When products are introduced into one nation from another, acceptance is far more likely if there are similarities between the two cultures. For example, when Johnson & Johnson tried to move its successful U.S. campaign for Affinity Shampoo to Spain, it did not understand the cultural differences between the two countries. Affinity was renamed Radiance and positioned as *the* shampoo for women over forty, the same campaign as used in the United States. But Spain's culture treats age differently than America's. A woman's age in Spain is a closely guarded secret, especially if she is over forty. According to the marketing director for Johnson & Johnson, "Nobody bought the product, fearing they would be identified with the age group it appealed to." Nearly two years after its introduction, Radiance held only a 0.2-percent market share.[13]

The connotations associated with body motions, greetings, colors, numbers, shapes, sizes, and symbols vary considerably across cultures. A few examples are shown in Table 22.3. For multinational marketers, these cultural differences have implications that pertain to product development, personal selling, advertising, packaging, and pricing.

12. Vern Terpstra, "Critical Mass and International Marketing Strategy," *Journal of the Academy of Marketing Science,* Summer 1983, pp. 269–282.
13. Laurel Wentz, "Local Laws Keep International Marketers Hopping," *Advertising Age,* July 11, 1985, p. 20.

Table 22.3 A sampling of cultural variations

Country/Region	Body Motions	Greetings	Colors	Numbers	Shapes, Sizes, Symbols
Japan	Pointing to one's own chest with a forefinger indicates one wants a bath. Pointing a forefinger to the nose indicates "me."	Bowing is the traditional form of greeting.	Positive colors are in muted shades. Combinations of black, dark gray, and white have negative overtones.	Positive numbers are 1, 3, 5, 8. Negative numbers are 4, 9.	Pine, bamboo, or plum patterns are positive. Cultural shapes such as Buddha-shaped jars should be avoided.
India	Kissing is considered offensive and not seen on television, in movies, or in public places.	The palms of the hands are placed together and the head is nodded for greeting. It is considered rude to touch a woman or shake hands.	Positive colors are bold colors such as green, red, yellow, or orange. Negative colors are black and white if they appear in relation to weddings.	To create brand awareness, numbers are often used as a brand name.	Animals such as parrots, elephants, tigers, or cheetahs are often used as brand names or on packaging. Sexually explicit symbols are avoided.
Europe	Raising only the index finger signifies a person wants two items. When counting on one's fingers, "one" is often indicated by thumb, "two" by thumb and forefinger.	It is acceptable to send flowers in thanks for a dinner invitation, but not roses (associated with sweethearts) or chrysanthemums (associated with funerals).	Generally, white and blue are considered positive. Black often has negative overtones.	The numbers 3 or 7 are usually positive. 13 is a negative number.	Circles are symbols of perfection. Hearts are considered favorably at Christmas time.
Latin America	General arm gestures are used for emphasis.	The traditional form of greeting is a hearty embrace followed by a friendly slap on the back.	Popular colors are generally bright or bold yellow, red, blue, or green.	Generally, 7 is a positive number. Negative numbers are 13, 14.	Religious symbols should be respected. Avoid national symbols such as flag colors.
Middle East	The raised eyebrow facial expression indicates "yes."	The word "no" must be mentioned three times before it is accepted.	Positive colors are brown, black, dark blues, and reds. Pink, violets, and yellows are not favored.	Positive numbers are 3, 7, 5, 9, while 13, 15 are negative.	Round or square shapes are acceptable. Symbols of 6-pointed star, raised thumb, or Koranic sayings are avoided.

Sources: James C. Simmons, "A Matter of Interpretation," *American Way*, April 1983, pp. 106–111; and "Adapting Export Packaging to Cultural Differences," *Business America*, Dec. 3, 1979, pp. 3–7.

Application

Understanding the Five Nations of Latin America

Although Latin America is composed of seventeen nations, marketing consultant Marlene L. Rossman believes that it can be divided into five distinct markets: Mexico, Brazil, Caribbean Latin America, European Latin America, and Indian Latin America. The five markets are based on demographical, sociological, and cultural differences. The only inherent similarity between these markets is the language of origin.

Americans have trusted stereotypes that have cost companies millions of dollars in lost sales. For instance, one major U.S. multinational food company successfully test-marketed its products in Mexico and then made a major investment decision to market those products in Brazil based on the Mexican success. After several years of losses, the error was obvious: what sells in Mexico has very little to do with consumer preferences in Brazil. When developing a marketing strategy for Latin America, therefore, it is important to understand the characteristics of Latin America's five markets:

Mexico's proximity and importance to the United States make it a major market. The country's 75 million inhabitants, including 15 million middle-class Mexicans, constitute a major opportunity for American marketers. Two-thirds of all Mexican exports go to the United States, while 6 to 7 percent of U.S. exports go to Mexico. American marketers must keep in mind that Mexicans are very proud of their country's economic progress and feel a strong sense of nationalism.

Brazil is the only Portuguese-speaking country on the South American continent and also the largest Latin American nation. Half of Brazil's population is under twenty years of age, not an uncommon situation in Latin America. Pent-up demand is enormous, particularly in the youth market. U.S. goods are highly valued, and Brazilians admire U.S. economic success.

Caribbean Latin America includes Puerto Rico, the Dominican Republic, Panama, Honduras, Caracas and coastal Venezuela, coastal cities of Colombia, and Cubans in Miami and Tampa, Florida. This market is characterized by a tropical climate, a fairly large black Creole population, and a small upper class that controls most of the industry and politics. The people are warm, open, and friendly and often admire the United States.

European Latin America includes Argentina, Chile, Uruguay, most of Colombia, southern Brazil, Costa Rica, and Lima, Peru. Argentina and Uruguay, especially, have very strong European ties. People are gracious, formal, and receptive to U.S. goods and services.

Indian Latin America includes Bolivia, Paraguay, Ecuador, and Peru (except Lima) in South America and Guatemala and El Salvador in Central America. Spanish is spoken in the capitals and large cities, but people in rural areas speak Indian dialects almost exclusively and are steeped in Indian tradition. Poverty and isolation make this a fairly difficult market to penetrate. (*Source: Marlene L. Rossman, "Understanding the Five Nations of Latin America,"* Marketing News, *Oct. 11, 1985, p. 10. Reprinted from* Marketing News, *published by the American Marketing Association.*)

A society's attitude toward the body also affects international marketers. The American custom of patting a child on the head would not be considered a sign of friendliness in the Orient, where the head has been held sacred. In contrast, the illustration of feet is regarded as despicable in Thailand.

An international marketer also must know a country's customs regarding male-female social interaction. Advertising that is based on the togetherness of married life could backfire in Japan and Western Europe, where husbands and wives often lead separate lives. In Italy it is unacceptable for a salesman to call on someone's wife if the husband is not home. In Thailand, some Listerine television commercials that portray boy-girl romantic relationships were unacceptable.

Social Forces

Marketing activities are primarily social in purpose; therefore, they are structured by the institutions of family, religion, education, health, and recreation. In every nation, these social institutions can be identified. By finding major deviations in institutions among countries, one can gain insights into the adaptation of marketing strategy. While football is a popular sport in the United States and is a major opportunity for many television advertisers, soccer is the most popular TV sport in Europe. Yet fan violence has caused major advertisers in the United Kingdom to have second thoughts about supporting such events with millions of advertising dollars. One advertising executive indicated that advertising on soccer matches is similar to placing advertisements in nude magazines in the United States.[14] The role of children in the family and a society's overall view of children also affect marketing activities. The use of cute, cereal-loving kids in advertising for Kellogg's is illegal in France. In the Netherlands, children are banned from confectionary advertisements and candymakers are required to place a little toothbrush symbol at the end of each confectionary spot.[15]

Economic Forces

Economic differences dictate many of the adjustments that must be made in marketing across national boundaries. The most prominent adjustments are caused by standards of living, availability of credit, discretionary buying power, income distribution, national resources, climate, and conditions that affect transportation.

In terms of the value of all products produced by a nation, the United States has the largest **gross national product (GNP)** in the world, $3,297.8 billion. GNP is an overall measure of a nation's economic standing, but it does not take into account the concept of GNP in relation to population (GNP per capita). The United States has a GNP per capita of $13,492. The aggregate GNP of a very small country may be low. Austria's, for instance, is $69.6 billion, but the GNP per capita, a measure of the **standard of living,** is $8,908. The Soviet Union (population 262,436,000) has one of the highest GNPs in the world ($1,843.4 billion) but has only a $6,490 GNP per capita.[16] This figure means that the average Soviet citizen has less discretionary income than do citizens in countries with higher GNPs per capita. Knowledge about per capita income, aggregate GNP, credit, and the distribution of income provides general insights into market potential.

Opportunities for international marketers are not limited to those countries with the highest incomes. Some nations are progressing at a markedly faster rate than they were a few years ago, and these countries—especially in Latin America, Africa, and the Middle East—have tremendous market potential for

14. Brian Oliver, "U.K. Soccer Advertising in Trouble," *Advertising Age,* July 8, 1985, p. 36.
15. Wentz, "Local Laws," p. 20.
16. *Statistical Abstract of the United States,* 1986, p. 842.

specific products. However, marketers must understand the political and legal environment before they can convert buying power into actual demand for specific products.

Technological Forces

Much of the marketing technology used in North America and other industrialized regions of the world may be ill suited for developing countries. In addition, the export of technology of strategic importance to the United States may require U.S. Department of Defense approval before foreign sales can occur. For example, the Soviet Union wanted to buy Boeing 747 jet engines, made by General Electric, for Russian airlines. When GE applied for the license to export these jet engines to the Soviet Union, its request was denied. Yet General Electric was licensed to sell these same engines to Israel for use on jet fighters.

Political and Legal Forces

A country's political system, national laws, regulatory bodies, national pressure groups, and courts all have great impact on international marketing. A government's policies toward public versus private enterprise, consumers, and foreign firms influence marketing across national boundaries. For example, the Japanese have developed many barriers to imports into their country. Even though they have announced that over the next few years tariffs on 1,853 items will be reduced, many nontariff barriers still make it difficult for American companies to export their products to Japan.[17] Until recently, companies exporting electronic equipment to Japan had to wait for the Japanese government to inspect each item. A government's attitude toward cooperation with importers has a direct impact on the economic feasibility of exporting to that country.

Figure 22.4 summarizes categories of political and legal risk in international markets. Political experts individually rated sixty-one countries according to (1) each nation's likelihood of restricting business and (2) its relative political instability. A "high" ranking on either scale means a greater than 30-percent chance of regime change or further business restriction. "Low" is defined as less than 20-percent risk. Thus China, whose regime is considered secure, nonetheless rates high on restrictions. Nevertheless, ITT is marketing its System 12 computer in China, as illustrated in Figure 22.5.

Differences in political and government ethical standards are illustrated by what the Mexicans call *la mordida,* "the bite." The use of payoffs and bribes is deeply entrenched in many governments. Since U.S. trade and corporate policy, as well as U.S. law, prohibits direct involvement in payoffs and bribes, American firms may have a hard time competing with foreign firms that engage in this practice. Some U.S. firms that refuse to make payoffs are forced to hire local consultants, public relations firms, or advertising agencies—which results in indirect payoffs. The ultimate decision about whether to give small tips or gifts where they are customary must be based on a firm's code of conduct. However, it is illegal for U.S. firms to attempt to make large payments or bribes to influence policy decisions of foreign governments. These actions are covered under the Foreign Corrupt Practices Act of 1977. The act also subjects all publicly held U.S. corporations to demanding internal control and record-keeping

17. Lee Smith, "Japan Wants to Make Friends," *Fortune,* Sept. 2, 1985, p. 84.

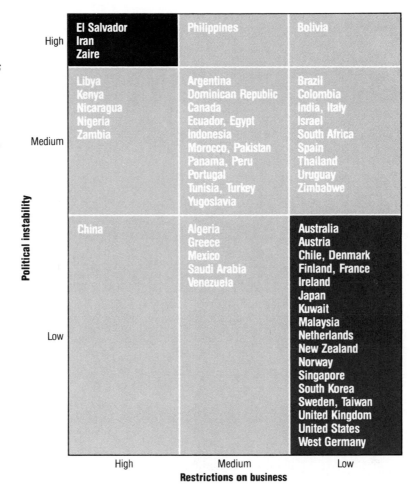

Figure 22.4

Sixty countries classified by instability and restrictions on business (Source: From Bob Donath, "Handicapping and Hedging the Foreign Investment," Industrial Marketing, *Feb. 1981, p. 58. Based on the Frost and Sullivan (F&S) World Political Risk Forecast)*

	High	Medium	Low
High	El Salvador Iran Zaire	Philippines	Bolivia
Medium	Libya Kenya Nicaragua Nigeria Zambia	Argentina Dominican Republic Canada Ecuador, Egypt Indonesia Morocco, Pakistan Panama, Peru Portugal Tunisia, Turkey Yugoslavia	Brazil Colombia India, Italy Israel South Africa Spain Thailand Uruguay Zimbabwe
Low	China	Algeria Greece Mexico Saudi Arabia Venezuela	Australia Austria Chile, Denmark Finland, France Ireland Japan Kuwait Malaysia Netherlands New Zealand Norway Singapore South Korea Sweden, Taiwan United Kingdom United States West Germany

Political instability (vertical axis) · **Restrictions on business** (horizontal axis: High, Medium, Low)

requirements related to their overseas operations. Failure to meet the requirements can result in civil or criminal prosecution of corporate officers, directors, employees, agents, or stockholders.[18]

Strategic Adaptation of Marketing Mixes

Strategic marketing planning is discussed in detail in Chapter 18. A planning aid discussed in that chapter is the plotting of competitive strengths and market attractiveness on a two-dimensional matrix. Such a device is most useful for analyzing products within the international context. As Figure 22.6 illustrates, each axis is a linear combination of factors that can be used to define a country's

18. Jyotic N. Prasad and C. P. Rao, "Foreign Payoffs and International Business Ethics Revisited," in *Marketing Comes of Age,* eds. David M. Klein and Allen E. Smith (Southern Marketing Association, 1984), pp. 260–264.

我们的
电话系统
能够不断地
扩增更新，
所以它能够
经久耐用。

能够经久耐用的电话系统原也甚多。

问题是，一个系统经过了很长的一段时间，就会逐渐过时。

尤其是，各个国家都在不断发展，需求在变，技术要求也在变。土耳其共和国正因为考虑到这些因素，才定购了三百四十万条 ITT SYSTEM 12™（系统12）线路。

不用说，SYSTEM 12 是一种全数字式的系统。

但最独特的还是我们握有专利的电信处理技术：全分布式控制。

这就是土耳其选择我们系统的理由。

全分布式控制使我们不必像一般数字式电话系统那样装用庞大的中心电子计算机。

而用散置在系统内的许多微处理机来分别进行控制。

SYSTEM 12在增加线路的同时，就可以增加它所需的控制系统。如要添加一些新的性能也一样方便。

随着土耳其的发展繁荣，SYSTEM 12 也能逐步加以扩增。当技术要求变化时，SYSTEM 12 也能随着作相应的改变。

更重要的是，我们的组合式设计保证了某一部分的故障不会牵连到整个系统。

这一些都是 SYSTEM 12 所以能真正经久耐用的原因。

不断发展，不断扩增，不断变化，不断更新。

SYSTEM 12 ITT

© 1985 ITT Corporation. 320 Park Avenue, New York, NY 10022, U.S.A.

Figure 22.5 *Advertisement for ITT's System 12 computer, promoted in the Chinese market despite many import restrictions (Source: Courtesy of ITT Corporation)*

attractiveness from a market view and to assess the level of competition in that country.[19] To develop a matrix, marketers must gather data for a specific product and country. Research style, methodology, and approach to data gathering vary by company.[20]

Once a U.S. firm determines foreign market potentials and understands the foreign environment, it develops and adapts its marketing mix. Creating and maintaining the marketing mix is the final step in developing the international marketing strategy. Only if foreign marketing opportunities justify the risk will a company go to the expense of adapting the marketing mix. Of course, in some situations new products are developed for a specific country. In these cases, there is no existing marketing mix and no extra expense to consider in serving the foreign target market.

19. Gilbert D. Harrell and Richard O. Kiefer, "Multinational Strategic Market Portfolios," *MSU Business Topics,* Winter 1981, p. 6.
20. David C. Pring, "Filling Overseas Gaps," *Advertising Age,* Oct. 26, 1981, pp. 5–18.

Part VII / Selected Applications

Figure 22.6

Matrix for plotting products in international marketing (Source: Adapted from Gilbert D. Harrell and Richard O. Kiefer, "Multinational Strategic Market Portfolios," MSU Business Topics, Winter 1981, p. 7. Reprinted by permission)

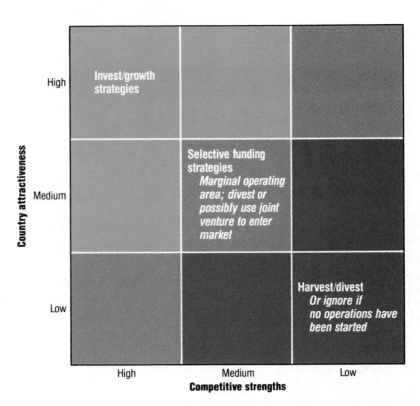

Product and Promotion

As shown in Figure 22.7, there are five possible strategies for adapting product and promotion across national boundaries: (1) keep product and promotion the same worldwide, (2) adapt promotion only, (3) adapt product only, (4) adapt both product and promotion, and (5) invent new products.[21]

Keep Product and Promotion the Same Worldwide

This strategy attempts to use in the foreign country the product and promotion that have been developed for the U.S. market, an approach that seems desirable wherever possible since it eliminates the expenses of marketing research and product redevelopment. Despite certain inherent risks that stem from cultural differences in interpretation, exporting advertising copy does provide the efficiency of international standardization.

Even multinational firms operating in less-developed countries are using standardization, despite wide economic and cultural differences. A recent survey of American and British firms marketing nondurable consumer products in less-developed countries revealed that approximately 70 percent of the firms maintained their original brand names. Only 10 percent used a new local name for their brands, while the remaining 20 percent either used another English brand name or translated the original name to the local language.[22]

21. Adapted from Warren G. Keegan, "Multinational Product Planning: Strategic Alternatives," *Journal of Marketing*, Jan. 1969, pp. 58–62; and Philip Kotler, *Marketing Management: Analysis, Planning and Control*, 5th ed. (Englewood Cliffs, N.J.: Prentice-Hall, 1984), pp. 455–456.
22. John S. Hill and Richard S. Still, "Brand Name Decisions in International Marketing: To Adapt or Not to Adapt—(That Is the Question)," in Klein and Smith, *Marketing Comes of Age*, pp. 161–163.

Figure 22.7

International product and promotion strategies Source: Adapted from Warren J. Keagan, "Multinational Product Planning Strategic Alternatives," Journal of Marketing, Jan. 1969, pp. 58–62. Published by the American Marketing Association)

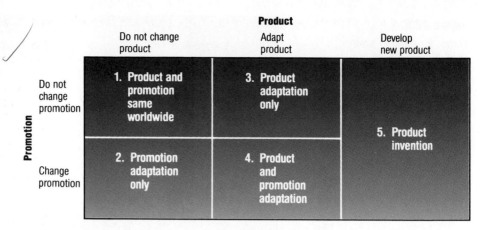

Global advertising embraces the same concept as global marketing, discussed earlier in this chapter. An advertiser can save hundreds of thousands of dollars by running the same advertisement worldwide. Playtex has combined its thirteen foreign intimate-apparel operations with its U.S. operation. Grey Advertising developed a global advertisement using models who have universal appeal. Clones of the same advertisement in different languages were used globally.[23]

Adapt Promotion Only

This strategy leaves the product basically unchanged but modifies its promotion. This approach may be necessary because of language, legal, or cultural differences associated with the advertising copy. The application on page 681 illustrates how legal restrictions could cause an adaptation in advertising.

As discussed earlier in this chapter, sales of Affinity Shampoo were hurt because the U.S. advertising campaign was translated directly into Spanish. Because of the sensitivity about Spanish women's ages, the advertising slogan had to be changed to appeal to "women who feel young regardless of their age."[24] Promotional adaptation is a low-cost modification compared with the cost of redeveloping engineering and production and the cost of physically changing products.

In general, the strategy of adapting only promotion infuses advertising with the culture of people who will be exposed to it. Often promotion combines thinking globally and acting locally: at company headquarters a basic global marketing strategy is developed, but promotion is modified to fit each market's needs. For example, in the U.S., Affinity Shampoo uses a Nancy Reagan look-alike in advertisements, but in England, where Nancy Reagan does not have a great following, a more independent-looking female character is used.[25]

Adapt Product Only

The basic assumption in modifying a product without changing its promotion is that the product will serve the same function under different conditions of use. Soap and detergent manufacturers have adapted their products to local

23. "Playtex Kicks Off a One-Ad-Fits-All Campaign," *Business Week,* Dec. 16, 1985, p. 48.
24. Laurel Wentz, "Local Laws Keep International Marketers Hopping," *Advertising Age,* July 11, 1985, p. 20.
25. "Global Brands Need Local Ad Flavor," *Advertising Age,* Sept. 13, 1984, p. 26.

Country	Restriction	Justification
France	No tourism advertising	Minimizes the public's spending outside the country
	No TV commercials for supermarket chains	Small grocers should not be driven out of business by the larger chains
Germany	Comparative advertising is heavily discouraged and must pass rigorous fairness tests	Comparative advertising is often felt to be misleading and deceptive
	Children cannot talk about product benefits or be appealed to in an ad	Children are not to be exploited or taken advantage of
Great Britain	Product categories banned from TV advertising: undertakers, the Bible, matrimonial agencies, fortune tellers, private detectives, contraceptives, and pregnancy tests	Whenever the Independent Broadcasting Authority receives 10 or more complaints about an ad/product, they ban it
Switzerland	People cannot be used in print and TV ads for alcoholic beverages	The consumption of alcohol should not be depicted as glamorous and socially demanded
Spain	Tobacco and alcohol (excluding wine and beer) are banned from TV	These products are not viewed as beneficial to the public

(*Source: Laurel Wentz, "Local Laws Keep International Marketers Hopping,"* Advertising Age, *July 11, 1985, p. 20. Reprinted with permission from* Advertising Age, *July 11, 1985. Copyright © 1985 Crain Communications, Inc.*)

water conditions and washing equipment without changing their promotions. Household appliances have been altered to use different types of electricity.

A product may have to be adjusted for legal reasons. Japan has some of the most stringent automobile emission requirements in the world. American automobiles that fail emission standards cannot be marketed in Japan.

Sometimes, products must be adjusted to overcome social and cultural obstacles. Jell-O introduced a powdered gelatin mix that failed in England because the English were used to buying gelatin in jelled form. Resistance to a product is frequently based on attitudes and ignorance about the nature of a new technology. It is often easier to change the product than to overcome technological biases.

Adapt Both Product and Promotion

When a product serves a new function in a foreign market, then both the product and its promotion need to be altered. In Europe, greeting cards provide a space for senders to write messages in their own words; and European greeting cards are cellophane wrapped, which also calls for a product alteration.

Figure 22.8

Strategies for international distribution and pricing

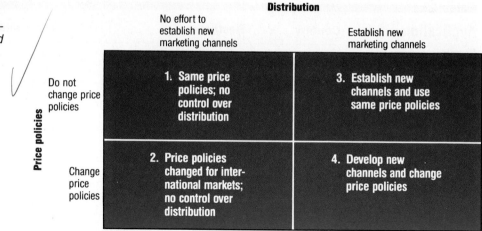

Both the product and the promotion must be changed because the product's function is different. Adaptation of both product and promotion is the most expensive strategy discussed thus far, but it should be considered if the foreign market appears large enough.

Invent New Products

This strategy is selected when existing products cannot meet the needs of a foreign market. General Motors has developed an all-purpose, jeeplike motor vehicle that can be assembled in underdeveloped nations by mechanics with no special training. The vehicle is designed to operate under varied conditions; it has standardized parts and is inexpensive. Colgate-Palmolive has developed an inexpensive, all-plastic, hand-powered washing machine that has the tumbling action of a modern automatic machine. The product, marketed in underdeveloped countries, was invented for households that have no electricity. Strategies that involve the invention of products are often the most costly, but the payoff can be great.

Distribution and Pricing

Decisions about the distribution system and pricing policies are important in developing an international marketing mix. Figure 22.8 illustrates different approaches to these decisions.

Distribution

A firm can sell its product to an intermediary that is willing to buy from existing market channels in the United States, or it can develop new international marketing channels. It must consider distribution both between countries and within the foreign country.

In determining distribution alternatives, the existence of retail institutions and wholesalers that can perform marketing functions between and within nations is one major factor. If a foreign country has a segmented retail structure consisting primarily of one-person shops or street vendors, it may be difficult to develop new marketing channels for such products as packaged goods and prepared foods. Quite often in Third World countries, certain channels of

Figure 22.9

Distribution of Bank-America Travelers Cheques sold throughout Asia; the registered mark "World Money®" conveys global acceptability (Source: Courtesy of BankAmerica)

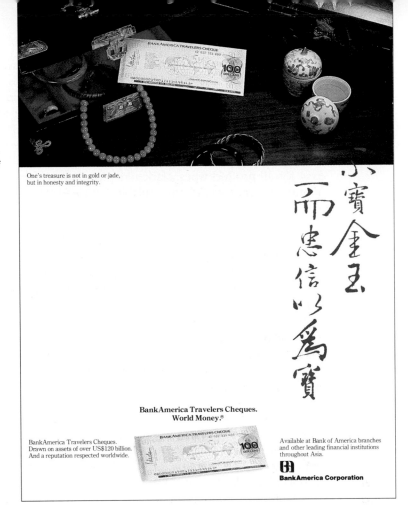

One's treasure is not in gold or jade, but in honesty and integrity.

小寶金玉
而忠信以為寶

**BankAmerica Travelers Cheques.
World Money.®**

BankAmerica Travelers Cheques.
Drawn on assets of over US$120 billion.
And a reputation respected worldwide.

Available at Bank of America branches
and other leading financial institutions
throughout Asia.

BankAmerica Corporation

distribution are characterized by ethnodomination. Ethnodomination is defined as a situation where an ethnic group occupies a majority position within a marketing channel. Consider the following examples: Indians own approximately 90 percent of the cotton gins in Uganda; the Hausa tribe in Nigeria dominates the trade in kola nuts, cattle, and housing; Chinese merchants dominate the rice economy in Thailand. Marketers must be sensitive to ethnodomination and recognize that the ethnic groups operate in subcultures that are unique in social and economic organization.[26]

If the product being sold across national boundaries requires service and information, then control of the distribution process is desirable. Figure 22.9 illustrates that BankAmerica Travelers Cheques are available at banks throughout Asia. Travelers cheques require personal service in sales and informing the customer of utilization and reimbursement if lost or stolen. American Express carefully controls the distribution of its travelers cheques. Caterpillar sells over half its construction and earth-moving equipment in foreign countries. Because it must provide services and replacement parts, Caterpillar has established its own dealers in foreign markets. Regional sales offices and technical experts

26. Douglass G. Norvell and Robert Morey, "Ethnodomination in the Channels of Distribution of Third World Nations," *Journal of the Academy of Marketing Science,* Summer 1983, pp. 204–215.

are also available to support local dealers. A manufacturer of paintbrushes, on the other hand, would be more concerned about agents, wholesalers, or other manufacturers that would facilitate the product's exposure in a foreign market. Control over the distribution process would not be so important for that product.

Several international marketing channels are available to American businesses (see Figure 22.10). These marketing channels are not all-inclusive, nor do they exist for all product types. Marketers planning to sell products across national boundaries must work with available intermediaries or bridge the gaps.

Pricing

The domestic and foreign price of products are usually different. The increased costs of transportation, supplies, taxes, tariffs, and other expenses necessary to adjust a firm's operations to international marketing can raise prices. A key decision is whether the basic pricing policy will change (as discussed in Chapter 15). If it is a firm's policy not to allocate fixed costs to foreign sales, then lower foreign prices could result.

American drug manufacturers have been accused of selling drugs in foreign markets at low prices (without allocating research and development costs), while charging American customers high prices that include all research and development expenses. The sale of U.S. products in foreign markets—or vice versa—at lower prices (when all costs have not been allocated or when surplus products are sold) is called **dumping.** Dumping is illegal in many countries if it damages domestic firms and workers.

A cost-plus approach to international pricing is probably the most common method used because of the compounding number of costs necessary to move products from the United States to a foreign country. Of course, our discussion of pricing policies in Chapter 15 points out that understanding consumer demand and the competitive environment is a necessary step in selecting a price.

The price charged in other countries is also a function of foreign currency exchange rates. Fluctuations of the international monetary market can change the prices charged across national boundaries on a daily basis. There has been a trend toward greater fluctuation (or float) in world money markets. A sudden variation in the exchange rate—which occurs when a nation devalues its currency, for example—can have wide-ranging effects on consumer prices. U.S. devaluation of the dollar in the 1970s resulted in lower prices for American products in foreign countries and higher prices for imports in the United States.

In the 1980s this trend was reversed. The strong dollar caused the prices of American exports to climb, while the price of many imported products declined. By early 1985, the dollar's exchange value was 90 percent over the average weighted 1970s price of other countries' currencies. The high value of the dollar eliminated many foreign markets for American exporters. After reaching a peak in early 1985, the dollar once again dropped, lowering the prices of American products in other countries. However, it takes time even after prices drop for foreign companies to reorient their purchasing habits away from established trade relationships. For larger American companies, the stakes can be enormous. Packaged goods companies such as Colgate-Palmolive, Procter & Gamble, and Bristol-Myers get as much as 50 percent of their revenues from overseas operations.[27]

27. "Who Wins from the Cheaper Dollar," *Fortune,* Aug. 19, 1985, p. 30.

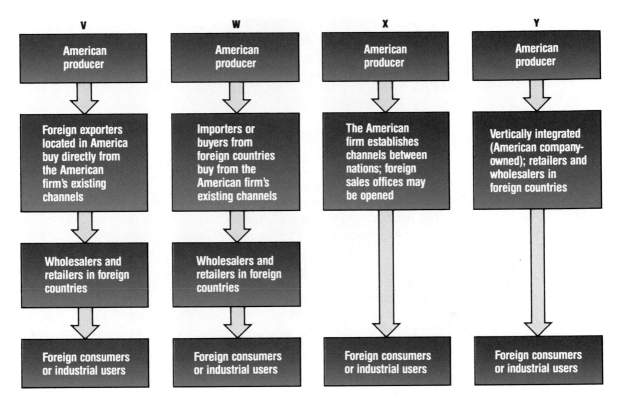

V	W	X	Y
American producer	**American producer**	**American producer**	**American producer**
Foreign exporters located in America buy directly from the American firm's existing channels	Importers or buyers from foreign countries buy from the American firm's existing channels	The American firm establishes channels between nations; foreign sales offices may be opened	Vertically integrated (American company-owned); retailers and wholesalers in foreign countries
Wholesalers and retailers in foreign countries	Wholesalers and retailers in foreign countries		
Foreign consumers or industrial users	Foreign consumers or industrial users	Foreign consumers or industrial users	Foreign consumers or industrial users

Figure 22.10 *Examples of international channels of distribution for an American firm*

Developing International Marketing Involvement

The level of commitment to international marketing is a major variable in deciding what kind of involvement is appropriate. A firm's options range from occasional exporting to expanding overall operations (production and marketing) into other countries. Here, we will examine exporting, licensing, joint ventures, and direct ownership as approaches to marketing across national boundaries.

Exporting

Exporting represents the lowest level of commitment to international marketing and the most flexible approach. A firm may find an exporting intermediary that can perform most marketing functions associated with selling to other countries. This approach entails minimum effort and cost. Modifications in packaging, labeling, style, or color may be the major expenses in adapting a product. There is limited risk in using export agents and merchants since there is no direct investment in the foreign country.

Export agents bring buyers and sellers from different countries together; they collect a commission for arranging sales. Export houses and export merchants purchase products from different companies, then sell them to foreign countries. They are specialists at understanding customers' needs in foreign countries.

Foreign buyers from companies and governments provide a direct method of exporting and eliminate the need for an intermediary. Foreign buyers encourage international exchange by contacting domestic firms about their needs and

Figure 22.11

Yoplait, a product produced in the United States under a license from a French company (Source: Used with permission of Yoplait USA, a division of General Mills, Inc.)

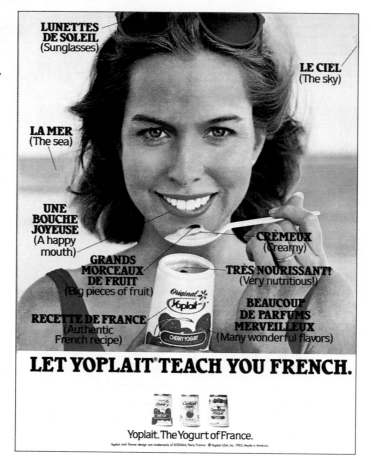

about the opportunities available in exporting. Domestic firms that want to export with a minimum of effort and investment seek out foreign importers and buyers.

Licensing

When potential markets are found across national boundaries—and when production, technical assistance, or marketing know-how is required—**licensing** is an alternative to direct investment. Exchanges of management techniques or technical assistance are primary reasons for licensing agreements. The licensee (the owner of the foreign operation) pays commissions or royalties on sales or supplies used in manufacturing. Figure 22.11 illustrates a French yogurt that is licensed for production in the United States. The Yoplait brand tries to maintain a French image. An initial down payment or fee may be charged when the licensing agreement is signed. Licensing is an attractive alternative to direct investment when the political stability of a foreign country is in doubt or when resources are unavailable for direct investment.

Licensing is especially advantageous for small manufacturers wanting to launch a well-known brand internationally. For example, all Spalding sporting products are licensed worldwide. The Questor Corporation owns the Spalding name but produces no products itself. Pierre Cardin has issued five hundred licenses and Yves St. Laurent two hundred to make their products.[28] Lowenbrau has used licensing agreements, including one with Miller in the United States, to increase sales worldwide without committing capital to build breweries.

Joint Ventures

In international marketing, a **joint venture** is a partnership between a domestic firm and a foreign firm or government. Joint ventures are often a political necessity because of nationalism and governmental restrictions on foreign ownership. They are assuming greater global importance because of cost advantages and the number of inexperienced firms entering foreign markets. In environments of scarce resources, rapid technological change, and massive capital requirements, joint ventures may be the best way for underdog firms to attain better positions in global industries. Such partnerships may be used to gain access to marketing channels, suppliers, and technology.[29]

Joint ventures are especially popular in industries that call for large investments, such as natural resources extraction or automobile manufacturing. Control of the joint venture can be split equally, or one party may control decision making. In one example of a joint venture, Toyota Motor Corporation and General Motors have joined to produce the Nova automobile. The major components of the car, the engine and transmission, come from Japan; many of the surface elements such as the grill, radio, seats, and tires are made in the United States. General Motors and other domestic auto manufacturers are faced with the dilemma that Japanese companies can produce cars at a cost advantage of $2,000 per unit. The joint venture with Toyota allows GM to provide import quality and price competitiveness in an American-branded product.[30]

Increasingly, once a joint venture succeeds, nationalism spurs a trend toward expropriating or purchasing foreign shares of the enterprise. On the other hand, a joint venture may be the only available means to enter a foreign market. American construction firms bidding for business in Saudi Arabia, for example, have found that joint ventures with Arab construction companies gain local support among the handful of people who make the contracting decisions.

Trading Companies

The purpose of a **trading company** is to provide a link between buyers and sellers in different countries. A trading company, as its name implies, is not involved in manufacturing or owning assets related to manufacturing. It buys in one country at the lowest price consistent with quality and sells to buyers in another country. An important function of trading companies is taking title to products and undertaking all of the activities necessary to move the products from the domestic country to a market in a foreign country. For example, major grain trading companies operating out of home offices in both the United States and overseas control a major portion of the world's trade in basic food commodities, which is valued at over $50 billion per year. These trading companies sell agricultural commodities that are homogeneous in nature and can be stored and moved rapidly in response to market conditions.

28. John A. Quelch, "How to Build a Product Licensing Program," *Harvard Business Review,* May–June 1985, pp. 186–187.
29. Cathryn Rudie Harrigan, "Joint Ventures and Global Strategies," *Columbia Journal of World Business,* Summer 1984, pp. 7–16.
30. Maralyn Edid, "The American Small Car Keeps Getting More Japanese," *Business Week,* June 24, 1985, p. 50.

Trading companies reduce risk for companies interested in getting involved in international marketing. A trading company will assist producers with information about products that meet quality and price expectations in domestic or international markets. Additional services a trading company may provide include consulting, marketing research, advertising, insurance, product research and design, legal assistance, warehousing, and foreign exchange.

In 1982, the Export Trading Company Act was passed to facilitate the efficient operation of trading companies in the United States. At least seventy-five major trading companies have been created to help American manufacturers build international markets. Besides allowing banks to invest in trading companies, the Export Trading Act created a new certification procedure that enables companies to apply for limited protection from antitrust laws when conducting export operations. A few major corporations have set up trading companies to market various lines of business abroad. The best known is Sears World Trade, which specializes in consumer goods, light industrial items, and processed foods. A trading company acts like a wholesaler, taking on much of the responsibility of finding markets while facilitating all marketing aspects of a transaction.

Direct Ownership

Once a company makes a long-term commitment to marketing in a foreign nation that has a promising political and economic environment, **direct ownership** of a foreign subsidiary or division is a possibility. Although most discussions of foreign investment concern only manufacturing equipment or personnel, the expenses of developing a separate foreign distribution system can be tremendous. The opening of retail stores in Europe, Canada, or Mexico can require a large investment in facilities, research expenditures, and management costs.

A wholly owned foreign subsidiary may be allowed to operate independently of the parent company so that management can have more freedom to adjust to the local environment. Cooperative arrangements are developed to assist in marketing efforts, production, and management. A wholly owned foreign subsidiary may export products to the home nation. Some American automobile manufacturers import cars built by their foreign subsidiaries. A foreign subsidiary offers important tax, tariff, and other operating advantages. One of the greatest advantages is the cross-cultural approach. A subsidiary usually operates under foreign management, so it can develop a local identity. The greatest danger in such an arrangement comes from political uncertainty—a firm may lose its foreign investment.

Summary

Marketing activities performed across national boundaries are usually significantly different from domestic marketing activities. International marketers must have an in-depth awareness of the foreign environment. The marketing strategy ordinarily is adjusted to meet the needs and desires of foreign markets.

Global marketing strategies are developed to expand a business beyond national boundaries and to achieve a corporate goal of long-term growth. The level of involvement in international marketing can range from casual exporting to globalization of markets. Although most firms adjust their marketing mixes for differences in target markets, some firms are able to standardize their marketing efforts worldwide. That is, they sell the same things in the same way everywhere.

Marketers must understand the complexities of the international marketing environment before they can formulate a marketing mix. Environmental aspects of special importance include cultural, social, economic, political, and legal forces. Cultural aspects of the environment that are most important to international marketers include customs, concepts, values, attitudes, morals, and knowledge. Social institutions influence human interaction. International marketers must understand such social institutions as family, religion, education, health, and recreation.

The most prominent economic forces that affect international marketing are those that can be measured by income and resources. Credit, buying power, and income distribution provide aggregate measures of market potential. The level of technology helps define economic development within a nation and indicates the existence of methods to facilitate marketing. The level of technology can dictate the structure of the marketing mix.

Political and legal institutions include the political system, national laws, regulatory bodies, national pressure groups, and courts. Foreign policies of all nations involved in trade determine how marketing can be conducted. Ethical standards and internal politics must be dealt with effectively; a firm must decide whether to use a domestic code of ethics or the foreign country's code of ethics.

After a country's environment has been analyzed, marketers must develop a marketing mix and decide whether to adapt product or promotion. Foreign distribution channels are nearly always different from domestic ones. The allocation of costs, transportation considerations, or the costs of doing business in foreign nations will affect pricing. Standardization of international marketing mixes is highly desirable, but most evidence indicates that standardization is regional at best.

There are several ways of getting involved in international marketing. Exporting is the easiest and most flexible method. Licensing is an alternative to direct investment. It may be necessitated by political and economic conditions. Joint ventures or partnerships are often appropriate when outside resources are needed or when there are governmental restrictions on foreign ownership. Trading companies are experts at buying products in the domestic market and selling to foreign markets, thereby taking most of the risk in international involvement. Direct ownership of foreign divisions or subsidiaries represents the strongest commitment to international marketing and involves the greatest risk.

Important Terms

International marketing
Multinational enterprise
Globalization of markets
Social institutions
Economic institutions
Political and legal institutions
Culture

Gross national product (GNP)
Standard of living
Dumping
Licensing
Joint venture
Trading company
Direct ownership

1. How does international marketing differ from domestic marketing?
2. What must marketers consider before deciding whether or not to become involved in international marketing?
3. Why are the largest industrial corporations in the United States so committed to international marketing?
4. Why was so much of this chapter devoted to an analysis of the international marketing environment?
5. A manufacturer recently exported peanut butter with a green label to a nation in the Far East. The product failed because it was associated with jungle sickness. How could this mistake have been avoided?
6. Relate the concept of reference groups (Chapter 3) to international marketing.
7. How do religious systems influence marketing activities in foreign countries?
8. Which is more important to international marketers, a country's aggregate GNP or its GNP per capita? Why?
9. If you were asked to provide a small tip (or bribe) to have a document approved in a foreign nation where this practice was customary, what would you do?
10. In marketing dog food to Latin America, what aspects of the marketing mix would need to be altered?
11. What should marketers consider as they decide whether to license or to enter into a joint venture in a foreign nation?

Cases

Case 22.1 Porsche AG[31]

In 1931, the company known today as Porsche AG was only a dream in the mind of Dr. Ferdinand Porsche. It was a dream that would quickly become a reality, however. The original company, called "Porsche Konstruktionsburo fuer Motoren-Fahrzeug-Luftfahrzeug und Wasserfahrzeugbau," accepted contracts from individuals and firms to design new automobiles, airplanes, and ships. Prototypes of each design were subsequently built by Porsche and thoroughly tested. If the firm that commissioned the work approved the design, it was then produced by one of the large manufacturing firms in Germany. In the early years, Porsche existed as a research and development company only.

The year 1945 brought the end of World War II, and a devastated Europe embarked on the long road to recovery. It was, however, the beginning of new tribulation for the Porsche family, culminating in Ferdinand Porsche's imprisonment by the French for alleged war crimes that, as later determined, were false accusations. Meanwhile Porsche's son, Dr. Ferry Porsche, started producing automobiles in Germany in the late 1940s.

Despite disappointments and hardships, a depressed economic climate, and personal tragedy, the Porsches built a strong and persevering company. By 1973, the firm had built and sold some 200,000 Porsches and had gained world recognition for its cars and their offer of "driving in its purest form." The company today is divided into three distinct segments located in three different subcities around Stuttgart. The factory is located in Zuffenhausen; testing, engineering, and design in Weissach; and marketing in Ludwigsburg.

31. Contributed by Lee Ann Heard, Texas A&M University Summer Intern for Porsche AG, Stuttgart, West Germany.

All of the voting shares of the company are in the hands of the Porsche family, to whom it is far more important to build the image and reputation of the company than to build sales and profits. When the family hired Porsche's current president, Peter Schutz, they set no goal for growth. They simply want the company to be independent and to be more of what it has been.[32]

Porsche is successful in markets with a high standard of living, a social climate favorable to people who want to show their success outwardly, and an economic climate conducive to the entrepreneur. According to Schutz, the Porsche customer has high personal goals, is not given to compromise, is not risk averse, does his homework, drives to achieve though always succeeding is not mandatory, and every time is his or her best shot. Porsche customers are doers and goers but they are not show-offs. "Getting there is not the point but rather the driving."[33]

To succeed, it is essential that Porsche AG also exhibit some of these qualities. Customers must be able to identify with the firm—to see in the company the same characteristics they see in themselves. A Porsche customer must be able to truthfully say, "If I were a car, I would want to be a Porsche." The following quote by Peter Schutz sums up his philosophy for Porsche:

> We must be world-class in terms of the way in which our customers are treated and the kind of people who represent us. Selling Porsche represents a long-term commitment to the customer, to his needs, to his wishes, to his problems ... Our most important asset is the nucleus of customers who just love Porsche. They love Porsche because Porsche fulfills a dream and need for them. We can survive a lot of other catastrophies but we can't risk alienating this nucleus of loyal customers. Our job as Porsche salesmen is to safeguard that asset. We must never lose contact with our customers. Our highest priority is the customer and when he or she walks in the door, phones, writes or stays away, then we must drop everything and act on these signals. Customers' wishes and problems are the salesman's raison d'etre. Customers never interrupt—they contribute.[34]

In 1985, slightly more than 50 percent of Porsche's sales came from the United States. This country and Germany combined represent 75 percent of sales. Germany, England, France, and the United States make up 85 percent of total sales. The other 15 percent of sales come from the rest of the European community, Japan, and Australia. Schutz indicates that all the cars Porsche builds are already sold and that the company has backlogs for every model and every market. If a dealer does have too many cars, Porsche will take them back and reallocate them to dealers that can move them. Schutz also believes the company could sell 30,000–32,000 cars in the United States if it had the production capacity, adding, "We always try to produce one less than the demand."[35] Total production for world markets in 1986 was approximately 50,000 cars.

The Porsche's enormous popularity is due to its reputation for outstanding performance. Not only are the cars produced in a painstaking fashion; Porsche AG also takes maintenance and repair very seriously. Mechanics servicing Porsches must be Porsche trained and, indeed, those mechanics receive five days of classroom instruction per year at the marketing center in Ludwigsburg. This

32. Peter Schutz and Jack Cook, "Porsche on Nichemanship," *Harvard Business Review,* March–April 1986, p. 100.
33. *Plan Your Success,* 2nd ed. (Stuttgart: Dr. Ing. h.c. = Porsche AG, 1985), p. 1.
34. *Plan Your Success,* p. 3.
35. Joseph M. Callahan and Lance A. Ealey, "Porsche's Schutz Reveals U.S. Marketing Plans," *Industries,* March 1985, p. 50.

constitutes more training than is provided by any other car company. Up until very recently, U.S. mechanics also flew to Germany every year for their training. However, in 1984, training centers were established in this country for that purpose. In addition, through advertising, Porsche encourages customers to trust the repair and maintenance of their Porsches only to Porsche experts. In this way, Porsche hopes to prevent the customer, regardless of nationality, from having an unsatisfactory experience with an unqualified mechanic. At the same time, the company is further distinguishing its product.

In Germany, 60 percent of all Porsches are picked up at the factory by their owners. While there are approximately 325 Porsche dealers in the United States, many Americans elect to pick up their cars in Stuttgart. Schutz spends considerable time visiting with customers when they pick up their cars and in this way has learned much about his customers.[36]

By remaining relatively small, Porsche AG has retained the flexibility that is often crucial in a successful firm's continuing ability to serve the customer. Today, the company is struggling to meet the overwhelming demand for its fine cars while preserving the unequaled quality that has made it great. The job at hand is to plan the future at Porsche. In the words of Dr. Ferry Porsche, "To do this, we have to, so to speak, keep our fingers on the public's pulse and expand the firm's technology to meet any oncoming challenge."[37]

Will Porsche try to expand into other geographic markets? That's doubtful, says Mr. Schutz. Porsche's primary market will remain North America and Western Europe. "From what I know, no significant growth is to be expected outside the U.S. in the forseeable future," he says. "We see a rather steady development in Europe."[38] On the other hand, Schutz indicates that the company is now undertaking the development of an airplane engine.[39]

Questions for Discussion

1. Porsche is a German company with over half its market in the United States. What are the implications for marketing strategy development?
2. When Peter Schutz joined Porsche as president he was committed not just to excellence in quality but also to winning auto races that the firm participated in. How does this decision relate to Porsche's marketing strategy?
3. Should Porsche produce a lower-priced automobile under $20,000? Should it be marketed in the United States, in Europe, or in both regions?

Case 22.2 Procter & Gamble's European Marketing[40]

During the 1950s and 1960s, Procter & Gamble expanded its operations to include a greater number of European countries. New operations were started in Switzerland, Holland, Italy, Germany, Greece, Austria, Spain, and Scandinavia. Today, consumers can purchase Procter & Gamble products in over 130 countries.

36. Schutz and Cook, "Nichemanship," p. 99.
37. John Bentley, *We at Porsche* (Garden City, N.Y.: Doubleday, 1976), p. 263.
38. "Porsche," *Ward's Auto World,* Jan. 1985, pp. 52–53.
39. Schutz and Cook, p. 101.
40. Portions of the information in this case are from Howard Sharman, "P&G on the Warpath Throughout Europe," *Advertising Age,* May 23, 1983, pp. 4, 54; Dagmar Mussey, "P&G Gambles on Shampoo Market in German Launch," *Advertising Age,* Oct. 3, 1983, p. 62; *Procter & Gamble's International Business,* 1980; and *The Procter & Gamble 1983 Annual Report.*

Despite worldwide economic problems and fluctuations of foreign currencies in relation to the U.S. dollar, Procter & Gamble's earnings from international operations have increased dramatically. About a third of Procter & Gamble's total business is done outside the United States. One-third of its employees work in operations abroad, and a fifth of the company assets are outside the United States. Procter & Gamble's international operations continue to be important to the growth of the company.

Procter & Gamble's overall marketing plan is to offer superior products that meet consumer needs. Previously, Procter & Gamble products that were used in different European countries often had different formulas based on consumer preferences. Now, however, the company is changing its approach for its European markets. The product mix will now stress "multinational" or worldwide brands. For instance, Ariel laundry detergent has been reformulated to be accepted and used in all countries. Some of the products included in Procter & Gamble's international product mix include:

Pampers/Luvs diapers
Dash/Bold/Ariel laundry detergents
Vizir liquid laundry detergent

Top Job laundry additive
Head & Shoulders shampoo
Crest toothpaste

In addition to being more adventuresome, the new approach involves being much more aggressive. Procter & Gamble has been nicknamed the "sleeping giant" in Europe. This nickname may soon become obsolete. Advertising and promotional expenditures recently have skyrocketed. Procter & Gamble has increased its promotional expenditures level to over five times the level of five years ago. The company now plans to advertise heavily and establish more versatile advertisements. It wants some of its advertisements to be usable in several different European countries. Recently, one of its advertising agencies used the same advertisement in France and Germany successfully. It also plans to use other promotional techniques extensively. For example, trial size samples were used to introduce Head & Shoulders shampoo in Germany. Finally, test marketing time has been cut drastically. Previously, Procter & Gamble test marketed products for a year or more. Vizir liquid detergent was launched nationally after being test marketed for a mere six months. Procter & Gamble is taking its foreign competitors by surprise and gaining market shares quite rapidly.

Questions for Discussion

1. Evaluate Procter & Gamble's decision to standardize its European marketing.
2. Is the marketing environment fairly consistent across most European countries?
3. Use back issues of the *Wall Street Journal* to find out the degree of variation in exchange rates in the currencies of countries mentioned in this case. Discuss how these fluctuations might affect Procter & Gamble's operations.

Appendix A
Careers in Marketing

Some General Issues

As noted in Chapter 1, between one-fourth and one-third of the civilian work force in the United States is employed in marketing-related jobs. Although there obviously are a multitude of diverse career opportunities in the field, the number of positions in its different areas varies. For example, millions of workers are employed in many facets of sales, but relatively few people work in advertising and marketing research.

Many nonbusiness organizations now recognize that they do, in fact, perform marketing activities. For that reason, marketing positions are increasing in government agencies, hospitals, charitable and religious groups, educational institutions, and similar organizations.

Even though financial reward is not the sole criterion for selecting a career, it is only practical to consider how much you might earn in a marketing job. Table A.1 illustrates some top twelve salary positions for middle managers in marketing. Note that all of these careers relate directly to marketing. A national sales manager may earn from $50,000 to $75,000 or an even higher salary. Brand managers make $30,000 to $65,000. A media manager could earn $30,000 to $55,000. Generally, entry-level marketing personnel earn more than their counterparts in economics and liberal arts, but not as much as people who enter accounting, chemistry, or engineering positions. Starting salaries for marketing graduates averaged $20,672 according to Northwestern University's 1986 Endicott Report. Marketers who advance to higher-level positions often earn high salaries, and a significant proportion of corporate executives have held marketing jobs before attaining top-level positions.

Another important issue is whether or not you can enjoy the work associated with a particular career. Since you will spend almost 40 percent of your waking hours on the job, you should not allow such factors as economic conditions or status to override your personal goals as you select a lifelong career. Too often, people do not weigh these factors realistically. You should give considerable thought to your choice of a career, and you should adopt a well-planned, systematic approach to finding a position that meets your personal and career objectives.

After determining your objectives, you should identify the organizations that are likely to offer desirable opportunities. Learn as much as possible about

Table A.1 Top salary ranges for middle managers in marketing

Position	Salary Range
Corporate Strategic Market Planner	$55,000–$75,000
National Sales Manager	50,000– 75,000
International Sales	45,000– 60,000
Advertising Accounts Executive	40,000– 60,000
Sales Promotion	40,000– 55,000
Purchasing Manager	35,000– 55,000
Product/Brand Manager	30,000– 55,000
Media Manager	30,000– 50,000
Retail Sales	20,000– 40,000
Distribution Management	40,000– 60,000

these organizations before setting up employment interviews. Job recruiters are generally impressed with applicants who have done their homework.

A brief, clearly written letter of introduction is needed when making initial contact with potential employers by mail. After an initial interview you should send a brief letter of thanks to the interviewer. The job of getting the right job is important, and you owe it to yourself to take this process seriously.

The Resume

The resume is one of the keys to being considered for a good job. By stating your qualifications, experiences, education and career goals, the resume provides the opportunity for a potential employer to assess your compatibility with the job requirements. For the employer's benefit and the individual's, the resume should be accurate and current.

To be effective, the resume can be targeted toward a specific position, as shown in Figure A.1. This document is only one example of an acceptable resume. The job target section is specific and leads directly to the applicant's qualifications for the job. Capabilities show what the applicant can do and that he or she has an understanding of the job's requirements. Skills and strengths should be highlighted in terms of how they relate to the specific job. The achievement section indicates success at accomplishing tasks or goals within the job market and at school. The work experience section includes educational background, which adds credibility to the resume but is not the major area of focus. The applicant's ability to function successfully in a specific job is the major emphasis.

Common suggestions for improving resumes include deleting useless information, improving organization, using professional printing and typing, listing duties (not accomplishments), maintaining grammatical perfection, and avoiding an overly elaborate or fancy format.[1]

1. Tom Jackson, "Writing the Targeted Resume," *Business Week's Guide to Careers*, Spring 1983, pp. 26–27.

```
┌─────────────────────────────────────────────────────────────────┐
│                          LORRAINE MILLER                          │
│                         2212 WEST WILLOW                          │
│                          (416) 862-9169                           │
│                                                                   │
│                                                                   │
│   EDUCATION:  B.A. Arizona State University  1987  Marketing      │
│                                                                   │
│   POSITION DESIRED:  PRODUCT MANAGER WITH AN INTERNATIONAL FIRM    │
│                      PROVIDING FUTURE CAREER DEVELOPMENT AT THE    │
│                      EXECUTIVE LEVEL.                              │
│                                                                   │
│   QUALIFICATIONS:                                                 │
│                                                                   │
│      * communicates well with individuals to achieve a common goal│
│                                                                   │
│      * handles tasks efficiently and in a timely manner           │
│                                                                   │
│      * knowledge of advertising, sales, management, marketing     │
│        research, packaging, pricing, distribution, and warehousing│
│                                                                   │
│      * coordinates many activities at one time                    │
│                                                                   │
│      * receives and carries out assigned tasks or directives      │
│                                                                   │
│      * writes complete status or research reports                 │
│                                                                   │
│   EXPERIENCES:                                                    │
│                                                                   │
│      * Assistant Editor of college paper                          │
│                                                                   │
│      * Treasurer of the American Marketing Association (student   │
│        chapter)                                                   │
│                                                                   │
│      * Internship with 3-Cs Advertising, Berkeley, CA             │
│                                                                   │
│      * Student Assistantship with Dr. Steve Green, Professor of   │
│        Marketing, Arizona State University                        │
│                                                                   │
│      * Achieved 3.6 average on a 4.0 scale throughout college     │
│                                                                   │
│   WORK RECORD:                                                    │
│   1984 – Present          Blythe and Co., Inc.                    │
│                              * Junior Advertising Account Executive│
│                                                                   │
│   1982 – Present          Assistantship with Dr. Steve Green      │
│                              * Research Assistant                 │
│                                                                   │
│   1980 – 1982             The Men                                 │
│                              * Retail sales and consumer relations│
│                                                                   │
│   1976 – 1980             Tannenbaum Trees, Inc.                  │
│                              * Laborer                            │
│                                                                   │
└─────────────────────────────────────────────────────────────────┘
```

Types of Marketing Careers

In considering marketing as a career, the first step is to evaluate broad categories of career opportunities in the areas of marketing research, sales, public relations, industrial buying, distribution management, product management, advertising, retail management, and direct marketing.[2] Keep in mind that the categories described here are not all-inclusive and that each of them encompasses hundreds of marketing jobs.

Marketing Research

Clearly marketing research and information systems are vital aspects of marketing decision making. The information about buyers and environmental forces that is provided through research and information systems improves a marketer's ability to understand the dynamics of the marketplace and to make effective decisions.

2. Much of this information is adapted from *Occupational Outlook Handbook*, 1978–1979 edition, U.S. Department of Labor, Bureau of Labor Statistics, Bulletin 1955.

Marketing researchers gather and analyze data relating to specific problems. Marketing research firms are usually employed by a client organization, which could be a provider of goods or services, a nonbusiness organization, the government, a research consulting firm, or an advertising agency. The activities performed include concept testing, product testing, package testing, advertising testing, test-market research, and new-product research.

A researcher may be involved in one or several stages of research, depending on the size of the project, the organization of the research unit, and the researcher's experience. Marketing research trainees in large organizations usually perform a considerable amount of clerical work, such as compiling secondary data from a firm's accounting and sales records and from periodicals, government publications, syndicated data services, and unpublished sources. A junior analyst may edit and code questionnaires or tabulate survey results. Trainees also may participate in primary data gathering by learning to conduct mail and telephone surveys, conducting personal interviews, and employing observational methods of primary data collection. As a marketing researcher gains experience, he or she may become involved in defining problems and developing hypotheses; designing research procedures; and analyzing, interpreting, and reporting findings. Exceptional personnel may assume responsibility for entire research projects.

Although most employers consider a bachelor's degree sufficient qualification for a marketing research trainee, many specialized positions require a graduate degree in business administration, statistics, or other related fields. Today, trainees are more likely to have a marketing or statistics degree than a liberal arts degree. Also, trainees who are capable of immediate productivity and more complex tasks are more desirable.[3] Courses in statistics, data processing, psychology, sociology, communications, economics, and English composition are valuable preparations for a career in marketing research.

The U.S. Bureau of Labor Statistics indicates that marketing research provides abundant employment opportunity, especially for applicants with graduate training in marketing research, statistics, economics, and the social sciences. In general, the value of information gathered by marketing information and research systems will become more important as competition increases, thus expanding the opportunities for prospective marketing research personnel.

The three major career paths in marketing research are with independent marketing research agencies/data suppliers, advertising agency marketing research departments, and marketing research departments in businesses. In a company where marketing research plays a key role, the researcher is often a member of the marketing strategy team. In marketing research agencies, one deals with many clients, products, and problems. Advertising agencies use research as an ingredient in developing and refining campaigns for existing or potentially new clients.[4]

Salaries in marketing research depend on the type, size, and location of the firm as well as the nature of the positions. Generally, starting salaries are somewhat higher and promotions are somewhat slower than in other occupations requiring similar training. Starting salaries of $21,000 to $25,000 per year are

3. Marcia Fleschner, "Evolution of Research Takes the Profession to New Heights," *Collegiate Edition Marketing News*, March 1986, p. 1.
4. "What It's Like to Work in Marketing Research Depends on Where You Work, Supplies, Ad Agency, Manufacturer," *Collegiate Edition Marketing News*, Dec. 1985, pp. 1 and 3.

typical. Experienced research personnel earn above-average salaries. In addition, the role of marketing in overall corporate planning is growing more important as companies seek marketing information for strategic planning purposes. Marketing research directors are reporting to higher levels of management than ever before, and the number of corporate vice presidents who receive marketing research as regular input in decision making has doubled in recent years.

Sales

Millions of people earn a living through personal selling. Chapter 13 defines personal selling as a process of informing customers and persuading them to purchase products through personal communication in an exchange situation. Although this definition describes the general nature of many sales positions, individual selling jobs vary enormously with respect to the type of businesses and products involved, the educational background and skills required, and the specific activities performed by sales personnel. Because the work is so varied, sales occupations offer a large number of career opportunities for people with a wide range of qualifications, interests, and goals. In terms of compensation, a sales career offers the greatest potential. The following sections describe what is involved in wholesale and manufacturer sales.

Wholesale Sales

Wholesalers perform a variety of activities to expedite transactions in which purchases are intended for resale or are used to make other products. Wholesalers thus provide services to both retailers and producers. They can help match producers' products to the needs of retailers and can provide accumulation and allocation services that save producers time, money, and resources. Some activities associated with wholesaling include planning and negotiating transactions; assisting customers with sales, advertising, sales promotion, and publicity; handling transportation and storage activities; providing customers with inventory control and data processing assistance; establishing prices; and giving customers technical, management, and merchandising assistance.

The background needed by wholesale personnel depends on the nature of the product that is handled. A drug wholesaler, for example, needs extensive technical training and product knowledge and may hold a degree in chemistry, biology, or pharmacology. A wholesaler of standard office supplies, on the other hand, may find it more important to be familiar with various brands, suppliers, and prices than to have technical knowledge about the products. A new wholesale representative may begin a career as a sales trainee or may hold a nonselling job that provides experience with inventory, prices, discounts, and the firm's customers. A college graduate usually enters the sales force directly out of school. Competent salespersons also transfer from manufacturer and retail sales positions.

The number of wholesale sales positions is expected to grow about as fast as the average for all occupations through 1987. Earnings for wholesale personnel vary widely because commissions often make up a large proportion of their incomes.

Manufacturer Sales

Manufacturer sales personnel sell a firm's products to wholesalers, retailers, and industrial buyers; they thus perform many of the same activities handled by wholesale salespersons. As is the case with wholesaling, the educational requirements for manufacturer sales depend largely on the type and complexity of the products and markets. Manufacturers of nontechnical products usually hire college graduates who have a liberal arts or business degree and provide them with training and information about the firm's products, prices, and customers. Manufacturers of highly technical products generally prefer applicants who have degrees in fields associated with the particular industry and market involved.

More and more sophisticated marketing skills are being utilized in industrial sales. Industrial marketing originally followed the commodity approach to complete a sale, whereby the right product is in the right place at the right time and for the right price. Now, there is a much stronger service attitude and emphasis on warranties and the entire support network such as parts and service availability.[5]

Employment opportunities in manufacturer sales are expected to experience average growth. Manufacturer sales personnel are well compensated and earn above-average salaries. Most of them are paid a combination of salaries and commissions, and the highest salaries are paid by manufacturers of electrical equipment, food products, and rubber goods. Commissions vary according to the salesperson's efforts, abilities, and sales territory and the type of products sold.

Public Relations

Public relations encompasses a broad set of communication activities designed to create and maintain favorable relations between the organization and its publics—customers, employees, stockholders, government officials, and society in general. Communication is basic to all public relations programs. To communicate effectively, public relations practitioners first must gather data about the firm's client publics to assess their needs, identify problems, formulate recommendations, implement new plans, and evaluate current activities.

Public relations personnel disseminate large amounts of information to the organization's client publics. Written communication is the most versatile tool of public relations, and good writing ability is essential. Public relations practitioners must be adept at writing for a variety of media and audiences. It is not unusual for a person in public relations to prepare reports, news releases, speeches, broadcast scripts, technical manuals, employee publications, shareholder reports, and other communications aimed at both organizational personnel and external groups. In addition, a public relations practitioner needs a thorough knowledge of the production techniques used in preparing various communications.

Public relations personnel also establish distribution channels for the organization's publicity. They must have a thorough understanding of the various media, their areas of specialization, the characteristics of their target audiences, and their policies regarding publicity. Anyone who hopes to succeed in public relations must develop close working relationships with numerous media personnel to enlist their interest in disseminating an organization's communications.

A college education combined with writing or media-related experience probably is the best preparation for a career in public relations. Most beginners

5. Nicholas Basta, "Marketing Managers," *Business Week's Guide to Careers*, Spring 1983, p. 46.

hold a college degree in journalism, communications, or public relations, but some employers prefer a business background. Courses in journalism, business administration, psychology, sociology, political science, advertising, English, and public speaking are recommended. Some employers require applicants to present a portfolio of published articles, television or radio programs, slide presentations, and other work samples. Manufacturing firms, public utilities, transportation and insurance companies, and trade and professional associations are the largest employers of public relations personnel. In addition, sizable numbers work for health-related organizations, government agencies, educational institutions, museums, and religious and service groups.

Although some larger companies provide extensive formal training for new personnel, most new public relations employees learn on the job. Beginners usually perform routine tasks such as maintaining files about company activities and searching secondary data sources for information that can be used in publicity materials. More experienced employees write press releases, speeches, and articles and help plan public relations campaigns.

Employment opportunities in public relations are expected to increase faster than the average for all occupations through the 1980s. One caveat is in order, however. Competition for beginning jobs is keen. The prospects are best for applicants who have solid academic preparation and some media experience. Those who land jobs in public relations can expect to earn above-average salaries.

Industrial Buying

Industrial buyers, or purchasing agents, are responsible for maintaining an adequate supply of the goods and services that an organization needs for operations. In general, industrial buyers purchase all items needed for direct use in producing other products and for use in the day-to-day operations. Industrial buyers in large firms often specialize in purchasing a single, specific class of products—for example, all petroleum-based lubricants. In smaller organizations, buyers may be responsible for purchasing many different categories of items, including such goods as raw materials, component parts, office supplies, and operating services.

An industrial buyer's main job consists of selecting suppliers who offer the best values in terms of quality, service, and price. When the products to be purchased are standardized, buyers may compare suppliers by examining catalogs and trade journals, making purchases by description. Buyers who purchase highly homogeneous products often meet with salespeople to examine samples and observe demonstrations. Sometimes, buyers must inspect the actual product before purchasing; in other cases, they invite suppliers to bid on large orders. Buyers who purchase specialized equipment often deal directly with manufacturers to obtain specially designed items made to specifications. After choosing a supplier and placing an order, an industrial buyer usually must trace the shipment to ensure on-time delivery. Finally, the buyer sometimes is responsible for receiving and inspecting an order and authorizing payment to the shipper.

Training requirements for a career in industrial buying relate to the needs of the firm and the types of products purchased. A manufacturer of heavy machinery may prefer an applicant who has a background in engineering; a service company, on the other hand, may recruit liberal arts majors. Although it is not generally required, a college degree is becoming increasingly important for buyers who wish to advance to management positions.

Employment prospects for industrial buyers are expected to increase faster than average through the 1980s. Opportunities will be excellent for individuals with a master's degree in business administration or a bachelor's degree in engineering, science, or business administration. In addition, companies that manufacture heavy equipment, computer equipment, and communications equipment will need buyers with technical backgrounds.

Distribution Management

A distribution (or traffic) manager arranges for the transportation of goods within firms and through marketing channels. Transportation is an essential distribution activity that permits a firm to create time and place utility for its products. It is the job of the distribution manager to analyze various transportation modes and to select the combination that minimizes cost and transit time while providing acceptable levels of reliability, capability, accessibility, and security.

To accomplish this task, a distribution manager performs a wide range of activities. First, the individual must choose one or a combination of transportation modes from the five major modes available: railways, motor vehicles, inland waterways, pipelines, and airways. Then the distribution manager must select the specific routes the goods will travel and the particular carriers to be used, weighing such factors as freight classifications and regulations, freight charges, time schedules, shipment sizes, and loss and damage ratios. In addition, this person may be responsible for preparing shipping documents, tracing shipments, handling loss and damage claims, keeping records of freight rates, and monitoring changes in government regulations and transportation technology.

Distribution management employs relatively few people and is expected to grow about as fast as the average for all occupations in the near future. Manufacturing firms represent the largest employers of distribution managers, although some traffic managers work for wholesalers, retail stores, and consulting firms. Salaries of experienced distribution managers vary but, in general, are much higher than the average for all nonsupervisory personnel.

Entry-level positions for distribution management are available in the $20,000–$25,000 per year salary range. Starting jobs are diverse, varying from inventory control, traffic scheduling, operations management, or distribution management. Inventory management is an area of great opportunity because many U.S. firms see inventory costs as high relative to foreign competition, especially that from the Japanese. Just-in-time inventory systems are designed by inventory control specialists to work with the bare minimum of inventory.[6]

Most employers prefer graduates of technical programs or seek people who have completed courses in transportation, logistics, distribution management, economics, statistics, computer science, management, marketing, and commercial law. A successful distribution manager must be adept at handling technical data and must be able to interpret and communicate highly technical information.

6. Nicholas Basta, "Inventory and Distribution," *Business Week's Guide to Careers*, Spring/Summer 1985, p. 23.

Product Management

In firms that use the product manager form of organization, the product manager occupies a staff position and is responsible for the success or failure of a product line. Product managers coordinate most of the marketing activities required to market a product; however, because they hold a staff position, they have relatively little actual authority over marketing personnel. Even so, they take on a large amount of responsibility and typically are paid quite well relative to other marketing employees. Being a product manager can be rewarding both financially and psychologically, but it also can be frustrating because of the disparity between responsibility and authority.

A product manager should have a general knowledge of advertising, transportation modes, inventory control, selling and sales management, sales promotion, marketing research, packaging, pricing, and warehousing. The individual must be knowledgeable enough to communicate effectively with personnel in these functional areas and to make suggestions and help assess alternatives when major decisions are being made.

Product managers usually need college training in an area of business administration. A master's degree is helpful, although a person usually does not become a product manager directly out of school. Frequently, several years of selling and sales management are prerequisites for a product management position, which often is a major step in the career path of top-level marketing executives.

Advertising

Advertising pervades our daily lives. As detailed in Chapter 14, business and nonbusiness organizations use advertising in many ways and for many reasons. Advertising clearly needs individuals with diverse skills to fill a variety of jobs. Creative imagination, artistic talent, and expertise in expression and persuasion are important to copywriters, artists, and account executives. Salesmanship and managerial ability are vital to the success of advertising managers, media buyers, and production managers. Research directors must have a solid understanding of research techniques and human behavior.

Advertising professionals disagree on the most beneficial educational background for a career in advertising. Most employers prefer college graduates. Some seek individuals with degrees in advertising, journalism, or business; others prefer graduates with broad liberal arts backgrounds. Still other employers rank relevant work experience above educational background.

"Advertisers look for generalists," says Kate Preston, a staff executive of the American Association of Advertising Agencies, "thus there are just as many economics or general liberal arts majors as MBAs. Many of the larger agencies want MBAs in their account management position, but there is a trend away from that at other agencies."[7]

A variety of organizations employ advertising personnel. Although advertising agencies are perhaps the most visible and glamorous of employers, many manufacturing firms, retail stores, banks, utility companies, and professional and trade associations maintain advertising departments. Advertising jobs also can be found with television and radio stations, newspapers, and magazines. Other businesses that employ advertising personnel include printers, art studios, letter shops, and package-design firms. Examples of specific advertising jobs

7. Nicholas Basta, "Marketing Managers," *Business Week's Guide to Careers*, Spring 1983, p. 40.

are advertising manager, account executive, research director, copywriter, media specialist, and production manager.

Employment opportunities for advertising personnel are expected to increase faster than average through the mid-1980s. However, general economic conditions strongly influence the size of advertising budgets and, hence, employment opportunities.

Retail Management

Although a career in retailing may begin in sales, there is more to retailing than simply selling. Many retail personnel occupy management positions. Besides managing the sales force, they focus on selecting and ordering merchandise, promotional activities, inventory control, customer credit operations, accounting, personnel, and store security.

The manner in which retail stores are organized varies. In many large department stores, retail management personnel rarely get involved with actually selling to customers; these duties are performed by retail salespeople. However, other types of retail organizations may require management personnel to perform selling activities from time to time.

Large retail stores offer a variety of management positions besides those at the very top. A few examples include assistant buyers, buyers, department managers, section managers, store managers, division managers, regional managers, and vice president of merchandising. The following describes the general duties of a few of these positions. The precise nature of duties will vary from one retail organization to another, though.

A section manager coordinates inventory and promotions and interacts with buyers, salespeople, and ultimate consumers. The manager performs merchandising, labor relations and managerial activities and can rarely expect to get away with as little as a forty-hour work week.

The buyer's task is more focused. In this fast-paced occupation, there is much travel, pressure, and need to be open-minded with respect to new and potentially successful items.

The regional manager coordinates the activities of several stores within a given area. Sales, promotions, and procedures in general are monitored and supported.

The vice president of merchandising has a broad scope of managerial responsibility and reports to the president at the top of the organization.

Traditionally, retail managers began their careers as salesclerks. Today, many large retailers hire college-educated people, put them through management training programs, and then place them directly into management positions. They frequently hire people with backgrounds in liberal arts or business administration. Sales and retailing provide the greatest employment opportunity for marketing students. Usually, a successful background in a variety of retailing jobs is needed for store managers.[8]

Retail management positions can be exciting and challenging. Competent, ambitious individuals often assume a great deal of responsibility very quickly and advance rapidly. However, compensation programs for entry-level positions (management trainees) are usually below average. In addition, a retail manager's

8. Kevin Higgins, "Economic Recovery Puts Marketers in Catbird Seat," *Marketing News*, Oct. 14, 1983, p. 8.

job is physically demanding and sometimes entails long working hours. Nonetheless, positions in retail management often provide numerous opportunities to excel and advance.

Direct Marketing

One of the most dynamic areas in marketing is direct marketing. Direct marketing involves activities by which the seller uses one or more direct media (telephone, mail, print, or television) to solicit a response. For example, Shell Oil uses its credit card billings (direct mail) to sell a variety of consumer products.

The telephone is a major vehicle for selling many consumer products, such as magazines. Telemarketing involves direct selling to customers using a variety of technological improvements in telephone services and is an estimated $91-billion-a-year industry creating jobs in sales, marketing strategy, and marketing technology. According to the American Telemarketing Association (Glenview, Ill.) $73 billion of the industry's sales come from business-to-business marketing, not from selling to consumers at home. In addition, the telemarketing industry has been growing by an average of 30 percent per year. Starting salaries in telemarketing range from $19,000 to $26,000.[9]

The use of direct mail catalogs appeals to market segments such as working women or people that find going to retail stores difficult or inconvenient. Newspapers and magazines offer great opportunity, especially in special market segments. *Golf Digest* for example is obviously a good medium for selling golfing equipment. Cable television provides many new opportunities for selling directly to consumers. Interactive cable will offer a new method to expand direct marketing by developing timely exchange opportunities for consumers.

The volume of goods distributed through direct marketing is a strong indicator of opportunity for careers in this growing area. H. B. Crandall, president of Crandall Associates, New York, has stated that job candidates with experience could "write their own ticket." He continued, "People with five years' experience are getting phenomenal salary offers. People with one year's experience are getting offers unheard of in any other marketing field."[10]

The most important asset in direct marketing is experience. Employers often look to other industries to locate experienced professionals. In a choice between an MBA or an individual with a direct marketing background, the experienced individual would be hired.[11] This preference means that if you can get an entry-level position in direct marketing, you will have a real advantage in developing a career.

Some of the jobs in direct marketing include buyers, like department store buyers, who select goods for catalog, telephone, or direct mail sales. Catalog managers develop marketing strategies for each new catalog that goes into the mail. Research/mail-list management involves developing lists of products that will sell in direct marketing and lists of names that will respond to a direct-mail effort. Order fulfillment managers direct the shipment of products once they are sold. Nearly all nonprofit organizations have fund raising managers who use direct marketing to obtain financial support.[12]

9. Nicholas Basta, "Telemarketing," *Business Week's Guide to Careers*, Dec. 1985, p. 27.
10. Higgins, "Economic Recovery," pp. 1, 8.
11. Ibid.
12. Nicholas Basta, "Direct Marketing," *Business Week's Guide to Careers*, March 1986, p. 52.

The executive vice president of the advertising agency Young & Rubicam, Inc., in New York has stated that direct marketing will have to be used "not as a tactic, but as a strategic tool."[13] Direct marketing's effectiveness is enhanced by periodic analysis of advertising and communications at all phases of contact with the consumer. Direct marketing involves all aspects of the marketing decision. It is becoming a more professional career area that provides great opportunity.

13. "Wonderman Urges: Replace Marketing War Muskets with the Authentic Weapon—Direct Marketing," *Marketing News*, July 8, 1983, pp. 1, 12.

Appendix B
Financial Analysis in Marketing

Our discussion in this book has focused more on fundamental concepts and decisions in marketing than on financial details. However, marketers must understand the basic components of selected financial analyses if they are to explain and defend their decisions. In fact, they must be familiar with certain financial analyses if they are to reach good decisions in the first place. We will therefore examine three areas of financial analyses: cost-profit aspects of the income statement, selected performance ratios, and price calculations.[1] To control and evaluate marketing activities, marketers must understand the income statement and what it says about the operations of their organization. They also need to be acquainted with performance ratios, which compare current operating results with past results and with results in the industry at large. In the last part of the appendix, we discuss price calculations as the basis of price adjustments. Marketers are likely to use all these areas of financial analysis at various times to support their decisions and to make necessary adjustments in their operations.

The Income Statement

The income, or operating, statement presents the financial results of an organization's operations over a period of time. The statement summarizes revenues earned and expenses incurred by a profit center, whether it is a department, brand, product line, division, or entire firm. The income statement presents the firm's net profit or net loss for a month, quarter, or year.

Table B.1 shows a simplified income statement for a retail store. The owners of the store, Rose Costa and Nick Schultz, see that net sales of 250,000 are decreased by the cost of goods sold and by other business expenses to yield a net income of $83,000. Of course, these figures are only highlights of the complete income statement, which appears in Table B.2.

1. We gratefully acknowledge the assistance of Jim L. Grimm, Professor of Marketing, Illinois State University, in writing this appendix.

Table B.1 *Simplified income statement for a retailer*

Stoneham Auto Supplies Income Statement for the Year Ended December 31, 1986

Net Sales	$250,000
Cost of Goods Sold	45,000
Gross Margin	$205,000
Expenses	122,000
Net Income	$ 83,000

The income statement can be used in several ways to improve the management of a business. First, it enables an owner or manager to compare actual results with budgets for various parts of the statement. For example, Rose and Nick see that the total amount of merchandise sold (gross sales) is $260,000. Customers returned merchandise or received allowances (price reductions) totaling $10,000. Suppose the budgeted amount was only $9,000. By checking the tickets for sales returns and allowances, the owners can determine why these events occurred and whether the $10,000 figure could be lowered by adjusting the marketing mix.

After subtracting returns and allowances from gross sales, Rose and Nick can determine net sales from the statement. They are pleased with this figure because it is higher than their sales target of $240,000. Net sales is the amount the firm has available to pay its expenses.

A major expense for most companies that sell goods (as opposed to services) is the cost of goods sold. For Stoneham Auto Supplies, it amounts to 18 percent of net sales. Other expenses are treated in various ways by different companies. In our example, they are broken down into standard categories of selling expenses, administrative expenses, and general expenses.

The income statement shows that the cost of goods sold by Stoneham Auto Supplies during fiscal year 1986 was $45,000. This figure was reached in the following way. First, the statement shows that merchandise in the amount of $51,000 was purchased during the year. In paying the invoices associated with these inventory additions, purchase (cash) discounts of $4,000 were earned, resulting in net purchases of $47,000. Special requests for selected merchandise throughout the year resulted in $2,000 of freight charges, which increased the net cost of delivered purchases to $49,000. Adding this amount to the beginning inventory of $48,000, the cost of goods available for sale during 1986 was $97,000. However, the records indicate that the value of inventory at the end of the year was $52,000. Since this amount was not sold, the cost of goods that were sold during the year was $45,000.

Rose and Nick observe that the total value of their inventory increased by 8.3 percent during the year.

$$\frac{\$52,000 - \$48,000}{\$48,000} = \frac{\$ 4,000}{\$48,000} = \frac{1}{12} = .0825 \text{ or } 8.3\%$$

Further analysis is needed to determine whether this increase is desirable or undesirable. (Note that the income statement provides no detail concerning the composition of the inventory held on December 31; other records provide this information.) If Nick and Rose determine that inventory on December 31 is excessive, they can implement appropriate marketing action.

Gross margin is the difference between net sales and cost of goods sold. Gross margin reflects the markup on products and is the amount available to pay all other expenses and provide a return to the owners.

Table B.2 *Operating statement for a retailer*

Stoneham Auto Supplies
income statement
for the year ended December 31, 1986

Gross Sales			$260,000
Less: Sales returns and allowances			10,000
Net Sales			$250,000
Cost of Goods Sold			
Inventory, January, 1 1986 (at cost)		$48,000	
Purchases	$51,000		
Less: Purchase discounts	4,000		
Net purchases	$47,000		
Plus: Freight-in	2,000		
Net cost of delivered purchases		$49,000	
Cost of goods available for sale		$97,000	
Less: Inventory, December 31, 1986			
(at cost)		52,000	
Cost of goods sold			$ 45,000
Gross Margin			$205,000
Expenses			
Selling expenses			
Sales salaries and commissions	$32,000		
Advertising	16,000		
Sales promotions	3,000		
Delivery	2,000		
Total selling expenses		$53,000	
Administrative expenses			
Administrative salaries	$20,000		
Office salaries	20,000		
Office supplies	2,000		
Miscellaneous	1,000		
Total administrative expenses		$43,000	
General expenses			
Rent	$14,000		
Utilities	7,000		
Bad debts	1,000		
Miscellaneous (local taxes, insurance,			
interest, depreciation)	4,000		
Total general expenses		$26,000	
Total expenses			$122,000
Net Income			**$ 83,000**

Appendix B / Financial Analysis in Marketing

Stoneham Auto Supplies had a gross margin of $205,000:

Net Sales	$250,000
Cost of Goods Sold	− 45,000
Gross Margin	$205,000

Stoneham's expenses (other than cost of goods sold) during 1986 totaled $122,000. Observe that $53,000, or slightly more than 43 percent of the total, is direct selling expenses.

$$\frac{\$53,000 \text{ selling expenses}}{\$122,000 \text{ total expenses}} = .434 \text{ or } 43\%$$

The business employs three salespersons (one full time) and pays competitive wages for the area. All selling expenses are similar to dollar amounts for fiscal year 1985, but Nick and Rose wonder whether more advertising is necessary, since inventory increased by more than 8 percent during the year.

The administrative and general expenses are also essential to operate the business. A comparison of these expenses with trade statistics for similar businesses indicate that the figures are in line with industry amounts.

Net income, or net profit, is the amount of gross margin remaining after deducting expenses. Stoneham Auto Supplies earned a net profit of $83,000 for the fiscal year ending December 31, 1986. Note that net income on this statement is figured before payment of state and federal income taxes.

Income statements for intermediaries and for businesses that provide services follow the same general format as that shown for Stoneham Auto Supplies in Table B.2. The income statement for a manufacturer, however, is somewhat different, in that the purchases section is replaced by a section called cost of goods manufactured. Table B.3 shows the entire cost-of-goods-sold section for a manufacturer, including cost of goods manufactured. In other respects, income statements for retailers and manufacturers are similar.

Selected Performance Ratios

Rose and Nick's assessment of how well their business did during fiscal year 1986 can be improved through selective use of analytical ratios. These ratios enable a manager to compare the results for the current year with data from previous years and with industry statistics. Unfortunately, comparisons of the current income statement with income statements and industry statistics from other years are not very meaningful, since factors such as inflation are not accounted for when comparing dollar amounts. More meaningful comparisons can be made by converting these figures to a percentage of net sales, as this section shows.

The first analytical ratios we will discuss, the operating ratios, are based on the net sales figure from the income statement.

Operating Ratios

Operating ratios express items on the income, or operating, statement as percentages of net sales. The first step is to convert the income statement into percentages of net sales, as illustrated in Table B.4.

Table B.3 *Cost of goods sold for a manufacturer*

Cost of Goods Sold

Finished goods inventory, January 1, 1986				$ 50,000
Cost of goods manufactured				
Work-in-process inventory, January 1, 1986			$20,000	
Raw materials inventory, January 1, 1986	$ 40,000			
Net cost of delivered purchases	240,000			
Cost of goods available for use	$280,000			
Less: Raw materials inventory, December 31, 1986	42,000			
Cost of goods placed in production		$238,000		
Direct labor		$32,000		
Manufacturing overhead				
Indirect labor	$12,000			
Supervisory salaries	10,000			
Operating supplies	6,000			
Depreciation	12,000			
Utilities	10,000			
Total manufacturing overhead		$ 50,000		
Total manufacturing costs			$320,000	
Total work-in-process			$340,000	
Less: Work-in-process inventory, December 31, 1986			22,000	
Cost of goods manufactured				$318,000
				$368,000
Cost of goods available for sale				
Less: Finished goods inventory, December 31, 1986				48,000
Cost of Goods Sold				**$320,000**

After making this conversion, the manager looks at several key operating ratios. These ratios include two profitability ratios (the gross margin ratio and the net income ratio) and the operating expense ratio.

For Stoneham Auto Supplies these ratios are determined as follows (see Tables B.2 and B.4 for supporting data);

$$\text{Gross margin ratio} = \frac{\text{gross margin}}{\text{net sales}} = \frac{\$205,000}{\$250,000} = 82\%$$

Table B.4 *Income statement as a percentage of net sales*

**Stoneham Auto Supplies income statement as a percentage
of net sales for the year ended December 31, 1986**

		Percentage of net sales
Gross Sales		103.8%
Less: Sales returns and allowances		3.8
Net Sales		100.0%
Cost of Goods Sold		
Inventory, January 1, 1986 (at cost)		19.2%
Purchases	20.4%	
Less: Purchase discounts	1.6	
Net Purchases	18.8%	
Plus: Freight-in	.8	
Net cost of delivered purchases		19.6
Cost of goods available for sale		38.8%
Less: Inventory, December 31, 1986 (at cost)		20.8
Cost of goods sold			18.0
Gross Margin			82.0%
Expenses			
Selling expenses			
Sales salaries and commissions	12.8%		
Advertising	6.4		
Sales promotions	1.2		
Delivery	0.8		
Total selling expenses		21.2%	
Administrative expenses			
Administrative salaries	8.0%		
Office salaries	8.0		
Office supplies	0.8		
Miscellaneous	0.4		
Total administrative expenses		17.2%	
General expenses			
Rent	5.6%		
Utilities	2.8		
Bad debts	0.4		
Miscellaneous	1.6		
Total general expenses		10.4%	
Total expenses			48.8
Net Income			**33.2%**

$$\text{Net income ratio} = \frac{\text{net income}}{\text{net sales}} = \frac{\$\ 83,000}{\$250,000} = 33.2\%$$

$$\text{Operating expense ratio} = \frac{\text{total expense}}{\text{net sales}} = \frac{\$122,000}{\$250,000} = 48.8\%$$

The gross margin ratio indicates the percentage of each sales dollar available to cover operating expenses and to achieve profit objectives. The net income ratio indicates the percentage of each sales dollar that is classified as earnings (profit) before payment of income taxes. The operating expense ratio indicates the percentage of each dollar needed to cover operating expenses.

If Nick and Rose feel that the operating expense ratio is higher than historical data and industry standards, they can analyze each operating expense ratio in Table B.4 to determine which expenses are too high. They can then take corrective action.

After reviewing several key operating ratios, in fact, managers will probably want to analyze all the items on the income statement. For instance, by doing so, Nick and Rose can determine whether the 8-percent increase in inventory was necessary.

Inventory Turnover

The inventory turnover rate, or stockturn rate, is an analytical ratio that can be used to answer the question, "Is the inventory level appropriate for this business?" The inventory turnover rate indicates the number of times that an inventory is sold (turns over) during one year. To be useful, this figure is then compared to historical turnover rates and industry rates.

The inventory turnover rate can be computed on cost as follows:

$$\text{Inventory turnover} = \frac{\text{cost of goods sold}}{\text{average inventory at cost}}$$

Rose and Nick would calculate the turnover rate from Table B.2 as follows:

$$\frac{\text{Cost of goods sold}}{\text{Average inventory at cost}} = \frac{\$45,000}{\$50,000} = 0.9 \text{ time}$$

They find that inventory turnover is less than once per year (0.9 time). Industry averages for competitive firms are 2.8 times. This figure convinces Rose and Nick that their investment in inventory is too large and that they need to reduce inventory.

Return on Investment

Return on investment (ROI) is a ratio that indicates management's efficiency in generating sales and profits from the total amount invested in the firm. For example, Stoneham Auto Supplies' ROI is 41.5 percent, which compares well with competing businesses.

We use Figures from two different financial statements to arrive at ROI. The income statement, already discussed, gives us net income. The balance sheet, which states the firm's assets and liabilities at a given point in time, provides the figure for total assets (or investment) in the firm.

The basic formula for ROI is

$$\text{ROI} = \frac{\text{net income}}{\text{total investment}}$$

For Stoneham Auto Supplies, net income for fiscal year 1986 is $83,000 (see Table B.2). If total investment (taken from the balance sheet for December 31, 1986) is $200,000, then

$$\text{ROI} = \frac{\$\ 83,000}{\$200,000} = 0.415 \text{ or } 41.5\%$$

The ROI formula can be expanded to isolate the impact of capital turnover and the operating income ratio separately. Capital turnover is a measure of net sales per dollar of investment; the ratio is figured by dividing net sales by total investment. For Stoneham Auto Supplies,

$$\text{Capital turnover} = \frac{\text{net sales}}{\text{total investment}}$$

$$= \frac{\$250,000}{\$200,000} = 1.25$$

ROI is equal to capital turnover times the net income ratio. The expanded formula for Stoneham Auto Supplies is

$$\text{ROI} = (\text{capital turnover}) \times (\text{net income ratio})$$

or

$$\text{ROI} = \frac{\text{net sales}}{\text{total investment}} \times \frac{\text{net income}}{\text{net sales}}$$

$$= \frac{\$250,000}{\$200,000} \times \frac{\$\ 83,000}{\$250,000}$$

$$= (1.25)(33.2\%) = 41.5\%$$

Price Calculations

An important step in setting prices is selecting a pricing method, as indicated in Chapter 16. The systematic use of markups, markdowns, and various conversion formulas helps in calculating the selling price and in evaluating the effects of various prices. The following sections provide more detailed information about price calculations than was offered in Chapter 15.

Markups

As indicated in the text, markup is the difference between the selling price and the cost of the item. That is, selling price equals cost plus markup. The markup must cover cost and contribute to profit; thus, markup is similar to gross margin on the income statement.

Markup can be calculated on either cost or selling price, as follows:

$$\text{Markup as a percentage of cost} = \frac{\text{amount added to cost}}{\text{cost}} = \frac{\text{dollar markup}}{\text{cost}}$$

$$\text{Markup as a percentage of selling price} = \frac{\text{amount added to cost}}{\text{selling price}} = \frac{\text{dollar markup}}{\text{selling price}}$$

Retailers tend to calculate the markup percentage on selling price.

Examples of Markup

To review the use of these markup formulas, assume that an item costs $10 and the markup is $5.

$$\text{Selling price} = \text{cost} + \text{markup}$$

$$\$15 = \$10 + \$5$$

Thus

$$\text{Markup percentage on cost} = \frac{\$5}{\$10} = 50\%$$

$$\text{Markup percentage on selling price} = \frac{\$5}{\$15} = 33\frac{1}{3}\%$$

It is necessary to know the base (cost or selling price) to use markup pricing effectively. Markup percentage on cost will always exceed markup percentage on price, given the same dollar markup, so long as selling price exceeds cost.

On occasion, we may need to convert markup on cost to markup on selling price, or vice versa. The conversion formulas are

$$\text{Markup percentage on selling price} = \frac{\text{markup percentage on cost}}{100\% + \text{markup percentage on cost}}$$

$$\text{Markup percentage on cost} = \frac{\text{markup percentage on selling price}}{100\% - \text{markup percentage on selling price}}$$

For example, if the markup percentage on cost is $33\frac{1}{3}$ percent, then the markup percentage on selling price is

$$\frac{33\frac{1}{3}\%}{100\% + 33\frac{1}{3}\%} = \frac{33\frac{1}{3}\%}{133\frac{1}{3}\%} = 25\%$$

If the markup percentage on selling price is 40 percent, then the corresponding percentage on cost would be

$$\frac{40\%}{100\% - 40\%} = \frac{40\%}{60\%} = 66\frac{2}{3}\%$$

Finally, we can show how to determine selling price if we know the cost of the item and the markup percentage on selling price. Assume that an item costs $36 and the usual markup percentage on selling price is 40 percent. Remember that selling price equals markup plus cost. Thus, if

$$100\% = 40\% \text{ of selling price} + \text{cost}$$

then

$$60\% \text{ of selling price} = \text{Cost}$$

In our example, cost equals $36. Then

$$0.6X = \$36$$

$$X = \frac{\$36}{0.6}$$

$$\text{Selling price} = \$60$$

Alternatively, the markup percentage could be converted to a cost basis as follows:

$$\frac{40\%}{100\% - 40\%} = 66\tfrac{2}{3}\%$$

Then the computed selling price would be as follows:

$$\text{Selling price} = 66\tfrac{2}{3}\% \text{ (cost)} + \text{cost}$$

$$= 66\tfrac{2}{3}\% \ (\$36) + \$36$$

$$= \$24 + \$36$$

$$= \$60$$

By remembering the basic formula—selling price equals cost plus markup—you will find these calculations straightforward.

Markdowns

Markdowns are price reductions on merchandise by a retailer. Markdowns may be useful on items that are damaged, or priced too high, or selected for a special sales event. The income statement does not express markdowns directly, for the change in price is made before the sale takes place. Therefore, separate records of markdowns are needed to evaluate the performance of various buyers and departments.

The markdown ratio (percentage) is calculated as follows:

$$\text{Markdown percentage} = \frac{\text{dollar markdowns}}{\text{net sales in dollars}}$$

In analyzing their inventory, Nick and Rose discover three special auto jacks that have gone unsold for several months. They decide to reduce the price of each item from $25 to $20. Subsequently, these items are sold. The markdown percentage for these three items is

$$\text{Markdown percentage} = \frac{3\,(\$5)}{3\,(\$20)} = \frac{\$15}{\$60} = 25\%$$

Net sales, however, include all units of this product sold during the period, not just those marked down. If ten of these items have already been sold at $25 each, in addition to the three items sold at $20, then the overall markdown percentage would be

$$\text{Markdown percentage} = \frac{3\,(\$5)}{10\,(\$25) + 3\,(\$20)}$$

$$= \frac{\$15}{\$250 + \$60} = \frac{\$15}{\$310} = 4.8\%$$

Sales allowances also are a reduction in price. Thus, the markdown percentages should also include any sales allowances. It would be computed as follows:

$$\text{Markdown percentage} = \frac{\text{dollar markdowns} + \text{dollar allowances}}{\text{net sales in dollars}}$$

Discussion and Review Questions

1. In what way does a manufacturer's income statement differ from a retailer's income statement?
2. Use the following information to answer questions a through c:

   Company TEA
   fiscal year ended June 30, 1987

Net Sales	$500,000
Cost of Goods Sold	300,000
Net Income	50,000
Average Inventory at Cost	100,000
Total Assets (total investment)	200,000

   a. What is the inventory turnover rate for TEA Company? From what sources will the marketing manager determine the significance of the inventory turnover rate?
   b. What is the capital turnover ratio for fiscal year 1987? What is the net income ratio? What is the return on investment (ROI)?
   c. How many dollars of sales did each dollar of investment produce for TEA Company in fiscal year 1987?
3. Product A has a markup percentage on cost of 40 percent. What is the markup percentage on selling price?

4. Product B has a markup percentage on selling price of 30 percent. What is the markup percentage on cost?
5. Product C has a cost of $60 and a usual markup percentage of 25 percent on selling price. What price should be placed on this item?
6. Apex Appliance Company sells twenty units of product Q for $100 each and ten units for $80 each. What is the markdown percentage for product Q?

Glossary

Accessory equipment Equipment used in production or office activities; does not become a part of the final physical product.

Accumulation A process through which an inventory of homogeneous products is developed that have similar production or demand requirements.

Administered pricing Process in which the seller sets a price for a product, and the customer pays that specified price.

Advertising A paid form of nonpersonal communication about an organization and/or its products that is transmitted to a target audience through a mass medium.

Advertising appropriation The total amount of money that a marketer allocates for advertising for a specific time period.

Advertising platform The basic issues or selling points that an advertiser wishes to include in the advertising campaign.

Advertising target The group of people toward which advertisements are aimed.

Agent Marketing intermediary who receives a commission or fee for expediting exchanges; represents either buyers or sellers on a permanent basis.

Aided recall test A post-test method of evaluating the effectiveness of advertising in which subjects are asked to identify advertisements they have seen recently; they are shown a list of products, brands, company names, or trademarks to jog their memory.

Allocation Breaking down large homogeneous inventories into smaller lots.

Allowance A concession in price to achieve a desired goal; for example, industrial equipment manufacturers give trade-in allowances on used industrial equipment to enable customers to purchase new equipment.

Approach The manner in which a salesperson contacts a potential customer.

Arbitrary approach A method for determining the advertising appropriation in which a high-level executive in the firm states how much can be spent on advertising for a certain time period.

Area sampling A variation of stratified sampling, with the geographic areas serving as the segments, or primary units, used in random sampling.

Artwork The illustration in an advertisement and the layout of the components of an advertisement.

Assorting Combining products into collections or assortments that buyers want to have available at one place.

Assortment A combination of similar or complementary products put together to provide benefits to a specific market.

Atmospherics The conscious designing of a store's space to create emotional effects that enhance the probability that consumers will buy.

Attitude Knowledge and positive or negative feelings about an object.

Attitude scale Measurement instrument that usually consists of a series of adjectives, phrases, or sentences about an object; subjects are asked to indicate the intensity of their feelings toward the object by reacting to the statements in a certain way; can be used to measure consumer attitudes.

Automatic vending Nonstore, nonpersonal retailing; includes coin-operated, self-service machines.

Average cost Total costs divided by the quantity produced.

Average fixed cost The fixed cost per unit produced; it is calculated by dividing the fixed costs by the number of units produced.

Average revenue Total revenue divided by quantity produced.

Average total cost The sum of the average fixed cost and the average variable cost.

Average variable cost The variable cost per unit produced; it is calculated by dividing the variable cost by the number of units produced.

B

Barter The trading of products.

Base-point pricing A geographic pricing policy that includes the price at the factory plus freight charges from the base point nearest the buyer.

Benefit segmentation The division of a market according to the benefits that customers want from the product.

Better Business Bureau A local, nongovernmental regulatory group supported by local businesses that aids in settling problems among specific business firms and consumers.

Bid pricing A determination of prices through sealed bids or open bids.

Bonded storage A storage service provided by many public warehouses in which the goods are not released until U.S. customs duties, federal or state taxes, or other fees are paid.

Brand A name, term, symbol, design, or combination of these that identifies a seller's products and differentiates them from competitors' products.

Brand-extension branding Type of branding in which a firm uses one of its existing brand names as part of a brand for an improved or new product that is usually in the same product category as the existing brand.

Brand manager A type of product manager responsible for a single brand.

Brand mark The element of a brand, such as a symbol or design, that cannot be spoken.

Brand name The part of a brand that can be spoken—including letters, words, and numbers.

Breakdown approach A general approach for measuring company sales potential based on a general economic forecast—or other aggregate data—and the market sales potential derived from it; company sales potential is based on the general economic forecast and the estimated market sales potential.

Breakeven point The point at which the costs of producing a product equal the revenue made from selling the product.

Broker A functional middleman who performs fewer functions than other intermediaries; the primary function is to bring buyers and sellers together for a fee.

Build up approach A general approach to measuring company sales potential in which the analyst initially estimates how much the average purchaser of a product will buy in a specified time period and then multiplies by the number of potential buyers; estimates are generally calculated by individual geographic areas.

Business analysis Provides a tentative sketch of a product's compatibility in the market place, including its probable profitability.

Buy-back allowance A certain sum of money given to a purchaser for each unit bought after an initial deal is over.

Buying allowance A temporary price reduction to resellers for purchasing specified quantities of a product.

Buying behavior The decision processes and acts of people involved in buying and using products.

Buying center The group of people within an organization who are involved in making organizational purchase decisions; these people occupy roles in the purchase decision process such as users, influencers, buyers, deciders, and gatekeepers.

Buying power Resources such as money, goods, and services that can be traded in an exchange situation.

Buying power index A weighted index consisting of population, effective buying income, and retail sales data. The higher the index number, the greater the buying power.

C

Captioned photograph A photograph with a brief description that explains the picture's content.

Cash-and-carry wholesaler Limited-service wholesaler that sells to customers who will pay cash and furnish transportation or pay extra to have products delivered.

Cash discount A price reduction to the buyer resulting from prompt payment or cash payment.

Catalog retailing A type of mail-order retailing in which selling may be handled by telephone or in-store visits and products are delivered by mail or picked up by the customers.

Catalog showrooms A form of warehouse showroom in which consumers shop from a mailed catalog and buy at a warehouse where all products are stored out of buyers' reach. Products are provided in the manufacturer's carton.

Causal study Research planned to prove or disprove that x causes y or that x does not cause y.

Cents-off offer A sales promotion device for established products in which buyers receive a certain amount off the regular price shown on the label or package.

Channel capacity The limit to the volume of information that a communication channel can handle effectively.

Channel conflict Friction between marketing channel members often resulting from role deviance or malfunction; absence of an expected mode of conduct that contributes to the channel as a system.

Channel cooperation A helping relationship among channel members that enhances the welfare and survival of all necessary channel members.

Channel of distribution *See* marketing channel.

Channel leadership Guidance provided by a channel member with one or more sources of power to other channel members to help achieve channel objectives.

Channel power The ability of one channel member to influence goal achievement of another channel member.

Clayton Act Passed in 1914, this act prohibits specific practices, such as price discrimination, exclusive dealer arrangements, and stock aquisitions, in which the effect may substantially lessen competition to tend to create a monopoly.

Client public The direct consumers of the product of a nonbusiness organization; for example, the client public of a university is its student body.

Closing The element in the selling process in which the salesperson asks the prospect to buy the product.

Coding process The process by which a meaning is placed into a series of signs that represent ideas.

Cognitive dissonance Dissatisfaction that may occur shortly after the purchase of a product, when the buyer questions whether he or she should have purchased the product at all or would have been better off purchasing another brand that was evaluated very favorably.

Combination compensation plan A plan by which salespeople are paid a fixed salary and a commission based on sales volume.

Commercialization A phase of new product development in which plans for full-scale manufacturing and marketing must be refined and settled, and budgets for the project must be prepared.

Commission merchant Agent often used in agricultural marketing who usually exercises physical control over products, negotiates sales, and is given broad powers regarding prices and terms of sale.

Communication A sharing of meaning through the transmission of information.

Community shopping center Shopping center that includes one or two department stores and some specialty stores, as well as convenience stores; serves several neighborhoods and draws consumers who are not able to find desired products in neighborhood shopping centers.

Company sales forecast The amount of a product that a firm actually expects to sell during a specific period at a specified level of company marketing activities.

Company sales potential The amount of a product that an organization could sell during a specified period.

Comparative advertising Advertising that compares two or more identified brands in the same general product class; the comparison is made in terms of one or more specific product characteristics.

Competition Generally viewed by a business as those firms that market products similar to, or substitutable for, its products in the same target market.

Competition-matching approach A method of ascertaining the advertising appropriation in which an advertiser tries to match a major competitor's appropriations in terms of absolute dollars or in terms of using the same percentage of sales for advertising.

Competition-oriented pricing A pricing method in which an organization considers costs and revenue secondary to competitors' prices.

Competitive advertising Advertising that points out a brand's uses, features, and advantages that benefit consumers and that may not be available in competing brands.

Competitive structure The model used to describe the number of firms that control the supply of a product and how it affects the strength of competition; factors include number of competitors, ease of entry into the market, the nature of the product, and knowledge of the market.

Component part A finished item ready for assembly or a product that needs little processing before assembly and that becomes a part of the physical product.

Comprehensive spending patterns The percentages of family income allotted to annual expenditures for general classes of goods and services.

Concentration strategy A market segmentation strategy in which an organization directs its marketing efforts toward a single market segment through one marketing mix.

Consumer buying behavior The buying behavior of ultimate consumers—those persons who purchase products for personal or household use and not for business purposes.

Consumer buying decision process The five-stage decision process consumers use in making purchases.

Consumer contest A sales promotion device for established products based on the analytical or creative skill of contestants.

Consumer Goods Pricing Act Federal legislation

that prohibits the use of price maintenance agreements among producers and resellers involved in interstate commerce.

Consumer jury A panel used to pretest advertisements, consisting of a number of persons who are actual or potential buyers of the product to be advertised.

Consumer market Purchasers and/or individuals in their households who intend to consume or benefit from the purchased products and who do not buy products for the main purpose of making a profit.

Consumer movement A social movement through which people attempt to defend and exercise their rights as buyers.

Consumer movement forces Focus on three different areas: product safety, disclosure of information, and protection of our environment. The major forces in the consumer movement are consumer organizations, consumer laws, consumer education, and independent consumer advocates.

Consumer product Product purchased for ultimate satisfaction of personal and family needs.

Consumer Product Safety Commission A federal agency created to protect consumers by setting product standards, testing products, investigating product complaints, banning products, and monitoring injuries through the National Electronic Surveillance System.

Consumer protection legislation Laws enacted to protect consumers' safety, to enhance the amount of information available, and to warn of deceptive marketing techniques.

Consumer sales promotion method Sales promotion method that encourages or stimulates customers to patronize a specific retail store or to try and/or purchase a particular product.

Consumer spending patterns Information indicating the relative proportions of annual family expenditures or the actual amount of money that is spent on certain types of goods or services.

Consumer sweepstakes A sales promotion device for established products in which entrants submit their names for inclusion in a drawing for prizes.

Containerization The practice of consolidating many items into one container, sealed at the point of origin and opened at the destination.

Convenience products Relatively inexpensive, frequently purchased items for which buyers want to exert only minimal effort.

Cooperative advertising An arrangement in which a manufacturer agrees to pay a certain amount of a retailer's media costs for advertising the manufacturer's products.

Copy The verbal portion of advertisements; includes headlines, subheadlines, body copy, and signature.

Corporate Strategy The strategy that determines the means for utilizing resources in the areas of production, finance, research and development, personnel, and marketing to reach the organization's goals.

Correlation methods Methods used to develop sales forecasts as the forecasters attempt to find a relationship between past sales and one or more variables, such as population, per capita income, or gross national product.

Cost comparison indicator Allows an advertiser to compare the costs of several vehicles within a specific medium relative to the number of persons reached by each vehicle.

Cost-oriented pricing A pricing policy in which a firm determines price by adding a dollar amount or percentage to the cost of a product.

Cost-plus pricing A form of cost-oriented pricing in which first the seller's costs are determined and then a specified dollar amount or percentage of the cost is added to the seller's cost in order to set the price.

Count and recount A sales promotion method based on the payment of a specific amount of money for each product unit moved from a reseller's warehouse in a given period of time.

Coupon A new-product sales promotion technique used to stimulate trial of a new or improved product, to increase sales volume quickly, to attract repeat purchasers, or to introduce new package sizes or features.

Credence service qualities Qualities of services that cannot be assessed even after purchase and consumption; for example, few consumers are knowledgeable enough to assess the quality of an appendix operation, even after it has been performed.

Culture Everything in our surroundings that is made by human beings, consisting of tangible items as well as intangible concepts and values.

Cumulative discount Quantity discount that is aggregated over a stated period of time.

Customary pricing A type of psychological pricing in which certain goods are priced primarily on the basis of tradition.

Customer forecasting survey The technique of asking customers what types and quantities of products they intend to buy during a specific period in order to predict the sales level for that period.

Customer orientation A marketer attempts to provide a marketing mix that satisfies the needs of buyers in the target market.

Cycle analysis   A method of predicting sales in which a forecaster analyzes sales figures for a period of three to five years to ascertain whether sales fluctuate in a consistent, periodic manner.

D

Dealer listing   An advertisement that promotes a product and identifies the names of participating retailers who sell the product.

Dealer loader   A gift, often part of a display, that is given to a retailer for the purchase of a specified quantity of merchandise.

Decline stage   The stage in a product's life cycle in which sales fall rapidly and profits decrease.

Decoding process   The stage in the communication process in which signs are converted into concepts and ideas.

Defensive advertising   Advertising used to offset or lessen the effects of a competitor's promotional program.

Demand-oriented pricing   A pricing policy based on the level of demand for the product—resulting in a higher price when demand for the product is strong and a lower price when demand is weak.

Demand schedule   The relationship, usually inverse, between price and quantity demanded; classically, a line sloping downward to the right, showing that as price falls, quantity demanded will increase.

Demographic factors   Personal characteristics such as age, sex, race, nationality, income, family, life-cycle stage, and occupation.

Demonstration   A sales promotion method used by manufacturers on a temporary basis to encourage trial use and purchase of the product or to actually show how the product works.

Department stores   A type of retail store having a wide product mix; organized into separate departments to facilitate marketing efforts and internal management.

Dependent variable   A variable contingent on, or restricted to, one or a set of values assumed by the independent variable.

Depression   A stage of the business cycle during which there is extremely high unemployment, wages are very low, total disposable income is at a minimum, and consumers lack confidence in the economy.

Depth (of product mix)   The average number of different products offered to buyers in a firm's product line.

Depth interview   Personal interview with an open, informal atmosphere; this interview may take several hours; used to study motives.

Derived demand   A characteristic of industrial demand that arises because industrial demand derives from the consumer demand.

Descriptive studies   Type of study undertaken when marketers see that knowledge of the characteristics of certain phenomena is needed to solve a problem; may require statistical analysis and predictive tools.

Direct-cost approach   An approach to determining marketing costs in which cost analysis includes direct costs and traceable common costs, but does not include nontraceable common costs.

Direct costs   Costs directly attributable to the performance of marketing functions.

Direct distribution channels   Distribution channels in which products are sold directly from producer to users.

Direct ownership   A long-run commitment to marketing in a foreign nation in which a subsidiary or division is owned by a foreign country through purchase.

Discount store   Self-service, general merchandise store positioned as having low prices.

Discretionary income   Disposable income that is available for spending and saving after an individual has purchased the basic necessities of food, clothing, and shelter.

Disposable income   After-tax income.

Distribution variable   The marketing mix variable in which marketing management attempts to make products available in the quantities desired with adequate service to a target market and to hold the total inventory, transportation, communication, storage, and material handling costs as low as possible.

Diversified growth   A type of growth that occurs in three forms, depending on the technology of the new products and the nature of the new markets the firm enters; the three forms are horizontal, concentric, and conglomerate.

Drop shipper   A limited-service wholesaler that takes title to products and negotiates sales but never physically handles products.

Dumping   The sale of products in foreign markets at lower prices than those charged in the domestic market (when all costs are not allocated or when surplus products are sold).

E

Early adopters   Individuals who choose new products carefully and are viewed as being "the people to check with" by persons in the early majority, late majority, and laggard categories.

Early majority Individuals who adopt a new product just prior to the average person; they are deliberate and cautious in trying new products.

Economic forces Forces that determine the strength of a firm's competitive atmosphere, and affect the impact of marketing activities because they determine the size and strength of demand for products.

Economic institutions An environmental force in international markets made up of producers, wholesalers, retailers, buyers, and other organizations that produce, distribute, and purchase products.

Economic order quantity (EOQ) The order size that minimizes the total cost of ordering and carrying inventory.

Effective buying income Similar to disposable income; it includes salaries, wages, dividends, interest, profits, and rents less federal, state, and local taxes.

Elasticity of demand The relative responsiveness of changes in quantity demanded to changes in price.

Encoding *See* Coding process.

Environmental analysis Process of assessing and interpreting the information gathered through scanning.

Environmental monitoring The process of seeking information about events and relationships in a company's environment to assist marketers in identifying opportunities and in planning.

Environmental scanning The collection of information regarding the forces in the marketing environment.

Equalized workload method A method of determining sales-force size in which the number of customers multiplied by the number of sales calls annually required to serve these customers effectively is divided by the average number of calls made annually by each salesperson.

Ethical pricing A form of professional pricing in which the demand for the product is inelastic and the seller is a professional who has a respsonsibility not to overcharge the client.

Exchange Participation by two or more individuals, groups, or organizations, with each party possessing something of value that the other party desires. Each must be willing to give up its "something of value" to get "something of value" held by the other, and all parties must be willing to communicate with each other.

Exclusive dealing contract Agreement in which resellers agree to buy all of a specific product from one supplier.

Exclusive distribution A type of market coverage in which only one outlet is used in a geographic area.

Executive judgment A sales forecasting method based on the intuition of one or more executives.

Experience curve pricing A pricing approach in which a company fixes a low price that high-cost competitors cannot match and thus expands its market share; this approach is possible when a firm gains cumulative production experience and is able to reduce its manufacturing costs to a predictable rate through improved methods, materials, skills, and machinery.

Experience service qualities Qualities of services that can be assessed only after purchase and consumption (taste, satisfaction, courtesy, and the like).

Experimentation Research in which those factors that are related to or may affect the variables under investigation are maintained as constants so that the effects of the experimental variables may be measured.

Expert forecasting survey Preparation of the sales forecast by experts, such as economists, management consultants, advertising executives, college professors, or other persons outside the firm.

Exploratory studies Type of research conducted when more information is needed about a problem and the tentative hypothesis needs to be made more specific; it permits marketers to conduct ministudies with a very restricted data base.

Extensive decision making Considerable time and effort spent by a buyer to seek out alternative products, search for information about them, and then evaluate them to determine which one will be most satisfying.

F

Facilitating agency Organization that performs activities that assist in performing channel functions but does not buy, sell, or transfer title to the product; can include transportation companies, insurance companies, advertising agencies, marketing research agencies, and financial institutions.

Family packaging A policy in an organization that all packages are to be similar or are to include one major element of the design.

Feature article A form of publicity that is up to three thousand words long and usually is prepared for a specific publication.

Federal Trade Commission Made up of five commissioners with the goal of preventing the free enterprise system from being stifled or fettered by monopoly or anti-competitive practices and providing the direct protection of consumers from unfair or deceptive trade practices.

Federal Trade Commission Act (1914) Established the Federal Trade Commission and currently regulates the greatest number of marketing practices.

Feedback The receiver's response to the decoded message.

Field warehouse Producer-controlled storage space that separates part of the inventory.

Fixed cost Cost that does not vary with changes in the number of units produced or sold.

F.O.B. (free-on-board) factory Part of price quotation; used to indicate who must pay shipping charges. For example: F.O.B. factory indicates the price of the merchandise at the factory, before it is loaded onto the carrier vehicle. Thus the buyer must pay for shipping.

Food broker Intermediary that sells food and other grocery products to retailer-owned and merchant wholesalers, grocery chains, industrial buyers, and food processors. Both buyers and sellers use food brokers to cope with fluctuating market conditions.

Franchising An arrangement in which a supplier (franchisor) grants a dealer (franchisee) the right to sell products in exchange for some type of consideration.

Free merchandise A sales promotion method aimed at retailers in which free merchandise is offered to resellers that purchase a stated quantity of product.

Free samples A new-product sales promotion technique used by marketers to stimulate trial of a product, to increase sales volume in early stages of the product's life cycle, or to obtain desirable distribution.

Freight absorption pricing Pricing for a particular customer or geographical area by which the seller absorbs all or part of the actual freight costs.

Freight forwarders Businesses that consolidate shipments from several organizations into efficient lot sizes, which increases transit time and sometimes lowers shipping costs.

Full-cost approach An approach to determining marketing costs in which cost analysis includes direct costs, traceable common costs, and nontraceable common costs.

Full-service wholesaler A marketing intermediary that provides most services that can be performed by wholesalers.

Functional discount *See* Trade discount.

Functional middleman Agent or broker who ne-

gotiates purchases and expedites sales but does not take title to the product; performs a limited number of marketing activities for a commission.

Functional modifications Changes that affect a product's versatility, effectiveness, convenience, or safety, usually requiring the redesigning of one or more parts of the product.

G

General merchandise wholesaler Full-service merchant wholesaler who carries a very wide product mix.

General public The indirect consumers of the product of a nonbusiness organization; for instance, the general public of a university includes alumni, trustees, parents of students, and other groups.

Generic brand A brand that indicates only the product category (such as *aluminum foil*) and does not include the company name and other identifying terms.

Gentlemen's pricing A form of professional pricing in which professionals feel they are "above" charging their customers on the basis of each service performed. For example, a doctor may charge a flat $35 for a physical exam.

Geographic pricing A form of pricing that involves reductions for transportation costs or other costs associated with the physical distance between the buyer and the seller.

Globalization of Markets To develop marketing strategies as if the entire world (or regions of it) were a single entity; products are marketed the same way everywhere.

Good A physical concrete something you can touch; a tangible item.

Government markets Markets made up of federal, state, county, and local governments, spending billions of dollars annually for goods and services to support their internal operations and to provide such products as defense, energy, and education.

Gross National Product (GNP) An overall measure of a nation's economic standing in terms of the value of all products produced by that nation for a given period of time.

Group interview A method to uncover people's motives relating to some issue, such as product usage, with an interviewer generating discussion on one or several topics among the six to twelve people in the group.

Growth state The product life cycle stage in which

sales rise rapidly; profits reach a peak and then start to decline.

H

Heterogeneous market   A market made up of individuals with diverse product needs for products in a specific product class.

Horizontal channel integration   The combining of institutions at the same level of operation under one management.

Hypothesis   A guess or assumption about a certain problem or set of circumstances, reasonable supposition that may be right or wrong.

I

Idea   A concept, philosophy, image, or issue.

Idea generation   The search by businesses and other organizations for product ideas that help them achieve their objectives.

Illustrations   Photographs, drawings, graphs, charts, and tables, used to encourage an audience to read or watch an advertisement.

Income   The amount of money received through wages, rents, investments, pensions, and subsidy payments for a given period.

Incremental productivity method   A plan by which a marketer should continue to increase the sales force as long as the additional sales increases are greater than the additional selling costs that arise from employing more salespeople.

Independent variable   Variable free from influence of, or not dependent on, other variables.

Individual branding   A branding policy in which each product is named something different.

Industrial buying behavior   *See* Organizational buying behavior.

Industrial distributor   Independent business organization that takes title to industrial products and carries inventories.

Industrial market   A market consisting of individuals, groups, or organizations that purchase specific kinds of products for direct use in producing other products or for use in day-to-day operations.

Industrial Marketing   A set of activities directed toward facilitating and expediting exchanges involving industrial markets and industrial products.

Industrial product   A product purchased to be used directly or indirectly to produce other products or to be used in the operations of an organization.

Industrial service   Intangible product that an organization uses in its operations, such as financial products and legal services.

Inelastic demand   A type of demand in which a price increase or decrease will not significantly affect the quantity demanded.

Inflation   A condition in which price levels increase faster than incomes, causing a decline in buying power.

Information inputs   The sensations that we receive through our sense organs.

In-home retailing   A type of nonstore retailing that involves personal selling in consumers' homes.

Innovators   The first consumers to adopt a new product; they enjoy trying new products and tend to be venturesome, rash, and daring.

Input-output data   A type of information, sometimes used in conjunction with the SIC system, that is based on the assumption that the output or sales of one industry are the input or purchases of other industries.

Institutional advertising   A form of advertising promoting organizational images, ideas, and political issues.

Institutional market   A market that consists of organizations that seek to achieve goals other than such normal business goals as profit, market share, or return on investment.

Integrated growth   The type of growth that a firm can have within its industry; three possible growth directions include forward, backward, and horizontal.

Intense growth   The type of growth that can take place when current products and current markets have the potential for increasing sales.

Intensive distribution   A form of market coverage in which all available outlets are used for distributing a product.

International marketing   Marketing activities performed across national boundaries.

Introduction stage   The stage in a product's lifecycle beginning at a product's first appearance in the marketplace, when sales are zero and profits are negative.

J

Joint demand   A characteristic of industrial demand that occurs when two or more items are used in combination to produce a product.

Joint venture A partnership between a domestic firm and foreign firms and/or governments.

Kinesic communication Commonly known as body language, this type of interpersonal communication occurs in face-to-face selling situations when the salesperson and customers move their heads, eyes, arms, hands, legs, and torsos.

Labeling An important dimensioin of packaging for promotional, informational, and legal reasons; regulated by numerous federal and state laws.

Laggards The last consumers to adopt a new product; they are oriented toward the past and suspicious of new products.

Late Majority People who are quite skeptical of new products; they eventually adopt new products because of economic necessity or social pressure.

Layout The physical arrangement of the illustration, headline, subheadline, body copy, and signature of an advertisement.

Learning A change in an individual's behavior that arises from prior behavior in similar situations.

Legal forces Forces that arise from the legislation and interpretation of laws; these laws, enacted by government units, restrain and control marketing decisions and activities.

Licensing (international) An arrangement in international marketing in which the licensee pays commissions or royalties on sales or supplies used in manufacturing.

Limited decision making The type of consumer decision making employed for products that are purchased occasionally and when a buyer needs to acquire information about an unfamiliar brand in a familiar product category.

Limited-line wholesaler Full-service merchant wholesaler who carries only a few product lines.

Limited-service wholesaler A marketing intermediary that provides only some marketing services and specializes in a few functions.

Line family branding A branding policy in which an organization uses family branding only for products within a line but not for all its products.

Long-range plan A plan that covers more than five years.

Mail-order retailing A type of nonpersonal, nonstore retailing that uses direct mail advertising and catalogs and is typified by selling by description. The buyer usually does not see the actual product until it is delivered.

Mail-order wholesaler Organization that sells through direct mail by sending catalogs to retail, industrial, and institutional customers.

Major equipment A category of industrial products that includes large tools and machines used for production purposes.

Manufacturer brand Brand initiated by a producer; makes it possible for a producer to be identified with its product at the point of purchase.

Manufacturers' agent An independent business person who sells complementary products of several producers in assigned territories and is compensated through commissions.

Marginal cost The cost associated with producing one more unit of a product.

Marginal revenue (MR) The change in total revenue that occurs after an additional unit of a product is sold.

Market An aggregate of people who, as individuals or as organizations, have needs for products in a product class and who have the ability, willingness, and authority to purchase such products.

Market attractiveness/business position model A two-dimensional matrix designed to serve as a diagnostic tool to highlight SBUs that have an opportunity to grow or that should be divested.

Market density The number of potential customers within a unit of land area, such as a square mile.

Marketing Individual and organizational activities that facilitate and expedite satisfying exchange relationships in a dynamic environment through the creation, distribution, promotion, and pricing of goods, services, and ideas.

Marketing audit A systematic examination of the objectives, strategies, organization, and performance of a firm's marketing unit.

Marketing channel A group of interrelated intermediaries who direct products to customers; also called channel of distribution.

Marketing concept Managerial philosophy that an organization should try to satisfy the needs of customers through a coordinated set of activities that at the same time allows the organization to achieve its goals.

Marketing control process Process that consists of establishing performance standards, evaluating actual performance by comparing it with established standards, and reducing the differences between desired and actual performance.

Marketing cost analysis A method for helping to control marketing strategies in which various costs are broken down and classified to determine which costs are associated with specific marketing activities.

Marketing data bank A file of data collected through both the marketing information system and marketing research projects.

Marketing environment Environment that surrounds both the buyer and marketing mix; consists of political, legal, regulatory, societal, consumer movement, economic, and technological forces. Environmental variables affect a marketer's ability to facilitate and expedite exchanges.

Market manager A person responsible for the marketing activities that are necessary to serve a particular group or class of customers.

Market opportunity An opportunity that arises when the right combination of circumstances occurs at the right time to allow an organization to take action toward generating sales from a target market.

Market requirement Related to customers' needs or desired benefits, the market requirement is satisfied by components of the marketing mix that provide benefits to buyers.

Market sales potential The amount of a product that would be purchased by specific customer groups within a specified period at a specific level of industrywide marketing activity.

Market segment A group of individuals, groups, or organizations that share one or more similar characteristics that make them have relatively similar product needs.

Market segmentation The process of dividing a total market into groups of people with relatively similar product needs, for the purpose of designing a marketing mix (or mixes) that more precisely matches the needs of individuals in a selected segment (or segments).

Market share A firm's sales in relation to total industry sales, expressed as a decimal or percentage.

Market test Stage of new product development that involves making a product available to buyers in one or more test areas and measuring purchases and consumer responses to promotion, price, and distribution efforts.

Marketing experimentation A set of rules and procedures under which the task of data gathering is organized to expedite analysis and interpretation.

Marketing function account Classification of costs that indicates which function was performed through the expenditure of funds.

Marketing information system (MIS) System that establishes a framework for the day-to-day managing and structuring of information gathered regularly from sources both inside and outside an organization.

Marketing intelligence Includes all data gathered as a basis for marketing decisions.

Marketing intermediary A member of a marketing channel, primarily merchants and agents, acting to direct products to buyers.

Marketing management A process of planning, organizing, implementing, and controlling marketing activities in order to facilitate and expedite exchanges effectively and efficiently.

Marketing mix Consists of four major variables including product, price, distribution, and promotion.

Marketing objective A statement of what is to be accomplished through marketing activities.

Marketing-oriented organization An organization that attempts to determine what target market members want and then tries to produce it.

Marketing plan The written document or blueprint for implementing and controlling an organization's marketing activities related to a particular marketing strategy.

Market planning cycle The five-step cycle that involves developing or revising marketing objectives relative to performance, assessing marketing opportunities and resources, formulating marketing strategy, developing the plan for implementation and control, and implementing the marketing plan.

Marketing program A set of marketing strategies that are implemented and used at the same time.

Marketing research The part of marketing intelligence that involves specific inquiries into problems and marketing activities to discover new information in order to guide marketing decisions.

Marketing strategy A plan for selecting and analyzing a target market and creating and maintaining a marketing mix.

Markup A percentage of the cost or price of a product added to the cost.

Markup pricing Pricing method through which the price is derived by adding a predetermined percentage of the cost to the cost of the product.

Mass merchandiser A retail operation that tends to offer fewer customer services than department stores and to focus their attention on lower prices, high turnover, and large sales volume; includes supermarkets and discount houses.

Materials handling Physical handling of products.

Maturity stage A stage in the product life cycle in which the sales curve peaks and starts to decline as profits continue to decline.

Mechanical observation devices Cameras, recorders, counting machines, and equipment to record movement, behavior, or physiological changes in individuals.

Media plan Plan that sets forth the exact media vehicles to be used and the dates and times that the advertisements are to appear.

Medium of transmission That which carries the coded message from the source to the receiver or audience; examples include ink on paper or vibrations of air waves produced by vocal cords.

Medium-range plans Plans that usually encompass two to five years.

Mega carrier A freight transportation company that provides many methods of shipment, such as rail, truck, and air service.

Merchandise allowance A sales promotion method aimed at retailers consisting of a manufacturer's agreement to pay resellers certain amounts of money for providing special promotional efforts, such as setting up and maintaining a display.

Merchant A marketing intermediary who takes title to merchandise and resells it for a profit.

Merchant wholesaler A marketing intermediary who takes title to products, assumes risk, and generally is involved in buying and reselling products.

Missionary salesperson Support salesperson, usually employed by a manufacturer, who assists the producer's customers in selling to their own customers.

Modified rebuy purchase A type of industrial purchase in which a new-task purchase is changed the second or third time, or the requirements associated with a straight rebuy purchase are modified.

Money refund A new-product sales promotion technique in which a consumer is mailed a specific amount of money by the producer when proof of purchase is established.

Monopolistic competition A market structure in which a firm has many potential competitors; to compete, the firm tries to develop a differential marketing strategy to establish its own market share.

Monopoly Market structure existing when a firm produces a product that has no close substitutes and/or when a single seller may erect barriers to potential competitors.

Motive An internal energizing force that directs a person's behavior toward his or her goals.

MRO items An alternative term for supplies that refers to the fact that supplies can be divided into maintenance, repair, and operating (or overhaul) items.

Multinational enterprise A firm that has operations or subsidiaries in several countries.

Multisegment strategy A market segmentation strategy in which an organization directs its marketing efforts at two or more segments by developing a marketing mix for each selected segment.

Multivariable segmentation Market division achieved by using more than one characteristic to divide the total market; this approach provides more information about the individuals in each segment than does single variable segmentation.

N

National Advertising Review Board A self-regulatory unit created by the Council of Better Business Bureaus and three advertising trade organizations; screens national advertisements to check for honesty and processes complaints about deceptive advertisements.

Natural account Classification of costs based on what the money is actually spent for; typically a part of a regular accounting system.

Negotiated pricing A determination of price through bargaining even when there are stated list prices and discount structures.

Negotiation Mutual discussion or communication of the terms and methods of an exchange.

Neighborhood shopping center Shopping center that usually consists of several small convenience and specialty stores and serves consumers who live less than ten minutes' driving time from the center.

New product Any product that a given firm has not marketed previously.

New product development A process consisting of six phases: idea generation, screening, business analysis, product development, test marketing, and commercialization.

News release A form of publicity that is usually a single page of typewritten copy containing fewer than three hundred words.

New-task purchase A type of industrial purchase in which an organization is making an initial purchase of an item to be used to perform a new job or to solve a new problem.

Noise A condition in the communication process existing when the decoded message is different from what was coded.

Nonbusiness marketing Marketing activities conducted by individuals and organizations to achieve some goal other than ordinary business goals such as profit, market share, or return on investment.

Noncumulative discount One-time price reduction based on the number of units purchased, the size of the order, or the product combination purchased.

Nonstore retailing Consumers purchase products without visiting a store.

Nontraceable common costs Costs that cannot be assigned to any specific function according to any logical criteria and thus are assignable only on an arbitrary basis.

O

Objective and task approach   One approach to determining the advertising appropriation; marketers first determine the objectives that a campaign is to achieve, then ascertain the tasks required to accomplish those objectives; the costs of all tasks are added to ascertain the total appropriation.

Observation method   Researchers record the overt behavior of subjects, taking note of physical conditions and events. Direct contact with subjects is avoided; instead, their actions are examined and noted systematically.

Odd-even pricing   A type of psychological pricing that assumes that more of a product will be sold at $99.99 than at $100.00, indicating that an odd price is more appealing than an even price to customers.

Oligopoly   Competitive structure existing when a few sellers control the supply of a large proportion of a product; each seller must consider the actions of other sellers to changes in marketing activities.

Open bids   Prices submitted by several, but not all, sellers; the amounts of these bids are not made public.

Opportunity cost   The value of the benefit that is given up by selecting one alternative rather than another.

Order getter   A type of salesperson who increases the firm's sales by selling to new customers and by increasing sales to present customers.

Order taker   A type of salesperson who primarily seeks repeat sales.

Organizational buying behavior   The purchase behavior of producers, government units, institutions, and resellers.

Overall family branding   A policy in which all of a firm's products are branded with the same name or at least a part of the name.

P

Patronage motives   Motives that influence where a person purchases products on a regular basis.

Penetration price   A lower price designed to penetrate the market and thus quickly produce a larger unit sales volume.

Percent of sales approach   A method for establishing the advertising appropriation in which marketers simply multiply a firm's past sales, forecasted sales, or a combination of the two by a standard percentage based on both what the firm traditionally has spent on advertising and on what the industry averages.

Perception   The process by which an individual selects, organizes, and interprets information inputs to create a meaningful picture of the world.

Perfect competition   Ideal competitive structure that would entail a large number of sellers, no one of which could significantly influence price or supply.

Performance standard   An expected level of performance against which actual performance can be compared.

Personal selling   A process of informing customers and persuading them to purchase products through personal communication in an exchange situation.

Personality   An internal structure in which experience and behavior are related in an orderly way.

Person-specific influences   Factors influencing the consumer buying decision process that are unique to particular individuals.

Persuasion   Convincing or prevailing upon an individual or organization in order to bring about an exchange.

Physical distribution   An integrated set of activities that deal with managing the movement of products within firms and through marketing channels.

PIMS (Profit Impact on Marketing Strategy)   A Strategic Planning Institute (SPI) research program that provides reports on the products of SPI member firms; these reports assist the member firms in analyzing marketing performance and formulating marketing strategies.

Pioneer advertising   A type of advertising that informs persons about what a product is, what it does, how it can be used, and where it can be purchased.

Point-of-purchase materials   A sales promotion method including such items as outside signs, window displays, and display racks used to attract attention, to inform customers, and to encourage retailers to carry particular products.

Political and legal institutions   Public agencies, laws, courts, legislatures, and government bureaus.

Political forces   Strongly influence the economic and political stability of our country not only through decisions that affect domestic matters but also through their authority to negotiate trade agreements and to determine foreign policy.

Population   All elements, units, or individuals that are of interest to researchers for a specific study.

Post-test   Evaluation of advertising effectiveness after the campaign.

Premiums   Items that are offered free or at a minimum cost as a bonus for purchasing.

Press conference   A meeting used to announce major news events.

Prestige pricing Setting prices at a high level to facilitate a prestige or quality image.

Pretest Evaluation of an advertisement before it actually is used.

Price The value placed on what is exchanged.

Price differentiation A demand-oriented pricing method in which a firm uses more than one price in the marketing of a specific product; differentiation of prices can be based on several dimensions, such as type of customers, type of distribution used, or the time of the purchase.

Price discrimination A policy in which some buyers are charged lower prices than other buyers, which gives those paying less a competitive advantage.

Price elasticity The percentage change in quantity demanded divided by the percentage change in price.

Price leaders Products sold at less than cost to increase sales of regular merchandise.

Price lining A form of psychological pricing in which an organization sets a limited number of prices for selected lines of products.

Price skimming A pricing policy in which an organization charges the highest possible price that buyers who most desire the product will pay.

Price variable A critical marketing mix variable in which marketing management is concerned with establishing a value for what is exchanged.

Pricing method A mechanical procedure for setting prices on a regular basis.

Pricing objectives Overall goals that describe the role of price in an organization's long-range plans.

Pricing policy A guiding philosophy or course of action designed to influence and determine pricing decisions.

Primary data Information observed and recorded or collected directly from subjects.

Private brand *See* Private distributor brand.

Private distributor brand A brand that is initiated and owned by a reseller.

Private warehouse A storage facility operated by a company for the purpose of distributing its own products.

Problem definition The first step in the research process toward finding a solution or launching a research study; the researcher thinks about how best to discover the nature and boundaries of a problem or opportunity.

Process materials Materials used directly in the production of other products; unlike component parts, they are not readily identifiable.

Procompetitive legislation Laws enacted to preserve competition.

Producer market Market that consists of individuals and business organizations that purchase products for the purpose of making a profit by using them

to produce other products or by using them in their operations.

Product Everything (both favorable and unfavorable) that one receives in an exchange; it is a complexity of tangible and intangible attributes including functional, social, and psychological utilities or benefits; a product may be a good, service, or idea.

Product adoption process The multistep process of buyer acceptance of a product, consisting of five stages: awareness, interest, evaluation, trial, and adoption.

Product advertising Advertising that promotes goods and services.

Product assortment A collection of a variety of products.

Product deletion Elimination of some products that no longer satisfy target market customers and contribute to achieving an organization's overall goals.

Product development A stage in creating new products that moves the product from concept to test phase and also involves the development of the other elements of the marketing mix (promotion, distribution, and price).

Product differentiation Using promotional efforts to differentiate a company's products from its competitors' products, hoping to establish the superiority and preferability of its products relative to competing brands.

Production orientation The viewpoint that increasing the efficiency of production is the primary means of increasing an organization's profits.

Production-oriented organization A firm that concentrates either on improving production efficiency or on producing high-quality, technically improved products; it has little regard for customers' desires.

Product item A specific version of a product that can be designated as a unique offering among an organization's products.

Product life cycle Course of product development, consisting of several stages: introduction, growth, maturity, and decline. As a product moves through these stages, the strategies relating to competition, pricing, promotion, distribution, and market information must be evaluated and possibly changed.

Product line A group of closely related products that are considered a unit because of marketing, technical, or end-use considerations.

Product manager Person who holds a staff position in a multiproduct company; responsible for a product, a product line, or several distinct products that are considered an interrelated group.

Product mix The composite of products that an organization makes available to consumers.

Product mix depth *See* Depth of product mix.

Product mix width   *See* Width of product mix.

Product modification   Refers to changing one or more of a product's characteristics.

Product portfolio analysis (BCG approach)   A strategic planning approach based on the philosophy that a product's market growth rate and its relative market share are important considerations in determining its market strategy.

Product portfolio approach   An approach to managing the product mix that attempts to create specific marketing strategies to achieve a balanced mix of products that will produce maximum long-run profits.

Product positioning   The decisions and activities that are directed toward trying to create and maintain the firm's intended product concept in customers' minds.

Product-specific spending patterns   The dollar amounts spent by families for specific products within a general product class.

Product variable   That aspect of the marketing mix dealing with researching consumers' product wants and planning the product to achieve the desired product characteristics.

Professional pricing   Pricing used by persons who have great skill or experience in a particular field or activity, indicating that a price should not relate directly to the time and involvement in a specific case; rather, a standard fee is charged regardless of the problems involved in performing the job.

Professional services   Complex and frequently regulated services that usually require the provider to be highly skilled; examples are accounting or legal services.

Projective technique   Test in which subjects are asked to perform specific tasks for particular purposes while, in fact, they are being evaluated for other purposes; assumes that subjects will unconsciously "project" their motives as they perform the tasks.

Promotion   The communication with individuals, groups, or organizations to directly or indirectly facilitate exchanges by influencing audience members to accept an organization's products.

Promotion mix   The specific combination of promotional methods used by an organization for a particular product.

Promotion variable   A major marketing mix component used to facilitate exchanges by informing an individual or one or more groups of people about an organization and its products.

Prospecting   Developing a list of potential customers for personal selling purposes.

Prosperity   A stage of the business cycle, during which unemployment is low and aggregate income is relatively high, which causes buying power to be high (assuming a low inflation rate).

Proxemic communication   A subtle form of interpersonal communication used in face-to-face interactions when either party varies the physical distance that separates them.

Psychological influences   Factors that operate within individuals to partially determine their general behavior and thus to influence their behavior as buyers.

Psychological pricing   Pricing method designed to encourage purchases that are based on emotional reactions rather than on rational responses.

Publicity   Nonpersonal communication in news story form, regarding an organization and/or its products, that is transmitted through a mass medium at no charge.

Public relations   A broad set of communication activities employed to create and maintain favorable relations between the organization and its publics—such as customers, employees, stockholders, government officials, and society in general.

Public warehouses   Business organizations that provide rented storage facilities and related physical distribution facilities.

Pull policy   Promotion of a product directly to consumers with the intention of developing strong consumer demand.

Purchasing power   A buyer's income, credit, and wealth available for purchasing products.

Push money   An incentive program designed to push a line of goods by providing additional compensation to salespeople.

Push policy   Promotion of a product only to the next institution down the marketing channel.

Q

Quality modification   A change that relates to a product's dependability and durability and usually is executed by alterations in the materials or production process employed.

Quality of life   The enjoyment of daily living, which is enhanced by leisure time, clean air and water, an unlittered earth, conservation of wildlife and natural resources, and security from radiation and poisonous substances.

Quantity discounts   Deductions from list price that reflect the economies of purchasing in large quantities.

Quota sampling   Nonprobability sampling in which the final choice of respondents is left up to the interviewers.

Rack jobbers Middlemen (also called service merchandisers) similar to truck wholesalers but who provide the extra service of cleaning and filling a display rack.

Random factor analysis A method of predicting sales in which an attempt is made to attribute erratic sales variations to random, nonrecurrent events, such as a regional power failure or a natural disaster.

Random sampling Type of sampling in which all the units in a population have an equal chance of appearing in the sample; probability sampling.

Raw materials Basic materials that become part of a physical product; provided from mines, farms, forests, oceans, and recycled solid wastes.

Real-estate brokers Brokers who, for a fee or commission, bring buyers and sellers together to exchange real estate.

Receiver The individual, group, or organization that decodes a coded message.

Recession A stage in the business cycle, during which unemployment rises and total buying power declines, stifling both consumers' and business persons' propensity to spend.

Reciprocity A practice unique to industrial sales in which two organizations agree to buy from each other.

Recognition test A post-test method of evaluating the effectiveness of advertising in which individual respondents are shown the actual advertisement and are asked whether they recognize it.

Recovery A stage of the business cycle, during which the economy moves from recession toward prosperity.

Recruiting A process by which the sales manager develops a list of applicants for sales positions.

Reference group A group with which an individual identifies so much that he or she takes on many of the values, attitudes, and/or behaviors of group members.

Regional issues Versions of a magazine that differ across geographic regions and in which a publisher can vary the advertisements and editorial content.

Regional shopping center Type of shopping center that usually has the largest department stores, the widest product mix, and the deepest product lines of all shopping centers in an area; usually at least 150,000 customers in their target area.

Regulatory forces Forces that arise from regulatory units at all levels of government; these units create and enforce numerous regulations that affect marketing decisions.

Reinforcement advertising An advertisement that tries to assure current users that they have made the right choice and tells them how to get the most satisfaction from the product.

Reliability Reliability exists when a sample is representative of the population; it also exists when repeated use of an instrument produces almost identical results.

Reminder advertising Advertising used to remind consumers that an established brand is still around and that it has certain uses, characteristics, and benefits.

Resale price maintenance laws (Fair trade laws) Enacted during the Depression, these state laws permitted manufacturers to set resale prices at which dealers within a state were supposed to sell a firm's products; lawmakers intended to stop large retailers from selling products at such low prices that smaller, financially weaker retailers could not compete.

Reseller market Market that consists of intermediaries, such as wholesalers and retailers, who buy finished goods and resell them for the purpose of making a profit.

Retail warehouse Smaller public warehouse that sells space to clients who operate retail stores out of the warehouse.

Retailer coupon A sales promotion method used by retailers when price is a primary motivation for consumers' purchasing behavior; usually takes the form of a "cents-off" coupon that is distributed through advertisements and is redeemable only at a specific store.

Retailing Focuses on the activities required for exchanges in which ultimate consumers are the buyers.

Robinson-Patman Act Directly influences pricing and promotions policies; the Act prohibits price differentials and promotional allowances that are discriminatory.

Role A set of actions and activities that a person in a particular position is supposed to perform, based on the expectations of both the individual and the persons around him or her.

Routine response behavior The type of decision making a consumer uses when buying frequently purchased, low-cost items that require very little search and decision effort.

S

Safety stock Inventory needed to prevent a stockout (running out of a product).

Sales analysis A process for controlling marketing strategies in which sales figures are used to evaluate performance.

Sales branches Similar to merchant wholesalers in their operations; they may offer credit, delivery, give promotional assistance, and furnish other services.

Sales contest A sales promotion method employed to motivate distributors, retailers, and sales personnel through the recognition of outstanding achievements.

Sales-force forecasting survey Estimation by members of a firm's sales force of the anticipated sales in their territories for a specified period.

Sales office Provides service normally associated with agents; owned and controlled by the producer.

Sales orientation A focus on increasing an organization's sales as the major way to increase profits.

Sales-oriented organization There is a general belief that personal selling and advertising are the primary tools used to generate profits and that most products—regardless of consumers' needs—can be sold if the right quantity and quality of personal selling and advertising are employed.

Sales promotion An activity and/or material that acts as a direct inducement, offering added value or incentive for the product, to resellers, salespersons, or consumers.

Sampling Selecting representative units from a total population.

Scientific decision making An approach that involves seeking facts on a systematic basis, and then applying decision making methods other than trial and error or generalization from experience.

Screening ideas A stage in the product development process in which the ideas that do not match organizational objectives are rejected and those with the greatest potential are selected for further development.

Sealed bids Prices submitted to a buyer, to be opened and made public at a specified time.

Search service qualities Tangible attributes of services that can be viewed prior to purchase.

Seasonal analysis A method of predicting sales in which an analyst studies daily, weekly, or monthly sales figures to evaluate the degree to which seasonal factors, such as climate and holiday activities, influence the firm's sales.

Seasonal discounts A price reduction that sellers give to buyers who purchase goods or services out of season; these discounts allow the seller to maintain steadier production during the year.

Secondary data Information compiled inside or outside the organization for some purpose other than the current investigations.

Segmentation variable A dimension or characteristic of individuals, groups, or organizations that is used to divide a total market into segments.

Selective distortion The changing or twisting of currently received information that occurs when a person receives information that is inconsistent with his or her feelings or beliefs.

Selective distribution A form of market coverage in which only some available outlets in an area are chosen to distribute a product.

Selective exposure Selection of some inputs to be exposed to our awareness, while ignoring many others because of the inability to be conscious of all inputs at one time.

Selling agents Intermediaries who market all of a specified product line or the entire output of a manufacturer; they have control over the manufacturer's marketing effort and may be used in place of a marketing department.

Service An intangible that is the result of applying human and mechanical efforts to people or objects.

Service Heterogeneity Because people typically perform services, there may be variation from one service provider to another or variation in the service provided by a single individual from day to day and from customer to customer.

Service Inseparability Because services normally are produced at the same time that they are consumed, the consumer frequently is directly involved in the production process.

Service Intangibility Since services are performances, they cannot be seen, touched, tasted, or smelled, nor can they be possessed.

Service Perishability Due to simultaneous production and consumption, unused capacity to produce services in one time period cannot be stockpiled or inventoried for future time periods.

Sherman Act Legislation passed in 1890 to prevent businesses from restraining trade and monopolizing markets.

Shopping product An item for which buyers are willing to put forth considerable effort in planning and making the purchase.

Short-range plans Plans that cover a period of one year or less.

Single-variable segmentation The simplest form of segmentation is achieved by using only one characteristic to divide—or segment—the market.

Situational factors The set of circumstances or conditions that exist when a consumer is making a purchase decision.

Social class An open aggregate of people with similar social ranking.

Social influences The forces that other people exert on one's buying behavior.

Social institutions An environmental force in international markets including the family, education, religion, health, and recreational systems.

Societal forces Forces that pressure marketers to provide high living standards and enjoyable lifestyles through socially responsible decisions and activities; the structure and dynamics of individuals and groups and the issues of concern to them.

Socioeconomic factors *See* Demographic factors.

Sorting activities The way channel members divide roles and separate tasks, including the roles of sorting out, accumulating, allocating, and assorting products.

Sorting out The first step in developing an assortment; it involves breaking down conglomerates of heterogeneous supplies into relatively homogeneous groups.

Source A person, group, or organization that has a meaning that it intends and attempts to share with a receiver or an audience.

Special-event pricing Advertised sales or price cutting to increase revenue or to lower costs.

Specialty-line wholesaler A merchant wholesaler that carries a very limited variety of products designed to meet their customers' specialized requirements.

Specialty product An item that possesses one or more unique characteristics that a significant group of buyers is willing to expend considerable purchasing efforts to obtain.

Specialty retailer A type of store that carries a narrow product mix with deep product lines.

Standard Industrial Classification (SIC) System A system developed by a federal government for classifying industrial organizations, based on what the firm primarily produces; also classifies selected economic characteristics of commercial, financial, and service organizations. Code numbers are used to classify firms in different industries.

Statistical interpretation Analysis that focuses on what is typical or what deviates from the average; it indicates how widely respondents vary and how they are distributed in relation to the variable being measured.

Stockout Condition that exists when a firm runs out of a product.

Storyboard A blueprint used by technical personnel to produce a television commercial; combines the copy with the visual material to show the sequence of major scenes in the commercial.

Straight commission compensation plan A plan by which a salesperson's compensation is determined solely by the amount of his or her sales for a given time period.

Straight rebuy purchase A type of industrial purchase in which a buyer purchases the same products routinely under approximately the same terms of sale.

Straight salary compensation plan A plan by which salespeople are paid a specified amount per time period.

Strategic business unit (SBU) A division, product line, or other profit center within its parent company that sells a distinct set of products and/or services to an identifiable group of customers and competes against a well-defined set of competitors.

Strategic marketing planning A process by which an organization can develop marketing strategies that, when properly implemented and controlled, will contribute to achieving the organization's overall goals.

Strategic market plan A comprehensive plan that takes into account not only marketing but also all other functional areas of a business unit that must be coordinated, such as production, finance, and personnel, as well as concern about the environment.

Strategy The key decision or plan of action required to reach an objective or set of objectives.

Stratified sampling Units in a population are divided into groups according to a common characteristic or attribute; then a probability sample is conducted within each group.

Style modification Modification directed at changing the sensory appeal of a product by altering its taste, texture, sound, smell, or visual characteristics.

Subculture A division of a culture based on geographic regions or human characteristics, such as age or ethnic background.

Superficial discounting A deceptive markdown sometimes called "Was-Is pricing" (the firm never intended to sell at the higher price); fictitious comparative pricing.

Supermarket A large, self-service store that carries broad and complete lines of food products, and perhaps some nonfood products.

Superstore A giant store that carries all food and nonfood products found in supermarkets as well as most products purchased on a routine basis; sales are much greater than discount stores or supermarkets.

Supplies (industrial) Items that facilitate an organization's production and operations, but they do not become part of the finished product.

Support personnel Members of the sales staff who facilitate the selling function but usually are not involved only with making sales.

Survey methods Include interviews by mail or by telephone and personal interviews.

Symbolic pricing A type of psychological pricing in which prices are set at an artificially high level to provide prestige or a quality image.

Syndicated data services External sources of information used by a marketer to study a marketing problem. Examples include American Research Bureau (ARB), Sell Area Marketing, Inc. (SAMI), the A. C. Nielsen Company Retail Index, the Market Research Corporation of America (MRCA); they collect general information that is sold to subscribing clients.

T

Tactile communication Interpersonal communication through touching.

Target market A group of persons for whom a firm creates and maintains a marketing mix.

Target public A collective of individuals who have an interest in or concern about an organization, a product, or a social cause.

Technical salesperson Support salesperson who directs his or her efforts toward the organization's current customers by providing technical assistance in system design, product application, product characteristics, or installation.

Technological forces Forces that influence marketing decisions and activities because they affect people's lifestyles and standards of living, influence their desire for products and their reaction to marketing mixes, and have a direct impact on maintaining a marketing mix by influencing all its variables.

Technology The knowledge of how to accomplish tasks and goals.

Technology assessment A procedure in which managers try to foresee the effects of new products and processes on the firm's operation, on other business organizations, and on society in general.

Telephone retailing A type of nonstore retailing based on a cold canvass of the telephone directory or a screening of prospective clients before calling.

Test marketing A limited introduction of a product in areas chosen to represent the intended market in order to determine probable buyers' reactions to various parts of a marketing mix.

Time series analysis A technique in which the forecaster, using the firm's historical sales data, tries to discover patterns in the firm's sales volume over time.

Total costs The sum of fixed costs and variable costs.

Total market approach Approach in which an organization designs a single marketing mix and directs it at an entire market for a specific product category.

Total revenue Price times quantity.

Traceable common costs Costs that can be allocated to specific activities indirectly, using one or several criteria, to the functions that they support.

Trade (functional) discount A reduction off the list price given to a middleman by a producer for performing certain functions.

Trademark A legal designation indicating that the owner has exclusive use of a brand or part of a brand and that others are prohibited by law from using it.

Trade mart *See* Trade show.

Trade name The legal name of an organization, rather than the name of a specific product.

Trade salesperson A type of salesperson not strictly classified as support personnel because he or she performs the order-taking function as well.

Trade sales promotion method A category of sales promotion techniques that stimulate wholesalers and retailers to carry a producer's products and to market these products aggressively.

Trade show Allows manufacturers or wholesalers to exhibit products to potential buyers and, therefore, assists in the selling and buying functions; these shows are commonly held annually at a specified location.

Trading company Companies that provide a link between buyers and sellers in different countries. Trading companies take title to products and provide all of the activities necessary to move the product from the domestic country to a market in a foreign country.

Trading stamps A sales promotion method used by retailers to attract consumers to specific stores and to increase sales of specific items by giving extra stamps to purchasers of those items.

Transfer pricing The type of pricing used when one unit in a company sells a product to another unit; the price is determined by one of the following methods: actual full cost, standard full cost, cost plus investment, or market-based cost.

Transit time The total time that a carrier has possession of the goods.

Transportation modes Railways, motor vehicles, waterways, pipelines, and airways used to move goods from one location to another.

Trend analysis Analysis that focuses on aggregate sales data, such as company's annual sales figures, over a period of many years to determine whether annual sales are generally rising, falling, or staying about the same.

Truck wholesaler Wholesaler that provides transportation and delivery products directly to customers for inspection and selection.

Tying contract An agreement by which a supplier agrees to sell certain products to a dealer on the condition that the dealer consent to purchase other products sold by the supplier.

U

Unaided recall test A post-test method of evaluating the effectiveness of advertising in which subjects are asked to identify advertisements that they have seen or heard recently but are not shown any clues to stimulate their memories.

Undifferentiated approach Occurs when an organization designs a single marketing mix and directs it at an entire market for a specific product; same as total market approach.

Unfair trade practices acts State laws, enacted in over half the states, that prohibit wholesalers and retailers from selling products below their costs or below their costs plus a certain percentage of markup.

Uniform geographic pricing Sometimes called "postage-stamp pricing," results in fixed average transportation; used to avoid the problems involved with charging different prices to each customer.

Unit loading The grouping of one or more boxes on a pallet or skid.

Universal product code (UPC) The standard source-symbol for marking primarily food-industry products to identify product characteristics and to facilitate pricing.

Universal vendor marking (UVM) A coding system in which a vendor marks merchandise for individual retailers with a machine-readable code containing such information as department, class, size, and color.

V

Validity Said to exist when an instrument does measure what it is supposed to measure.

Variable cost A cost that varies directly with changes in the number of units produced or sold.

Vending *See* Automatic vending.

Venture team An organizational unit established to create entirely new products that may be aimed at new markets.

Vertical channel integration Combining two or more stages of a marketing channel under one management.

Vertical marketing systems Centrally controlled, professionally managed, vertically integrated marketing channels. *See also* Vertical channel integration.

W

Warehouse showroom A type of retail store with high volume and low overhead. Lower costs are effected by shifting some marketing functions to consumers who must transport, finance, and perhaps store merchandise.

Warranty Document that specifies what the producer will do if the product malfunctions.

Wealth The accumulation of past income, natural resources, and financial resources.

Wheeler-Lea Act Makes unfair and deceptive acts or practices unlawful regardless of whether they injure competition.

Wheel of retailing A hypothesis which holds that new types of retailers usually enter the market as low-status, low-margin, low-price operators who eventually evolve into high-cost, high-price merchants.

Wholesaler An intermediary that buys from a producer or another intermediary and sells to another reseller; performs such marketing activities as transportation, storage, and information gathering necessary to expedite exchanges.

Wholesaling All marketing transactions in which purchases are intended for resale or are used in making other products.

Width (of product mix) The number of product lines offered by a company.

Z

Zone prices Regional prices that vary for major geographic zones as the transportation costs differ.

Name Index

Abdul-Jabbar, Kareem, 240
Abell, Derek F., 538n, 534n, 539n, 554(illus.)
Abrams, Bill, 47n, 225n
Adam computer, 510
ADM Corn Sweeteners, 359, 360(illus.)
Adolph Coors Company, 25, 26, 283-284, 416(table),
    431(illus.)
Advil, 243
Affinity Shampoo, 672, 680
Aim toothpaste, 408
Air Jordan shoes, 213, 230, 231, 380
Ajax cleaning products, 220
Albaum, Gerald S., 319n, 671(table)
Albertson's, Inc., 326(table)
Alderson, Wroe, 52n, 273n, 274n, 283n, 295n, 317n
Alexander, Ralph S., 206n, 266n
Alka-Seltzer, 166
Allen-Edmonds shoes, 215
Allen Solly, 339
Alliance automobiles, 527
Allied department stores, 325(table)
Allstate, 330, 638
Almay, 595
Alpine White with Almonds candy bar, 669
Alsop, Ronald, 163n, 221n, 240, 331n, 400n, 652n
American Airlines, 494
American Bar Association, 515
American Brands, 416(table)
American Broadcasting Co., 414(table)
American Cancer Society, 12, 13(illus.), 419, 644
American Council of Life Insurance, 38(illus.)
American Cyanamid, 414(table)
American Express card, 56, 57(illus.)
American Express Co., 330, 415(table), 683
American Express Travel Related Services Company,
    Inc., 57n
American Greetings Corporation, 234(illus.), 235,
    242-243
American Home Products, 415(table)

American Honda Motor Co., 414(table), 511,
    512(illus.)
American Motors Corp., 414(table), 527
American Newspaper Publishers Association, 628
American Postal Workers Union, 644
American Standard, 304
American Stores Co., 326(table)
American Telephone & Telegraph. See AT&T
American Television & Communications, 481
AMF Voit, Inc., 288-289
AMR Inc., 414(table)
Amstel Light beer, 291
Amtrak, 369
Anchor Hocking glassware, 214
Anderson, Carol H., 649n
Anheuser-Busch Co., 221, 290, 291, 416(table)
Ansoff, H. I., 559(illus.)
A & P (The Great Atlantic and Pacific Tea Company,
    Inc.), 326(table)
Apparel Mart, 307
Apple Computer, Inc., 386, 412, 414(table), 480, 558-
    559
Apple IIc computer, 510
Aqua Clear drinking water, 595
Arbitron Ratings Co., 165(table)
Archer Daniels, 360(illus.)
Ariel laundry detergent, 693
Arm & Hammer, 220, 409
Arrid deodorants, 220
Arthur H. Froman & Company, 305
Aspinwall, Leo, 280n
Assael, Henry, 127n
Associated Dry Goods department stores, 325(table)
Astro automobiles, 411
Athlete's Foot, 328
AT&T (American Telephone and Telegraph),
    34(illus.), 35-36, 200(illus.), 202, 330, 416(table),
    433, 519(illus.), 657
AT&T Information Systems, Inc., 35

Austin, Albert A., 564
Avery, Robert B., 56n
Avis, 330, 333, 595
Avon Products, 329, 470-471
Awake, 535
Aziza, 238

Bagozzi, Richard P., 7n
Bailey, Earl, 97n, 99n, 100n, 101n
Banana Republic, 546
Bank America Travelers Cheques, 683 and *illus.*
Banks, Howard, 69n, 494n
Banting, Peter M., 610n
Barban, Arnold M., 425n, 427(table)
Barbetta, Frank, 159n
Bardi, Edward, 354n
Barks, Joseph V., 354n, 356n
Barksdale, Hiram C., Jr., 610n
Baskin-Robbins, 209, 332 and *illus.*
Bateson, John E. G., 630n
Batus Inc., 416(table)
Bayer, Tom, 438n, 535n
Bayer AG, 415(table)
Bayer aspirin, 215
Bay State Machine Company, 106-107
B. Dalton bookstores, 280, 479
Beam, Alex, 538n
Beatrice Co., 415(table), 594-596
Beckenstein, Alan R., 517n
Beckman, Theodore N., 294n, 359n
Beck's beer, 290(table)
Beecham Group p.l.c., 416(table)
Beef Industry Council, 407 and *illus.*
Behavior Scan, 179
Belk, Russell, 631n
Bell, Martin L., 241(illus.), 480n, 589n
Bell Atlantic, 559, 560(illus.)
Bell Communications, 658
Bellizzi, Joseph A., 322n, 618n
BellSouth Corporation, 656-658
BellSouth Services Incorporated, 657-658
Bell System, 35
Beman, Lewis, 351n, 352n
Bennett, Roger C., 237n
Bennigans Tavern and Restaurant, 32-33, 475
Benoit, Joan, 380
Benson & Hedges, 464
Bentley, John, 692n
Bergiel, Blaise J., 649n
Berkman, Harold W., 129(table)
Berkowitz, Eric N., 653n
Bernstein, Aaron, 494n
Berry, Dick, 147n
Berry, Jon, 535n

Berry, Leonard L., 130n, 316n, 328n, 629n, 630n, 631(illus.), 631n, 636, 638n, 642n
Best, Roger, 319n
Best Products, 328(table)
Betty Crocker, 214
Bic disposable lighters, 400, 401
Bic pens, 484
Bic 2000 lighter, 401
Big Boy restaurants, 583
Billig, Stephen M., 183n
Biospherics, 625
Bivens, Jacquelyn, 327n
Black & Decker, 544, 668, 669
Blackwell, Roger D., 110n, 129(table), 279(illus.)
Blank, Author, 344
Blankenship, Albert B., 175n
Block, Alex Ben, 541n
Bloomingdale's, 324
Blue Stratos cologne, 462
BMW of North America, Inc., 482 and *illus.*
Boeing, 558, 614
Boeing 747 jet engines, 676
Bold detergent, 209, 220, 285
Bolton, Philip, 344n
Bonoma, Thomas V., 306n
Bonus detergent, 209
Borkum Riff smoking tobacco, 304
Borrus, Amy, 230n
Bose Corporation, 24
Boston Consulting Group, 550, 551(illus.), 557
Boswell, Dan A., 579n
Boundary Waters, 339
Bourgeois, Jacques C., 666n
Boyd, Harper W., Jr., 171(table)
Brackett, Bruce, 146n
Bradlees, 328(table)
Brauer, Molly, 325n
Breakfast Bake Shop line, 312
Breen, George E., 175n
Bristol-Myers Co., 231, 415(table), 684
Brody, Jane E., 110n
Brokaw Hospital (Normal, Illinois), 659, 662
Brookfield Zoo (Chicago), 651 and *illus.*
Brooks, Douglas G., 619n
Brown, Ellen, 243n
Brown, James R., 603n
Brown, John A. department stores, 280
Brown, S. W., 630n, 641n
Brown & Williamson, 551
Brylane, 315
Budweiser beer, 290
Buell, Barbara, 246n, 258n, 538n
Bulkeley, William, 546n
Bullock's, 324
Burger King, 33, 360, 437-438, 532

Burke, James E., 232
Burke Marketing Services, Inc., 165(table), 166(illus.)
Bush, Alan J., 185n
Bush, Ronald F., 321n, 322(illus.)
Bush Industries, Inc., 207
Buss, W. Christian, 666n
Buzzell, Robert D., 239n
Bylinski, Gene, 624n
Byrne, John A., 494n

Cabbage Patch Kids, 242
California Cooler, Inc., 211, 267
Callahan, Joseph M., 691n
Calvin Klein, 137, 339
Camaro automobiles, 411
Camel cigarettes, 217
Campbell Soup Company, 415(table), 418(illus.), 563-566
Campbell's soups, 223
Canon Inc., 259, 414(table)
Cara, Irene, 439
Cardin, Pierre, 686
Care Bears, 242
Carling O'Keefe, Ltd., 283
Carper, Jean, 169
Carr, Fitzhugh L., 188n
Carson Pirie Scott department stores, 325(table)
Carter Hawley Hale Stores, 325(table), 339
Cartier watches, 219
Casual Corner, 339
Caterpillar China Limited, 623-624
Caterpillar Tractor Company, 52, 618, 622-624, 623(illus.), 683-684
Cavalier automobiles, 411
Cavusgil, S. Tamer, 648(table), 648n
CBS Inc., 414(table)
Celebrity automobiles, 411
Cerruti, Nino suits, 319, 320(illus.)
Certified Grocers of California, Ltd., 297
C. F. Hathaway, 124, 125(illus.)
Chanel, Inc., 27(illus.)
Chanel No. 5 perfume, 27(illus.)
Chang, Dae R., 239n
Charlie, 91
Chase, Richard B., 641n
Cheer detergent, 209, 220, 285
Chemical Bank, 579
Chemlawn, 630
Chesebrough-Ponds, Inc., 237, 238, 416(table)
Chevette automobiles, 411
Chevrolet automobiles, 411
Chevrolet Motor Division, 239(illus.)
Chevron, 667(table)
Chicago Apparel Mart, 306(illus.)

Chicken McNuggets, 22, 539
Chih Kang Wang, 381n
Children's World, 105
Chinon Industries, 259
Chonko, Lawrence B., 191n
Choudhury, Pravet, 22n
Chrysler Corporation, 270, 271(illus.), 414(table), 666
Chunky Fisherman's Chowder, 564
Church's, 252
Citgo Petroleum Corp., 343, 542, 543
Citibank, 638, 639(illus.)
Citicorp, 667(table)
Citrus Hill orange juice, 281, 535
Clark Equipment Company, 612
Classic Revlon, 91
Clorox Co., 416(table)
Close-Up toothpaste, 251
Clovermill Associates, Inc., 516(illus.)
Coca-Cola Company, 162, 180, 186, 215-216, 218, 220, 221, 251-252, 333, 398-400, 416(table), 538, 584
Coen, Robert J., 417(table)
Cogenic Energy Systems Inc., 154
Cohen, Arthur I., 340n
Cohen, Dorothy, 427(table)
Coke, 221, 398-400, 489
Coke Classic, 221, 399
Coleco Industries, 510
Colgate-Palmolive Co., 220, 416(table), 682, 684
Columbia Pictures Industries, Inc., 538
Commodore International, 510
Common Cause, 644
Connor, Patrick E., 581n
Consolidated Freightways, Inc., 354 and *illus.*
Consumer Product Safety Commission, 662
Continental Airlines, 27, 480
Continental Baking Company, 312
Continental Cablevision of Boston, 481
Cook, Jack, 691n, 692n
Cooper, Philip D., 649n, 650(table), 653(table)
Cooper, Robert G., 237n
Coors, Adolph Company, 25, 26, 283-284, 416(table), 432(illus.)
Corona beer, 290(table)
Corvette automobiles, 238, 239(illus.)
Cosby, Bill, 398
Cosmair Inc., 416(table)
Cosse, Thomas J., 236n
Cotter & Co., 416(table)
County Seat, 328
Cox, Jonathan M., 307n
Coyle, John J., 354n
CPC International, 415(table)
Crabtree, Larry D., 182n
Cracker Jacks, 464
Crane Co., 304

Cravens, David W., 557n
Creamy Natural Soups, 564
Crest toothpaste, 204, 209, 251, 408
Crimmins, Ed, 466n
Crocker, Betty, 214
Cross, James S., 206n
Cross pens, 484
Crowley, Ayn E., 322n
Crown, Judith, 535n
Crown Clothing, Inc., 134-135
Crown Plaza, 217
Crown Zellerback Corporation, 361-362
Crowther of Lyon Lodge, 323(illus.)
Crum & Forster, 544
Crunch Bar, 240
CSX Corporation, 357, 358(illus.)
Cuccio, Angela, 495n
Culligan's Aqua Clear drinking water, 595
Cunningham, John D., 238
Cunon, John J., 283n
Curley, Jim, 369n
Curley, John, 280n, 475n
Curran, John J., 26n
Curtis Mathes Corporation, 641

Dahl, Jonathan, 22n
Dairy Queen, 333
Dallas Market Center, 307
Dallas Trade Mart, 307
Dalton, B. bookstores, 280, 479
D'Amato, Nancy, 218n
Daniels & Associates, 481
Daniel Starch, 428
Dart & Kraft, 415(table)
Dash detergent, 209, 220
Datril, 231
Datsun, 218
Davidson, William R., 294n, 359n
Davis, Bob, 300n
Dawson, Gaye C., 283n
Day, George S., 550n, 551(illus.), 553(illus.)
Day, Verne, 411
Day Bridge Learning Centers, 105
Days Inns of America, Inc., 267-268, 321
Dayton-Hudson Corp., 280, 325(table), 339
Dayton's department store, 280
De Bruicker, E. Steward, 213n, 253n
Decorative Center, 307
Deep Dish Danish, 565
Delano, Frank, 218n
Delco Electronics, 24
Deli's, 565
Del Monte canned fruits and vegetables, 217
Del Monte Corp., 225

Delozier, M. Wayne, 381n
Delta Air Lines, 414(table), 614
Dennison KYBE Corporation, 300
Densmore, Max L., 315n
DHL, 364(illus.)
Diamond I corporate jet, 269, 270(illus.)
Diamond's department store, 280
Die-Hard battery, 216
Diet Coke, 180, 221, 398
Diet Dr Pepper, 376(illus.), 377-378
Dillard department stores, 325(table)
Dillman, Don A., 187(table)
Diners Club card, 56
Disney theme parks, 636
Dobryzynski, Judith, 319n
Dr Pepper, 163, 333, 438-439, 489
Dr Pepper Company, 376(illus.), 377-378
Dodds, Lynn Strongin, 230n
Dodge Challenger, 270
Dodge Colt, 270, 271(illus.)
Dolecheck, Maynard M., 193n
Donath, Bob, 677(table)
Donnelly, J. H., 630n, 634n, 642, 648(table), 648n
Dos Equis beer, 290(table)
Double Stuff, 217
Downs, Philip E., 320n
Doyle, Peter, 607n, 609n
Dreisbach, Bruce R., 172n
Dreyfuss, Joel, 330n
Drucker, Peter F., 243n
Dumaine, Brian, 253n, 362n, 498n
Dun & Bradstreet, 605, 607
Dunkin, Amy, 238n, 278n, 325(table), 339n
Dunn, Dan T., Jr., 237n
Dunn, William, 105n
Dunn, S. Watson, 425n, 427(table)
du Pont de Nemours, E. I., 118, 414(table), 667(table)
Duz detergent, 209
Dworkin, Peter, 267n

Ealey, Lance A., 691n
Eastern Airlines, 414(table), 558
Eastman Kodak Company, 160(illus.), 162, 258-259, 414(table), 441, 538, 669
Eccles, Robert G., 490n
Edid, Maralyn, 687n
Edmondson, Brad, 11n, 110n, 583n
Edwards, Paul L., 411
E. I. du Pont de Nemours, 118, 414(table), 667(table)
Eklund, Christopher S., 544n, 564n
El-Ansary, Adel I., 338(illus.), 338n, 284n
Electra lighter, 400, 401
Electrolux, 329

Electronic Data Systems Corp., 142
Elephant Memory Systems disks, 300
Eli Lilly and Company, 69-70
Elkins, John, 22n
Elliehausen, Gregory E., 56n
Elms Inn, 474(illus.)
Embassy Suite, 217
Engel, James F., 110n, 129(table)
English, Mary M., 462n
Enis, Ben M., 558n, 634n
Enrick, Norbert L., 100n, 101n
Episcopal Church, 652
Esher, M. C., 116(illus.)
Esprit de Corp, 278
Etherea Fine Fragrances, 91
Ethernet computer, 71
Eutwisle, Nancy, 362n
Evans, 345
Excel automobiles, 665
Ex-Cell-O Corporation, 99
Express Mail, 403, 626(illus.), 627
Exxon, 216, 667 and *table*
E-Z-Go outdoor equipment, 310

Fahey, Liam, 540n
Fairchild perfume, 531
Family Casserole line, 26
Family World, 321
Fannie May Candy Shops, 317
Fannin, Rebecca, 231n
Federal Express, 370 and *illus.*, 402(illus.), 403, 404, 627, 628
Federated Department Stores, 325(table), 339, 536-537
Fern, Edward F., 603n
Ferrari, 79
Ferrell, O. C., 15(table), 48n, 191n, 273(table), 549n, 630n
F. G. Montabert Company, 136(illus.), 137-138
Fidelity Investments, 633
Figuia, James S., 179n
Fila boutiques, 328
Filiatrault, Pierre, 114n
Fink, Peter L., 233
Finney, E. Robert, 143n
Firestone, 216
First Software Corporation, 145(illus.)
Fisher, Ann B., 635n
Fisher, Maria, 116n
501 Jeans, 30-32
Fleming wholesalers, 293, 294(table), 307, 362
Florida State Department of Commerce, 445(illus.)
Foote, Cone and Bending/Direct Market, 140(illus.)
Foot Locker, The, 328

Forbis, John L., 618n
Ford Motor Company, 25(illus.), 330, 414(table), 667(table)
47th Street Photo, 325, 327
Foster, J. Robert, 350(illus.), 350n, 351(illus.)
Foster, Thomas A., 348n, 356n, 362n
Franco-American, 563
Franco's Hidden Harbor, 475
Frary, Julie, 98n
Fresca, 398
Frey, Albert Wesley, 432(table)
Friedman, Jack, 380n
Frisbee discs, 288, 289
Frohman, Alan L., 541n, 542n
Froman, Arthur H. & Company, 305
Fruit Bars, 248
Fruit Roll-Ups, 248
Fuji, 259
Fuller Brush Company, 329

Gabel, H. Landis, 517n
Gable, Myron, 340n
GAF Corporation, 144(illus.)
Gage, Theodore, 289n
Gail, Brenda L., 230
Gain detergent, 209, 285
Galek, Thomas, 283n
Gallup & Robinson, 428
Gap, The, Inc., 278(illus.), 328, 538-539
Gardner, Fred, 438n
Garino, David P., 225n
Garroway, Thomas Ltd., 331
Gaski, John F., 285n
Gates, Roger, 185n
Gemco, 328(table)
General Electric, 220, 259, 414(table), 544, 552-553, 666, 676
General Foods Corp., 15, 122-123, 236, 331, 409, 415(table), 461, 535
General Grocer, 216
General Mills, 214, 248, 249(illus.), 415(table), 686(illus.)
General Motors Acceptance Corporation, 411
General Motors Corp., 24-25, 142, 163, 414(table), 480, 483, 526-527, 541, 647, 667(table), 682, 687
Georgaff, David M., 540n
George, William R., 630n, 634n, 638n, 640n, 648n, 648(table)
George R. Lyons Company, 305
Gerber, 208
G. Heileman Brewing Company, 291
Gibson, Christopher C., 129(table)
Gillette Co., 246, 416(table)
Gillette Cricket lighter, 400

Gilley, Mickey, 439
Gilman, Hank, 339n, 495n
Glacial Confections Inc., 213(illus.)
Glaskowsky, J. Nicholas, 357(table)
Glass, David, 367
Glazer, Eugene G., 258-259
Gleem toothpaste, 209
Glynn, Karen, 182n
Godiva, 563
Godiva chocolate stores, 317
Godzilla II, 378
Goizueta, Roberto C., 398, 399
Gold, Howard, 256n
Gooden, Dwight, 231
Goodrich, 216
Goodyear Tire & Rubber Co., 216, 414(table)
Gorman, Ronald H., 283n
Gottlieb, Carrie, 211n
Grainger, W. W., 609
Grand Metropolitan p.l.c., 416(table)
Gray, Daniel H., 533n
Great Atlantic and Pacific Tea Company, Inc. (A & P),
    326(table)
Great Start Breakfasts, 564-565
Greenfield, Joseph, 327
Green Giant, 216
Green Giant vegetables, 32
Gresham, Larry G., 48n, 191n
Grether, E. T., 42n
Greyhound Corp., 415(table)
Grimm, Jim L., 225n
Grossman, Elliot S., 97n, 99n, 100n, 101n
GTE Corp., 15, 16(illus.), 416(table)
Guaranteed Emergency Transportation Service, 356
Guastafson, Thomas A., 56n
Guiltinan, Joseph P., 203n, 317n, 550n, 635(table)
Guiness beer, 290(table)
Gulf & Western Industries, 414(table)
Gun Owners of America, 644
Guton, Janet, 123n

Häagen Dazs ice cream, 32
Haas, Robert W., 604n
Hacker-Pschorr beer, 291
Haggerty, Betsy, 39n, 369n, 373n
Haimann, Theo, 581n
Hair, Joseph F., Jr., 185n, 321n, 322(illus.)
Hall, Peter, 105n
Hall, Ronald E., 343
Hallmark Cards, Inc., 234(illus.), 235, 240
Halston Enterprises, Inc., 79, 80(illus.), 84(illus.), 595
Hammermill, 615-616, 617(illus.)
Hammond, John S., 534n, 539n, 554(illus.)
Hampton, William J., 231n

Hampton Inns, 217
Hampton perfume, 531
Hanes, 331
Hansotia, Behram J., 539n
Happy Cat, 312
Happy Dog, 312
Happy Kitten, 312
Hardin, David K., 162n
Hargrove, Earnestine, 610n
Harley-Davidson Motor Co., 221, 386, 507
Harrell, Gilbert D., 323n, 678n
Harrigan, Cathryn Rudie, 687n
Harrington, Lisa H., 363n
Harris, Paul, 651n
Harrison, E. Frank, 578n
Harrold, David T., 581n
Harry Winston, Inc., 319, 321(illus.)
Hartley, Robert F., 332n, 336(illus.)
Hartley, Steven W., 653n
Hasbro Inc., 416(table)
Hawes, Jon M., 220n, 335n
Hawkins, Chuck, 494n
Hawkins, Del, 319n
Haworth, Inc., 603, 604(illus.)
Haynes, Joel B., 320n
Head & Shoulders shampoo, 693
Health Insurance Association of America, 38(illus.)
Health-tex, 335
Heany, Donald F., 238n
Heard, Lee Ann, 690n
Hearty Chews, 312
Heath Company, 552
Hechinger, 345
Heileman, G. Brewery Company, 291
Heineken, 289, 290(table), 291
Heinz, H. J., Co., 415(table)
Heller, Walter H., 294n
Hemphill, Gary A., 438n
Herlin Press, Inc., 542 and *illus.*
Hershey Foods Corporation, 108(illus.), 109-110,
    415(table), 513(illus.), 539(illus.), 540
Hertz, 333
Heskett, J. L., 357(table)
Heublein, Inc., 267
Hewlett-Packard Company, 264(illus.), 265, 618
Heydt, Bruce, 356n
HF-5 tractor/mower, 311
Hicks, Herbert G., 250(illus.)
Higgins, Kevin T., 289n, 532n, 541n, 549(table), 644n,
    647n
Hill, John S., 679n
Hill, Richard M., 206n, 237n
Hilton Hotels Corporation, 537(illus.), 537-538
Hippel, Eric von, 244n
Hiram Walker, Inc., 304

Hise, Richard, 340n
H. J. Heinz Co., 415(table)
Hlavacek, James D., 237n, 364n, 612n
Hodges, Harold M., Jr., 129(table)
Hofer, C.W., 536(table)
Holiday Inns, Inc., 216-217, 321, 333
Hollander, Stanley C., 336n
Hollis, Benny, 193-196
Home Depot, Inc., 344-345
Homefurnishing Mart, 307
Homelite outdoor equipment, 310, 311
Home Style Soups, 564
Honda automobiles, 527, 665
Honda motorcycles, 123, 507, 511
Honda power equipment, 208, 209(illus.)
Hopkins, David, 242n
Horan, Ray, 158
Hostess line, 312
Hotpoint, 218
Houghton Mifflin, 479
Houston, Franklin S., 334n
Houston Symphony Orchestra, 645 and *illus.*
Howard, John A., 111n
Howard Johnson's, 321
H & R Block, 333, 630, 636
Hudson's department store, 280, 324
Hughs, Kathleen A., 27n
Hume, Scott, 437n
Hunt, Shelby D., 191n
Hurwood, David, 97n, 99n, 100n, 101n
Hutt, Michael D., 323n

IBM (International Business Machines), 35, 70, 98, 159, 240, 259, 330, 414(table), 440(illus.), 442, 510, 667(table), 669
IBM computers, 440(illus.)
IC Industries, 415(table)
IGA (Independent Grocers' Alliance), 216, 285
Illinois Wesleyan University, 654
IMS International, 165(table)
Inbound Logistics, 371
Independent Grocers' Alliance (IGA), 216, 285
Information Resources, 165(table)
Ingrassia, Lawrence, 244n, 280n
Instamatic camera, 258-259
International Business Machines. *See* IBM
International Coffee Organization, 26
International Silver, 335
ITT Corporation, 416(table), 667
ITT System 12 computer, 676, 678(illus.)
ITT World Communications, 667
Ivie, Robert, 357(table)
Ivory Shampoo, 286
Izod, 137

Jacobs, Sanford L., 524n
Jacobsen, 311
Jacobsen Turf outdoor equipment, 310, 311
Jacuzzi, Giocondo, 157
Jacuzzi, Incorporated, 157-158
Jaguar automobiles, 204
James, Frank E., 221n
J. C. Penney Co., 121, 216, 269, 285, 318, 324, 416(table)
Jell-O, 409, 681
Jell-O Pudding Pops, 123
Jereski, Laura Konrad, 594n
Jerrey, Gay, 115n, 261n
Johnson, Howard, 321
Johnson, James C., 359n, 361n
Johnson, S. C. & Son, 416(table)
Johnson & Johnson, 231-233, 415(table), 457, 672
Jones, Ana Loud, 340n
Jordan, Michael, 213, 230, 380
Joseph E. Seagram & Sons, Inc., 100, 267, 416(table)
JVC, 256

Kallen, Barbara, 221n
Karger, Theodore, 254n
Karin beer, 290
Karo, Alan, 594n
Kaufman, Sylvia, 315n
Keagan, Warren J., 680(illus.)
Kearns, David T., 271n
Keegan, Warren G., 679n
Kellogg Co., 280, 415(table), 675
Kelly, J. Patrick, 340n, 638n, 640n
Kenmore, 216
Kennedy, James H., 398n
Kentucky Fried Chicken, 252, 280, 333, 539
Keppler, Herbert, 258-259
Kesselman-Turkel, Judi, 464n
Kidde, Walter and Company, 158
Kiefer, Richard O., 678n, 679(illus.)
Kimberley-Clark Co., 415(table)
Kinder-Care, 105-106
King, Michael, 252n
King, William K., 540n
Kingsford Company, 463(illus.)
Kinney Shoe Corp., 328
Kirby vacuum cleaners, 329
Kirkpatrick, C. A., 423n
Kleiman, Carol, 23n
Klein, Calvin, 137, 339
Klein, David M., 225n, 679n
Klinkerman, Steve, 543n
K mart Corp., 52, 121, 216, 285, 319, 325, 328(table), 415(table), 532
Kodak, 160(illus.), 162, 258-259, 414(table), 441, 538, 669

Stratton, Felecia, 369n
Strawberry Shortcake, 242
Stroh Brewery Company, 291, 379(illus.), 416(table)
Stroud, Ruth, 380n
Stuart Reed, 339
Stuckey's, 117-118
Sugar-Free Dr Pepper, 376(illus.), 377, 439
Sulerno, Steve, 614n
Summe, Gregory L., 213n, 253n
Summey, John H., 182n, 649n, 650(table), 653(table)
Sun Company, 379(illus.)
Sunkist, 331
Supermarkets General Corporation, 326(table)
Super Valu, 292(illus.), 293, 294(table), 307
Sure Fire lighter, 401
Suzy Q, 312
Swan, John E., 236n
Swandby, Richard K., 307n
Swanson, 563, 564, 565
Swayne, Linda E., 618n
Sweeney, Robert E., 579n
Swire, Donald J., 557n
SX-70 camera, 258-259
Sylvania, 216

Tab, 221, 251-252, 398
Talarzyk, W. Wayne, 294n, 359n
Talley, Walter J., 449n
Talmadge, Candice, 169n
Tandy Corp., 414(table)
Tanzer, Andrew, 539n
Tappan, 666
Target discount stores, 121, 280, 325, 328(table)
Taylor, Alex, III, 258n, 259n, 538n
Taylor, Raymond E., 172n
Taylor, Ronald D., 182n, 649n, 650(table), 653(table)
Tecate beer, 290(table)
Technics compact disc player, 204
Telephone Marketing Resources, 330
Tender Vittles, 312
Terpstra, Vern, 666n, 672n
Texaco, 667(table)
Texaco Chemical Company, 607, 608(illus.)
Texas Instruments 994 computers, 327
Textron, Inc., 158, 310-311
T.G.&Y., 328(table)
Therrien, Lois, 230n
Thomas, Lewis, 65
Thomas Garroway, Ltd., 331
Thornton, Jeannye, 105n
Those Characters from Cleveland, 242
3B microcomputers, 35
3M Corporation, 620 and *illus.*
3M floppy disks, 259

Ticer, Scott, 537n
Tide detergent, 209, 220, 285, 636
Time Inc., 330, 414(table)
Time magazine, 388
Timex, 52
Today's Family, 234(illus.)
Tokai Seiki, 400
Tompkins, Doug, 278
Tomy Corporation, 385 and *illus.*
Tonka's Pound Puppies, 242
Topmost brand, 216
Toshiba, 259
Totten, Jeffrey W., 225n
Touchstar system, 658
Toy, Stewart, 252n
Toyota Motor Corporation, 527, 687
Toyota Motor Sales Co., 414(table)
Toys Я Us, 328(table)
Trac II, 246
Tracy, Eleanor Johnson, 246n
Traffic management, 363
Transamerica Corporation, 543-544, 545
Trans World Airlines, 414(table)
Travelers Corporation, 10 and *illus.*, 638
TreeSweet Products Company, 535
Tropicana orange juice, 535
Trudeau, Terry, 659-663
Turf Cat, 311
Tylenol, 218, 231-233, 243

UAL Inc., 414(table)
Udell, Jon G., 610n
Ultima II, 91
Ultra Brite toothpaste, 218
Ultra-Lite lighter, 400
Unilever U. S., 416(table)
Union Carbide Corp., 414(table), 414(table)
Union Pacific Railroad, 355 and *illus.*
Uni-Royal, 216
United Parcel Service, 301, 305, 357, 369, 402(illus.), 403-404, 602, 627, 628, 650
U. S. Air Force, 14
U. S. Army, 8, 651
U. S. Commerce Department, 665
U. S. Geological Survey, 651
U. S. Government, 415(table)
U. S. Postal Service, 301, 403, 626(illus.), 627-628, 650
United States Tobacco Company, 304
United Way, 12, 13(illus.)
UNIX, 34(illus.), 35, 36
Urbanski, Al, 489n
USAIR, Inc., 520
USA Today, 548

Van Heusen, 335
Van Muching and Company, 291, 416(table)
Vaughn, Ronald L., 190n
Vectra Personal Computer, 264(illus.)
Vegetables in a Pastry, 565
Victoria's Secret, 315
Visa, 56
Visine eye freshener, 381-382
Viswanathan, R., 182n
Vizir liquid detergent, 693
Vlasic foods, 565
Volkswagen, 79
Volkswagen of America, 414(table)
Volvo, 162
Vulcan-Hart, 147(illus.)

Walker, Hiram, Inc., 304
Walker, Kelly, 652n
Wall Drug Store, 319
Wal-Mart Stores, Inc., 89, 121, 325, 328(table), 366-369, 368(illus.), 532, 541
Walsh, Doris, 386n
Walter Kidde and Company, 158
Walters, C. Glenn, 295n, 317n
Warner Communications, 414(table)
Warner-Lambert Co., 415(table)
Warshaw, M. R., 202n
Warsteiner Brewery, 291
Warsteiner Importers Agency, 291
Webster, Frederick E., Jr., 151n, 152(illus.)
Weigand, Robert E., 284n
Weight Watcher's foods, 223
Weiher, Steve, 479n
Weiner, Elizabeth, 219n
Wendy's, 252, 532
Wendy's International, 415(table)
Wentz, Laurel, 672n, 675n, 680n, 681n
Wescon Products, 610
Westfall, Ralph, 171(table)
Westheimer, Ruth, 378
Westinghouse Electric Corp., 304, 554
Wetterau, Ted C., 307n
Wetterau wholesalers, 293, 294(table), 307
Whalen, Bernie, 162n, 185n, 260n, 666n
Wham-O Manufacturing Company, 288, 289
Whatchamacallit candy bar, 110
Whitman Chocolates, 331
Wickes Furniture, 326

Wiessler, David, 105n
Wilcox, James B., 191n
Wilkinson Sword, 253, 254(illus.)
Williams, Monci Jo, 221n, 532n
Wm. Wrigley Jr. Co., 415(table)
Wilstein, Steve, 559n
Wind, Yoram, 151n, 152(illus.), 238n, 533n, 545n, 546n, 557n
Winn-Dixie Stores, Inc., 326(table)
Winston cigarettes, 217
WJIM-TV, 44
Wonder bread, 312
Wood, Donald F., 359n, 361n
Woods, Bob, 507n
Woodside, Arch G., 350(illus.), 350n, 351(illus.)
Woolco, 338
Woolworth, 338
World Book Encyclopedia, 329
World Trade Center, 307
Worthy, Ford S., 665n
Wrangler, 137, 335
Wrigley, Wm., Jr. Co., 415(table)
Wylie, Kenneth, 347n

Xerox Corporation, 70-71, 170, 259, 271, 414(table), 544, 669
Xerox Learning Systems, 452

Yamaha, 507
Yankelovich, Skelly, and White, 169
Yoplait USA, 686 and *illus.*
Yves St. Laurent, 687

Zayre, 328(table)
Zeithaml, Carl P., 37n
Zeithaml, Valarie A., 37n, 316n, 629n, 630n, 631(illus.), 631n, 638n, 642n
Zenith, 552
Zenith Data Systems, 140(illus.), 552
Zeren, Linda, 214n, 218n
Ziegler, Lou, 335n
Ziegler, Mel, 546
Ziegler, Pat, 546
Ziegler, William L., 390n, 458n, 460n
Zinszer, Paul H., 284n
Zonana, Victor F., 212n

Subject Index

Basic electronic cash register (Basic ECR), 362
BCG. *See* Boston Consulting Group
B. Dalton bookstores, 479
Benefit segmentation, 92
Bennigan's Restaurants, 475
Better Business Bureaus, 46
Bid pricing, 619
Big Boy restaurants, 583
Birdyback services, 357
Bonded storage, 359
Boston Consulting Group (BCG), 550-552
Brand(s), 214, 216-218
  generic, 219-220
  manufacturer, 216
  private distributor, 216
  registration of, 218-219
Brand decision, 126, 126-127(table)
Brand-extension branding, 220, 221
Branding, 214-221
  benefits of, 215-216
  brand-extension, 220
  counterfeit, 219
  generic, 219-220
  generic terms and, 219
  individual, 220
  line family, 220
  overall family, 220
  policies for, 219-221
  private-label, 339
  selecting and promoting brands and, 218-219
  types of brands and, 216-218
Brand manager, 236
Brand mark, 214
Brand name, 214
Breakdown approach, to company sales potential, 96
Breakeven analysis, 507-509
Breakeven point, 507, 508(illus.)
Bribes, in international marketing, 676-677
Brokers, 266-267, 301, 302, 305
  services provided by, 303(table)
Buildup approach, to company sales potential, 96-97
Business analysis, for new products, 244-245
Business cycles, 59-60
Business position, 552-554
Buy-back allowances, 464
Buyers' perceptions, 116-119
  pricing decisions and, 485-486
Buying allowances, 465
Buying behavior, 110. *See also* Consumer buying
    behavior; Organizational buying behavior
Buying center, in organizational buying, 151
Buying power, 53-55
Buying power index, 54

Cable television, 481

California Cooler, Inc., 267
Capability
  of firm, 541-544
  of transportation, 355-356
Capacity, of communication channels, 383
Captioned photograph, 430
Car license plate survey, 182
Cash-and-carry wholesalers, 299-300
Cash cows, 550-551
Cash discounts, 488
Cash flow, as pricing objective, 481
Catalog retailing, 331-332, 546
Catalog showrooms, 326
Causal studies, 174
Cents-off offers, 464
Channel, marketing. *See* Marketing channels
Channel capacity, in communication, 383
Channel conflict, 283-284
Channel cooperation, 283
Channel leadership, 268, 284-285
Channel of distribution. *See* Marketing channels
Channel power, 284-285
Chemical Bank, 579
Chesebrough-Ponds, Inc., 238
Chevrolet, 411
City size, as segmentation variable, 87-89
Class. *See* Social class
Clayton Act, 41
  pricing decisions and, 487
Client publics, 648
Closing, in personal selling, 446
CMSA. *See* Consolidated metropolitan statistical area
Coca-Cola, 162, 221
Coding process, in communication, 381
Cogenic Energy Systems Inc., 154
Cognitive dissonance, postpurchase, 114
Coleco Industries, 510
Combination compensation plan, 454
Commercial(s), channel capacity and, 383
Commercialization
  managing products after, 252
  for new products, 248-251
Commission merchants, 303-304
Commodore International, 510
Communication(s)
  channel capacity and, 383
  coding process and, 381
  decoding process and, 382
  defined, 381
  feedback and, 383
  kinesic, 389
  within marketing unit, 578-579
  medium of transmission of, 382
  noise in, 382-383
  in personal selling, 389

physical distribution and, 361-363
promotion and, 381-384
proxemic, 389
receiver of, 382
source of, 381
tactile, 389
Community shopping centers, 334-335
Compact disks, 497-498
Company sales forecast, 97-102
correlation methods in, 101
executive judgment in, 98
market tests in, 101
multiple forecasting methods in, 101-102
surveys for, 98-100
time-series analysis for, 100
Company sales potential, 96-97
Comparative advertising, 407
Compensation for salespersons, 453-454, 455(table)
Competition, 50
monitoring, 52-53
monopolistic, 51 and *table*
perfect, 51 and *table*, 486-487
price and nonprice, 477-479
pricing decisions and, 486-487
tools of, 52
Competition-matching approach, to advertising
appropriation, 414-415
Competition-oriented pricing, 509, 510, 520
Competitive advertising, 407
Competitive forces, assessment of, 50-53
Competitive strategies, 558-560
Competitive structures, 50-51, 51(table)
Competitors, prices of, 509, 510
Component parts, 206-207
Comprehensive spending patterns, 57-58
Computer market, 510
Concentration strategy, 78-79
Conflict in marketing channel, 283-284
Consolidated metropolitan statistical area (CMSA), 89, 90(illus.)
Consumer(s), 53-59
buying power of, 53-55
perceptions of, 116-119, 485-486
spending patterns of, 57-59
willingness to spend, 55-57
Consumer awareness, 13-14
Consumer buying behavior, 110
decision process in, 111-114
evaluation of alternatives in, 113
information search in, 113
person-specific influences on, 114-116
postpurchase evaluation and, 114
problem recognition in, 112
psychological influences on, 116-124
purchase stage in, 113-114

social influences on, 124-131
understanding, 131
Consumer contests, 464
Consumer credit, 54, 56
Consumer jury, 427
Consumer movement, 47-48
Consumer products, 203
classification of, 203-205
marketing channels for, 268-269
see also Product(s)
Consumer protection legislation, 42
Consumer sales promotion methods, 390, 460
Consumer sweepstakes, 464
Containerization, 357, 361
Control
of inventory, 349-352
of marketing activities, 579-582
of nonbusiness marketing activities, 653-654
Convenience products, 204
Cooperation, in marketing channels, 283
Cooperative advertising, 465-466
Coordination
of marketing activities, 577-578
of transportation, 357
Copy, advertising, 422-424
Corporate strategy, 532-533
strategic market planning and, 544
Correlation methods, in company sales forecasting, 101
Cost(s)
of advertising, 413-416
analysis of, 585-588
common, 586
determining, 586
direct, 586
fixed, 504
marginal, 504
of marketing, 14
opportunity, 652
pricing decisions and, 484
of promotional methods, 394
relationships among, 505(table)
total, 504
of transportation, 354-355
variable, 504
Cost-oriented pricing, 517-518
Cost-plus pricing, 517
Count and recount promotion, 465
Coupons, 462
dangers of, 461
Credence qualities, 630-631
Credit
consumer, 54, 56
importance to organizational buyers, 146

Cultural influences
  on consumer buying behavior, 130-131
  on international marketing, 672-675, 673(table)
Culture, defined, 130
Cumulative discounts, 488
Customary pricing, 512-513
Customer(s)
  as basis for sales analysis, 585
  organizing marketing unit by, 575-576
  perceptions of, 116-119, 485-486
  size of, as segmentation variable, 93
Customer forecasting survey, 98-99
Customer orientation, 17
Cycle analysis, 100

Daniels & Associates, 481
Data
  primary, 173
  secondary, 173, 188-190
  see also Information search; Information sources
Data bank, marketing, 166-167
Data collection, 173-174, 180-190. See also Marketing
  research
Data processing, physical distribution and, 361-363
Dealer listings, 466
Dealer loaders, 466
Decision making
  consumer. See Consumer buying behavior
  information needs and, 167-170, 170-171(table)
  scientific, 169, 171(table)
Decline stage in product life cycle, 213-214
  marketing strategy for products in, 255-256
Decoding process, in communication, 382
Defensive advertising, 407-408
Demand
  advertising to stimulate, 405-407
  derived, 149
  elasticity of, 501-503, 503(illus.)
  fluctuations in, 150, 501
  for industrial products, 149-150
  inelasticity of, 149
  joint, 150
  pricing and, 500-503, 518-520
Demand curve, 500-501, 501(illus.)
Demand-oriented pricing, 518-520
Demographic factors
  baby-boom generation and, 117
  in consumer buying behavior, 114-115
  in market segmentation, 81-87
Demonstrations, 460-461
Density, of market, 88-89
Department stores, 324
Dependent variable, 178
Depression, 60

Depth interview, 120
Derived demand, 149
Description, as method of organizational buying, 148
Descriptive studies, 173-174
Direct cost(s), 586
Direct-cost approach, 586
Direct distribution channels, 611
Direct ownership, in international marketing, 688
Discount(s)
  cash, 488
  cumulative and noncumulative, 488
  functional and quantity, 488
  seasonal, 488-489
  trade, 488
Discounting, 488-489
  dangers of, 461
  superficial, 516
Discount stores, 325
Discretionary income, 53
Disposable income, 53
Distribution
  of declining products, 255
  exclusive, 281, 282
  in growth stage, 253
  intensive, 281
  of mature products, 254
  selective, 281
  see also Marketing channels; Physical distribution
Distribution variable, 25-26
Diversified growth, marketing strategy and, 559-560
Dogs, products as, 550-551
Dollar volume sales analysis, 583
Drop shippers, 301
Dr Pepper, 377-378
Dumping, in international marketing, 684
Dun & Bradstreet, 607

Early adopters, 386
Early majority, 386
Eastman Kodak, 162, 441
Economic developers, 647
Economic forces, 22, 50-60
  assessment of competitive forces and, 50-53
  consumer demand and buying behavior and, 53-59
  in international marketing, 675-676
Economic institutions, 672
Economic order quantity (EOQ), 351
ECR. See Electronic cash register
Effective buying income, 54
Effectiveness, 18
  of control, 581
Efficiency, 18
EFT. See Electronic funds transfer
Electronic cash register (ECR), 362, 363

basic, 362
sophisticated, 362
Electronic funds transfer (EFT), 363
Encoding, in communication, 381
Endorsers, athletic, 380
Environment, 11. *See also* Marketing environment
Environmental analysis, 37
Environmental forces
    in international marketing, 672-677
    organizational buying behavior and, 155
    strategic market planning and, 536
Environmental monitoring, 540-541
Environmental scanning, 37
Equalized workload method, for determining sales
        force size, 449-450
Ethical issues, 48-50
    foreign payoffs and, 676
    in marketing research, 190-191
Ethnicity, as segmentation variable, 84-85
Evaluation
    of advertising effectiveness, 427-428
    in consumer buying behavior, 113, 114
    in organizational buying behavior, 153, 154
    of performance, 580-581, 582-588
    postpurchase, 114, 154
    of price and ability to purchase, 500
    of sales-force performance, 458
    see also Test marketing
Exchange, 9(illus.), 9-11
Exclusive distribution, 281, 282
Executive judgment, in company sales forecasting, 98
Experience curve pricing, 516-517
Experience qualities, 630
Experimentation, in marketing research, 178-179
Expert forecasting survey, 100
Exploratory studies, 173
Exporting, 685-686. *See also* International marketing
Extensive decision making, 11

Facilitating agencies, functions of, 275-280
Factory outlet mall, 335-336
Family branding, 220
Family influences, on consumer buying behavior,
        124-126
Family packaging, 223
FCC. *See* Federal Communications Commission
Feature article, 430
Federal Communications Commission (FCC), 44
Federal Express, 403, 404, 628
Federal regulatory agencies, 43-44, 45(illus.)
Federal Trade Commission (FTC), 43-44
    powers of, 41
    Robinson-Patman Act and, 41
Federal Trade Commission Act, 41

pricing decisions and, 487
Feedback, in communication, 383
Field order takers, 447
Field settings, for marketing research, 179
Field warehouses, 359
Finance companies, 305
Fishyback services, 357
Fixed costs, 504
Fleming wholesalers, 362
F.O.B. (free-on-board) factory, 489
Focus-group interviews, 185
Follow up, in personal selling, 446
Food brokers, 302
Food wholesalers, 293, 362
Forecasting. *See* Sales forecasting
Foreign currency exchange rates, pricing in
        international marketing and, 684
Foreign marketing. *See* International trade
47th Street Photo, 327
Forward integration, 560
Franchising, 332-334
Franco's Hidden Harbor, 475
Free merchandise, 465
Free samples, 462
Freight absorption pricing, 490
Freight forwarders, 357
Froman, Arthur H. and Company, 305
FTC. *See* Federal Trade Commission
Full-cost approach, 586
Full-service wholesalers, 297-299
Function, organizing marketing unit by, 573-574
Functional accounts, analysis of, 587-588
Functional discount, 488
Functional middlemen, 301
Functional modifications of products, 240

General Foods, 461
General merchandise wholesalers, 298
General publics, 648
Generic brands, 219-220
Generic terms, as brand names, 219
Geographic location
    as basis for sales analysis, 584
    as segmentation variable, 87-89, 92
Geographic pricing, 489-490
Globalization of markets, 668-669
GNP. *See* Gross national product
Goods, 12
Government markets, 140-142
Government regulation. *See* Regulatory forces
Grainger, W.W., 609
Gross national product (GNP), international
        comparison of, 675
Group interview, 120

Marketing environment, 19(illus.), 21-23
  economic and competitive forces in, 50-60
  examining and dealing with, 36-38
  laws and their interpretation in, 39-43
  politics and, 38-39
  regulatory forces in, 43-46
  societal forces in, 46-50
  technological forces in, 60-65
Marketing experimentation, 178
Marketing function accounts, 586
Marketing information system (MIS), 163-167
  defined, 163
Marketing intelligence, for international marketing,
  670-672
Marketing intermediaries, 266-267
Marketing management, 18-28, 547
  environmental forces and, 21-23
  internal organizational factors and, 20-21
  marketing mix development and, 24-28
  target market selection and, 23
  tasks of, 19, 20(illus.)
Marketing mix, 19, 19(illus.)
  development of, 24-28
  industrial, 608-620
  in international marketing, 677-684
  for nonbusiness marketing, 649-652
  for retailing, 339-340
Marketing myths, 15(table)
Marketing objectives, pricing decisions and, 483
Marketing opportunity analysis, 19-23
  environmental forces and, 21-23
  internal organizational factors and, 20-21
Marketing planning, 547
  cycle of, 547-548
  duration of, 549
  marketing strategy and, 545-550
  see also Strategic market planning
Marketing program, 535
Marketing research, 164-165, 172-191
  data collection in, 173-174
  defined, 163
  designing, 176-179
  ethics of, 190-191
  hypotheses in, 173
  interpretation of findings of, 174-175
  observation methods in, 187-188
  problem definition and location in, 172-173
  reporting findings of, 175-176
  secondary data collection in, 188-190
  steps in, 172, 173(illus.)
  survey methods in, 180-187
Marketing strategy, 19, 23, 23-28, 533
  for declining products, 255-256
  in growth stage, 252-256
  marketing planning and, 545-550

for mature products, 253-255
for nonbusiness marketing, 646-652
packaging and, 224-225
for retailing, 337-340
for services, 634-642
see also Strategic market planning
Market manager, 236
Market opportunity, 538-539. See also Marketing
  opportunity analysis
Market requirements, 539
Market Research Corporation of America (MRCA),
  190
Market sales potential, 96
Market segmentation approach, 77-95
  choosing variables for, 81
  concentration strategy for, 78-79
  conditions for effectiveness of, 80-81
  for consumer markets, 81-92
  multisegment strategy for, 79-80
  for organizational markets, 92-94
  single-variable or multivariable segmentation in,
    94-95
Market share, as pricing objective, 480-481
Market share analysis, of sales, 584
Market tests
  in company sales forecasting, 101
  see also Test marketing
Markup pricing, 518
Marriott Corporation, 441-442, 583
Mass merchandisers, 324-328
Materials handling, 361, 362
Mattel, 571-572
Maturity stage in product life cycle, 212-213
  marketing strategy for products in, 253-255
MC. See Marginal cost
Meat industry, 616
  market research and, 169
Mechanical observation devices, 188
Media plan
  characteristics, advantages and disadvantages of
    major media and, 420-421(table)
  developing, 416-419
Medium of transmission, in communication, 382
Medium-range plans, 549
Megacarrier, 354
Merchandise, free, 465
Merchandise allowances, 465
Merchandising, 339
  scrambled, 339-340
Merchants, 266
  commission, 303-304
Merchant wholesalers, 297
Message, advertising, 419, 422-425
Metropolitan statistical area (MSA), 89
Middlemen, functional, 301

Miniwarehouse mall, 336
MIS. *See* Marketing information system
Missionary salespersons, 447-448
Modified rebuy purchase, 148
Money refunds, 463
Monopolistic competition, 51 and *table*
Monopoly, 50, 51(table)
   pricing decisions and, 486
   see also Procompetitive legislation
Montabert, F. G. Company, 137-138
Montfort, 616
Montgomery Ward, 546
Motivating
   of marketing personnel, 578
   of salespersons, 454
Motive(s)
   in consumer buying behavior, 120-121
   defined, 120
   patronage, 120
   as segmentation variable, 91
Motorola, 665
MR. *See* Marginal revenue
MRCA. *See* Market Research Corporation of America
MSA. *See* Metropolitan statistical area
Multinational enterprises, 667-668, 667(table). *See also* International marketing
Multisegment strategy, 79-80
Multivariable segmentation, 94-95, 95(illus.)

Nabisco Brands, Inc., 217
National Advertising Review Board, 46
Natural accounts, 586
   analysis of, 587
Nature Company, 546
Negotiated pricing, 619
Negotiation
   as method of organizational buying, 148
   in nonbusiness marketing, 643
Neighborhood shopping centers, 334
New-product development, 238, 242-251
   business analysis for, 244-245
   commercialization and, 248-251
   development stage of, 245
   idea generation for, 243-244
   for international marketing, 682
   screening ideas for, 244
   test marketing and, 245-246, 247(table)
New-product sales promotion techniques, 462-463
News release, 430
New-task purchase, 148
Nielsen, A. C. Company, Retail Index published by, 189-190
Nike, 380
Nikolaisen's Restaurant, 475

Noise, in communication, 382-383
Nonbusiness marketing, 643-654
   business marketing compared with, 643-644
   controlling activities of, 653-654
   controversial nature of, 644-645
   objectives of, 645-646
   strategies for, 646-652
Noncumulative discounts, 488
Nonpersonal sales, 330-332
Nonprice competition, 478-479
Nonstore retailing, 329-332
   nonpersonal sales in, 330-332
   personal sales in, 329-330
Nontraceable common costs, 586

Objections, in personal selling, 445
Objective and task approach, to advertising appropriation, 413
Observation methods, in marketing research, 187-188
Odd-even pricing, 512
Oligopoly, 51 and *table*
   pricing decisions and, 486
Open-ended questions, 186-187
Opportunity, 538-539. *See also* Marketing opportunity analysis
Order getters, 446-447
Order takers, 447
Organization(s) (businesses)
   advertising to promote, 415
   goals of, strategic market planning and, 537-538
   internal factors in, 20-21
   marketing-oriented, 572
   marketing's place in, 572-573
   objectives of, pricing decisions and, 483
   opportunities and resources of, 538-544
   production-oriented, 572
   sales-oriented, 572
   type of, as segmentation variable, 92-93
   using marketing, 12
Organization (process)
   to manage products, 236-237
   of marketing activities, 572-576
Organizational (industrial) buying behavior, 142-155
   buyer characteristics and, 143
   buyer concerns and, 143-147
   buying center and, 151
   demand and, 149-150
   influences on, 155
   methods of, 148
   stages in, 152-154
   stages of, 152(illus.)
   transaction characteristics and, 142-143
   types of purchases and, 148-149
Organizational markets. *See* Industrial markets

demand and, 500-503, 518 520
demand, cost, and profit relationships and, 504-509
experience curve, 516-517
factors affecting, 482-487
freight absorption, 490
geographic, 489-490
in growth stage, 253
for industrial markets, 487-491, 618-620
in international marketing, 684
markup, 518
of mature products, 255
method for, 517-520
negotiated, 619
in nonbusiness marketing, 652
objectives of, 479-482
odd-even, 512
pioneer, 509-511
policy for, 509-517
prestige, 513
professional, 514-515
promotional, 515-516
psychological, 511-514
of services, 640-641
setting objectives for, 499
special-event, 515-516
transfer, 490
uniform geographic, 489
Primary data, 173
Primary metropolitan statistical area (PMSA), 89
Private distributor brands, 216
Private label branding, 339
Private warehouses, 359, 360-361
Problem children, products as, 550-551
Problem definition, in marketing research, 172-173
Problem recognition
  in consumer buying behavior, 112
  in organizational buying behavior, 152
Process materials, 207
Procompetitive legislation, 39-42, 40(table)
Procter & Gamble, 286
Producer(s), wholesalers' services for, 295-296
Producer markets, 138-139
Product(s), 12
  advertising to promote, 415
  as basis for sales analysis, 585
  branding and, 214-221
  consumer, 203-205
  convenience, 204
  declining, 255
  defined, 202-203
  in growth stage, 252-253
  industrial, 206-208, 603, 608-610
  in international marketing mix, 679-682
  labeling and, 225
  managing after commercialization, 252

mature, 253-255
in nonbusiness marketing, 649-650
organizing marketing unit by, 574
organizing to manage, 236-237
packaging and, 222-225
physical characteristics of, 226
premium- and lower-priced, 484-485
promotion mix and, 393-394
quality of, 146
service, 635, 637
shopping, 204
specialty, 204-205
supportive services and, 226-227
tangibility of, 629
unsought, 205
see also New-product development
Product adoption process, 249-250
  promotion and, 384-387
Product advertising, 415
Product assortments, 317
Product deletion, 240-241
Product differentiation, 76
Production orientation, 16-17
Product item, 208
Product life cycles, 210-214
Product line, 208, 209
  depth of, 208
  width of, 208-209
Product manager, 236
Product mix, 208-209
Product mix management, 237-251
  modification of products and, 238-240
  new-product development and, 242-251
  product deletion and, 240-241
Product modification, 238-240
Product portfolio approach, 237-238, 550-552
Product positioning, 251-252
Product quality, 146
  modifications of, 239
  as pricing objective, 482
Product-related variables, in market segmentation, 91-92
Product specifications, in organizational buying behavior, 153
Product use(s)
  advertising to increase, 409
  as segmentation variable, 93-94
Product variable, 24-25
Professional pricing, 514-515
Profit
  breakeven analysis and, 507-509
  as pricing objective, 480
Projective techniques, 120-121
Promotion, 378-396
  communication process and, 381-384

Promotion (Continued)
  cost and availability of methods for, 394, 396
  of declining products, 255
  in growth stage, 253
  of industrial products, 614-618
  in international marketing mix, 679-682
  of mature products, 255
  methods of, 394, 396
  for nonbusiness marketing, 651-652
  product adoption process and, 384-387
  promotion mix and, 387-396
  role of, 378-380
  sales. *See* Sales promotion
  of services, 638-640
Promotional pricing, 515-516
Promotion mix, 387-396
  ingredients of, 387-390
  selecting ingredients of, 391-396
Promotion variable, 26-27
Prospecting, in personal selling, 444
Prosperity, in business cycle, 59-60
Proxemic communication, in personal selling, 389
Psychographic variables, in market segmentation, 89, 91
Psychological influences, on consumer buying behavior, 116-124
Psychological pricing, 511-514
Publicity, 429-434
  advertising compared with, 429-430
  kinds of, 430
  limitations of, 434
  in promotion mix, 390
  requirements for program of, 431-432
  unfavorable, 433-434
  uses of, 430-431, 432(table)
Public relations, 429
Public warehouses, 304-305, 359, 361
Pull policy, in promotion, 391-392
Purchase(s)
  modified rebuy, 148
  new-task, 148
  organizational, 148-149
  straight rebuy, 148-149
Purchase decision, 126, 126-127(table)
Purchase stage
  in consumer buying behavior, 113-114
  in organizational buying behavior, 154
Purchasing power, 476
Push money, 466
Push policy, in promotion, 391

Quality, 146
  modifications of, 239
  as pricing objective, 482

Quality of life, 47
Quantity discounts, 488
Question(s)
  open ended, 186-187
  to overcome objectionable nature of subject, 187(table)
Questionnaires, in market research, 186-187
Quota sampling, 177

Rack jobbers, 300-301
Radio copy, 423
Random factor analysis, 100
Random sampling, in marketing research, 176-177
Raw materials, 206
Raytheon Company, 666
Real-estate brokers, 302
Rebuy purchase
  modified, 148
  straight, 148-149
Recall tests, aided and unaided, 428
Recession, 60
Reciprocity, in organizational sales, 143
Recognition test, 428
Recovery, 60
Recruiting, of salespersons, 450-451
Reference-group influence, on consumer buying behavior, 126-128
Refunds, 463
Region, organizing marketing unit by, 574-575
Regional shopping centers, 335
Regulatory forces, 22, 43-46
  federal agencies and, 43-44, 45(illus.)
  nongovernmental agencies and, 45-46
  pricing decisions and, 487
  state and local agencies and, 44-45
Reinforcement advertising, 409
Reliability
  of research, 176
  of transportation, 355
Reminder advertising, 409
Research. *See* Marketing research
Reseller markets, 139-140
  sales promotion techniques aimed at, 464-466
Resources, of firm, 541-544
Responsibility, social, 48-50. *See also* Ethical issues
Restaurants, pricing changes in, 475
Retailer(s)
  sales promotion techniques used by, 460-462
  wholesalers' services for, 296
Retailer coupons, 460
Retailing, 316-340
  developing store image and atmosphere and, 318-324
  franchising and, 332-334

major types of stores and, 324-329
nature of, 316-318
nonstore, 329-332
planned shopping centers and, 334-336
strategy for, 337-340
wheel of, 336-337
Retailing mix, 339-340
Return on investment, as pricing objective, 480
Reynolds, R. J. Industries, Inc., 217
Robinson-Patman Act, 41-42, 490, 618
pricing decisions and, 487
Role(s)
in consumer buying behavior, 124-126
defined, 124
Routine response behavior, 11

Safety stock, 350
Sale(s)
advertising to reduce fluctuations in, 409-410
to current customers, 446
measurement of, 583-584
new-business, 446-447
nonpersonal, 330-332
organizational, 142-143
personal, 329-330
Sales analysis, 582-585
Sales branches and offices, 304-307
Sales contests, 466
Sales force
advertising to improve effectiveness of, 408-409
see also Salespersons
Sales-force forecasting survey, 99-100
Sales force management, 448-458
compensation and, 453-454, 455(table)
controlling and evaluating performance and, 458
creating sales territories and, 454-458
establishing objectives and, 448-449
motivation and, 454
recruitment and selection in, 450-451
size of force and, 449-450
training and, 451-453
Sales force recognition program, 457
Sales forecasting, 95-102
accuracy of, 98
company sales forecasts and, 97-102
company sales potential and, 96-97
market sales potential and, 96
Sales offices, 304-307
Sales orientation, 17
Salespersons
compensation of, 453-454, 455(table)
missionary, 447-448
sales analysis based on, 584-585
technical, 448

trade, 448
types of, 446-448
see also Sales force; Sales force management
Sales presentation, 444-445
Sales promotion, 458-466
consumer, 390, 460
dangers of, 461
methods for, 460-466
nature of, 458-459
objectives of, 459
in promotion mix, 390
of services, 639
trade, 390, 460
Sales territories, 454-458
routing and scheduling and, 457-458
shape of, 456
size of, 455-456
SAMI. See Sell Area Marketing, Inc.
Sample(s), free, 462
Sampling
area, 177
in marketing research, 176-177
as method of organizational buying, 148
quota, 177
random, 176-177
stratified, 177
Sanyo, 256
SBU. See Strategic business unit
Scientific decision making, 169, 171(table)
Scrambled merchandising, 339-340
Screening, of new-product ideas, 244
Search qualities, 630
Sears, Roebuck & Co., 546
Seasonal analysis, 100
Seasonal discounts, 488-489
Secondary data, 173
SECR. See Sophisticated electronic cash register
Security, of transportation, 356
Segmentation. See Market segmentation approach
Segmentation variables, 81
age as, 83
city size as, 87-89
customer size as, 93
ethnicity as, 84-85
geographic location as, 92
income as, 84
for industrial markets, 92-94
lifestyle as, 91
marital status as, 85-87
motives as, 91
organizational type as, 92-93
population as, 97
product use as, 93-94
sex as, 83
Selective distortion, 118

Tactile communication, in personal selling, 389
Tangibility
    of aspects of services, 635
    of products, 629
Target, advertising, 410-411
Target market(s)
    evaluation of price and ability to spend by, 500
    industrial, 603-608
    market segmentation approach to identifying, 77-95
    measuring sales potential of, 95-102
    for nonbusiness marketing, 647-649
    promotion and, 392
    selecting, 73, 75
    total market approach to identifying, 75-77
Target public, 648
Technical salespersons, 448
Technology, 23, 60-65
    adoption and use of, 65
    changing, 64-65
    defined, 61-62
    impact of, 62-63
    in international marketing, 676
Technology assessment, 65
Telephone retailing, 329-330
Telephone surveys, 183
Television copy, 423-424
Territories, for sales force, 454-458
Test drives, 386
Test marketing, 245-246, 247(table)
Theft, during physical distribution, 359
Time series analysis, in company sales forecasting, 100
Total cost, 504
Total market (undifferentiated) approach, 75-77
Traceability, of transportation services, 356
Traceable common costs, 586
Trade allowances, 461
Trade discount, 488
Trademark, 214
Trade marts, 305-307
Trade name, 214
Trade salespersons, 448
Trade sales promotion methods, 390, 460
Trade shows, 305-307
Trading companies, in international marketing, 687-188
Trading stamps, 461-462
Training, for sales force, 451-453
Transaction(s), industrial, 142-143
Transfer pricing, 490
Transit time, 355
Transmission medium, in communication, 382
Transportation, 352-357
    accessibility of, 356
    capability of, 355-356

coordinating, 357
cost of, 354-355
modes of, 352-354, 353(table)
ranking of modes by selection criteria for, 357(table)
reliability of, 355
security of, 356
selection criteria for, 354-357, 357(table)
traceability of, 356
transit time and, 355
Transportation companies, 305
TreeSweet Products Company, 535
Trend analysis, 100
Truck wholesalers, 300

Unaided recall test, 428
Undifferentiated market approach, 75-77
Uniform geographic pricing, 489
United Parcel Service, 403-404, 602, 628
U. S. Army, 11
U. S. Department of Commerce, 647, 665
U. S. Postal Service, 403, 627-628
Unit loading, 361
Universal product code (UPC), 363
Universal vendor marking (UVM), 363
Unsought products, 205
UPC. *See* Universal product code
UVM. *See* Universal vendor marking

Validity of research, 176
Variable costs, 504
Vending machines, 330
Venture team, 237
Vertical channel integration, 278-280
Vertical marketing systems (VMS), 279-280
Volvo, 162

Warehouse(s)
    field, 359
    private, 359, 360-361
    public, 304-305, 359, 361
Warehouse showrooms, 326
Warehousing, physical distribution and, 357-361
Warranty, 226-227
Wheeler-Lea Amendment, 41
    pricing decisions and, 487
Wheel of retailing hypothesis, 336-337
Wholesalers, 294
    activities of, 295(table), 295-296
    cash-and-carry, 299-300
    classifying, 296-304
    drop shippers and, 301